Microsoft® Office 2000 8 in 1

by Joe Habraken

201 West 103rd Street, Indianapolis, Indiana 46290 USA

To my wonderful wife, Kim. Everyone should have such a fantastic partner to go through life with.

Copyright © 1999 by Que Corporation

International Standard Book Number: 0-7897-1840-5

Library of Congress Catalog Card Number: 98-86835

Printed in the United States of America

First Printing: May 1999

01   00   99   4   3   2   1

Interpretation of the printing code: The rightmost double-digit number is the year of the book's printing; the rightmost single-digit, the number of the book's printing. For example, a printing code off 99-1 shows that the first printing of the book occured in 1999.

Executive Editor
Jim Minatel

Acquisitions Editors
Jill Byus
Don Essig
Jenny Watson

Development Editor
Jill Hayden

Managing Editor
Thomas F. Hayes

Project Editor
Sossity Smith

Copy Editors
Barbara Hacha
Kay Hoskin
Julie McNamee
Kelli Martin
Anne Owen

Indexers
Joy Dean Lee
Rebecca Salerno
Larry Sweazy

Technical Editor
Coletta Witherspoon

Proofreader
Jeanne Clark

Layout Technician
Darin Crone

Acknowledgments

Creating books like this takes a real team effort. I would like to thank Jenny Watson, our acquisitions editor, who worked very hard to assemble the team that made this book a reality and kept us all on track as the book evolved toward completion. I would also like to thank Jill Hayden who served as the developmental editor for this book and who came up with many great ideas for improving its content. Also a tip of the hat and a thanks to Coletta Witherspoon, who as the technical editor for the project did a fantastic job making sure that everything was correct and suggested a number of additions that made the book even more technically sound. Finally, a great big thanks to our project editor, Sossity Smith, who ran the last leg of the race and made sure the book made it to press on time—what a great team of professionals.

Trademarks

All terms mentioned in this book that are known to be trademarks have been appropriately capitalized. Que cannot attest to the accuracy of this information. Use of a term in this book should not be regarded as affecting the validity of any trademark or service mark.

About the Author

Joe Habraken is a best-selling author whose publications include *The Microsoft Access 97 Exam Guide, The Complete Idiot's Guide to Microsoft Access 2000, Easy Publisher 2000, Sams Teach Yourself Microsoft Publisher 2000 in 10 Minutes,* and *Sams Teach Yourself Microsoft Outlook 2000 in 10 Minutes.* Joe has a master's degree in communication (American University, Washington, D.C.) and nearly two decades of experience as an educator, author, and consultant in the information technology field. He is a Microsoft Certified Professional who teaches computer software seminars across the country. He currently serves as the lead instructor for the Networking Technologies program at Globe College in St. Paul, MN.

Contents

Part II: Word   141

Part III: Excel 317

Part IV: Access   439

Part VI: Outlook   685

PartVIII: FrontPage/PhotoDraw 1047

Introduction

Congratulations! You are about to harness the incredible features and tools of Microsoft Office 2000 Premium Edition. Office 2000 provides you with all the applications that you need for your personal use or to run your small business: word processing, spreadsheets, databases, personal information management, Web site creation and much, much more. This book is designed to get you up and running quickly on all the Office applications, such as Word, Excel, Access, PowerPoint, and Outlook, and to make it easy for you to use their basic and a number of their advanced features. There is also a section on Windows that will help you become familiar with the Windows graphical user interface and the Internet Explorer Web browser. You'll learn the ins and outs of surfing the Web and using the Windows Channel Bar.

Microsoft Office 2000 Premium Edition provides you more software applications than Office 97, the previous version. You will find familiar applications like Word and Excel, and you will also find new additions like FrontPage and PhotoDraw. The Premium Edition of Office includes the following applications:

- **Word**—A versatile word processing application that enables you to create every possible type of document from simple letters to newsletters to reports that include charts and tables.

- **Excel**—A powerful spreadsheet program that enables you to create simple worksheets or specialty worksheets like invoices and financial statements. Excel provides all the tools and formulas for doing simple math or special statistical and financial calculations.

- **PowerPoint**—An easy-to-use presentation application that enables you to create eye-catching and impressive slideshows that can be shown from your computer monitor or other video output device. PowerPoint also enables you to print presentation outlines and speaker's notes for your presentations.

- **Access**—A relational database application that is extremely powerful yet very straightforward to use. Access provides a number of database wizards that will help you create your own databases quickly and efficiently.

- **Outlook**—A personal information manager that will help you keep organized. Outlook not only helps you manage your contacts, appointments, and tasks, it also serves as your email and fax client.

- **Publisher**—A desktop publishing application that enables you to create a variety of personal items, such as greeting cards and banners, and business documents such as business cards, brochures, and flyers. Publisher provides wizards and templates, making it easy to create and lay out any type of publication.

- **FrontPage**—A Web design tool that provides wizards to create several different kinds of Web sites. You can quickly create a personal, business, or other type of Web site using FrontPage and include graphics and navigational tools such as hyperlinks.

- **PhotoDraw**—An easy-to-use, yet full featured graphics studio that enables you to create your own images and modify and enhance nearly any existing image file. You can touch up photos, add special effects to a scanned image, or even create your own images using PhotoDraw's design tools and templates.

Using This Book

Microsoft Office 2000 8 in 1 is designed to help you learn the eight applications in the Office suite and gain a good understanding of how to work with applications in the Windows environment (an entire section of the book is devoted to Windows). All the most important and useful tasks are covered in this book and the short, concise lessons make it easy for you to learn a particular feature quickly.

This book is organized into eight sections. The first section covers Windows and Internet Explorer. Each of the subsequent sections (sections 2–7) covers a particular Office application: Word, Excel, Access, PowerPoint, Outlook, and Publisher. A special bonus section, FrontPage/PhotoDraw, covers features in FrontPage and PhotoDraw that will help you create and customize your own Web sites.

Appendixes are also included in the book that walk you through the Office installation process, assist you in becoming familiar with the new Office Help system, and show you how to integrate the Office applications and share information between them. You will find that the book is designed for you either to work through the various lessons sequentially or skip around to get help with a particular feature or set of features in a particular application.

Conventions Used in This Book

Each of the lessons in this book includes step-by-step instructions for performing specific tasks. To help you as you work through these steps and help you move through the lessons easily, additional information is included and identified by the following icons:

Term New or unfamiliar terms are defined to help you as you work through the various steps in the lesson.

Tip Read these tips for ideas that cut corners and confusion.

CAUTION

Caution This icon identifies areas where new users often run into trouble; these hints offer practical solutions to those problems.

In addition to the icons discussed, the following conventions are also used:

Text you should type	Information you need to type appears in **bold type**.
Items you select	Commands, options, and icons you are to select and keys you are to press also appear in **bold type**.

Tell Us What You Think!

As the reader of this book, *you* are our most important critic and commentator. We value your opinion and want to know what we're doing right, what we could do better, what areas you'd like to see us publish in, and any other words of wisdom you're willing to pass our way.

As the Executive Editor for the General Desktop Applications team at Que Publishing, I welcome your comments. You can fax, email, or write me directly to let me know what you did or didn't like about this book—as well as what we can do to make our books stronger.

Please note that I cannot help you with technical problems related to the topic of this book, and that due to the high volume of mail I receive, I might not be able to reply to every message.

When you write, please be sure to include this book's title and author as well as your name and phone or fax number. I will carefully review your comments and share them with the author and editors who worked on the book.

Fax: 317-581-4666

Email: `office-que@mcp.com`

Mail: Executive Editor
       General Desktop Applications
       Que Publishing
       201 West 103rd Street
       Indianapolis, IN 46290 USA

Windows

Working in Windows 98

In this lesson, you'll learn how to start and shut down Windows 98. You will also learn how to use the mouse (including how to use the Microsoft IntelliMouse) and the Windows Start button.

Starting Windows 98

Windows 98 should start automatically every time you turn on your computer. When Windows 98 starts, it prepares your computer for use, a process called booting the computer.

Next you'll see a logon dialog box. This dialog box contains either two or three text boxes. The User Name box should already contain your name or the name under which your computer is presently registered. The box marked Domain, if it's there, should also be filled in already with the name of the domain your system administrator wants you to use. The box marked Password should be blank, except for a blinking cursor (in Windows this cursor is called the insertion point). Type your password and press **Enter**. (If you are part of a network and don't know what your password is, consult your network system administrator.) As you type, Windows inserts asterisks in place of your letters in the Password box as a security measure. These aren't the characters you're actually typing—they just represent the fact that you are typing characters, in case anyone is peeking over your shoulder.

CAUTION

Remember That Password You must know your password to access a network using Windows 98. If you don't log on to Windows 98 with your password, you won't have access to any local area network (LAN) that might be available. However, if you really need to get into Windows 98, but you don't need to be on the network, you can press **Esc** when you see the logon dialog box. Keep in mind that if you are using Windows 98 at home and are not connected to a network, you may not be prompted for a password.

CAUTION

I See a Startup Menu If you are first prompted with a numbered menu with the header "Windows 98 Startup Menu" instead of the logon dialog box, you are either being asked to choose from one of several configurations your system administrator has set up for you, or something peculiar may have happened the last time you tried to shut down Windows 98. Contact your administrator, if you have one, to find out which number you should choose in this instance. Otherwise, you should probably just pick the **Normal** option to boot as if nothing out of the ordinary happened. Most Windows 98 users won't see this menu.

In a moment you'll see the Welcome to Windows 98 dialog box. This dialog box gives you the opportunity to register your copy of Windows 98 with Microsoft, connect to the Internet, tour Windows 98 features, or run maintenance tasks on your Windows 98 system. If you don't want this dialog box to appear each time you start Windows 98, you can deselect the check box in the lower-left corner of the dialog box. To close the box, use the mouse to click the **Close** button (the × in the upper-right corner of the box). (If you are unfamiliar with using a mouse, you may want to skip ahead to the "Using the Mouse" section in this lesson and read it now.)

In a few moments, you'll see the Windows 98 Desktop, which should appear similar (although perhaps not identical) to Figure 1.1. The term desktop is used metaphorically here. It symbolizes how the objects you work with in Windows are arranged and managed, like the papers and other objects on your desk in the real world.

Windows 98 offers you a choice of two desktops: the Classic Desktop and the Active Desktop. You'll learn more about the Active Desktop and how to switch between it and the Classic Desktop in Lesson 2, "Navigating the Windows 98 Desktop."

Figure 1.1 The Classic Windows 98 Desktop is designed to resemble a real-world desk.

Using the Mouse

A mouse is a device that you use to manipulate objects in Windows. As you move the mouse on its pad, the mouse pointer onscreen moves in tandem. The mouse pointer, which is often referred to simply as a pointer, is the small symbol (such as an arrow) that moves on the screen when you move the mouse.

Because the mouse is such a simple device, mechanically speaking, there are only a few gestures you'll ever need to perform with it:

- To point to an object on the screen, move the mouse pointer directly over that object. You point to an object when you are preparing to do something to it.
- To click an object to which your mouse pointer is currently pointing, you press the left mouse button once and quickly release it. Generally, you click an object to issue a command, open a program, or select an object.
- To right-click an object, point to it and then press and release the right mouse button. When you right-click an object, Windows and many applications display a menu called a *context menu*, which lists commands that pertain to that object.

- To drag an object from place to place, you first point to it and then click and hold down the mouse button—don't release it yet. Next, you move the pointer in the direction you want to drag the object. When the pointer is in the position where you want the object to appear, you release the mouse button. (If you want to drag a word or paragraph, you have to select it first.) The process of dragging an object to a new place is called *drag and drop.* You might use drag and drop to move a file from one directory to another or to move a paragraph within a word processing document. Normally, a drag operation involves the left mouse button; however, Windows 98 and some Windows programs employ *right-drags* (using the right mouse button) that bring up a context menu after the button is released.

- To double-click an object, you point to it and then press and release the left mouse button twice rapidly. Double-clicking is the standard method in the Windows Classic Desktop for starting an application or selecting an object from a dialog box and immediately closing the box (dismissing it).

How Using the Mouse Is Different in Web Style

When you turn on Windows 98's new Web Style option, the way your mouse operates changes dramatically. For instance, to select an object, instead of clicking once on that object with the left mouse button, you point to it, stop the mouse completely, and wait for Windows to recognize that the pointer has stopped (about a third of a second by default). Windows then highlights the object you selected.

CAUTION

Using Windows 95? If you're using Windows 95 and have not installed Internet Explorer 4 or later, you don't have access to the new Web Style or its related features. You can download Internet Explorer 4 (and the soon-to-be-available version 5) from the Microsoft Web site at http://www.microsoft.com. Installing one of the later versions of Internet Explorer adds the Active Desktop components to your Windows installation and enables you to take advantage of the Web Style desktop discussed in this lesson.

Also, double-clicking is replaced entirely with single-clicking, thus treating each object as though it were a hyperlink. With the Web Style option turned on, you can single-click a file to open it. The optional Web Style setting is covered in greater detail in Lesson 7, "Working with Drives, Folders, and Files."

Using the IntelliMouse

Because Microsoft is the manufacturer of both Windows 98 and the IntelliMouse pointer device, Microsoft has provided extra support for the IntelliMouse. This Microsoft-brand pointer has a small, gray, vertical wheel between its two buttons. This wheel is used for scrolling, and it can also be clicked—to act as a third button of sorts. Windows applications that can work with the IntelliMouse driver (especially Microsoft-brand software) can make use of the IntelliMouse wheel. Here are the basics:

- To scroll slowly, rotate the wheel up or down.
- To scroll more quickly, click the wheel once and then move the mouse in the direction in which you want to scroll. Click the wheel again to turn off the automatic scrolling.
- To zoom in or out, press the **Ctrl** key as you rotate the wheel up (to zoom in) or down (to zoom out).

By rotating the wheel in Microsoft Excel 2000, for instance, you can use the wheel to pan through a worksheet the way a camera pans a scene. Using the wheel more like a button, you can hold it down and then move the mouse in the direction you want to scroll. Or you can press the **Ctrl** key while rotating the wheel up or down to increase or decrease, respectively, the zoom factor of the active worksheet.

Using the Start Menu

Almost every operation you initiate in Windows 98 begins with the Start button, located in the lower-left corner of the screen. You can start programs, change Windows features, locate files, shut down Windows, and perform other operations with the commands you'll find on the Start menu, as shown in Figure 1.2. Most of the commands available on the Windows 98 Start menu are also available on the Windows 95 Start menu (unless otherwise noted).

When you click the **Start** button, the Start menu appears. The following are brief descriptions of the commands that are displayed:

- If you have a connection to the Internet, you can use the **Windows Update** command to update your version of Windows periodically (this is for Windows 98 users only; Windows 95 does not have an Update command available). This command connects you to the Microsoft Windows Update Web site.

- **Programs** displays a categorized listing of the applications (programs) available on your system. Navigate through the various categories or submenus that appear until you find the program you intend to start.

- **Favorites** brings up a list of the documents, channels, and Internet links you have previously selected for convenient access from this command.

- **Documents** displays a list of documents that have recently been accessed or created with your applications. You can click one of these entries to open the document in the associated application.

- **Settings** displays a short list where you can access, among other things, the Control Panel. In the Control Panel you can change the major characteristics of the operating system, such as display properties, printer status, and computer setup.

- **Find** helps you locate files, folders, or computers on your system or on your company's network. You can also use the Find command to locate Web pages on the Internet or people's email addresses.

- **Help** brings up the Windows 98 (or Windows 95) Help system, which provides information on the various aspects of Windows 98, including quick pointers on using the operating system.

- **Run** enables you to enter a program's executable filename, either by typing it in or by browsing for it in your file directories. One case in which you might use the Run command is to initiate the setup command for a new software program.

- **Log Off** enables you to log off your company's network and log back on under a different user profile (a set of customized configuration settings). You might use this command when you share your computer with a coworker (this command is not available on computers that use the initial version of Windows 95; the command is available on computers running the Windows 95 OSR2 version).

- **Shut Down** provides the means for shutting down Windows safely. You can also use this command to restart (reboot) your computer when needed.

As you select commands from some parts of the Start menu, additional menus are displayed. When you select **Programs**, for example, a listing of the programs installed on your computer and your program groups are displayed.

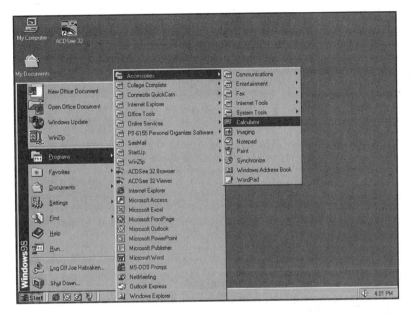

Figure 1.2   The Start menu is displayed when you click the Start button.

Shutting Down Windows 98

When it is time for you to turn your computer off, don't just flip the Off switch. Doing so might damage your computer files. You need to shut down Windows 98 first and then let the system tell you when it's okay to flip the Off switch. To shut down Windows 98 and prepare to turn off your machine, do the following:

1. Close all your open applications, making sure that any documents you're currently working on are saved.

2. Click the **Start** button.

3. From the **Start** menu, select **Shut Down**. Windows displays the dialog box shown in Figure 1.3.

4. Make sure that the **Shut Down** option button is selected, and then click **OK**. Windows initiates its shut-down procedure and soon informs you that it is safe to turn off your computer. A number of newer computers (purchased in the last year) automatically power down. All you have to do is shut off your monitor to complete the shutdown process.

Figure 1.3   Select Start, then Shut Down to open the Shut Down Windows dialog box.

Some computers enable you to suspend their operations, which means to switch them into low-power mode, maintaining just the central processor without the peripherals, hard drive, or display. The Power Management options in Windows enable you to maintain what you're currently doing on your computer with the minimum amount of power necessary. Using the Power Management options is an alternative to shutting down your computer and restarting your programs from scratch when you want to work again. If your computer supports *standby mode*, the Stand By command appears just above Shut Down on the Start menu. For more information on Power Management, see Lesson 6, "Customizing the Appearance of Windows 98."

Other Shut Down Options

The Shut Down menu provides additional options. Here's when to use them:

> **Restart**—You might need to restart your computer after making a system configuration change (such as changing the screen resolution), or to refresh the internal resources of Windows. You'll find that running multiple applications at once often causes a severe drain on your system's resources. By restarting your PC, you can remove all programs from memory and refresh your system.

TIP   **The Old Ctrl+Al+Delete**   In the early days of PCs, users restarted their PCs by pressing **Ctrl+Alt+Delete**. This "three-finger salute" is used in Windows 98 to bring up a dialog box that enables you to close a program (end a task) without shutting down the entire system, or to initiate an emergency shutdown when your system locks up.

> **Restart in MS-DOS mode**—Programs written for the MS-DOS operating system will most likely run in Windows 98 without your having to switch to MS-DOS mode. Many DOS programs are displayed in their own windows and won't interfere with other Windows functions or

applications. However, some "legacy" applications (programs that were originally created for use on an earlier operating system, such as MS-DOS), especially graphically intense games, require you to shut down "Windows mode" to eliminate the constraints that Windows places on running programs.

CAUTION

Don't Just Shut Down While in MS-DOS mode, don't shut down your computer by just turning it off. Instead, when you're ready to turn off your computer, first return to Windows mode by typing **exit** at the command prompt and pressing **Enter**. Windows responds with the message **Windows is now restarting**. Soon the entire operating system is restarted. From there, you can initiate the regular Windows shutdown procedure outlined earlier.

Logging On as a Different User

Windows 98 enables multiple users to share the same computer while maintaining the individual preferences of each user. This is accomplished by setting up passwords for each user and having each user enter that password, thus logging on, when Windows 98 is started. Logging on also affects your network connection—meaning that you will be logged off the network and then logged back on as a different user when you follow this procedure.

By the way, logging on again doesn't require a complete shutdown of the system, but it closes all running applications—so make sure you save your work and shut down your programs before proceeding. To log on as a different user, follow these steps:

1. Click the **Start** button.
2. From the Start menu, select **Log Off** (your username will appear after log off), as shown in Figure 1.4. The Log Off Windows dialog box appears and the Windows desktop is dimmed.
3. To log off the system, click **Yes**. The system pauses for a moment, and then the Welcome to Windows dialog box appears.
4. Enter the username and password you want to use in the dialog box, and then click **OK**.

Each user who logs on to a particular Windows-based system can set screen and Windows attributes that are saved in a profile file. This enables each user to customize the look and feel of the Windows environment. You can create new users for your computer in the Windows Control Panel (click **Start**, then point at

Settings, then click **Control Panel**). Double-click the **Users** icon in the Control
Panel to add or remove users on your computer.

Figure 1.4 Log off Windows without shutting down.

In this lesson, you learned about the major components of the Windows 98
Desktop and how the mouse is used to manipulate those components. You also
saw how to start, restart, and shut down Windows 98. In the next lesson, you
learn the difference between the Classic and the Active Desktops, along with
how to use the taskbar and the toolbars.

Navigating the Windows 98 Desktop

In this lesson, you learn how to turn on the Active Desktop and how to switch back to the Classic Desktop when needed. You also learn how to use the Windows taskbar and the toolbars.

Understanding the Windows 98 Desktop

The Windows 98 Desktop appears when you start Windows. The desktop holds objects, shown as icons, that you use to start applications; copy, move, and delete files; connect to the Internet; and perform other functions. The Classic Windows Desktop is shown in Figure 2.1. You'll learn how to use the desktop components listed in Table 2.1 later in this lesson.

Web Integration and the Active Desktop

One of the most important features of Windows 98 is the Active Desktop, shown in Figure 2.2. The Active Desktop combines the aspects of the Classic Desktop with some of the features of a Web browser.

Web Browser   A Web browser is a program used to view Web pages on the World Wide Web. Web pages often contain graphics, text, animation, and other special elements, and a Web browser is designed to display these elements properly. Popular Web browsers include Microsoft's Internet Explorer and Netscape Communication Corporation's Netscape Communicator.

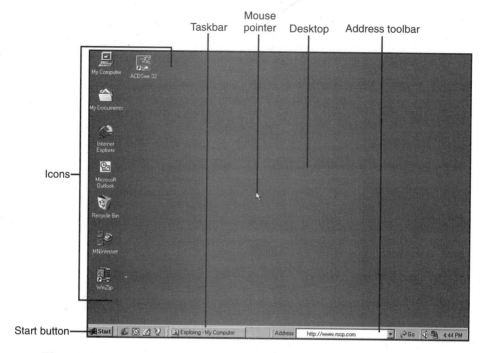

Figure 2.1 Perform functions by selecting icons on the Classic Windows Desktop.

Table 2.1 Elements of the Windows 98 Desktop

Element	Description
Mouse pointer	Indicates the current position of the mouse.
Icons	Shortcuts to folders, files, programs, and other items you work with.
Desktop	The launch pad for your application and your workspace.
Taskbar	Enables you to switch between open windows.
Address toolbar	One of several add-on toolbars that provide convenient access to Windows features that you use often.
Start button	Gives you quick access to your computer's settings and applications via a cascading menu system.

With the Active Desktop, you can have up-to-date Web content at your fingertips without the hassle of constantly logging on to the Internet, starting your Web browser, and selecting a Web page to view. For example, you might want to display current stock prices, news, weather, or updates from your company's intranet.

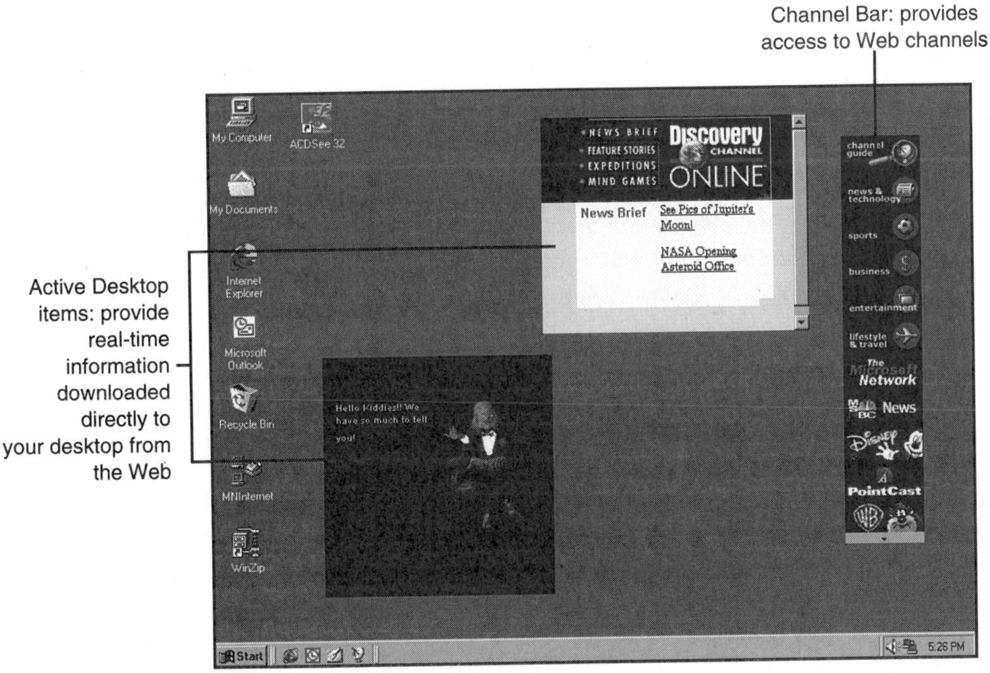

Channel Bar: provides
access to Web channels

Active Desktop
items: provide
real-time
information
downloaded
directly to
your desktop from
the Web

Figure 2.2 The Active Desktop can display Web pages in addition to the Classic Desktop content.

The Active Desktop can also affect how you browse your files and folders. Unlike the Classic Desktop—in which you usually double-click to open a folder or file—with the Active Desktop, you single-click instead. This feature (called Web Style) enables you to open files and folders more quickly. (You'll learn more about this feature in Lesson 7, "Working with Drives, Folders, and Files.")

Even though the Active Desktop is an integral part of the Windows 98 operating system, you can add the same features and functionality to your Windows 95 installation. Internet Explorer 4 (and the soon-to-be-available Internet Explorer 5) adds the Active Desktop and all its features to the Windows 95 Desktop.

Download Internet Explorer 4 or later from Microsoft at http://microsoft.com. A download link on the Microsoft home page provides you with a list of all the Web browsers (and their versions) available for download.

Turning On the Active Desktop

By default, the Classic Desktop is displayed when you first start Windows. You can switch to the Active Desktop at any time. Remember—the two desktops offer many of the same features, except that the Active Desktop enables you to display and access Web content more easily. Also, with the Active Desktop, the Web Style option that enables you to single-click to open files and folders is turned on initially (although you can turn it off if you like). You can also use the Web Style option with the Classic Desktop.

To turn on the Active Desktop, follow these steps:

1. Right-click an open area of the desktop. A shortcut menu appears.

2. Click **Active Desktop**. A cascading menu appears with more options.

3. From the cascading menu, select **View As Web Page**. The Active Desktop is displayed.

That's it! When the Active Desktop option is initially turned on, you won't see much of a change. The Channel bar appears, and with it, you can subscribe to the channels you want to display. You'll learn how to do that in Lesson 9, "Subscribing to Channels and Working Offline." Also, the Web Style option is now turned on, meaning that you can single-click a particular icon to open or activate it. If you don't want to use the Web Style option with Active Desktop, follow these steps:

1. Right-click an open area of the desktop. A shortcut menu appears.

2. Click **Active Desktop**. A cascading menu appears with more options.

3. From the cascading menu, select **Customize My Desktop**.

4. On the **Web** tab of the Display Properties dialog box, click the **Folder Options** button.

5. When asked if you want to close the Display Properties dialog box and go to the Folder Options dialog box, click **Yes**.

6. In the Folder Options dialog box (see Figure 2.3), select **Classic Style**, and then click **OK**. This enables you to use the Active Desktop but removes the single-click readiness of the Web style.

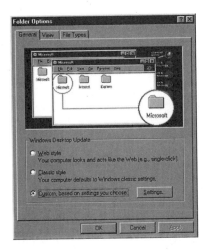

Figure 2.3 The Folder Options dialog box enables yout to turn off the Web Style option of the Windows Active Desktop.

CAUTION

Internet Connection Required   Because the Active Desktop's main duty is to display Web content, it requires that you be connected to the Internet to be effective—if not all the time, then at least when you initially turn the option on. If you haven't yet established an Internet connection for your PC, the Connection Wizard appears to help guide you through the process.

You don't have to have the icons on the desktop appear when you're using the Active Desktop; you may find that they just add clutter. To remove them, follow these steps:

1. Right-click the desktop and select **Properties**. The Display Properties dialog box appears.

2. Click the **Effects** tab on the Display Properties dialog box, and then select the check box to **Hide Icons When the Desktop Is Viewed as a Web Page**.

3. Click **OK**. When you switch to the Classic Desktop, the icons reappear.

Switching Back to the Classic Desktop

After using the Active Desktop for a while, you might want to switch back to the Classic Desktop. Switching back and forth between the two desktops doesn't remove any customization or channel selections you have made.

To switch back to the Classic Desktop, follow these steps:

1. Right-click an open area of the desktop. A shortcut menu appears.
2. Select **Active Desktop**. A cascading menu appears.
3. Click **View As Web Page** (this click actually deselects the option). This removes the check mark in front of the command, turning the option off. Your desktop is now set to the Classic Desktop mode.

If the Web Style option is turned on in Active Desktop, it remains on when you switch to Classic Desktop. To turn it off, follow these steps:

1. Right-click an open area of the desktop. A shortcut menu appears.
2. Click **Active Desktop**. A cascading menu appears with more options.
3. From the cascading menu, select **Customize My Desktop**.
4. On the **Web** tab of the Display Properties dialog box, click the **Folder Options** button.
5. When asked if you want to close the Display Properties dialog box and go to the Folder Options dialog box, click **Yes**.
6. In the Folder Options dialog box (refer to Figure 2.3), select **Classic Style**, and then click **OK**. This enables you to remove the single-click readiness of the Web style.

If you decide to switch back to the Active Desktop, the Web Style option won't be turned on because you turned it off while using Classic Desktop. To turn it back on, return to the Folders Options dialog box using the technique previously outlined, and select the **Web Style** option button. Then click **OK** to return to the desktop.

Using the Taskbar

At the bottom of the desktop is the taskbar. In addition to the Start button, the taskbar can contain several other elements, as shown in Figure 2.4.

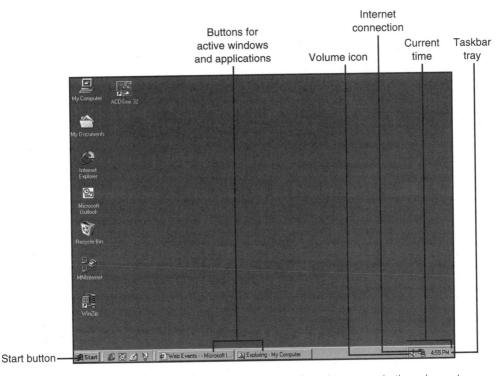

Figure 2.4 The Windows taskbar contains the Start button and other elements.

- **Start button**—With the Start button, you can select commands to open programs, customize Windows, locate files, and search the Internet.

- **Active programs and open windows**—Your currently running programs and any open windows, such as folder windows, appear as buttons on the taskbar. To switch to an open program or window, simply click its button.

- **Taskbar toolbars**—You can also add to the taskbar several toolbars that provide quick access to popular programs and functions, such as Web addressing. These toolbars include Address, Links, Desktop, and Quick Launch. In addition, you can create your own toolbars. See Lesson 4, "Using Toolbars, Menus, and Dialog Boxes," for help.

- **Taskbar tray**—At the far right of the taskbar is the taskbar tray—a status area that supplies you with the current time. Icons also occasionally appear in the tray to update you on the status of various things, such as your Internet connection status, whether you have new email messages in your inbox, and so on.

The taskbar initially appears at the bottom of the desktop; however, you can move it to the top, the left side, or the right side by simply clicking it, holding down the left mouse button, and dragging it where you want it.

You can also hide the taskbar and then cause it to appear only when needed. Hiding the taskbar gives you more room on your desktop for viewing your programs. To hide the taskbar, follow these steps:

1. Click the **Start** button. The Start menu appears.
2. Select **Settings**. A cascading menu appears.
3. Select **Taskbar & Start Menu**. The Taskbar Properties dialog box, shown in Figure 2.5, appears. (You can also right-click the taskbar and select **Properties** to display the Taskbar Properties dialog box.)

Figure 2.5 The Auto Hide option is found in the Taskbar Properties dialog box.

4. Click the **Auto Hide** check box to turn on this option.
5. Click **OK**. Click anywhere on the desktop. The taskbar disappears. To make it reappear, move the mouse pointer toward the taskbar's former location. The taskbar reappears.

TIP **Quick Hide** You can also hide the taskbar by dragging it out of sight. Just move the mouse pointer to the top edge of the taskbar (the pointer changes to a black, two-headed arrow) and drag the top of the taskbar down and out of sight. To bring the taskbar back in view, position the pointer along the bottom edge of the screen so that the two-headed arrow activates. Then drag the taskbar back into view.

Using Windows 98 Toolbars

Windows 98 comes with several toolbars that you can use to access the Internet and your programs more quickly. Some of these toolbars initially appear on the taskbar. You can remove them and place them on the desktop for more convenient access.

A toolbar is a bar of buttons that represent various commands. When you click the appropriate button, the associated command is carried out. Just like the toolbars you often find in Windows programs, a Windows 98 toolbar might contain text boxes in which you can type a command or list boxes from which you can make a selection.

Here are the Windows 98 toolbars:

- **Address**—Type an Internet address here, such as the address of a Web page, and press **Enter**; Internet Explorer opens to display the location you entered.

- **Links**— Provides access to some popular Internet Explorer links (Web sites).

- **Desktop**—Displays the icons that appear on your desktop, enabling you to access them when the desktop is covered with open windows.

- **Quick Launch**—Provides easy access to Internet Explorer, Outlook Express, your desktop, and the Active Channel Viewer.

- **Custom**—Enables you to create your own toolbars. For more information on creating toolbars, see Lesson 4. To display a toolbar, follow these steps:

    1. Right-click the taskbar and point at **Toolbars** on the shortcut menu that appears.

    2. Click the toolbar you want to display. The toolbar appears on the taskbar.

To use a toolbar, simply click one of its buttons. If the toolbar has a text box (such as the one on the Address toolbar), click inside the text box and type your information (in this case, the address of the Web page you want to display).

To remove a toolbar from the taskbar, right-click the taskbar, point at **Toolbars,** and then click the toolbar you want to remove (you are, in effect, deselecting it).

You can move or adjust the amount of space the toolbar takes up on the taskbar by dragging its handle—the ridge that appears on the toolbar's left edge.

Or, if you like, you can drag a toolbar off the taskbar and onto the desktop. Click anywhere on the toolbar, press and hold down the left mouse button, and then drag the toolbar onto the desktop, releasing the mouse button when the toolbar is in position. After the toolbar appears on the desktop, you can resize it the same as any other window. See Lesson 4 for help. To close a toolbar that is on the desktop, click the **Close** (×) button in the upper-right corner of the window.

In this lesson, you learned the differences between the Classic Desktop and the Active Desktop. In addition, you learned how to switch between the two, as needed. You also learned how to use the taskbar and the Windows 98 toolbars. In the next lesson, you learn how to work with and within the windows found in the Windows environment.

Working Within a Window

In this lesson, you learn how to open, close, resize, move, arrange, and scroll through the contents of a window.

What Is a Window?

A *window* is a box on your screen that contains items such as icons, files, folders, and even applications. Depending on your preferences, one or more windows can occupy a part of your screen or the entire screen. Figure 3.1 shows the parts of a typical window.

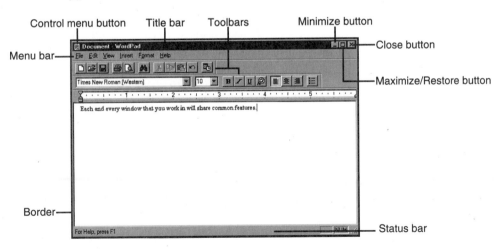

Figure 3.1 A typical window contains icons, files, folders, and other items.

Table 3.1 describes the elements you see in a typical window.

Table 3.1 Elements of a Typical Window

Element	Description
Control menu button	Provides a menu with commands for controlling the window's size, closing the window, and moving the window. Generally the control box contains the identifying icon for the program that uses this window. For example, in Figure 3.1, the icon for WordPad serves as the control button. On an Active Desktop item (a window that contains Web content), the control button looks like a down arrow.
Border	The frame that surrounds the window. You can resize a window by stretching its border. Place the mouse pointer on any window edge to view the resizing tool.
Title bar	Displays the title of the window, which includes the name of the program (if applicable) and the name of its active file. You can use a window's title bar to drag the window to a new location on the desktop (when it's not maximized).
Minimize button	Removes the window from the desktop. A button for the application will be available on the taskbar. Click this button to restore the window to the desktop.
Maximize/Restore button	Share the same position on the right of the window's title bar. To make the window cover the entire desktop, click the **Maximize** button (an open rectangle). When the window is maximized, the button becomes the Restore button (two overlapping rectangles); click the **Restore** button to return the window to its former size.
Close button (×)	Closes (exits) a window and its associated program.
Vertical scrollbar	Used to view data hidden above or below the displayed data. Click the scroll arrows at the top and bottom of the vertical scrollbar to move up and down through the information in the window.
Horizontal scrollbar	Used to view data hidden to the left or right of the displayed data. Click the scroll arrows at the left and right edges of the horizontal scrollbar to move left and right through the information in the window.

Element	Description
Menu bar	Contains the main categories of commands you give to an application. When you click one of these main categories, its list of associated commands drops down, and you can select a command or pull up a submenu from that list.
Toolbars	Used in most applications, they contain buttons you can click to perform common commands such as printing, opening, and saving a document.
Status bar	Alerts you to changes in the program and provides other useful information about the currently active application.

Opening a Window

Generally, a window opens automatically when you launch an application or when you open a document within that application.

When you launch an application from the Start menu, from a Windows Explorer listing (discussed in Lesson 7, "Working with Drives, Folders, and Files"), or from its icon on the desktop (double-click it), the application responds by opening its own program window. For an application such as WordPad, which comes with Windows 98, the window that pops up is empty, ready for you to enter text into it and save that text as a document file.

Applications such as Microsoft Word, Excel, and other, more sophisticated programs enable you to work on more than one document or worksheet at a time. Each subsequent Word document that you open resides in its own program window. Each document is represented by a button on the Windows taskbar. You switch between these open windows (even though they are in the same application) by clicking the appropriate button on the taskbar. For more about working with multiple documents in a program such as Word, see Lesson 3, "Editing Documents," in the Word section of this book.

CAUTION

Office 2000 Changes the Way You Look at Windows   In the past, Windows applications such as Word or Excel would support several open document windows, all "living" inside the one application window. In Office 2000, even though you may start out running one occurrence of the Word application, you end up with several Word windows (one for each document) running on the Windows Desktop.

Switching Between Windows

Before you work with the contents of a window, that window must be active. For example, to use a particular program, you must activate the window in which it's contained. Regardless of how many windows you have open at the time, you can only have one active window. The active window appears with a brighter title bar than the other open windows (typically blue under the standard Windows 98 default Desktop settings).

Several ways exist to activate a window (in other words, to switch from one window to another); you can do any of the following:

- Click any part of the open window.
- Press **Alt+Tab** to hop through the list of open windows (don't release the **Alt** button until you have selected the icon for the window you want to activate).
- Click the window's button on the taskbar.

Sizing a Window

A window can be maximized (made to cover the desktop) or minimized (removed from the desktop, but still available as a button on the taskbar). To maximize a window, click its **Maximize** button (refer to Figure 3.1). When the window is maximized, this button changes to the Restore button. Click the **Restore** button to restore the window to its former size. Maximizing applications enables you to concentrate on a particular document or other item and also gives you the maximum amount of desktop space available in which to work. On the other hand, when you're working with more than one application at the same time, you might want to see all their respective windows simultaneously. In that case, leave them at their restored size.

The Minimize button removes the window from the desktop without closing the application that is running inside it. To restore the window so that you can start using the program again, click that program's button on the taskbar.

Minimizing All Windows

To minimize all your windows at once so that only the desktop is visible, do the following:

1. Right-click an empty portion of the taskbar (where there are no minimized application buttons).

2. From the shortcut menu that appears, select **Minimize All Windows**. All the windows currently on the desktop are minimized.

To restore your windows, right-click the taskbar again and select **Undo Minimize All**.

If you're currently displaying the Quick Launch toolbar on your taskbar, you can also use it to minimize all your open windows. Simply click the **Show Desktop** button.

CAUTION

My Web Windows Are Still There! Using the Minimize All Windows command doesn't affect the Active Desktop items (the windows that contain Web content) you might be displaying on your Active Desktop. To remove them temporarily, switch back to the Classic Desktop. Right-click the desktop, select **Active Desktop**, and then select **View as Web Page** to turn the option off. To return to the Active Desktop, repeat these steps.

Sizing a Window's Borders

When a window is not maximized, you can change its size by dragging its border. When you stretch or shrink a window, you can move one side or corner at a time. Here's how:

1. Move the mouse pointer to one edge or corner of the window. The pointer changes to a black, two-headed arrow.

CAUTION

No Arrow? If you don't see a two-headed arrow when you move the mouse pointer to a window's border, the window size probably can't be changed.

2. While the pointer is a two-headed arrow, click and hold down the left mouse button.

3. Drag the mouse pointer in the direction you want to stretch or shrink the window. As you're dragging, the window size changes.

4. When the window is the size you want, release the mouse button.

Can't Resize a Window? Many applications' windows have minimum applicable sizes. So if the window doesn't budge, but the pointer continues to move, the window is as small as it can be.

CAUTION

Using Scrollbars

Scrollbars are used to display contents that extend beyond the window's current viewing area. Figure 3.2 shows a window with both horizontal and vertical scrollbars.

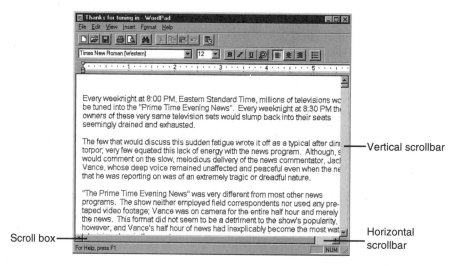

Figure 3.2 Use scrollbars to view different parts of a large document.

Here's how you use scrollbars:

- To move by a small amount, click the arrow at either end of the scrollbar that points in the direction you want to move.

- To move by a larger amount, click the open space on either side of a horizontal scroll box, or above or below a vertical scroll box.

- To move quickly through a document, drag the scroll box along the scrollbar to whatever position you choose. Many Windows programs move the contents of the window as you move the scroll box; others wait until you release the button to execute the move. Some programs provide a ScreenTip that displays the relative page number in the document as you drag the scroll box. The ScreenTip enables you to quickly scroll to the exact page you want.

Moving a Window

The title bar displays the name of the program being used by the window, as well as the name of the current active document. The supplemental function of the title bar is as a handle of sorts. To move a window onscreen, click and drag the window's title bar. When you move a window in Windows 98, the contents of the window follow your movements. If you want to switch back to the Windows 95 method (which displays only the window outline as you move), right-click the desktop, select **Properties**, click the **Effects** tab, and turn off the option to **Show Window Contents While Dragging**.

Can't Move a Maximized Window? You can't move a window that's been maximized. There's no place for it to go.

CAUTION

You can also move Active Desktop items, such as the one shown in Figure 3.3. Here's how:

1. Move the mouse pointer toward the top of the Active Desktop item. A title bar should appear.
2. Click this title bar and drag the window wherever you like.
3. Release the mouse button. The window is repositioned.

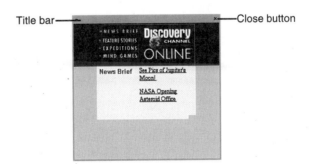

Figure 3.3 Moving an Active Desktop item is similar to moving any other window.

Arranging Windows on the Desktop

When you have more than one window open simultaneously—say, three or four—and all are pertinent to the job you're working on, stretching and shrinking all of them so that they fit precisely might be inconvenient. Thankfully, Windows 98 has a few ways for you to automatically arrange several windows without the drag-and-drop maneuver.

CAUTION

Multiple Document Windows in an Office 2000 Application Are Treated as Separate Program Windows If you are running one of the Office 2000 applications such as Word or Excel and use the cascade or tile commands, you will find that the various documents you opened in the application are treated as separate program windows and are arranged with the other windows present on the desktop.

Cascading Windows

All the windows in a cascaded set overlap one another so that the upper and left borders are always visible—not unlike the way you would fan out a hand of gin rummy. Figure 3.4 shows a set of five cascaded windows.

Figure 3.4 Cascaded windows overlap each other.

Here is how you can make Windows automatically cascade all open windows on the desktop:

1. Right-click an empty portion of the taskbar.

2. From the shortcut menu that appears, select **Cascade Windows**. The windows on the desktop are arranged in an overlapping, cascaded group. Remember, however, that the Cascade Windows command doesn't affect Active Desktop items.

Tiling Windows

By comparison, each window in a tiled set (whether the tiling is horizontal or vertical) doesn't overlap in any way. Figure 3.5 shows four windows, this time tiled horizontally.

If you have a large number of windows open, tiling can result in rather small windows.

Figure 3.5   Tiled windows do not overlap.

To tile your open windows, right-click an empty portion of the taskbar and select either **Tile Windows Horizontally** or **Tile Windows Vertically**. The Tile commands don't affect Active Desktop items.

Closing a Window

When you're finished with a window, you should close it. This frees up system resources for other activity. Closing a program's window is the same as exiting the program.

Some windows immediately close when you click the Close (×) button; other windows—especially programs with open files—might ask if you want to save information before closing the window. This gives you an opportunity to save your open files before exiting the program. You can also close a window from the taskbar; just right-click the program's button and select **Close**.

You can also close Active Desktop items by clicking their Close buttons (refer to Figure 3.3). Closing an Active Desktop item temporarily removes it from the Active Desktop. To get the window back, follow these steps:

1. Right-click the desktop and select **Active Desktop** from the shortcut menu.
2. Select **Customize My Desktop**. This opens the Display Properties dialog box.
3. Click the **Web** tab, and then click in the box in front of the Active Desktop item you want to redisplay. A check mark appears in front of the window you select.
4. Click **OK**. The item reappears on the desktop.

In this lesson, you learned the various parts of a window. You also learned how to move, resize, minimize, maximize, and close a window. In addition, you learned how to operate scrollbars and how to arrange windows on the Windows 98 Desktop. In the next lesson, you learn how to use toolbars and select menu commands.

Using Toolbars, Menus, and Dialog Boxes

In this lesson, you learn how to use the toolbars that come with many Windows programs, how to create new toolbars, how to select commands from menus, and how to select options using all types of dialog box elements, such as text boxes, list boxes, option buttons, and check boxes.

Using Windows Toolbars

Not every Windows program uses a toolbar, but many do. A *toolbar* is a collection of buttons that represent commands. When you click a button, the associated command is executed by the computer program. Keep in mind as you work with a particular toolbar that the way the toolbar functions is determined by the actual purpose of the utility or application you are working with. For instance, Windows Explorer and My Computer are tools designed to help you see what is on your computer and to assist you in managing files, folders, and drives. The toolbar buttons available in these types of programs reflect the various commands available in the program. The toolbars that you find in Windows applications such as Microsoft Word, Excel, or Access are geared to the commands available in those particular applications. For instance, Word provides you with several toolbars that relate to working with text and graphics.

Windows Toolbars Versus Windows Applications Toolbars Don't assume that every toolbar operates in the same manner. The ins and out of a particular toolbar are related to the application in which it appears.

CAUTION

In this lesson, you'll learn how to use the toolbars included with many Windows programs, such as Windows Explorer and My Computer. If you want to learn how to use some of the other Windows 98 toolbars, see Lesson 2, "Navigating the Windows 98 Desktop."

Because toolbars offer access to the most common commands, you will find that toolbars in different programs contain some of the same buttons. Figure 4.1 shows Windows Explorer and its toolbars.

The Cut button is a commonly available toolbar button. It enables you to select an item and then cut (or remove) it from the current location. In the Explorer window, this toolbar button may be used to remove files or folders. You can then go to a new location (a different folder or drive) and use the Paste button to paste the items into the new location. Cut and Paste not only manipulate items found in the Explorer window, but they are found on Office applications' toolbars as well, where they are used to cut and move text or other items within the application.

Clipboard A tool provided by Windows that holds any cut or copied text temporarily in memory so you can paste it to another location, document, or application.

As you work with different toolbars, you may find that a toolbar button behaves somewhat differently, depending on which toolbar it is chosen from. Toolbar buttons also vary in how they help you execute a particular command. In some cases, you must select an item first (such as text, a graphic, and so on) and then invoke the command by clicking the appropriate button. The Cut command is a good example of this type of toolbar button. Other toolbar buttons are used to turn a particular attribute or feature on or off. For instance, in a program such as Word or Excel, you may want to bold new text that you are typing in a document or worksheet. You must click the **Bold** button on the toolbar first (to turn on the bold), and then type the appropriate text. To turn off the bold, click the **Bold** button a second time. The Explorer toolbar also provides buttons that help you navigate the drives, files, and folders on your computer. Click the **Back** button once, for instance, and you are taken back to the previous folder (or Web page) that you were perusing. A drop-down arrow to the right of the button enables you to access a drop-down list that shows the most recent folders (or Web pages) in Windows Explorer's history buffer (the folders or Web pages you most recently visited). You then choose the directory you want to move back to by clicking it in the list.

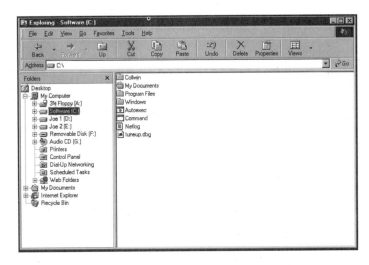

Figure 4.1 Windows Explorer and its toolbars.

As you can see, the buttons on the toolbar vary in how they relate to a particular command. The Cut button, clicked once, invokes an actual command, but the Back button not only can be clicked to return to the previous location (executing a command), but it also provides a drop-down list that gives you a list of options (folders that you could return to). Other buttons, such as the Address box, don't enable you to invoke a particular command with a click, but offer you a drop-down list box from which you can make choices. When you select the Address box, you are provided with the hierarchy of the current folder. You choose the folder you want Windows Explorer to move to by clicking it.

Common Toolbars

Many Windows programs, such as Windows Explorer and My Computer, use the same standard toolbars: Standard buttons, Address boxes, and Links. The purpose of the buttons on each of these toolbars is explained in Tables 4.1, 4.2, and 4.3. (Note the Links toolbar buttons link to Web pages, and the contents of the toolbar may vary.)

Table 4.1 The Standard Buttons Toolbar

Button	Name	Purpose
Back	Back	Displays the previous folder.
Forward	Forward	Redisplays the folder viewed immediately before the Back button was pressed.
Up	Up	Moves up in the folder hierarchy.
Cut	Cut	Moves the selected file or folder to the Clipboard.
Copy	Copy	Copies the selected file or folder to the Windows Clipboard.
Paste	Paste	Pastes the contents of the Clipboard into the current folder.
Undo	Undo	Undoes the last action.
Delete	Delete	Removes the selected file or folder.

CAUTION

Understand the Ramifications of Delete Deleting items inadvertently can be one of the scariest and most counterproductive tasks that you perform in Windows. Windows 98 (and Windows 95) provides you with a second chance if you've deleted something that you realize you really needed. See Lesson 8, "Managing Files and Folders," for tips and information on deleting files and folders and using the Recycle Bin to recover them.

	Properties	Displays the properties of the selected file or folder.
	Views	Enables you to select the way in which files and folders are displayed.

TIP   **New Clipboard Functions**   In the past, the Windows toolbar could hold only one item at a time, and this item (file, folder, text, graphic, whatever) would be displaced the next time you used Copy or Cut. Office 2000 has updated the concept of the Clipboard and provides a new Clipboard that can hold multiple items. See Lesson 3, "Editing Documents," in the Word section of this book for a look at the new, improved Office 2000 Clipboard.

Table 4.2 The Address Toolbar

Name	Purpose
Address	Enables you to enter or select the address of the folder you want to view.

Table 4.3 The Links Toolbar

Name	Purpose
Best of the Web	Displays links to some of the best pages on the Web in categories such as Business, Computers & Internet, and Entertainment.
Channel Guide	Displays a listing of channels to which you can subscribe.
Customize Links	Displays a page that shows you how to customize the Links bar.
Free HotMail	Displays the hotmail from the Microsoft (a free Web-based email service) Web page.
Internet Start	Displays the Microsoft Internet Start Web page.
Microsoft	Displays the Microsoft Web page.
Internet Explorer	Displays the Internet News Explorer Web page.
Windows Update	Displays the Windows Update Web page.

Moving Toolbars

Not all toolbars in Windows can be moved from place to place. A clear signal that a toolbar can be moved is the presence of a handle on the toolbar—a single ridge near the left edge of the toolbar (or the top edge of a vertical toolbar). You might want to move a toolbar to a different location for short-term convenience. For example, you might want to move a toolbar into the work area to make it easier to work with a particular bit of text or a graphic image.

Here are some general methods for moving toolbars:

- To move a toolbar into the work area, click an empty space on the toolbar (a space not occupied by a button) and drag the toolbar wherever you like. Typically, the toolbar then takes on a more rectangular shape, which you can adjust as you might adjust the size of a window.

- To move a toolbar under another toolbar, drag the toolbar by its handle until you have it positioned under the toolbar that will appear above the toolbar you are moving. Release the mouse button and the toolbar appears in its new location. This enables you to "stack" toolbars so that all their commands are in the same relative area of the window, making it easier for you to click commands with your mouse.

- To adjust the boundaries between two toolbars that are horizontally adjacent to each other (for example, the Address and the Links toolbars in Windows Explorer), position the pointer between the two toolbars so that it changes to a black, two-headed arrow. Then drag the border in either direction.

- To swap positions between two toolbars sharing the same line (such as the Address and Standard toolbars in Windows Explorer), click the handle of one of the toolbars. Then drag the handle just past the handle of the other toolbar.

Creating a Toolbar

You can create your own toolbar by selecting **New Toolbar** from the Toolbars menu. Select the folder whose contents you want to display as a toolbar, or type in the address of a Web page, and then click **OK**. If you select a folder, a toolbar with icons representing the contents of that folder appears. You can then click an icon for a document, for example, to open that document with its associated program. If you enter the full address of a Web page, starting with **http://**, that page appears on the toolbar itself. To see the page, drag the toolbar off the taskbar.

Keep in mind that the toolbars you create are only temporary. If you close one, you'll need to create it again to get it back. If, however, you keep the toolbar open, it remains open and active even if you restart your PC.

Using Menus

The menu bar is a Windows program's chief device for presenting you with its available commands. Menu bars are typically placed just under the title bar in a window (see Figure 4.2), although some programs enable you to move the menu bar to a different position onscreen (Windows Explorer is one such example).

When you open one of the menus on a menu bar, a list of related commands drops down. You can select any of the commands on the menu. Here are a few examples of what typically happens when you choose a command:

- Most commands are executed by the program immediately after you select them. Cut and Paste are classic examples. When you select them, the program carries them out without delay and without asking you anything else.

- If a command has a right-pointing arrow, a submenu (a pull-down or cascading menu) with additional choices appears. For example, in Windows Explorer, if you open the **File** menu and select **New**, a sub-menu appears. The submenu in this case lists various objects, such as folder, shortcut, or bitmap image, that you select to answer the question "New *what*?"

- If a command is followed by an ellipsis (...), the command requires more information from you before it can be executed. Thus, when you select such a command, a dialog box appears with several options from which you can choose or a blank text box that you use to type in the appropriate information. For example, in Microsoft Word, you select the **File** menu and then select **Open**. The Open dialog box appears, enabling you to set parameters related to the opening of a file into the Word application window.

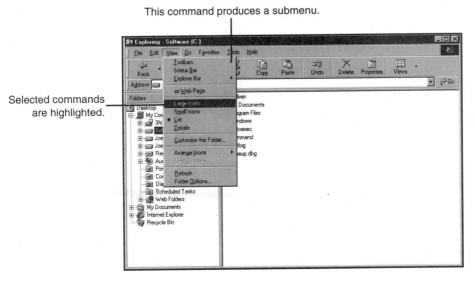

Figure 4.2 Select an item on the menu bar to open the menu.

Choosing Menu Commands

To select a menu command with the mouse, you click one of the menus so that it drops down, and then you click one of the menu commands. If a submenu is involved, it appears to the right of that command (or to its left if there's no room to the right). At that point, just move the mouse pointer onto the submenu and click the command you want.

If you don't see the command you need, you can move the pointer to another menu category, without clicking, to have its menu drop down instead. Or, if you change your mind altogether, you can click anywhere outside the menu area to close it. Office 2000 also provides a new twist related to the commands that you find on the menus provided in Windows applications such as Word and Excel. The new adaptive menus show you the commands that you've used most recently. The toolbars in the Office 2000 applications also use this same strategy for providing you the commands you use most often. For more about the adaptive menus found in the Office 2000 applications, see Lesson 1 in the Word, Excel, or PowerPoint sections of this book.

To use the keyboard to select a menu command, press and hold down the **Alt** key as you press the underlined letter of the menu command. For example, to open the File menu, press **Alt+F**. After the menu is opened, press the underlined letter of the command you want. For example, to select the **Open** command from the File menu, press the letter **O**. You can also press the **up-arrow** and **down-arrow** keys on the keyboard to move the highlight line to the command you want, and then press **Enter** to select the command.

Using Shortcut Keys

Many commands provide another method for you to select them with the keyboard—without having to open the menu first. For example, the common commands Cut, Copy, and Paste have shortcut key combinations that you can press to select them: **Ctrl+X** for Cut, **Ctrl+C** for Copy, and **Ctrl+V** for Paste. To issue the Copy command, for example, press and hold down the **Ctrl** key as you press the letter **C**. Shortcut keys are listed next to their corresponding commands on menus. For a complete listing of the shortcut keys associated with the program you're using, consult that program's Help system, under the terms shortcut keys or keyboard shortcuts.

Using Shortcut Menus

As an alternative to using the menu bar or toolbars, you can issue commands to many Windows programs by using a right-click method, which brings up a shortcut menu. With this method, you point to the item onscreen that is the object of your command—for instance, a highlighted sentence or a row of cells in a worksheet. You then right-click. If the program supports shortcut menus, one pops up onscreen, as shown in Figure 4.3. From there, you can click a menu command to issue that command to the program, or click outside the menu area to close it.

Figure 4.3 Right-click to access common commands with a shortcut menu.

You will find that the great thing about the shortcut menus is that the commands that are provided relate directly to the item on which you right-clicked.

 Default Command On the shortcut menu shown in Figure 4.3, the command **Open** is bold. This means that **Open** is the default command—the command that will be executed if you double-click this object (in this case, the Windows folder).

Shortcut menus are available outside applications, as well. For example, if you right-click the desktop, a shortcut menu appears from which you can select commands that arrange your icons, switch you between the Active and Classic Desktops, and change the desktop's properties.

When a Dialog Box Appears

A dialog box typically appears after you select a menu command marked with an ellipsis (…). The ellipsis tells you that the command you selected requires more information from you before the program can execute it. The dialog box provides the means by which you can tell the program which options to use with the command.

41

Selecting Dialog Box Options

Windows uses a handful of standardized elements that work the same way for any dialog box you encounter. To move through the objects in the dialog box using the keyboard, press the **Tab** key. To back up to the previous element, press **Shift+Tab**. Here's a listing of the elements and how to use them:

- **Text box**—A box into which you type text, such as the name of a file, the key number on the back of the Windows 98 CD, or a password to access the Windows 98 Desktop. To replace existing text, drag over it to highlight the text, and then type what you want to replace it. Figure 4.4 shows a dialog box that contains a text box control.

- **List box**—A rectangle that lists several choices, the way a menu does. If more entries are in the list than can be shown at once, a scrollbar appears along the right and/or bottom edges. For a list box that supports multiple choices (such as a file list), to select more than one item at a time, hold down the **Ctrl** key and click each item. You can also hold down the **Shift** key and click the first and last items in a range to select all the items in that range. A list box is shown in Figure 4.4.

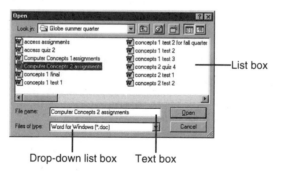

Figure 4.4 A text box and a list box both provide options.

- **Drop-down list box**—A variation of a standard list box; the list is revealed when you click the down arrow. To select something from the list, click it. You can't change or add to the items in the list. Figure 4.4 shows a drop-down list box.

- **Combo box**—A hybrid of the text box and list box. The top line of a combo box works like a regular text box, featuring a blinking cursor. You may type a choice into this box or choose one from the list below the text line. A combo box supports only one choice at a time.

- **Check box**—Click the box next to the item you select to place a check mark in the box. Check boxes may be grouped together. If they are, you can choose more than one option. Figure 4.5 shows a group of check boxes.

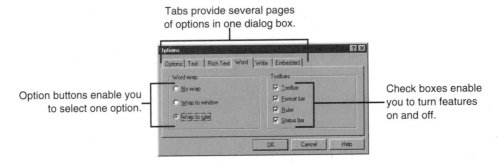

Tabs provide several pages of options in one dialog box.

Option buttons enable you to select one option.

Check boxes enable you to turn features on and off.

Figure 4.5 This tabbed dialog box features check boxes and option buttons.

- **Option button**—This type of button is also known as a radio button. You click the circle or label beside an item to select it. Unlike the check box, you can choose only one option in the set. Figure 4.5 shows a dialog box with a set of option buttons.

- **Command button**—The most common button in a dialog box. The OK and Cancel buttons are command buttons. After making selections in a dialog box, click **OK** to issue the command with the options you selected, or click **Cancel** to not issue the command. Most dialog boxes have a default command button, which is generally the OK button. Press **Enter** at any time while the dialog box is active to activate the default command button; press **Esc** to close the dialog box without issuing the command.

TIP   **Keyboard Shortcut** If a dialog box contains controls whose labels have certain letters underlined, holding down the **Alt** key while pressing the underlined letter immediately moves the focus to the labeled element and selects (or deselects) it. To immediately reverse the selection, press the spacebar or the underlined letter.

Tabbed Dialog Boxes

Many dialog boxes have *tabs* that compartmentalize information into multiple pages. A tabbed dialog box looks a little like a file drawer where you would thumb through the tabs sticking up to find the folder you want. A tabbed dialog box is shown in Figure 4.5.

To change pages in a dialog box, click one of the tabs. Using the keyboard, press **Ctrl+Tab** to move to the next tabbed page in the sequence, or press **Shift+Ctrl+Tab** to move to the previous one.

In this lesson, you learned how commands are issued to Windows programs. You studied the operation and arrangement of toolbars onscreen. You examined the role played by the menu bar in all Windows applications, and you were introduced to the shortcut menu, which provides a convenient alternative to the menu bar. Finally, you learned how to make selections in a dialog box using the most common elements: text boxes, list boxes, drop-down list boxes, check boxes, option buttons, and command buttons. In the next lesson, you learn how to access Help.

Using Windows 98 Help

In this lesson, you learn about the Windows 98 Help system, including the Contents, Index, Search, and What's This features.

Getting Help in Windows 98

Help is always close at hand in Windows. When you press **F1** while viewing files from My Computer or Windows Explorer, or when another Windows program is active, the Help system is activated. The Help window that appears usually coincides with whatever action you were performing. You can also activate Help by clicking the **Start** button and selecting the **Help** command.

The Help window appears with two panes. The left one is used to navigate Help, and the right one displays information on a help topic. Also included are five buttons:

- **Hide/Show**—Hides (or redisplays) the left Help pane (the Table of Contents).
- **Back**—Returns you to a previously viewed Help page.
- **Forward**—After you've used Back, this button redisplays a previously viewed Help page.
- **Options**—Displays a list of Help options.
- **Web Help**—Provides a link to Microsoft Help on the World Wide Web.

TIP **Quick Dialog Help** In addition to pressing F1 to activate Help, most dialog boxes feature a Help button that you can click to get help in choosing the options in that dialog box.

In this lesson, you'll learn how to navigate the Windows 98 Help system to locate the information you're looking for.

Help consists of three parts:

- **Contents**—A table of contents you can browse through
- **Index**—Similar to the index in the back of a book
- **Search**—Enables you to search the Help system for a particular word or phrase

You'll learn how to use these three features in this lesson.

Do You Use the Web Style Desktop? Help is written for the Classic Style Desktop, in which you double-click a filename to open it. If you use the Web Style Desktop, take note that when Help tells you to double-click, you'll need to single-click.

CAUTION

Using the Contents Feature

Using the Contents feature is similar to using the table of contents in a book. Here you'll find the major categories of Help. If you select a topic, it expands to display subtopics from which you can choose, as shown in Figure 5.1. The book icons represent topics and subtopics; document icons represent actual Help pages. Selecting a document displays information on that topic in the right pane.

Follow these steps to use the Contents feature:

1. If needed, press **F1** or click the **Start** button and select **Help** to display the Help dialog box.
2. Click a topic that has a book icon, and it expands to reveal subtopics.
3. If needed, click a subtopic to expand it.
4. Click a topic that has a document icon to display its contents in the right pane of the Help window (see Figure 5.1).
5. Depending on the topic, you may be presented with the following options in the right pane of the Help window:

- **Click Here**—Click this link to launch related applications and wizards.
- **Related Topics**—If you click this link, a small window appears from which you can select a related topic.

6. To close Help, click the **Close** (×) button in the upper-right corner of the Windows Help window.

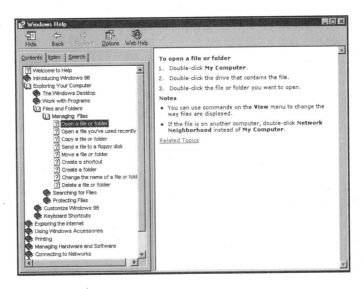

Figure 5.1 When you select a topic, it expands.

Using the Index Feature

Help's Index feature is similar to an index you might find at the back of a book. To use it, you type in the word you're looking for, and it appears in a list, as shown in Figure 5.2. Select a topic from this list, and it's displayed in the right pane.

Follow these steps to use the Index feature:

1. Type a word or phrase in the text box. As you type, Help searches the Index for a match, so you might not actually have to type the entire word you're looking for.

2. Double-click the topic in the list that you would like to display. The topic appears in the right pane. (A dialog box of selections may appear; if so, select the subtopic you want and click **Display**.)

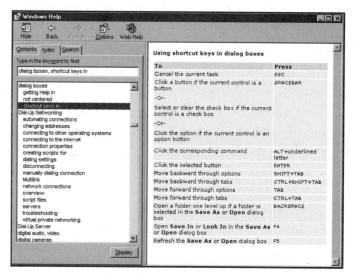

Figure 5.2 Use the Index to locate a specific word or phrase.

Using the Search Feature

Another avenue for getting help in Windows is the Search tab. Although the Index feature enables you to search for a match to a word or phrase within a particular topic heading, Search enables you to search for a match within the contents of the topic itself, expanding the possibility of locating a match. If you have trouble finding the help you need using the Contents and Index features, try using Search. Follow these steps:

1. Type the word or phrase you want to search for in the text box, and then press **Enter** or click **List Topics**.
2. A list of topics is displayed. When you double-click a topic, it appears in the right pane, as shown in Figure 5.3.

Using the What's This? Feature

Many Windows dialog boxes include a What's This? button (often a question mark symbol). After you click it, you can click any option within that dialog box and view a description of it. This feature lets you quickly decide which options within a dialog box you want to use.

When a dialog box includes a What's This? button (shown in Figure 5.4), follow these steps to use the What's This? feature:

1. Click the **What's This?** button. The mouse pointer changes to show a question mark along side it.

2. Click any option within the dialog box. A description of that option appears.

3. After reading the description, click anywhere in the dialog box to remove the dialog box from the screen and turn off the What's This? feature.

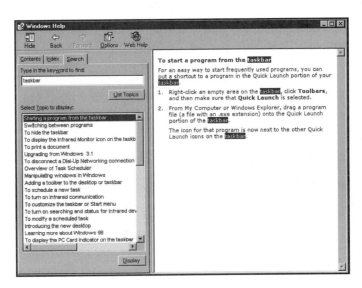

Figure 5.3 Search enables you to search the text within Help topics.

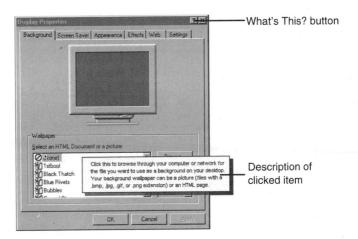

Figure 5.4 The What's This? feature helps you identify which dialog box options you might want to use.

TIP **Quick Description** To display a description of a particular part of the current dialog box, just right-click the item and select **What's This?** from the shortcut menu that appears.

Using Web Help

For users who have access to the Internet, Windows 98 includes a Web Update feature that can be used for Windows 98 support.

The Windows Update site, like many Web sites, may change its content frequently, so the specific steps to follow and the selections available at the time you access the site may vary from those described in this lesson.

To locate answers to common Windows questions, follow these general steps:

1. Connect to the Internet if you are not already connected.
2. Click the **Start** button and select **Windows Update**. Internet Explorer starts and connects to Microsoft's Update site.
3. Click **Support**. You might be asked if you would like to register. Click **Yes** and follow the instructions in the Registration Wizard that appears.
4. You may see a security warning. Click **Yes** to continue.
5. Select a topic that interests you from the **My Search Is About** list.
6. Type the keywords for the item you want help with in the **I Want to Search For** text box.
7. Click **Find** to start the search.

You might also want to click the **How To** or the **Glossary** links displayed on the Web page. They provide additional help; How To describes how to search for information, and Glossary defines terms used in Windows.

In this lesson, you learned how to use the Windows Help system, including its Contents, Index, Search, and What's This? features. In the next lesson, you learn how to customize the appearance of Windows 98 to suit your needs.

Customizing the Appearance of Windows 98

In this lesson, you learn various ways in which you can customize Windows 98 to fit your needs.

Arranging Icons on the Desktop

The icons on your Windows Desktop provide quick access to the programs you use most often. However, if the icons are placed on the desktop haphazardly, it becomes difficult for you to find a particular icon when you need it.

One way to arrange the Windows Desktop is to manually drag each icon to a position. But to arrange the icons on the desktop in neat rows quickly and automatically, follow these steps:

1. Right-click the desktop and select **Arrange Icons** from the shortcut menu.

2. Select a command from the cascading menu that appears:

   - **By Name** arranges the icons alphabetically.
   - **By Type** arranges the icons by their type (their filename extension).
   - **By Size** arranges the icons by the size of their files.
   - **By Date** arranges icons by their file date (the date they were created or changed).
   - **AutoArrange** arranges icons automatically. If you add an icon to the desktop, it's automatically arranged with the other icons in neat rows.

You can also arrange your icons in neat rows by right-clicking the desktop and selecting **Line Up Icons**.

> **TIP** **Icons and the Active Desktop**   You can completely remove icons from the Active Desktop and avoid the problem of having to arrange them all the time. Right-click the desktop and select **Properties**. Click the **Effects** tab and select the **Hide Icons When the Desktop Is Viewed as a Web Page** option.

Changing the Desktop's Wallpaper

Initially, the desktop is a solid teal color. Instead of a plain color, you can use a graphic as wallpaper to cover the background. In some cases, depending on where you bought your computer or whether Windows 98 was already installed on the computer, your desktop may already be outfitted with wallpaper. These graphic files are bitmap images with the .bmp file extension. You can choose a Windows graphic or use one of your own. You can create your own wallpaper files in the Windows Paint program or some other drawing application. Just make sure you save the file as a bitmap picture with the extension .bmp. (If you want to change the color of your desktop background but you don't want to use a graphic or a pattern, see the section "Changing Windows's Colors.")

> **TERM** **Bitmap Image**   A bitmap image is a picture with a specific graphic format that stores the image as a series of pixels or dots.

You can also choose a pattern to use as your Windows background (but you can't use both a wallpaper graphic and a pattern). You can even edit these patterns to customize the look of your desktop, if you like.

Follow these steps to select a graphic for your Windows Desktop:

1. Right-click the desktop and select **Properties** from the shortcut menu that appears. The Display Properties dialog box, shown in Figure 6.1, appears.

2. Make sure the **Background** tab on the Display Properties dialog box is selected. Scroll through the **Wallpaper** list and select a particular graphic. A preview of your selection appears at the top of the dialog box.

   If you'd like to use your own graphic as a background (perhaps something you've downloaded from the Internet), click **Browse** and select the graphic from the list. You can use .bmp, .gif, and even .jpg images.

3. To determine how the wallpaper will sit on the desktop, click the **Display** drop-down list and choose one of the following options:

- **Tile** arranges the graphic across the desktop in neat rows.
- **Center** places the graphic image in the center of the desktop.
- **Stretch** does just what the name implies: It stretches the graphic image so that it fills the entire desktop.

4. To place the graphic on your desktop, click **Apply**. This enables you to test the look and feel of the wallpaper without closing the Display Properties dialog box. If you don't like the result, select another graphic from the list and click **Apply** again.

5. When you're satisfied with your selection, click **OK**.

CAUTION

Big Wallpaper File Slowing Down Your System?   Because it takes computer resources to display your wallpaper on the desktop, you may find that your system just doesn't run as fast when it constantly has to draw that big picture (yes, every time you maximize or minimize a window, the desktop is refreshed, meaning the wallpaper is redrawn). If you find that your system seems slower, remove the wallpaper or go with a pattern instead.

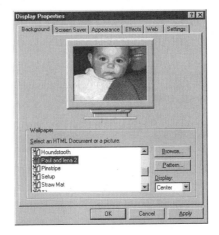

Figure 6.1   Wallpaper your desktop with a nice graphic.

Follow these steps to select a pattern for your Windows Desktop:

1. Right-click the desktop and select Properties. The Display **Properties** dialog box appears (refer to Figure 6.1).

2. If you were previously using a graphic (wallpaper) for your background, select **None** from the Wallpaper list.

3. Click the **Pattern** button. The Pattern dialog box, shown in Figure 6.2, appears.

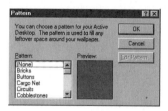

Figure 6.2   You can use a pattern as a background for your desktop.

4. Select a pattern from the list. To edit the pattern, click **Edit Pattern**. Otherwise, skip to step 6.

5. Click within the **Pattern** box to change the pattern one pixel at a time (a pixel is one dot). You can give your variation a new name by typing that name in the **Name** text box. Naming your new pattern makes it available to you in the future so that you don't have to modify one of the default patterns if you switch to a new pattern and then want to switch back to the previous, custom pattern. When you're through, click **Change** to save your changes. Then click **Done** to return to the Pattern dialog box.

6. In the Pattern dialog box, click **OK**.

7. To test the pattern on your desktop, click **Apply**. If you don't like the result, follow steps 3 through 6 to select another pattern, and click **Apply** again.

8. When you're satisfied with your selection, click **OK**.

Adding a Screen Saver

Screen savers originated a number of years ago when it was necessary to keep the image on the monitor active or risk the possibility of a static image being permanently burned onto the screen (kind of like a tattoo). Although recent monitor technology has negated the need for screen savers as a preventative measure, they are still a great form of cheap entertainment; you will find that screen savers are still quite popular and provide you with a way to liven up your screen when you aren't at your desk (and potentially hide your work from casual observers).

CAUTION **Have an Energy Saving Monitor?** Newer monitors have a feature that enables them to automatically turn themselves off after so many minutes of inactivity. So if you've set up a screen saver on your computer, even that will halt activity when the monitor's power-saving features take over.

Several screen savers come with Windows 98 (and Windows 95). You can also purchase any number of screen savers, or download a very large (and free) number of screen savers from various sites on the World Wide Web.

To turn on the Windows 98 screen saver, follow these steps:

1. Right-click the desktop and select **Properties** from the shortcut menu. The Display Properties dialog box appears.

2. Click the **Screen Saver** tab. The Screen Saver page appears, as shown in Figure 6.3.

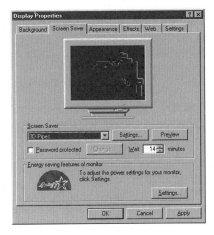

Figure 6.3 Windows 98 offers several screen savers from which you can choose.

3. Select the screen saver you want to use; just click the **Screen Saver** drop-down arrow and scroll through the list. A preview of the selected screen saver appears at the top of the dialog box in the mini-monitor.

4. In the **Wait** box, use the click arrows or enter the number of minutes of inactivity you want Windows to wait before initiating the screen saver.

5. Some screen savers have settings that you can change related to the particular screen saver. Click **Settings** to access the options available

(for instance, the Scrolling Marquee screen saver enables you to change the text that appears on the screen, along with its size and color). Make your changes for the particular screen saver, and then click **OK** to return to the Display Properties dialog box.

6. If you want to protect your PC from unauthorized use when you're away from your desk, click the **Password Protected** check box and then click the **Change** button; enter a password, and then click **OK**. You then have to enter this password to gain access to your system whenever the screen saver is initialized.

7. When you've completed selecting and setting your screen saver, click **OK**.

 TIP   To save energy when your PC is not in use, you can have your monitor (and the hard disks) put themselves into "suspended animation" (see your computer's documentation to see whether your computer and monitor embrace these power management features). To access the Power Management options, follow steps 1 and 2 of the previous steps to open the Display Properties dialog box and then the Screen Saver tab. In the **Energy Saving Features of Monitor** section of the dialog box, click the **Settings** button. After you set the Power Management options, they will function whether or not you use a screen saver.

Changing Colors in Windows

Windows uses a particular color scheme by default. This color scheme determines the color of the title bars of active and inactive windows, the color of the desktop, the style of the window text, the size and spacing of icons, and so on. You can select a different color scheme entirely, or change only the colors of individual elements. Here's what to do:

1. Right-click the desktop and select **Properties**. The Display Properties dialog box appears.

2. Click the **Appearance** tab (see Figure 6.4).

3. Click the **Scheme** drop-down list and select a color scheme. A preview of the scheme appears at the top of the dialog box.

4. If you want, you can change the color and style of individual Windows elements. Click the **Item** drop-down list and select the element you wish to change. Then select the new color using the **Color** drop-down box. You can preview your color scheme on the desktop and any open windows present

on the desktop by clicking the **Apply** button. If you don't like what you see, change the color options and then click **Apply** again.

5. When you're through making selections, click **OK**.

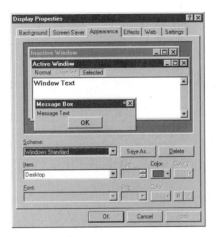

Figure 6.4 Customize the appearance of Windows in the Appearance tab.

Changing the Icons Display

When you first install Windows 98, your desktop has several icons for basic Windows items, such as My Computer and the Recycle Bin. You can change these icons if you want. In addition to changing the icons on the desktop, you can also elect to show larger icons and to display those icons using the entire spectrum of colors available to your monitor.

TIP **More Space Required?** If you want to adjust the amount of space between icons, do so with the Appearance tab, as explained in the previous section.

To change the icon options, follow these steps:

1. Right-click the desktop and select **Properties**. The Display Properties dialog box appears.

2. Click the **Effects** tab. The desktop icon options reside on this particular tab (see Figure 6.5).

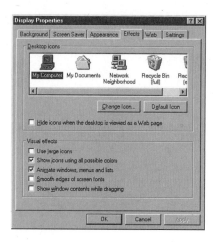

Figure 6.5 Visual options are available on the Effects tab.

3. To change one of the desktop icons, click it in the dialog box and then click **Change Icon**. Windows opens a file of default icons from which you can choose. Select one and click **OK**. (If you have another icon file you want to use instead, click **Browse** to select the file first.)

4. If you want to use large icons, or if you want to display your icons using all possible colors, select those options.

5. When you're finished, click **OK**. Your new icons (or a change of icon size) appear on the Windows Desktop.

TIP   Hide Those Icons If you use the Active Desktop and want to hide the icons from view, right-click the desktop and select **Properties** from the shortcut menu. Click the **Effects** tab and select the option **Hide Icons When the Desktop Is Viewed as a Web Page**.

Changing Screen Resolution

Screen resolution settings are identified by the number of pixels (or dots) used horizontally and vertically. For example, 640×480 resolution uses 640 pixels horizontally and 480 pixels vertically. The 640×480 resolution is typically the lowest you can use. In addition to the number of pixels, you can control the range of colors your monitor uses. The more colors, the better the display of certain graphics, but this takes up more video memory.

For Office 2000, Go with 800×600 Unless you have a monitor with a viewing space of less than 14 inches on the diagonal, you will probably want to set your screen resolution at 800×600. This optimizes the size of your application windows and provides you with the best working environment for the Office 2000 applications.

CAUTION

To change your screen resolution, follow these steps:

1. Right-click the desktop and select **Properties**. The Display Properties dialog box appears.

2. Click the **Settings** tab, shown in Figure 6.6.

3. To change to a higher resolution, drag the **Screen Area** slider (on the right side of the dialog box) toward **More**. To switch to a lower resolution, drag the slider toward **Less**. As you move the slider in either direction, you will see the actual resolution (under the slider bar) that you have selected.

4. When you have completed your resolution selection, click **Apply**. This enables you to get a quick preview of the new settings.

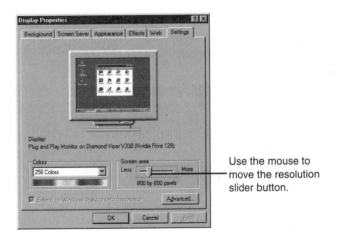

Use the mouse to move the resolution slider button.

Figure 6.6 Changing the resolution affects how items are displayed onscreen.

5. Click **OK** when you've made your final selection.

TIP **Change Often?** If you change your screen resolution often, you can place an icon on the taskbar for fast access to the Display Properties dialog box. To place an icon on the taskbar, click the **Advanced Properties** button and select the **Show Settings Icon on Task Bar** option.

When you use a higher resolution, the images might become clearer, but your icons and text become smaller. This is because with more pixels onscreen, the relative size of each pixel is smaller. To compensate for this, you can choose the **Large Fonts** option—just click the **Advanced** button on the **Settings** tab of the Display Properties dialog box. This opens the Properties dialog box for your video card. Use the **Font** drop-down box on the **General** tab of this dialog box to edit the settings for font size. And remember that you can also return to the Display Properties dialog box and select the **Effects** tab. On the Effects tab, you can change the size of the desktop icons so that they match the larger font size you chose using the Advanced options.

Changing the Number of Screen Colors

You can also manipulate the number of colors that are used for your display. The more colors you use, the better screen images and graphics appear.

CAUTION

Slower Performance   Older, slower computers can sometimes suffer a performance hit if you select the maximum number or a high number of colors. As with other settings, however, such as resolution, you can change your color settings and then give them a trial run to see whether your computer seems to be running slower.

The number of colors available for your system is dictated by the graphics card that is installed in your computer. Most newer systems support a wide variety of color possibilities. You often have the option of selecting from 16 colors all the way up to 16 million colors.

To set the number of screen colors, follow these steps:

1. Right-click the desktop and select **Properties**. The Display Properties dialog box appears.

2. Click the **Settings** tab.

3. Click the **Colors** drop-down box arrow and select the number of colors for your display (see Figure 6.7).

4. A Compatibility Warning dialog box appears, letting you know that changing the number of colors may cause some programs to run improperly. At this point, you can choose to **Go with the New Settings and**

Restart the Computer or **Apply the New Settings Without Restarting**
(select your choice using the appropriate option button). After you've
made your selection, click **OK**.

Figure 6.7   You can choose the number of colors used by your display.

**Some Software Requires a Certain Number of Colors to
Operate**   This is particularly true of many games and graphics programs.
Check the box or documentation that came with the software to determine the
optimal setting for number of colors.

CAUTION

If you chose to restart the computer, Windows 98 shuts down and your system
is restarted. The new color scheme will be available after the system restarts
Windows. If you chose to apply the colors without restarting, your system will
seem to hiccup slightly (the screen will go black for just a second), and the new
screen colors will be in force. If you find that your system runs slower or that
you would like to change the number of colors, follow the steps outlined above.

In this lesson, you learned how to customize Windows by arranging icons,
changing the background, selecting a screen saver, changing colors, changing
how icons are displayed, and selecting a different screen resolution. In the next
lesson, you learn to work with drives, folders, and files in the Windows environment.

Working with Drives, Folders, and Files

In this lesson, you learn various ways to manage, view, and sort your files, folders, and disk drives using both My Computer and Windows Explorer.

Understanding Drives, Folders, and Files

Most computers come with at least two disk drives: the hard disk drive and the floppy disk drive. The hard disk drive provides large-capacity storage for your programs and the data files you create. Windows itself is also stored on the hard disk drive. The floppy disk drive enables you to transfer small amounts of data from one computer to another easily.

The drives are assigned letters so that the computer can tell them apart. Typically, the hard disk is drive C: and the floppy disk drive is A:. Your PC might have more than one hard disk, or the hard disk might be divided into separate partitions. If so, the additional drives are labeled D:, E:, and so on. If your PC has more than one floppy disk drive, it is labeled B:. If your PC has a CD-ROM drive, it's assigned the first available drive letter, such as D: or E:.

Typically, a new folder is created for each program you install on the hard disk. You can create additional folders to organize your data into manageable units, just as you might organize your work papers into various folders within your file cabinet.

Files are placed into each folder, just as you might place individual pieces of paper into a file folder. Two basic file types exist: program files (files that are used to run an application) and data files (files that contain data created by an application). You can mix both types within a folder if you want.

Filenames under Windows 98 can contain up to 255 characters, with a three-character extension. Although you can't use some characters (/ \ ; * ? > < |), this still gives you a fair amount of freedom in assigning your files names that will help you later identify their purpose, such as "Sales for 4th Quarter 1997." Note that filenames can include letters, numbers, and also spaces.

Extension   A file's extension identifies its purpose. For example, a filename that ends with the extension .txt contains only text. A filename that ends in .exe is a program file, and a filename that ends in .bmp is a bitmap graphic file. Many other file types exist, but you don't need to learn them because Windows specifies the type of file in the Type column in both My Computer and Explorer.

Naming Restrictions   If you still use old DOS programs, you'll have to restrict the names for the files you create with those programs to eight characters or less (no spaces). These older programs don't recognize the longer filenames used by Windows 98. You should also restrict the names you give to the folders you use with those programs to eight characters or less.

Using My Computer

Windows 98 offers two programs with which you can view your files, folders, and drives: My Computer and Windows Explorer. Both are remarkably similar, as you'll soon see. My Computer is shown in Figure 7.1.

As you'll learn in upcoming lessons, you use both My Computer and Windows Explorer in the same way:

- To start My Computer, double-click its icon on the desktop.
- To display the contents of a drive or folder, double-click the appropriate icon in the My Computer window. A new window opens, displaying the contents of the drive or folder you selected.
- To jump back to the previous window (typically a drive or the parent folder of the currently selected folder—the parent is the folder in which the current folder resides), click the **Up** button.

- You can also move from folder to folder or to a different drive by selecting it from the Address drop-down list box. Select the **Address** drop-down arrow and select the drive or folder you wish to view.

- To return to a recently displayed folder (in its own window), open the **File** menu and select the folder from the list near the bottom of the menu.

- To refresh the display (for example, if you switch disks in a drive and you want to display the contents of the new disk), press **F5** or select the **View** menu and choose **Refresh**.

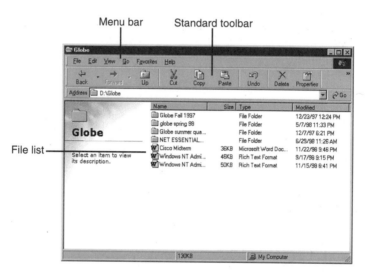

Figure 7.1   You can view your files, folders, and drives with My Computer.

You will find that My Computer and the other tool for viewing and manipulating folders and files in windows—the Windows Explorer—enable you to do pretty much the same things (locate files, copy files, create new folders, and so on). But they are quite different in the way they operate. My Computer opens a new window each time you double-click a drive or folder icon, and My Computer does not include a complete folder list (called the All Folders list) in a separate panel on the left as Explorer does. You will also find that Windows Explorer does all its work in one application window, and it displays drives and folders in a tree structure. Folders, inside of drives, are depicted as branching limbs.

TIP **Close All Those My Computer Windows with One Click** To close all the windows that you opened as you've worked with My Computer to locate a folder or file, hold down the **Shift** key on the keyboard and then click the **Close** (×) button of the last window you opened. All the open windows close.

Using Windows Explorer

On first inspection, Windows Explorer looks a lot like My Computer, as you can see from Figure 7.2. However, Explorer contains the All Folders list, which supplies an expandable (and collapsible) view of the drives and folders contained on your computer. Explorer also provides you with a great search tool—the Find command—that makes it easy for you to locate folders and files. You'll learn how to search for files and folders in the next lesson.

To use Explorer, follow these steps:

1. To start Explorer, open the **Start** menu, select **Programs**, and then select **Windows Explorer**.

 TIP **Start Explorer with a Right-Click** You can also quickly start Windows Explorer by right-clicking the **My Computer** icon. Select **Explore** from the shortcut menu that appears.

2. From the **All Folders** list (on the left side of the Explorer window), select a folder or file to view by clicking it.

3. If a folder in the All Folders list is preceded by a plus sign, it contains subfolders. To display them, click the **plus** sign. To hide them again, click the **minus** sign that appears. You are, in effect, expanding (with the plus) and collapsing (with the minus) the folder tree of your computer.

4. To view the contents of any folder in the All Folders list, click the folder; its contents a Windows Explorerppear in the right pane of the Explorer window.

5. If you want to change the size of either of the panes in the Explorer window, place your mouse on the vertical bar that divides them and drag it to a new position.

Address toolbar   Standard toolbar

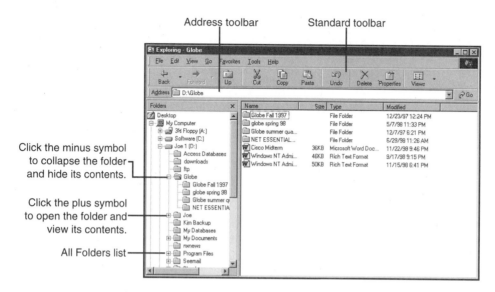

Click the minus symbol
to collapse the folder
and hide its contents.

Click the plus symbol
to open the folder and
view its contents.

All Folders list

Figure 7.2 Windows Explorer enables you to view and work with files, folders, and drives.

TIP   Faster Exploration If you have a Windows keyboard with a key that shows the Windows logo, then you can use a shortcut to launch the Windows Explorer. Press and hold down the **Windows** key (much like the Shift or Ctrl keys), and then press the **E** key and release both keys.

Understanding Web Style Versus Classic Style

If you use the Active Desktop, you might be interested in using the Web style option within My Computer and Explorer. With Web style, the purpose of clicking and double-clicking is changed. Instead of clicking to select a file, you simply point to it. And instead of double-clicking to open a file, you click it. This change affects not only Explorer, but My Computer and the desktop, as well.

TIP   Install Internet Explorer 5 to Take Advantage of the Active Desktop in Windows 95 To download and install Microsoft Internet Explorer 5 from Microsoft's Web site, go to www.microsoft.com and then click the download link to find the download page for the most recent version of Internet Explorer.

In addition, if you change to Web style and then use My Computer, each folder you open is displayed in the same window instead of separate windows. If you want to use Web style's single-click method for selecting and opening folders and files, but want to retain the use of multiple windows in My Computer, then use the Custom option, as explained in the tip later in this lesson.

To change to Web style:

1. Select the **View** menu, and then select **Folder Options**.
2. Click the **General** tab. On the General tab, select the option button for the **Web Style**.

To complicate matters somewhat, you can also set up Explorer and My Computer to view folders as Web pages. Each subfolder and file are shown as icons, as shown in Figure 7.3. To display a folder in Web view, select the **Views** button drop-down arrow and select **As Web Page**.

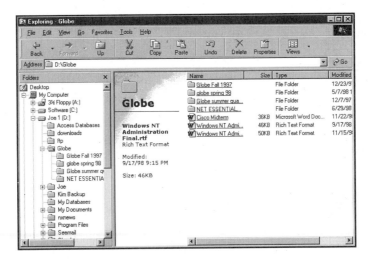

Figure 7.3 In Web style, point at a file to view a description. To open the file, click it once as you would a link to any Web page.

Here are some tips on using Web style:

- To open a subfolder, you click it, just as you might click a link within a Web page.
- To select a file, point to it. A description of the file appears.
- You can browse the Web using Explorer or My Computer. Simply type the address of the page you want to view in the **Address** list box.

If you don't want to use Web style, you can select Classic style, which provides you with the more typical environment of having to double-click items you wish to open or display.

TIP   **I Want It My Way!**   When you select the Custom option on the General tab, you can choose the options to use with the style you selected, such as single-clicking or double-clicking, and the opening of a new window when you view a folder.

Changing the Look and Feel of Windows Explorer

As you've already seen, My Computer and Windows Explorer are remarkably similar. All tasks can be performed in either program (unless noted). However, for clarity, you will see only Windows Explorer in the following figures.

The main difference between the My Computer and Windows Explorer displays is the presence of the All Folders list in Explorer (see Figure 7.4). You can easily remove this list to provide more room for the file listing by opening the **View** menu and selecting **Explorer bar,** and then selecting **None**. Or you can simply click the **Close** button (the ×) at the top of the All Folders list.

If you want to display the All Folders list but you would like it to take up less room, you can resize the All Folders panel by dragging the bar that separates it from the file list.

Not in My Computer!   You can't display the All Folders panel in My Computer. It is strictly a Windows Explorer option.

CAUTION

Changing the File List Display

In Figure 7.4, files are displayed using large icons. This is just one of many ways in which you can list your files. To change the File List display, open the **View** menu and select the view option you want: **Large Icons**, **Small Icons**, **List**, or **Details** (which provides the file's name, size, type, and date of last modification, as shown in Figure 7.5). The current option appears with a dot next to it on the View menu.

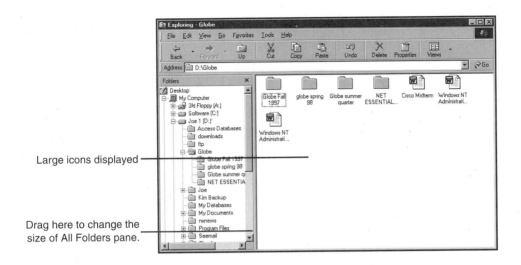

Large icons displayed

Drag here to change the size of All Folders pane.

Figure 7.4 The All Folders list provides quick access to your folders.

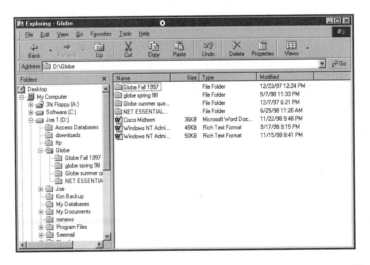

Figure 7.5 The Details view provides information about each item on the File List.

TIP **Quick View** If the Standard Buttons toolbar is displayed, you can use its Views button to change views. Click the **Views** button's down arrow and select the file list view you want. (If the Standard Buttons toolbar isn't displayed, see the section "Working with Toolbars" later in this chapter for help.)

Normally, file extensions such as .doc, .txt, .bat, and so on do not appear in the file list. If you want to see the extensions, open the **View** menu, select **Folder Options**, and click the **View** tab in the Folder Options dialog box. Then click the **Hide File Extensions for Known File Types** option to deselect it (this removes the check mark next to the option). To display hidden files (system files such as WIN.ini, AUTOEXEC.bat, and so on), click the **Show All Files** option; its check mark is removed, turning off this view option, as well.

Sorting Files by Name, Type, Size, or Date

As shown in Figure 7.4, files are displayed in alphabetical order, with folders appearing at the top of the file list. To change the order of the list, follow these steps:

1. Select the **View** menu, and then select **Arrange Icons**.

2. Select the sort option you want to use from the cascading menu that appears: **By Name**, **By Type**, **By Size**, or **By Date**.

- **By Name** arranges the icons alphabetically.
- **By Type** arranges the icons by their type (their filename extension).
- **By Size** arranges the icons by the size of their files.
- **By Date** arranges icons by their file date (the date they were created or changed).

3. If you've selected either the Large Icons or Small Icons view (click **View** and then select **Large Icons** or **Small Icons**), you are also given the AutoArrange option on the Arrange Icons cascading menu. Click **AutoArrange** to quickly line up the icons shown in the right pane of the Explorer window.

 TIP **Fast Arrangement** If you're using the Details view, you can quickly sort the file list by any column by clicking that column's header. For example, click the **Modified** header to sort the files by date.

Replacing the All Folders List

In Windows 98 and Windows 95 where Internet Explorer 5 has been installed, you can replace the All Folders list with other Explorer bar panels:

- **Search** displays a Search page that enables you to search the Internet. You'll learn more about this in Lesson 10, "Using Internet Explorer 5.0, " when we discuss Internet Explorer 5.

- **Favorites** displays a list of your favorite Internet sites. You add to this list just as you would within Internet Explorer.

- **History** displays a list of previous Internet sites you've visited. To visit a site, click it, and it's displayed in the file list window. The History list is displayed in Figure 7.5.

- **Channels** displays a list of channels you can subscribe to. See Lesson 9, "Subscribing to Channels and Working Offline," for more information.

 TIP **Web Pages in Explorer?** In Windows 98, both My Computer and Explorer can be used as Web browsers of sorts. With the help of the Explorer bar panels such as Search, Favorites, and History, you can quickly display your favorite Internet sites within the Explorer or the My Computer window.

To display the Explorer bar panels in either My Computer or Explorer, select the **View** menu and then point at **Explorer bar**. Then select the panel you want to display from the cascading menu that appears (remember, you cannot display the All Folders list in My Computer, but you can display any of the others listed here).

Previewing Files

You can preview the contents of a file by right-clicking it, then selecting Quick View from the shortcut menu. You can use this technique to view graphics files, Word document files, Excel worksheet files, and many other file types.

If you're viewing the folder as a Web page and you select a file, it is automatically previewed in the left panel. For example, if you select a graphics file, the graphic is displayed in the left panel, along with other file information such as the file size and date of last modification.

Working with Toolbars

Both My Computer and Explorer come with several toolbars that enable you to work with your files more easily. Initially, the Standard Buttons toolbar is displayed, along with the Address and Links toolbars, as shown in Figure 7.6.

To display a toolbar, follow these steps:

1. Open the **View** menu and select **Toolbars**.

2. Select the toolbar you want to display from the cascading menu (currently displayed toolbars have a check mark next to them):

- **Standard Buttons**—This toolbar provides file management commands such as copying and deleting. You'll learn the purpose of each of these buttons later in this lesson.

- **Address**—This toolbar enables you to type in an Internet address for display in the file list area. You can also select local addresses (such as a different drive) from the Address list.

- **Links**—This toolbar provides quick access to popular locations on the Internet, such as Microsoft's home page.

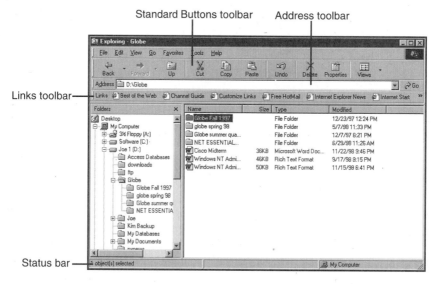

Figure 7.6   Toolbars provide quick access to common commands.

TIP **No Words** To display only icons on the Standard Buttons toolbar (instead of icons and text), open the **View** menu, select **Toolbars**, and then select **Text Labels**.

To use a toolbar, click the button that represents the command you want to execute. To use the **Address toolbar**, click its drop-down arrow (on the far right of the text box), and type the address of the site you want to view or select an address from the drop-down list.

To avoid crowding the toolbars on one line, you can display one toolbar under another. Click the tool-bar's grab handle and drag it to its new location.

The Standard Buttons Toolbar

The Standard Buttons toolbar appears in both Explorer and My Computer. Table 7.1 lists each button and its purpose. For more information on the Windows toolbars and how to use them, see Lesson 4, "Using Toolbars, Menus, and Dialog Boxes."

Table 7.1 The Buttons on the Standard Buttons Toolbar

Button	Name	Purpose
Back	Back	Redisplays a previously displayed folder.
Forward	Forward	After you use Back, this button displays the original folder.
Up	Up	Moves up one level in the folder hierarchy.
Cut	Cut	Moves the selected file or folder to the Clipboard.
Copy	Copy	Copies the selected file or folder.
Paste	Paste	Copies the file or folder from the Clipboard to the current location.

continues

Table 7.1 Continued

Button	Name	Purpose
Undo	Undo	Undoes the last action.
Delete	Delete	Deletes the selected file or folder.
Properties	Properties	Displays the properties of the selected file or folder.
Views	Views	Lets you change the file list display.

In this lesson, you were introduced to both My Computer and Explorer. You learned how to use Explorer to view and sort your files and folders and how to customize its display. You also learned the differences between Web style and Classic style. In the next lesson, you learn how to delete, copy, and move your files and folders.

Managing Files and Folders

In this lesson, you learn how to create, delete, rename,
and find files and folders. Also you'll learn how to copyand move files and folders.

Creating a Folder

Windows 98 provides a My Documents folder for your data files (this folder is created when you install Windows 98 or 95 on your computer), but you might prefer to organize your files by creating subfolders within the My Documents folder. Alternatively, you might want to create your own folders somewhere else on your hard drive. Open Windows Explorer (select the **Start** button, then point at **Programs**, then select **Windows Explorer**) or double-click the **My Computer** icon to open the My Computer window. Either of these folder-and-file-management tools can be used to create a new folder. Here's how to create the new folder:

1. Select the drive where you want to create the new folder. If the new folder will be a subfolder in a particular folder, double-click the parent folder to open it. For example, double-click the **My Documents** folder to create a subfolder inside it.

2. Select the **File** menu, and then point at **New**.

3. Select **New Folder** from the cascading menu that appears. A folder is created on the current drive or in the current folder.

4. Type a name for the folder and then press **Enter**. You can give the folder any name, up to 255 characters long, including spaces.

Some Characters Can't Be Used in File Names Although Windows 98 and 95 provide you with the capability to create long file-names that can include spaces, some characters are still considered illegal. You can't use the following characters: \ / : * ? " < > |.

Deleting a File or Folder

When you delete a file or folder, it's placed in the Recycle Bin. This gives you a chance to reconsider your deletion and get files back that you accidentally deleted.

Insurance Policy Even with the Recycle Bin, it's still possible to lose a file. So you might want to back up your files to disks before you delete them.

To delete a file or folder, follow these steps:

1. Select the file(s) or folder(s) you want to delete.

TIP **Select More Than One File or Folder for Deletion** To select a contiguous group of files or folders, click the first item and then hold down the **Shift** key and click the last item in the group. To select noncontiguous files or folders, click the first item, and then hold down the **Ctrl** key and click subsequent items.

2. Click the **Delete** button on the Standard Buttons toolbar, or press the **Delete** key on the keyboard. The Confirm File Delete dialog box appears.

3. Click **Yes** to delete the file(s) or folder(s).

I Didn't Mean to Delete That! If you notice right away you've made a mistake deleting a file or folder, click the **Undo** button on the Standard Buttons toolbar or open the **Edit** menu and select **Undo** to restore the file. Otherwise, read the next section to learn how to retrieve your file or folder.

Emptying the Recycle Bin

After a file or folder is sent to the Recycle Bin, it stays there until you empty the Recycle Bin (or restore the file or folder to its original location). This means that files or folders placed in the Recycle Bin are not discarded when you exit Windows and shut down your system.

To retrieve a file or folder from the Recycle Bin, follow these steps:

1. Open the **Recycle Bin**, shown in Figure 8.1, by double-clicking its icon on the desktop.

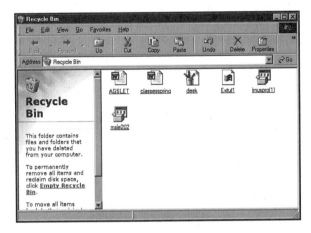

Figure 8.1 Deleted items are moved to the Recycle Bin.

2. In the Recycle Bin window, select the items (files or folders) you want to restore.

3. Select the **File** menu and select **Restore**. The items you selected are removed from the Recycle Bin and restored to their original locations on your computer.

Not All Files Can Be Restored The Recycle Bin can't be used to restore files that were deleted from a floppy disk or a removable drive such as a JAZ or ZIP disk. These files aren't moved to the Recycle Bin when you delete them from these drives. So be careful when removing files from a floppy disk or other removable drive.

CAUTION

Although it may be quite soothing to know that files and folders that you delete are actually stockpiled for you in the Recycle Bin, you should periodically empty the Recycle Bin to free up space on your hard drive. Emptying the Recycle Bin removes the already deleted files and folders completely from your computer.

To empty the Recycle Bin, follow these steps:

1. Double-click the **Recycle Bin** icon to open the Recycle Bin.

2. Select the **File** menu and select **Empty Recycle Bin**. Or, if the Recycle Bin is displayed as a Web page, click the **Empty Recycle Bin** link.

If you want to remove only one or two items from the Recycle Bin, you can. Select them from the file list and click the **Delete** button on the Standard Buttons toolbar in the Recycle Bin window, or press the **Delete** key on the keyboard.

 TIP   **Empty It Quickly**   You can actually empty the Recycle Bin without opening it. Right-click the **Recycle Bin** icon and select **Empty Recycle Bin** from the shortcut menu that appears.

Bypassing the Recycle Bin

You can delete files or folders without sending them to the Recycle Bin. This saves you the step of emptying the bin later to actually get rid of the files. However, it also removes your "safety net." And you won't have the option of restoring a file or files later. Here's what to do:

1. Select the file or folder you want to permanently delete.

2. Right-click to bring up the shortcut menu.

3. Press and hold down the **Shift** key.

4. Select **Delete** from the shortcut menu.

5. Click **Yes** to confirm. The file is deleted from your computer; it is not sent to the Recycle Bin.

You can turn off the Recycle Bin for all your file deletions if you want, although it might be dangerous to do so because you'll have no way to restore accidentally deleted files. To turn off the Recycle Bin, right-click its icon on the desktop and select **Properties** from the shortcut menu. Select the **Do Not Move Files to the Recycle Bin** option and click **OK**. Now deleted files will be completely removed from your system when you first delete them.

Renaming a File or Folder

You might want to rename a file or folder if it turns out that the original name you chose doesn't clearly identify the purpose of the file or folder. To rename a file or folder, open the Windows Explorer or the My Computer window, and then follow these steps:

1. Select the file or folder you want to rename. (You can rename only one object at a time.)

2. Select the **File** menu and select **Rename**. The file or folder name with be highlighted.

3. Type the new name for the selected file or folder and press **Enter**. Be sure to type the same file extension as before. For example, if the filename ended in .doc, be sure to use .doc at the end of the filename you type.

If you're using the Classic style option, you can actually click the file to select it, and then, after a moment, click its name. The name will be highlighted and an insertion point will appear in the filename. Type in a new name or make changes to the current name as required, and then press **Enter** when you have finished. The new filename you typed replaces the previous filename.

Searching for a File

With all the space that a large hard drive can provide, it's not that hard to misplace a file (or files). In Windows Explorer (My Computer does not provide the Find feature), you can search for your lost files by entering a complete or partial name, the date the file was created, the file type, or the file's size. You can even look for some matching text within the file.

If you're unsure of the exact spelling of a filename, you can use wildcards when entering a filename to search for. Two wildcards can be used: an asterisk (*) represents multiple characters, and a question mark (?) represents a single character in the filename. Table 10.1 lists some sample uses of wildcards.

Table 10.1 Examples of Wildcard Use

Wildcard Entered	Search Results
sales*.doc	sales95.doc, sales 96.doc, sales.97.doc
sales.*	sales.doc, sales.xls, sales.ppt
sales?.doc	sales1.doc, sales2.doc, sales3.doc
sales??.doc	sales11.doc, sales12.doc
sa*.xls	sailing.xls, sales97.xls, sam.xls
sa*.*	sailing.xls, sales97.doc, sam.ppt

To search for a file or folder, follow these steps:

1. In Explorer, open the **Tools** menu and select **Find**. Then select **Files** or **Folders** from the cascading menu that appears. The Find: All Files dialog box appears, as shown in Figure 8.2.

Type a filename for the search

Select a drive or folder

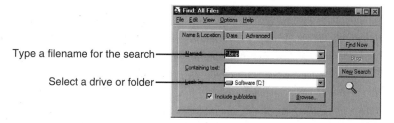

Figure 8.2 Search for a lost file in the Find: All Files dialog box.

TIP **Anywhere, Anytime** You can initiate a search without starting Explorer. Click the **Start** button and select **Find**. Then select **Files** or **Folders**.

2. Type the name you want to search for in the **Named** text box. You can use wildcards if you like. If you've searched for this file recently, you can select it from the drop-down list box.

3. If you want to search for a file that contains a particular phrase, type that phrase in the **Containing Text** text box.

4. Select the folder in which you want to search from the **Look In** drop-down list box, or click **Browse** to select it from a list in the Browse for Folder box.

To search a drive, such as drive C:, select it instead. To search an entire drive (all the folders and subfolders it contains), make sure that the **Include Subfolders** check box is selected.

5. To search for a file with a particular creation date or last modification date, click the **Date** tab. Then select the date options you want.

6. To search for a file of a particular type or size, click the **Advanced** tab and select the options you need.

7. When you're through selecting options, click **Find Now**. The results appear in a pane under the Find dialog box, as shown in Figure 8.3.

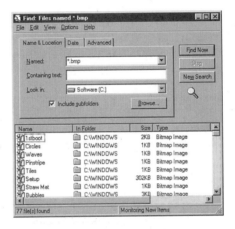

Figure 8.3   Windows lists the results of your search.

8. If you didn't get the results you wanted, you can modify your search criteria and click **Find Now** again. Or, to clear the criteria you've set and start over, click **New Search**.

You can also use the Find command to locate people and sites on the Internet. (For more information on searching the Web, see the "Searching the Web" section in Lesson 10, "Using Internet Explorer 5.0.")

Selecting Multiple Files and Folders

When you work in Windows Explorer or My Computer you will be manipulating files and performing tasks using copy, cut, and paste. Before you can copy or move a file or folder, however, you must select it. When you select a file or folder, it becomes highlighted. You can select more than one file or folder at a time to move or copy multiple files or folders in one step.

To select a file or folder, do the following:

- Click the file or folder you want to select.
- If you have the Web style option turned on, point at the file you want to select. After a second or so, the file is highlighted so that you'll know it's selected.

To select contiguous files or folders (files or folders listed next to each other; see Figure 8.4), do one of the following:

- Click the first file or folder in the list, and then press and hold the **Shift** key as you click the last file you want to select.
- If you're using the Web style option, point at the first file or folder you want to select, and then press and hold the **Shift** key as you point to the last file you want to select.

Contiguous files

Noncontiguous files

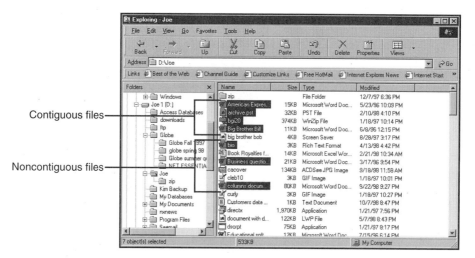

Figure 8.4   You can select multiple files or folders to copy or move.

To select noncontiguous files or folders (files or folders that are not listed next to each other; refer to Figure 8.4), do one of the following:

- Click the first file or folder you want to select, and then press and hold the **Ctrl** key as you click each additional file or folder.
- If you're using the Web style option, point at the first file or folder you want to select, and then press and hold the **Ctrl** key as you point to each additional file or folder.

Copying and Moving Files and Folders

After the files or folders you want to work with are selected, you can copy or move them as needed. When you copy a file or a folder, the original file or folder remains as is (it remains at the current location), and a copy is placed in the location you choose. Thus, two copies of the file or folder exist.

When you move a file or folder, it is removed from its original location and then placed in the new location you select. In this scenario, only one copy of the file or folder exists.

The simplest way to copy or move a file or folder is to use drag-and-drop. Basically, you drag the object to its new location and then drop it where you want it. Dragging simply means to place the mouse on an item, hold down the left mouse button, and then drag the item to a new location. When you place the item on the new folder or drive you wish it to be moved to, release the left mouse button. To drag and drop successfully, you must be able to see within the My Computer or Explorer window both the original location of the file or folder and the location to which you want to copy or move it (see Figure 8.5). If you can't see both locations, you can still copy or move your files, but you'll want to use the copy and paste or cut and paste methods, as explained later in this section.

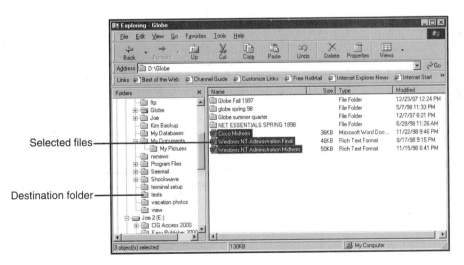

Figure 8.5 To make drag-and-drop easier, make sure both the original location and the destination location are visible.

TIP **For Easy Drag-and-Drop, Use Explorer** Because you can display the file hierarchy in Explorer's All Folders list, it's easy to arrange things so that you can see both the original and the final location of your files. So try using Explorer when attempting to drag and drop files to copy or move them.

Copying Files and Folders

To copy a file or folder from one location to another location on the same drive, follow these steps:

1. Select the file(s) or folder(s) you want to copy.

2. Start dragging the file(s) or folder(s) to its new location. Before dropping it at the new location, press and hold down the **Ctrl** key.

3. Release the mouse button first, and then the **Ctrl** key.

The reason you must hold down the Ctrl key is that you want to copy the file from the original location to a second location on the same drive. Dragging the file and dropping it without the use of the Ctrl key actually moves the file, which means the file is removed from the original location and placed in the second location. To simply move the file, follow the steps outlined without using the Ctrl key. When you drag a file that resides on a drive to another drive (for example, when you drag a file from the C: drive to the A: drive), you do not have to hold down the Ctrl key to copy the file from the original drive (C:) to the destination drive (A:). Although this may seem a little confusing at first, just remember that the Ctrl key (which begins with the letter "c," the same as copy) is required to drag and copy a file from one place to another on the same drive.

CAUTION **Already There?** If the file already exists in the location you're trying to copy it to, you'll see a warning telling you so. You can overwrite the existing file with the copy by clicking **Yes** in the warning dialog box that appears.

If the destination location for a copied file is not visible in the Explorer window, you can follow these steps to copy your files or folders:

1. Select the file(s) or folder(s) you want to copy.

2. Click the **Copy** button on the Standard Buttons toolbar, or open the **Edit** menu and select **Copy**.

3. Open the drive or folder you wish to copy the item to in the Explorer window.

4. Click the **Paste** button, or open the **Edit** menu and select **Paste**. The file is copied to the specified location.

Moving Files and Folders

To move a file or a folder from a location on one drive to a location on another drive, follow these steps:

1. Select the file(s) or folder(s) you want to move.

2. Start dragging the file(s) or folder(s) to its new location. Before dropping it at the new location, press and hold down the **Shift** key.

3. Release the mouse button first, then the **Shift** key. The file is moved from the original drive to the destination drive. If you are moving a file or folder from one location to another on the same drive, you don't have to hold down the Shift key. This use of the Shift key in moving files is similar to the use of the Ctrl key when you want to copy files, as discussed in the "Copying Files and Folders" section earlier in the lesson.

 TIP **When to Drag and Drop Using Ctrl or Shift** To move files between two locations on the same drive, drag the file to the new location. To move a file from one drive to another drive, remember to hold down the **Shift** key. To copy a file from one drive to another drive, just drag and drop. To copy a file onto a new location on that same drive, you must hold down the **Ctrl** key as you drag the file.

If the destination location is not visible in the Explorer window, you can follow these steps to move your files or folders:

1. Select the file(s) or folder(s) you want to move.

2. Click the **Cut** button on the Standard Buttons toolbar, or open the **Edit** menu and select **Cut**.

3. Select the folder or drive you want to move to.

4. Click the **Paste** button, or open the **Edit** menu and select **Paste**.

 Oops! If you copy or move the wrong files or folders, you can undo your mistake by clicking the **Undo** button on the Standard Buttons toolbar or by opening the **Edit** menu and selecting **Undo**.

CAUTION

Copying or Moving Files with a Right-Click

Although dragging and dropping using the left mouse button (and the Ctrl or Shift key when required) is a straightforward method for copying and moving files in the Windows Explorer window, you can also copy or move files using the same dragging action, but with a slight twist. You hold down the right mouse button instead of the left mouse button and drag the file or folder to a new location. Using the right-drag method requires an additional step; you must select **Move** or **Copy** from a shortcut menu that appears.

The advantage of this method is that you don't have to remember if you need to hold down the Ctrl key or the Shift key when you execute the drag. A shortcut menu enables you to select the **Move** or **Copy** option.

To copy or move a file or folder (or files and folders) with the right mouse button, follow these steps:

1. Select the files you want to move or copy in the Windows Explorer window (select the files in the right pane of the Explorer window).
2. Point to one of the selected files and press down the right mouse button.
3. Drag the files to a location shown in the All Folders list in the left pane of the Explorer window. Release the mouse button. A shortcut menu appears.
4. Select **Copy Here** or **Move Here** from the shortcut menu, as needed. The file (or files) are copied or moved to the new location you specified.

Creating Shortcuts

Rather than actually copying or moving a file into another folder, you can create a shortcut to it. A shortcut is an icon that points to the real file, wherever it might actually be. Shortcuts are used to open files and programs without having to select them from the Start menu or from their permanent location on the hard disk. You'll find most shortcuts on your desktop, although they can exist anywhere.

To create a shortcut, follow the steps in the preceding section for right-dragging: Select the file you want to create a shortcut to, click and hold down the right mouse button, and then drag the file to its final destination. When you release the mouse button, select **Create Shortcut(s) Here** from the pop-up menu that appears.

Shortcuts, by the way, appear as normal icons, except that they also have a tiny bent arrow in their bottom-left corner. This arrow tells you that the icon is a shortcut and not an actual file. Thus, you can safely delete a shortcut icon without accidentally deleting any real file.

To use your shortcut, double-click (or click) it. The program associated with that file opens automatically.

Using Send To

If you often copy files to a disk or to a particular folder, you can use the Send To menu option to perform that task more quickly. The Send To option is available in Windows Explorer and My Computer, and the command is found on either tool's File menu.

To use the Send To menu option, follow these steps:

1. Select the file(s) or folder(s) you want to send.

2. Open the **File** menu and select the **Send To** command. A list of possible destinations appears on a cascading menu.

3. Select the destination for the file(s) or folder(s) from the **Send To** menu.

The Send To menu option contains these destinations, among others, depending on how your computer is configured:

- **Floppy Drives**—Enables you to copy files to available floppy disk drives.
- **Desktop as Shortcut**—If you send a file to the desktop, it appears as a shortcut icon. You can then open the file by clicking (or double-clicking) it.
- **Mail Recipient**—Enables you to create a quick email message with the file you select attached to it.
- **My Briefcase**—Places the file in your Briefcase, for eventual transfer to your laptop PC.
- **My Documents**—Moves the file to the My Documents folder.

You can add your own destinations to the Send To menu if you wish; the best place to add destinations to Send To is the Windows Explorer. After opening Windows Explorer, double-click the drive that holds the Windows 98 (or Windows 95) software files (double-click it in the **All Folders** List on the left side of the Explorer window). This is typically your C: drive. After you open the drive, double-click the **Windows Folder** icon to open the Windows folder. You will find a **Send To** folder inside the Windows folder. Drag your destination folders into this folder (see Figure 8.6).

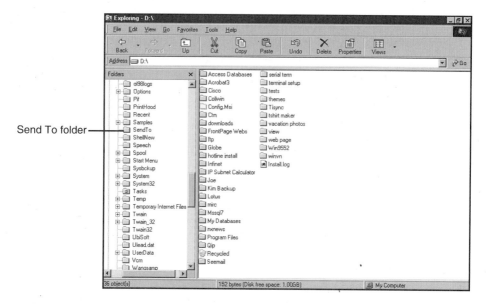

Send To folder

Figure 8.6   To add destinations to the Send To menu, open the **Send To** folder in Windows Explorer and drag new locations (folders) to the Send To folder.

To add destinations, follow these steps:

1. Select the destination you want to add. For example, select the folder you want to add to the menu.

2. Press and hold down the right mouse button as you drag the folder to the **Send To** folder (which is shown in the Windows Explorer All Folders list).

3. Select **Create Shortcut(s) Here** from the shortcut menu that appears.

The next time you click the Windows Explorer File menu and then point at Send To, your new destination shortcuts will appear on the Send To menu.

In this lesson, you learned how to create, rename, delete, and find files and folders. You also learned how to select, copy, and move files and folders. In the next lesson, you learn about some of the Windows Internet-related features, such as Internet channels and working offline.

Subscribing to Channels and Working Offline

In this lesson, you'll learn about the Web and how it fits into Windows 98. In addition, you'll learn how to display Web content on your desktop and how to customize that display to fit your needs.

Internet Basics

The Internet is a vast worldwide network of networks that connects various businesses, government offices, universities, research centers, and so on. Through the Internet, you can access data from these networks, such as scientific research, sales and product information, and travel and weather data.

You connect to the Internet through an Internet service provider (ISP). You can connect to an ISP via a modem (called a dial-up connection) or through your company's network (a direct connection).

The Internet has several "on ramps"—different software tools—that enable you to access the information on the Internet. These Internet tools include email clients, File Transfer Protocol (FTP) clients, Telnet clients, and World Wide Web browsers (such as Internet Explorer).

The World Wide Web (WWW) supports the transmission of graphics, sound, animation, and formatted text—unlike other parts of the Internet, which are strictly text based. Thus, the part of the Internet you'll visit most often will probably be the Web. To view Web pages (the documents that make up the World Wide Web), you need a Web browser. Windows 98 comes with Internet Explorer, a popular Web browser from Microsoft; however, you might want to use Netscape Communicator from Netscape Communication Corporation instead. Both are compatible with Windows 98. In Lesson 10, "Using Internet Explorer 5.0," you'll learn how to use Internet Explorer. If you decide to use Netscape Communicator, you'll find that the general Web searching techniques described in this lesson and Lesson 10 apply to it as well.

 TIP   **Office 2000 Introduces Internet Explorer 5**   Windows 98 (as of the publication of this book) ships with Internet Explorer 4. The Office 2000 software includes Internet Explorer 5, the latest version of this powerful Web browser. You will find that the browser features discussed in this chapter take advantage of the new features provided by Internet Explorer 5.

Most Web browsers (including Internet Explorer and Netscape Communicator) have components that handle the non-WWW elements of the Internet, so you won't have to install a bunch of special programs to send and receive email or visit newsgroups.

What Are Subscriptions and Channels?

Windows 98's Active Desktop (and Windows 95's Active Desktop when Internet Explorer 5 has been installed on your computer) is designed to help you quickly access information from the World Wide Web. You can access new Web content in real-time or download updated Web information at selected intervals from Web sites. Some information can be displayed on the desktop in the form of stock market tickers, sports scores, or other real-time news formats. This type of information is called *push* content because it is automatically updated by a particular source and then pushed directly to your desktop (if you maintain your online connection).

The Active Desktop also displays the Internet Explorer Channel bar, which contains a listing of Web channels. These Web channels differ from regular Web sites (which contain fairly static information), in that they typically provide information that is being updated at regular intervals. This updated information can be downloaded to your computer at specific intervals, or in a more constant fashion if you have a connection to the Internet that is online all the time. The great thing about channels is that you can also download new information to your PC from a channel and then read it offline (when you are not connected to your Internet service provider). See the section "Adding a Channel" for information on adding new channels to the Channel bar.

One way to receive updated Web content in Windows (Internet Explorer plays an important part in this process) is to subscribe to a particular Web site. This *subscription* can then be set up to automatically download the new Web content directly to your desktop in the Internet Explorer window. When the information is updated depends on options that you set when you create the subscription to a particular Web site. The main purpose of subscribing to a particular Web site is so you can then view the current content of the site offline. The content is placed on your computer so that you don't have to be connected to the Internet as you read through the information on the site.

You can subscribe to any Web page that you place in your Favorite folder when you are using Internet Explorer. You can also add Web channels to the Internet Explorer Channel bar on the Active Desktop (adding a channel to the Channel bar is, in effect, subscribing to that particular channel). Just keep in mind that regular Web sites you subscribe to don't update their content all that often. Whereas Web channels (special Web sites) are, by design, constantly updating their Web content to provide you with new information.

Pay to Play? Currently, it costs you nothing to use most channels, although that might change in the future.

CAUTION

Fox News Browser is an example of a channel to which you might subscribe by adding it to your Channel bar. It provides you with constant updates of important news stories. You can select from many kinds of channels using the Channel bar. Channels can be displayed in a full-screen window and often contain more multimedia features (sound, animation, and so on) than typical Web sites.

Some Web channels can be set up so that they provide updated information displayed as a screen saver on your computer. This is a great way to get sports scores, stock market updates, and other useful (and fun) information. These special screen savers do require that you be connected to the Internet when they are activated. They are another example of push content sent directly to your desktop. The Screen Saver option appears when you subscribe to the channel offering this service. Select it if you want to view the push content in this manner. You can also subscribe to conventional Web pages; this enables you to download and view content from the Web page offline and to be notified when the content on the page has changed. Such a page can automatically be downloaded to your system once a day (or following whatever schedule you prefer). After the page has been updated for the day, its content doesn't change until the next scheduled update takes place.

Subscribing to a Web Site

Subscribing to a Web site is straightforward. When you subscribe to a particular site, you are automating the process of downloading updated information from the site. This is particularly useful for sites that you read often, such as news sites or online magazines.

Subscribing to a Site Means Making the Content Available Offline
The term subscription is often a point of confusion when you are working with Web sites and channels. Subscribing to a regular Web site simply means that you make the content of this site available offline and download new content at periodic intervals. When you add a channel to your Channel bar, you can also set up the special channel site so that content can be viewed offline.

To subscribe to a Web site, follow these steps:

1. Connect to your Internet service provider if necessary (if you're on a corporate network, you are probably constantly connected to the Internet). Double-click the **Internet Explorer** icon on the Windows Desktop. The Explorer window opens.

2. Go to the Web site that you want to subscribe to (you can type the Web site address into the **Address** box or use the **Search** button on the Explorer toolbar to locate the Web site).

3. After the site is open in the Internet Explorer window, select the **Favorites** menu, then select **Add to Favorites**. The Add Favorite dialog box appears (see Figure 9.1).

4. Click the **Make Available Offline** check box in the Add Favorite dialog box.

5. To customize the subscription settings for this site, click the **Customize** button. The Offline Favorite Wizard appears. The first screen of the wizard explains how the wizard helps you set up the site for offline viewing. After reading the information, click **Next** to continue.

6. The next screen of the Offline Favorite Wizard asks if you want any links contained on the subscribed site to also be available for viewing offline (see Figure 9.2). Click the **Yes** or **No** option button, then click **Next** to continue.

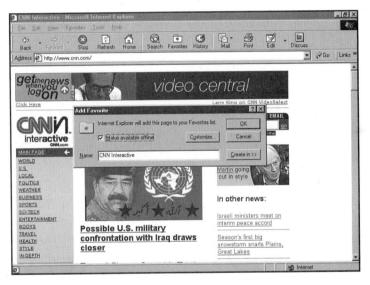

Figure 9.1   To subscribe to a Web site, open the Web site in Internet Explorer and then add it to your Favorites list.

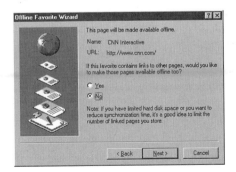

Figure 9.2   You have the option of making links provided on the subscribed, favorite site also available for offline viewing.

CAUTION

Downloading Web Content for Offline Viewing Takes Up Hard Drive Space   When you subscribe to a particular Web site and set up the offline viewing features, you are, in effect, asking for a lot of material to be downloaded to your hard drive. If you also select the option to have links on a subscribed site made available for offline viewing, you are adding to the amount of material that must be placed on your computer. The purpose of viewing material offline is to enable you to connect to the Internet periodically and then view the most recent material. If hard drive space is at a premium on your computer, however, you may want to connect to the Internet and view sites online, in the more typical fashion.

7. The next screen asks how you would like to synchronize this page, meaning how often you would like new content downloaded to your computer. Two selections are available (after making the appropriate selection, click **Next** to continue):

- **Only When I Choose Synchronize from the Tools Menu**— Selecting this choice means that you completely control when the new content is downloaded to your computer (updates would be performed when you select **Tools**, then **Synchronize** in the Internet Explorer window). If you choose this option, skip step 8 below.

- **I Would Like to Create a New Schedule**—This option enables you to set up a schedule that dictates when the downloading of new material (synchronization) takes place.

8. If you chose to create a new schedule, the next wizard screen enables you to set up the schedule. In the **Every** box, use the click arrows to set the number of days. In the **Time** box, set the time. You can also type a name for the scheduled update in the **Name** box (see Figure 9.3). Click **Next** to continue.

9. The last wizard screen prompts you to supply a username and password if you are subscribing to a secure Web site. If you are subscribing to a corporate Web site for your company, this may be the case. Supply the necessary information, and then click **Finish**.

10. You return to the Add Favorite dialog box. Click **OK** to complete the process.

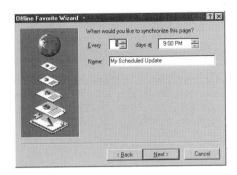

Figure 9.3 Set the day and time intervals for your subscribed Web site's synchronization download schedule.

 TIP **Subscribe to Web Sites Already on Your Favorites List** If you would like to subscribe to a Web site already on your Favorites list (meaning you want to view the content offline), click the **Favorites** button on the Explorer toolbar. The Favorites pane appears on the left side of the Explorer window. Right-click any favorite and then select **Make Available Offline**. The Offline Favorite Wizard appears; follow the steps already detailed in this section to set up the site for offline viewing.

After you've set up a site for offline viewing, its content will either be downloaded according to the synchronization schedule that you set, or you can synchronize the content by selecting **Tools**, then selecting **Synchronize**. The Items to Synchronize dialog box appears. Each site that you subscribed to appears in the Synchronization window (channels that you've set up to be viewed offline also appear). To synchronize the content of these Web sites for offline viewing, click the **Synchronize** button.

If you decide you want to remove a site from the synchronization list and no longer make it available for offline viewing, right-click the site in the **Favorites** list in the Internet Explorer window. The **Make Available Offline** menu selection will have a check mark next to it. Click this menu item to remove the check mark. The site is now no longer offline and its new content will not be downloaded when you synchronize your subscribed sites.

Adding a Channel

As already mentioned, channels are special Web sites. When you add them to your Channel bar, you make them easily accessible right from your Active Desktop. Clicking a Channel icon in the Channel bar loads the selected channel Web site into your Internet Explorer Web browser. Channels are different from regular Web sites in that they can also provide you with the option of adding Active Desktop items.

These items (such as the Discover Channel Online, the CBS Sportsline Score Center, and the Crypt Keeper Desktop component shown in Figure 9.4) can be added when you open a particular channel in the Internet Explorer (using the Channel bar or your Favorites list on the Start menu). Channels that provide this function have a special button marked **Add to Active Desktop** located somewhere on their Web pages. Click this button and the channel's Active Desktop component is added to your Windows Desktop.

Be advised that Active Desktop items (stock tickers, news update windows, and other special items) are not available for all channels that you add to the Channel bar. Some of the special content that you receive from channel sites will still be directed to your Internet Explorer Web browser when you select the particular channel on the Channel bar. Adding Active Desktop items is discussed later in this lesson in the section "Adding Active Desktop Items."

To add a channel to the Channel bar, follow these steps:

1. If needed, change to the Active Desktop by right-clicking the desktop, pointing at **Active Desktop** on the shortcut menu, and then selecting **View as Web Page**. The Internet Explorer Channel bar appears on the desktop.

2. If the Channel bar doesn't appear on your desktop, display it by right-clicking the desktop, and then pointing at **Active Desktop** on the shortcut menu that appears. Then click **Customize My Desktop**. The Display Properties dialog box appears. On the **Web** tab, click the **Internet Explorer Channel Bar** check box. To close the dialog box and return to the desktop, click **OK**.

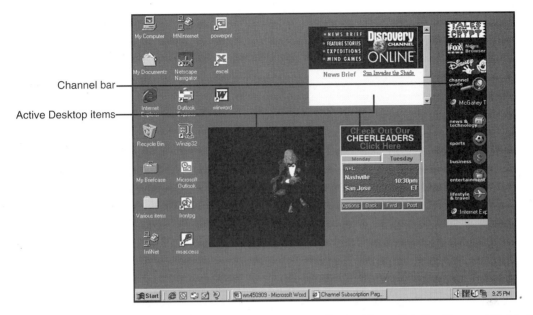

Channel bar

Active Desktop items

Figure 9.4 To add a new channel to the Channel bar, click the **Channel Guide** icon.

3. To view a list of channels and video and audio content available on the Web, click the **channel guide** icon on the Channel bar. The Internet Explorer window opens (wait a moment for the Web events Redirect screen to be cleared from the Browser window) and you are taken to the Microsoft Web Events site. This site provides you with access to various Web video and sound events that you can add to your channels list or to your favorites list (depending on the type of site that is accessed by a particular link). To view a list of sites (and channels) in a particular category, click any of the categories listed on the right side of the guide page, such as **business** (see Figure 9.5).

4. The guide page for the category that you selected appears. Each category page contains of list of Web sites. To go to a particular site click the link provided. For instance, you may choose to open the link to CNN Financial News provided on the Business category page.

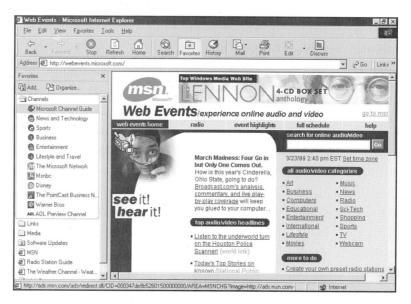

Figure 9.5 Channels providing audio and video Web content can be accessed using the Web Events category pages.

TIP **Search for Web Events and Channels** You can also search for specific Web events or channels by using the **search for online audio/video** search box found at the top of each of the Web Event category pages. Enter your search text in the search box and then click **Go**.

5. Once you've clicked a link, you are taken to a Web page for that particular channel (it appears on the right side of the Internet Explorer window (see Figure 9.6, which shows the channel page for CNN Financial news). The channel pages typically contain links to video and audio events such as live news programs or other Web media events. To add the current channel to your Channel bar, click the **Add** button on the top left of your favorites pane (see Figure 9.6).

TIP **Shop Around** You can try out the video and audio links on any of the channel pages before you actually add the site to your Channel bar. Click any of the links provided to view or hear that content.

Figure 9.6   You can quickly add Web channels to your favorite list by clicking the Add button on the Favorites pane.

6. The Add Favorites dialog box appears (the same dialog box that was used for adding a regular Web site to your list of favorites. Double click the channels folder to open it). If you want to have access to content on this channel when you are offline, remember to click the **Make Available Offline** check box. Then click **OK** to add the channel to your Favorites list (under the Channel folder) and your Channel bar.

Immediately after adding the channel to your Favorites list (and your Channel bar), you can access the site at your convenience. If you want to add more channels, click the **Back** button on the Internet Explorer toolbar to return to the category pages.

Adding Active Desktop Items

Some channels also provide special Active Desktop items that can be placed directly on the Active Desktop. Then these items, which can range from a window that displays news headings to a scoreboard that provides sports scores, update their content automatically (when you are connected to the Internet). This enables you to keep up-to-date on certain information while you work on your computer.

To add an Active Desktop item to your desktop, follow these steps:

1. Click the **channel guide** icon on the Channel bar. The Internet Explorer window opens and the Web events Redirect screen appears. Click the active desktop items link under the *Hunting around for Active Desktop components?* message. The Microsoft Active Desktop Component Web page appears.

2. Select the category of Active Desktop components you want to view such as **news**. (choose from news, sports, entertainment, travel, weather, cool utilities). A list of channels providing desktop components appears (see Figure 9.7).

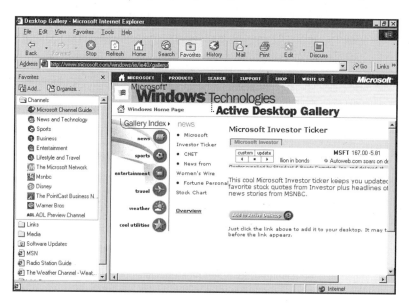

Figure 9.7   The Active Desktop Components page provides links to several categories of desktop items.

3. Click a component link (such as the **Microsoft Investor Ticker** link shown in Figure 9.7).

4. A preview of the Active Desktop item will appear in the left pane of your Browser window. To add the component to your desktop, click the **Add to Active Desktop** icon (see Figure 9.8).

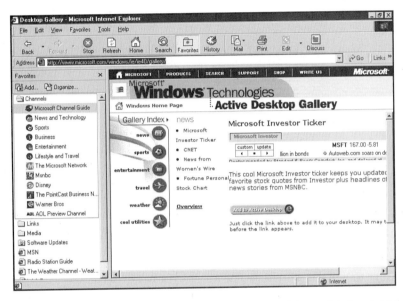

Figure 9.8   View a preview of a particular component and then click the Add to Active Desktop icon to add it to your desktop.

5. A dialog box appears, asking you if you want to add an Active Desktop item to your desktop. Click **Yes** to continue.

6. A second dialog box appears, letting you know that you've chosen to make a particular Active Desktop item (it shows the address of the channel site where the content originates) part of your Active Desktop. Click **OK**. The Synchronizing dialog box appears and synchronizes the content of the Active Desktop component.

After synchronization, the new Active Desktop item appears on your Active Desktop. Figure 9.9 shows the C/net Channel's Active Desktop component Search.com. You can search for items on the Web right from your Active Desktop.

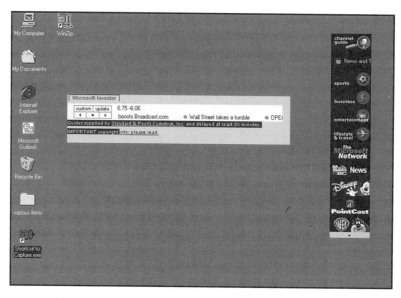

Figure 9.9 You can add any number of Active Desktop items to your Active Desktop.

Obviously, too many Active Desktop items can really clutter your desktop (as well as put a lot of demand on your Internet connection when they download new information). You can easily remove any Active Desktop item.

Right-click your desktop, and then click **Properties** on the shortcut menu that appears. The Display Properties dialog box appears. Click the **Web** tab on the dialog box. Active Desktop items that you've added to your desktop are listed on the Web tab (see Figure 9.10). Their positions on the desktop are also shown in the desktop window at the top of the dialog box (it looks like a miniature monitor).

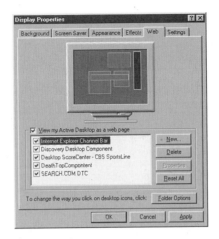

Figure 9.10 Active Desktop items that you've added to your desktop are listed on the Web tab of the Display Properties dialog box.

To remove an item from the Active Desktop, click the check box for the item. This removes the check mark from the box and also removes the item from the Active Desktop. When you have completed removing items (or adding items that you previously removed), click the **OK** button to close the dialog box. When you return to the Desktop, the items you removed will no longer be on the Desktop.

In this lesson, you learned about the Internet as it relates to the Active Desktop. You learned how to add channels and Active Desktop items to your desktop, and you learned how to subscribe to static Web pages. You also learned how to adjust schedules for updating Web content and how to remove Web items from your Active Desktop. In the next lesson, you learn how to use Internet Explorer 5 to locate and view pages on the Web.

Using Internet Explorer 5.0

*In this lesson, you set up an Internet
connection and browse the Web with Internet Explorer 5.*

Installing Explorer 5.0

Office 2000 comes with Internet Explorer 5.0 and several of its accompanying components, such as Outlook Express. During your first installation of Office 2000 from the CD-ROM, you are prompted by a dialog box to install Internet Explorer 5.0. Follow the appropriate prompts and install the software. For more information on installing Office 2000 and its components, see Appendix A, "Installing Microsoft Office 2000."

This lesson assumes you are using Internet Explorer 5.0. If you are using version 4.0, you can still do most of the same things, but the procedures are a little different in some cases.

Assembling Your Account Information

If you already have an account with an Internet service provider (ISP—the company that provides your Internet service), you need to have some information handy. Make sure you have it ready before you set up your connection in Windows. If you don't have some of this information, contact your ISP and ask.

Username and password—for example, fwempen@provider.com

Local phone number to dial—for example, 555-3948

Domain Name Server (DNS) address—for example, 349.78.33.78

Internet Protocol (IP) address—for example, 391.29.495.39

Name of incoming mail server—for example, pop.provider.com

Name of outgoing mail server—for example, smtp.provider.com

Name of news server—for example, news.provider.com

If you don't already have an account, the Internet Connection Wizard helps you set up one.

Running the Connection Wizard

The Connection Wizard creates a Dial-Up Networking connection that dials your ISP and sends the correct settings that enable you to connect to the Internet. It also configures Outlook Express, the program that manages your email and newsgroups, and Internet Explorer, the program that lets you browse the Web.

Follow these steps:

1. Select the **Start** button, and then point at **Programs** on the Startup menu that appears. On the Programs menu, point at **Internet Explorer** and then select **Connection Wizard**. The Connection Wizard starts.

2. Click the **Next** button to begin.

3. On the first screen of the Connection Wizard, choose one of the three options presented:

    - **I want to choose an Internet service provider and set up a new Internet account.** Choose this if you are starting from scratch, with no account.

    - **I want to set up a new connection on this computer to my existing Internet account using my phone line or a local area network (LAN).** Use this if you have an account but have not used it from this computer.

    - **I already have an Internet connection set up on this computer, and I do not want to change it.** Use this if you already have connected to your account with this computer.

4. After making your selection, click **Next**.

Depending on which of these options you choose, the Wizard takes different paths at this point. If you choose the first option, it asks for the first three digits of your phone number and your area code, and dials a special number that downloads a list of service providers with a local access number in your area. (This is called the Microsoft Internet Referral Service.)

CAUTION

Not the Only Providers   The companies shown by the Microsoft Internet Referral Service (the MIRS, not the IRS) have paid a fee to be listed. There might be a good, economical service provider in your area that is not listed there. It might pay to shop around before selecting one of these providers.

If you choose the second option in step 3, you are prompted for information about how you plan to connect (phone line or LAN), and it walks you through creating the appropriate dial-up connection if needed. Just follow the prompts, entering any information for which it asks. When asked about Advanced settings, most people should answer **No**. Answer **Yes** only if your service provider has given you something you need to type when you connect or a specific IP or DNS address that you need to use every time. (Don't worry about what those are; just ask your service provider if you need to use them. The Advanced options let you fill in this information.)

If you choose the third option in step 3, the Connection Wizard checks to make sure that the existing connection has all the right stuff, and then quickly ushers you out of the program.

Using the Internet Explorer 5.0 Browser

To use Internet Explorer to browse the Internet, you must have your Internet connection started. (In other words, your modem or LAN must be connecting you.) You can either start this connection before or after you start Internet Explorer. (With a LAN, you are probably always connected, so you don't need to worry about establishing the connection.)

To dial the connection first (assuming you are connecting with a modem), follow these steps:

1. Double-click the **My Computer** icon on the desktop. And then in the My Computer window, double-click **Dial-Up Networking**.

2. In the Dial-Up Networking window that appears, you see the Make New Connection icon and an icon for your dial-up connection. Double-click the icon for your dial-up connection to your service provider. A dialog box appears showing the ID/password, phone number, and modem to use (see Figure 10.1).

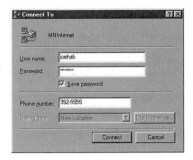

Figure 10.1 You can establish your connection first through Dial-Up Networking.

3. Enter any missing information (for example, your password) and click **Connect**.

4. Wait until the connection dialog box disappears and a connection icon appears next to the clock on the taskbar tray (the far right of the taskbar), indicating the connection is active.

5. Double-click the **Internet Explorer** icon on your desktop to open Internet Explorer.

To open Internet Explorer before establishing your Internet connection, follow these steps:

1. Click the **Internet Explorer** icon on your desktop (or the **Internet** icon if you have that one instead). If you are not connected, a warning appears to that effect.

CAUTION

IE 5 Not Set Up to Dial? If you see a warning box that says Internet Explorer cannot open the Internet site, and a blank page loads in the browser, perhaps you do not have Internet Explorer configured to start a dial-up connection when you launch Explorer. In IE 5, select the **Tools** menu, and then click **Internet Options**. In the Internet Options dialog box that appears, click the **Connection** tab and make sure the **Dial Default Connection When Needed** check box is selected and that your **Internet Dial In** account is shown and selected in the text box directly above the check box.

2. Click **Connect** in the warning box. The Dial-Up Connection dialog box appears. It might start dialing automatically; if it doesn't, fill in any missing information, and then click **Connect**.

When the connection is made, Internet Explorer begins loading the Microsoft home page immediately (see Figure 10.2).

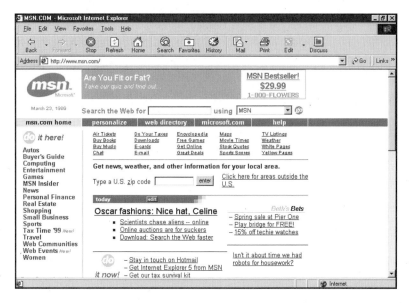

Figure 10.2 After you're connected to the Internet, Internet Explorer can be launched to open your home page.

Browsing with Hyperlinks

On most Web pages, one or more pictures or bits of underlined text are hyperlinks. This means you can click them to jump to other pages. For example, in Figure 10.3, on the Macmillan Publishing home page, almost everything you see is a hyperlink. Both text and graphics can serve as hyperlinks. The mouse pointer turns into a hand when it's over a hyperlink.

Going to a Specific Site

If, for example, someone gives you a Web address (a URL, or Uniform Resource Locator) to investigate, you can type it directly in the Address box located at the top of the screen. In Figure 10.3, for example, you would click and drag to select the current address (http://www.mcp.com) and type over it. Try http://www.microsoft.com if you don't have another address handy.

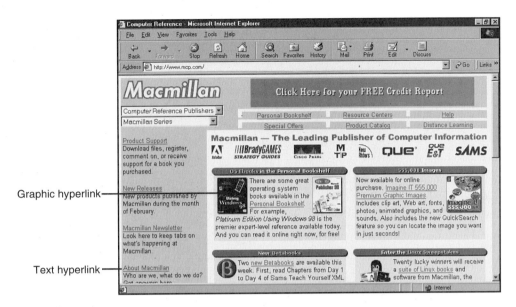

Graphic hyperlink

Text hyperlink

Figure 10.3 Click hyperlinks to jump to related pages.

Using Back and Forward

When you are on one page and then you click a hyperlink to move to another page, you are going "forward." The Forward button is unavailable because the browser doesn't know where you might be going next. You can return to the last page you previously visited by clicking the Back button. When you click Back, the Forward button becomes available because it knows what comes next after the page you are now seeing; you can click Forward to return forward.

Notice that both the Back and Forward buttons have down-pointing arrows. Click one of these arrows to open a drop-down list of all the places you have been during this session, and click the one you want. For instance, to return to a site you visited recently, click the **Back** drop-down arrow and select a site, as shown in Figure 10.4.

TIP **Getting Back Home** You can quickly return to your home page by clicking the **Home** button on the Internet Explorer toolbar.

109

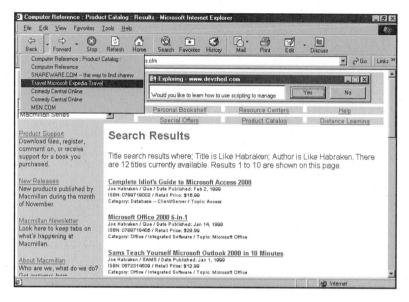

Figure 10.4 Use the Back (or Forward) drop-down list to scan and jump to previously visited pages.

If you want to set your own home page for Internet Explorer, open that page in the Internet Explorer window (any site you like). Then follow these steps:

1. Select the **Tools** menu, and then select **Internet Options**.
2. On the **General** tab of the Internet Options dialog box, the address of the current Web page appears in the Address box. To make the site your home page, click the **Use Current** button.
3. When you have completed making your selection, click **OK** to close the Internet Options dialog box.

Searching for Sites

Finding specific information on the Web can be a real struggle (especially considering the number of sites available on the Web); however, a number of search engines exist that can help you find exactly what you are looking for. These search engines vary slightly in how they operate and have names like HotBot, Infoseek, and Lycos. The great thing about Internet Explorer is that you can access a number of the best search engines available on the Web using the same Search command.

Click the **Search** button on the Explorer toolbar. A Search panel appears, as shown in Figure 10.5.

Several option buttons appear at the top of the Search panel and enable you to select the type of item you are looking for, such as a particular Web site, a person's address, information on a company, and so on. Click the appropriate option button. After selecting the type of item you want to search for, you then need to enter the actual search parameters.

When you are searching for a Web site, enter a keyword or keywords that pertain to the subject you are looking for. If you are searching for a person, provide information like the person's last name, the city they live in, and so on. You enter the search criteria (keywords or other information) in the various text boxes that appear in the middle of the Search panel. Figure 10.5 shows a search that has been set up to find Web sites that contain information on *computer books*. After you have entered your search parameters, click the **Search** button.

 TIP **Different Search Engines** Narrow your search by choosing a search engine specific to information you seek.

Internet Explorer plugs you into the most popular search engines on the Web. If you want to set the search engines that are used by the Search panel in the Explorer window, click the **Customize** icon (the second icon from the right) at the top of the Search panel. A Customize Search Settings page opens. The page is broken down into five parts: Find a Web Page, Find a Person's Address, Find a Company, and Find a Map. Scroll down to the search type for which you want to select the search engines. For instance, in the Find a Web Page section, you can select between nine different search engines to conduct this type of search by selecting some or all of the check boxes provided for the various search engines. After you have customized your search options, go ahead and run your search in the Search panel.

The results of your search appear as hyperlinks in the Search panel. To view the Web site associated with a particular hyperlink, click the link. The Web page appears in the Internet Explorer window, as shown in Figure 10.6.

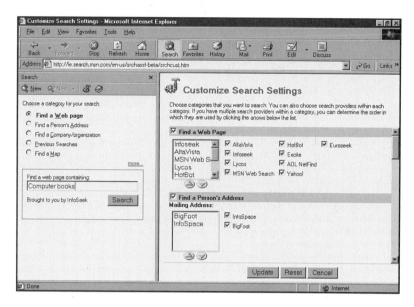

Figure 10.5 Select a search category using the option buttons, and then type your search parameters in the Search panel.

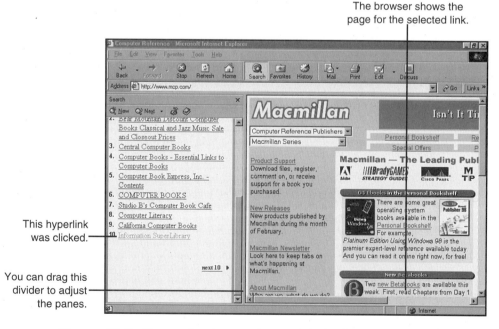

The browser shows the page for the selected link.

This hyperlink was clicked.

You can drag this divider to adjust the panes.

Figure 10.6 The results of a search appear in the Search panel. Click any link to view the associated Web page.

If you find that your search didn't provide the results you anticipated, run the search again using different keywords (click the **New** button at the top of the Search panel to clear the panel and start a new search). Or click the **Customize** button at the top of the Search panel and change the search engine that was used for the search.

Accessing Your Computer Through Internet Explorer

You can also use Internet Explorer to view the various files and folders found on your computer. Internet Explorer actually provides you with the same kind of functionality for viewing and manipulating files you have when you use Windows Explorer or My Computer (for discussions of Windows Explorer and My Computer, see Lesson 7 "Working with Drives, Folders, and Files").

To view your computer's drives and folders in the Internet Explorer window, click the **View** menu and then point at **Explorer Bar**. Select **Folders** from the cascading menu that appears. The Folders list appears on the left side of the Internet Explorer window. To view the contents of a particular drive or folder, click the drive or folder in the Folders list (see Figure 10.7).

Figure 10.7 You can view the drives and folders on your computer in the Internet Explorer window.

You can also copy and move files or folders on your computer using Internet Explorer. Select the appropriate file or folder in the Internet Explorer window, and then use the appropriate commands on the Edit menu (Cut or Copy, and then Paste) to copy or move the items as needed. When you want to return to the Web, use any of the navigation buttons, such as Back or Home, to return to a particular Web page.

In this lesson, you learned how to connect to the Internet and use Internet Explorer 5.0. In the next lesson, you learn to add, manage, and remove your favorite Web sites from the Internet Explorer Favorites List.

Creating and Managing Internet Explorer Favorites

*In this lesson, you learn to add, manage, and remove
your favorite Web sites from the Internet Explorer Favorites list.*

Adding Internet Explorer Favorites

Microsoft Internet Explorer makes it easy for you to return to your favorite Web sites. It's just a matter of going to the site and then adding it to the Internet Explorer Favorites list. You can then access this list and quickly go to a site of your choice.

To add a Web site to your Favorites list, follow these steps:

1. Go to the Web site you want to add to the Favorites list, as shown in Figure 11.1. You can type the site's address in the **Address** box or use **Search** to locate the site, as described in Lesson 10, "Using Internet Explorer 5.0."

2. Select the **Favorites** menu, and then select **Add to Favorites**. The Add Favorite dialog box appears. The Add Favorite dialog box offers options related to adding the current site to your Favorites list:

   - **Make Available Offline**—Click this check box if you want to have the content on this site downloaded to your computer periodically so you can view the site offline. For more information on viewing sites offline, see the section "Subscribing to a Web Site" in Lesson 9, "Subscribing to Channels and Working Offline."

- **Name**—Type a name for the site (if you want to change the default listing) in this box.

- **Create In**—If you want to place the Favorite listing in an existing folder, click the **Create In** button (you can also create a new folder to hold the item). The Add Favorite dialog box expands and shows existing folders available (see Figure 11.2). Double-click the folder you want to place the listing in.

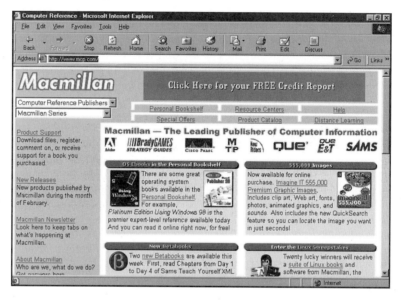

Figure 11.1   Go to the Web site you want to add to your Favorites list.

3. Select the options you want to use, as discussed earlier, and then click **OK** to add the site to the Favorites list (if you don't select any of the options, the Web site is placed on the main Favorites list).

TIP   Create a Folder for the Web Site Address   If you want to create a folder to hold the listing, click the **New Folder** button in the expanded Add Favorite dialog box. The Create New Folder dialog box appears. Type a name for the folder, and then click **OK**.

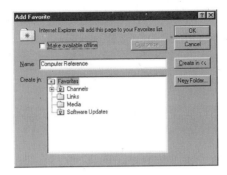

Figure 11.2 You can set options for the current Web site's listing on the Favorites list, including a folder selection for the site.

Using the Favorites List

After you've added a site or sites to the Favorites list, you can quickly access them at any time. Internet Explorer actually provides you with two different ways to view your Favorites list and select the site you want to go to.

To access your favorites from the Favorites menu, follow these steps:

1. Select the **Favorites** menu.

2. Select the site you want to go to from the menu.

TIP **Access a Folder Holding an Address** If you placed the site address in a folder on the Favorites list, point at the folder and select the site you want to go to.

After you select the site from the list, the site's address appears in the Internet Explorer Address box. You then are taken to the site.

You can also open up a Favorites pane on the left side of the Internet Explorer window. This enables you to easily view your favorites and then select from the list as needed.

To open the Favorites pane, follow these steps:

1. Click the **Favorites** button on the Internet Explorer toolbar. The Favorites pane appears on the left side of the Explorer window (see Figure 11.3).

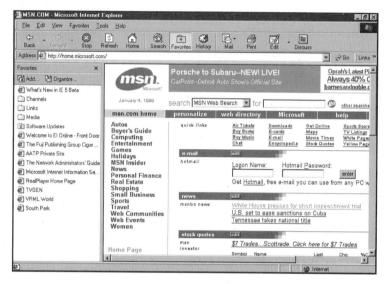

Figure 11.3 The Favorites pane enables you to view all your favorites.

2. Select the site you want to go to from the list.

When you have finished working with the Favorites pane, click the **Close** (×) button in its upper-left corner to close the pane.

TIP **Add a Web Site Address from the Favorites Pane** If you have the Favorites pane open, you can add your current Web site to the list. Click the **Add** button at the top of the pane, and the Add Favorites dialog box appears.

Organizing Your Favorites

You might find that over time you end up with a fairly large Favorites list. In fact, when you click on the Favorites menu, the list is so large that you have to scroll through the possibilities to find the site you want to access.

You can organize your favorites into folders that make it easier for you to view the sites in the Favorites list. For instance, you might want to take all the sites related to comedy or humor and place them in a Comedy folder. You also might want to delete sites from your Favorites list that you don't visit anymore or that are no longer available.

To organize the sites in your Favorites list, follow these steps:

1. Select the **Favorites** menu, and then select **Organize Favorites**. The Organize Favorites dialog box appears (see Figure 11.4). This dialog box offers you several options for managing the sites on your Favorites list:

   - **Create Folder**—Click this button to create a new folder to hold a site (or sites). The Create New Folder dialog box appears. Type a name for the folder, and then click **OK**. The folder appears on the Favorites list.

   - **Rename**—Select a site on the list, and then click **Rename**. Type a new name for the selected site.

   - **Delete**—Select a site, and then click the **Delete** button to remove the site from your Favorites list. You are asked to confirm the deletion; click **Yes**.

   - **Move to Folder**—Select a site, and then click the **Move to Folder** button. The Browse for Folder dialog box appears. Select the folder you want to place the site address in, and then click **OK**.

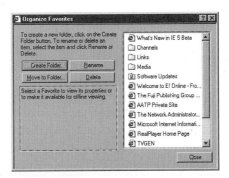

Figure 11.4 The Organize Favorites dialog box enables you to manage the sites you placed on your Favorites list.

2. When you have completed organizing your Favorites list, click **Close** to close the Organize Favorites dialog box.

TIP   **Organize Your Favorites from the Favorites Pane**   If you have the Favorites pane open, you can access the Organize Favorites dialog box; click the **Organize** button at the top of the pane.

In this lesson, you learned how to add Web site addresses to your Favorites list. You also learned how to use the Favorites list and how to manage Web addresses on the list. In the next lesson, you learn to download files using Internet Explorer.

Downloading Files Using Internet Explorer

In this lesson, you learn how to download software files from the Web using Internet Explorer.

Getting Software on the Web

As you explore the Web with Internet Explorer, you might find that the World Wide Web not only is a huge collection of informational Web sites, but it also provides you with the capability to download files from software libraries and then use these software applications on your computer. These software products come in two flavors: *shareware* and *freeware*.

 Shareware   Typically a fully operational program that asks you to send the programmer of the product a certain fee. Sometimes shareware products operate only for a limited time (a month or so) so you can use the software and then decide if you want to keep using it by paying the programmer. Some shareware is called "nag-ware" because it will constantly remind you that you need to pay the author of the program if you want to keep using it.

 Freeware   Programs you can download and use for free. These are usually add-on programs or other specialty programs written by someone who needed a particular application. They then share it with anyone who would like to use the program.

The software applications available on the Web range from Web browser add-ons (such as those discussed in Lesson 13, "Using Internet Explorer Add-Ons") to full-blown applications. You can find just about everything possible: word processors, home finance programs, drawing programs, email packages—you name it, it's probably available for downloading from the Web.

Locating the Best Sites

There are quite a few Web sites on the Web that you can download files from. These sites range from catchall sites that contain a wide variety of different types of software to sites that contain specific categories of software, such as Internet-related applications.

You can start your own search for software sites using the Search feature in Internet Explorer (see Lesson 10, "Using Internet Explorer 5.0," for more information on the Search feature). When you are asked to provide keywords for your search, type **freeware** or **shareware**. If you are looking for a specific category of applications such as games, type **freeware games**. This type of search provides you with a number of links to different shareware and freeware sites on the Web.

Several Web sites exist that are considered the best sites to find and download software from the Web. These sites vary in content, but usually have the latest and greatest freeware and shareware products available first. Table 12.1 lists some of these sites.

Table 12.1 Web Sites Containing Freeware and Shareware

Web Site	Type of Software	URL Address
Shareware.com	A large collection of shareware and freeware in nearly all categories. Shareware.com has its own search engine for locating files.	www.shareware.com
TUCOWS	The Ultimate Collection of Winsock Software (thus the name TUCOWS) contains Internet-related shareware and freeware. TUCOWS rates each software product.	www.tucows.com

Web Site	Type of Software	URL Address
Stroud's Consummate Winsock Collection	Another collection of Internet-related shareware and freeware applications. Stroud's provides a review of each application available on the site.	cws.internet.com
Microsoft	Microsoft provides updates and patches for all its products (such as Windows 98 and the Office 2000 applications), and freeware tools and trial software applications for downloading.	www.microsoft.com
Winfiles.com	This site provides downloads related to Windows. They are updated Windows device drivers, Windows add-ons, and a number of other files.	www.winfiles.com/
CNET Gamecenter.com	If you have time for some "play," this site has demo versions and shareware/ freeware games you can download. It provides games reviews and other information for gamers.	www.gamecenter.com/

CAUTION

Be Careful Downloading from Obscure or Unfamiliar Sites Most of the sites that offer shareware and freeware (particularly those listed in Table 12.1) make sure that the files they offer are virus free. Not all sites, however, spend the time and effort necessary to make sure that the files they contain are virus and error free. You download at your own risk, so try to use sites that claim to provide virus-free files.

Downloading Files

Actually downloading files is really just a matter of locating the specific file on a site, and then letting Internet Explorer take over, so that it pulls the file off the site and places it on your computer. Downloadable files are typically listed on the site as hyperlinks. Selecting a particular hyperlink either begins the download process or takes you to a Web page where links are provided for the actual download.

To download a file from a Web site, follow these steps:

1. Go to the Web site you want to download a file from (such as Stroud's, shown in Figure 12.1).

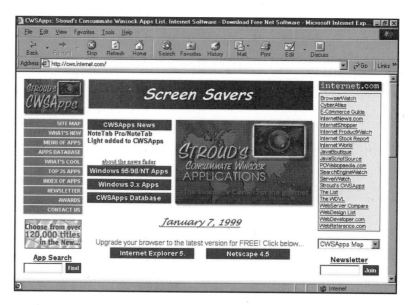

Figure 12.1 Go to the Web site you want to download a file from.

2. Select the type of software or the operating system you use to see a list of files available (in the case of Stroud's, click the Windows 95/98/NT link on the Main page).

3. Most sites provide a list of software categories for you to choose from (see Figure 12.2). For instance, if you want to download a virus scanner from the Stroud site, click the **Virus Scanners** category hyperlink.

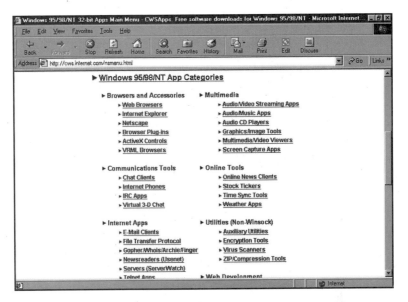

Figure 12.2 Most sites provide categories of software applications for you to choose from.

4. Scroll down through the list of files provided. Many of the applications available on the site are rated, and reviews are available. When you find the application you want to download, click on the download link (typically the title of the software, as shown in Figure 12.3).

5. After you click the download link, the File Download dialog box appears. Click **OK** to begin the download.

6. The Save As dialog box appears. Choose the folder and drive on your computer that you want to have the file saved on. Then click **Save**.

A download dialog box appears that keeps you apprised of the download of the selected file. The time that it takes to actually download the file depends on your modem speed and the size of the file. After the file download is complete, the File Download dialog box tells you that the download is complete. Click **Close** to close the dialog box.

Installing a Downloaded Application

After the file has been downloaded to your computer, you can install the software. Because most software you download from the Web has been compressed to speed up download times, you need to have WinZip or some file compression/decompression utility installed on your computer (see the following definition).

Click here for download.

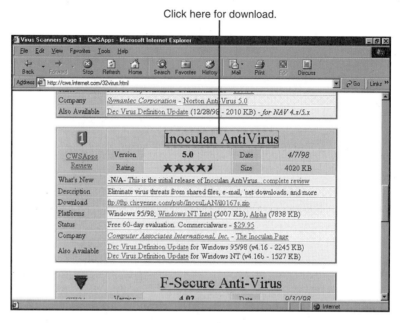

Figure 12.3 Click the software title to start the download of the application.

 WinZip WinZip is a tool that is used to "zip" (compress) and "unzip" (decompress) files that you download from the Web. Files that you download are typically zipped so they don't take up a lot of space on the Web server that stores them and so you can download them faster. You can download WinZip from Stroud's, Shareware.com, and the WinZip site at www.winzip.com.

Unzipping a Downloaded File

Unzipping downloaded files from the Web is usually a very straightforward process that can be done using Windows Explorer (and a zip utility such as WinZip to unzip the files). The file you downloaded is actually a group of files called an *archive*. This archive contains all the files you need to install the application you downloaded. Zip archives appear as a single file icon in Windows Explorer.

To unzip an application you've downloaded from the Web, follow these steps:

1. Close the Internet Explorer window and any other applications you have running. You can also disconnect from your Internet service provider (you don't need to be online to install the software).

2. Right-click on the **My Computer** icon on your Windows desktop and choose **Explore** from the shortcut menu that appears (Windows Explorer opens).

3. In the left pane of the Internet Explorer window, click the drive that the downloaded file resides on.

4. In the right pane of Internet Explorer, double-click the folder that holds the file.

5. Locate the downloaded file and double-click it.

6. If the file was zipped and you've installed WinZip, the WinZip window (click **I Agree** to get passed the opening WinZip screen) opens, showing the contents of the zipped file you downloaded (see Figure 12.4). To unzip the files found in the compressed zip file, click the **Extract** button on the WinZip toolbar.

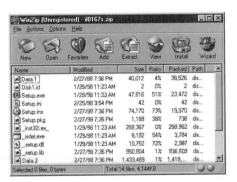

Figure 12.4 WinZip opens the compressed file archive you downloaded.

7. Specify a folder in the Extract dialog box that you want WinZip to place the extracted files in (such as your Windows Temporary folder; see Figure 12.5).

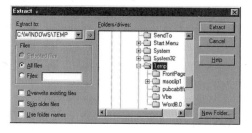

Figure 12.5 Specify a folder where you want the zipped software files placed.

8. Click **Extract** to extract the files to the specified folder.

CAUTION

Some Downloaded Files Are Zipped, and Some Are Not Some applications you download from the Web aren't zipped but are contained in auto-executable compressed files. Just double-click their icons in the folders that they were downloaded to. This begins the installation process.

Installing the Unzipped Application

After you've unzipped the file archive to a particular folder, you can then use the Windows Run dialog box to actually install the software. The installation process for the software you downloaded is the same or very similar to software that you bought on disk or on a CD.

To install the application from the unzipped file archive, follow these steps:

1. Click the Windows **Start** menu, and then click **Run**. The Run dialog box opens.

2. Click the **Browse** button to locate the installation file that installs the downloaded software. The Browse dialog box appears.

3. Use the **Look In** drop-down box to locate the drive that holds the unzipped files, and then open the folder that holds the files. A setup or installation file typically is found among the unzipped files (see Figure 12.6).

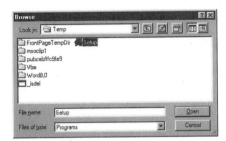

Figure 12.6 Locate the installation file that installs the downloaded application.

4. Click the **Setup** or **Install** file, and then click the **Open** button to close the Browse dialog box.

5. Click **OK** in the Run dialog box to begin the installation. Typically a Welcome screen appears to help you walk through the software installation. Click **Next** to continue (see Figure 12.7).

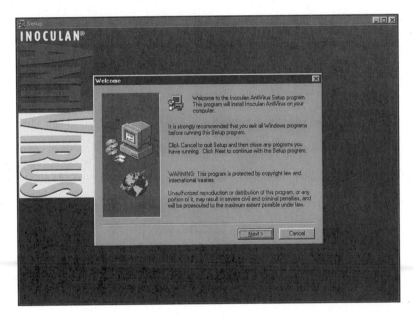

Figure 12.7 Follow the screen prompts to install your downloaded software.

6. Follow the prompts to complete the installation of the software (such as choosing a folder to install the application into).

7. When you have completed the installation, click **Finish**.

After the application is installed on your computer, you can start it by clicking the Start button, pointing at Programs, and then clicking the icon for that particular application. Some applications also install a shortcut icon on the desktop that you can use to start the application. You can now use the software as you would any other software application.

Remember that you might be bound to certain restrictions when you are using shareware products. For instance, you might be limited to a 30-day trial period. If you have any questions regarding the software, the best place to start is the help system provided with the particular application.

In this lesson, you learned how to download files from the World Wide Web using Internet Explorer. You also learned how to install a downloaded application. In the next lesson, you learn to take advantage of Internet Explorer add-ons such as Media Player, VRML Viewer, and Macromedia Shockwave.

Using Internet Explorer Add-Ons

*In this lesson, you learn how to use Internet Explorer add-ons
such as Windows Media Player, VRML Viewer, and Macromedia Shockwave.*

Understanding Internet Explorer Add-Ons

Internet Explorer provides you with a robust, full-featured Web browser, as you
saw in Lessons 10 through 12 of this part of the book; it's great for surfing the
World Wide Web, searching for your favorite Web sites, and downloading files
and software. Believe it or not, you can extend and enhance the capabilities of
Explorer with browser add-ons—applications that work with Internet Explorer
to allow you to view special Web content.

Browser Add-On A mini-program that runs in conjunction with the Browser
and that supplies you with additional Web tools, such as a viewer for special
content like VRML Viewer or Macromedia Shockwave.

Add-ons enhance your Web interactions in a variety of ways. For instance,
Windows Media Player enables you to play sound and video files on the Web.
Other add-ons like VRML Viewer enable you to view three-dimensional objects
and actually visit three-dimensional worlds on the Web. Macromedia Shockwave
enables you to view interactive multimedia content that has been placed on a Web
page.

Playing Video and Sound Files with Windows Media Player

Many sites on the Web provide video and sound files you can play. To play these files, click on the appropriate link, and Windows Media Player opens. The video or audio file is played within the Media Player window. While not an add-on for Internet Explorer, Media Player is actually an add-on to the operating system itself (Windows 98 or Windows NT). And because Internet Explorer is tightly integrated with your Windows operating system, it takes advantage of this media utility to play any special media files it finds on the Web.

Media Player supports most of the sound and video formats found on the Web. You can play video files such as .avi, .mov, and others. A number of sound formats, including .wav, are also supported.

Media Player can also be used to play real-time video and audio feeds from the Web. For example, a number of sites, such as CNN (www.cnn.com) and FOX News (www.foxnews.com), provide live video and audio feeds you can view or listen to by using Media Player.

To use Windows Media Player, follow these steps:

1. Go to any site that provides links to audio or video content using Internet Explorer. Many sites offer live news broadcasts and other media content you can view using Media Player (for a sample of Media Player content, go to http://www.microsoft.com/windows/windowsmedia/techshowcase/jukebox2/default.htm).

2. Click a link to the video (or audio) content. In some cases, you click a **Play** button on a video box showing a frame of the video that plays.

3. The Media Player window opens (see Figure 13.1). You might have to wait a moment for the video to begin playing. After the video (or audio) has finished playing, click the **Close** (×) button in the upper corner of the Media Player window to close it.

CAUTION

Playing Audio Content Does Not Open the Media Player Video Box   When you play audio content, don't be alarmed by the "look" of the Media Player. It won't open a provide video box at the top of the player. It still provides the control box, however, that allows you to start, stop, or rewind the content and play it again.

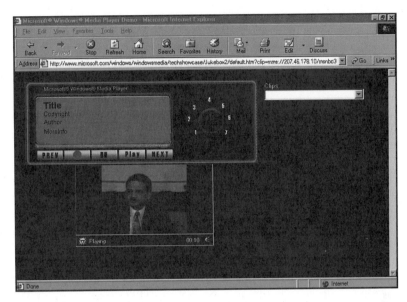

Figure 13.1 You will find a large number of sites on the Web that provide video and audio content.

Using VRML Viewer

Another add-on that allows you to view special Web content is VRML Viewer. VRML has enabled programmers to turn the Web into a three-dimensional wonderland. You can use VRML to create three-dimensional objects and three-dimensional worlds that you can view as you browse the Web. You not only can view these worlds, but, with VRML, you also can move three-dimensional objects and navigate through a three-dimensional world.

VRML Virtual Reality Modeling Language (VRML) is used to create virtual worlds and objects that can be viewed with a special VRML add-on for Internet Explorer.

The VRML Viewer comes with the Internet Explorer 5 installation files found on the Office 2000 CD-ROM. If you do a typical installation of Office 2000 and Internet Explorer, the VRML add-on should be installed (for more about adding components to the Office installation, see Appendix A, "Installing Microsoft Office 2000").

TIP **Download the Most Recent Version of Internet Explorer** If you want to make sure you have the latest version of Internet Explorer and add-ons such as VRML Viewer installed on your computer, you can go to the Windows 98 Update site. Make sure you are connected to the Internet, click the Windows **Start** button, and then click **Windows Update**.

Manipulating Three-Dimensional Objects

To use VRML Viewer, you must locate a Web page that contains VRML content. VRML objects on the Web range from entire worlds to movable objects. A good site to test out your VRML Viewer is the Microsoft VRML site at http://www.microsoft.com/vrml/content.htm. This page has links to a number of VRML objects and worlds.

1. Open the http://www.microsoft.com/vrml/content.htm site using Internet Explorer. Click the **Offworld Exploits** link shown in Figure 13.2.

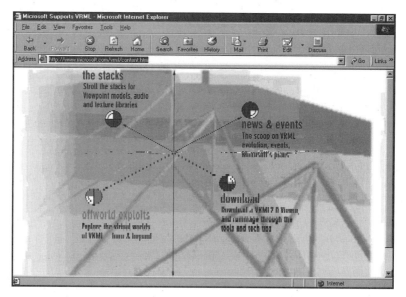

Figure 13.2 Microsoft offers a page of links to a number of VRML objects.

2. The Offworld page appears. This page contains a link to a library of VRML objects called the Array. Click the head for the Array link to continue.

3. On the Array page, select any of the 3D objects shown, such as the virtual chess board.

4. After you have selected a 3D object and it appears in your Web browser, place the mouse on the object, press the left button, and then push the mouse toward the object. Your view zooms in toward the three-dimensional forklift (see Figure 13.3).

5. You can rotate the object by clicking the **Study** tool on the left side of the VRML Viewer.

6. When you tire of the VRML object you've chosen, press the **Back** button on the Explorer toolbar and try out some of the other VRML objects listed on the Array page.

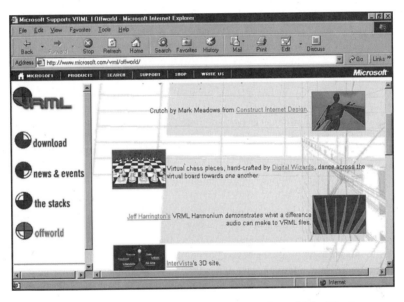

Figure 13.3 Microsoft's Array provides links to a number of 3D objects.

Controlling Movement in 3D Space

To get a really good feel of how sophisticated VRML can be, it makes sense to visit one of the three-dimensional VRML worlds. A three-dimensional world also is a good place to try out all VRML Viewer's tools and learn how to control your movements in 3D space. A good place to preview some of the best VRML worlds is the ZDnet Web site at `www.zdnet.com/devhead/resources/showcase/search/vrml.html`. This site has links to a number of VRML worlds.

135

TIP **Use Search to Find Other VRML Worlds** After you've exhausted the VRML links at www.zdnet.com/devhead/resources/showcase/search/vrml.html, use the Internet Explorer search feature to locate others. Another good site for VRML worlds is www.virtpark.com/theme/proteinman/.

To use VRML Viewer to explore a VRML world, follow these steps:

1. Use Internet Explorer to go to http://www.zdnet.com/devhead/resources/showcase/search/vrml.html. Click one of the VRML world links on this page, such as the Water Tank link. You are taken to a page that describes the VRML world.

2. To load the VRML world, click the **Play** button.

3. After the VRML World loads (see Figure 13.4), you can use VRML Viewer movement controls to move around. All the controls are used by selecting the control and then dragging the mouse (holding down the left mouse button) in a particular direction. Controls are marked by the first initial of the control name (such as *W* for Walk). See Table 13.1 for a complete list of controls.

4. After you've gotten a good feel or how to move in 3D space, click the **Back** button and explore some of the other VRML worlds provided on the Web page.

Table 13.1 VRML Viewer Movement Controls

Control	Description
Walk	Enables you to move forward and backward with the mouse.
Pan	Enables you to slide to the left or the right.
Turn	Enables you to swing to the left or the right.
Roll	Enables you to rotate the VRML object (in this case, it turns the room upside down).
Goto	Enables you to click on a part of the VRML space. You are moved toward the item until you click somewhere else in the space.
Study	Enables you to rotate a VRML object in any direction.
Zoom Out	Enables you to zoom out to see the entire virtual world.
Straighten Up	Puts you back on an even keel, as if you were standing upright (things can get pretty tilted with some of the controls).

Control	Description
View	Enables you to totally shift your perspective to either the left or right.
Restore	Gets the view back to where you started (this can be helpful, especially if you flipped your virtual world upside down).

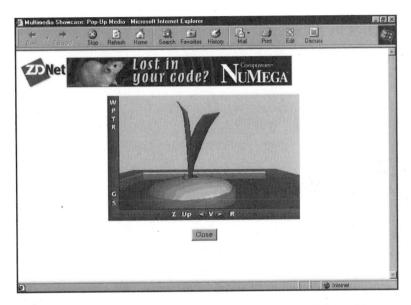

Figure 13.4 You can practice moving in 3D space using a VRML world.

 TIP **Jump Start the VRML World** If the VRML world you've chosen takes a long time to load and seems to hang up during the loading process, click the **Refresh** button on the Internet Explorer toolbar. This might help load the VRML file.

 CAUTION **VRML Problems** VRML files can be very large and aren't always completely compatible with every VRML Viewer available. You might find times when a VRML world or object doesn't appear correctly. In the worse-case scenario, a VRML file can lock up Internet Explorer. Press **Ctrl+Alt+Delete**, and then shut down Internet Explorer to close the Browser window.

Using Shockwave

You already know that you can play and view audio, video, and multimedia files on the Web using Windows Media Player. Going to the next step and adding interactivity to special content on the Web increases the possibilities for learning and fun on the Web a thousandfold.

Macromedia, the company that developed interactive multimedia authoring tools like Macromedia Director and AuthorWare, has developed a way to get interactive multimedia onto the Web: a product called Shockwave.

When you have the Shockwave add-on for Internet Explorer installed on your computer, you can interact with multimedia content on Web sites. This content is regular interactive multimedia (developed in Director or AuthorWare) that has been *shocked* for the Web. Shocked content can be used to provide interactive games, even educational content on the Web.

 Shocked   Multimedia programs that have been converted to Web content using Shockwave.

You can download the latest version of Shockwave from the Macromedia Web site at www.macromedia.com/. After you've installed this add-on, you're ready to take advantage of shocked content on the Web (for more about downloading and installing applications from the Web, see Lesson 12, "Downloading Files Using Internet Explorer").

A number of Web sites have also started using Shockwave Flash content for short animations and other multimedia events on their Web pages. You might also want to download and install Flash when you visit the Macromedia Web site. To view shocked content on the Web, follow these steps:

1. Use the Internet Explorer to go to Macromedia's Shockzone at www.macromedia.com/shockzone/ssod/ (see Figure 13.5).

2. Click the **Archive** link on this page.

3. You are taken to an archive page that provides links to the months of several years. Click any of these months (see Figure 13.6) to view a list of sites of the day for that particular month.

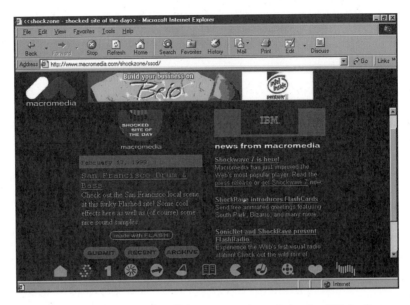

Figure 13.5 The Shockzone offers links to a number of shocked Web sites.

4. Select a link to a particular site to load the shocked content. Directions for how to interact with the content (such as shocked games) appears on that page.

Patience Some shocked content can take a seemingly long time to load into your Web browser window; at times, you have to be very patient.

CAUTION

While you might find some of the shocked content on the Web frivolous and even idiotic, there are sites that are attempting to use shocked content for educational and information purposes. Use your favorite search engine and see what kind of shocked content you can find.

In this lesson, you learned how play special content on the Web. You used Media Player to play video content, and you explored 3D content using VRML Viewer. You also viewed shocked content using Shockwave. In the next lesson, you learn to start Microsoft Word and become with the Word application window.

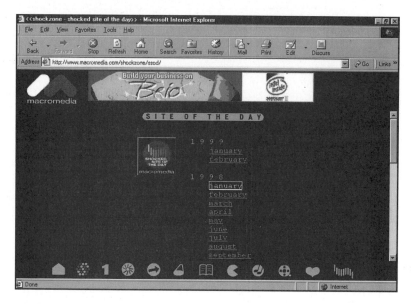

Figure 13.6   You can view the shocked sites of the day for a particular month and year.

Word

Working in Word

1

*In this lesson, you learn to start Microsoft Word
and navigate the Word window. You also learn to use
common tools such as the menus, toolbars, and dialog boxes.*

Starting Word

Microsoft Word 2000 is an efficient and full-featured word processor that
provides you with all the tools you need to produce a tremendous variety
of document types—everything from simple documents, such as memos and
outlines, to complex documents, such as newsletters and Internet-ready HTML
pages. You create your Word documents in the Word window, which provides
you with easy access to all the tools you need to create all your documents.

Before you can take advantage of Word's slick document processing features,
you need to open the Word application window. To start the Word program,
follow these steps:

1. From the Windows Desktop, click **Start**, and then point at **Programs**.
   The Programs menu appears (see Figure 1.1).
2. To start Word, click the **Word** icon. The Word program window appears.

 TIP **Use the Office Toolbar** If you installed the Office toolbar during the Office
installation, it appears on your Windows Desktop. Click the **Word** icon on the
toolbar to quickly start Word.

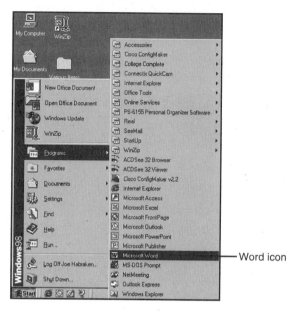

Word icon

Figure 1.1 Open the Programs menu and click the Word icon to start Word.

Understanding the Word Environment

When you start the Word program, the Word application window greets you (see Figure 1.2). You create your documents in the Word window. The Word window also provides you with items that help you navigate and operate the application itself.

TIP **Control the View** If your view differs from the view shown in Figure 1.2 (the Normal view), or if you don't see all the Word window elements shown in the figure (particularly the ruler), you can change your view easily. Select **View**, then choose the menu selection (such as **Normal** or **Ruler**) that matches your view to the figure.

You will notice that the largest area of the window is currently blank; this is where you will create your new document. All the other areas—the menu bar, the toolbar, and the status bar—either provide a fast way to access the various commands and features that you use in Word or supply you with information concerning your document, such as what page you are on and where the insertion point is currently located in your document.

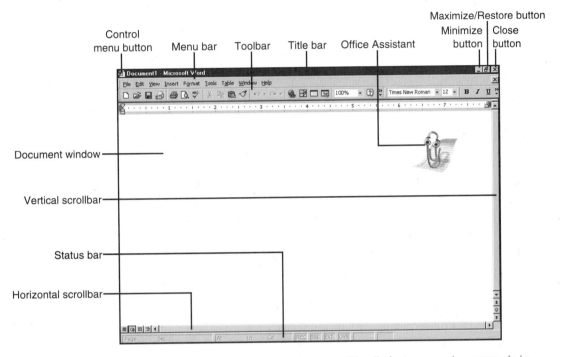

Figure 1.2   Create your documents and access Word's features and commands in the Word window.

Table 1.1 describes the elements you see in the Word application window.

Table 1.1   Elements of the Word Window

Element	Description
Title bar	Includes the name of the application and the current document, as well as the Minimize, Maximize, and Close buttons.
Control menu button	Opens the Control menu, which provides such commands as Move, Size, Minimize, and Close.
Minimize button	Reduces the Word window to a button on the taskbar; to restore the window to its original size, click the button on the taskbar.

continues

Table 1.1 Continued

Element	Description
Maximize/Restore button	Enlarges the Word window to cover the Windows Desktop. When the window is maximized, the Maximize button changes to a Restore button that you can click to return the window to its previous size.
Close (×) button	Closes the Word program.
Menu bar	Contains menus of commands you can use to perform tasks in the program.
Toolbar	Includes icons that serve as shortcuts for common commands, such as Save, Print, and Spelling.
Status bar	Displays information about the current page number, the document section that you are located in, and the current location of the insertion point (the line and column). The status bar also shows you other information, such as whether you have turned on the typeover mode by pressing the Insert key on the keyboard.
Document window	This is where you type and format your documents.
Scrollbars	The horizontal scrollbar is used to scroll your view of the current document from left to right or vice versa. The vertical scrollbar is used to scroll up and down through the current document.
Office Assistant	The Office Assistant provides you with the help you need to get the most out of Word. Click the Assistant when you need help.

Using Menus and Toolbars

Word provides you with several ways to access the commands and features you use as you create your documents. You can access these commands by using the menus on the menu bar and the buttons on the various toolbars that Word supplies.

You can also access a number of Word commands using shortcut menus. These menus are accessed by right-clicking a particular document element. The shortcut menu appears with a list of commands related to the item you are current working on, such as a word or a paragraph.

The Word Menu Bar

The Word menu bar gives you access to all the commands and features that Word provides. Like all Windows applications, Word's menus are found below the title bar, and are activated by clicking a particular menu choice. The menu then opens, providing you with a set of command choices.

Word 2000 (and the other Office 2000 applications) has adopted a new menu system that provides you with the capability to quickly access the commands you use most often. When you first choose a particular menu, you will find a short list of menu commands. As you use commands, Word adds them to the menu list.

You will find that this personalized strategy is also embraced by the toolbar system. As you use commands, they are added to the toolbar. This provides you with customized menus and toolbars that are, in effect, personalized for you.

To access a particular menu, follow these steps:

1. Select the menu by clicking its title (such as **View**), as shown in Figure 1.3. The most recently used commands appear; wait just a moment for all the commands on a particular menu to appear.

2. Select the command on the menu that invokes a particular feature (such as **Header and Footer**).

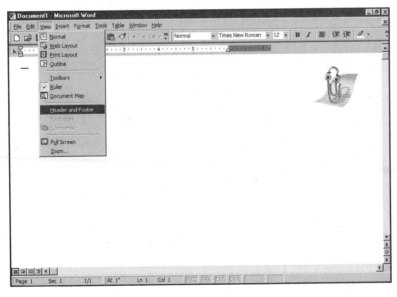

Figure 1.3 Select a particular menu to view, and then point to a Word command.

You will find that a number of the commands found on the menu are followed by an ellipsis (...). These commands, when selected, open a dialog box that requires you to provide Word with additional information before the particular feature or command can be used. More information about working with dialog boxes is included later in this lesson.

Some of the menus also contain a submenu or cascading menu that you use to make your choices. The menu commands that produce a submenu are indicated by an arrow to the right of the menu choice. In cases where a submenu is present, you point at the command (marked with the arrow) on the main menu to open the submenu.

You will find that the menu system itself provides you with a logical grouping of the Word commands and features. For instance, commands related to files, such as opening, saving, and printing, are all found on the File menu.

 TIP   **Activating Menus with the Keyboard**   You can also activate a particular menu by holding down the **Alt** key and then pressing the keyboard key that matches the underscored letter in the menu's name. This underscored letter is called the hotkey. For instance, to activate the File menu in Word, you would press **Alt+F**.

If you find that you would rather have access to all the menu commands (rather than accessing only those you've used recently), you can turn off the personalized menu system. To do this, follow these steps:

1. Click the **Tools** menu, then click **Customize**.
2. In the Customize dialog box, click the **Options** tab.
3. To show all the commands on the menus, clear the **Menus Show Recently Used Commands First** check box.
4. Click **OK** to close the dialog box.

Shortcut Menus

A fast way to access commands related to a particular document element is to select that document object and then right-click. This opens a shortcut menu that contains commands related to the particular object you are working with.

TERM   **Object**   Any element found in a document, such as text, a graphic, a hyperlink, or other inserted item.

For instance, if you select a line of text in a document, right-clicking the selected text (see Figure 1.4) opens a shortcut menu with commands such as **Cut**, **Copy**, and **Paste**, or it provides you with quick access to formatting commands such as **Font** and **Paragraph**.

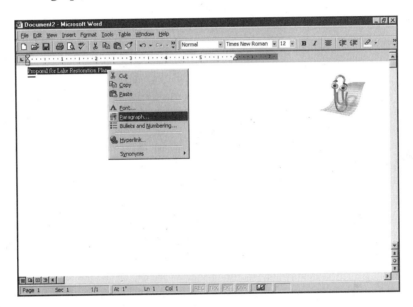

Figure 1.4   You can quickly access Word commands using shortcut menus.

Word Toolbars

The Word toolbars provide you with a very quick and straightforward way of accessing commands and features. When you first start Word, you are provided with the Standard and Formatting toolbars, which reside as one continuous toolbar found directly below the menu bar.

To access a particular command using a toolbar button, click the button. Depending on the command, you see an immediate result in your document (such as the removal of selected text when you click the **Cut** button), or a dialog box appears, requesting additional information from you.

TIP **Finding a Toolbar Button's Purpose** You can place the mouse pointer on any toolbar button to view a description of that tool's function.

Word offers several toolbars; many of them contain buttons for a specific group of tasks. For example, the Drawing toolbar provides you with buttons that give you access to tools that enable you to draw graphical elements in your documents (such as text boxes, lines, and rectangles).

To place additional toolbars in the Word window, right-click any toolbar currently shown and select from the list that appears. You will find that specific toolbars exist for working with tables, pictures, and the World Wide Web.

You can also easily add or remove buttons from any of the toolbars present in the Word window. Each toolbar is equipped with a **More Buttons** button that you can use to modify the buttons shown on that particular toolbar.

To add or remove buttons from a toolbar, follow these steps:

1. Click the **More Buttons** button on any toolbar; a drop-down area appears.
2. Click **Add or Remove Buttons**. A list of all the buttons for the current toolbar appears, as shown in Figure 1.5.

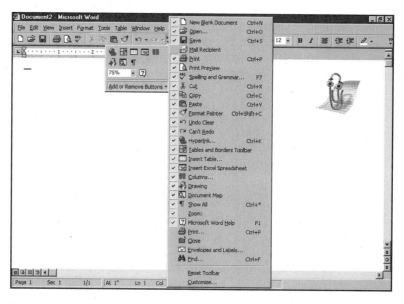

Figure 1.5 You can easily add or remove buttons from a toolbar using the button list.

3. To add a button, click the button. A check mark appears to the left of the button. To remove a button, click it to remove the check mark.

4. When you have completed your changes to the current toolbar, click outside the button list to close it.

You will find that the Word toolbars provide you with a quick fix whenever you need to fire off a particular command. Buttons exist for all the commands that are available on the Word menu system.

TIP   **Missing Toolbar Buttons?**   If you can't find a particular toolbar button because of the limited space for the Standard and Formatting toolbars, click the **More Buttons** button on either toolbar.

TIP   **Give the Standard Toolbar More Space**   Another way to provide more space for buttons on the toolbars is to drag the Formatting toolbar below the Standard toolbar. Then both toolbars have the width of the screen to display buttons. Place the mouse on the vertical handle just to the left of the Style button on the Formatting toolbar and drag the Formatting toolbar underneath the Standard toolbar.

Understanding Dialog Boxes

When you are working with the various commands and features found in Word, you will invariably come up against dialog boxes. Dialog boxes are used when Word needs more information from you before it can complete a particular command or take advantage of a special feature. Dialog boxes always appear when you select a menu command that is followed by an ellipsis. Dialog boxes also appear when you invoke the same commands using the appropriate toolbar button.

The way that you provide information in the dialog box can vary. Some dialog boxes require that you type a text entry in a text box. Other dialog boxes provide you with a list of choices on a drop-down menu, and still others enable you to make your selection by clicking a particular option button.

Figure 1.6 shows the Page Setup dialog box. This dialog box enables you to make selections using check boxes, drop-down lists, and option buttons, and you can even type margin values into certain boxes.

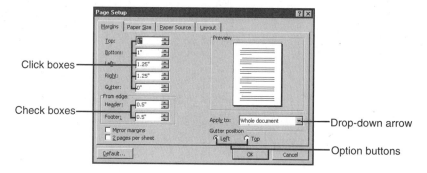

Click boxes

Check boxes

Drop-down arrow

Option buttons

Figure 1.6 Dialog boxes ask you for additional information regarding a particular Word command or feature.

Dialog boxes vary, however, and each may use a different way to get you to supply the needed information for a particular Word feature. In most cases, when you complete your selections in a dialog box, you click the **OK** button to close the box and complete the command you originally started with a menu choice or toolbar button.

Exiting Word

When you have completed your initial survey of the Word application window or whenever you have completed your work in the program, you will want to exit the software. More than one way exists to close the Word window, which is the same as exiting the program.

You can exit Word by selecting the **File** menu, then **Exit**. Or you can close Word with one click of the mouse by clicking the Word **Close** (×) button in the upper-right corner of the application window.

When you close Word, you may be prompted to save any work that you have done in the application window. If you were just experimenting as you read through this lesson, you can click **No**. The current document will not be saved, and the Word application window closes. All the ins and outs of saving your documents are covered in Lesson 2, "Creating a New Document."

In this lesson, you learned how to start Word and explored the various parts of the Word window. You also learned how to work with the menu system, toolbars, and dialog boxes. Finally, you also learned how to exit the Word program. In the next lesson, you learn how to create a new document and save your work.

Creating a
New Document

*In this lesson, you learn to start a new
document and enter text. You also learn to take advantage of
Word document templates and the Word document wizards.*

Starting a New Document

When you choose to start a new document in Word, you can take three routes:
You can create a blank new document, create a document using a Word *template*,
or create a document using one of the Word *wizards*, such as the Fax or Envelope
Wizard. The amount of assistance you get in creating your new document is
greatly increased when you choose the template or wizard option.

Template   A blueprint for a document that may already contain certain
formatting options and text.

Wizard   A feature that guides you step-by-step through a particular process
in Word, such as creating a new document.

When you create a new document from scratch, you are actually using a
template—the Word Blank Document template. Documents based on the Blank
Template do not contain any "pre-made" text (as some of the other templates
do), and the formatting contained in the document will reflect the default
settings you have chosen for margins, fonts, and other document attributes

(for more information on default Word settings involving font and document attributes, see Lesson 6, "Changing How Text Looks," and see Lesson 10, "Working with Margins, Pages, and Line Spacing," respectively).

You have already seen in Lesson 1 that Word automatically opens a new blank document for you when you start the Word software. You can also open a new document when you are already in the Word application window.

To open a new document, follow these steps:

1. Select **File**, then **New**. The New dialog box will open as shown in Figure 2.1.

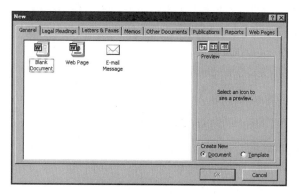

Figure 2.1   When you choose New on the File menu, the New dialog box opens.

2. Make sure that the General tab is selected on the New dialog box and then double-click the Word **Blank Document** icon. A new document will appear in the Word application window.

 TIP   **Toolbar Shortcut**   The easiest way to open a new document is to click the **New** button on the Word toolbar. A new blank document will appear in the Word window.

 CAUTION   **What Happened to My Previous Document?**   If you were already working on a document, the new document will, in effect, open on top of the document you were previously working on. You can get back to the previous document by clicking the appropriate document icon on the Windows taskbar.

Entering Text

After you have opened a new document, you are ready to start entering text. You will notice that a blinking vertical element called the *insertion point* appears in the upper-left corner of your new document. This is where new text will be entered.

Begin typing text from the keyboard. The insertion point moves to the right as you type. When you come to the end of a line, continue to type; you don't have to press the Enter key at the end of each line to return the insertion point to the left margin (you probably remember having to press return on an electric typewriter to return the carriage to the left side of the paper; this isn't necessary in Word or most other computer-based word processors). The text will automatically wrap to the next line for you (see Figure 2.2). This feature is called *word wrap*.

Word Wrap As you type within a paragraph, Word automatically breaks the line of text at the right margin and wraps the text to the next line.

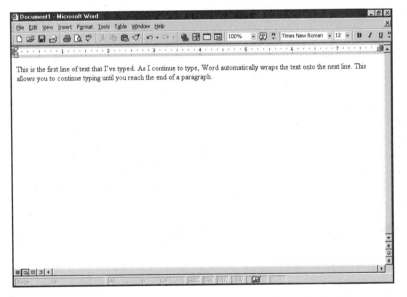

Figure 2.2 Enter your text at the insertion point. Text will automatically wrap to a new line as you type.

When you do reach the end of a paragraph in Word, you will have to press the **Enter** key to manually insert a line break. If you wish to view the manually placed line breaks (called paragraph marks) in your document, click the **Show/Hide** button on the Word standard toolbar. If the Show/Hide button is not visible on the Word toolbar, click **More buttons**. A drop-down box of other buttons like the Show/Hide button will appear. Click the button to turn on the feature and add the button to the toolbar.

 How Word Views Paragraphs Word considers any line or series of lines followed by a line break (created when you press the **Enter** key) a separate paragraph. This concept becomes very important when you deal with paragraph formatting issues such as line spacing, indents, and paragraph borders.

Using Document Templates

You don't have to base your new documents on a blank template. Instead, you can take advantage of one of the special document templates that Word provides. These templates make it easy for you to create everything from memos to newsletters.

Templates contain special text and document attributes; therefore, the look and layout of the document you create using a template are predetermined by the options contained in the template. This can include margins, fonts, graphics, and other document layout attributes.

To base a new document on a Word template, follow these steps:

1. Select the **File** menu, then click **New**. The New dialog box opens.
2. Several template category tabs are available on the **New** dialog box. These tabs include categories such as Legal Pleadings, Letters and Faxes, Memos, and Reports. Select the category tab for the type of document you wish to create. For instance, to create a new memo, click the **Memos** tab.
3. The Memos tab contains templates for different memo types, such as those shown in Figure 2.3. To start a new document based on one of the templates, such as Elegant Memo, double-click the document template.
4. The new document based on the template will appear as shown in Figure 2.4.

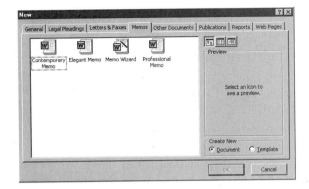

Figure 2.3 The document category tabs on the New dialog box contain templates for different document types.

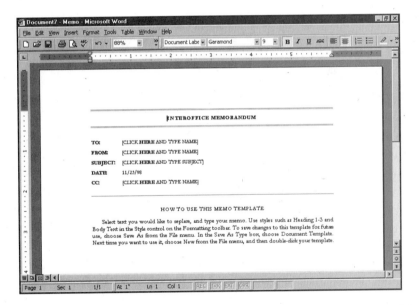

Figure 2.4 The new document contains text and formatting attributes derived from the template.

Most new documents based on templates already contain text, such as headings, as well as a variety of document layouts and text attributes, such as a particular font. For instance, the document based on the Elegant Memo template already contains the layout for a memo, and it automatically enters the current date in the memo for you.

Text can easily be entered into the document using the Click Here and Type boxes that are placed in the document. Just click anywhere on the bracketed box and type the text you wish to enter.

Many templates (the Elegant Memo template, for example) contain text that gives you advice on how to use the template. Any of this explanatory text can be selected and removed or replaced with your own text (for more about selecting and editing text, see Lesson 3, "Editing Documents").

Using Word Wizards

If you find that you would like even more help as you create a new document, you can use any of a number of Word document wizards. These wizards actually walk you through the document creation process, and in many cases, they make sure that you enter the appropriate text in the proper place in the new document.

The wizards are found on the same tabs that housed the templates located in the New dialog box. The wizards can be differentiated from templates by a small "Wizard's wand" that appears on the wizard icon.

To create a new document using one of the wizards, follow these steps:

1. Select the **File** menu, then click **New** to open the New dialog box.
2. In the New dialog box, select the category tab (such as Letters and Faxes) for the new document you wish to create.
3. To start the document creation process using the wizard, double-click the appropriate wizard icon (for example, the Fax Wizard on the Letters and Fax tab).

When you double-click the wizard icon, the Wizard dialog box will open with an introductory screen and outline the document creation process for the type of document you wish to create. For example, the Fax Wizard shown in Figure 2.5 details the Fax creation process on the left side of the Fax Wizard dialog box.

If you find that you need help as you work with the wizard, you can click the Office Assistant button on the Wizard screen. The Office Assistant will appear with context-sensitive help related to the Wizard screen on which you are current working (for help using the Office Assistant, see Appendix B, "Using the Office 2000 Help System").

To move to the next step in the document creation process, click the **Next** button at the bottom of the Wizard screen.

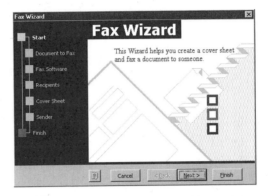

Figure 2.5 The various document wizards, such as the Fax Wizard, outline the new creation process and then walk you through the steps of creating the document.

The various document wizards walk you through the entire document creation process. In the Fax Wizard, for example, you are asked to select what fax software you will use to send the fax and to specify the recipient or recipients of the fax, as shown in Figure 2.6 (for more about using the Fax Wizard, see Lesson 15, "Faxing and Emailing Documents").

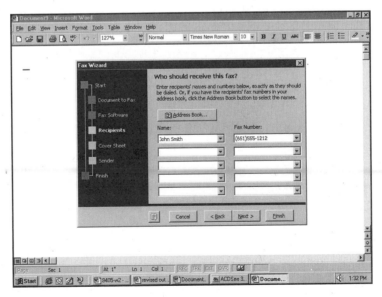

Figure 2.6 The Fax Wizard asks you to specify to whom you want to send the fax.

After completing the steps for document creation, close the wizard by clicking the **Finish** button. A new document appears in the Word window based on the choices you made as the wizard walked you through the document creation process. Figure 2.7 shows a new document created using the Fax Wizard.

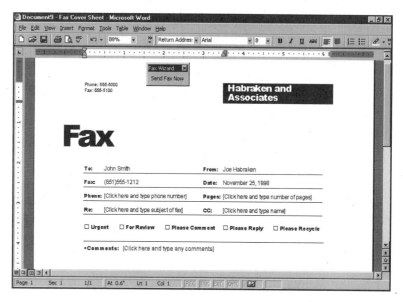

Figure 2.7 The Fax Wizard helps you input the appropriate information in your fax cover page and provides the formatting for the new document.

The wizards you use will vary in "look and feel" depending on the type of document you are trying to create. For instance, the Resume Wizard produces a decidedly different product than the Envelope Wizard does. A good rule to follow is to read each of the wizard screens carefully. Remember that you can always back up a step by clicking the **Back** button if you find that you've made an inappropriate choice.

Saving a Document

Whether you create your new document using the blank template, a Word template, or a document wizard, you will still want to save the new document. Saving your work is one of the most important aspects of working with any software application. If you don't save your Word documents, you will lose all your hard work when you exit the Word application.

To save a document, follow these steps:

1. Click the **Save** button on the Word toolbar or select the **File** menu, then **Save**. The first time you save your new document, the Save As dialog box will appear.

2. Type a file name into the File Name box. If you wish to save the file in a format other than a Word document (.doc), click the **Save as Type** drop-down arrow and select a different file type.

3. To save the file to a different location (the default location is My Documents), click the **Save In** drop-down arrow. After you select a particular drive, the folders on that drive will appear.

4. Double-click any folder in the Save In box to open the folder.

5. After you have specified a name and a location for your new document, select the **Save** button to save the file. You will be returned to the Word document window.

As you edit and enhance your new document, you will want to save changes that you make. To save changes to a document that has been saved under a file name, just click the **Save** button.

If you would like to keep a backup of a document (a version of the document as it appeared the last time you saved it) each time you save changes to it, you need to set the backup option in the Save As dialog box the first time you save the document.

1. Click the **Tools** command on the Save As dialog box toolbar and then select **General Options**.

2. In the General Options dialog box, click the **Always Create Backup Copy** check box and then click **OK** to return to the Save As dialog box.

3. Name your file and save it for the first time to an appropriate location.

Now, when you use the Save command to save changes you've made to the document, a backup copy of the file (with the extension .wbk) will be created. This backup copy is the previous version of the document before you made the changes. Each subsequent saving of the document will replace the backup file with the previous version of the document.

Closing a Document

When you have completed working with a document, you will probably want to save your changes and then close the document. To close a document, select the **File** menu, then select **Close**. You can also close a document by clicking the **Close** (×) button on the right side of the document window. If you are working with multiple documents, closing one of the documents does not close the Word application. If you wish to completely end your Word session, select the **File** menu, then select **Exit**. You will be asked to save any documents that have been changed but not saved. Click **Yes** to save these files. Then the Word application will close.

Opening a Document

Opening an existing document is a straightforward process. You will find that the Open dialog box shares many of the attributes that you saw in the Save As dialog box.

To open an existing Word file, follow these steps:

1. Select the **File** menu, then **Open**. The Open dialog box appears.
2. Click the **Look In** drop-down arrow to select the drive on which the file is located. The folders on the drive appear.
3. Double-click the folder that contains the file. The files in that folder are listed.
4. To open the file, click the file, then click the **Open** button. The file appears in a Word document window.

You can also double-click a file in the Open dialog box to quickly open it in Word. Remember that if you are working with text files or documents that have been saved in a format other than the Word document format (.doc), you will have to select the file type in the **Files of Type** drop-down box.

In this lesson, you learned how to create a new blank document and base a new document on a Word template. You also learned how to create a new document using the Word wizards, how to open an existing document, and how to save your documents. In the next lesson, you learn to edit your document and delete, copy, and move text. You also learn how to save your document under a new file name.

Editing
Documents

*In this lesson, you learn to do basic text editing in Word,
including moving and copying text; you work with the mouse
and keyboard to move your document; and you learn to save
existing documents under a new filename.*

Adding or Replacing Text and Moving in the Document

After you have completed a draft of your document, you will probably find
yourself in a situation where you want to add and delete text in the document
as you edit your work. Word makes it very easy for you to add new text and
delete text that you don't want. You will also find that, whether you use the
mouse or the keyboard to move around in your document as you edit, Word
offers a number of special keystrokes and other tricks that make moving within
the document a breeze. Figure 3.1 highlights some of these tools and Word
screen areas.

Adding New Text

You actually have two possibilities for adding text to the document: *insert* and
typeover. To insert text into the document and adjust the position of the existing
text, place the mouse pointer where you want to insert the new text; the mouse
pointer becomes an *I-beam* (it looks like a capital "I"). Click the mouse to place
the insertion point at the chosen position using the I-beam as your guide.

I-beam: Used to place the
insertion point in the document

Vertical Scrollbar: Scroll
up and down in a document

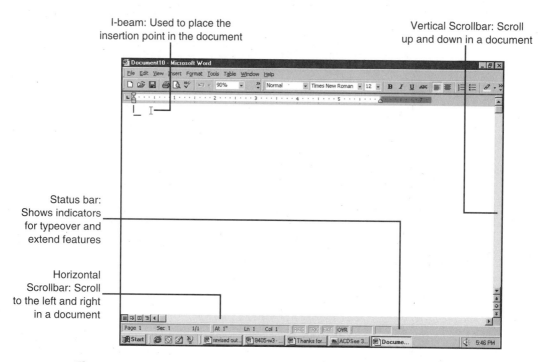

Status bar:
Shows indicators
for typeover and
extend features

Horizontal
Scrollbar: Scroll
to the left and right
in a document

Figure 3.1   A number of different tools and approaches are available for editing
and selecting text in Word and moving around in your Word documents.

I-beam   This is the shape that the mouse pointer takes on when you place
it over any text in a Word document. Use it to place the insertion point at a
particular position in a document.

Type your new text. It is added at the insertion point and existing text
(the text to the right of the inserted text) is pushed forward in the document.

Replacing Text

If you want to add new text to a document and simultaneously delete text to the
right of the insertion point, use the mouse to place the insertion point where you
want to start typing over the existing text. Press the **Insert** key on the keyboard
and add your new text. The added text types over the existing text, deleting it
(see Figure 3.2). You will also find that when you switch to the Typeover mode
using the **Insert** key, the Word status bar displays the message OVR. This means
that you are currently in the typeover mode.

New text replacing current text

Typeover indicator

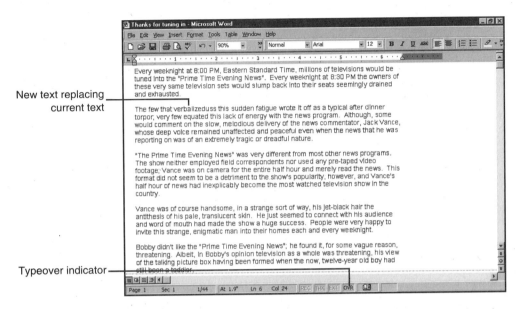

Figure 3.2 When you are in the typeover mode, existing text is overwritten by the new text. Notice that OVR appears on the Word status bar.

Insert Mode The default text mode in Word, new text is added at the insertion point and existing text is pushed forward in the document so that it remains as part of the document.

Typeover Mode Press the **Insert** key to enter this mode; new text is added at the insertion point and types over the existing text, deleting it.

When you have completed entering text in the typeover mode make sure that you switch back to the insert mode. Press the **Insert** key again (it toggles Word between the Insert and Typeover modes) and the OVR message on the status bar is dimmed.

CAUTION **Undo that Typeover**   If you inadvertently type over text in a document because you are in the typeover mode, click the **Undo** button on the toolbar to return the deleted text to the document. Remember to press **Insert** to toggle the feature off.

Moving Around the Document

Whether you are a mouse aficionado or prefer to stick close to your keyboard, Word provides you with a number of shortcuts and tools for moving around a document that you are trying to edit.

When you use the mouse you can move to a different position in the current page by placing the mouse pointer (the I-beam) over a particular text entry and then clicking. This places the insertion point where you clicked.

You can also use the mouse to move through your document via the vertical and horizontal scrollbars. For instance, clicking on the up scroll arrow on the vertical scrollbar moves you up through the document. Clicking on the down scroll arrow moves you down through the document. If you want to move to a relative position in your document by dragging the scroll box to a particular place on the vertical scrollbar. For instance, if you wanted to move half-way through the document, you would drag the scroll box to the half-way position on the vertical scrollbar.

The vertical scrollbar also provides a Previous Page and Next Page button (the double-up arrow and double-down arrow buttons on the bottom of the scrollbar) that can be used to move to the previous page and next page, respectively. Use the mouse to click the appropriate button to move in the direction that you want in your document.

The horizontal scrollbar operates much the same as the vertical scrollbar, however it only offers you the ability to scroll to the left and right of a document page. This is particularly useful however, if you have zoomed in on a document and want to scrutinize an area of the page in great detail.

You should be aware, that using the mouse to change your position in a document using the vertical scrollbar may allow you to view a different portion of a page or a different part of the entire document, however, it does not move the insertion point to the current page or position. To actually place the insertion point, you have to move to a specific place or position in the document and then click the mouse I-beam where you want to place the insertion point.

When you're typing or editing text, you may find that the fastest way to move through the document is with the help of the keyboard shortcuts shown in Table 3.1. Keeping your hands on the keyboard, rather than reaching out for the mouse, may prove to be a more efficient way to move in a document while you compose or edit.

Table 3.1 Using the Keyboard to Move Through the Document

Key Combination	Movement
Home	Move to the beginning of a line
End	Move to the end of a line
Ctrl+Right arrow	Move one word to the right
Ctrl+Left arrow	Move one word to the left
Ctrl+Up arrow	Move to the previous paragraph
Ctrl+Down arrow	Move to the next paragraph
Ctrl+. (period)	Move to the next sentence
PgUp	Move up one window
PgDn	Move down one window
Ctrl+PgUp	Move up one page
Ctrl+PgDn	Move down one page
Ctrl+Home	Move to the top of a document
Ctrl+End	Move to the bottom of a document

Selecting Text

Having a good handle on the different methods for selecting text in a document makes it easy for you to take advantage of a number of features including deleting text, moving text, and formatting text. You can select text with either the mouse or the keyboard. You will find that both methods have their own pluses and minuses as you work on your documents.

Selecting Text with the Mouse

The mouse is an excellent tool for selecting text in your document during the editing process. You can double-click a word to select it and also use different numbers of mouse clicks (quickly pressing the left mouse button) or the mouse in combination with the Shift key to select sentences, paragraphs, or other blocks of text. You can also hold the left mouse button down and drag it across a block of text that you want to select.

How you use the mouse to select the text depends on whether the mouse pointer is in the document itself or along the left side of the document in the *selection bar*. The selection bar is the white space on the left edge of your document window, just before your text paragraphs begin. When you place the mouse in the selection bar, the mouse pointer becomes an arrow (as opposed to placing the mouse in the document where the pointer appears as the I-beam).

Selecting text lines and paragraphs from the selection bar makes it easy for you to quickly select either a single line or the entire document. Table 3.2 shows you how to select different text items using the mouse. Figure 3.3 shows the mouse pointer in the selection bar with a selected sentence.

Table 3.2   Using the Mouse to Quickly Select Text in the Document

Text Selection	Mouse Action
Selects the word	Double-click a word
Selects Text Block	Click and drag
Or	Click at beginning of text, and then hold down Shift key and click at the end of text block
Selects line	Click in selection bar next to line
Selects multiple lines	Click in selection bar and drag down through multiple lines
Selects the sentence	Hold Ctrl and click a sentence
Selects paragraph	Double-click in selection bar next to paragraph
Or	triple click in the paragraph
Selects entire document	Hold down Ctrl and click in selection bar

You will find these mouse manipulations are particularly useful when you are editing the document. Selected text can be quickly deleted, moved, or copied.

Selecting Text with the Keyboard

You can also select text using the keyboard. Press the F8 Function key to turn on the extend (select) feature. EXT appears on the Word Status bar.

To select text using the extend feature, use the arrow keys to move to characters, words, or sentences you want to select. You can also quickly select words by pressing F8 and then pressing the Spacebar. To select an entire sentence, turn on the extend feature and then press the period (.) key. Entire paragraphs can be selected using this method by pressing the **Enter** key. To turn off the extend feature, press the **Esc** key.

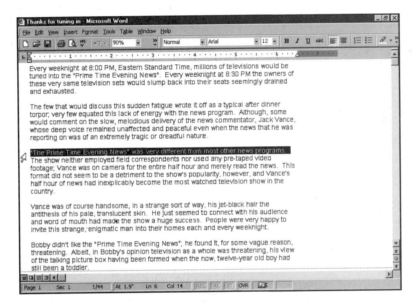

Figure 3.3 Place the mouse pointer in the selection bar to quickly select a line, paragraph, or other text block.

Deleting, Moving, and Copying Text

Another important aspect of editing is being able to delete, move, or copy text in your document. Each of these tasks can be easily accomplished in Word and makes use of the mouse or the keyboard to select the text that you want to delete, move, or copy. Then it's just a matter of invoking the correct command to delete, move, or copy the selected text.

Deleting Text

Deleting text can actually be accomplished in more than one way. The simplest way to remove characters as you type is with the Backspace or Delete keys. With no selected text:

- **Delete**—Deletes the character to the right of the insertion point.
- **Backspace** —Deletes the character to the left of the insertion point.

You will probably find, however, that when you delete text you want to remove more than just one character, so use the keyboard or the mouse to select the text you want to delete. After the text is selected, press the Delete key. The text is then removed from the document.

You can also delete text and replace it with new text in one step. After the text is selected, type the new text. It replaces the existing text.

CAUTION

Delete and Cut Are Different   When you do not need to have access to an edited text block again, use the **Delete** key. In instances where you want to remove text from a particular place in the document, but may want to place it somewhere else use the **Cut** command on the **Edit** menu.

Copying and Pasting Text

When you copy text an actual copy of the selected text is placed on the Windows Clipboard. The Clipboard isn't a place so much as a part of the computer's memory. This piece of memory temporarily holds anything you copy to it. Word 2000 has the capability to hold multiple items on the Clipboard. When multiple items are held on the Clipboard, the Clipboard box opens when the Paste command is invoked. This provides you with a selection of the items that currently reside on the Clipboard.

Use the following steps to copy and paste text in your document:

1. Using the mouse or keyboard select the text that you want to copy.
2. Select the **Edit** menu, and then select **Copy**, or press **Ctrl+C** to copy the text.
3. Place the insertion point in the document where you want to place a copy of the copied text.
4. Select the **Edit** menu, and then select **Paste**. A copy of the text is inserted at the insertion point.

TIP   **Use the Copy, Cut, and Paste Icons**   To quickly access the copy, cut, and paste features use the Copy, Cut, and Paste icons on the Word toolbar, respectively.

Moving Text

You can also use the Clipboard to move text. Using the Clipboard to move text in your document is very similar to copying text.

To move text in a document follow these steps:

1. Using the mouse or keyboard select the text that you want to move.

2. Select the **Edit** menu, and then select **Cut**, or press **Ctrl+X** to cut the text from its current position.

3. Place the insertion point in the document where you want to move the text.

4. Select the **Edit** menu, and then select **Paste**. The text is moved to the new location (defined by the insertion point).

You can also select the text and just drag it to a new location. After the text is selected, place the mouse on the text block and press the left mouse button (hold the left mouse button). A Move pointer appears as shown in Figure 3.4.

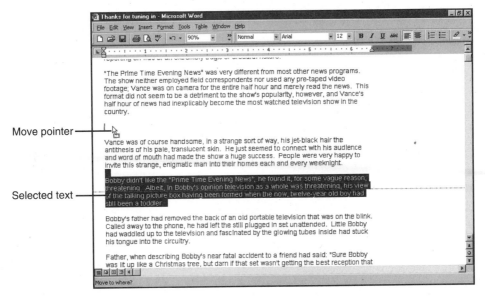

Figure 3.4   Drag a block of selected text to a new location with drag and drop.

Drag the Move pointer to the new location for the text. A dotted insertion point appears in the text. Place this insertion point in the appropriate position and release the mouse button. The text is moved to the new location.

Using the Save As Command

After editing a particular document, you may want to save the edited version under a new filename. Word makes it easy for you to save multiple versions of the same document or documents using the **Save As** command.

To save your document with a new filename follow these steps:

1. Select **File**, and then select **Save As**.

2. In the Save As dialog box type the new filename in the Filename box.

3. Click **Save**. The file is saved under the new name.

Opening and Switching Between Multiple Documents

Word also provides you with the ability to open multiple documents on the Windows desktop. This is particularly useful when you want to copy and paste (or cut and paste) between documents.

To open multiple documents in Word, you use the Open command. To open a document from the current document, select the **File** menu, and then select **Open**. The Open dialog box appears. Use the **Look In** drop-down box to choose the drive that holds the file and then double-click the appropriate folder to locate the file. When located, select the file and then click **OK**.

The Word document opens on top of the document that you were previously working in. The newly opened document resides in a Word application window exactly the same as the document you already had open. Word documents occupying separate Word application windows is a new feature of Word 2000 and the other applications found in Office 2000. If you look at the Windows taskbar, buttons for both the newly opened document and the previously opened document are available.

To switch between the Word documents, click the appropriate button on the Taskbar. You can also open additional Word documents and additional buttons (for the newly opened documents) appear on the Taskbar. Click a button to switch to that particular Word window.

Copying and Moving Text Between Documents

You can copy and move text easily between documents. All you have to do is open the appropriate documents and then use the methods already discussed for copying or moving text. You can even use drag and drop to move inform ation from one document to another.

To copy information from one document to another follow these steps:

1. Open the document you want to copy the information from; click the **File** menu, and then click **Open**. Select the document from the Open dialog box and then click **Open**.

2. Open the document that you want to copy the information to by using step 1.

3. To switch back to the document that contains the text you want to copy, click the document's button on the Taskbar or Select the Windows menu and then the name of the document.

4. Select the text you want to copy and then select the **Edit** menu, and then select the **Copy** command.

5. Click the document's button on the Windows Taskbar or on Word's **Window** menu to switch to the document that you want to paste the text into.

6. Select the **Edit** menu, and then select **Paste**. The text is pasted into your document.

You can also use the steps outlined to move text from one document to another by substituting the Cut command for the Copy command. If you want you can also use drag and drop to move text from one document to another. Working with multiple document windows can be tricky. For more information on using the Windows Taskbar and working with multiple Windows on the desktop, see Lesson 2 "Navigating the Windows 98 Desktop" in Part I.

In this lesson, you learned basic editing techniques including the deleting, copying, and moving of text. You also learned to move around your documents and various ways to select text. You also worked with multiple documents and copied text from one document to another. In the next lesson you learn how to use the AutoText feature and add special characters to your documents.

Adding Document Text with AutoText and Using Special Characters

In this lesson, you learn to quickly add repeating text elements to your documents using the AutoText feature. You also learn to add special characters to your document, such as the copyright symbol.

Understanding AutoText

AutoText provides you with a way to build a library of words and text phrases that you use often in your documents. An AutoText entry can consist of a company name, your name, or an entire paragraph that you commonly place in your documents.

AutoText makes it easy for you to quickly insert items from your AutoText list into any document. Creating AutoText entries is also very straightforward.

Creating AutoText Entries

You can create an AutoText entry using text from an existing document, or you can type the text that you want to add to the AutoText list in a blank document. It's then just a matter of copying the text to your AutoText list.

To create an AutoText entry, follow these steps:

1. Type the text you want to use for the AutoText entry or open the document containing the text that will serve as the AutoText entry.

2. Select the text.

3. Select the **Insert** menu, point at **AutoText**, then select **New** from the cascading menu. The Create AutoText dialog box will appear as shown in Figure 4.1.

TIP   **AutoText Isn't on My Insert Menu**   Remember that Word 2000 uses a personalized menu system that places your most recently used commands on the various menus. If you click a menu and don't see a particular command, wait for a moment; the menu will expand and provide a list of all the commands available on that particular menu.

Figure 4.1   Type a name for your new AutoText entry in the Create AutoText dialog box.

4. Type the name that you will use to retrieve this AutoText entry in the text box provided (for one-word text entries, the selected text can also serve as the entry name).

5. After providing the name for the AutoText entry, click **OK**.

Your selected text is added to the AutoText list. You can repeat the above procedure and add as many text items to the AutoText list as you want.

Inserting AutoText Entries

After you add an AutoText entry or entries to the list, you can insert them into any Word document. One method of inserting an AutoText entry into the current document is to pull the entry directly from the AutoText list.

To insert an AutoText entry into a document, follow these steps:

1. Place the insertion point in the document where you want to insert the AutoText entry.

2. Select the **Insert** menu, point at **AutoText**, then select **AutoText**. The AutoCorrect dialog box will appear as shown in Figure 4.2.

Figure 4.2 Insert your AutoText entries from the AutoCorrect dialog box.

3. The AutoText tab of the AutoCorrect dialog box displays a list of the AutoText entries that you have added to the AutoText list (a number of default entries provided by Word are also listed). Select the entry you want to insert and then click **Insert**. Or double-click any entry on the list to insert it into the document. The AutoText entry is inserted into your document. An alternative to manually inserting AutoText into the document is using the AutoComplete feature to automatically insert an entry into your document. For instance, if you have an entry in your AutoText list that reads "Super Computer Company," you can automatically insert this entry into your document by beginning to type the entry. As you type the first few letters in the AutoText entry, an Auto-Complete box appears containing the complete AutoText entry, as shown in Figure 4.3.

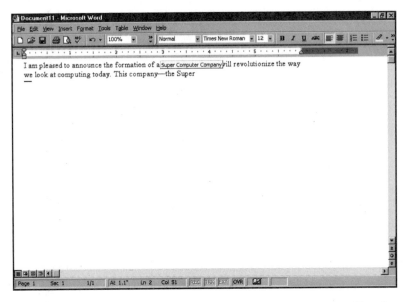

Figure 4.3   AutoComplete automatically places entries from your AutoText list into your documents.

To insert the entry into the document press the **Enter** key. You find that AutoComplete also helps you enter items that are not included on your AutoText list into your document. These items include the current date, days of the week, and names of months.

TIP   **Use the AutoText Toolbar to Quickly Insert AutoText Entries** Right-click any toolbar and then select **AutoText** from the menu. To add an entry into the current document, click the **All Entries** button on the AutoText toolbar and select your AutoText from the list.

Deleting AutoText Entries

You can easily delete items on the AutoText list when you no longer have a need for them. This is done on the AutoText tab of the AutoCorrect dialog box.

177

To delete an AutoText entry, follow these steps:

1. Select the **Insert** menu, point at **AutoText**, then select **AutoText** from the cascading menu. The AutoCorrect dialog box appears.
2. Select any of the entries in the AutoText list.
3. Click **Delete** to remove the entry from the list.

After you have completed your deletion of AutoText entries, click **OK** to close the AutoText dialog box.

Using Special Characters and Symbols

Special characters and symbols are characters that can't be found on your keyboard and are not part of what is considered to be the standard character set. Characters such as the u with an umlaut (it's very important in German words) are considered special characters, and an item such as the trademark symbol is an example of a symbol.

A number of special characters and symbols exist. Table 4.1 lists some of the commonly used special characters and symbols.

Table 4.1 Common Special Characters and Symbols

Special Character or Symbol	Use
Copyright symbol	Used in a copyright notice in a document ©.
Trademark symbol	Placed to the right of official trademarks placed in a document ™.
Em dash	Used to bracket asides or sudden changes in emphasis in a sentence—rather than using a comma. It appears as a long dash.
En dash	Slightly shorter than an em dash, this dash is commonly used to separate numbers from capital letters, such as Figure B–1.
Wingdings	A group of special icons ☺ that can be used in your documents for emphasis or as bullets.
Foreign language characters	Characters that include special accents, such as À.

The basic special characters and symbols are held in three groups:

- **Symbol**—This group contains mathematical symbols, arrows, trademark and copyright symbols, and letters from the Greek alphabet.
- **Normal Text**—This group provides you with special characters containing accents and other special marks.
- **Wingdings**—Special icons and symbols for almost any purpose.

Additional special character sets may be available to you depending on which fonts have been installed on your computer.

Inserting Special Characters and Symbols

Special characters and symbols can be easily inserted into your documents by using the Insert Symbol feature. To insert a special character or symbol, follow these steps:

1. Place the insertion point in your document where you want to insert the special character or symbol. Select **Insert**, then **Symbol**. The Symbol dialog box appears as shown in Figure 4.4.

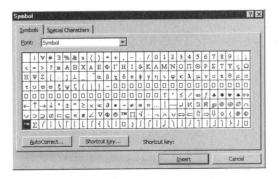

Figure 4.4   The Symbol dialog box gives you access to Symbols and Special Characters that you can insert into your document.

2. To insert a symbol, make sure the Symbol tab is selected on the dialog box (if you want to insert a special character, go to step 5). Use the Font drop-down box to select the Symbol set from which you want to choose your symbol.

3. After you select the Symbol set (such as normal text, Symbol, Wingdings, or other font family available), click to select the symbol you want to insert.

4. After selecting the symbol, click the **Insert** button.

5. If you want to insert a special character, such as the copyright symbol or an em dash, click the **Special Characters** tab on the Symbol dialog box.

6. Select the special character, then click **Insert**.

7. When you have completed inserting your symbol or special character, click the **Close** button on the Symbol dialog box.

My Key Combination Turns into a Symbol   The Word AutoCorrect feature is set up to replace a number of character combinations with special characters. You can override these changes made by the AutoCorrect feature

CAUTION   by immediately pressing the **Backspace** key. For more on AutoCorrect see Lesson 5, "Using Proofreading Tools."

After you've inserted the symbol or special character into the document, you can continue typing or editing your text. Symbols and special characters give your document a finished, typeset look.

In this lesson, you learned how to create an AutoText entry list and insert AutoText entries into your documents. You also learned to add special characters to your documents. In the next lesson, you learn to use the document proofing tools provided in Word.

Using Proofreading Tools

In this lesson, you learn to check your documents for errors such as misspellings and improper grammar. You work with the spell checker and grammar checker and learn how to find synonyms with the thesaurus, proof your document as you type, and use the AutoCorrect feature.

Proofing as You Type

Word offers several excellent features for helping you to create error-free documents. Each of these features—the spell checker, the grammar checker, and the thesaurus—will be explored in this lesson. Word also gives you the option of checking your spelling and grammar automatically as you type. And the AutoCorrect feature will automatically make some proofing changes for you (for more about AutoCorrect, see "Working with AutoCorrect" in this lesson).

Proofing as you type simply means that errors in spelling and grammar can be automatically flagged as you enter text into your document. This enables you to quickly and immediately correct errors as you build your document.

When you proof as you type, spelling errors—words not found in the Word dictionary file or in your custom dictionary file—will be flagged with a wavy red line. Errors in grammar will be likewise underlined with a way green line. Spelling and grammar errors marked in this way can be corrected on-the-fly, or you can correct them collectively by running the spelling and grammar checking features after you have finished entering all the text. For information on using the Spelling and Grammar Checker on a completed document, see the section "Using the Spelling and Grammar Checker," later in this lesson.

The Proof as you type features are on in Word by default. To change the defaults associated with the automatic spelling and grammar checking features (or turn them off completely), follow these steps:

1. Select the **Tools** menu, then choose **Options**. The Options dialog box opens.

2. Make sure the **Spelling and Grammar** tab is selected as shown in Figure 5.1.

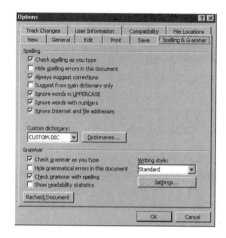

Figure 5.1 You can turn the automatic spelling and grammar checking options on or off in the Options dialog box.

3. To turn on the automatic spelling checker, click the **Check Spelling as You Type** check box in the Spelling area of the dialog box.

4. To turn on the automatic grammar checker, click the **Check Grammar as You Type** check box in the Grammar area of the dialog box (near the bottom).

Obviously, if you find the wavy lines in your document distracting, you can also clear either of these check boxes (or both) to turn these features off. After you have finished making your selections in the Options dialog box, click **OK**.

Now, as you type, suspected misspellings and grammatical errors will be flagged with the appropriate colored wavy line. To correct words flagged as misspelled, follow these steps:

1. Place the mouse pointer on the flagged word and click the right mouse button. A shortcut menu will appear as shown in Figure 5.2.

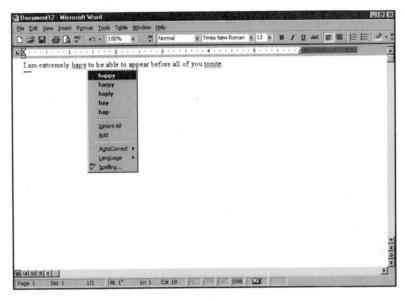

Figure 5.2 Right-click any flagged word to get a list of suggested spellings.

2. If Word provides a list of suggestions, select the correct spelling for the word from the list. The word will be corrected with the correctly spelled word.

- If the flagged word is correctly spelled but is not in the dictionary files, you have three other options: you can click **Ignore All** and the wavy red line will be removed from all occurrences of the word.

- Or you can add the word to the dictionary file; click **Add**. All occurrences of the word will have the wavy red line removed, and when you add the word to a document in the future, the word will be considered spelled correctly and not flagged.

- If you find that you constantly misspell the word as it currently appears in your document, you can add the word to the AutoCorrect list. Point to **AutoCorrect**. Suggested spellings will be listed. Select a spelling from the list; the incorrect spelling and the correct spelling will be entered in the AutoCorrect list. The word will be corrected, and the next time you type the word incorrectly, it will be automatically corrected.

183

> **TIP** **Automatically Corrected Spelling Errors** Some of your misspelled words are automatically corrected as you type. This is done by the AutoCorrect feature that uses a list of common spelling errors and typos to correct entries in your documents. For expanding the AutoCorrect list and other associated information, see the section "Working with AutoCorrect" later in this lesson.

Correcting grammatical errors as you type is very similar to correcting spelling errors that are flagged in the document. Suspected grammatical errors will be marked with a green wavy line.

To correct a suspected grammatical error, follow these steps:

1. Right-click text strings marked with the green wavy line.
2. The shortcut menu that appears may offer you a list of grammatically correct phrases. Select the phrase that corrects your text entry.
3. If your text is not incorrect grammatically, click **Ignore**.

As soon as you make a selection from the shortcut menu or click **Ignore**, the shortcut menu will close. You can then continue working on your document.

Using the Spelling and Grammar Checker

If you do not wish to correct spelling and grammatical errors as you type, you can run the Spelling and Grammar feature after you have completed typing your document. Waiting to correct the document until you have finished composing all your text enables you to concentrate on getting your thoughts down interruption free. You can then check the entire document upon completion.

To use the Word Spelling and Grammar feature, follow these steps:

1. Select **Tools**, then **Spelling and Grammar**, or click the **Spelling and Grammar** button on the toolbar. The Spelling and Grammar dialog box appears as shown in Figure 5.3.
2. Words not found in the dictionary will be flagged, and the text that the word is contained in will be displayed in the Not in Dictionary box.

You can manually correct the highlighted word in the box and then click **Change** to correct the word in the document. Other options available for the flagged word are

- Select the appropriate selection for the flagged word from the Suggestion box and click **Change**. If you want to correct all occurrences of the misspelled word (assuming you have consistently misspelled it), click **Change All**.

- You can also choose to ignore the flagged word if it is correctly spelled. Click **Ignore** to ignore this occurrence of the word, or click **Ignore All** to ignore all occurrences of the word in the document.

- You can also add the word to the dictionary; click **Add**.

- If you would rather add the misspelled word and an appropriate correct spelling to the AutoCorrect feature, click **AutoCorrect**; the word will be corrected and future insertions of the word with the incorrect spelling will be automatically corrected.

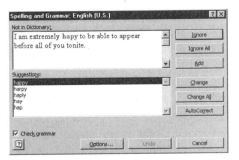

Figure 5.3 The Spelling and Grammar dialog box displays the suspected spelling and grammar errors in your document and offers you options for correcting them.

3. Whichever selection you make, the word will be dealt with appropriately and the Spell checker will move on to the next flagged word. Make your selection either to correct or to ignore the word, as previously outlined.

If the Check Grammar check box in the Spelling and Grammar dialog box is selected, Word will also check the grammar in your document. Word actually checks different syntax and grammar parameters, such as subject-verb agreement and passive sentence structure.

When the Spelling and Grammar dialog box flags a grammatical error in the document, the suspected error appears in the text box at the top of the Spelling and Grammar dialog box with a heading that describes the type of error. Figure 5.4 shows a sentence fragment that has been caught by the grammar checker.

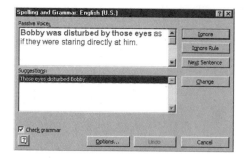

Figure 5.4   The grammar checker will flag suspected grammar errors and offer suggestions and possible fixes for the problem.

To correct flagged grammatical errors, follow these steps:

Suggested corrections, if available, will appear in the Suggestions box. In the case of the fragment, the suggestion is to consider revising the fragment. In other cases, more suggestions with actual sentence revisions may appear in this box. Select the appropriate revision and click **Change**.

You are also presented with different ignore options for flagged grammatical errors:

- You can choose to ignore the suspected grammatical error by clicking **Ignore**. This will ignore the currently flagged error.
- In some cases, **Ignore All** will also be an option. If you click **Ignore All**, all occurrences of this same grammatical error will be ignored by the grammar checker in the rest of the document.
- Word also provides you with the option of ignoring the grammar rule that was used to flag the current grammatical error; click **Ignore Rule** to do this throughout the document. This means that any error (not just the current error) that is flagged because of that particular rule will not be flagged as a grammatical error.

When you have dealt with the suspected error, the Spelling and Grammar feature moves on to the next suspected error in the document. Use the options discussed to deal with grammatical errors that are flagged.

Finding Synonyms Using the Thesaurus

The Word thesaurus provides you with a tool that can be used to find synonyms for the words in your document. Synonyms are words that mean the same thing. Because the thesaurus can generate a list of synonyms for nearly any word in your document, you can avoid the constant use of a particular descriptive adjective (such as "excellent") and actually add some depth to the vocabulary that appears in your document.

TIP   **The Thesaurus Also Lists Antonyms**   Depending on the word you select to find synonyms for using the thesaurus, you may find that a list of antonyms—words that mean the opposite—are also provided. Antonyms will be marked with (antonym) to the right of the suggested word.

TERM   **Synonyms**   Words that have the same or similar meanings.

To use the thesaurus, follow these steps:

1. Place the insertion point on the word for which you want to find a synonym.

2. Select the **Tools** menu, point at **Language**, then select **Thesaurus**. The Thesaurus dialog box will appear as shown in Figure 5.5.

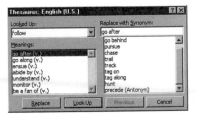

Figure 5.5   The Thesaurus dialog box offers a list of synonyms for the selected word.

3. To replace the word with a synonym, select the synonym in the synonym list and then click **Replace**.

4. You can also choose to see a list of synonyms for any of the words listed in the synonym list. Select the word and then click **Look Up**.

After you have selected a synonym and clicked **Replace**, the word is replaced in the document and the Thesaurus dialog box closes.

TIP   **Right-Click for Synonyms**   A quick way to get a list of synonyms for a word is to right-click a word in your document and then select **Synonyms** from the shortcut menu. A list of synonyms will appear. Select the appropriate word on the list to replace the currently selected word.

Working with AutoCorrect

AutoCorrect provides you with a way to automatically correct words that you constantly and consistently misspell. For instance, if you always spell aardvark as ardvark, you can set up AutoCorrect to correct this spelling error every time you type it.

You've already seen that the Spelling feature provides you with the option of placing misspelled words into the AutoCorrect library. You can also manually enter pairs of words (the incorrect and correct spelling) in the AutoCorrect dialog box.

To place words in the AutoCorrect list, follow these steps:

1. Click the **Tools** menu, then click **AutoCorrect**. The AutoCorrect dialog box will appear as shown in Figure 5.6.

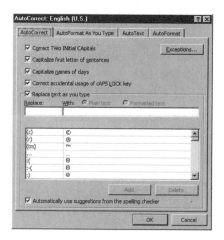

Figure 5.6   The AutoCorrect feature enables you to build a list of commonly misspelled words for automatic correction.

2. Enter the word as you misspell it in the **Replace** box. In the **With** box enter the correct spelling of the word.

3. Click **Add** to add the entry to the AutoCorrect list.

4. When you have completed adding entries, click **OK** to close the dialog box.

Now when you misspell the word, it will be corrected for you automatically. An example is "misspelled." If you happen to type the word with only one "s" (which I seem to do all the time), the word is automatically corrected and the missing "s" is added. You can also use the AutoCorrect dialog box to delete AutoCorrect entries that you do not use or that inadvertently correct items that you wish to have in your document.

 TIP **Override the AutoCorrect Feature** If you type a text entry that is changed by the AutoCorrect feature, immediately press the **Backspace** key. This will return the word to the text you originally entered.

In this lesson, you learned how to proof your documents as you type. You also learned to use the Spelling and Grammar feature and select synonyms for words in your document using the thesaurus. You also explored the use of the Auto-Correct feature. In the next lesson, you learn how to change the look of your documents using fonts and how to align text in your documents.

Changing How
Text Looks

*In this lesson, you learn basic ways to change the look of your
text. You work with fonts and learn how to change font attributes.
You also work with text alignment, such as centering and right justification.*

Understanding Fonts

When you work in Word, you want to be able to control the look of the text in
the documents that you create. The size and appearance of the text is controlled
for the most part by the font or fonts you choose to use in the document. Each
available font has a particular style or typeface. A variety of fonts exists, such as
Arial, Courier, Times New Roman, CG Times, Bookman Old Style, and so on; the
fonts you can choose from depend on the fonts that have been installed on your
computer (Windows 98 and 95 provide most of the font families that applications
such as Microsoft Word use; you will also find that additional fonts are added to
your computer when you install Office 2000, particularly when you install applications such as PowerPoint and Publisher). Each font has a particular look and
feel that makes it unique.

TIP   **Keep Your Business Documents Standard**   The standard point size
for most business documents is 12 point, which is 1/6 of an inch tall. So when
selecting a new font, make sure that you use 12 point for documents such as
business letters and memos.

You have the ability to change the font or fonts used in a document whenever
you have the need, and you can also manipulate the size of the characters and
their attributes, including bold, underlining, and italic. You can select a new font
before you begin typing your document, or you can select text and change its
fonts and text attributes at any time.

Changing Font Attributes

The easiest way to change font attributes is through the use of the buttons provided on the Word Formatting toolbar. Figure 6.1 shows the Word Formatting toolbar with some of the most common font attribute buttons displayed.

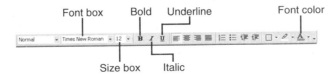

Figure 6.1 The Word Formatting toolbar gives you quick access to control the font attributes in your documents.

You can quickly change the font of selected text by clicking the **Font** box and selecting a new font from the list that appears. Other attributes, such as bold, italic, and underline, only require that you select the text and then click the appropriate button once to add that attribute to the text. For example, you may want to apply special formatting to a heading so that it stands out from rest of the text. You can do that by adding bold to the text.

To bold text in a document, follow these steps:

1. Select the word or other text to be bold.
2. Click the **Bold** button on the Formatting toolbar. The text appears in bold.
3. Click another part of the document to deselect the text and view the results of your formatting.

You can use this same technique to underline and italicize text in your documents.

I Don't Have Those Buttons on My Toolbar Click the **More Buttons** drop-down arrow and select **Add or Remove Buttons**; then select the buttons from the drop-down list that you want to add to the Formatting toolbar. If you don't see the Formatting toolbar at all, right-click any of the toolbars and select **Formatting** on the menu that appears.

CAUTION

You can also use the various font buttons to select font attributes for new text you type into a new document or insert into an existing document. Select the appropriate font attributes on the Formatting toolbar and then type the text. To turn off a particular attribute, such as bold or italic, click the appropriate button a second time. To change to a new font or size, use the appropriate drop-down box.

When you are typing in a document, you might find that selecting font attributes from the toolbar actually slows you down because you must remove one hand from the keyboard to use the mouse to make your selection. You can also turn on or off a number of the formatting attributes using shortcut keys on the keyboard. Table 6.1 shows some of the common keyboard shortcuts for formatting attributes.

Table 6.1 Font Attribute Shortcut Keys

Attribute	Shortcut Keys
Bold	Ctrl+B
Italic	Ctrl+I
Underline	Ctrl+U
Double underline	Ctrl+Shift+D
Subscript	Ctrl+equal sign (=)
Superscript	Ctrl+Shift+plus sign (+)

To use any of the shortcut key combinations, press the keys shown simultaneously to turn the attribute on and then repeat the key sequence to turn the attribute off. For instance, to turn on bold while you are typing, press the **Ctrl** key and the **B** key at the same time. Press these keys again to turn the bold off.

Working in the Font Dialog Box

Although the Formatting toolbar certainly provides the quickest avenue for controlling various font attributes such as the font and the font size, you can access several more font attributes in the Font dialog box. The Font dialog box gives you control over common attributes such as font, font size, bold, and so on, and it also provides you with control over special font attributes such as superscript, subscript, and strikethrough.

To open the Font dialog box, select the **Format** menu, and then select **Font**. The Font dialog box appears, as shown in Figure 6.2.

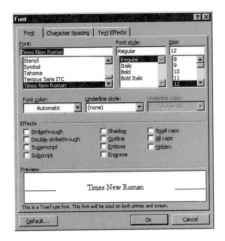

Figure 6.2 The Font dialog box provides you with control over a number of font attributes not found on the Formatting toolbar.

As you can see, the Font dialog box enables you to choose from a number of font attributes. You can control the font, the font style, and other character attributes such as strikethrough, superscript, and shadow.

- To change the font, click the **Font** drop-down box and select the new font by name.
- To change the font style to italic, bold, or bold italic, make the appropriate selection in the **Font Style** box.
- To change the size of the font, select the appropriate size in the **Size** scroll box.
- For underlining, click the **Underline Style** drop-down box and select an underlining style.
- To change the color of the font, click the **Font Color** drop-down box and select a new color.
- To select any special effects, such as strikethrough, superscript, or shadow, select the appropriate check box in the lower half of the dialog box.

As you make the various selections in the Font dialog box, a sample of what the text will look like appears in the Preview box at the bottom of the dialog box. After you have made all your selections in the Font dialog box, click **OK**.

TIP   **Change the Default Font**   To change the default font that you use for your documents (documents created using the template you are currently basing your document on), select the font attributes in the Font dialog box, then click the **Default** button at the lower left of the dialog box, then click **Yes**.

Aligning Text

Another important basic attribute of the text in your documents is how that text is aligned on the page. When you first start typing in a new document, all the text begins at the left margin and moves to the right as you type; this means the default alignment for text is left justified. Left-justified text is characterized by text that is straight or aligned on the left and has a ragged right edge.

Text that serves a special function in a document, such as a heading, will probably stand out better in the document if it is aligned differently than the rest of the text. Word makes it easy for you to change the alignment of any text paragraph. Several alignment possibilities are available:

- **Left Justified**—The default justification for normal text, aligned on the left.
- **Right Justified**—Text is aligned at the right margin, and text lines show a ragged left edge.
- **Center**—The text is centered between the left and right margins of the page.
- **Full Justification**—The text is justified on both the left and the right, so text is aligned at both the right and the left margins.

Remember How Word Sees a Paragraph   Any text followed by a paragraph mark—created when you press the **Enter** key—is considered a separate paragraph in Word.

CAUTION

Figure 6.3 shows examples of each of the alignment possibilities.

The easiest way to change the alignment of text in the document is to use the alignment buttons on the Formatting toolbar. A button exists in the Paragraph dialog box for each of the alignment possibilities. Table 6.2 shows the buttons and their functions.

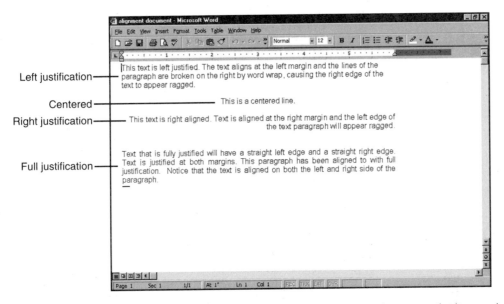

Figure 6.3 You can align the text in your document to suit your particular needs on a document page.

Table 6.2 Alignment Icons on the Formatting Toolbar

Button	*Justification*
	Align left
	Center
	Align right
	Justify (full justification)

These justification buttons can be used to align new text or selected text. Again, if you are typing new text with a particular justification, your selected justification will still be in force even after you press Enter. You must change the justification as needed.

Aligning Text with Click and Type

Word also offers a very fast and easy way to align new text. You can use the mouse pointer to quickly designate how you want a new line of text justified on the page.

To use the Click and Type feature, make sure that you are in the Print Layout or Web Layout view. The feature is not available in the Normal view. To switch to the Print Layout or Web Layout view, select **View**, and then the appropriate view from the View menu.

Click and Type Option Must Be On   To use Click and Type, you must also make sure that it is selected on the **Edit** tab of the Options dialog box (select **Tools**, **Options** to open this dialog box).

To use Click and Type to align your new text, follow these steps:

1. Move the mouse pointer toward the area of the page where you want to place the insertion point:

 • Center (the centering pointer appears)

 • Right (the align-right pointer appears)

2. After the mouse pointer shows the centering or right-align icon, double-click in the document. The insertion point moves to the selected justification.

3. Type your new text.

After you've typed the centered or right-aligned text and you've pressed **Enter** to create a new line, you can return to left justification by placing the mouse on the left of the line (the align-left icon appears on the mouse pointer) and double-clicking.

In this lesson, you learned how change the font and font size in your document and work with various font attributes, such as bold, italic, and underline. You also learned how to align text in your document and worked with the various justification options. In the next lesson, you learn how to use borders and colors to emphasize text in your documents.

Using Borders and Colors

*In this lesson, you learn how to use borders
and colors to emphasize text in your documents.*

Adding Borders to Text

You've already learned that there are a number of different font attributes,
such as font size, bold, italic, and underline, that you can use to emphasize and
otherwise denote certain text in your document (see Lesson 6, "Changing How
Text Looks"). You also learned that alignment such as centering can be used to
set off certain text lines on a page. Word provides you with the ability to add
borders to your text and even place a shadow on the edge of the border for
greater emphasis.

A border can be placed around any text paragraph (any line followed by a
paragraph mark). This means that one line of text or a number of lines of text
can have a border placed around them.

 TIP ¶ **Remember How Word Views a Paragraph** Whenever you type a
line or a number of lines of text and then press Enter, you are placing an
end-of-paragraph mark at the end of the text. Word views any line or lines
followed by a paragraph mark as a separate paragraph. If you need to view the
paragraph marks in your document, click the **Show/Hide** button on the Word
Standard toolbar.

To place a border around a text paragraph, follow these steps:

1. Place the insertion point in the paragraph that you want to place the border around. If you want to place a border around multiple paragraphs, select the paragraphs.

2. Select the **Format** menu, and then **Borders and Shading**. The Borders and Shading dialog box will appear, as shown in Figure 7.1.

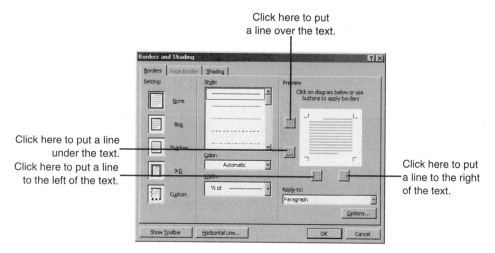

Click here to put
a line over the text.

Click here to put a line
under the text.
Click here to put a line
to the left of the text.

Click here to put
a line to the right
of the text.

Figure 7.1 The Borders and Shading dialog box enables you to place a border around your text.

3. Make sure the **Borders** tab is selected on the dialog box. You are provided with several settings for how the border should appear around the text.

4. In the Setting area of the dialog box, select the type of box you want around your text: choose **Box**, **Shadow**, **3-D**, or **Custom** by clicking the appropriate setting sample. The Custom option enables you to create a border that uses different line styles for the various sides of the border.

TIP **Removing a Border from a Paragraph** If you want to remove the border from a paragraph, choose **None** in the Setting area of the Borders and Shading dialog box.

5. Several line styles are available for your border. Click the **Style** scroll box to scroll through the various line styles and then click the style you want to use.

6. To change the color of the border lines, click the **Color** drop-down arrow and select a color from the color palette that appears.

7. As you select the various parameters for your border (in cases where you have selected Box, Shadow, or 3-D as the border setting), you can view a preview of the border in the Preview box. The Preview box also makes it easy for you to place an incomplete border around a paragraph in cases where you might only want a line above or below the text (refer to Figure 7.1).

8. When you have completed selecting the settings for the border, click the **OK** button. The border will appear around the paragraph or paragraphs (if you selected more than one) in the document, as shown in Figure 7.2.

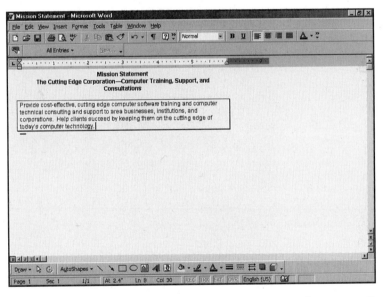

Figure 7.2 A border appears around the selected paragraph after you set the border parameters in the Borders and Shading dialog box.

Borders Around More Than One Paragraph If you select several paragraphs that are using the same style and indents (for more about styles, see Lesson 10, "Working with Margins, Pages, and Line Spacing," and for more about indents see Lesson 8, "Working with Tabs and Indents"), Word places one border around all the paragraphs. If you want separate borders around the paragraphs, assign a border to them one at a time.

CAUTION

You also can quickly place a border around a paragraph or other selected text by using the Tables and Borders toolbar. Right-click any of the currently shown toolbars and select **Tables and Borders** from the toolbar list. The Tables and Borders toolbar will appear in the document window.

 To apply a border to a paragraph, make sure the insertion point is in the paragraph, then click the **Borders** drop-down button on the Tables and Borders toolbar. Select the type of border you want to place around the text from the border list provided.

Placing a Border Around a Page

If you find that you would like to place a border around an entire page or pages in your document, you will want to use the Page Border feature.

Follow these steps to place a border around the entire page:

1. Open the Borders and Shading dialog box (click the **Format** menu, then select **Borders and Shading**) and click the **Page Border** tab.

2. Select the **Border** setting and style as you would for a paragraph border.

3. Click the **Apply To** list drop-down arrow and select one of the following:

   - **Whole Document** places a border around each of the pages in the document.

   - **This Section** places a border around each of the pages in the current section of the document.

   - **This Section-First Page Only** places a border around the first page of the current section.

   - **This Section-All Except First Page** places a border around each of the pages of the current section except the first page of the section.

To put a border around pages in a section, you must place sections in your document. Sections enable you to break a large document into smaller parts that can have radically different formatting attributes. For more about sections and how to create them, see Lesson 21, "Working with Larger Documents."

Adding Shading to the Paragraph

You can place a color or grayscale pattern behind the text in a paragraph or paragraphs. This color or pattern is called shading and can be used with or without a border around the text.

To add shading to text, you must select the text for a particular paragraph—just make sure the insertion point is in the paragraph. After you've designated the text that you want to place the shading behind, follow these steps:

1. Select **Format**, then **Borders and Shading**. The Borders and Shading dialog box will appear.
2. Select the **Shading** tab, as shown in Figure 7.3.

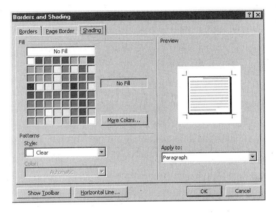

Figure 7.3 You can apply shading to a paragraph or selected text.

3. To select a fill color, click one of the colors on the color palette in the **Fill** area.
4. To select a pattern for the fill color, click the **Style** drop-down arrow and select a pattern from the list.
5. Use the **Apply To** drop-down arrow to designate whether the current paragraph or selected text should be shaded.
6. When you have completed your selections, click **OK**.

Your selected text or paragraph will now be shaded.

Changing Font Colors

When you use the shading options, you might find that the current text color does not show up that well on the fill color or pattern that you selected. You can quickly change the font color for selected text anywhere in your document.

To change the color of text, follow these steps:

1. Select the text that you want to change to a different font color.
2. Select the **Format** menu, then select **Font**. The Font dialog box will appear.
3. In the Font dialog box, click the **Font Color** drop-down arrow and select the color you want to use.
4. When you have completed your selection, click **OK**.

You might find that you have to play around with the fill color and the font color to get an ideal combination on the page. You might even have to print out a sample page to see if the colors work well on an actual printed page. Intensity of color will vary for some color printers. You might also find that bolding the text that you've placed a fill color behind might make the text more readable.

In this lesson, you learned how to place a border around your text and place shading behind text. You also learned how to change the font color for selected text. In the next lesson, you learn how to set tabs and indents in your documents.

Working with Tabs and Indents

In this lesson, you learn how to set and use tabs and indents in your documents.

Aligning Text with Tabs

While the left and right alignment of text in your document is governed by the margins set in the document, there are times when you want to align the text to emphasize a list of items or otherwise offset text from the rest of the items on the page. In Lesson 6, "Changing How Text Looks," you worked with centering and justification as a way to change the alignment of text. Another way to align text in a document is using tabs. Tabs are set every half-inch by default in a new document. Every time you press the Tab key on the keyboard you offset the text line from the left margin one tab stop.

You can use tab stops to align text lines in columns. Word gives you complete control over where the tab stops are set in your document. Word also provides you with different tabs that enable you to align text in different ways:

- **Left Tab** aligns the beginning of the text line at the tab stop.
- **Center Tab** centers the text line at the tab stop.
- **Right Tab** right justifies the text line at the tab stop.
- **Decimal Tab** lines up numerical entries at their decimal point.

Each of these tab types makes it easy for you to create lists that are offset from other text elements in the document. Your tab stops fall between the left and right margins on each page of the document. Each paragraph in the document can potentially have a different set of tab stops with different kinds of tabs set at the stops.

One way to set tabs in your document is using the Tabs dialog box. Select the **Format** menu, and then select **Tabs**. The Tabs dialog box requires that you specify a tab position in the Tab stop position box and then click the appropriate option button to select the type of tab you want to create at the tab stop (see Figure 8.1). After you have specified a position and a tab type, add the tab by clicking **Set**.

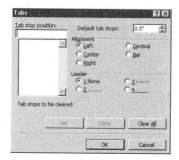

Figure 8.1 You can set and remove Tab stops in the Tabs dialog box.

After you have completed setting your tabs, click **OK**. You will find that the Tabs dialog box is not necessarily the best place to quickly set the tabs for your documents. It does not really provide you with a visual display of how the tabs will look in the document. However, if you are creating tabs that will include leading characters (such as dot leaders often seen in a table of contents) and you want to precisely set the tab positions to previously determined settings, the Tabs dialog box gives you complete control over all the settings.

Setting Tabs on the Ruler

An excellent alternative to setting tabs in the Tabs dialog box is to use the Word Ruler and actually set the tabs on the ruler itself. This allows you to visually check the position of the tab stops and makes it easy for you to change the type of tab at a particular tab stop and delete unwanted tabs.

To view the Ruler in the Word document window, select **View**, and then **Ruler**. The Ruler appears at the top of your document.

TIP **Quickly View the Ruler** If the Ruler is not displayed in the Word window, place the mouse pointer at the top of your current document, below the toolbars. If you wait for just a moment, the Ruler will drop down onto the document. This allows you to view current tab settings. When you remove the mouse, the Ruler will fold up.

To set a tab on the Ruler, click the **Tab** button on the far left of the Ruler to select the tab type (Left, Center, Right, or Decimal). Each time you click the Tab button you are cycled to the next tab type. If you go past the type of tab you want to set, keep clicking until the tab type appears on the Tab button.

After you have the appropriate tab type selected on the Tab button, place the mouse pointer on the ruler where you want to create the tab stop. Click the mouse and the tab is placed on the ruler. It's that simple.

Figure 8.2 shows the Ruler with each of the tab types set. The figure also shows how text aligns at each of the tab types.

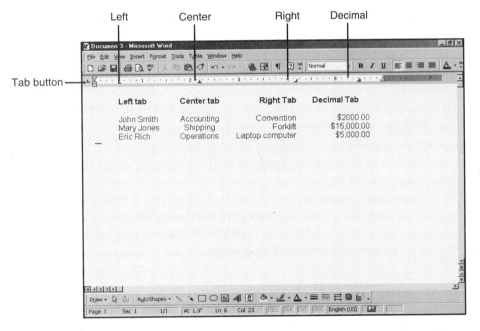

Figure 8.2   Setting tabs on the Ruler allows you to view their position and type.

TIP   **Moving or Removing Tabs**   If you want to delete a tab on the Ruler, use the mouse to drag the tab off the Ruler. If you need to reposition a particular tab, drag it to a new location on the Ruler.

I Adjust the Tabs But it Only Works for One Line   Remember that Word treats each line followed by a paragraph mark as a separate paragraph. When you adjust the tab positioning on the ruler, it only affects the paragraph containing the insertion point. To adjust the tabs for a number of paragraphs, select all the lines and then adjust the tabs on the Ruler.

Working with Indents

While tabs enable you to align text at various tab stops on the Ruler, you may want to indent or offset lines and paragraphs from the left or right margins. Word provides you with different indent settings that indent the text at a particular setting on the Ruler.

Indent   The offset of a particular paragraph or line of text from the left or right margin.

 The easiest way to indent a paragraph from the left margin is to use the **Increase Indent** button on the Formatting toolbar. Place the insertion point in the paragraph you want to indent and then click the **Increase Indent** button on the toolbar.

 Each time you click the button you are increasing the indent one half inch. You can also decrease the left indent on a particular paragraph. Click the **Decrease Indent** button on the Formatting toolbar.

Setting Indents on the Ruler

You can also indent a paragraph from both the left and right margins using the Ruler. The Ruler has a left and right indent marker on the far left and far right, respectively (see Figure 8.3).

To indent a paragraph from the left margin, use the mouse to drag the **Left Indent** marker to the appropriate position. Grab the marker at the very bottom, because the top of the marker is the First Line indent marker. These two markers will separate if you don't grab both markers together at the bottom. You can also indent a paragraph from the right margin using the Right Indent marker. Slide the marker to the appropriate position on the ruler to create your indent.

Figure 8.3 shows a paragraph indented from the both the left and right margins.

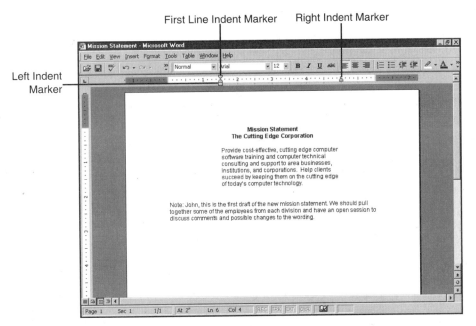

Figure 8.3 The Left and Right Indent markers can be used to indent paragraphs from the left and right margins, respectively.

Creating Hanging Indents

The hanging indent is a special kind of indent. In this type of indent the text (a single line or multiple lines) that wraps under the first line of the paragraph is indented more than the first line. Hanging indents are created by separating the First Line Indent Marker from the Left Indent Marker on the ruler.

To create a hanging indent follow these steps:

1. Place the insertion point in the paragraph that you want to indent.

2. Drag the Left Indent marker (drag it by the bottom of the marker) to the position to which you want to indent the second and subsequent lines of the paragraph.

3. Drag the First Line Indent marker (drag it by the top of the marker) back to the position that decreases its indent as needed.

Figure 8.4 shows a paragraph with a hanging indent. You can increase or decrease the offset between the first line and the rest of the paragraph by dragging either the First Line Marker or the Left Indent Marker.

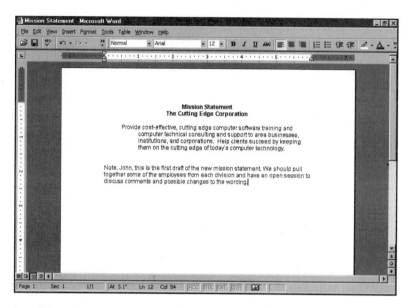

Figure 8.4   Hanging indents enable you to offset the indent on the first line of a paragraph and the remainder of the paragraph.

In this lesson, you learned to set tabs in your document using the Tabs dialog box and the Ruler. You also learned how to set indents for your paragraphs. In the next lesson you learn how to change the view of your document in the Word window.

Examining Your Documents in Different Views

In this lesson, you learn to examine your document using the different document displays offered in Word.

Changing the Document Display

Word provides you with a number of different viewing possibilities as you work on your documents in the Word application window. Each of these display modes provides a different look at your document. For instance, the Normal view provides you with a look at all the font and paragraph formatting in the document, but does not give you a view of the document as it would appear on the printed page. This type of view is supplied by the Print Layout View.

Using the different document views to your advantage can help you create great looking documents in Word. Special views are supplied for creating outlines and creating Web pages in Word. You can take advantage of these different views using the View menu. Table 9.1 shows the various views available to you and, in general terms, what they are best used for.

Table 9.1   The Word Views

View	Typical Use
Normal	Use for general word processing tasks
Web Layout	Use for designing HTML documents and viewing Web pages
Print Layout	Use for document layout and documents containing graphics and embedded or linked objects
Outline	Use to view document as outline
Full Screen	Use when you want to use the entire screen to view the document

The Normal View

The Normal view provides you with a view that is perfect for most word processing tasks. It is the default view for Word and to change to the Normal view (from any of the other views), select **View**, and then **Normal**.

 TIP   **Switch to Normal with a Click**   You can also change from view to view in Word using the View toolbar in the lower left corner of the Word window. To go to the Normal view, click the **Normal** icon.

This view displays character and paragraph formatting that you place in the document (see Figure 9.1). Normal view, however, does not display the document headers and footers or show graphics in the document as they will print. Also, items created using the Drawing toolbar are not displayed in the Normal view.

In the Normal View you will see:

- Page breaks appear as dashed lines.
- Headers and footers displayed in a header/footer-editing pane (when **Header and Footer** is selected on the View menu). Only the header or footer can be edited at this point.
- Footnotes and endnotes displayed in a footnote or endnote editing pane (when **Footnotes** is selected on the View menu). Only the footnote or endnote can be edited at this point.
- Margins and column borders are not displayed in this view.

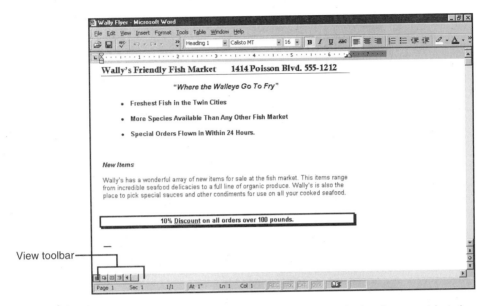

Figure 9.1 The Normal view shows all the formatting in the document but does not show graphics, margins, and other special elements as they will appear on the printed page.

Web Layout View

The Web Layout view is perfect for designing *HTML* documents that you will use as a Web page. The Web Layout view displays your document as it would appear in your Web browser window. To switch to the Web Layout view, select **View**, and then **Web Layout**.

HTML Hypertext Markup Language—This document format is used for the creation of Web pages for the World Wide Web. The special document format is read using a Web browser or some other application (such as Word) that can display HTML documents.

In the Web Layout view, text is wrapped to fit in the window and graphics are placed as they will appear online. Any backgrounds present on the page are also seen in this view. Figure 9.2 shows a Web page in the Web Layout View.

Switch to Web Layout View Quickly   To switch to the Web Layout View, click the Web Layout icon on the View toolbar.

The Web Layout view is the perfect view for designing your personal Web pages or viewing Web pages using the Web Page Wizard (for more about Word and the Web see Lesson 22, "Word and the World Wide Web").

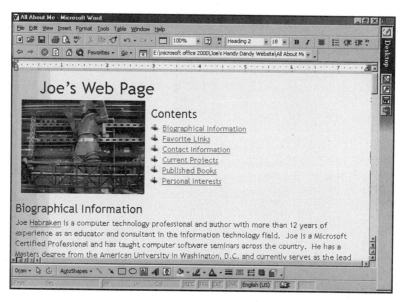

Figure 9.2   The Web Layout view allows you to look at and edit your HTML documents as they will appear in a Web browser.

Print Layout View

The Print Layout view shows your document exactly as it will appear on the printed page. Working in this view allows you to fine-tune your document and work with graphic placement and text formatting as you prepare your document for printing.

To switch to the Print Layout view, select **View**, and then **Print Layout**. This view allows you to view headers, footers, footnotes, endnotes, and the margins in your document. You will also find that graphics are positioned and sized as they will appear on the printed page. Figure 9.3 shows the same document that appeared earlier in Figure 9.1. Notice that in the Page Layout view the margins of the document and (more importantly) a graphic in the document appears.

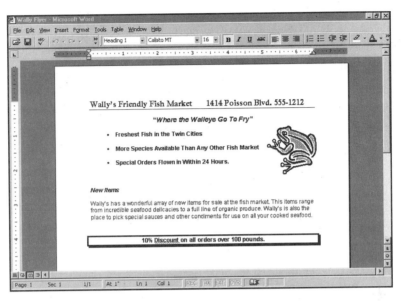

Figure 9.3   The Print Layout view allows you to fine-tune your document for printing.

TIP   **Switch to Print Layout View Quickly**   To switch to the Print Layout View, click the Print Layout icon on the View toolbar.

Outline View

The Outline view allows you to create and edit your document in an outline format. Using the Word built-in heading styles is the key to creating the document in this view (for more about styles see Lesson 10, "Working with Margins, Pages, and Line Spacing"). Each heading (Heading 1, 2, 3, and so on) is treated as a different level in the outline. For instance, a heading assigned the Heading 1 style would be a Level 1 heading in the outline. You can promote and demote headings using the appropriate buttons on the Outline toolbar (a special toolbar that appears when you are in the Outline view).

You can also collapse and expand the outline to better organize your document. Collapsing the document to all Level 1 Headings allows you to ignore the body text in the document and concentrate on the overall organization of the document.

TIP **Move a Heading and Associated Text** You can also drag a heading to a new position and the subheading and body text associated with the heading moves to the new position as well. This makes it very easy for you to reorganize the text in your document.

To change to the Outline view, select **View**, and then click **Outline**. You can easily select a heading and the text that is subordinate to it by clicking on the plus symbol (+) to the left of the text (see Figure 9.4). After the text is selected it can be dragged to a new position.

When you have completed creating and editing a document in the Outline view, you can switch to any of the other views (such as the Print Layout view) to see your document in a more typical format.

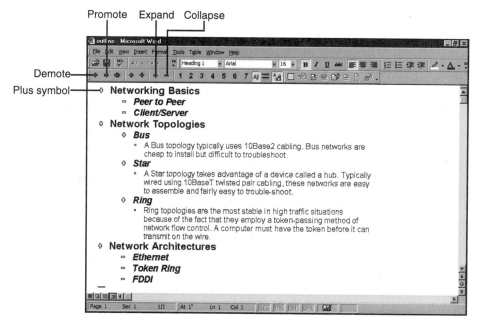

Figure 9.4 The Outline view makes it very easy to organize your document by collapsing and expanding different levels.

TIP **Switch to Outline View Quickly** To switch to the Outline view, click the Outline icon on the View toolbar.

Using the Full Screen View

In situations where you want to concentrate on the text and other items in your document, it would be great to be able to clear all the clutter from the screen (the toolbars, scrollbars, and other Word tools) and just view your document. For instance, you may be proofreading a particular page and want to place as much of the page's text on the screen as you can. You can switch to a view where your document occupies all the space available on the screen. Select **View**, and then **Full Screen**.

You can still add or edit the text in your document when you are in the Full Screen view. You can also quickly return to the previous view you were using (such as Normal view or Print Layout view), before you switched to the Full Screen view. Click the **Close Full Screen** box that appears in the document window and you will be returned to the previous view.

Zooming In and Out on Your Document

You can use the Zoom command to zoom in and out on your documents. This allows you to increase the magnification of items on the page such as small fonts or allows you to step back (zoom out) from the document to view its general layout.

You can use Zoom in any of the Word views. In the Normal, Web Layout, and Outline view the effect of zooming in or out really just changes the magnification of the onscreen elements. When you use Zoom In and Out on the Print Layout view, you get a very good look at how the document is laid out on the printed page.

To zoom in or out on your current document, select **View**, and then select **Zoom**. The Zoom dialog box appears (see Figure 9.5).

A series of option buttons is used to change the zoom setting for the current document. When you click a particular option button (such as the **200%** option button), you are given a preview of this magnification in the Preview box.

You can also set a custom zoom level in the **Percent** box. Use the click arrows in the box to increase or decrease the current Zoom percent. When you have selected the zoom level for the current document, click **OK**.

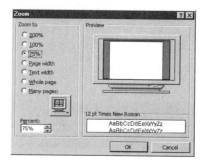

Figure 9.5 The Zoom dialog box can be used to change the current zoom level of your document.

TIP **View Multiple Pages on your Screen** You can also use the Zoom dialog box to view two or more pages at the same time, when you are in the Print Layout view. Click the **Many Pages** option button and then click the **Computer** icon below the option button. Drag over the page boxes to select the number of pages you want to display, and then click **OK**.

You can also quickly change the zoom level in your current document using the Zoom drop-down box on the Word Standard toolbar. Click the drop-down arrow on the **Zoom** box and select the appropriate zoom level. If you want to set a custom zoom level, select the current zoom percentage on the Zoom box and then type your own value.

Working with the Document Map

The Document Map view is somewhat similar to the Outline view in that it gives you a quick reference to the overall structure of your document. A special pane appears in the document window (on the left) that shows the headings in your document. The Document Map can be used to quickly move from one area of a document to another by clicking on the appropriate heading.

To open the Document Map, select **View**, and then **Document Map**; the Map pane appears in the Document window (see Figure 9.6). You can change the width of the Document Map pane by placing the mouse on the border between the pane and your document. The Mouse arrow changes to a sizing tool, a double-headed arrow. Drag the sizing tool to create a custom Document Map width.

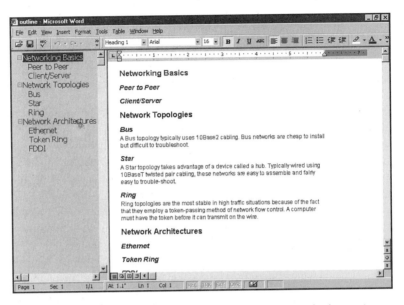

Figure 9.6 The Document Map makes it easy to jump to a particular part of a document by clicking the appropriate heading.

The Document Map pane is available in any of the Word views. When you want to close the Document Map, select **View**, and then **Document Map** to deselect it.

Splitting the Document Window

Another useful way to view your documents is to split the current document window into two panes. This allows you to view the same document in both panes—particularly useful when you want to view two different parts of the same document.

You can use the two panes to drag and drop information from one part of a document into another. Remember that changes you make in either of the Split panes will affect the document.

To split the document screen into two panes, select **Window, Split**. A Horizontal split appears across the document window. Notice that as you move the mouse in the document window the split bar moves with it. Place the mouse where you want to split the document window and then click the left mouse button.

A set of vertical and horizontal scrollbars appears for each of the panes in the split window (see Figure 9.7). Use the scrollbars in each pane as needed.

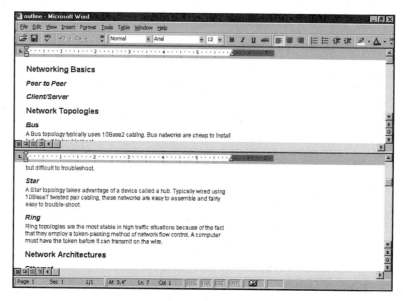

Figure 9.7 You can split the document screen to view different areas of a long document.

When you have completed working in the split document window, select **Window**, and then **Remove Split**. The Splitter bar is removed from the document.

TIP **Split a Window Using the Splitter Bar** You can also split a document window by manually dragging the Splitter bar down into the document window. Place the mouse just above the Up arrow on the Vertical scrollbar on the Splitter bar. Your mouse becomes a Splitter sizing tool. Drag to split the window as needed, and then click the mouse to set the bar.

In this lesson, you learned to take advantage of the various views offered to you by Word. You also learned to zoom in and out on your document and split the document window. In the next lesson, you learn how to work with margins, line spacing, and line breaks.

Working with Margins, Pages, and Line Spacing

In this lesson, you learn how to set margins, insert page breaks into your documents, and control line spacing and line breaks in your documents.

Setting Margins

Margins control the amount of white space between your text and the edge of a printed page. Four different margins—Left, Right, Top, and Bottom—can be set for your pages. The default margin settings for documents based on the Word Normal template are shown in Table 10.1.

Table 10.1 Default Margin Settings for the Normal Template

Margin	Setting (in inches)
Left	1.25
Right	1.25
Top	1
Bottom	1

You can change any of the margin settings for your document or a portion of your document at any time. The Page Setup dialog box provides you with access to all these margin settings.

To change the margin settings for your document, follow these steps:

1. Select **File**, then **Page Setup**. The Page Setup dialog box appears as shown in Figure 10.1.

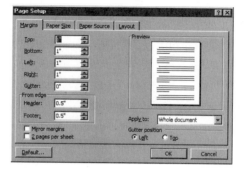

Figure 10.1 The Margins tab of the Page Setup dialog box allows you to set your document margins.

TIP **Margins Can Be Different for Different Parts of the Document**
You can set different margin settings for different portions of your document. The easiest way to do this is to divide your document into sections. Each section can then have a different set of margins. For information on creating sections in your documents, see Lesson 21, "Working with Larger Documents."

2. Click the **Margins** tab if necessary. Use the click arrows in the **Top**, **Bottom**, **Left**, or **Right** margin boxes to increase or decrease the current setting. Or double-click in any of the boxes and type in a new value.

3. After you have selected the new margin settings, you can apply the margins to the entire document, to a section of the document (this option is only available if you have more than one section in the document), or to the document from the current page forward in the document. Using the last choice allows you to have different margin settings in the same document without requiring you to divide the document into sections (for more about sections, see Lesson 21). Click the **Apply To** drop-down box and select **Whole Document** (the default setting), **This Point Forward**, or **This Section** (if available).

4. After you have completed selecting your new margin settings and the amount of the document that they will affect, click **OK**.

TIP **Set a Gutter for Bound Documents** Whether your document will be bound or placed in a 3-ring binder, set a value in the Gutter box to provide extra space for the binder. Since documents printed on both sides of the paper are meant to open with facing pages, select the **Mirror Margins** button to add a gutter to the left margin for the odd pages and to the right margin for the even pages.

The new margins take effect in your document. The best way to view how these margins will look when you print the document is to switch to the Print Layout view (if you are not already in this view). Select **View**, then **Print Layout**. The margins you've selected appear on the top, left, right, and bottom of your document in the Word document window.

When you are in the Print Layout view, you can also adjust the margins in your document using the Ruler. To view the Ruler, select **View**, then **Ruler**.

In the Print Layout view, horizontal and vertical rulers appear in the document window. The margins appear as shaded areas on the edge of the respective ruler. For instance, the left margin is a gray-shaded area on the left side of the Horizontal Ruler (see Figure 10.2).

TIP **Open the Page Setup Dialog Box Using the Ruler** Double-click any of the margins shown on the Vertical or Horizontal Ruler. This opens the Page Setup dialog box.

To adjust a margin, place the mouse pointer between the gray margin and the white document area on the ruler. A margin-sizing arrow appears. Drag the gray margin to increase or decrease the respective margin. Figure 10.2 shows the margin-sizing arrow on the top margin on the Vertical Ruler.

Controlling Paper Types and Orientation

Other page attributes that you need to control in your documents are the paper size and the page orientation. Word's default settings assume that you will print to paper that is a standard 8.5 by 11 inches. The default page orientation is portrait, meaning that the maximum distance from the left-to-right of the page is 8.5 inches.

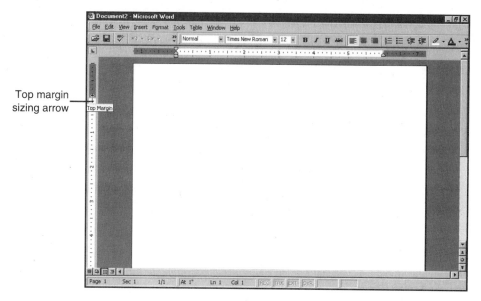

Top margin
sizing arrow

Figure 10.2   Drag the respective margin-sizing arrow to increase or decrease a margin.

You can select different paper sizes, which is particularly important if you want to print to envelopes or a different paper size, such as legal-size paper. You can also change the orientation of your page from portrait to landscape, where the page is rotated to the right and the distance between the left and right edges on a standard sheet of paper would be 11 inches.

Paper size and page orientation are both set in the Page Setup dialog box. Follow these steps to edit the settings for these page attributes:

1. Select **File**, then **Page Setup**. The Page Setup dialog box opens.
2. Click the **Paper Size** tab on the dialog box (see Figure 10.3).
3. To select a new paper size, click the **Paper Size** drop-down box and select the paper type. For nonstandard paper sizes, select **Custom Size** in the **Page Size** box, then place the paper's width in the **Width** box and its height in the **Height** box.
4. To change the orientation of the page from portrait to landscape (or, vice versa), click the **Portrait** or the **Landscape** option button as needed.
5. In the Apply To drop-down box, select **Whole Document** to apply the new settings to the new document, **This Point Forward** to apply the settings

to the document from the current page forward, or **This Section** to apply the new settings to the current document section.

6. When you complete editing the settings, click **OK**.

Inserting Page Breaks

As you create your document, Word automatically starts a new page when you fill the current page with text or other document items (such as graphics, tables, and so on). You can insert your own page breaks in the document as needed. These types of page breaks are often referred to as *hard*, or manual, page breaks.

To insert a page break into your document, follow these steps:

1. Place the insertion point in the document where you want to force a page break.

2. Select **Insert**, then **Break**. The Break dialog box appears.

3. Make sure the Page Break option button is selected, and then click **OK**.

A page break is placed in your document. In the Normal view, the page break appears as a dashed line across the page, with "Page Break" denoted at the center of the line. In the Print Layout view, you can move to the new page by clicking the **Next Page** button on the bottom of the vertical scrollbar.

Use the Keyboard to Place a Page Break   You can also place a page TIP   break in your document using the keyboard. Hold down the **Ctrl** key and then press the **Enter** key.

Changing Line Spacing

Another setting that greatly influences the amount of white space on the page is line spacing. When you consider whether you want your text single-spaced or double-spaced, those text attributes are controlled by changing the line spacing.

Line spacing can be set for each paragraph in the document or for selected text. Setting line spacing for a blank document allows you to set a default line spacing for all text paragraphs that will be placed in the document.

To set the line spacing for a new document, a paragraph, or selected text, follow these steps:

1. Select **Format**, then **Paragraph**. The Paragraph dialog box will appear (see Figure 10.4).

2. Make sure the **Indents and Spacing** tab on the dialog box is selected.

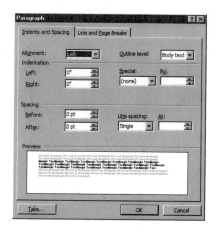

Figure 10.4   The Paragraph dialog box allows you to control the line spacing in your text.

3. To change the line spacing, click the Line Spacing drop-down box and select one of the following choices:

   - **Single**—Spacing accommodates the largest font size found on the lines and adds a small amount of white space (depending on the font used).

   - **1.5**—The line spacing is one-and-a-half times greater than single spacing.

   - **Double**—Twice the size of single line spacing.

   - **At Least**—(the default setting) Line spacing will adjust to accommodate the largest font on the line and special items, such as graphics.

   - **Exactly**—All lines are equally spaced, and special font sizes or items such as graphics are not accommodated. These items will appear cut off in the text. You can accommodate these items by using the Multiple box described next to shift all the text lines to a higher spacing percentage that accommodates special items.

- **Multiple**—You specify the line spacing by a particular percentage. This feature is used in conjuction with the Exactly option to set a line spacing percentage that accommodates special font sizes or graphics found in the document. For instance, if you want to decrease the line spacing by 20%, you enter the number 0.8. Increasing the line spacing by 50%, you enter 1.5.

4. The line spacing option selected in step 2 is influenced by the point size entered in the At box (this only applies when you have selected At Least, Exactly, or Multiple). Use the click arrows to increase or decrease the point size of the line spacing if needed.

TIP   **Set Spacing Before and After a Paragraph**   You can also set special spacing **Before** and **After** a particular paragraph. This is particularly useful for headings or other special text items.

5. When you complete setting the line spacing parameters, click **OK**.

If you find that you don't like the new line spacing settings for a particular paragraph, click the **Undo** button on the Standard toolbar to reverse the changes that you have made.

In this lesson, you learned to set margins for your documents, change the paper size and page orientation, and place page breaks in your documents. You also learned how to control line spacing in your paragraphs. In the next lesson, you learn how to create and apply styles to the text in your documents.

Working with Styles

In this lesson, you learn how to create text and paragraph styles. You also learn to edit your styles and take advantage of the styles in the Style Gallery.

Understanding Styles

Word Styles provide an excellent way to manage the character and paragraph formatting in a document. A *style* is a grouping of formatting attributes identified by a style name. You can create styles for text that contains character-formatting attributes such as bold, italic, or a particular font size; these types of styles are called *character styles*. You can also create styles for paragraphs that include paragraph attributes, such as alignment information, indents, and line spacing; this type of style is called a *paragraph style*.

 TIP **View the Styles in a Document** To view the style names displayed in the left margin of the document, make sure that you are in the Normal view. Then select the **Tools** menu and click **Options**. Enter a width in the Style area width box (such as 1 inch or more). Then click **OK**. The style names will appear in the style area pane on the left of your document.

Word also includes a number of built-in styles that you can take advantage of in your documents, such as the heading styles. (The heading styles are also very useful when you are building a document in the Outline view; see Lesson 21, "Working with Larger Documents.") Styles are particularly useful because, if you use them to format text or paragraphs in the document, you can change the attributes saved in the style at any time. These changes will immediately take effect on all the text that has been assigned that style.

Updating the look of text or the layout of paragraphs by editing a style allows you to quickly edit the look of text in your document. Using styles also provides you with a way to make certain categories of text, such as headings or figure captions, look uniform throughout the document without having to assign each of the character or paragraph attributes.

Before you create a style, it's important to know how to select a style for a particular paragraph. For instance, you may want to assign one of Word's default styles (such as a heading style) to text in your document; follow these steps:

1. Place the insertion point in the paragraph to which you want to assign the style.
2. Click the **Style** drop-down box on the Formatting toolbar.
3. Select a style from the drop-down list.

The style is assigned to your text paragraph.

CAUTION

Paragraph Styles Versus Text Styles   Paragraph styles (the more commonly used option) assign both character and paragraph attributes to the paragraph containing the insertion point. Text styles affect only the word or text string you select before you apply the style.

Creating Text Styles

Creating text styles is extremely easy. Select the text you wish to emphasize with special character formatting, and assign it all the character attributes (font type, bold, underline, italics, and so on) that you wish to include in the style. You may assign the attributes using either the Font dialog box (by selecting **Format**, and then **Font**) or the appropriate buttons on the Formatting toolbar.

Make sure that the text is selected and then follow these steps to create the style:

1. Select **Format**, and then **Style**; the Style dialog box will appear (see Figure 11.1).
2. To create the new style, click the **New** button. The New Style dialog box will appear.
3. Click the **Style Type** drop-down box and select **Character** for the style type.

227

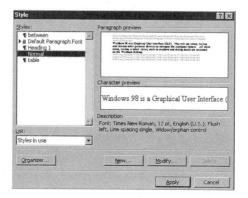

Figure 11.1 The Style dialog box is the starting place for creating, editing, and managing the styles in your documents.

4. Look in the Description area of the dialog box. Note that the new style will be based on the current style (the default paragraph style or the normal style), plus the additional text attributes that you assigned to your selected text.

5. Type a name for your new style in the Name box (see Figure 11.2).

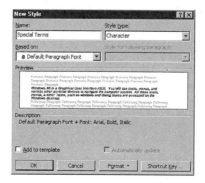

Figure 11.2 In the New Style dialog box, you specify the type of style you want to create and name the new style.

6. If you want to have the style automatically update when you manually make changes to text in a paragraph that has been assigned the style, click the **Automatically Update** check box. Now all paragraphs using the style will change their formatting if you change any of the formatting attributes in any paragraph using the style.

7. Click **OK** to conclude the style creation process. You will be returned to the Style dialog box. Notice that your new style now appears in the Styles list on the left side of the dialog box.

8. Click **OK** again to return to your document.

You can now assign the new character style to text in your document as needed. Simply select the text that you want to assign the character style to and then select the **Style** drop-down box on the Formatting toolbar. Select a style from the list provided. The style will be applied to the selected text.

You can also quickly assign a character style to selected text by selecting the style from the Style list box. Click the **Style** list drop-down arrow on the Formatting toolbar and select the appropriate style for the text. You can also assign paragraph styles and built-in styles to text using the Style list.

Creating Paragraph Styles

Creating paragraph styles is very similar to creating character styles. Apply the formatting that you wish to include in the style to a paragraph (you can use alignment settings, indents, all the paragraph attributes that you are familiar with). Make sure that the insertion point is in the paragraph and then follow these steps to create the style:

1. Select **Format**, then **Style**; the Style dialog box will appear.

2. Click the **New** button. The New Style dialog box will appear.

3. Type a name in the **Name** box for the style and make sure that the style type is set to Paragraph in the Style type box.

4. Click **OK** to return to the Style dialog box. The style is now available on the Style list. Click **OK** to close the Style dialog box. You can now apply the style to any paragraph in the document by placing the insertion point in the paragraph. Then select the style in the Style dialog box or select the style from the Style list on the Formatting toolbar.

Editing Styles

You can also edit the attributes found in any of your styles or the default styles in the document. Styles are edited via the Style dialog box. Remember, however, that when you edit a style, all the text that the style was applied to will reflect the new text and paragraph attributes of the edited style.

To edit a style, follow these steps:

1. Select **Format**, then **Style**; the Style dialog box will appear.

2. Select the style you want to edit in the Style list and then click **Modify**. The Modify Style box will appear as shown in Figure 11.3.

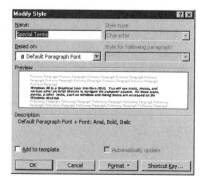

Figure 11.3   The Modify Style box allows you to edit the name of a style and modify all the attributes found in the style.

3. To modify the style, select the **Format** button. A menu appears allowing you to modify the following attributes in the style:
   - Font
   - Paragraph
   - Tabs
   - Borders
   - Language
   - Frame
   - Numbering

4. Select one of the choices provided in the Format box. The appropriate dialog box will appear to edit the settings for the chosen attributes. For instance, if you want to modify the font attributes for the style, click the **Format** arrow, then select **Font** from the list provided. The Font dialog box will appear, as shown in Figure 11.4.

5. When you have finished modifying the Font attributes for the style, click **OK**. You will be returned to the Modify Style dialog box.

6. Modify other attributes of the style as needed by clicking the **Format** arrow and making the appropriate choice from the list.

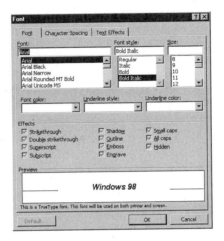

Figure 11.4 Selecting Font on the style Modify list opens the Font dialog box.

7. When you have completed your style modifications, click **OK** in the Modify Style dialog box.

8. You will be returned to the Style dialog box (refer to Figure 11.1). You can click **Apply** to apply the changes to all occurrences of the style in your document. You can now edit other styles, or return to the document by clicking **OK**.

TIP **You Can Delete Unwanted Styles** You can delete styles that you've created that you no longer need. Open the Style dialog box (select **Format**, then select **Style**), select the style in the Style list, and then click the **Delete** button. The style will be removed from the Style list.

Using the Style Organizer

You can also copy styles from other documents and templates. This provides you with an easy way to add already existing styles to the current document.

To copy styles from another document or template, follow these steps:

1. Select **Format**, then **Style**; the Style dialog box will appear.

2. Click the **Organizer** button. The Organizer dialog box will appear, as shown in Figure 11.5.

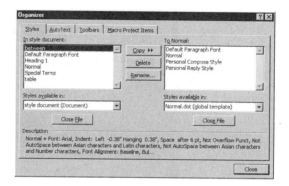

Figure 11.5   The Organizer dialog box makes it easy for you to copy a style from one document to another.

3. The styles in the current document will appear on the left side of the Organizer dialog box. On the right side of the Organizer dialog box, the styles in the template your document is based upon will be listed. To open a new document or template and copy styles from it, click the **Close** button on the right side of the Organizer dialog box. This closes the current template.

4. Click **Open** on the right side of the Organizer dialog box. The Open dialog box will appear. Locate the document or template that you want to copy the styles from. Double-click the file in the Open dialog box to open the file.

5. You will be returned to the Organizer dialog box, and the styles for the recently opened template or document will be listed on the right side of the dialog box. To copy a style or styles, select the style and click the **Copy** button. The style will be copied to the styles in your current document.

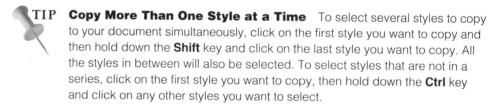

TIP   **Copy More Than One Style at a Time**   To select several styles to copy to your document simultaneously, click on the first style you want to copy and then hold down the **Shift** key and click on the last style you want to copy. All the styles in between will also be selected. To select styles that are not in a series, click on the first style you want to copy, then hold down the **Ctrl** key and click on any other styles you want to select.

6. You can also copy styles from your document to the document shown on the right side of the dialog box. When you have completed your copying of styles, click **Close** to close the Organizer dialog box.

As you can see, the Organizer makes it very easy for you to share the styles that you create between your documents.

In this lesson, you learned to create and assign character and paragraph styles. You also learned to modify your styles and learned how to copy styles from one document to another using the Organizer dialog box. In the next lesson, you learn how to use AutoFormat to quickly change the way the text and paragraphs look in your documents. With AutoFormat, Word examines the text and paragraph formatting you are assigning to your document and applies an appropriate Word style.

Using AutoFormatting to Change Text Attributes

In this lesson, you learn how to quickly change the look of your text with AutoFormat and apply text attributes automatically as you type.

Understanding AutoFormatting

AutoFormat is a great feature that helps you create professional-looking documents. AutoFormatting actually examines the text elements that you have placed in your document (such as headings, tables, lists, regular body text, and other items). It then automatically formats these elements using an appropriate Word style. Even though this formatting is automatic, can accept or reject the changes made by AutoFormatting. You can also make additional changes to the document as you see fit by using other styles or font and paragraph formatting attributes (for more about styles, see Lesson 11, "Working with Styles").

You will also find that AutoFormat does more than just apply styles to your document elements. It can remove extra line breaks between paragraphs and apply the hyperlink styles to email addresses or Web addresses that you place in your documents (for more about hyperlinks, see Lesson 22, "Word and the World Wide Web").

You can use AutoFormat in two different ways. You can turn on AutoFormatting, so items are formatted as you type, or you create a new document and then use AutoFormat to format the entire document at once.

Formatting as You Type

You can have your document elements formatted as you type. However, this feature requires that you supply Word with certain cues so that the correct formatting is applied to the text. For instance, if you turn on AutoFormat As You Type, and want to create a bulleted list that is automatically formatted by the AutoFormat feature, you must begin the bulleted line with a dash, an asterisk, or a lowercase "o," so Word knows to apply the bulleted list formatting.

To turn on the AutoFormat As You Type feature, follow these steps:

1. Select **Tools, AutoCorrect**. The AutoCorrect dialog box appears.
2. Select the **AutoFormat As You Type** tab on the dialog box (see Figure 12.1).

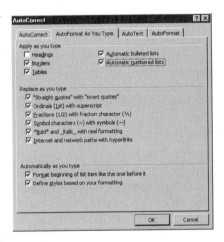

Figure 12.1 The AutoFormat As You Type tab of the AutoCorrect dialog box allows you to select which document elements will be formatted automatically as you type.

3. A series of check boxes on the AutoFormat As you Type tab allows you to select which document elements will be formatted as you type. Again, you need to type certain characters for a particular element to be recognized by, and then formatted by, the AutoFormat feature.

   - **Headings**—Select this check box to have all document heads formatted with the Heading 1–9 styles.

   - **Borders**—Select this check box to have borders automatically placed between paragraphs. You must type 3 dashes (-) for a thin border,

3 underscores (_) for a bold line, or 3 equal signs (=) for a double-line border.

- **Tables**—Select this check box to automatically create tables. You must type a series of plus symbols (+) and dashes (-) to signify the number of columns (+) and the distance between the columns (-).

- **Automatic Bulleted Lists**—Select this check box to create bulleted lists automatically. Start each line in the list with an asterisk (*), a dash (-), or a lowercase "o."

- **Automatic Numbered Lists**—Select this check box to create numbered lists. Start a line with a letter or number and it will be turned into a numbered list item. Paragraphs following the first numbered line will be numbered sequentially if the **Format Beginning of List Item Like the One Before It** check box is selected.

Other AutoFormatting check boxes also include features that will format your quotation marks, ordinals (1st), and fractions (1/2). Select (or deselect) the various AutoFormatting as you type options and then click **OK** to close the dialog box.

TIP **Create Styles as You Type** If you select the Define Styles Based on Your Formatting check box, Word will take your character and paragraph formatting attributes and turn them into styles. You can then use the created styles to format other paragraphs.

Now you can AutoFormat as you type. For instance, you may want to begin a bulleted list in your document; begin a line with a dash (-). Although formatting as you type may seem like a real time saver, there is the additional burden on you to remember which special characters will automatically begin a particular formatting type, such as the plus (+) and dash (-) to start a new table.

Applying AutoFormat to a Document

The alternative to AutoFormatting as you type is to create the document and then format it after the fact with AutoFormat. Waiting to format a document until after its completion allows you to concentrate on the document content as you type. You can then concentrate on the look and feel of the document by selecting from the various AutoFormatting options. Heads, numbered or bulleted lists, and other items you have designated throughout the text will be identified and formatted.

To AutoFormat a document, follow these steps:

1. Select **Format, AutoFormat**. The AutoFormat dialog box appears (see Figure 12.2).

Figure 12.2 The AutoFormat dialog box allows you to immediately format the document or review each of the suggested formatting changes.

2. You can increase the accuracy of the formatting process by choosing a particular document type. Click the Document type drop-down arrow and select from the document types listed on the drop-down list (the default setting is **General Document**).

3. Now you can AutoFormat the document. If you want to AutoFormat the current document without reviewing the formatting changes, click the **AutoFormat Now** option button, and then click **OK**. The document will be automatically formatted.

4. If you want to review the AutoFormatting process after the changes are made, click the **AutoFormat and Review Each Change** option button. Then click **OK**.

5. The document will be formatted, and then the AutoFormat/Review Changes dialog box will appear. At this point, you can choose to **Accept All** or **Reject All** using the appropriate button in the dialog box. If you want to review the formatting changes in the document, click the **Review Changes** button. The Review AutoFormat Changes dialog box will appear (see Figure 12.3).

Figure 12.3 This dialog box enables you to review each of the formatting changes made in the document.

237

6. Click the **Find** (forward) button (this button has a right pointing arrow) to begin the review process.

7. When you are asked to review a particular change (the change will appear in the Changes box), either select **Reject** to reject the change, or click the **Find** button to skip to the next formatting change in the document. You can also choose to **Accept All** or **Reject All** using the appropriate button in the dialog box.

8. When you reach the bottom of the document, Word notifies you that it can start searching for changes at the top of the document. To end the process, click **Cancel**. Click **Cancel** to close the two subsequent dialog boxes as well.

You can now save your document to save the automatic formatting changes that have been made.

Changing AutoFormat Options

You can customize certain options related to the AutoFormat feature. This dialog box can be reached by selecting the **Tools** menu, and then **AutoCorrect**. Make sure that the **AutoFormat** tab is selected.

The options that you have control over on the AutoFormat tab are similar to those found on the AutoFormat As You Type tab. You can choose check boxes that will automatically format headings, lists, and so on (see Figure 12.4).

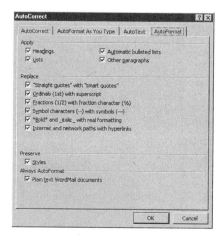

Figure 12.4   You can set the various options for AutoFormatting on the AutoFormat tab of the AutoCorrect dialog box.

You can also choose to have Word retain the style that you have already placed in the document (prior to running AutoFormat). Select the **Styles** check box to do so.

Once you selected the options you wish to set for AutoFormat, select **OK**. You can now run AutoFormat, and your options will be in force as your document is formatted.

In this lesson, you learned to AutoFormat your text as you typed and also to use AutoFormat to format a completed document. In the next lesson you learn how to add headers, footers, and page numbers to your documents.

Adding Headers, Footers, and Page Numbering

In this lesson, you learn how to add headers, footers, and page numbers to your documents.

Understanding Headers and Footers

Another aspect of creating a document is using headers and footers to insert information that you want repeated on every page of the document or in the pages of a particular document section.

Header   The header resides inside the top margin on the page; it holds information such as the date or draft number that appears at the top of every page of the document or at the top of every page in a section of a document.

Footer   The footer resides inside the bottom margin of the page; it holds information such as the page number or other information that appears at the bottom of every page of the document or at the bottom of every page in a section of a document.

Headers and footers provide you with a way to include a document title, the current date, or the current page number on the top or bottom of each page in the document. Headers can include text, graphics, or other imported objects.

Adding Headers and Footers

You can add a header or footer to a document in any view. To add a header or footer, follow these steps:

1. Select **View**, then **Header and Footer**. You will temporarily be switched to the Print Layout mode and placed in the header area of the document (see Figure 13.1). The regular text area is dimmed and unavailable while you work in the header or footer box.

2. Type your text in the header area as appropriate (using Word formatting options the same as you would for regular document text). If you want to create a footer, click the **Switch Between Header and Footer** button on the Header and Footer toolbar, which is also available in the document window.

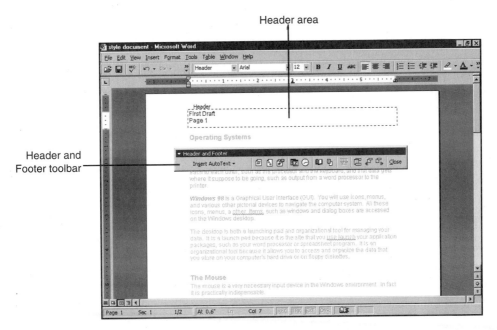

Figure 13.1 The header area of the page is where you type your header text. The Header and Footer toolbar provides you with tools to insert page numbers, the date, and to switch between your headers and footers.

3. You can add a page number, the current date, the current time, and other elements using the appropriate buttons on the Header and Footer toolbar (see Table 13.1).

4. In cases where you need to align or format the text, use the appropriate buttons on the Word Formatting toolbar as you would for text on the document page.

5. When you have completed entering your header and footer text, click the **Close** button on the Header and Footer toolbar.

You are returned to your document text. In the Normal view you are not able to see your header or footer. In the Print Layout view, header and footer text appears dimmed.

You can edit your headers and footers by selecting **View**, then **Header and Footer**. Move to the appropriate header or footer using the navigation buttons on the Header and Footer toolbar shown in Table 13.1. To quickly enter a header or footer box in the Print Layout view, double-click the header or footer text.

Table 13.1   The Header and Footer Toolbar Buttons

Button	Purpose
	Inserts the page number.
	Inserts the page count or number of total pages.
	Edits the format of the page number.
	Inserts the current date.
	Inserts the current time.
	Opens the Page Setup dialog box to the Layout tab where you can change the header and footer settings.
	Hides the document text while you work on your header and footer.
	Sets up the next header the same as the current header (or footer).

Button	Purpose
	Switches between your header and footer.
	Moves to the previous header or footer in the document.
	Moves to the next header or footer in the document.

Several toolbar choices, such as Same as Previous and Move to Previous or Next (header or footer) relate to documents that have a number of sections and so have different headers or footers in the same document. You can also have more than one header or footer in the document if you choose to have different headers or footers for odd- and even-numbered pages.

Using Odd- and Even-Page Headers and Footers

By default, the Header and Footer layout settings in Word assume that one header or footer is shown on all the pages of a document (except in cases where the document is divided into more than one section; each section can have different headers and footers). You can change the header and footer settings so that different headers and/or footers appear on the odd and even pages of your document (or the odd and even pages of a document section).

To change the layout settings for Word Headers and Footers, follow these steps:

1. If you are already in a header or footer and the Header and Footer toolbar is available in the document window, click the **Page Setup** button.

TIP Changing Header and Footer Layout When You Aren't in the Header or Footer To get to the Header/Footer layout options when you don't have the header or footer displayed, select **File**, then **Page Setup**. The Page Setup dialog box appears. Make sure the **Layout** tab is selected.

2. In the Page Setup dialog box, click the **Different Odd and Even** check box to enable odd and even headers and/or footers in the current document (or document section).

3. If you want to have a header or footer (or none) on the first page of your document that is different from subsequent pages in the document, click the **Different First Page** check box (see Figure 13.2).

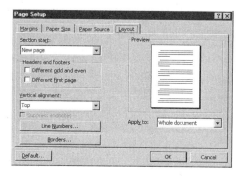

Figure 13.2 On the Layout tab of the Page Setup dialog box, you can select whether to have different odd- and even-page headers/footers or a different header/footer on the first page of the document.

4. Click **OK** to close the Page Setup dialog box. If you are returned to your document, select **View**, and then **Header and Footer** to add the odd- or even-page headers to the document. If you were already in the Header and Footer view when you exited the Page Setup dialog box, you will be returned to the current header and footer.

5. When you have completed adding your odd- and even-page headers and/or footers or your first page and subsequent page headers, click the **Close** button on the Header and Footer toolbar.

Odd- and even-page headers and footers are set up exactly the way you would typically set up a header or footer in the document. Use the **Show Next** or **Show Previous** button to move between the odd- and even-page headers or footers.

Adding Page Numbering to a Document

Headers and footers enable you to place repeating information in your documents, including the date, other important text, and most important—page numbers. In cases where you want to place only page numbers on your document pages, you can forego the Header and Footer command and quickly add page numbers via the Insert menu.

To place page numbers in your document, follow these steps:

1. Select **Insert**, then **Page Numbers**. The Page Numbers dialog box appears (see Figure 13.3).

Figure 13.3 Use the Page Numbers dialog box to select the position and alignment of page numbers in your document.

2. To select the position for your page numbers, select the **Position** drop-down arrow and select **Top of Page (Header)** or **Bottom of Page (Footer)**.

3. You can select the alignment for the page numbers using the **Alignment** drop-down box. Select **Center, Left,** or **Right** to position the page numbers. In cases where you are using mirror margins on a document that will be printed on both sides of the paper, select **Inside** or **Outside** (relative to the binding) to position your page numbers.

4. To select the format for your page numbers, click the **Format** button. The Format dialog box appears.

5. Use the **Number Format** drop-down box to choose the format for your page numbers (Arabic numerals—1, 2, 3—is the default). When you have selected your number format, click **OK** to return to the Format dialog box.

6. Click **OK** to close the Page Numbering dialog box.

The page numbers are placed in your document according to your positioning and formatting choices. You can edit the page numbers and add text if you want by selecting **View**, then **Header and Footer**. The page numbers you placed in the document appear in the header or footer area of the document, depending on your position settings in the Page Numbers dialog box.

In this lesson, you learned to place headers and footers in your documents. You also learned how to add page numbering to your documents using the Insert menu. In the next lesson, you learn to print your documents and work with the various print options.

Printing Documents

In this lesson, you learn to preview your documents and then print them.

Sending Your Document to the Printer

 When you have completed a particular document and are ready to generate a hard copy, Word makes it easy for you to get your document to the printer. In fact, you have three choices. You can send the document directly to the printer (no questions asked) by clicking the **Print** button on the Standard toolbar. You can open the Print dialog box (select **File**, then **Print**) and set any print options that you desire, such as printing a particular range of pages or printing multiple copies of the same document. You also have the option of previewing your hard copy before printing. This enables you to view your document exactly as it will appear on the printed page.

 To preview your document before printing, click the **Print Preview** button on the Word Standard toolbar. The Print Preview window opens for the current document (see Figure 14.1).

You will find that the Print Preview window provides several viewing tools that you can use to examine your document before printing.

- **Zoom In or Out**—In the Print Preview window, the mouse pointer appears as a magnifying glass. Click once on your document to zoom in, and then click a second time to zoom out. To turn this feature off (or on again), click the **Magnifier** button.
- **Zoom by Percentage**—You can change to different zoom levels on the current document by using the **Zoom** drop-down arrow.

- **View Multiple Pages**—You can also zoom out and view several pages at once in the Preview window. Click **Multiple Pages** and then drag to select the number of pages to be shown.

- **Shrink to Fit**—In cases where you have a two-page document and only a small amount of text appears on the second page, you can condense all the text to fit on the first page only; click the **Shrink to Fit** button.

When you have completed viewing your document in the Print Preview mode, you can click the **Print** button to print the document, or if you wish to edit the document before printing, click the **Close** button on the toolbar.

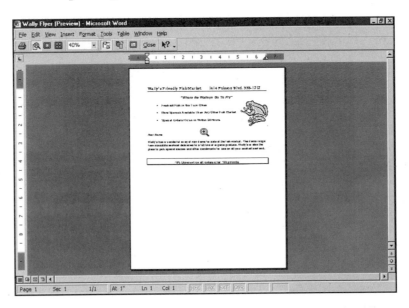

Figure 14.1   The Print Preview mode enables you to view your document as it will print.

Changing Print Settings

In some situations, you may wish to print only the current page or a certain range of pages. These options are controlled in the Print dialog box. The Print dialog box supplies you with a number of options, including the printer to which you send the print job, the number of copies, and the page range to be printed.

To open the Print dialog box, select **File**, then **Print**. The Print dialog box is shown in Figure 14.2.

247

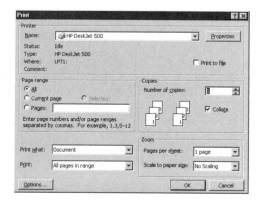

Figure 14.2 The Print dialog box gives you control over the various print options for your document.

Depending on your home or office situation, you may have your computer connected to more than one printer (especially if you are on a network). The Print dialog box has a drop-down box that lists all the printers to which you have access. To select a printer other than the current printer, click the drop-down arrow in the **Name** box and choose your printer from the list.

The Print dialog box also enables you to select the range to be printed. This range can consist of a page, a group of specific pages in a sequence, or all the pages in the document.

- **All Pages**—To print all the pages in the document, make sure the **All** option button is selected.
- **Current Page**—To print a single page, click the **Current Page** option button (this prints the page that the insertion point was parked on).
- **Page Range**—To designate a range of pages, click the **Pages** option button and type the page numbers in the Pages box.

You can also choose to print all the pages in a chosen range or only print the odd or even pages. Click the **Print** drop-down box (near the bottom left of the dialog box) and select **All Pages in Range**, **Odd Pages**, or **Even Pages,** as required.

Another print option worth mentioning is the Zoom print option in the Print dialog box. This feature enables you to place several document pages on one sheet of paper. To use Zoom print, click the **Pages per Sheet** drop-down box in the **Zoom** area of the Print dialog box and select the number of document pages you want to place on a sheet of paper. To select a scale for the print job (the scale is the relative size of the mini-pages on the printout page, such as 8.5 by 11 inches or legal size), click the **Scale to Paper Size** drop-down box.

After you select these two options, proceed with your print job. Be advised, however, that the more pages you place on a single sheet, the smaller the text appears.

 TIP   Specifying Page Ranges   To print a continuous range of pages, use the 1-5 format (where 1 is the start and 5 is the end of the range). For pages not in a continuous range, use the 5,9,11 format (where each distinct page number to be printed is separated by a comma). You can also mix the two formats.

Printing Multiple Copies

You can also choose to print multiple copies of your document. In the **Copies** area of the Print dialog box, use the increment buttons in the **Number of Copies** box to select the number of copies you want to print. You can also double-click inside the **Number of Copies** box and type in a particular value for the number of copies you want to print.

Printing Special Document Items

You can print special items that you have placed in your document, such as comments, styles, and AutoText entries. When you choose to print one of these items, you are supplied with a page or pages separate from the main document that list the comments, styles, or other items you've selected.

Select the **Print What** drop-down arrow and select from the list of items supplied (**Document**, **Document Properties**, **Comments**, **Styles**, **AutoText Entries**, or **Key Assignments**). If you wish to print more than one of these optional items with the document printout, you must select them in the Print Options dialog box.

Selecting Paper Trays, Draft Quality, and Other Options

Several additional print options are also available to you from the Print dialog box. To access these options, click the **Options** button on the bottom left of the Print dialog box (see Figure 14.3).

Figure 14.3 In the Print options dialog box, you can select or deselect certain options associated with your print job.

The Print options dialog box, using a series of check boxes, gives you control over the output of the print job as well as other options. You can also select the paper tray in your printer that you wish to use for the print job (this is very useful in cases where you have a specific tray for letterhead, envelopes, and so on). Several of these options are described in Table 14.1.

Table 14.1 Print Options on the Print Dialog Box

Option	Purpose
Draft Output	Prints the document faster with less resolution.
Reverse Print Order	Prints pages last to first, collating your document on printers that output documents face up.
Background Printing	Prints the document quickly to a memory buffer so that you can work while the output is actually sent out to the printer.
Document Properties	Prints the document properties.
Comments	Prints any comments in the document.

When you have completed selecting the various options for the printing of your document, click the **OK** button. You are returned to the Print dialog box. When you are ready to print the document, click **OK**.

In this lesson, you learned how to preview and print your document. You also learned how to set various print options. In the next lesson, you learn how to fax and email documents.

Faxing and Emailing Documents

15

In this lesson, you learn to fax and email documents from Word.

Understanding Faxes and Email in Word

The capability to send faxes and email directly from Word is actually an extension of Word's printing capabilities and its tight integration with your Windows default email client, respectively. When you fax a document in Word, you are actually sending the current document and a cover page (if you've selected these particular options using the Fax Wizard, which controls the process) to your modem. Your modem accepts the print job the same as your printer normally would. The big difference, however, is that the hard copy of the document is actually printed out on the fax machine that receives the document from you.

Emailing a Word document directly from Word is also a case of computer "sleight of hand," and Word actually calls on your default email package (such as Outlook or Outlook Express) to attach the current document to an email message. You supply the recipient's email address, and the email (with your document as an attachment) is sent via your Internet service provider (again using your modem) or over your corporate network using your email server.

 Email Attachment   Any file, including a Word document, that is attached to an email message.

Sending a Document As a Fax

To send a document from Word as a fax, your computer must be set up to send and receive faxes. This means that your computer must have a modem and some sort of fax service installed, such as Microsoft Fax (or other fax service software that enables you to send faxes using your computer's modem). For information on setting up Microsoft Fax on your computer, see Lesson 23, "Managing Faxes with Outlook," in Part VI, "Outlook."

The great thing about faxing directly from Word and your computer is that you negate the need for a hard copy of your document and access to a standard fax machine. To send the current document as a fax, follow these steps:

1. Select **File**, then point to **Send To**, then select **Fax Recipient** from the cascading menu. The Word Fax Wizard starts (see Figure 15.1).

Figure 15.1 The Fax Wizard walks you through the process of sending the current document as a fax.

2. The Fax Wizard walks you through the process of sending the current document as a fax. Click **Next** to continue the process.

3. On the next wizard screen, a series of option buttons enables you to select whether to send the current document, send a cover sheet with the document, or send just a cover sheet with a note. Choose the appropriate option buttons (see Figure 15.2), then click **Next** to continue.

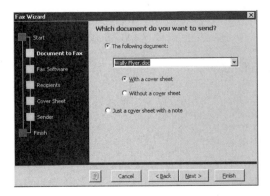

Figure 15.2   You can select whether to send the current document with a cover sheet or just send a cover sheet with a note.

4. On the next screen you select your fax service. Microsoft Fax is the default. If you use a different fax program on your computer, select the **A Different Fax Program Which Is Installed on This System** option button, and then select your fax program from the **Fax Service** drop-down list. Then click **Next** to continue.

5. On the next screen, enter the recipient and the fax number in the appropriate boxes. If you have the recipient listed in your email program Address Book, click the **Address Book** button and select the person from the Address Book list. Depending on the email package you are using, it may include an Address Book feature that enables you to enter information on clients and friends, including their email addresses, home addresses, and even their fax and phone numbers. If a fax number is listed in the Address book (as it is in Microsoft Outlook), all you have to do is select the recipients from the Address Book for your Word fax, and the fax numbers are entered for you automatically. When you have completed entering the recipient information for the fax, click **Next** to continue.

6. On this screen, select the type of layout you wish to use for your Fax cover page. Select the option button for either **Professional**, **Contemporary,** or **Elegant**. When you select each of the option buttons, a preview of the layout is shown on the screen. When you have selected your cover sheet layout, click **Next** to continue.

7. On the next screen, input the information regarding who the fax is from (such as your name, fax number, and so on). When you have entered this information, click **Next**.

8. On the final screen of the Fax Wizard, you are given advice on what to do if the fax doesn't send. Click **Finish**.

The cover sheet that you designed for the fax is displayed in the Word window. Fill in any information that is required and then click the **Send Fax Now** button. Your fax is sent using the fax service you selected.

Emailing Documents from Word

If you have an *email client* (software for sending and receiving email) on your computer, you can send Word documents as attachments. This means that you can send a typical email message to a specific email address or addresses and include your Word document. If you use Microsoft Outlook as your email client, you will find that Outlook enables you to send your Word document directly from the Word application window, as detailed next. This is because Outlook and Word are tightly integrated members of the Office Suite (for more about working with Microsoft Outlook, see Part VI of this book).

 Email Client   The email program installed on your computer that you use to send and receive email.

Typically, when you attach a document or other file to an email message, the attached file is represented by an icon in the email message (or some other area of the message). To send your current Word document as an email attachment, follow these steps:

1. Open the file that you want to send as an email attachment.

2. Select **File**, point to **Send To**, and then select **Mail Recipient**.

 TIP   Connect with Your Internet Service Provider   If you use an Internet service provider to connect to the Internet (and your email server), you may wish to dial into your provider before attempting to send email.

3. Your email client software starts. If you use Microsoft Outlook as your email client, a box appears at the top of the Word window containing an area for the recipient's email address (To), a copy area (CC), and a box for the subject (which will be the current filename), as shown in Figure 15.3. The Outlook toolbars also appear in the Word window. Your document appears in the document window.

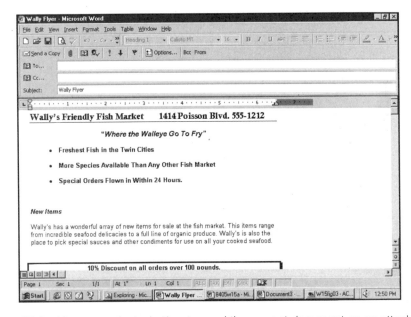

Figure 15.3 You can select whether to send the current document as an attachment on an email message.

4. Fill in the recipient address (in the **To** box) for the email message and edit the **Subject** line if you wish. (The subject line in the email is a copy of the first line of text that appears in the document you've attached to the email message. Changing the subject line does not affect the text in the document.)

5. When you are ready to send the email message, click **Send Copy**.

Your Word document is sent as an email message. When the recipient of the message reads the email message in Outlook, he or she will be able to open the message directly, as if looking at a Word document. Other email recipients will be able to open the document by double-clicking the Word document icon that appears in the message. This starts Microsoft Word and opens the document in the Word window. The recipient can save the document to a new location using **Save As**, or print the document.

CAUTION

Outlook Express Opens a Separate Window If you use Outlook Express as your email client, a separate window opens for the email message. Your Word document appears as an attachment—an icon in the email message. Fill in the recipient's address in the **To** box, and then add other information as needed. Then click **Send** to send your Word document as an email attachment.

CAUTION

Email Attachments Can Be Tricky in Some Cases Some email client software does not have the capability to correctly encode or decode attachments, so you may end up with mixed results.

In this lesson, you learned to fax and email documents from within Word. In the next lesson, you learn how to create numbered and bulleted lists.

Creating Numbered and Bulleted Lists

In this lesson, you learn to create and edit numbered and bulleted lists.

Understanding Numbered and Bulleted Lists

You can add emphasis to a list of points or delineate a list of items in a document by adding numbers or bullets to the items in the list. Numbered lists are great for steps or points that should be read in order. Bulleted lists work best when you want to separate and highlight different items or points in a list, but the items do not have to appear in any particular order.

The style and look of the numbers or bullets that you apply to a list can easily be edited, and you can even change the starting number for a numbered list. The list will then renumber itself automatically. Also, as you add new lines to numbered or bulleted lists, the items are automatically set up with the same numbering style (with the proper number in the list sequence) or bullet style.

Creating a Numbered or a Bulleted List

You can create numbered or bulleted lists from scratch or add numbers or bullets to an existing list.

To create a new numbered list, follow these steps:

1. Place the insertion point where you want to begin the numbered list in your document.

2. Select **Format**, then **Bullets and Numbering**. The Bullets and Numbering dialog box appears.

3. For a numbered list, select the **Numbered** tab (see Figure 16.1).

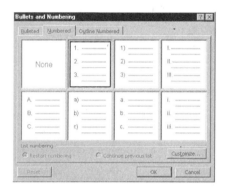

Figure 16.1 Use the Numbered tab on the Bullets and Numbering dialog box to select a number style for your numbered list.

  TIP **Quickly Start a Numbered or Bulleted List Using the Formatting Toolbar** To start a numbered or bulleted list using the default number or bullet style, click the **Numbering** or **Bullets** button on the Formatting toolbar. To turn off the numbers or bullets, click the appropriate button on the toolbar.

4. On the **Numbered** tab, click the style box for the particular style that you want to use for the numbers in the list. If you want to customize any of the default styles offered, select the style box and then click the **Customize** button. The Customize Numbered List dialog box appears (see Figure 16.2).

5. Use this dialog box to change the number style, the format, the start number, the font for the numbers, or the number position. A preview of your changes is shown on the right side of the dialog box.

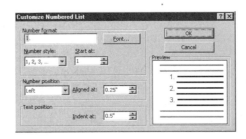

Figure 16.2   The Customize Numbered List dialog box enables you to set the number style, format, and start number for the list.

   6. When you have selected your options for the number style for your list, click **OK**. You are returned to the Bullets and Numbering dialog box. Click **OK** to return to the document.

You can also easily create a bulleted list using the Bullets and Numbering dialog box; follow these steps:

   1. To start a bulleted list, open the Bullets and Numbering dialog box, as previously discussed (select **Format**, then **Bullets and Numbering**). Click the **Bulleted** tab.

   2. Select the bullet style you want to use by clicking the appropriate box (see Figure 16.3). If you need to customize your bullet style, click the **Customize** button.

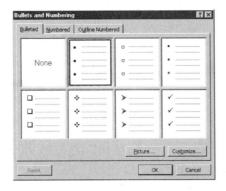

Figure 16.3   Use the Bulleted tab to select the bullet style for your bulleted list.

   3. When you are ready to begin the bulleted list, click **OK** to close the Bullets and Numbering dialog box.

You can choose from a number of special bullets, called Picture Bullets, that Word provides for your bulleted lists. These minigraphics can really add emphasis to your bulleted lists. To select a picture to use as your bullet, click the **Picture** button on the **Bulleted** tab of the Bullets and Numbering dialog box. After selecting your picture from the list, click **OK** to return to the Bullets and Numbering dialog box.

Adding Items to the List

After you've turned on numbering or bulleting, you will notice that a number or a bullet appears at the beginning of the line that holds the insertion point. Type the text for this numbered or bulleted item.

Press the **Enter** key to begin a new line. The numbering (sequentially) or bulleting continues with each subsequent line. Just add the needed text and press **Enter** whenever you are ready to move to the next new item in the list.

 You can turn off the numbering or bulleting when you have finished creating your list. Click the **Numbering** button or the **Bullets** button, respectively, on the Formatting toolbar.

Creating a Numbered or a Bulleted List from Existing Text

You can also add numbers or bullets to existing text. Select the text list, as shown in Figure 16.4, then select **Format**, and **Bullets and Numbering**. Select the appropriate tab on the Bullets and Numbering dialog box and select the style of bullets or numbers you want to use.

When you have completed making your selection, click **OK**. The numbers or bullets appear on the text list.

 TIP **Add Numbers or Bullets with a Click** You can quickly add numbers or bullets to an existing list. Select the list of items and click the **Numbering** or **Bullets** buttons, respectively, on the Formatting toolbar.

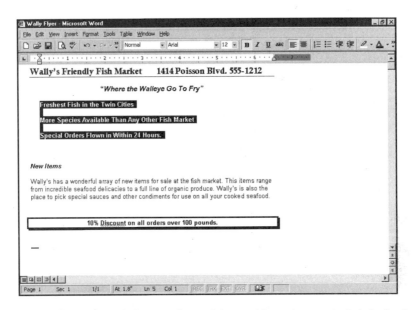

Figure 16.4 Select an existing text list and then add numbers or bullets to the list.

Customizing the Way Numbers and Bullets Look

You have complete control over the look of the numbers and bullets used in your lists. You can change the look of the numbers or bullets before you build your list or after the fact, which requires only that you select the existing numbered or bulleted list.

To change the numbers or the bullet format, follow these steps:

1. Select **Format**, then **Bullets and Numbering**, or right-click the selected list and select **Bullets and Numbering** from the shortcut menu.

2. Click the **Numbered** tab on the Bullets and Numbering dialog box to select a new style for your numbers. If you want to customize the style, click the **Customize** button. In cases where you want to remove the numbers from the list, choose **None** on the Numbered tab.

3. Use the **Bulleted** tab on the Bullets and Numbering dialog box to select a new style for your bullets. If you want to customize the style, click the **Customize** button. If you want to use a picture for the bullet, click the **Picture** button.

When you have finished editing your number or bullet style, click **OK** in the Bullets and Numbering dialog box. The new number or bullet style takes effect in your selected list.

Creating Multilevel Lists

You can also create multilevel lists by using the numbering and bullet feature. Multilevel lists merely contain two or more levels within a particular list. For instance, a multilevel list might number primary items in the list, but secondary items (which fall under a particular primary item) in the list are denoted by sequential letters of the alphabet. Figure 16.5 shows a numbered, multilevel list.

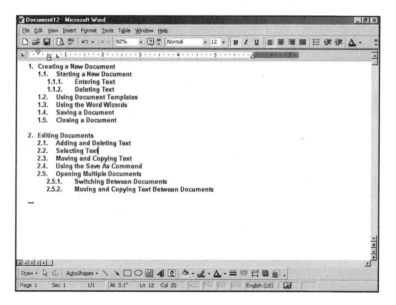

Figure 16.5 A multilevel numbered list uses several levels of numbering, like an outline does.

To create a multilevel list, follow these steps:

1. Place the insertion point where you want to begin the list, or select text in an already existing list.
2. Select **Format**, then **Bullets and Numbering**. The Bullets and Numbering dialog box opens.
3. Click the **Outline Numbered** tab to view the multilevel options (see Figure 16.6).

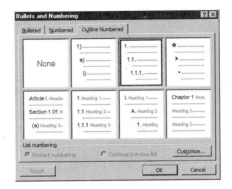

Figure 16.6   Use the Outline Numbered tab to select the outline style for your multilevel list.

4. Select the style of multilevel list you want to use in your document.

5. After customizing the list options in the Customize Outline Numbered list, click **OK** to return to the Outline Numbered tab.

6. Click **OK** to close the Bullets and Numbering dialog box and return to the document.

7. To enter first-level items in the list, type the item (it will be automatically numbered as is appropriate). Press **Enter** to move to the next line.

8. To demote the next line to the next sublevel (the next level of numbering), press the **Tab** key. Then type your text. Press **Enter** to move to the next line.

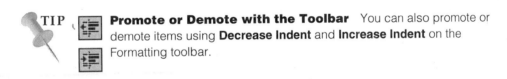

TIP   **Promote or Demote with the Toolbar**   You can also promote or demote items using **Decrease Indent** and **Increase Indent** on the Formatting toolbar.

9. If you decide to promote a line that you have demoted using the **Tab**, make sure the insertion point is on the line, and then press **Shift+Tab**. When you have finished with the current line, press **Enter** to continue.

 When you have completed your list, you can turn off the numbering by clicking the **Numbering** button on the Formatting toolbar (this deactivates numbering).

In this lesson, you learned how to create numbered, bulleted, and multilevel lists. In the next lesson, you learn how to work with Word tables.

263

Using Word Tables

17

In this lesson, you learn to create and format tables in your Word document. You also learn to place math formulas in a table.

Understanding Tables and Cells

A Word table is made up of columns and rows—a tabular format. The intersection of a row and a column in a table is often referred to as a *cell*. It is within the cell that you enter the information that is contained in a particular place in the table. You will find that tables provide much more flexibility for arranging text in a tabular format, much more so than trying to set up the columns and rows using tab settings (for more information on setting tabs in Word, see Lesson 8, "Working with Tabs and Indents").

TERM   **Cell**   A table cell is the intersection of a column and row.

Word makes it easy for you to create a table of any size with any number of columns and rows in your document and then easily edit it. These editing capabilities are not restricted to the text that is in the rows and columns, but also includes a number of formatting options related to the table itself, such as row and column attributes and the capability to easily add or delete rows and columns from the table.

Word also offers you several approaches for actually placing the table in the document. You can insert the table into the document or actually draw the table using the Draw Table command.

Inserting a Table

One option for placing a table into your document is inserting the table. Inserting a table enables you to select the number of rows and columns in the table. The height and the width of the rows and columns are set to the default (one line space [based on the current font height] for the row height and 1.23 inches for the column width). Using the Insert command for a new table provides you with the simplest way to select the number of rows and columns for the table. Also, to place the table, you need only to place the insertion point at the position where the new table is to be inserted.

Inserted tables are static; you can move them to a new location in a document only by selecting the entire table and then using cut and paste. If you wish to have better control over the placement of the table, you might want to draw a table (as described in the next section). This type of table can be dragged to any location in the document because it is created inside a movable frame.

To insert a table into your document, follow these steps:

1. Place the insertion point in the document where you want to place the table; select **Table**, then point at **Insert**. Select **Table** from the cascading menu. The Insert Table dialog box appears (see Figure 17.1).

Figure 17.1 The Insert Table dialog box enables you to specify the number of columns and rows for your new table.

2. Use the click arrows in the **Number of Columns** text box to set the number of columns. Use the click arrows in the **Number of Rows** text box to set the number of rows.

3. If you wish to set the number of columns and rows as the default for subsequent tables, click the **Set as Default for New Tables** check box. When you have completed your settings for the table, click **OK**.

The table is inserted into your document.

 TIP   **Use the Toolbar to Insert a Table**   Click the **Insert Table** button on the Standard toolbar, and then drag down and to the right to select the number of rows and columns (a column and row counter shows you the number selected). Release the mouse to insert the table.

Drawing a Table

An alternative to inserting a table in your document is to draw the table. This method creates a table that resides inside a table cell. (This is not the same thing as the intersection of a column and a row, but a movable box that the table lives inside of—much like a frame. It can be dragged to any position in the document.) You actually draw the table with a drawing tool and use the tool to add rows and columns to the table.

When you draw the table, you will find that it is created without any rows or columns. You then must manually insert the rows and columns using the Table Drawing tool. Although you can build a highly customized table using this method, you will find that it is not as fast as inserting a table with a prescribed number of rows and columns, as described in the previous section.

To draw a table in your document, follow these steps:

1. Select **Table**, then **Draw Table**. The mouse pointer becomes a "pencil" drawing tool. The Tables and Borders toolbar also appears in the document window.

2. Click and drag to create the table's outside borders (its box shape). Release the mouse when you have the outside perimeter of the table completed.

3. To add rows and columns to the table, use the pencil to draw (hold down the left mouse button and drag the mouse) the row and column borders (see Figure 17.2).

 4. When you have completed your table, click the **Draw Table** button on the Tables and Borders toolbar to deactivate the button.

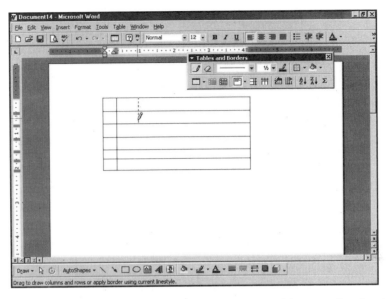

Figure 17.2   You can "draw" a table in your document and then use the drawing tool to place the row and column borders in the table.

The Tables and Borders toolbar provides you with buttons that enable you to edit the attributes of the table. You will find several of the buttons on the Tables and Borders toolbar useful for customizing your table:

- **Distribute Rows Evenly**—This button makes the row heights in the table all the same.
- **Distribute Columns Evenly**—This button makes all the column widths consistent.
- **Eraser**—This button enables you to turn on the eraser; drag it across any row or column line in the table to erase it.
- **Line Style**—This drop-down box enables you to change the weight and style of the row or column lines you create.

You will also find that the table can be moved anywhere on the document page (it's not anchored in one place like tables that are placed on the page using the Insert Table command). Place the mouse on the upper-left edge of the table and a Move icon (a four-headed arrow) appears. Drag the icon to a new location on the page. When you release the mouse, the table is placed in the new location.

Entering Text and Navigating in a Table

Entering text into the table is very straightforward. Click in the first cell of the table (the first column and first row of the table) and enter the appropriate text. To move to the next cell, press the **Tab** key. You can continue to move through the cells in the tables by pressing **Tab** and entering your text. If you wish to back up a cell, press **Shift+Tab**. This moves you to the cell to the left of the current cell and selects any text entered in that cell.

Several other keyboard combinations are useful as you work in your table:

- **Alt+Home** takes you to the first cell in the current row.
- **Alt+Page Up** takes you to the top cell in the current column.
- **Alt+End** takes you to the last cell in the current row.
- **Alt+Page Down** takes you to the last cell in the current column.

Of course, you can use the mouse to click any cell of the table at any time.

Deleting text in the table is really no different from deleting text in your document. Select text in the table and then press **Delete** to remove it. If you want to delete text in an entire row, but you want to keep the row in the table, place the mouse pointer at the left edge of the particular row. The mouse arrow pointer appears in the selection area. Click to select the entire row. When you press Delete, all the text in the cells in that particular row are deleted. You can also use a Column pointer (a solid black arrow; place the mouse at the top of any column) to select a column and delete text using the Delete key.

Inserting and Deleting Rows and Columns

You also have complete control over the number of rows and columns in your table. You can delete empty or filled rows and columns depending on your particular need.

To insert a row or column in the table, place the insertion point in a cell that is in the row or column next to where you wish to place a new row or column. The options available to you are found by selecting **Table**, then pointing at **Insert**. Your options can be selected from a cascading menu:

- **Rows Above**—Insert a new row above the selected row.
- **Rows Below**—Insert a new row below the selected row.
- **Columns to the Left**—Insert a new column to the left of the selected column.
- **Columns to the Right**—Insert a new column to the right of the selected column.

You can also easily delete columns or rows from your table. Select the rows or columns and then select the **Table** menu. Point at **Delete**, and then select **Columns** or **Rows** from the cascading menu, as appropriate. The columns or rows selected are removed from the table.

TIP **Add Multiple Rows or Columns** To add multiple rows, first select the number of cells down a column to specify the number of rows to add. To add multiple columns, first select the number of cells across a row to specify how many columns to add.

TIP **Quick Select Multiple Columns** To select several cells, drag the mouse across them. You can also click the first cell in the series and then hold down the **Shift** key as you click the last cell you wish to select.

Formatting a Table

Formatting a table can involve several things: You can change the width of a column or the height of a row, and you can also format the various table borders with different line weights or colors. Some of the table attributes can be modified directly on the table, but other attributes are best handled by modifying settings in the Table Properties dialog box or by using the AutoFormat dialog box.

Modifying Cell Size

An important aspect of working with your rows and columns is adjusting column widths and row heights to fit the needs of the information that you place inside the table cells. Both of these formatting tasks are mouse work. However, in cases where you would like to enter an actual value for all the column widths or row heights, you can use the Table Properties dialog box discussed in this section.

Place the mouse pointer on the border between any columns in your table. A sizing tool appears (see Figure 17.3). Drag the sizing tool to adjust the width of the column.

 TIP   **Use the Ruler as Your Guide**   You can also use the column border markers on the ruler to adjust the width of a column or columns in your table. This provides a method of sizing columns using the ruler as a measurement guide. Drag the marker on the ruler to the appropriate width. To view the ruler, select **View**, then **Ruler**.

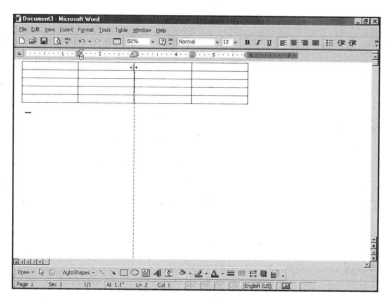

Figure 17.3   Use the Column sizing tool to adjust the width of a column.

 Be Careful When Sizing Columns If a Cell Is Selected   If a cell is selected anywhere in a column and you attempt to drag the sizing tool to change the column width, only the width of the row holding the selected cell is changed. Make sure no cells are selected if you wish to size the entire column.

CAUTION

You can also adjust the column widths and the row heights in the table using the Table Properties dialog box. If you wish to adjust the row or column attributes for just one row or column, make sure the insertion point is in that row or column.

If you want to adjust the values for the entire table, click anywhere in the table, and then choose the **Table** menu, point at **Select**, then choose **Table**. This selects the entire table.

Follow these steps to open the dialog box and adjust the various properties associated with the current table:

1. Select **Table**, then **Table Properties**. The Table Properties dialog box appears.
2. To adjust column widths using the dialog box, select the **Column** tab.
3. Make sure the **Specify Width** check box is selected, and then use the width click arrows to adjust the width (see Figure 17.4).

Figure 17.4 Adjust your column widths using the Column tab of the Table Properties dialog box.

4. If you wish to change the width of the next column, click the **Next Column** button. The **Previous Column** button enables you to adjust the width of the previous column.
5. When you have completed adjusting column widths, click the **OK** button.

You can also adjust row heights in a like manner. Use the **Row** tab of the Table Properties dialog box. A Specify Height box can be used to specify the row height, and Previous Row and Next Row buttons can be used to specify the row for which you want to adjust the height.

TIP **Working with Drawn Tables** If you've created your table using the Draw Table command and then inserted your rows and columns with the Drawing tool, you might find it faster to align any irregularly sized elements (such as rows or columns) with the mouse rather than the Table Properties dialog box.

TIP **Align Your Inserted Table Using the Table Properties Dialog Box** If you've created your table using the **Table Insert** command, it cannot be dragged to a new position. Realign your table using the **Left**, **Center**, and **Right** alignment buttons on the **Table** tab of the Table Properties dialog box.

Formatting Table Borders

Formatting your table borders is a matter of selecting the cells (or the entire table) and then selecting the formatting parameters. After you've selected the appropriate cells, select the **Format** menu, then select **Borders and Shading**.

TIP **Select the Entire Table** A fast way to select the entire table is to place the insertion point in the table and then select **Table**, point at **Select**, and then select **Table**.

The Borders and Shading dialog box appears. Select the style of border that you want to place on the selected area of the table.

To select the border style, choose from one of the following:

- **Box**—This places a box around the outside of the table.
- **All**—This places a box around the table, gridlines inside the table, and also applies any shadow and color parameters that have been set in Word.
- **Grid**—This places a border around the table and places a border (grid) on the row and column lines.
- **Custom**—When you select **Custom**, you must then specify on the Preview table the border lines you want to format. To change the style, color, and width of your border lines, use the line **Style**, **Color**, and **Width** drop-down boxes to select the options for your border lines. When you have completed your selections, click **OK** to return to the table.

The border options that you selected are used to format the cells that you selected in the table (for more about using borders and shading in your documents and tables, see Lesson 7, "Using Borders and Colors").

Automatically Formatting the Table

You can also format your table in a more automatic fashion using the Table AutoFormat feature. This feature enables you to select from a list of premade table formats (much like an entire package of formats) that will format the borders, provide text and background colors in the cells, and even select a particular font for the text contained in the cells.

To AutoFormat your table, click any cell of the table and then follow these steps:

1. Select **Table**, then **AutoFormat**. The Table AutoFormat dialog box appears (see Figure 17.5).

2. To preview the various formats provided, click a format in the **Formats** scroll box. A preview of the format is shown.

3. When you have found the format that you wish to use, select the format and then click **OK**.

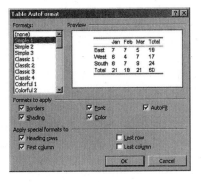

Figure 17.5 The Table AutoFormat dialog box enables you to select a format style for your entire table.

 TIP **Select the Table Items You Wish to Format with AutoFormat** The AutoFormat dialog box provides several check boxes (Borders, Shading, Font, Color, and so on) that can be deselected if you don't want your AutoFormat selection to format these particular items in your table.

In this lesson, you learned how to create, edit, and format tables. In the next lesson, you learn how to create columns in your documents.

Creating Columns in a Document

In this lesson, you learn to create and edit column settings in your document.

Understanding Word Columns

Word makes it very easy for you to insert and format columns for newsletters, brochures, and other special documents. You are given complete control over the number of columns, column widths, and the space between the columns. You can insert columns for the entire page run of a document or place columns in a particular document section (to learn about Word sections, see Lesson 21, "Working with Larger Documents").

The columns that you work with in Word are called newspaper or "snaking columns." This means that if you have two columns on a page and fill the first column the text will 'snake' over into the second column and continue there. This format is typical of your daily newspaper.

TIP **For Side-By-Side Columns Use a Table** If you want to create columns that allow you to place paragraphs of information side by side in a document, place the text in a table that is not formatted with a visible border. This gives you great control over the text in the various columns that you create (see Lesson 17, "Using Word Tables," for more about tables).

Creating Columns

You can format a new document for columns or you can select text and then apply column settings to that specific text. When you apply column settings to any selected text, Word automatically places the text (now in the number of columns you selected) in its own document section with a section break above and below the text. This allows you to switch from text in regular paragraphs (one column that covers all the space between the left and right margins) to text placed in multiple columns. You can also then turn off the columns and return to text in paragraphs with very little effort on your part. Figure 18.1 shows a document that contains a section of text in paragraphs followed by text in columns, followed by text in paragraphs (three different sections in the same document). Sections are covered in Lesson 21.

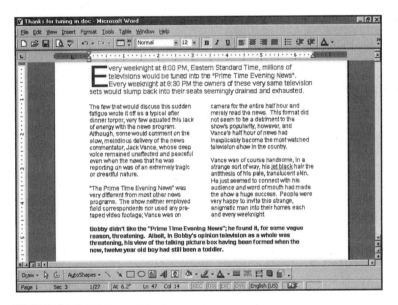

Figure 18.1 Documents can contain text in paragraphs and text in columns as needed.

To place additional columns in a document follow these steps:

1. Place the insertion point where you want the columns to begin or select the text that you want to format with the columns.

2. Select **Format**, then click **Columns**, and the Columns dialog box appears (Figure 18.2).

3. To select the number of columns you want to place in the document, you can choose from several preset options or specify a number of custom columns.

- **Presets**—Click one of the Preset buttons such as Two to create that number of equal width columns separated by a half-inch space.

- **Number of Columns Box**—You can also select your own custom number of columns using the **Number of Columns** click box. Below this click box in the Width and Spacing box, you can specify the width for each column and the distance between each of the columns.

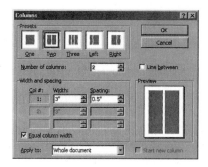

Figure 18.2 The Columns dialog box allows you to set the number of columns and column options for the columns that you place into your document.

4. If you want to place a vertical line between the column, select the **Line between** check box.

5. You can apply these new columns to the entire document (if you've selected text it only applies to that text) or click the **Apply to** drop-down box and select **This Section** or **This Point Forward**. If you choose This Point Forward, the columns will be placed in the document from the insertion point to the end of the document (in their own section).

6. When you have completed selecting your column options, click **OK**.

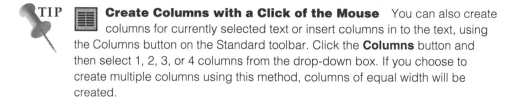

TIP **Create Columns with a Click of the Mouse** You can also create columns for currently selected text or insert columns in to the text, using the Columns button on the Standard toolbar. Click the **Columns** button and then select 1, 2, 3, or 4 columns from the drop-down box. If you choose to create multiple columns using this method, columns of equal width will be created.

Editing Column Settings

If you want to edit any of the column settings in your document such as column number or column width, you can return to the Column dialog box to change any of the options.

1. Make sure that you click in the document section that contains the columns that you want to modify.

2. Select **Format**, and then **Columns**. The Column dialog box appears.

3. Edit the various settings as needed. When you have completed your selections, click **OK**.

Inserting a Column Break

Because you are working with continuous, newspaper-type column settings, there may be times when you want to force a column break in a column. This allows you to balance the text between columns or end the text in a column at a particular point and force the rest of the text into the next column.

1. Place the insertion point in the column text where you would like to force the break.

2. Select **Insert**, and then **Break**. The Break dialog box appears.

3. Select the **Column break** option button.

4. Click **OK** to place the break in the column.

 TIP **Use the Keyboard to Insert a Column Break** You can also quickly place a column break in a column by pressing **Ctrl + Shift + Enter**.

The text at the break is moved into the next column in the document. Column breaks in the Print Layout view appear as they will print and you'll notice that all the column borders show in this view. In the Normal view, multiple columns are displayed as a single continuous column. The column break is shown as a dotted horizontal line labeled as Column Break.

Removing Column Breaks

Removing column breaks is very straightforward. Methods do vary, however, depending on the view that you are currently in.

In the Print Layout mode, place the insertion point at the beginning of the text just after the break and then press **Backspace**. This removes the break from the document.

In the Normal view you can actually see the Column Break line (it appears as a dashed line). Select the break line with the mouse and then press **Delete**.

In this lesson, you learned to create and edit column settings in your documents. In the next lesson, you learn to add graphics to your documents.

Adding Graphics
to Documents

In this lesson, you learn how to insert graphics such as clip art into your document and how to use the Word drawing tools to create your own graphics.

Inserting a Graphic

Adding a graphic to your document is really just a matter of identifying the place in the document where you would like to place the picture and then selecting a specific graphic file. Word provides you with a large clip-art gallery of ready-made graphics (in the metafile format .wmf), and you can also place images into your document that you find on the World Wide Web, that you receive attached to email messages, or that you scan into your computer using a scanner.

Word also embraces a number of graphic file formats, including the following file types:

- CompuServe GIF (.gif)
- Encapsulated PostScript (.eps)
- Various paint programs (.pcx)
- Tagged Image File format (.tif)
- Windows bitmap (.bmp)
- JPEG file interchange format (.jpg)
- WordPerfect graphics (.wpg)

To add a graphic file (a picture other than one of the Word clip art files), you insert the image via the Insert menu.

Follow these steps to add a graphic to your document:

1. Place the insertion point where you want to place the graphic in the document.
2. Select **Insert**, then point at **Picture**, then select **From File** on the cascading menu. The Insert Picture dialog box appears.
3. Use the **Look In** box to locate the drive and folder that contains the picture file. After you locate the picture, click the file to view a preview (see Figure 19.1).

Figure 19.1 You can preview your graphical images before inserting them into your document.

4. After you select the picture you want to insert into the document, click **Insert** in the lower-right corner of the Insert Picture dialog box.

The picture is placed in your document, and the Picture toolbar appears in the document window. The Picture toolbar provides several tools you can use to modify and edit the graphics in your document. See the "Modifying Graphics" section in this lesson.

TIP **Add a Graphic with Copy and Paste** You can also copy a graphic from any Windows graphic program that you are running to the Windows Clipboard and then paste it into your Word document.

Using the Word Clip Art

If you don't have a collection of your own pictures and graphics to place in your document, don't be dismayed; Word provides a large collection of clip art images you can use to liven up your documents. The clip art library is organized by theme. For instance, if you want to peruse the animal clip art that Word provides, you can select the **Animal** theme.

To insert Word clip art into your document, follow these steps:

1. Place the insertion point where you want to place the graphic in the document.

2. Select **Insert**, then point at **Picture**, then select **ClipArt** on the cascading menu. The Insert ClipArt dialog box appears (see Figure 19.2).

Access the Microsoft
clip art online Web site.

Return to
the category listing.

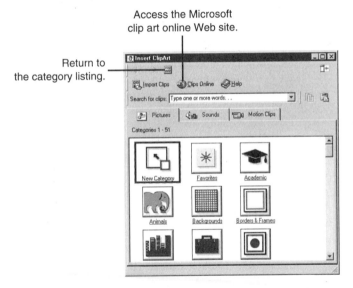

Figure 19.2 The Insert ClipArt dialog box gives you access to the Word clip art gallery.

3. Click a particular clip-art category, such as the **Business** category. A portfolio of the available clip art images appears (see Figure 19.3).

Word also provides sound and video files that you can place in your documents. Select a particular category and then select the **Sounds** or **Motion Clips** tab to view the items available in the particular category.

These clip art items are meant to be viewed on the computer, so they won't do you much good on a printout of your document. But they can enliven online material that you create in Word.

Figure 19.3   Click a particular clip art category to view the clip art images.

4. To return to the list of clip art categories, click the **All Categories** button on the dialog box. You can then select another category of images to view.

5. When you have located the clip art you want to place in the document, click the image. An image drop-down box appears. Select **Insert Clip** (the first icon on the box) to place the image in your document.

If used appropriately, pictures and clip art can definitely improve the look and feel of your documents, particularly special documents such as flyers, newsletters, and brochures. If you find the clip art library provided doesn't have what you need, click the **Clips Online** button in the Insert ClipArt dialog box. Your Web browser opens and you go to Microsoft's online clip-art library, which offers additional clip-art images for your use.

Images and Copyright   Clip-art images such as those that ship with Microsoft Word are considered "free" images and can be used in any of your Word documents. Other images that you find on the World Wide Web might be copyrighted. Find out if you have the right to use an image before using it.

CAUTION

Modifying Graphics

You can modify the images you place in your documents. An invaluable tool for modifying images is the Picture toolbar. It provides buttons that enable you to modify a number of picture parameters. You can also easily crop and resize your graphics.

When you click a picture (a picture file or Word clip art) in the document, the Picture toolbar automatically appears. You can use the toolbar to adjust the brightness or contrast of the image. You can also add a border to the graphic or adjust other picture properties. Word's Picture toolbar offers a large number of possibilities. Table 19.1 provides a listing and a description of the most commonly used buttons on the Picture toolbar.

Table 19.1   The Picture Toolbar Buttons and Their Purpose

Button	Click To
	Insert a new picture at the current picture position.
	Change the image to grayscale or black and white.
	Crop image (after selecting, you must drag the image border to a new cropping position).
	Select a line style for the image border (you must first use the **Borders and Shading** command to add a border to the image).
	Control how text wraps around the image (square, tight, behind image, and so on).
	Open the Format Picture dialog box.
	Reset the image to its original formatting values.

You can select from a number of formatting options for your picture when you select the **Format Picture** button; this opens the Format Picture dialog box (see Figure 19.4).

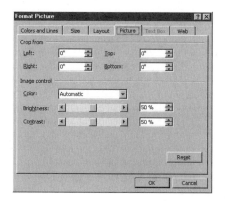

Figure 19.4   The Format Picture dialog box offers several ways to modify your picture.

You can change the color and lines, size, nearby text layout, and cropping of the picture by selecting the appropriate tab and then selecting the options you want to use to format your picture.

After making formatting changes to the picture using the Format Picture dialog box, click **OK** to return to your document.

TIP   **Resize or Crop with the Mouse**   Select the picture and then drag the resizing handles (the black boxes on the picture borders) to increase or decrease the size of your picture. If you want to crop the picture, hold down the **Shift** key as you drag any of the resizing handles.

You can delete a picture you no longer want in the document by clicking the picture and then pressing the **Delete** key on the keyboard. You can also move or copy the picture to another place in the current document—or to another document—using the **Cut** or **Copy** and **Paste** commands(for more general information about moving, copying, and pasting items in Word, see Lesson 3, "Editing Documents").

Using the Word Drawing Toolbar

You can also create your own graphics in your documents using the drawing tools provided on the Word Drawing toolbar. This toolbar provides you with a number of tools, including line, arrow, rectangle, oval, and text box tools. You can also use the appropriate tools to change the fill color on a box or circle, to change the line color on your drawing object, or to change the arrow style on arrows you have placed on the page.

To display the Drawing toolbar, select **View**, point at **Toolbar**, and then select **Drawing** from the toolbar list.

TIP **Quickly Access Toolbars** You can also right-click any toolbar in the Word window to access the toolbar list; then select **Drawing**.

The Drawing toolbar appears at the bottom of the document window just above the Word status bar. Figure 19.5 shows the Drawing toolbar and the tools available on it.

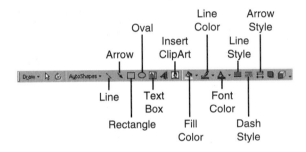

Figure 19.5 The Drawing toolbar makes it easy for you to create your own graphics in your documents.

 Word provides you with an add-on program called WordArt that enables you to create special text effects in your document. You can create text that wraps around a circle, as well as a number of other special text "looks." In Word, click the **WordArt** button on the Drawing toolbar to start the WordArt program. WordArt can also be used in other Office programs, such as PowerPoint, to create visually exciting text items. For more about WordArt, see Lesson 8, "Adding and Modifying Slide Text," in the PowerPoint section of this book.

Creating a New Object

 To draw a particular object, click the appropriate button on the toolbar. Then drag the mouse to create the object in your document. To draw a square or circle, click the **Rectangle** tool or the **Oval** tool and hold down the **Shift** key as you draw the object with the mouse. If you find that you aren't very good at actually drawing graphic objects, click the **AutoShapes** pop-up list and select a particular object shape from the list provided.

Modifying Drawn Objects

 You can also control the various attributes for a particular object that you've drawn. You must first select the object using the selection pointer (click the **Select Objects** tool, then click the object). You can manipulate the object's line style, fill color, and line color. Just choose the appropriate tool on the toolbar and then make your selection from the list of possibilities.

You can also size and move objects that you draw. Select an object and then use the sizing handles to increase or decrease the size of the particular object. If you want to move the object to a new position, place the mouse pointer in the middle of the selected object and drag it to a new position.

If you draw several objects that are related, you can select all the objects at once and drag them together to a new location. Select the first object, then hold down the **Shift** key and select subsequent objects, as needed. When you drag any of the objects to a new location, all the selected objects move together.

At times you will want to delete a particular object from your document. Simply select the object and then press **Delete** to remove it.

You will find that the Drawing toolbar provides you with all the tools (except artistic ability) you need to create fairly sophisticated custom images. A little practice with the various tools will go a long way in helping you create objects that add interest to your documents.

Inserting Images from Scanners and Other Sources

You can also place images into your Word documents that do not currently exist as a picture or clip art file. You can actually attach to a particular *input device*, such as a scanner or digital camera, and then have it scan an image or take a picture on-the-fly that is then inserted into your document.

 Input Device Any device, such as a scanner or a digital camera, that is attached to your computer and can be used to acquire a picture.

Word enables you to acquire images from an attached scanner, a digital camera, or other device such as a video camera. All you have to do is set up the device so that it works on your computer, and Word will have no problem using it to capture a particular image.

If you plan on using a scanner to capture the image, make sure the scanner is on and you have placed the picture on the scanner plate.

To insert an image from an attached device, follow these steps:

1. Place the insertion point in the document where you like to insert the image.
2. Select the **Insert** menu, point at **Picture**, then click **From Scanner or Camera**. The Insert Picture from Camera or Scanner dialog box appears.
3. Click the **Device** drop-down box and select the device you want to capture the picture from (this is only necessary if you have more than one device attached).
4. Click the **Insert** button. The device scans the image or takes a picture (if you are using an attached camera) and places the image in your document.

In this lesson, you learned how to insert pictures and clip art into your documents and edit the images. You also learned how to create your own graphics using the Word Drawing tools. In the next lesson, you learn how to set up a mail merge in Word.

Creating Personalized Mass Mailings

In this lesson, you learn how to create form letters,
envelopes, and mailing labels for mass mailings using the Word merge feature.

Understanding the Mail Merge Feature

Word makes it easy for you to take a list of names and addresses and merge them with a form letter, envelope template, or mailing label type. This enables you to quickly create items for mass mailings that appear to be customized for each person on the mailing list.

The Word merge feature walks you through the process of creating the main document that provides the repeating elements for the merge (such as the body text of a form letter) and placing the appropriate merge fields in the document.

 TERM   **Merge Fields**   Codes that serve as place holders in your main document; for instance, {FirstName} is an example of a merge field code that serves as a holding place for the first name information that is pulled from the data source.

Word also helps you create the data source that provides the information to be merged into the form letters or envelopes. Each merge field code in the main document relates to a piece of information in the data source document, such as first name or street address, and the merge field gets its name from that particular field. You can easily create form letters, envelopes, and mailing labels for mass mailings during the merge process. You can even create all three of these items using the same Word data source (meaning the same names and addresses).

Data Source   The information such as a list of names and addresses to be merged into the form letter, envelope, or label that serves as the main document. Data sources in Word typically take the form of a table, with each row in the table containing the name and address of a different individual.

The best way to understand how the various elements of the merge process, the main document, data source, and field codes relate is to actually perform a merge. Working through a merge that creates form letters for all the people listed in a data source is a good place to start.

Before jumping into the merge process, however, you might want to type the body of the letter that you are going to use as the main document in the merge. This enables you to get the body of the letter down, spell check it, and proof the document before merge codes are placed in it.

Creating a form letter for a mail merge in Word simply means that you create the body text for the letter, add the current date to the letter, and place any other unchanging elements—such as a closing—on the document.

After you have the body of the form letter ready to go on the screen (see Figure 20.1), you can then begin the merge process.

Specifying the Main Document

The first step in the merge process is to specify a main document for the merge. In this case, we are using the form letter that is already open in the Word window. To begin the merge process and designate a main document for the merge, follow these steps:

1. Open the form letter that you want to use as the main document (if it's not already open in the Word window).
2. Select **Tools**, and then **Mail Merge**. The Mail Merge Helper dialog box opens, as shown in Figure 20.2.

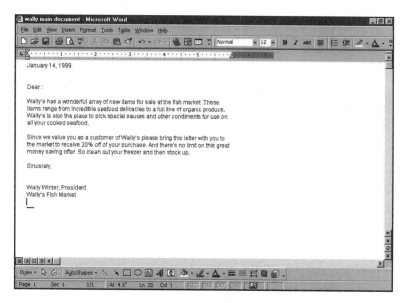

Figure 20.1   Create your form letter and then begin the merge.

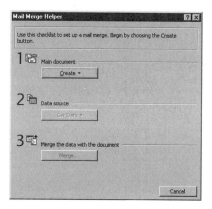

Figure 20.2   The Mail Merge Helper walks you through the steps of merging your main document with a data source.

3. Under step 1 of the dialog box (Main document), click the **Create** button. Select **Form Letters** from the Create list.

TIP   **Creating Lists from a Mail Merge**   If you want to make a list of the data source information, choose the **Catalog** as your main document type. Any blank document page can be set up as a catalog with the merge fields separated by tabs.

4. A dialog box appears (see Figure 20.3) that asks if you want to use the Active Window or create a New Main Document for the merge. Because you opened your form letter or other main document in step 1, select **Active Window**.

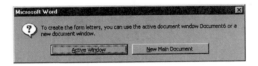

Figure 20.3   Select Active Window to designate the currently open document as the main document for the merge.

CAUTION **The Edit Button Appears**   After you select the Active Window, an Edit button appears next to the Create button. You can edit your main document now if necessary. However, if you haven't specified the data source, merge field codes still are unavailable.

Creating the Data Source

The next step in the process is to open or create a data source, and then place the merge fields designated in the data source into the appropriate areas of your main document (such as the name and address of the recipient below the date in the form letter). You can create the data source as a table before you begin the merge process (or use a database file from Microsoft Access as your data source). Figure 20.4 shows a table that serves as a data source. Notice that the first row of the table contains the fields that serve as the merge codes.

You can also create a data source from scratch as you perform step 2 in the merge process. To create a data source using the Mail Merge Helper, follow these steps:

1. In the Mail Merge Helper dialog box, click the **Get Data** button in the step 2 area.

2. Select **Create Data Source** from the drop-down menu that appears (you can also select **Open Data Source** and specify a data source table you've already created). The Create Data Source dialog box appears, as shown in Figure 20.5.

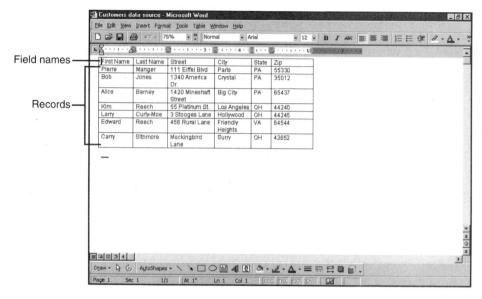

Figure 20.4 A table of names and addresses with appropriate field headings can be used as your merge data source.

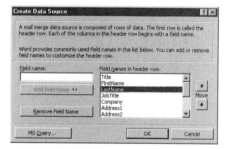

Figure 20.5 Select the fields you want to use in your data source file.

3. Select any fields you do not want to include in the data source, such as title or job title, and then click the **Remove Field Name** button. If you want to add your own fields, type the field name in the **Field Name** box, and then click **Add Field Name**. Click **OK** after you have added or removed fields from the field list.

4. After you exit the Create Data Source dialog box, the Save As dialog box appears. Enter a name or specify a location for the new data source file, and then click **Save**.

5. After you save the file, a dialog box appears asking you if you want to edit the data source or the main document. Click **Edit Data Source** to add information to the data source (people's names and addresses). The Data Form dialog box appears (see Figure 20.6).

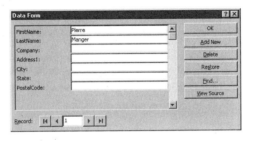

Figure 20.6 Enter your data into the data form.

There's No Data Form Box If your main document is a mailing label or envelope you created using a wizard, Word opens the data source file itself, which takes the form of a table (refer to Figure 20.6). Enter one row of information for each record, and then click the **Mail Merge Main Document** button on the Database toolbar to return to the main document. Then proceed with inserting the field codes.

6. Enter the data for the first person on your mailing list into the appropriate field boxes. When you have completed entering the information, click **Add New** to add another record. When you have completed adding all the records, click **OK**. The Data Form dialog box closes, and you are returned to the main document for the merge.

Record A record represents one row of data from your data source table; for example, all the information you have stored about one person on your mailing list.

Inserting the Field Codes

After you have specified the main document and either opened or created the data source, you are returned to the main document, ready to insert the field merge codes. A Merge toolbar appears at the top of the document that provides you with tools you can use to complete the merge process.

To place the merge codes into the document, follow these steps:

1. Place the insertion point in the main document where you want to place the first merge field. For example, to place the first name in a form letter, place the insertion point four lines below the date in the letter.

2. To insert the first merge field, click the **Insert Merge Field** button on the Merge toolbar and select the appropriate merge field.

3. Move the insertion point to the position where you want to place the next merge field (if you've placed the First Name field at the top of the letter, press the **Spacebar**, and then insert the **Last Name** merge field).

4. Insert all merge fields as needed. Figure 20.7 shows a form letter main document containing name and address merge fields.

Figure 20.7 Use the Insert Merge Field button on the Merge toolbar to insert the merge fields into your main document.

After you've inserted all the needed merge fields, you are ready to complete the mail merge process. At this point, you can also make any content changes to the main document (your form letter) if needed. You can also add fields to the data source (and then insert them in the main document as needed), which is discussed in the next section.

Editing the Data Source

If you find that you've forgotten a field or need to add information to the data source before you perform the merge, you can open the data source for editing. Follow these steps:

1. Click the **Mail Merge Helper** button on the Merge toolbar in the main document.

2. Click the **Edit** button in the Data Source area of the Mail Merge Helper dialog box and select the data source file from the drop-down list. The Data Form dialog box appears.

3. Use the Data Form dialog box to add new information. If you need to edit or add a field, click the **View Source** button. The data source file opens. Edit the table as needed (field names are in the top row). New fields can be added by inserting a new column into the data source.

4. Click **OK** to save changes to the data source. If you have added a new field, it is now available for use in your main document (click the **Insert Merge Field** button).

Merging the Documents

After you've designated a main document and a data source file, and placed the merge fields into your main document, you are ready to complete the merge process by merging the main document with the data source. You have a choice on how you complete the merge. You can send the merged documents directly to the printer, or you can have a new merge document created.

Sending the merge directly to the printer can be risky if the merge was set up incorrectly. Having a merge document created enables you to view the merged pages and make sure that the merge worked correctly. Creating a new document from the merge means you end up with a document of multiple pages. If you have a thousand individuals listed in your data source, you end up with a form letter or envelope for each individual, meaning a thousand pages.

CAUTION

I Have a Lot of Records in My Data Source Because the merge can create a very large document (especially if you have a lot of records in your data source), you might want to close other applications you are running so all your computer's memory is available for the new file that is created. After the merge document has been created, make sure you save the file immediately. You can then view it at your leisure and print out all or some of the pages as needed.

 To complete the merge, make sure you are in the main document window; click the **Merge to Printer** button on the Merge toolbar if you want to send the merge results directly to the printer.

 If you want to create a new document from the merge results, click the **Merge to New Document** button.

When you click the Merge to New Document button, a new document is created containing a separate page for each record found in the data source document (see Figure 20.8).

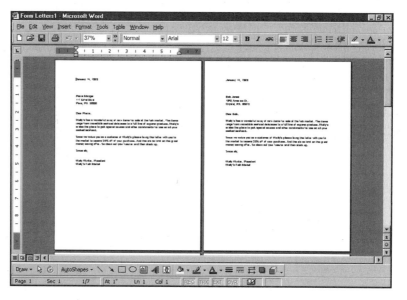

Figure 20.8 The merge document contains a separate page (in the case of form letters) for each record in the data source document.

After reviewing the form letters or other items created by the merge process, you can send them to the printer. You can also save the merged document by selecting **File**, and then **Save**. Provide a name and a location for the document in the Save As dialog box, and then click **Save**.

Creating Envelopes and Mailing Labels

The procedure for using the merge feature discussed in this lesson assumes that you are using a form letter as your main document and creating copies of the letter for each person listed in the data source. You can also use the merge feature to create other document types such as envelopes and labels. The procedure for creating envelopes and mailing labels is almost exactly the same. In either case, you use the appropriate wizard to create the document type (envelope or mailing label), and then you are walked through the entire merge process. The steps that follow discuss the Envelope Wizard, but you can use the same steps to create mailing labels using the Mailing Label Wizard (just make sure to select the Mailing Label Wizard when you are in the New dialog box discussed in the steps that follow).

To start the Envelope Wizard, follow these steps:

1. Select **File**, and then **New**; the New dialog box appears.

2. In the New dialog box, select the **Letters and Faxes** tab, and then double-click the **Envelope Wizard**.

3. You are prompted by the Office Assistant to select if you want to create one envelope or to create envelopes for a mailing list. Choose the latter and click **OK**.

4. The Mail Merge Helper appears. Envelope automatically is chosen for you as the main document type.

5. In the Mail Merge Helper dialog box, click the **Get Data** button in the step 2 area.

6. Open an existing data source or create a new data source if required (as discussed earlier in this lesson). After specifying the data source, a message box appears letting you know that Word needs to set up your main document (meaning it needs to format it as an envelope). Click **Set Up Main Document** in the message box.

7. The Envelope Options dialog box appears (see Figure 20.9). Use the **Envelope Size** drop-down box to specify the type of envelope you want to create. Then click **OK**. The Envelope Address dialog box appears.

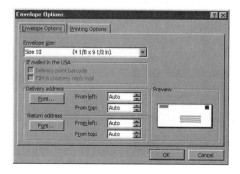

Figure 20.9 Select the type of envelope you want to use for the merge.

8. Insert the merge fields into the Envelope Address dialog box using the **Insert Merge Field** button. Remember to place spaces or line breaks between the fields as needed. After inserting the merge fields, click **OK**. The Mail Merge Helper dialog box appears.

9. You can now complete the merge; click the **Merge** button. A Merge dialog box appears (see Figure 20.10).

10. Use the **Merge To** drop-down box to create a new document or send the merged document (the envelopes) directly to the printer. When you have made your selection, click the **Merge** button.

Figure 20.10 Create a new document or send the merge directly to the printer.

If you choose to have a new document created by the merge process, your envelopes appear in the Word window (see Figure 20.11). You can take a look at the various envelopes to make sure that the merge worked correctly, and then send the documents to the printer.

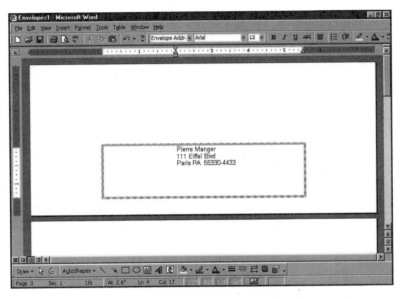

Figure 20.11   Your personalized envelopes appear in the Word window.

As stated earlier, you can follow these same steps to create mailing labels; be advised that the only difference is the actual names of the dialog boxes that appear (mailing label versus envelope). You also select your label type by Avery number (Avery is a label company that standardized label types for computer printers).

In this lesson, you learned to create a main document, a data source document, and then to perform a mail merge. In the next lesson, you learn to work with larger documents in Word, place sections in documents, and create a table of contents for a document.

Working with Larger Documents

21

In this lesson, you learn how to work with larger documents, including inserting section breaks and building a table of contents. You also learn how to create a master document in the Word Outline view.

Adding Sections to Documents

Large documents that are made of up several parts (such as a cover page, table of contents, bibliography, charts, tables, and so forth) probably require that the different parts contain dramatically different formatting options. These options can include margins, column settings, page orientation, and other page attributes. The simplest way to handle documents that require different formatting and layout attributes in their various parts is to divide the document into sections. A *section* is a defined portion of the document that can then contain its own set of formatting options. You can divide a document into as many sections as you require.

 TERM **Section** A portion of a document (defined as a separate section) that can then be formatted differently from the rest of the document or other sections of the document.

When you first begin a new document, the document consists of one section with consistent page formatting throughout the document. If you look at the status bar in a new document, you will find that it says "Sec 1," which means that the insertion point is currently in Section 1 of the document (which is actually the entire run of the document).

Sections are defined in your document as section breaks (which means a certain position in the document serves as the break between the existing section and the new section you insert). To place additional section breaks in a document, follow these steps:

1. Place the insertion point where you would like to insert the new section break.

2. Select **Insert**, then **Break**. The Break dialog box appears. In the lower half of the Break dialog box, several section break types are available (see Figure 21.1).

Figure 21.1 Select your section break in the Break dialog box.

- **Next Page**—A page break is placed in the document, and the new section begins on this new page.
- **Continuous**—The new section starts at the insertion point and continues for the rest of the document.
- **Even Page**—The new section starts on the next even-numbered page.
- **Odd Page**—The new section starts on the next odd-numbered page.

3. Select the option button for the type of section break you wish to place in the document.

4. Click **OK** to insert the new section into the document.

Your new section break appears in the document. In the Normal view, the section break appears as a double horizontal line marked with the text "Section Break" and the type of section you selected (in the Print Layout, the section that you are in can be determined by the section number displayed on the status bar).

After you have the new section in the document, you can apply page formatting to it as needed. (For more about changing page formatting attributes such as margins, page numbering, and columns, see Lessons 9, "Examining Your Documents in Different Views," 13, "Adding Headers, Footers, and Page Numbering," and 18, "Creating Columns in a Document," respectively.)

If you want to delete a section break, place the mouse pointer in the selection area and select the section break the same as you would any other line of text. After the section break is selected, press the **Delete** key to remove it.

Creating a Table of Contents

Another aspect of working with larger documents is the need for a table of contents. Having a reference such as a table of contents for readers of your document enables them to quickly and easily find a particular part of the document. Creating a table of contents in Word is actually very straightforward, as long as you use appropriate headings to differentiate parts of your document such as chapters or sections.

For instance, you can use either Word's built-in heading styles (Heading 1, Heading 2, Heading 3, and so forth) to format the different levels of headings in the document, such as section levels or chapter levels, or you can create your own styles and use them consistently to format the various headings that you use in the document.

A good example is a document that is divided into parts and then further subdivided into chapters (each part contains several chapters). If you use Word's heading styles to format the different division levels in the document, you would use Heading 1 for the parts (Part I, Part II, and so forth) and Heading 2 for the chapter titles. By assigning these built-in styles to your different headings (or by using different level heading styles that you create yourself), you can generate a table of contents that shows two levels (parts and chapters) because Word can pinpoint a particular heading level by the style that you've assigned to it (for more about working with and creating styles, see Lesson 11, "Working with Styles").

After you've placed your various headings for parts, chapters, or other divisions into your document and assigned a particular style to each group of headings, you are ready to use the Word Table of Contents feature to generate the actual table of contents.

CAUTION

Be Consistent When Assigning a Style to Chapter Headings
For the Word Table of Contents feature to be able to find all the headings for a particular document division, such as a chapter, you must assign the same Word style (one of the styles found in the style list) to all the chapter headings.

To create a table of contents using the Word heading styles or styles you've created, follow these steps:

1. Create a blank page at the beginning of your document for your table of contents (or create a new section in which to place your table of contents).

2. Select **Insert**, then **Index and Tables**. The Index and Tables dialog box appears (see Figure 21.2).

3. Select the **Table of Contents** tab, if necessary.

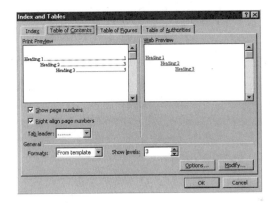

Figure 21.2   The Table of Contents tab on the Index and Tables dialog box is where you specify the options for your new table of contents.

4. The Table of Contents tab provides you with a Print and Web view of the table of contents (TOC) hierarchy for the Word built-in heading styles. If you used the Word heading styles to format and specify the various division levels in your document, you can skip down to step 7. If you used your own styles for your part or chapter headings, click the **Options** button.

5. The Table of Contents Options dialog box appears. This is where you specify the styles you used to format the various TOC levels in your document. Scroll down through the available styles list. To specify a style as a TOC level, type the level number (1, 2, 3, and so on) in the appropriate style's TOC level box.

6. When you have selected the styles that serve as your various TOC levels, click **OK** to return to the Table of Contents tab.

7. Use the various check boxes on the tab to select or deselect options for the table of contents. After you've specified options such as right align, page numbers, and the tab leader style, you are ready to generate the table of contents; click **OK**.

Your new table of contents appears in the document (see Figure 21.3). You can add a title to the table of contents (such as *Table of Contents*) and format the text as needed. If you want to remove the table of contents from the document, place the mouse pointer in the selection area to the left of the table of contents. Click to select the TOC. Press the **Delete** key to remove it from the document.

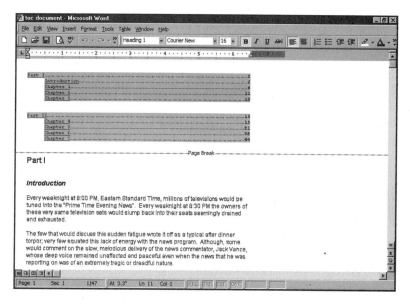

Figure 21.3 The table of contents is generated at the insertion point in your document.

TIP **Use the TOC to Quickly Move to a Particular Chapter** A real slick feature associated with a table of contents in your document is that you can use it to quickly jump to a particular part of your document. For instance, if you wanted to move to the beginning of Chapter 3 in the document, click the Chapter 3 notation in the table of contents. Word bumps you down to the beginning of Chapter 3.

Creating a Master Document

A feature that can prove to be very handy for long documents, especially documents where you created the various parts or chapters as separate documents, is the Master Document feature. A *master document* is really an outline that contains links to the various subdocuments that make up the entire document. This feature enables you to combine several files and then print them as one continuous document. This is particularly useful when you want to sequentially number the pages in the different chapter files as if they were all part of the same document.

 TIP **Jump Quickly to a Subdocument in a Master Document** You can use the Subdocument titles listed in the Master document to quickly jump to a particular subdocument. Just double-click the particular subdocument listing.

To create a master document, follow these steps:

1. Open a new Word document.
2. Change to the Outline view; select **View**, then **Outline**.
3. You build your master document the same as you would an outline (for additional information on navigating the Outline view, see Lesson 9, "Examining Your Documents in Different Views"). Place a title at the top of the outline, as needed. Now you can designate the subdocuments that make up the master document.

  The heading level that you choose for a particular subdocument dictates how the subdocument title is treated if you generate a table of contents from the master document outline. To add a subdocument to the master document, first use the **Promote** or **Demote** buttons on the Outline toolbar to specify the correct heading level for the subdocument.

 After you've selected the heading level at which you will link the subdocument, click the **Insert Subdocument** button on the Outline toolbar (see Figure 21.4).

 TIP **Create Subdocuments from Scratch** You can create subdocuments on-the-fly. Use the **Create Subdocument** button on the Outline toolbar and create your new subdocument as you would any new Word document. This new file is then linked to the main document as a subdocument.

Figure 21.4 The Insert Subdocument dialog box enables you to select the file you will use as the subdocument in your master document.

After you've inserted the various subdocuments into the master document, you can collapse or expand the various levels of the outline the same as you would any document outline that you create in the Outline view.

TIP **Master Documents Are Great for Collaboration** If you work on a network where documents can easily be shared, you can use master documents to build reports and other important files that are created by more than one person. Create a master document specifying the subdocuments that compose it. As participants complete their chapter or chapters, a link to the master document is already available, making it easy for you to print out a complete report including all the specified subdocuments.

In this lesson, you learned how to create sections in a document, generate a table of contents, and create a master document from various subdocuments. In the next lesson, you learn how to create Web pages using Word and add Web site hyperlinks to Word documents.

Word and the World Wide Web

*In this lesson, you learn how to work with Word's
capability to build World Wide Web pages, and you learn to add
hyperlinks to your documents that quickly take you to a particular Web page.*

What Is the World Wide Web?

The Internet is a global network of interconnected computer systems that provides
several ways for users to communicate with each other, such as electronic mail
(email), Internet Relay Chat, and more important—the World Wide Web (WWW).
The Web is actually the newest onramp to the Internet, and it enables you to
quickly move from computer to computer (no matter the distance between the
computers) by hopping from Web page to Web page using a Web browser (such
as Microsoft Internet Explorer).

The sites that you view on the Web are made up of linked documents created
in the *HTML* (Hypertext Markup Language) programming language. Your Web
browser is able to translate HTML into a format that is viewable (and usable) on
your home or office computer.

 TERM   **HTML**   Hypertext Markup Language is the coding system used to create Web
pages for the WWW.

In the Web's infancy, the creation of a Web site required a pretty good understanding of the HTML language so that the various elements of the Web pages
included on the Web site were coded with the appropriate HTML tag. In very

basic terms, tagging Web page headings, pictures, or other elements with HTML codes is not unlike using a Word style to format a particular line of text or paragraph.

Word 2000 makes it very easy for you to create Web pages for the WWW; you can create your own personal Web site or create Web pages for use on your corporate Web site. Word even provides a wizard that walks you through the steps of Web page creation.

Saving a Word Document as a Web Page

One way to create an HTML file from a Word document is to create the document in Word (as a typical document) and then save it in the HTML file format. This strategy enables you to use all of Word's familiar layout features and create a document that looks good when it is viewed online using a Web browser.

Even if you save the document in the HTML file format, you can still open it in Word and edit the document when needed. To save a Word Document as an HTML file, follow these steps:

1. Create the document as you would any other Word document. You can include graphics, links to objects, and so on.
2. Select **File**, then **Save As Web Page**. The Save As dialog box appears.
3. Select the location where you would like to save the HTML file using the **Save In** drop-down box. Also type a name for your HTML document in the **File Name** box (the format of the document HTML has already been selected for you in the File of Type box).

   If you are on a corporate network that has an Internet Web Server (a computer that "hosts" the company's Web site), or if you are supplied Web space on your Internet service provider's Web server, you can save your HTML document directly to the server itself. All you need to know is the FTP address of the server (something like ftp.webserver.com). In the **Save In** drop-down box, select **Add/Modify FTP Locations**. The Add/Modify FTP Locations dialog box appears. Type in the name of the FTP site and provide your username and password. When you click **OK**, the FTP site is added to the list of folders in the Save In drop-down box. Select the FTP site as the location to which you save the file. Then click **OK** to save the file.

Saving Files Directly to a Web Server If you save to the Web server of an Internet service provider, make sure that you are connected to the Internet via your dial-in service before you attempt to save the HTML file directly to the FTP location.

CAUTION

4. Click **Save** to save the HTML document to the specified location.

TIP **Batch Process a Folder of HTML Files** After you create several Web pages in Word and want to place them on the Web server that you use to get your site on the Net, you can upload an entire folder of files using the Web Publishing Wizard. See Part VIII, "FrontPage/PhotoDraw," for more information on saving files to a Web site.

Even though your file is now in the HTML format, you can still open the document in Word and edit the document as needed. Figure 22.1 shows a document in the HTML format open in the Word window.

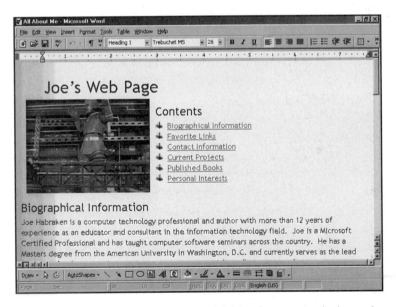

Figure 22.1 Use Word's various desktop publishing features to design a document and then save it as HTML for use on your Web site.

Creating a Web Site with a Wizard

If you would like more assistance in formulating and laying out a complete Web site that would look good and work well on the WWW, you can take advantage of the Word Web Page Wizard. The wizard walks you through the Web site creation process and helps you choose various themes and layouts for your new Web page or pages.

To create a Web page using the wizard, follow these steps:

1. Select **File**, then **New**. In the New dialog box, click the **Web Pages** tab (see Figure 22.2).

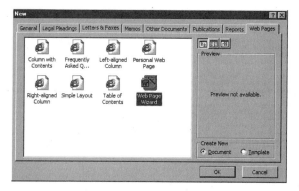

Figure 22.2   Double-click the Web Page Wizard icon on the Web Pages tab to begin the process of creating a Web page.

2. Several types of Web page templates reside on the Web Pages tab. To start the Web Wizard, double-click the **Web Page Wizard** icon.

3. The Web Page Wizard dialog box appears in the Word document window. To begin, click **Next**.

4. This wizard screen asks that you enter a name for your Web site and select a Web site location (the computer or server you wish to save the file to). If you are saving the file directly to a Web server, use the appropriate FTP address. Otherwise, save it to an appropriate folder on your computer (see Figure 22.3). Then click **Next** to continue.

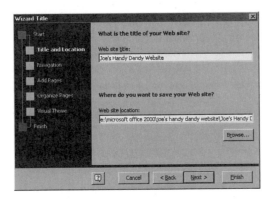

Figure 22.3 Specify a name and a location for your new Web site.

5. On the next screen, select the navigational setup for your page. You can choose to have a frame on the left side of the Web page by selecting the **Vertical Frame** option button, or on the top of the Web page by selecting **Horizontal Frame**. If you don't want a navigational frame on your main Web page, select the **Separate Page** option button. After making your selection, click **Next** to continue.

Frame A separate area or pane in the Web page window that typically contains navigational links. When you click a particular link in the frame, the Web page referenced appears in the main part of the Web page window.

6. On the next page, you can determine how many pages you would like in your new Web site (see Figure 22.4). The default is a Personal Web page (the main page for the site) and two blank pages. To add additional blank pages, click **Add New Blank Page**. You can also add existing files to your Web site by clicking **Add Existing File** and then selecting the appropriate file in the Add Existing File dialog box. Click **OK** to return to the wizard. When you have selected the number of pages or files you want to have in your Web site, click **Next** to continue.

7. On the next wizard screen, you can arrange your link pages in the order you want them to appear on the Web site. Select a particular page in the list and then use the **Move Up** or **Move Down** button to change the position of the page. When you have organized your pages, click **Next** to continue.

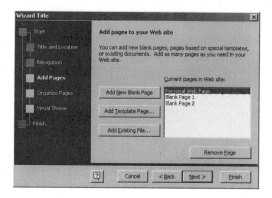

Figure 22.4 Specify the number of pages you would like in your new Web site.

8. On the next wizard screen, you can select a theme for your new Web site (see Figure 22.5). Themes provide colors and design elements for your new Web pages. To look at the list of themes available, click the **Browse Themes** button. Click a particular theme to see a preview. When you have selected the theme you want to use, click **OK** to return to the wizard. Then click **Next** to continue.

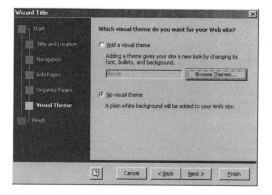

Figure 22.5 Select a theme, and Word provides colors and design elements that make your page look great.

 TERM   **Theme** A predetermined set of colors and design elements that you can use for your Web pages. Word provides a number of themes for your use.

9. The final screen of the Web Page Wizard appears. Click **Finish** to end the process and view your new Web page in the Word window.

Your new Web page consists of premade links, design elements, and various topic areas that contain placeholder text (see Figure 22.6). You have to fill in the information gaps to customize the Web pages created for your use. If you need to add additional pages to the Web site or want to remove pages, you can rerun the wizard at any time.

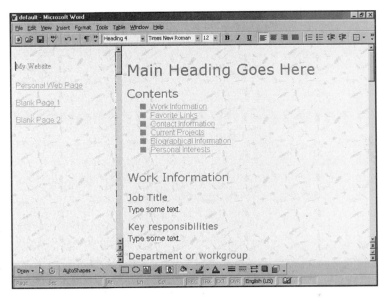

Figure 22.6   Fill in the various blanks and insert information as needed in your Web page's placeholder text.

You can also change the theme for your Web site if you want. Select **Format**, then **Themes**, and then select a new theme from the list. Click **OK** to return to your Web page.

Creating a Web Page from Scratch

You can also create your Web pages from scratch, which means you have to add the various elements (pictures, hyperlinks, and so on) that make up the page. This is also a requirement for blank pages that you have included in a Web site generated by the Web Page Wizard.

To create a Web page from scratch, follow these steps:

1. Select **File**, then **New**. In the New dialog box, click the **General** tab if necessary.

2. Double-click the **Web Page** template. Your new Web document opens in the Web Layout view.

3. Add the various elements to your document as required. For headings on your Web page, use the heading styles provided in the **Style** drop-down box on the Word Formatting toolbar (or create your own styles or modify the styles available, if you want).

4. After adding the text and other elements to the new Web document, save the file. It is automatically saved in the Web document (HTML) format.

Adding Hyperlinks to a Document

An important aspect of creating Web pages is being able to insert a hyperlink into a particular document. Hyperlinks really provide the main navigational tool for the Web. If you've spent any time on the Web at all, you know that you move from site to site using hyperlinks.

You can also designate graphics you create and pictures that you place on your Web pages as hyperlinks. Rather than clicking a text link, you click a picture, and it takes you to the referenced Web site.

 Hyperlink   A hyperlink references another Web page or site. Hyperlinks can appear as text or graphics on a Web page. When the hyperlink is clicked, you are taken to that page or site.

 TIP   Hyperlinks Can Reference Regular Documents and Files
Hyperlinks don't have to reference Web pages or Web sites. They can be used to link typical Word documents together. For instance, you can use a hyperlink to open another Word file on your hard drive.

When you create Web pages using the Web Page Wizard, hyperlinks are automatically created in your Web documents. They appear as underlined text elements. They also appear in a particular color. After you use a hyperlink, it appears in a different color when you return to the page containing it. This lets you know that you've used that particular link before.

To place a hyperlink in a Word document, follow these steps:

1. Select the text or other items that will serve as the hyperlink.

2. Select **Insert**, then **Hyperlink**. The Insert Hyperlink dialog box appears (see Figure 22.7).

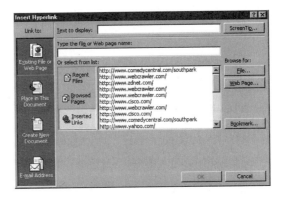

Figure 22.7 Enter the Web site address or the local filename for the new hyperlink in the Insert Hyperlink dialog box.

3. Enter the Web site address (URL—Uniform Resource Locator name—such as www.mcp.com) in the **Type the File or Web Page Name** box.

4. Click **OK**. You return to your document. The hyperlink is underscored and appears in a different color, denoting it as a hyperlink.

5. Repeat steps 2–4 as necessary to create all the hyperlinks for your document.

You can also create nontext hyperlinks. To make a picture, button, or other design element a hyperlink, right-click the object and then select **Hyperlink** from the shortcut menu. Enter the address for the Web site in the **Web Page Name** box of the Insert Hyperlink dialog box. Click **OK**. Now when you click the picture hyperlink, you are taken to the referenced Web address.

Previewing Your Web Pages

You can preview your Web pages in the Internet Explorer Web browser as you work on them. This enables you to get a Web-based view of how your pages are turning out. In the Internet Explorer window, you can also check out any hyperlinks that you've placed on your Web page.

To preview your Web page in Internet Explorer, follow these steps:

1. Select **File**, then **Web Page Preview**. Microsoft Internet Explorer opens with your Web page in its window.

2. Test your hyperlinks and other command elements as needed.

3. When you have completed viewing your Web page in Internet Explorer, click the **Close** (×) button on the upper-right corner of the window. You return to the Word window and your document.

Creating Web pages in Word can really be quite easy (and very satisfying) because you are working in an environment that you use to create a variety of other, more "typical," documents.

In this lesson, you learned how to create Web pages and Web sites for the World Wide Web. You also learned how to place hyperlinks into a Word document. In the next lesson, you learn how to start Microsoft Excel and become familiar with the Excel Workbook window.

Buttons button at the end of each toolbar and then click the toolbar button you want. You can move the Formatting toolbar to its own row if you wish, see the upcoming section "Moving Toolbars" for help.

- To view the name of a tool, position the mouse pointer over it. A ScreenTip appears, displaying the name of the tool (as shown in Figure 4.1).

- To get help with the command associated with a particular tool, select **Help,** and then **What's This?** or press **Shift+F1.** The mouse pointer changes to a question mark. Move the question mark pointer over a tool and click it. A Help window appears, explaining the tool's use.

Off Duty If a tool appears grayed, then it is currently unavailable. Tools become unavailable when they are not applicable to your current activity.

CAUTION

Turning Toolbars On and Off

By default, Excel displays just the Standard and Formatting toolbars. If you find that you don't use these toolbars, you can turn one or both of them off to free up some screen space. In addition, you can turn on other toolbars (although most toolbars appear on their own when you perform a related activity).

Follow these steps to turn a toolbar on or off:

1. Open the **View** menu and choose **Toolbars.** A cascading menu appears.

2. A check mark next to a toolbar's name indicates that the toolbar is currently being displayed. To turn a toolbar on or off (whichever it's not), simply click its name in the list to add or remove the check mark.

TIP **Quick View** To display a hidden toolbar quickly, right-click on an existing toolbar and select the toolbar you want to display from the shortcut menu that appears.

Because the Drawing toolbar is popular with many users, Microsoft provides an additional way to display it when needed. Just click the **Drawing** button on the Standard toolbar to turn it on. (If the Standard and Formatting toolbars are sharing the same row, you'll need to click the **More Buttons** button on the Standard toolbar, then click the **Drawing** button.)

Moving Toolbars

After you have displayed the toolbars you need, you can position them within the work area where they will be more convenient. For example, you might want to move the Formatting toolbar under the Standard toolbar so you can access all of its buttons easily. Figure 1.3 shows an Excel window with three toolbars in various positions on the screen.

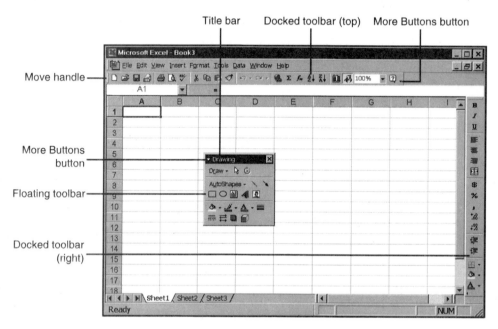

Figure 1.3   Three toolbars in various positions.

Here's how to move a toolbar:

1. Click a toolbar's move handle. (If the toolbar is floating in the middle of the window, click its title bar instead.)

2. Hold down the mouse button as you drag the toolbar where you want it. You can drag a toolbar to a side or bottom of the window (to a dock) or let it float anywhere in the window.

If you drag a floating toolbar to a docking area at the top or bottom of the screen, it turns back into a horizontal toolbar. By dragging the toolbar to a side docking area, it will turn into a vertical toolbar. (If you drag it back into the work area at a later time, the toolbar will resume its former shape.)

 TIP **Quickly Dock a Toolbar** To quickly dock a floating toolbar, double-click its
title bar.

Customizing the Toolbars

Because you use toolbars often, it makes sense to customize them to the way you work. The most common task you'll want to perform is adding and removing buttons from a toolbar, so that it contains only the tools you really use. Here's how:

1. To add or remove buttons on a toolbar, click **More Buttons**. On a floating toolbar, the More Buttons button is the down arrow at the left end of the title bar (see Figure 1.4). A cascading menu appears.

2. Click **Add or Remove Buttons**. Another menu appears.

3. Buttons that already appear on the toolbar have a check mark in front of them. If you click one of these buttons, the check mark disappears, and the button is removed from the toolbar.

   If you click a button that does not have a check mark, then a check mark appears, and the button is added to the toolbar.

You can place additional buttons in your toolbar's Add or Remove Buttons collection by selecting **Customize** from the **Add or Remove Buttons** menu in step 2 above. Then follow these steps:

1. On the **Commands** tab, select a category from the **Categories** list. (For example, to add the Clear Contents button to a toolbar, select the **Edit** category.) You can add menus to a toolbar as well; you'll find them listed at the bottom of the Categories list.

2. After you've selected the proper category, click the command you want in the **Commands** list, and drag it off the dialog box and onto the toolbar.

Remove a button from a toolbar by dragging it off the toolbar while the Customize dialog box is still open.

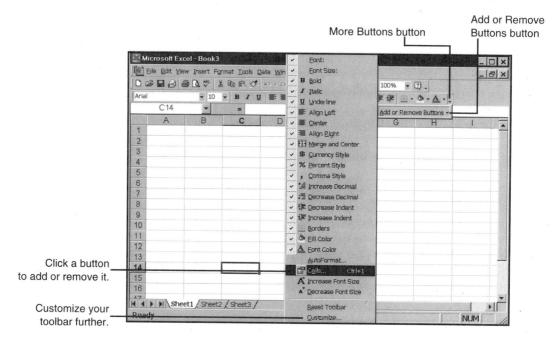

Figure 1.4 Adding and removing buttons from your toolbars is easy.

I Messed Up My Toolbar! To return a toolbar to its default settings (the way it was before you or someone else changed it), select the **Reset** toolbar command from the **Add or Remove Buttons** menu.

CAUTION

Exiting Excel

To exit Excel and return to the Windows 98 desktop, perform either of these two steps:

- Open the **File** menu and select **Exit**.

  or

- Click the **Close** (×) button in the upper-right corner of the Excel window.

If you changed the workbook in any way without saving the file, Excel displays a prompt asking if you want to save the file before exiting. Select the desired option.

In this lesson, you learned how to start and exit Excel. You also learned about the elements of the Excel workbook window and learned to work with and customize the Excel toolbars. In the next lesson, you learn how to create, open, and save your Excel workbook files.

Creating a New Workbook

In this lesson, you learn how to create new workbooks and opening existing workbook files. You also learn how to save your workbooks and change the name of a saved workbook file.

Starting a New Workbook

When creating a new workbook, you can start with a blank canvas, or you can use a template to create a more complete workbook. A *template* is a predesigned workbook that you can modify to suit your needs. Excel contains templates for creating invoices, expense reports, and other common worksheets.

Here's how you create a new workbook:

1. Open the **File** menu and select **New**. The New dialog box appears. As you can see in Figure 2.1, this dialog box contains two tabs: General and Spreadsheet Solutions.

2. To create a blank workbook, click the **General** tab and click the **Workbook** icon.

   To create a workbook from a template, click the **Spreadsheet Solutions** tab. You'll see icons for several common worksheet types. Click the icon for the type of workbook you want to create. If that template has not yet been installed, you'll be prompted to insert the Office 2000 CD. Follow the onscreen instructions.

3. Once you've made your selection, click **OK** or press **Enter**. A new workbook opens onscreen with a default name in the title bar. Excel numbers its files sequentially. For example, if you already have Book1 open, the Workbook title bar will read Book2.

Spreadsheet
Solutions tab   Worksheet icons

General tab —

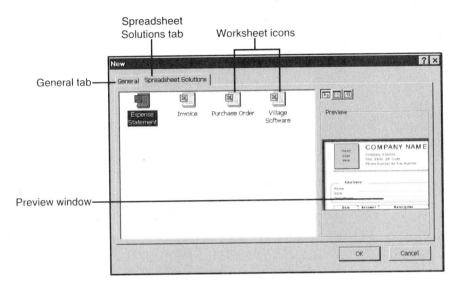

Preview window —

Figure 2.1   Click the icon for the type of worksheet you want to create.

 TIP   **Instant Workbook**   If you want to create a blank workbook (instead of creating one from a template), you can bypass the New dialog box by simply clicking the **New** button on the Standard toolbar. Excel opens a new workbook window without displaying the New dialog box.

Saving and Naming a Workbook

Whatever you type into a workbook is stored only in your computer's tempo-rary memory. If you exit Excel, that data will be lost. Therefore, it is important to save your workbook files to a disk regularly.

The first time you save a workbook to a disk, you have to name it. Follow these steps to name your workbook:

 1. Open the **File** menu and select **Save**, or click the **Save** button on the Standard toolbar. The Save As dialog box appears (see Figure 2.2).

Select a drive and folder

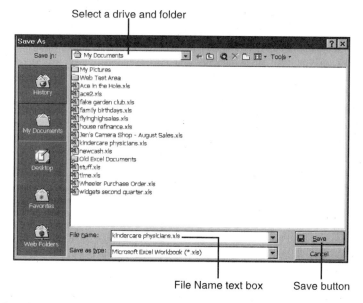

File Name text box   Save button

Figure 2.2 Name a workbook in the Save As dialog box.

2. Type the name you want to give the workbook in the **File name** text box. You can use up to 218 characters, including any combination of letters, numbers, and spaces (for example, Fourth Quarter Sales 1998).

3. Normally, Excel saves your workbooks in the My Documents folder. To save the file to a different folder or drive (such as a network drive), select it from the **Save in** list.

TIP **Set a New Default Directory**   You can change the default to your own private directory if you want. Open the **Tools** menu, select **Options**, and click the **General** tab. Click in the **Default File Location** text box and type a complete path for the drive and directory you want to use. Click **OK**.

CAUTION

The Folder I Want to Save In Doesn't Exist!   No problem—just create it! To create a new folder, click the **Create New Folder** button on the toolbar of the Save As dialog box, type a name for the new folder, then press **Enter**.

4. Click the **Save** button or press **Enter**.

To save an open file you have saved previously (and named), all you need to do is click the **Save** button. (Or you can press **Ctrl+S** or use the **File, Save** command.) Excel automatically saves the workbook and any changes you entered without displaying the Save As dialog box.

> **TIP**   **Save a Workspace**   After opening several workbooks and arranging them onscreen, you can save the arrangement as a workspace to quickly reopen and arrange these same workbooks at a later time. To save a workspace, open the **File** menu and select **Save Workspace**. Give the arrangement and name and click **OK**. To open the workspace later on, click the **Open** button and select **Workspaces** from the **Files of Type** list.

Saving a Workbook Under a New Name

Sometimes you might want to change a workbook but keep a copy of the original workbook, or you may want to create a new workbook by modifying an existing one. You can do this by saving the workbook under another name or in another folder—the original file remains unchanged, in its original location. The following steps show how you do that:

1. Open the **File** menu and select **Save As**. You'll see the Save As dialog box, just as if you were saving the workbook for the first time.
2. To save the workbook under a new name, type the new filename over the existing name in the **File Name** text box.
3. To save the new file on a different drive or in a different folder, select the drive letter or the folder from the **Save In** list.
4. To save the new file in a different format (such as Lotus 1-2-3 or Quattro Pro), click the **Save as Type** drop-down arrow and select the desired format.
5. Click the **Save** button or press **Enter**.

Opening an Existing Workbook

If you have a workbook you've previously saved that you would like to work on, you must open the file first, before you can make any changes. Follow these steps to open an existing workbook:

1. Open the **File** menu and select **Open**, or click the **Open** button on the Standard toolbar. The Open dialog box shown in Figure 2.3 appears.

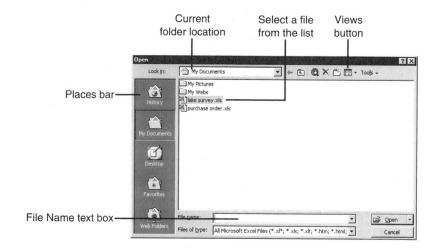

Figure 2.3 Find the file you want to open in the Open dialog box.

2. If the file is not located in the current folder, open the **Look In** drop-down list box and select the correct drive and folder.

Alternatively, you can switch to several common folders by clicking the appropriate icon on the Places bar:

- **History**—This folder contains links to up to 50 of your most recently used documents.

- **My Documents**—The default folder for your Office programs; you'll probably find most of your documents here.

- **Desktop**—From here, you can access any folder on your computer.

- **Favorites**—If you use certain files a lot, you can save them to the Favorites folder, and then quickly open them by clicking this icon.

- **Web Folders**—This folder contains links to folders on your company's intranet, or on the Internet. You can use this icon to quickly open documents you've published on the Web or on your company's intranet.

3. Select the file you want to open in the files and folders list. Or, type the name of the file in the File Name box. (As you type, Excel highlights the first filename in the list that matches your entry; this is a quick way to move through the list.)

TIP **Open a Web File**   If you know a Web file's location, you can type it in the **Filename** text box, such as `http://www.fakeinternetcompany.com/Sales/Widgets/firstqtr.xls`. If you're not sure of a file's location, you can browse the Web by clicking the **Search the Web** button.

4. To see a preview of the workbook before you open it, click the **Views** button and select **Preview**. Excel displays the contents of the workbook in a window to the right of the dialog box.

5. Click **Open** or press **Enter**.

There are other open options, if you click the arrow on the Open button:

- To open the workbook as a read-only file (to prevent you from accidentally changing data), click the arrow and select **Open Read-Only**.
- To open a copy of the workbook so that you can create a similar workbook without changing the original, click the arrow and select **Open as Copy**.
- To open an HTML document in your Web browser instead of within Excel, click the arrow and select **Open in Browser**.

TIP **Recently Used Workbooks**   If the workbook you want to open is one of your four most recently used workbooks, you'll find it listed at the bottom of the File menu. Just open the **File** menu and select it from the list. To open other recently used documents, use the **History** folder in the Open dialog box.

You can also open a specific workbook when you first start Excel. Just click the **Start** button on the Windows taskbar and select **Open Office Document**. Select the workbook you want to open and click **Open**. Excel starts with the workbook you selected open and ready to edit.

Closing Workbooks

When you close a workbook, Excel removes it from the screen. To close a workbook, follow these steps:

1. If the window you want to close isn't currently active, make it active by clicking its button on the Windows taskbar.

2. Click the **Close** (×) button in the upper-right corner of the workbook. (There are two Close buttons: The one on top closes Excel; the one below it closes the current workbook window.)

TIP **It's Closing Time!** If you have more than one workbook open, you can close all of them at once by holding down the **Shift** key, opening the **File** menu, and selecting **Close All**.

In this lesson, you learned how to create new workbooks, save workbooks, open existing workbooks, and close a workbook. In the next lesson, you learn how to enter text and data into your Excel worksheets.

Entering Data into the Worksheet

In this lesson, you will learn to enter different date types into an Excel worksheet.

The Data Types

There are many types of data that you can enter into your worksheets including text, numbers, dates, times, formulas, and functions. In this lesson, you'll learn how to enter text, numbers, dates, and times. In Lessons 13, "Performing Simple Calculations," 14, "Copying Formulas," and 15, "Performing Calculations with Functions," you'll learn how to enter formulas and functions.

Entering Text

Text is any combination of letters, numbers, and spaces. By default, text is automatically left-aligned in a cell.

To enter text into a cell:

1. Select the cell in which you want to enter text.
2. Type the text. As you type, your text appears in the cell and in the Formula bar, as shown in Figure 3.1.
3. Press **Enter**. Your text appears in the cell, left-aligned. (You can also press **Tab** or an arrow key to enter the text and move to another cell.) If you've made a mistake and you want to abandon your entry, press **Esc** instead.

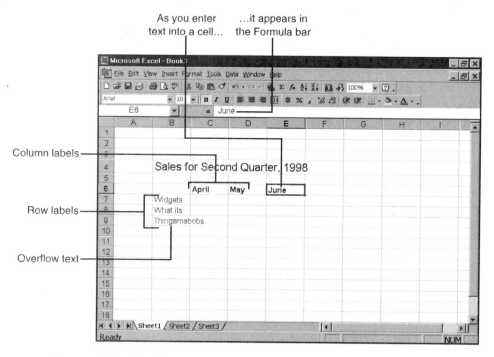

Figure 3.1 Data that you enter also appears in the Formula bar as you type it.

CAUTION

But It Doesn't Fit! When text does not fit into a cell, it "overflows" into the next cell, provided that cell is empty. If it is not, then the text is cut off. To expand a cell to display the data, you widen the column it's in: Move the mouse pointer to the right edge of the column's heading, then double-click. See Lesson 10, "Inserting and Removing Cells, Rows and Columns," for more help.

TIP

Entering Numbers as Text To enter a number that will be treated as text (such as a ZIP code), precede the entry with a single quotation mark ('), as in '46220. The single quotation mark is an alignment prefix that tells Excel to treat the following characters as text and left-align them in the cell.

Tips on Entering Column and Row Labels

Column and row labels identify your data. Column labels appear across the top of the worksheet beneath the worksheet title (if any). Row labels are entered on the left side of the worksheet.

Column labels describe what the numbers in a column represent. Typically, column labels specify time intervals such as years, months, days, quarters, and so on. Row labels describe what the numbers in each row represent. Typically, row labels specify data categories, such as product names, employee names, or income and expense items in a budget.

When entering your column labels, enter the first label and then press the **Tab** key instead of pressing Enter. This will move you to the next cell on the right so you can enter another column label. When entering row labels, use the down-arrow key instead of the Tab key.

If you need to enter similar data (such as a series of months or years) as column or row labels, there's a way to enter them quickly. See the section, "Entering a Series of Numbers, Dates, and Other Data," later in this lesson.

Adding Comments to Cells

While not really considered cell content (such as labels and values), you can add comment to particular cells. These comments allow you to associate information with a cell that will not print (by default) with the worksheet.

Comments are similar to placing a Post-it note on a cell, reminding you that there is an outstanding issue related to that cell. For instance, if you need to check the value that you've placed in a particular cell to make sure that it's accurate, you can place a comment in the cell (see Figure 3.2). Cells containing comments are marked with a red triangle in the upper-right corner of the cell. To view a comment, place the mouse pointer on the comment triangle.

To insert a comment into a cell, follow these steps:

1. Click on the cell where you want to place the comment.
2. Select **Insert**, then select **Comment**. A comment box will appear next to the cell.
3. Type your information in the comment box.
4. Click anywhere else in the worksheet to close the comment box.

You can also easily remove comments from cells. Select the cell, and then select **Edit** and point at **Clear**. Select **Comments** on the cascading menu to remove the comment.

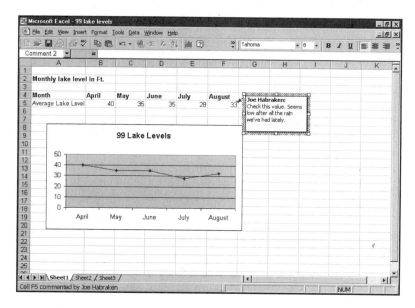

Figure 3.2 Data that you enter also appears in the Formula bar as you type it.

Entering Numbers

Valid numbers can include the numeric characters 0–9 and any of these special characters: + – / . , ( ) $ %. This means that you can include commas, decimal points, dollar signs, percent signs, and parentheses with the numbers that you enter into your worksheet.

Although you can include punctuation when you type your entries, you may not want to. For example, instead of typing a column of dollar amounts complete with dollar signs, commas, and decimal points, you could type just the numbers, such as 700 and 81295, and then *format* the column with currency formatting. Excel would then change your entries to $700.00 and $81,295.00 or to $700 and $81295, depending on the number of decimal points you specify. By not entering the dollar signs, commas, and decimal points yourself, you save time, and give yourself the ability to change the format later on if you like. See Lesson 7, "Changing How Numbers and Text Look," for more information on how to format numbers.

To enter a number:

1. Select the cell into which you want to enter a number.

2. Type the number. To enter a negative number, precede it with a minus sign or surround it with parentheses. To enter a fraction, precede it with a 0, as in 0 1/2. Note that you must type a space between the 0 and the fraction.

3. Press **Enter**, and the number appears in the cell, right-aligned.

CAUTION

Pound Signs Giving You a Pounding Headache? If you enter a number and it appears in the cell as all pound signs (#######) or in scientific notation (such as 7.78E+06), the cell just isn't wide enough to display the entire number. To fix it, double-click on the right border of the column's heading. The column expands to fit the largest entry. See Lesson 10 for more help on changing column widths.

Entering Dates and Times

After you enter a date or time into a cell, Excel converts the date into a number that reflects the number of days between January 1, 1900, and that date. Even though you won't see this number (Excel displays your entry as a normal date), the number is used whenever you use this date in a calculation.

Follow these steps to enter a date or time:

1. Select the cell into which you want to enter a date or time.

2. To enter a date, use the format MM/DD/YY or the format MM-DD-YY as in 5/9/98 or 5-9-98.

To enter a time, be sure to specify AM or PM, as in 7:21 p or 8:22 a.

CAUTION

Day or Night? Unless you type AM or PM after your time entry, Excel assumes that you are using a 24-hour military clock. Therefore, 8:20 is assumed to be AM, not PM. So if you mean PM, type the entry as 8:20 PM (or 8:20 p). Note that you must type a space between the time and the AM or PM notation.

3. Press **Enter**. As long as Excel recognizes the entry as a date or time, it appears right-aligned in the cell. If Excel doesn't recognize it, it's treated as text and left-aligned.

After you enter your date or time, you can format the cells to display the date or time exactly as you want it to appear, as September 16, 1998, and 16:50 (military time), for example. If you're entering a column of dates or times, you can format the entire column in one easy step. To format a column, click the column header to select the column. Then open the **Format** menu and select **Cells**. On the **Numbers** tab, select the date or time format you want (see Lesson 7).

Copying (Filling) the Same Data to Other Cells

You can copy (fill) an entry into surrounding cells by performing the following steps:

1. Click the fill handle of the cell whose contents you want to copy (see Figure 3.3).

2. Drag the fill handle down or to the right to copy the data to adjacent cells. A bubble appears to let you know exactly what data is being copied.

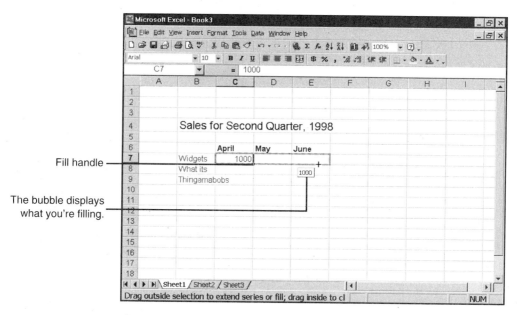

Figure 3.3 Drag the fill handle to copy the contents and formatting into neighboring cells.

Watch That Fill! Existing data (if any) in the adjacent cells to which you fill will be replaced by the data you're copying.

CAUTION

Entering a Series of Numbers, Dates, and Other Data

Entering a *series* (such as January, February, and March or 1998, 1999, and 2000) is similar to filling a cell's contents. As you drag the fill handle of the original cell, Excel analyzes the first entry and creates a series of entries based on it. For example, if you type Monday in a cell, and then drag the cell's fill handle over some adjacent cells, you'll create the series Monday, Tuesday, Wednesday.... As you drag, the bubble lets you know exactly what you're filling so that you can stop at the appropriate cell to create exactly the series you want.

If you're filling a number, a month, or other item that might be interpreted as a series (such as January, February, and so on), and you *don't* want to create a series—you just want to copy the contents of the cell exactly—then press and hold the **Ctrl** key as you drag the fill handle.

Entering a Custom Series

If you want to create a series such as 10, 20, 30, and so on, and Excel doesn't create the series when you drag the fill handle, or it creates the wrong series, here's what to do:

1. Enter the first value in the series in one cell.
2. Enter the second value in the series in the next cell.
3. Select both cells by clicking on the first cell and dragging over the second cell.
4. Drag the fill handle as usual. Excel will analyze the two cells, see the pattern, and recreate it.

Entering the Same Data in a Column Over and Over

Entering the same values over and over in a column is easy. When you type the first few letters of an entry, AutoComplete intelligently completes the entry for you based on the entries you've already made in that particular column. (AutoComplete works with data entered in columns only, not rows.) For example, suppose you want to enter the countries of origin for a series of packages. You type the name of a country once, and the next time you start to type that entry, AutoComplete inserts it for you.

By default, AutoComplete is always turned on, so you don't have to worry about that. Follow these steps to try out AutoComplete:

1. Type **England** into a cell and press the down-arrow key to move to the next cell down. Type **Spain** and press the down-arrow key again. Then type **Italy** and press the down-arrow key.

2. Type **e**, and "England" appears in the cell. Press **Enter** to accept the entry. (Likewise, if you type **i** or **s**, "Italy" or "Spain" will appear.)

3. If you'd like to try an alternative method of using AutoComplete, right-click a cell and select **Pick From List** from the shortcut menu. Excel shows you a PickList of entries (in alphabetical order) that it has automatically created from the words you've typed in the column.

4. Click a word in the PickList to insert it in the selected cell.

In this lesson, you learned how to enter different types of data and how to automate data entry. In the next lesson, you learn how to navigate from worksheet to worksheet, and move within an Excel worksheet.

Getting Around In Excel

*In this lesson, you learn the basics of moving
around in a worksheet, and within a workbook.*

Moving from Worksheet to Worksheet

By default, each workbook starts off with three worksheets. You can add or
delete worksheets from the workbook as needed. Because each workbook
consists of one or more worksheets, you need a way of moving from worksheet
to worksheet easily. Use one of the following methods:

- Click the tab of the worksheet you want to go to (see Figure 4.1). If the tab
  is not shown, use the tab scroll buttons to bring the tab into view, and then
  click the tab.

  or

- Press **Ctrl+PgDn** to move to the next worksheet or **Ctrl+PgUp** to move to
  the previous one.

Moving from Workbook to Workbook

Sometimes you may have several workbooks open at a time. (If you need help
opening a workbook, see Lesson 2, "Creating a New Workbook.") When you're
working with several workbooks, you often need to switch back and forth to
view or edit their contents. In Excel 2000, each workbook has its own button on
the Windows taskbar, as shown in Figure 4.2. To switch between workbooks,
simply click the button for the workbook you want.

Worksheet tabs   Drag to display more tabs

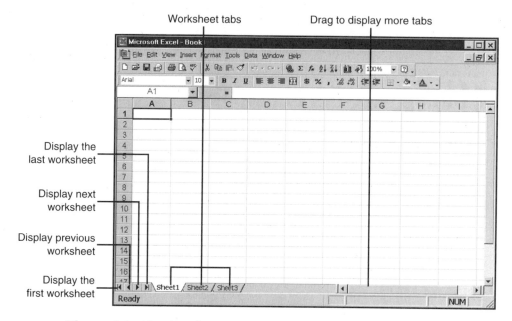

Display the
last worksheet

Display next
worksheet

Display previous
worksheet

Display the
first worksheet

Figure 4.1   Use the tabs to move from worksheet to worksheet.

TIP   **Don't Like the Taskbar Method?**   Open the **Window** menu and select the name of the workbook to which you want to switch; or Press **Ctrl+F6** to move from one workbook window to another.

Moving Within a Worksheet

In order to enter your worksheet data, you need some way of moving to the various cells within the worksheet. Keep in mind that the part of the worksheet displayed onscreen is only a small piece of the actual worksheet.

Using the Keyboard

To move around the worksheet with your keyboard, use the keys listed in Table 4.1.

Table 4.1 Moving Around a Worksheet with the Keyboard

To Move	Press This
One cell in the direction of the arrow	↑,↓,←, →
If the current cell is	Ctrl+↑, Ctrl+↓,
blank, moves to the *next cell* in the direction of the arrow that contains data. If the current cell contains data, moves to the *last cell* in the direction of the arrow that contains data.	Ctrl+←, Ctrl+→
Up one screen.	PgUp
Down one screen.	PgDn
Leftmost cell in a row (column A).	Home
Upper-left corner of a worksheet (cell A1).	Ctrl+Home
Lower-right corner of the data area (the area of the worksheet that contains data).	Ctrl+End

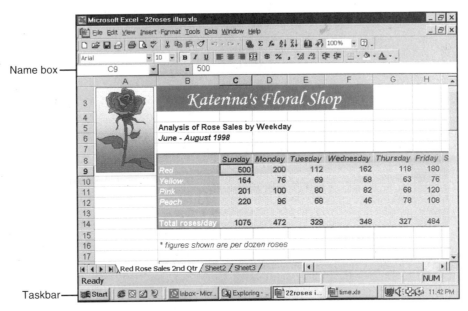

Figure 4.2 You can now switch between workbooks using the Windows taskbar.

345

TIP **Move to a Specific Cell** To move quickly to a specific cell on a worksheet, type the cell's address (the column letter and row number; for example, C25) in the Name box at the left end of the Formula bar and press **Enter** (see Figure 4.2).

 TIP **...On a specific worksheet** Type the worksheet's name, an exclamation point, and then the cell address (such as **sheet3!C25**) and press **Enter** to move to a specific cell on a specific worksheet.

Using a Mouse

To scroll through a worksheet with a mouse, follow the techniques listed in Table 4.2.

Table 4.2 Moving Around a Worksheet with the Mouse

To...	Click This
Move the selector to that cell.	Any visible cell.
View one more row, up or down.	Up or down arrows on the vertical scrollbar.
View one more column left or right.	Left or right arrows on the horizontal scrollbar.
Move through a worksheet quickly. As you drag, aScreenTip displays the current row/column number.	The scrollbar and drag it.

 Size Matters The size of the scroll box changes to represent the amount of the total worksheet that is currently visible. So, if the scroll box is large, you know you're seeing almost all of the current worksheet in the window. If the **CAUTION** scroll box is small, most of the worksheet is currently hidden from view.

Using the IntelliMouse

If you use the Microsoft IntelliMouse, you can move through a worksheet even more quickly than you can with a conventional mouse. Here's how:

To...	Do This...
Scroll a few rows (scroll up and down)	Rotate the wheel in the middle of the mouse forward or back.
Scroll faster (pan)	Click and hold the wheel button, and then drag the mouse in the direction in which you want to pan (scroll quickly). The farther away from the origin mark (the four-headed arrow) you drag the mouse, the faster the panning action. To slow the pan, drag the mouse back toward the origin mark.
Pan without holding the wheel	Click the wheel once, and then move the mouse in the direction in which you want to pan. (You'll continue to pan when you move the mouse until you turn panning off by clicking the wheel again.)
Zoom in and out	Press the Ctrl key as you rotate the middle wheel. If you zoom out, you can click on any cell you want to jump to. You can then zoom back in so you can see your data.

In this lesson, you learned how to move through a worksheet, and to move from workbook to workbook. In the next lesson, you learn how to change your view of a worksheet.

Changing How You View Your Worksheet

In this lesson, you learn about the various ways in which you can view your worksheets.

Magnifying and Reducing the Worksheet View

There are many ways to change how your worksheet appears within the Excel window. Changing the view has no effect on how your worksheets will look when printed (unless you choose to hide data onscreen), but changing the view and getting a different perspective helps you see your data more clearly. For example, you can enlarge or reduce the size of it in order to view more or less of the worksheet at one time.

To enlarge or reduce your view of the current worksheet, use the Zoom feature. Simply click the **Zoom button** on the Standard toolbar and select the zoom percentage you want to use, such as 25% or 200%. If you want to zoom by a number that's not listed, just type the amount in the Zoom box and press **Enter**. In addition, you can enlarge a specific area of the worksheet by selecting it first, opening the **Zoom** menu, and choosing **Selection**.

TIP **Fast Zoom** If you use the Microsoft IntelliMouse, you can zoom in and out quickly by pressing and holding the **Ctrl** key as you move the wheel forward or back.

You also can display your worksheet so that it takes up the full screen—eliminating toolbars, Formula bar, status bar, and so on—as shown in Figure 5.1. To do so, open the **View** menu and select **Full Screen**. To return to Normal view, click **Close Full Screen**.

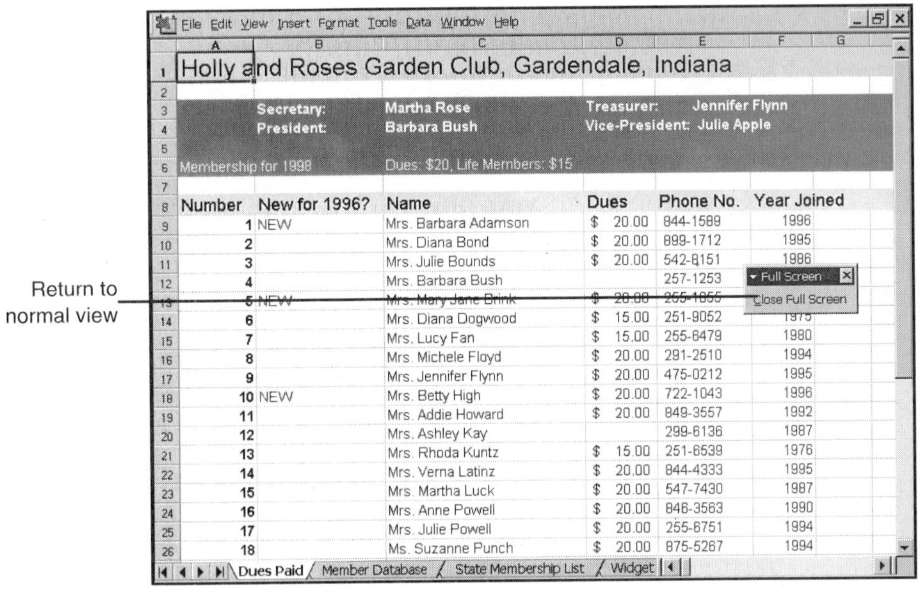

Return to normal view

Figure 5.1   View your worksheet in a full window.

Freezing Column and Row Labels

As you scroll through a large worksheet, it's often helpful to freeze your column and row labels so that you can view them with related data. For example, as you can see in Figure 5.2, it's helpful to view the column and row headings in order to understand the data in the cells.

To freeze row or column headings (or both), follow these steps:

1. Click the cell to the right of the row labels and/or below any column labels you want to freeze. This highlights the cell.

2. Open the **Window** menu and select **Freeze Panes**.

Play around a little, moving the cursor all around the document. As you do, the row and/or column headings remain locked in their positions. This enables you

349

to view data in other parts of the worksheet without losing track of what that data represents. To unlock headings, open the **Window** menu again and select **Unfreeze Panes**.

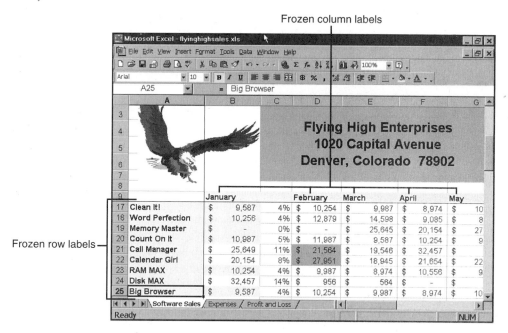

Figure 5.2 As you scroll, the frozen headings remain in place.

Splitting Worksheets

Sometimes when you're working with a large worksheet, you find yourself wanting to view two parts of it at one time in order to compare data, or to copy or move it. To view two parts of a worksheet, you *split* it. Figure 5.3 shows a split worksheet.

Follow these steps to split a worksheet:

1. Click and hold either the vertical or the horizontal split box.

2. Drag the split bar into the worksheet window.

3. Drop the split bar to divide the window at that location. When you scroll, the two panes automatically scroll in synch. For example, if you split the worksheet horizontally and then scroll right or left, the two panes are in synch.

To remove the split, drag it back to its original position on the scroll bar, or simply double-click the split bar.

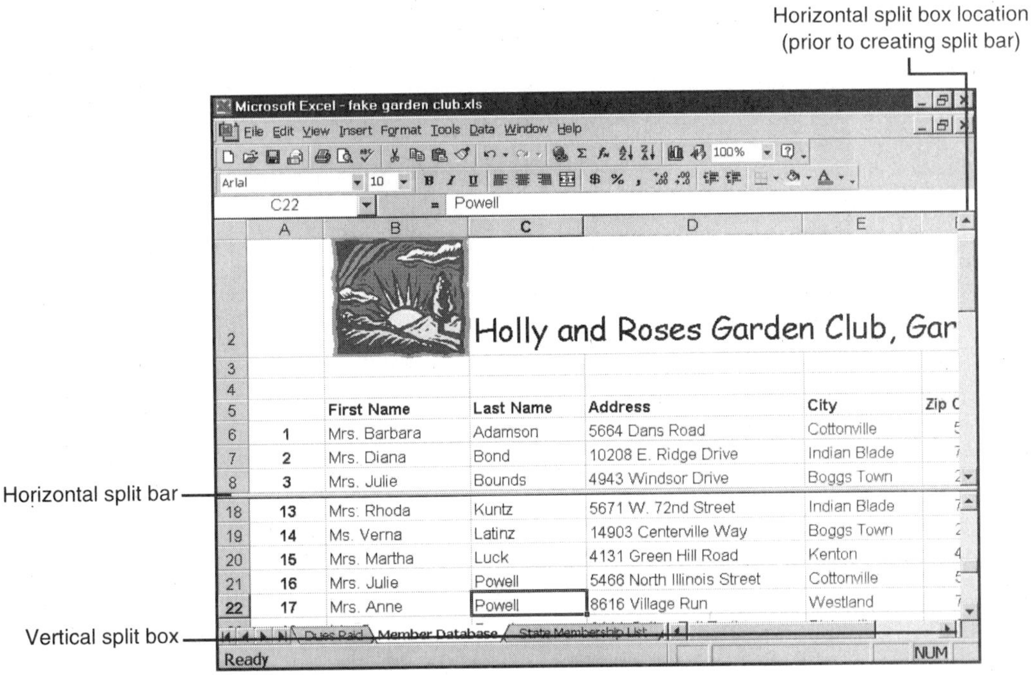

Figure 5.3 Split a worksheet to view two parts at one time.

Hiding Workbooks, Worksheets, Columns, and Rows

For those times when you're working on top-secret information, you can hide workbooks, worksheets, columns, or rows from prying eyes. For example, if you have confidential data stored in one particular worksheet, you can hide that worksheet, yet still be able to view the other worksheets in that workbook. You can also hide particular columns (see Figure 5.4) or rows within a worksheet—even an entire workbook if you want.

351

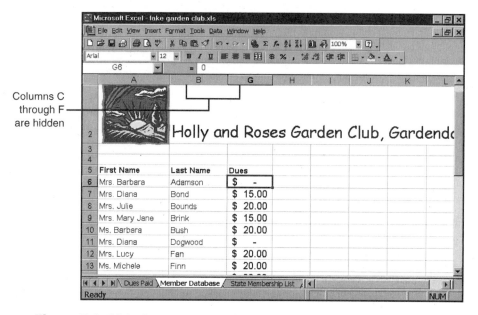

Columns C through F are hidden

Figure 5.4 Hide data to prevent it from being viewed, printed, or changed.

In addition to hiding data in order to prevent it from appearing on a report, you might hide it to prevent it from accidentally being changed. When data is hidden, it cannot be viewed, printed, or changed. (This is unlike the other changes you've learned about in this chapter, which just modify the worksheet view, such as zooming the worksheet.)

Use these methods to hide data:

- To hide a row or a column in a worksheet, click a row or column heading to select it. Then right-click within the row or column, and select **Hide** from the shortcut menu that appears.

- To hide a worksheet, click its tab to select it. Then open the **Format** menu, select **Sheet**, and select **Hide**.

- To hide an entire workbook, open the **Window** menu and select **Hide**.

TIP **Hide More Than One** To select several worksheets, press and hold **Ctrl** while you click each tab. To select several rows or columns, press and hold **Ctrl** while you click each heading.

Of course, whenever you need to, you can easily redisplay the hidden data. To redisplay hidden data, select the hidden area first. For example, select the rows, columns, or sheets adjacent to the hidden ones. Then repeat the previous steps, selecting **Unhide** from the appropriate menu.

CAUTION

You Can't Hide It Completely!   It's easy to undo the command to hide data, so you can't really hide data completely as a means of security. If you give the workbook file to someone else, for example, he could unhide and view the data you have hidden.

In this lesson, you learned how to change the view of your worksheet, freeze column and row headings, and hide data. In the next lesson, you will learn how to edit worksheets by correcting data. You will also learn to use the spell checker and AutoCorrect.

Editing Worksheets

In this lesson, you learn how to change data and how to undo those
changes if necessary. You also learn how to search for data and replace it
with other data, to spell check your work, as well as how to copy, move, and delete data.

Correcting Data

After you have entered data into a cell, you can make changes to it in either
the Formula bar or in the cell itself.

To make changes to a cell:

1. Select the cell in which you want to edit data.

2. To begin editing, click in the Formula bar. If you want to edit within the
   cell itself, press F2 or double-click the cell. This puts you in Edit mode;
   the word Edit appears in the status bar.

3. Press ← or → to move the insertion point within the entry. Press the
   Backspace key to delete characters to the left of the insertion point; press
   the Delete key to delete characters to the right. Then type any characters
   you want to add.

4. Click the **Enter** button on the Formula bar or press Enter on the keyboard
   to accept your changes.

   Or, if you change your mind and you no longer want to edit your entry,
   click the **Cancel** button or press **Esc**.

2. To accept the suggestion in the Change to box, click **Change**. Or, click **Change All** to change all occurrences of the misspelled word.

3. If the suggestion in the Change to box is not correct, you can do any of the following:

- Select a different suggestion from the Suggestions box, and then click **Change** or **Change All**. (You can display additional words in the Suggestions list by clicking **Suggest**.)

- Type your own correction in the Change to box, and then click **Change** or **Change All**.

- Click **Ignore** to leave the word unchanged.

- Click **Ignore All** to leave all occurrences of the word unchanged.

- Click **Add** to add the word to the dictionary so Excel won't flag it as misspelled again.

- Click **AutoCorrect** to add a correctly spelled word to the AutoCorrect list, so that Excel can correct it automatically as you type.

4. You may see a message asking you if you want to continue checking spelling at the beginning of the sheet. If so, click **Yes** to continue. When the spelling checker can't find any more misspelled words, it displays a prompt telling you that the spelling check is complete. Click **OK** to confirm that the spelling check is finished.

Correct Something Incorrectly?   If you mistakenly select the wrong option, you can click the **Undo Last** button in the Spelling dialog box to undo the last change you made.

CAUTION

Copying Data

When you copy or move data, a copy of that data is placed in a temporary storage area called the Clipboard. This Clipboard allows you to copy data anywhere, even into documents created by other programs. When you copy, the original data remains in its place and a copy of it is placed where you indicate.

What Is the Clipboard? The Clipboard is an area of memory that is accessible to all Windows programs. The Clipboard is used to copy or move data from place to place within a program or between programs. The techniques that you learn here are the same ones used in all Windows programs.

CAUTION

Follow these steps to copy data:

1. Select the cell(s) that you want to copy. You can select any range or several ranges if you want. (See Lesson 9, "Working with Ranges.")

2. Click the **Copy** button on the Standard toolbar. The contents of the selected cell(s) are copied to the Clipboard.

3. Select the first cell in the area where you would like to place the copy. (To copy the data to another worksheet or workbook, change to that worksheet or workbook first.)

4. Click the **Paste** button. Excel inserts the contents of the Clipboard at the location of the insertion point.

Watch Out! When copying or moving data, be careful not to paste the data over existing data (unless, of course, you intend to).

CAUTION

You can copy the same data to several places by repeating the **Paste** command. Data copied to the Clipboard remains there until you copy or cut (move) something else (unless you clear the Office Clipboard, which also clears the Windows Clipboard)—see the "Using the Office Clipboard to Copy or Move Multiple Items" section in this lesson.

TIP **Don't Forget the Shortcut Menu** When cutting, copying, and pasting data, don't forget the shortcut menu. Simply select the cells you want to cut or copy, right-click, and choose the appropriate command from the shortcut menu that appears.

Using Drag and Drop

The fastest way to copy something is to drag and drop it. Select the cells you want to copy, hold down the **Ctrl** key, and drag the border of the range you selected (see Figure 6.3). When you release the mouse button, the contents are copied to the new location. (If you forget to hold down the Ctrl key, Excel moves the data instead of copying it.) To insert the data between existing cells, press **Ctrl+Shift** as you drag.

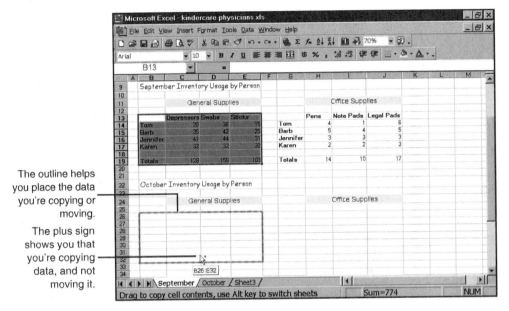

The outline helps you place the data you're copying or moving.

The plus sign shows you that you're copying data, and not moving it.

Figure 6.3 Dragging is the fastest way to copy or move data.

To drag a copy to a different sheet, press **Ctrl+Alt** as you drag the selection to the sheet's tab. Excel switches you to that sheet, where you can drop your selection in the appropriate location.

Moving Data

Moving data is similar to copying except that the data is removed from its original place and placed in the new location.

To move data, follow these steps:

1. Select the cells you want to move.

 2. Click the **Cut** button.

3. Select the first cell in the area where you would like to place the data. To move the data to another worksheet, change to that worksheet.

4. Click **Paste**.

359

Using Drag and Drop to Move Data

To move data quickly, use the drag and drop feature. Select the data to be moved, and then drag the border of the selected cells to its new location. To insert the data between existing cells, press **Shift** while you drag. To move the data to a different worksheet, press the **Alt** key and drag the selection to the worksheet's tab. You're switched to that sheet, where you can drop your selection at the appropriate point.

Using the Office Clipboard to Copy or Move Multiple Items

The Office Clipboard allows you to copy or move multiple bits of data (up to 12 separate items) to any of your other Office programs. For example, you could copy several parts of your Excel worksheet (maybe data stored on separate worksheets), a graphic, and even a chart from a PowerPoint slide, and then paste them all into a Word document. Actually, you can copy data from any document, but you can only paste the multiple items into an Office document. If you try to paste data into a non-Office document, you'll paste only the last item you copied (which is the same as if you were using only the Windows Clipboard).

What a Drag!   You can't use the drag-and-drop feature to copy or move data to the Office Clipboard.

CAUTION

To use the Office Clipboard:

1. Display the Clipboard toolbar (see Figure 6.4) by opening the **View** menu, selecting **Toolbars**, then selecting **Clipboard**.

Figure 6.4   The new Office Clipboard toolbar holds several cut or copied items at once.

2. Select the item you want to copy or move, then click the **Copy** button or the **Cut** button on the Standard toolbar of any Office program (and most other programs as well), or just use the **Edit, Copy** and **Edit, Cut** commands in any program.

What About the Windows Clipboard? When you're copying items to the Office Clipboard, the last item you copy or move is also placed on the Windows Clipboard. So if you try to paste something to a non-Office program, **CAUTION** the last item is all that will be pasted.

3. After you're done collecting the items you want to copy or move, switch to any Office program, and click the **Paste All** button on the Clipboard toolbar.

To paste only a single item from the Office Clipboard, just click that item. (To clear the Office Clipboard and start over, click the **Clear Clipboard** button. This clears the Windows Clipboard as well.)

There are a few things to keep in mind when using the Office Clipboard to paste multiple items. One, if you select a cell that contains a formula, and you paste it into another program's document, such as Word, you will not paste the formula itself, but the result of the formula (the value currently shown in the cell). Two, if you select multiple ranges in Excel and then paste them, they'll be pasted along one column. And three, if you've copied a drawing or clip art picture to the Office Clipboard, you will not be able to use the Paste All button while in Excel. (You can still paste an individual item by clicking it.)

Deleting Data

To delete the data in a cell or range of cells, just select them and press **Delete**. However, Excel offers additional options for deleting cells:

- With the **Edit, Clear** command, you can delete just the formatting of a cell (or an attached comment), without deleting its contents. The formatting of a cell includes the cell's color, border style, numeric format, font size, and so on. You'll learn more about this option in a moment.

- With the **Edit, Delete** command, you can remove cells and then shift surrounding cells over to take their place. This option is covered in Lesson 10, "Inserting and Removing Cells, Rows, and Columns."

To use the Clear command to remove the formatting of a cell or a note, follow these steps:

1. Select the cells you want to clear.
2. Open the **Edit** menu and select **Clear**. The Clear submenu appears.
3. Select the desired clear option: **All** (which clears the cells of all contents, formatting, and notes), **Formats**, **Contents**, or **Comments**.

In this lesson, you learned how to edit cell data and undo changes. In addition, you learned how to spell check your worksheet and how to copy, move, and delete data. In the next lesson, you will learn how to insert columns and rows into your worksheet, and to remove them when needed. You also will learn to change how numbers look using the style buttons as well as how to change text attributes with toolbar buttons.

Changing How Numbers and Text Look

In this lesson, you learn how to customize the appearance of numbers
in your worksheet and how to customize your text formatting to achieve the look you want.

Using the Style Buttons to Format Numbers

The Formatting toolbar (just below the Standard toolbar) contains several
buttons for applying a format to your numbers, including the following:

Button	Name	Example/Description
$	Currency Style	$1,200.90
%	Percent Style	20.90%
J	Comma Style	1,200.90
+.0 .00	Increase Decimal	Adds one decimal place
.00 +.0	Decrease Decimal	Deletes one decimal place

To use one of these buttons, select the cell you want to format and then click the desired button. If you want to use a format other than the ones on the Formatting toolbar, or if you'd like more control over the exact format you use, read on to the next section, Formatting Values.

TIP **A Conditional Format** If you want to apply special formatting to cells that meet certain conditions (such as all values that are larger than 1,000), use conditional formatting. See Lesson 8, "Adding Cell Borders and Shading," for more information.

Formatting Values

Numeric values are usually more than just numbers. They represent a dollar value, a date, a percent, or some other value. If the Style buttons on the Formatting toolbar do not offer the exact format you want for your numbers, don't worry. Through the Format Cells dialog box, Excel offers a wide range of number formats listed in Table 7.1.

Table 7.1 Excel's Number Formats

Number Format	Examples	Description
General	10.6 $456,908.00	Excel displays your value as you enter it. In other words, this format displays currency or percent signs only if you enter them yourself.
Number	3400.50 −120.39	The default Number format has two decimal places. Negative numbers are preceded by a minus sign, but they can also appear in red and/or parentheses.
Currency	$3,400.50 −$3,400.50	The default Currency format has two decimal places and a dollar sign. Negative numbers appear with a minus sign, but they can also appear in red and/or parentheses.

Number Format	Examples	Description
Accounting	$ 3,400.00 $ 978.21	Use this format to align dollar signs and decimal points in a column. The default Accounting format has two decimal places and a dollar sign.
Date	11/7	The default Date format is the month and day separated by a slash; however, you can select from numerous other formats.
Time	10:00	The default Time format is the hour and minutes separated by a colon; however, you can opt to display seconds, AM, or PM.
Percentage	99.50%	The default Percentage format has two decimal places. Excel multiplies the value in a cell by 100 and displays the result with a percent sign.
Fraction	1/2	The default Fraction format is up to one digit on either side of the slash. Use this format to display the number of digits you want on either side of the slash and the fraction type (such as halves, quarters, eighths, and so on).
Scientific	3.40E+03	The default Scientific format has two decimal places. Use this format to display numbers in scientific notation.
Text	135RV90	Use Text format to display both text and numbers in a cell as text. Excel displays the entry exactly as you type it.
Special	02110	This format is specifically designed to display zip codes, phone numbers, and Social Security numbers correctly, so that you don't have to enter any special characters, such as hyphens.
Custom	00.0%	Use Custom format to create your own number format. You can use any of the format codes in the Type list and then make changes to those codes. The # symbol represents a number placeholder, and 0 represents a zero placeholder.

After deciding on a suitable numeric format, follow these steps to apply it:

1. Select the cell or range that contains the values you want to format.

2. Open the **Format** menu and select **Cells**. The Format Cells dialog box appears, as shown in Figure 7.1.

3. Click the **Number** tab.

4. In the Category list, select the numeric format category you want to use. The sample box displays the default format for that category.

5. Make changes to the format as needed.

6. Click **OK** or press **Enter**. Excel reformats the selected cells based on your selections.

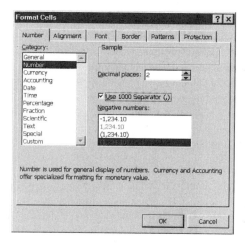

Figure 7.1 Apply a numeric format in the Number tab of the Format Cells dialog box.

You can also change the Number format of a cell by using the shortcut menu: Select the cell, right-click to display the shortcut menu, and choose **Format Cells**.

That's Not the Date I Entered! If you enter a date in a cell that is already formatted with the Number format, the date will appear as a value that represents the number of days between January 1, 1900 and that date. Change the cell's formatting from a Number format to a Date format and select a date type.

CAUTION

How Do I Get Rid of a Format?   To remove a number format from a cell (and return it to General format), select the cell whose formatting you want to remove, open the **Edit** menu, select **Clear**, and select **Formats**.

CAUTION

Copying Formats with Format Painter

After applying a format to a cell, you can easily copy that format to other cells. This works whether you're copying numeric or text formatting, or shading or borders, as you'll learn in upcoming lessons. Here's how to copy a format from one cell to another:

1. Select the cell(s) that contain the formatting you want to copy.

2. Click the **Format Painter** button on the Standard toolbar. Excel copies the formatting. The mouse pointer changes into a paintbrush with a plus sign next to it.

3. Click on one cell, or drag over several cells to which you want to apply the copied formatting.

4. Release the mouse button, and Excel copies the formatting and applies it to the selected cells.

TIP   **Faster Painter**   To paint several areas with the same formatting at one time, double-click the **Format Painter** button to toggle it on. When you're through, press **Esc** or click the **Format Painter** button again to return to a normal cursor.

How You Can Make Text Look Different

When you type text into a cell, Excel automatically formats it in the Arial font, which is readable, but not very fancy. You can change your text to improve its appearance or to set it apart from other text by changing its font, font style, color, alignment and size. (The higher the point size, the bigger the text is. There are approximately 72 points in an inch.)

TIP   **What's a Font?**   A font is a set of characters that have the same typeface, which means they are of a single design (such as Times New Roman).

To change the default font, follow these steps:

1. Select **Tools**, then click **Options** to open the Options dialog box.
2. Click the **General** tab.
3. Make your selection in the Standard Font area.
4. When you click the **OK** button, Excel makes your preference the default font.

Figure 7.2 shows a worksheet after some attributes have been changed for selected text. The worksheet title is merged and centered over several cells to give it importance. The column labels use bold and underlined attributes so that they stand out against the worksheet data. The row labels, on the other hand, are more subdued, using only italics.

Figure 7.2 Format your chart's text to improve readability.

Changing Text Attributes with Toolbar Buttons

A faster way to enter font changes is to use the Formatting toolbar shown in Figure 7.3.

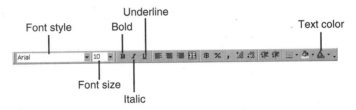

Figure 7.3 Use the Formatting toolbar to quickly make font changes.

To use the Formatting toolbar to change text attributes, follow these steps:

1. Select the cell or range that contains the text whose look you want to change.

2. To change the font or font size, pull down the appropriate drop-down list and click the font or size you want. You can also type the point size in the Font Size box.

3. To add an attribute (such as bold or underlining), click the desired button. When selected, a button looks like it has been pressed in. You can add more than one attribute to the same text, making it bold and italic, for example.

 TIP **Change Before You Type** You can activate the attributes you want *before* you type text. Unlike in a word processor where you must turn attributes on and off, in Excel, selecting formats for cells in advance of typing your data has no effect on the unselected cells; data in unselected cells will be the default type.

 TIP **Font Shortcuts** You can apply certain attributes quickly by using keyboard shortcuts. First select the cell(s), and then press **Ctrl+B** for bold, **Ctrl+I** for italic, **Ctrl+U** for single underline (accounting style), or **Ctrl+5** for strikethrough.

369

Aligning Text in Cells

When you enter data into a cell, that data is aligned automatically. Text is aligned on the left, and numbers are aligned on the right. Both text and numbers are initially set at the bottom of the cells. However, you can change both the vertical and the horizontal alignment of data in your cells.

Follow these steps to change the alignment:

1. Select the cell or range you want to align. If you want to center a title or other text over a range of cells, select the entire range of blank cells in which you want the text centered, including the cell that contains the text you want to center.

2. Pull down the **Format** menu and select **Cells**, or press **Ctrl+1**. The Format Cells dialog box appears.

3. Click the **Alignment** tab. The alignment options appear in front (see Figure 7.4).

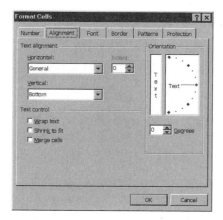

Figure 7.4 Set the Alignment options on the Alignment tab of the Format Cells dialog box.

4. Choose from the following options to set the alignment:

   • **Horizontal** lets you specify a left/right alignment in the cell(s). (The **Center Across** selection centers a title or other text within a range of cells.)

   • **Vertical** lets you specify how you want the text aligned in relation to the top and bottom of the cell(s).

   • **Orientation** lets you flip the text sideways or print it from top to bottom (instead of left to right).

- **Wrap text** tells Excel to wrap long lines of text within a cell without changing the width of the cell. (Normally, Excel displays all text in a cell on one line.)
- **Shrink** to fit shrinks the text to fit within the cell's current width. If the cell's width is adjusted, the text increases or decreases in size accordingly.
- **Merge** cells combines several cells into a single cell. All data is overlaid, except for the cell in the upper-left corner of the selected cells.

5. Click **OK** or press **Enter**.

A quick way to align text and numbers is to use the alignment buttons in the Formatting toolbar. The following buttons enable you to align the text:

Button	Name	Description
	Align Left	Places data at left edge of cell
	Align Right	Places data at right edge of cell
	Center	Centers data in cell
	Merge and Center	Centers data in selected cell range

Excel also enables you to indent your text within a cell. If you're typing a paragraph worth of information into a single cell, for example, you can indent that paragraph by selecting left alignment from the Horizontal list box in the Format Cells dialog box (as explained earlier). After selecting left alignment, set the amount of indent you want with the Indent spin box in the Format Cells dialog box.

In addition, you can add an indent quickly by clicking the following buttons on the Formatting toolbar:

Button	Name	Description
	Decrease Indent	Removes an indent or creates a negative indent.
	Increase Indent	Adds an indent.

Using the Format Cells Dialog Box

If you want to change a lot of different text attributes at once, use the Format Cells dialog box:

1. Select the cell or range that contains the text you want to format.

2. Open the **Format** menu and choose **Cells**, or press **Ctrl+1**. (You can also right-click the selected cells and choose **Format Cells** from the shortcut menu.)

3. Click the **Font** tab. The Font options jump to the front, as shown in Figure 7.5.

4. Select the options you want.

5. Click **OK** or press **Enter**.

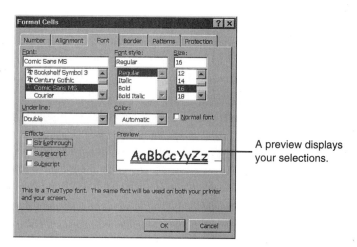

A preview displays your selections.

Figure 7.5 Access the Font tab to change several font attributes at once.

In this lesson, you learned how to format numbers and to copy formatting from one cell to another. As well, you learned how to customize your text formatting to achieve the look you want. In the next lesson, you learn how to add borders and shading to the cells in your worksheet.

Adding Cell Borders and Shading

In this lesson, you learn how to add a professional touch to your worksheets by adding borders and shading.

Adding Borders to Cells

As you work with your worksheet onscreen, you'll notice that each cell is identified by gridlines that surround the cell. By default, these gridlines do not print; even if you choose to print them, they appear washed-out. To create well-defined lines on the printout (and onscreen, for that matter), you can add borders to selected cells or entire cell ranges. A border can appear on all four sides of a cell or only on selected sides, whichever you prefer.

CAUTION

The Gridlines Don't Print?   It's true, gridlines do not print by default. But if you want to try printing your worksheet with gridlines first just to see what it looks like, open the **File** menu, select **Page Setup**, click the **Sheet** tab, check the **Gridlines** box, and click **OK**.

CAUTION

Text Underlining or a Cell Border?   A text-formatted underline is placed under the text—within the cell's borders. A cell-formatted border along the bottom of the cell also appears under the text. Which is right? Whichever one you like best.

To add borders to a cell or range, perform the following steps:

1. Select the cell(s) around which you want a border to appear.

2. Open the **Format** menu and choose **Cells**. The Format Cells dialog box appears.

3. Click the **Border** tab to see the Border options shown in Figure 8.1.

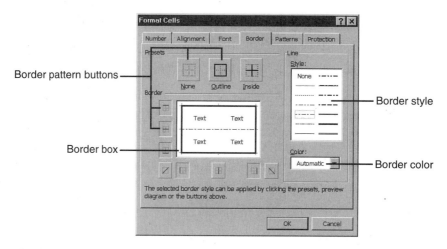

Border pattern buttons

Border box

Border style

Border color

Figure 8.1 Choose border options from the Format Cells dialog box.

4. Select the desired position, style (thickness), and color for the border. You can click inside the **Border** box itself, or you can click a preset **border pattern** button to add your border.

5. Click **OK** or press **Enter**.

When adding borders to a worksheet, hiding the gridlines onscreen gives you a preview of how the borders will look when printed. To hide gridlines, open the **Tools** menu, select **Options**, click the **View** tab, and remove the check mark from the Gridlines check box. Selecting this option has no effect on whether or not the gridlines actually print, only on whether or not they are displayed onscreen. If you want gridlines to print, apply cell borders to selected cells, or use the Page Setup dialog box, as described in Lesson 12, "Printing Your Workbook."

TIP **Use the Toolbar** Select the cells around which you want the border to appear, and then click the **Borders** drop-down arrow in the Formatting toolbar to select a border.

Adding Shading to Cells

For a simple but dramatic effect, add shading to your worksheets. With shading, you can add a color or gray shading to the background of a cell. You can add shading at full strength, or partial strength by selecting a *pattern*, such as a diagonal. Figure 8.2 illustrates some of the effects you can create with shading.

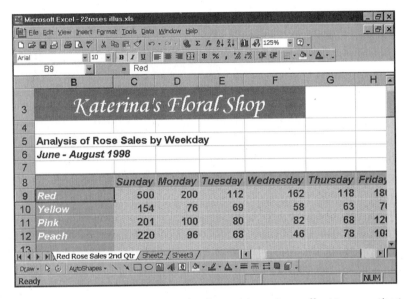

Figure 8.2   Solid color or dot-pattern shading add a unique effect to your chart.

Follow these steps to add shading to a cell or range. As you make your selections, keep in mind that if you plan to print your worksheet with a black-and-white printer, your pretty colors may not be different enough to create the effect you want. Select colors that contrast well in value (intensity), and use the Print Preview command (as explained in Lesson 12) to view your results in black and white before you print.

1. Select the cell(s) you want to shade.
2. Open the **Format** menu and choose **Cells**.
3. Click the **Patterns** tab. Excel displays the shading options (see Figure 8.3).
4. Click the **Pattern** drop-down arrow to see a grid that contains colors and patterns.

5. Select the shading color and pattern you want to use. The Color options let you choose a color for the overall shading. The Pattern options let you select a black or colored pattern that is placed on top of the cell shading color (the background color) you selected. A preview of the result appears in the Sample box, but keep in mind that the result will vary if you are using a black-and-white printer.

6. When you like the results you see, click **OK** or press **Enter**.

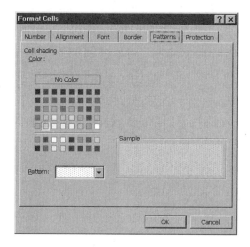

Figure 8.3   Choose colors and patterns from the Pattern tab of the Format Cells dialog box.

 TIP **Add Cell Shading with the Toolbar**   Select the cells you want to shade. Click the **Fill Color** drop-down arrow on the Formatting toolbar, then click the color you want to use.

 If the shading is too dark for the cell data to be easily read, consider using the **Font Color** button (just to the right of the **Fill Color** button) to select a lighter color for the text.

Using AutoFormat

Tired of trying to select the right shading, border, text color, and font to make your data professional looking? Well, to take some of the pain out of formatting,

Excel offers the AutoFormat feature. AutoFormat provides you with a number of predesigned table formats that you can apply to a worksheet.

To use predesigned formats, perform the following steps:

1. Select the cell(s) that contain the data you want to format.

2. Open the **Format** menu and choose **AutoFormat**. The AutoFormat dialog box appears, as shown in Figure 8.4.

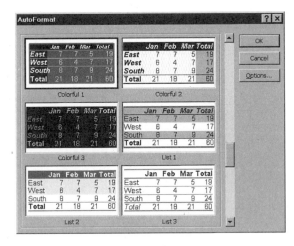

Figure 8.4 Select a predesigned format from the AutoFormat dialog box.

3. Scroll through the list and click the predesigned format you want to use.

4. To exclude certain elements from an AutoFormat, click the **Options** button and choose the formats you want to turn off.

5. Click **OK**, and Excel formats your table to make it look like the one in the preview area.

If you're upgrading from an older version of Excel, you'll find AutoFormat even easier to use, with large pictures that show you what each format really looks like.

CAUTION

Yuck! I Chose That? If you don't like what AutoFormat did to your worksheet, click the **Undo** button.

377

Applying Conditional Formatting

If you want to highlight particular values in your worksheet, you can use conditional formatting. For example, if you want to highlight all sales figures under a particular value, you could apply a conditional red shading.

To apply conditional formatting, follow these steps:

1. Select the first cell to which you want to apply conditional formatting. (Select only one cell; after you're done, you can copy the formatting to additional cells.)

2. Open the **Format** menu and select **Conditional Formatting**. The Conditional Formatting dialog box appears, as shown in Figure 8.5.

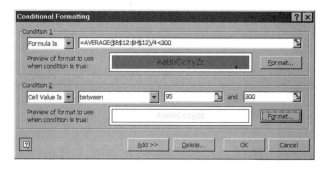

Figure 8.5   Apply formats conditionally to highlight certain values.

3. To apply a format based on the value found in a selected cell, choose **Cell value is** from the Condition 1 list.

To apply a format based on the result of a formula that involves cells outside the range of cells to which you want to apply the conditioning, select **Formula is** from the Condition 1 list.

4. In the Condition 1 text box, enter the value or formula you want to use as the condition that determines when Excel can apply the formatting you select.

If you selected **Cell value is** in step 3, you can still enter a formula in the text box, but the formula must result in a value. For example, you could enter:

Cell value is   **greater than**   **=C22*.25**

If you choose **Formula is** in step 3, the formula you enter must result in a true or false value. For example, if you wanted to format some cells based on whether or not a corresponding value in column A is less than 20% of projected sales (cell D12), you could use this formula:

Formula is   **=A1<20%*$D$12**

5. Click the **Format** button and select the format you want to apply when the conditions are met. Click **OK** to return to the Conditional Formatting dialog box.

6. You can add more conditions by clicking **Add** and repeating steps 3 to 5.

7. When you finish adding conditions, click **OK**.

 After applying the conditional formatting to the first cell, click the **Format Painter** button, and then drag over any additional cells to which you want to copy the conditional formatting.

In this lesson, you learned some ways to enhance the appearance of your worksheets with borders and shading. In the next lesson, you learn how to work with ranges and cells.

Working with Ranges

In this lesson, you learn how to select and name ranges.

What Is a Range?

A range is a rectangular group of connected cells. The cells in a range may all be in one column, or one row, or any combination of columns and rows, as long as the range forms a rectangle, as shown in Figure 9.1. A range also can be a single cell.

Ranges are referred to by their *anchor points* (the upper-left corner and the lower-right corner). For example, the ranges shown in Figure 9.1 include C10:I14, B16:I16, and H20.

Learning how to use ranges can save you time. For example, you can select a range and use it to format a group of cells with one step. You can use a range to print only a selected group of cells. You can also use ranges in formulas.

Selecting a Range

To select a range using the mouse, follow these steps:

1. Move the mouse pointer to the upper-left corner of a range.

2. Click and hold the left mouse button.

3. Drag the mouse to the lower-right corner of the range and release the mouse button. The cells are highlighted on the chart and the selected range appears in the formula bar.

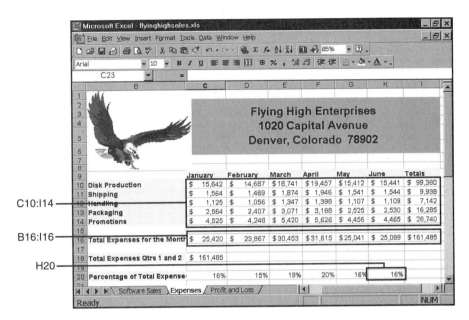

Figure 9.1 A range is any combination of cells that forms a rectangle.

Techniques that you can use to quickly select a row, a column, an entire worksheet, or several ranges, are shown in Table 9.1.

Table 9.1 Selection Techniques

To Select This	Do This
Several ranges	Select the first range, hold down the **Ctrl** key, and select the next range. Continue holding down the **Ctrl** key while you select additional ranges.
Row	Click the row heading number at the left edge of the worksheet. You also can press **Shift+Spacebar**. To select several adjacent rows, drag over their headers. To select non-adjacent rows, press **Ctrl** as you click each row's header.
Column	Click the column heading letter at the top edge of the worksheet. You also can press **Ctrl+Spacebar**.

continues

Table 9.1 Continued

To Select This	Do This
Entire worksheet	Click the **Select All** button (the blank rectangle in the upper-left corner of the work-sheet, above row 1 and left of column A). You also can press **Ctrl+A**.
The same range on several	Press and hold **Ctrl** as you click the worksheets you want to use, and then select the range in the usual way.
Range that is out of view	Press **Ctrl+G** (**Go To**) or click in the **Name** box on the Formula bar, and type the address of the range you want to select. For example, to select the range R100 to T250, type **R100:T250** and press **Enter**.

TIP **Deselecting a Selection** If you decide not to select a range, you can remove the range selection by clicking any cell in the worksheet.

Selected cells are not highlighted in reverse video, as in previous versions of Excel, but in a slightly grayed tone, so you can still read your data.

Naming Ranges

Up to this point, you have used cell addresses to refer to single cells and ranges. Although that works, it is often more convenient to name important cells with more recognizable names. For example, say you want to determine your net income by subtracting expenses from income. You can name the cell that contains your total income "INCOME," and name the cell that contains your total expenses "EXPENSES." You can then determine your net income by using the formula:

```
=INCOME-EXPENSES
```

Giving important cells memorable names will make adding formulas to your worksheet more logical and easier to manage. You can also use a range name or cell name to jump to a specific part of the worksheet by typing the name in the Name box on the Formula bar, or by selecting it from the Name list. This technique not only displays the range you want, but selects it, too. In addition, you can use named cell ranges to help you create charts, as explained in Lesson 16, "Creating Charts."

Follow these steps to name a range:

1. Select the range you want to name (the cells must be located on the same worksheet). If you want to name a single cell, then simply click it.

2. Click in the **Name** box on the left side of the Formula bar (see Figure 9.2).

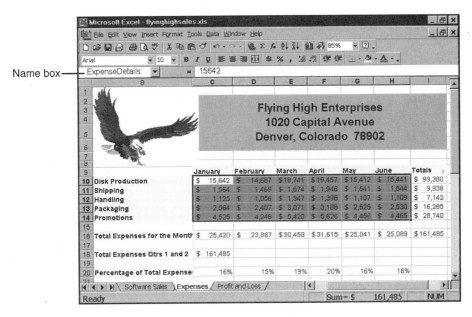

Figure 9.2   Naming a selected range makes it easier to manage.

3. Type a range name using up to 255 characters. Valid names can include letters, numbers, periods, and underlines, *but no spaces*. In addition, a number cannot be used as the first character in the range name, and a range name cannot look like a cell address such as B14.

4. Press **Enter**.

To see your list of range names, click the **Name** box drop-down arrow (on the Formula bar). To quickly select a named range, open the **Name** list and choose the range you want.

You may also name a range using the Define Name dialog box, which enables you to see the range to which a name refers, and to adjust that range if needed.

Follow these steps:

1. Select the range of cells to be named.

2. Open the **Insert** menu, then select **Name**.

3. Choose **Define**. This displays the Define Name dialog box shown in Figure 9.3.

4. Type a name in the Names in workbook text box and click **OK**.

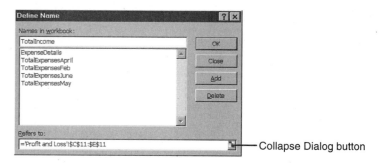

Figure 9.3 The Define Name dialog box is where you delete a range name.

To see the cell address currently assigned to the range name, click a range name in the Names in workbook list. The cell address appears in the Refers to text box. To adjust the range to which the name refers, type a new range or click the **Collapse Dialog** button and select a range in the worksheet.

This dialog box also lets you delete range names. Just click a name in the Names in workbook list and click the **Delete** button.

You can also use the Define Name dialog box to assign a name to a constant value, such as 120%, or a formula. Just type a name in the Names in workbook text box, then type the value or formula in the Refers to text box and click **OK**.

In this lesson, you learned how to select and name ranges to help manage your data. In the next lesson, you learn how to copy, move, and delete ranges of cells, rows, and columns.

Inserting and Removing Cells, Rows, and Columns

10

In this lesson, you learn how to rearrange the data in your worksheet by adding and removing cells, rows, and columns. You also learn how to adjust the width of your columns and the height of your rows to make the best use of the worksheet space.

Inserting Rows and Columns

Inserting entire rows and columns in your worksheet is easy. Here's what you do:

1. To insert a single row or column, select the cell to the right of where you want to insert a column, or below where you want to insert a row.

To insert multiple columns or rows, select the number of columns or rows equal to the number you want to insert. To select columns, drag over the column letters at the top of the worksheet. To select rows, drag over the row numbers.

2. Open the **Insert** menu and select **Rows** or **Columns**. Excel inserts row(s) above your selection; column(s) to the left of your selection. The inserted rows or columns contain the same formatting as the cells you selected in step 1,

TIP **Fast Insert** To quickly insert rows or columns, select one or more rows or columns, right-click one of them, and choose **Insert** from the shortcut menu.

Removing Rows and Columns

When you delete a row in your worksheet, the rows below the deleted row move up to fill the space. When you delete a column, the columns to the right shift left.

Follow these steps to delete a row or column:

1. Click the row number or column letter of the row or column you want to delete. You can select more than one row or column by dragging over the row numbers or column letters.

2. Open the **Edit** menu and choose **Delete**. Excel deletes the row(s) or column(s) and renumbers the remaining rows and columns sequentially. All cell references in formulas are updated appropriately, unless they are absolute ($) values (see Lesson 13, "Performing Simple Calculations," for more information on absolute values).

Merging Cells

In Excel 2000, you can merge the data in one cell with adjacent cells (that are blank) to form a big cell that is easier to work with. Merging cells is especially handy when creating a decorative title for the top of your worksheet (see Figure 10.1 for an example).

To create a title with merged cells, follow these steps:

1. Type the title you want to use for your heading in the upper-left cell of the range. If you have a multiline title, press **Alt+Enter** to insert each new line.

2. Select the range in which you want to place your title.

3. Open the **Format** menu and select **Cells**. The Format Cells dialog box appears.

4. Click the **Alignment** tab.

5. Click the **Merge Cells** check box. You may also want to make adjustments to the text within the merged cells. For example, you may want to select **Center** in the Vertical drop-down list to center the text vertically within the cell.

6. Click **OK** when you're done. The selected cells are merged into a single cell, which you can format as needed.

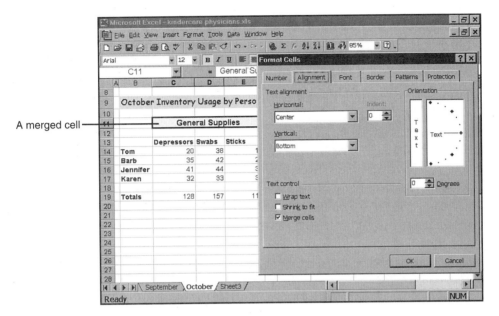

 Figure 10.1 Merge several cells to form a larger single cell.

You can quickly merge selected cells and center the data in the left-most cell by clicking the **Merge and Center** button on the Formatting toolbar.

Inserting Cells

Sometimes you need to insert information into a worksheet, right in the middle of existing data. Inserting cells will cause the data in existing cells to shift down a row or over a column to create a space for the new cells.

 Watch Your Formulas! If your worksheet contains formulas that rely on the contents of the cells being shifted, the calculations may be thrown off. After inserting cells, double-check any formulas in your worksheet that might be **CAUTION** affected.

To insert a single cell or a group of cells, follow these steps:

1. Select the area where you want the new cell(s) inserted. Excel will insert the same number of cells as you select.

2. Open the **Insert** menu and choose **Cells**. The Insert dialog box appears.

387

3. Select **Shift Cells Right** or **Shift Cells Down**.

4. Click **OK**. Excel inserts the cell(s) and shifts the data in the other cells.

 TIP   **Drag Insert**   A quick way to insert cells is to select the number of cells you want, hold down the **Shift** key, and then drag the fill handle up, down, left, or right to set the position of the new cells. (The fill handle is the little box in the lower-right corner of the selected cell or cells—see Figure 10.2.)

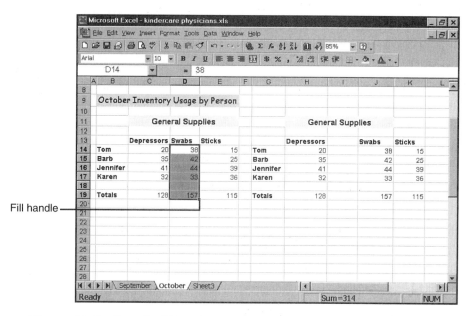

Figure 10.2   Drag the fill handle to quickly insert cells.

Removing Cells

In Lesson 6, "Editing Worksheets," you learned how to clear the contents and formatting of selected cells. That technique merely removed what was inside the cells. But you might want to eliminate the cells completely. When you do, Excel removes the cells and adjusts the data in surrounding cells to fill the gap.

If you want to remove the cells completely, perform the following steps:

1. Select the cell or range of cells you want to remove.

2. Open the **Edit** menu and choose **Delete**. The **Delete** dialog box appears.

3. Select **Shift Cells Left** or **Shift Cells Up**.

4. Click **OK**. Surrounding cells are shifted to fill the gap left by the deleted cells.

Adjusting Column Width and Row Height with a Mouse

Row height is automatically adjusted as you change the size of text. However, if a column's width is not as large as its data, then the data might be displayed as ########. You must adjust the width of the column in order for the data to be displayed. You can adjust the width of a column or the height of a row by using a dialog box, or by dragging with the mouse, as detailed in the following steps:

1. To change the height or width of two or more rows or columns, select them first by dragging over the row or column headings. To change a single column or row, skip this step and continue to step 2.

2. Position the mouse pointer over one of the row heading or column heading borders to change the mouse arrow to a resizing tool, as shown in Figure 10.3. (Use the right border of the column heading to adjust column width; use the bottom border of the row heading to adjust the row height.)

3. Drag the border to the size you need it to be.

4. Release the mouse button, and Excel adjusts the row height or column width.

 TIP **Change More Than One Column or Row at a Time**   Drag over the desired row or column headings, and then double-click the bottommost or rightmost heading border.

 TIP **AutoFit Your Cells**   To quickly make a column as wide as its widest entry using Excel's AutoFit feature, double-click the right border of the column heading. To make a row as tall as its tallest entry, double-click on the bottom border of the row heading.

Arrow becomes
a resizing tool

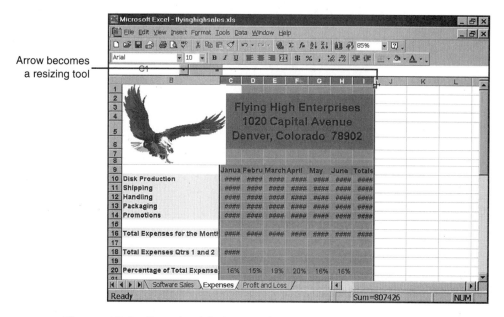

Figure 10.3 Drag the right border of any column to change its width.

Using the Format Menu for Precise Control

You can change a column's size by dragging the border of a row or column. As you drag, a ScreenTip displays the current measurement of the column or row. Even so, you cannot control the size of your column or row as precisely as you can by entering specific sizes with a dialog box.

To change the column width or row height through a dialog box, follow these steps:

1. Select the column(s) or row(s) you want to change. To change the width of a single column or row, select any cell in that column/row.

2. Open the **Format** menu, select **Column** (or **Row**), and then select **Width** (or **Height**). A dialog box similar to the one shown in Figure 10.4 appears.

Figure 10.4 To define the column width precisely, use the dialog box.

3. Type the desired width (or height). When entering the width for a column, enter the number of characters you want the column's width to be. When entering the height of a row, enter the height you want in points.

4. Click **OK** or press **Enter** to put your changes into effect.

In this lesson, you learned how to insert and delete cells, rows, and columns. As well, you learned how to change the row height and column width. In the next lesson, you learn how to select, insert, delete, and move your worksheets.

Managing Your Worksheets

In this lesson, you learn how to add
and delete worksheets within workbooks.
You also learn how to copy, move, and rename worksheets.

Selecting Worksheets

By default, each workbook consists of three worksheets whose names appear on tabs at the bottom of the Excel window. You can add or delete worksheets as desired. One advantage to having multiple worksheets within a workbook is that it enables you to organize your data into logical chunks. Another advantage to having separate worksheets for your data is that you can reorganize the worksheets (and the associated data) in a workbook easily.

Before we go into the details of inserting, deleting, and copying worksheets, you should know how to select one or more worksheets. Here's what you need to know:

- To select a single worksheet, click its tab. The tab becomes highlighted to show that the worksheet is selected.

- To select several neighboring worksheets, click the tab of the first worksheet in the group, and then hold down the **Shift** key and click the tab of the last worksheet in the group.

- To select several nonneighboring worksheets, hold down the **Ctrl** key and click each worksheet's tab.

If you select two or more worksheets, they remain selected until you ungroup them. To ungroup worksheets, do one of the following:

- Right-click one of the selected worksheets and choose **Ungroup Sheets**.
- Hold down the **Shift** key and click the tab of the active worksheet.
- Click any tab.

Inserting Worksheets

When you create a new workbook, it contains three worksheets. You can easily add additional worksheets to a workbook.

Follow these steps to add a worksheet to a workbook:

1. Select the worksheet you want to follow the inserted worksheet. For example, if you select **Sheet2**, the new worksheet (which will be called Sheet4 because the workbook already contains 3 worksheets) will be inserted in front of Sheet2.

2. Open the **Insert** menu.

3. Select **Worksheet**. Excel inserts the new worksheet, as shown in Figure 11.1.

 TIP **Shortcut Menu** A faster way to work with worksheets is to right-click the worksheet tab. This brings up a shortcut menu that lets you insert, delete, rename, move, copy, or select all worksheets.

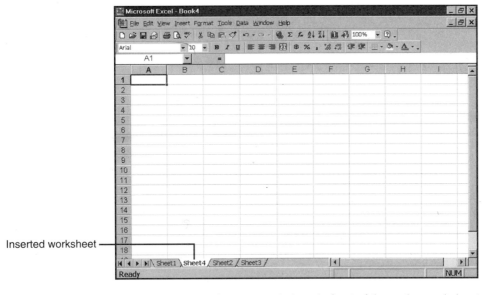

Inserted worksheet

Figure 11.1 Excel inserts the new worksheet in front of the active worksheet.

393

TIP   **Start with More**   You can change the number of worksheets Excel places in a new workbook by opening the **Tools** menu, selecting **Options**, clicking the **General** tab, and then changing the number in the **Sheets in new workbook** option. Click **OK** to save your changes.

Deleting Worksheets

If you plan to use only one worksheet, you can remove the two other worksheets. Here's how you remove a worksheet:

1. Select the worksheet(s) you want to delete.

2. Open the **Edit** menu.

3. Click **Delete Sheet**. A dialog box appears, asking you to confirm the deletion.

You Could Lose Data, Too!   If the worksheet you selected contains any data, you'll lose the data as well, so be careful when deleting worksheets.

CAUTION

4. Click the **OK** button. The worksheet(s) are deleted.

Moving and Copying Worksheets

You can move or copy worksheets within a workbook or from one workbook to another. Here's how:

1. Select the worksheets you want to move or copy. If you want to move or copy worksheets from one workbook to another, be sure the target workbook is open.

2. Open the **Edit** menu and choose **Move or Copy Sheet**. The Move or Copy dialog box appears, as shown in Figure 11.2.

3. To move the worksheets to a different workbook, make sure that workbook is open, then select that workbook's name from the To book drop-down list. If you want to move or copy the worksheets to a new workbook, select **(new book)** in the To book drop-down list. Excel creates a new workbook and then copies or moves the worksheets to it.

Figure 11.2 The Move or Copy dialog box asks where you want to copy or move a worksheet.

4. In the Before sheet list box, choose the worksheet you want to follow the selected worksheets.

5. To move the selected worksheet, skip to step 6. To copy the selected worksheets instead of moving them, select the **Create a Copy** option.

6. Select **OK**. The selected worksheets are copied or moved as specified.

Moving a Worksheet Within a Workbook by Dragging and Dropping

A fast way to copy or move worksheets within a workbook is to use drag and drop. First, select the tab of the worksheet(s) you want to copy or move. Move the mouse pointer over one of the selected tabs, click and hold the mouse button, and drag the tab where you want it moved. To copy the worksheet, hold down the **Ctrl** key while dragging. When you release the mouse button, the worksheet is copied or moved.

Moving a Worksheet Between Workbooks by Dragging and Dropping

You can also use the drag and drop feature to quickly copy or move worksheets between workbooks.

1. Open the workbooks you want to use for the copy or move.

2. Choose **Window**, then choose **Arrange** and select the **Tiled** option.

3. Click **OK** to arrange the windows so that a small portion of each one appears onscreen.

4. Select the tab of the worksheet(s) you want to copy or move.

5. Move the mouse pointer over one of the selected tabs, click and hold the mouse button, and drag the tab where you want it moved. To copy the worksheet, hold down the **Ctrl** key while dragging.

6. When you release the mouse button, the worksheet is copied or moved.

Changing Worksheet Tab Names

By default, all worksheets are named "SheetX," where X is a number starting with the number 1. So that you'll have a better idea of the information each sheet contains, you should change the names that appear on the tabs. Here's how to do it:

1. Double-click the tab of the worksheet you want to rename. The current name is highlighted.

2. Type a new name for the worksheet and press **Enter**. Excel replaces the default name with the name you type.

In this lesson, you learned how to insert, delete, move, copy, and rename worksheets. In the next lesson, you learn how to add headers and footers, preview, and print your workbook.

Printing Your Workbook

*In this lesson, you learn how to preview your print jobs,
repeat row and column headings on pages, and add headers
and footers to your worksheets. You also learn how to print an
entire workbook or a portion of it and how to print a large worksheet.*

Previewing a Print Job

After you've finished a particular worksheet and want to send it to the printer, you may want to take a quick look at how the worksheet will look on the printed page. You will find that worksheets don't always print the way that they look on the screen. To preview a print job, open the **File** menu and select **Print Preview**, or click the **Print Preview** button on the Standard toolbar. Your workbook appears as it will when printed, as shown in Figure 12.1.

TIP   **A Close-Up View**   Zoom in on any area of the preview by clicking it with the mouse pointer (which looks like a magnifying glass). Or use the **Zoom** button at the top of the Print Preview screen.

When you have finished previewing your worksheet, you can print the worksheet by clicking the **Print** button or return to the worksheet by clicking **Close**.

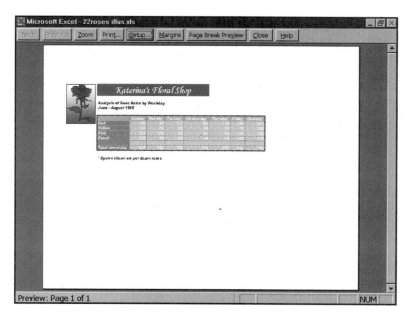

Figure 12.1 By previewing the worksheet, you can determine which page layout attributes need adjusting.

Changing the Page Setup

After you preview your worksheet, you may want to adjust page attributes or change the way the page is set up for printing. For instance, you may want to print the column and row labels on every page of the printout. This is particularly useful for large worksheets that span several pages so that you don't have to keep looking back to the first page of the printout to determine what the column headings were.

Printing column and row labels and other worksheet page attributes, such as scaling a worksheet to print out on a single page or adding headers or footers to a worksheet printout, are handled in the Page Setup dialog box. To access this dialog box, open the **File** menu and choose **Page Setup** (see Figure 12.2).

The following sections provide information on some of the most common page setup attributes that you will work with before printing your Excel worksheets.

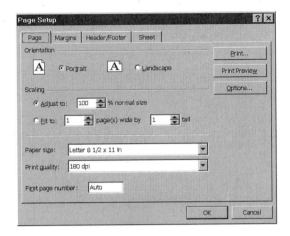

Figure 12.2 Access the Page Setup dialog box to make sure your page is set to print correctly.

Printing Column and Row Labels on Every Page

Excel provides a way for you to select labels and titles that are located on the top edge and left side of a large worksheet and to print them on every page of the printout. This option is useful when a worksheet is too wide to print on a single page. If you don't use this option, the extra columns or rows will be printed on subsequent pages without any descriptive labels.

Follow these steps to print column or row labels on every page:

1. Open the **File** menu and choose **Page Setup**. The Page Setup dialog box appears.
2. Click the **Sheet** tab to display the Sheet options.
3. To repeat column labels and a worksheet title, click the **Collapse Dialog** button to the right of the Rows to Repeat at Top text box.
4. Drag over the rows you want to print on every page, as shown in Figure 12.3. A dashed line border surrounds the selected area, and absolute cell references with dollar signs ($) appear in the Rows to Repeat at Top text box.

399

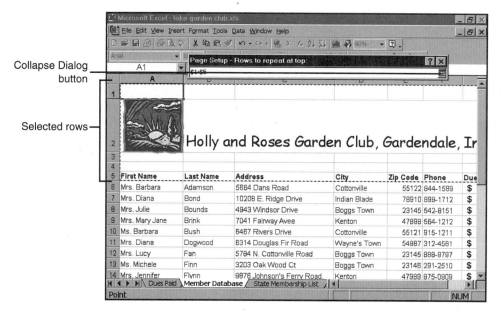

Figure 12.3 Select the headings you want to print on every page.

5. Click the **Collapse Dialog** button to return to the Page Setup dialog box.

6. To repeat row labels that appear on the left of the worksheet, click the **Collapse Dialog** button to the right of the Columns to Repeat at Left text box. Excel reduces the Page Setup dialog box.

7. Select the columns that contain the row labels you want to repeat.

8. Click the **Collapse Dialog** button to return again to the Page Setup dialog box.

9. To print your worksheet, click **Print** to display the Print dialog box. Then click **OK**.

Select Your Print Area Carefully If you select rows or columns to repeat, and those rows or columns are part of your print area, the selected rows or columns may print twice. To fix this, select your print area again, leaving out the rows or columns you're repeating.

CAUTION

400

TIP **Access Print Preview from Other Dialog Boxes** Page Setup and Print dialog boxes also include a Preview button, so you can check any last minute changes you made in either dialog box without having to close the box first.

Scaling a Worksheet to Fit on a Page

If your worksheet is too large to print on one page even after you change the orientation and margins, you might consider using the **Fit To** option. This option shrinks the worksheet to make it fit on the specified number of pages. You can specify the document's width and height.

Follow these steps to scale a worksheet to fit on a page:

1. Open the **File** menu and choose **Page Setup**. The Page Setup dialog box appears.
2. Click the **Page** tab to display the Page options.
3. In the Fit to XX Page(s) Wide by XX Tall text boxes, enter the number of pages into which you want Excel to fit your data.
4. Click **OK** to close the Page Setup dialog box and return to your worksheet. Or click the **Print** button in the Page Setup dialog box to display the Print dialog box, and then click **OK** to print your worksheet.

Adding Headers and Footers

Excel enables you to add headers and footers to print information at the top and bottom of every page of the printout. The information can include any text, as well as page numbers, the current date and time, the workbook filename, and the worksheet tab name.

You can choose the headers and footers suggested by Excel, or you can include any text plus special commands to control the appearance of the header or footer. For example, you can apply bold, italic, or underline to the header or footer text. You can also left-align, center, or right-align your text in a header or footer (see Lesson 7, "Changing How Numbers and Text Look").

To add headers and footers, follow these steps:

1. Open the **File** menu and choose **Page Setup**. The Page Setup dialog box appears. Click the **Header/Footer** tab on the dialog box (see Figure 12.4).

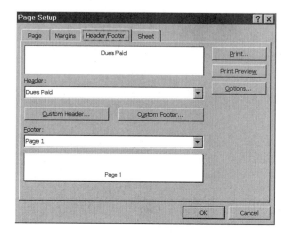

Figure 12.4 Add headers and footers with Header/Footer options.

2. To select a header, click the **Header** drop-down arrow. Excel displays a list of suggested header information. Scroll through the list and click a header you want. The sample header appears at the top of the Header/Footer tab.

 TIP **Don't See One You Like?** If none of the suggested headers or footers suit you, click the **Custom Header** or **Custom Footer** button and enter your own information.

3. To select a footer, click the **Footer** drop-down arrow. Excel displays a list of suggested footer information. Scroll through the list and click a footer you want. The sample footer appears at the bottom of the Header/Footer tab.

4. Click **OK** to close the Page Setup dialog box and return to your worksheet. Or click the **Print** button to display the Print dialog box, and click **OK** to print your worksheet.

CAUTION

Don't Want Headers or Footers Anymore? To remove the header and/ or footer, choose **(none)** in the **Header** and/or **Footer** lists.

Printing Your Workbook

After adjusting the page settings for the worksheet and previewing your data, it is time to print. You can print selected data, selected sheets, or the entire workbook.

To print your workbook, follow these steps:

1. If you want to print a portion of the worksheet, select the range you want to print (see Lesson 9, "Working with Ranges," for help). To print only a chart, click it. If you want to print one or more worksheets within the workbook, select the sheet tabs (see Lesson 11, "Managing Your Worksheets"). To print the entire workbook, skip this step.

2. Open the **File** menu and select **Print** (or press **Ctrl+P**). The Print dialog box appears, as shown in Figure 12.5.

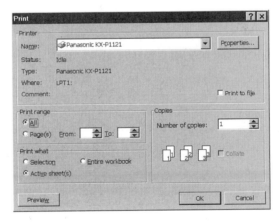

Figure 12.5 Select your printer and a page range to print in the Print dialog box.

TIP   **Print Using the Default Settings**   If you click the **Print** button (instead of using the **File** menu and clicking **Print**), Excel prints your current worksheet without letting you make any selections.

3. Select the options you would like to use:

- **Page Range** lets you print one or more pages. For example, if the selected print area contains 15 pages and you want to print only pages 5–10, select Page(s), and then type the numbers of the first and last page you want to print in the **From** and **To** boxes.

- **Print What** enables you to print the currently selected cells, the selected worksheets, or the entire workbook.

- **Copies** enables you to print more than one copy of the selection, worksheet, or workbook.

- **Coliate** enables you to print a complete copy of the selection, worksheet, or workbook before the first page of the next copy is printed. This option is available when you print multiple copies.

4. Click **OK** or press **Enter**.

While your job is printing, you can continue working in Excel. If the printer is working on another job that you (or someone else, in the case of a network printer) sent, Windows holds the job until the printer is ready for it.

Sometimes you might want to delete a job while it is printing or before it prints. For example, suppose you think of other numbers to add to the worksheet or realize you forgot to format some text; you'll want to fix these things before you print the file. To display the print queue and delete a print job, follow these steps:

1. Double-click the **Printer** icon on the Windows taskbar, and the print queue appears, as shown in Figure 12.6.

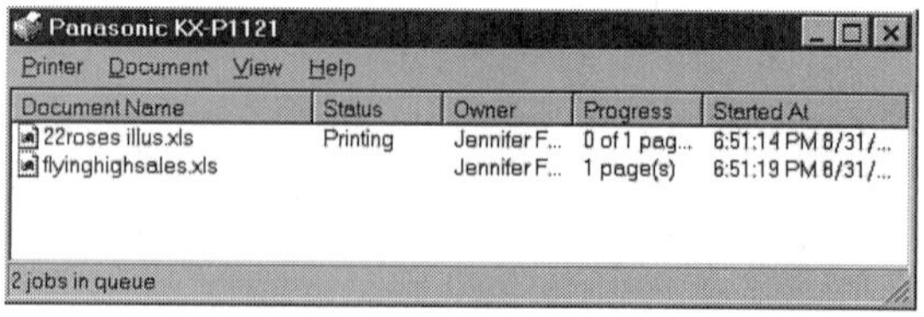

Figure 12.6   To stop a document from printing, use the print queue.

2. Click the job you want to delete.

3. Open the **Document** menu and select **Cancel Printing**, or just press **Delete**.

   To delete all the files from the print queue, open the **Printer** menu and select **Purge Print Documents**. This cancels the print jobs but doesn't delete the files from your computer.

Selecting a Large Worksheet Print Area

You do not have to always print an entire worksheet; instead, you can easily tell Excel what part of the worksheet you want to print by selecting the print area yourself. If the area you select is too large to fit on one page, no problem—Excel just breaks it into multiple pages. When you do not select a print area yourself, Excel prints either the entire worksheet or the entire workbook, depending on the options set in the Print dialog box.

CAUTION

Double Vision! When deciding which cells to select for your print area, make sure you *do not include the title, the subtitle, and the column and row labels in the print area.* If you do, Excel may print the labels twice. Instead, print your titles and headings on each page of your printout by following the steps in the previous section, "Printing Column and Row Labels on Every Page."

To select a print area, follow these steps:

1. Click the upper-left cell of the range you want to print.

2. Drag downward and to the right, until the range you want is selected.

3. Open the **File** menu, select **Print Area**, and select **Set Print Area**.

To remove the print area so you can print the entire worksheet again, open the **File** menu, select **Print Area**, and select **Clear Print Area**.

You can also select your print area from within the Page Setup dialog box, shown in Figure 12.7. Follow these steps:

1. Open the **File** menu and select **Page Setup**.

2. Click the **Sheet** tab, then click the **Collapse Dialog** button to the right of the Print Area text box.

3. Select the range you want to print, then click the **Collapse Dialog** button again to return to the Page Setup dialog box.

4. Make any other changes you want and click **Print**.

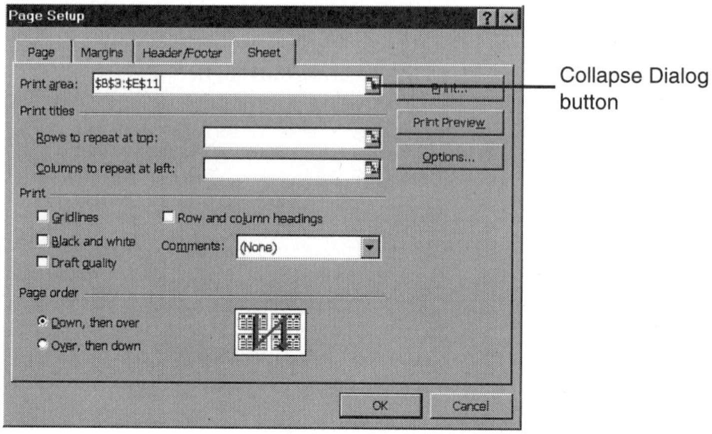

Figure 12.7 Select a print area from within the Page Setup dialog box.

Adjusting Page Breaks

When you print a workbook, Excel determines the page breaks based on the paper size, the margins, and the selected print area. To make the pages look better and to break information in logical places, you may want to override the automatic page breaks with your own breaks. However, before you add page breaks, try these options:

- Adjust the widths of individual columns to make the best use of space (see Lesson 10, "Inserting and Removing Cells, Rows, and Columns").
- Consider printing the workbook sideways using Landscape orientation.
- Change the left, right, top, and bottom margins to smaller values.

After trying these options, if you still want to insert page breaks, Excel offers you an option of previewing exactly where the page breaks appear and then adjusting them. Follow these steps:

1. Open the **View** menu and select **Page Break Preview**.

2. If a message appears telling you how to adjust page breaks, click **OK**. Your worksheet is displayed with page breaks, as shown in Figure 12.8.

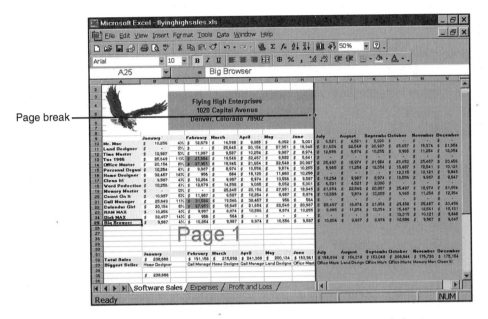

Page break —

Figure 12.8 Check your page breaks before printing your worksheet.

3. To move a page break, drag the blue line to the desired location.

   To delete a page break, drag it off the screen.

   To insert a page break, move to the first cell in the column to the right of where you want the page break inserted, or move to the row below where you want the break inserted. For example, to insert a page break between columns G and H, move to cell H1. To insert a page break between rows 24 and 25, move to cell A25. Then open the **Insert** menu and select **Page Break**. A dashed line appears to the left of the selected column or above the selected row.

4. To exit Page Break Preview and return to your normal worksheet view, open the **View** menu and select **Normal**.

In this lesson, you learned how to print all or part of your workbook, as well as how to print a large worksheet. You also learned to adjust page setup attributes such as column and row labels and headers and footers. In the next lesson, you learn how to create calculations with formulas.

Performing Simple Calculations

In this lesson, you learn how to use formulas to calculate results in your worksheets.

Understanding Excel Formulas

You can use Excel formulas to perform simple calculations on the data you enter. With formulas, you can perform addition, subtraction, multiplication, and division using the values contained in various cells.

Formulas typically consist of one or more cell addresses or values and a mathematical operator, such as + (addition), – (subtraction), * (multiplication), or / (division). For example, if you want to determine the average of the three values contained in cells A1, B1, and C1, you would type the following formula in the cell where you want the result to appear:

```
=(A1+B1+C1)/3
```

TIP **Start Right** Every formula must begin with an equal sign (=). If you don't type an = when you enter a formula, Excel may interpret what you type as a date or a label.

Figure 13.1 shows several formulas in action. Study the formulas and their results. Table 13.1 lists the mathematical operators you can use to create formulas.

Type the formula here...   ...and the result appears in the cell

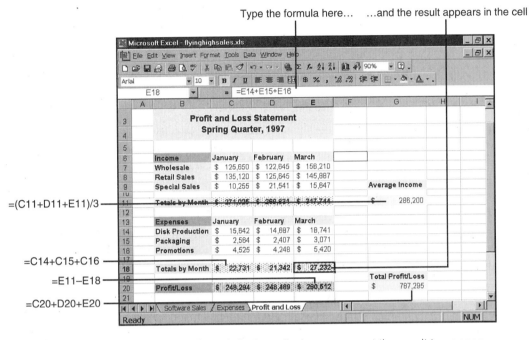

Figure 13.1 Type a formula in the cell where you want the result to appear.

Table 13.1 Excel's Mathematical Operators

Operator	Performs	Sample Formula	Result
^	Exponentiation	=A1^3	Enters the result of raising the value in cell A1 to the third power.
+	Addition	=A1+A2	Enters the total of the values in cells A1 and A2.
–	Subtraction	=A1–A2	Subtracts the value in cell A2 from the value in cell A1.
*	Multiplication	=A2*3	Multiplies the value in cell A2 by 3.
/	Division	=A1/50	Divides the value in cell A1 by 50.
	Combination	=(A1+A2+A3)/3	Determines the average of the values in cells A1 through A3.

Order of Operations

Excel performs the operations within a formula in the following order:

1st   Exponential and equations within parentheses

2nd   Multiplication and division

3rd   Addition and subtraction

For example, given the formula =C2+B8*4+D10, Excel computes the value of B8*4, then adds that to C2, and then adds D10. Keep this order of operations in mind when you are creating equations because it determines the result.

If you don't take this order into consideration, you could run into problems when entering your formulas. For example, if you want to determine the average of the values in cells A1, B1, and C1, and you enter =A1+B1+C1/3, you'll get the wrong answer. The value in C1 will be divided by 3, and that result will be added to A1+B1. To determine the total of A1 through C1 first, you must enclose that group of values in parentheses: =(A1+B1+C1)/3.

Entering Formulas

You can enter formulas in either of two ways: by typing the formula or by selecting cell references.

To type a formula, perform the following steps:

1. Select the cell in which you want the formula's calculation to appear.

2. Type the equal sign (=), or click the **equal** icon in the Formula bar.

3. Type the formula. The formula appears in the Formula bar.

4. Press **Enter** or click the **Enter** button on the Formula bar, and Excel calculates the result.

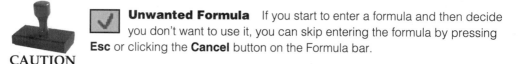

Unwanted Formula   If you start to enter a formula and then decide you don't want to use it, you can skip entering the formula by pressing **Esc** or clicking the **Cancel** button on the Formula bar.

CAUTION

TIP **Name That Cell** If you plan to use a particular cell in several formulas, you can give it a name, such as "Income." Then you can use the name in the formula, as in =Income+$12.50.

To enter a formula by selecting cell references, take the following steps:

1. Select the cell in which you want the formula's result to appear.

2. Type the equal sign (=) or click the **equal** icon on the Formula bar.

3. Click the cell whose address you want to appear first in the formula. You can also click on a cell in a different worksheet or workbook. The cell address appears in the Formula bar.

4. Type a mathematical operator after the value to indicate the next operation you want to perform. The operator appears in the Formula bar.

5. Continue clicking cells and typing operators until the formula is complete.

6. Press **Enter** or click the **Enter** button on the Formula bar to accept the formula.

CAUTION **Error!** If ERR appears in a cell, make sure that you did not commit one of these common errors: dividing by zero, using a blank cell as a divisor, referring to a blank cell, deleting a cell used in a formula, or including a reference to the cell in which the answer appears.

TIP **Natural Language Formulas** Excel lets you refer to row and column labels when entering a formula. For example, if you had a worksheet with the row labels "Revenues," "Expenses," and "Profit," and you had column labels for each month, you could enter a formula such as =Jan Profit+Feb Profit or =Revenues–Expenses.

Calculating Results Without Entering a Formula

Using a feature Excel calls AutoCalculate, you can view the sum of a range of cells simply by selecting the cells and looking at the status bar, as shown in Figure 13.2. You can also view the average, minimum, maximum, and count of a range of cells. To display something other than the sum, right-click the status bar and select the option you want from the shortcut menu that appears.

411

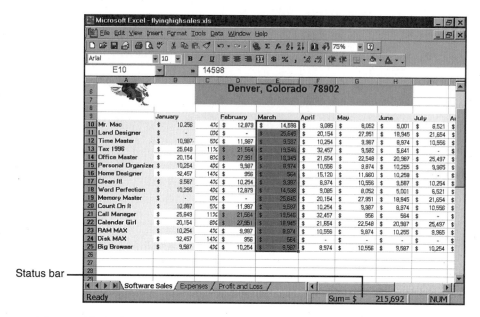

Figure 13.2 View a sum in the Status bar without entering a formula.

Where's the Status Bar? If the status bar is not visible on your screen, you can display it by opening the **View** menu and placing a check next to it by clicking **Status Bar**.

CAUTION

Displaying Formulas

Normally, Excel does not display the actual formula in a cell. Instead, it displays the result of the calculation. You can view the formula by selecting the cell and looking in the Formula bar. However, if you're trying to review all the formulas in a large worksheet, it would be easier if you could see them all at once (and even print them). If you want to view formulas in a worksheet, follow these steps:

1. Open the **Tools** menu and choose **Options**.

2. Click the **View** tab.

3. In the Window Options area, click to select the **Formulas** check box.

4. Click **OK**.

TIP **Keyboard Shortcut** To toggle between viewing formulas and viewing values, hold down the **Ctrl** key and press `` ` ``, the accent key (most likely located to the left of the 1 key; it has the tilde ~ on it). When you no longer need to view formulas, press **Ctrl+`** again.

Editing Formulas

Editing a formula is the same as editing any entry in Excel. Here's how you do it:

1. Select the cell that contains the formula you want to edit.

2. Click in the Formula bar or press **F2** to enter Edit mode.

TIP **In-Cell Editing** To quickly edit the contents of a cell, double-click the cell. The insertion point appears inside the cell, and you can make any necessary changes.

3. Press the left arrow key ← or right arrow → key to move the insertion point. Then use the **Backspace** key to delete characters to the left, or use the **Delete** key to delete characters to the right. Type any additional characters.

4. When you finish editing the data, click the **Enter** button on the Formula bar or press **Enter** to accept your changes.

Another way to edit a formula is to click the **Edit Formula** button on the Formula bar. When you do, the Formula bar expands to provide you with help. Make your changes to the formula and then click **OK**.

In this lesson, you learned how to enter and edit formulas. In the next lesson, you learn how to copy formulas, when to use relative and absolute cell addresses, and how to change Excel's settings for calculating formulas in the worksheet.

Copying Formulas

In this lesson, you learn how to copy formulas, use relative and absolute cell references, and change calculation settings.

Copying Formulas

When you copy a formula, the formula is adjusted to relate to the cell to which it is copied. This is called *relative addressing*, because the addresses of the cells in the original formula are adjusted to reflect their new column or row. For example, if you copy the formula =C2+C3 from cell C4 to cell D4 (a different column), the formula is adjusted to column D: it becomes =D2+D3. This allows you to copy a formula (such as one that totals monthly expenses for January) to a range of cells (such as the February, March, and April columns).

You can copy formulas using the Copy and Paste buttons (see Lesson 6), but there's a faster way:

1. Click the cell that contains the formula you want to copy.
2. Press **Ctrl** and drag the cell's border to the cell to which you want to copy your formula.
3. Release the mouse button, and Excel copies the formula to the new location.

If you want to copy a formula to a neighboring range of cells, follow these steps:

1. Click the cell that contains the formula you want to copy.
2. Move the mouse pointer over the fill handle.
3. Drag the fill handle across the cells into which you want to copy the formula.

TIP **Fast Copy** If you want to enter the same formula into a range of cells, select the range first. Then type the formula for the first cell in the range and press **Ctrl+Enter**.

CAUTION

Get an Error? If you get an error after copying a formula, verify the cell references in the copied formula. See the next section, "Using Relative and Absolute Cell Addresses," for more details.

Using Relative and Absolute Cell Addresses

As I mentioned at the beginning of this lesson, when you copy a formula from one place in the worksheet to another, Excel adjusts the cell references in the formulas relative to their new positions in the worksheet. For example, in Figure 14.1, cell C16 contains the formula =C10+C11+C12+C13+C14, which computes the total expenses for January. If you copy that formula one column over to cell D16 (to determine the total expenses for February), Excel automatically changes the formula to =D10+D11+D12+D13+D14. Because you copied the formula to a different column (from C to D), Excel adjusts the column letter in the cell addresses. If you had copied the same formula two rows down to cell C18, then the formula would be changed to =C12+C13+C14+C15+C16; all the cell addresses would be adjusted by two rows. This is how relative cell addresses work.

Sometimes you may not want the cell references to be adjusted when you copy formulas. That's when absolute cell references become important.

CAUTION

Absolute Versus Relative An *absolute reference* is a cell reference in a formula that does not change when copied to a new location. A *relative reference* is a cell reference in a formula that is adjusted when the formula is copied.

In the example shown in Figure 14.1, the cells C20, D20, E20, and F20 contain formulas that calculate the percentage of total expenses for that month. Each formula uses an absolute reference to cell C18, which contains the total expenses for quarters 1 and 2. (The formulas in C20, D20, E20, and F20 divide the sums from row 16 of each column by the contents of cell C18.) If you copied the formula from C20 to the range D20:F20 without defining the formula as absolute, the cell references would adjust incorrectly, and you would get an error message.

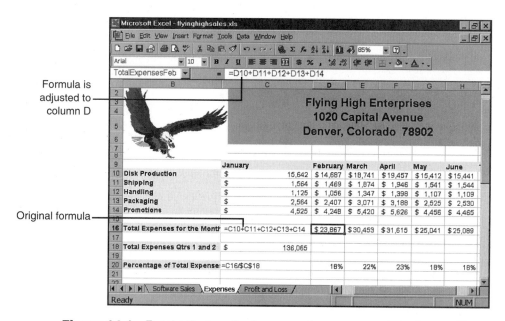

Figure 14.1 Excel adjusts cell references when you copy formulas to different cells.

To make a cell reference in a formula absolute, you add a $ (dollar sign) before the letter and before the number that make up the cell address. For example, in Figure 14.1, the formula in C20 reads as follows:

=C16/$C$18

The address, $C$18 refers to cell C18, which contains the total expenses for quarters 1 and 2. When you copy this formula to column D, it adjusts to become:

=D16/$C$18

If you hadn't used absolute cell references, the formula would have changed to =D16/D18. Since cell D18 is empty, the formula would have resulted in an error. To enter absolute cell addresses, you can type the dollar signs yourself, or just press **F4** after typing the cell address.

Some formulas use mixed references. For example, the column letter might be an absolute reference, and the row number might be a relative reference, as in the formula $A2/2. If you entered this formula in cell C2 and then copied it to cell D10 (one column over and eight rows down), the result would be the formula $A10/2. The row reference (row number) would be adjusted by eight rows, but the column reference (the letter A) would not be adjusted at all.

Mixed References A reference that is only partially absolute, such as A$2 or $A2. When a formula that uses a mixed reference is copied to another cell, only part of the cell reference (the relative part) is adjusted.

Recalculating the Worksheet

Excel recalculates the formulas in a worksheet every time you edit a value in a cell. However, on a large worksheet, you may not want Excel to recalculate until you have entered all of your changes. For example, if you are entering a lot of changes to a worksheet that contains many formulas, you can speed up the process by changing from automatic to manual recalculation. To change the recalculation setting, take the following steps:

1. Open the **Tools** menu and choose **Options**.

2. Click the **Calculation** tab to display the options shown in Figure 14.2.

3. Select one of the following Calculation options:

- **Automatic**—This is the default setting. It recalculates the entire workbook each time you edit or enter a formula.

- **Automatic except tables**—This automatically recalculates everything except formulas in a data table.

- **Manual**—This option tells Excel to recalculate only when you say so. To recalculate manually, click the Calc Now (F9) button. When this option is selected, you can turn the Recalculate before save option off or on.

4. Click **OK**.

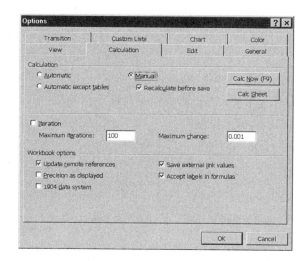

Figure 14.2 Change your calculation setting in the Options dialog box.

In this lesson, you learned how to copy formulas. You also learned when to use relative and absolute cell addresses and how to change recalculation settings. In the next lesson, you learn how to use Excel's Function Wizard to insert another type of formula, called a function.

Performing Calculations with Functions

In this lesson, you learn how to perform calculations with functions and how to use Excel's Function Wizard to quickly insert functions in cells.

What Are the Functions?

Functions are complex ready-made formulas that perform a series of operations on a specified range of values. For example, to determine the sum of a series of numbers in cells A1 through H1, you can enter the function =SUM(A1:H1) instead of entering =A1+B1+C1 and so on.

Every function consists of the following three elements:

- The = sign, which indicates that what follows is a function (formula).
- The function name, such as SUM, that indicates which operation will be performed.
- A list of argument(s) in parentheses, such as (A1:H1), which in this case indicates the range of cells whose values the function should use. The argument for a function can be a range of cells, an address, or a range name, such as APRSALES. Some functions use more than one argument, separated by commas, as in (A1,B1,H1).

You can enter functions either by just typing them into a cell or by using the Function Wizard, as you see later in this lesson. Table 15.1 shows Excel's common functions that you use most often in your worksheets.

Table 15.1 Excel's Most Common Functions.

Function	Example	Description
AVERAGE	=AVERAGE(B4:B9)	Calculates the mean or average of a group of numbers.
COUNT	=COUNT(A3:A7)	Counts the numeric values in a range. For example, if a range contains some cells with text and other cells with numbers, you can count how many numbers are in that range.
COUNTBLANK	=COUNTBLANK(B4:B10)	Counts all cells in a range that are not blank. Cells that contain zero are not counted, nor are cells that contain "" (empty text).
IF	=IF(A3>=100,A3*2,A2*2)	Allows you to place a condition on a formula. In this example, if A3 is greater than or equal to 100, the formula A3*2 is used. If A3 is less than 100, the formula A2*2 is used instead.
MAX	=MAX(B4:B10)	Returns the maximum value in a range of cells.
MIN	=MIN(B4:B10)	Returns the minimum value in a range of cells.
PMT	=PMT(.0825/12,360,18000)	Calculates the monthly payment on a 30-year loan (360 monthly payments) at 8.25% a year (.0825/12 a month) for $180,000.
PMT	=PMT(.07/12,60,10000)	Calculates the monthly deposit needed to accumulate $10,000 at an annual rate of 7 percent (.07/12 a month) over five years (60 months).
SUM	=SUM(A1:A10)	Calculates the total in a range of cells.

Function	Example	Description
SUMIF	=SUMIF(B2:B4,>100,A2:A4)	Calculates the total of the range for each corresponding cell in sum range that matches specified criteria. This example adds the cells in the range A2:A4 whose corresponding cell in column B is greater than 100.

Enter Text Right   When entering text into a formula, be sure to surround it with quotation marks, as in "Seattle." For example, if you wanted to total cells in column C that are next to a cell that contains the word "Indiana," you might use

CAUTION   this formula:

=SUMIF(B3:B10,"Indiana",C3:C10)

Using AutoSum

Because SUM is one of the most commonly used functions, Excel provides a fast way to enter it—you simply click the **AutoSum** button in the Standard toolbar. Based on the currently selected cell, AutoSum guesses which cells you want summed. If AutoSum selects an incorrect range of cells, you can change the selection.

To use AutoSum, follow these steps:

1. Select the cell in which you want the sum inserted. Try to choose a cell at the end of a row or column of data; doing so will help AutoSum guess which cells you want added together.

2. Click the **AutoSum** button in the Standard toolbar. AutoSum inserts =SUM and the range address of the cells to the left of or above the selected cell (see Figure 15.1).

3. If the range Excel selected is incorrect, drag over the range you want to use, or click in the Formula bar and edit the formula.

4. Click the **Enter** button in the Formula bar or press Enter. Excel calculates the total for the selected range.

The SUM function
appears in the
Formula Bar.

AutoSum selects
a range to sum.

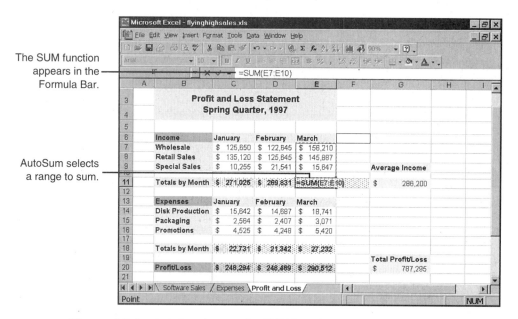

Figure 15.1 AutoSum inserts the SUM function and selects the cells it plans to total.

TIP **Quick AutoSum** To bypass the step where Excel displays the SUM formula and its arguments in the cell, select the cell in which you want the sum inserted and double-click the **AutoSum** button on the Standard toolbar.

Using the Function Wizard

Although you can type a function directly into a cell just as you can type formulas, you'll find it easier to use the Function Wizard. The Function Wizard leads you through the process of inserting a function. The following steps walk you through using the Function Wizard:

1. Select the cell in which you want to insert the function. (You can insert a function by itself or as part of a formula.)

2. Type = or click the **Edit Formula** button on the Formula bar. The Formula Palette appears, as shown in Figure 15.2.

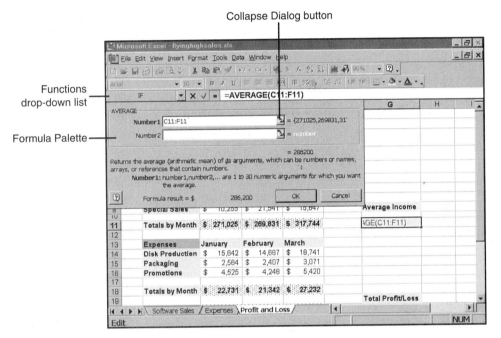

Figure 15.2 The Function Wizard helps you enter functions.

3. Select the function you want to insert from the Functions list by clicking the arrow on the Functions drop-down list (see Figure 15.2). If you don't see your function listed, select **More Functions** at the bottom of the list.

4. Enter the arguments for the formula. If you want to select a range of cells as an argument, click the **Collapse Dialog** button shown in Figure 15.2.

5. After selecting a range, click the **Collapse Dialog** button again to return to the Formula Palette.

6. Click **OK**. Excel inserts the function and argument in the selected cell and displays the result

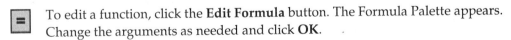

To edit a function, click the **Edit Formula** button. The Formula Palette appears. Change the arguments as needed and click **OK**.

TIP **What's This Function?** If you'd like to know more about a particular function, click the **Help** button in the Formula Palette. When the Office Assistant appears, click **Help with this feature**. Then click **Help on selected function**.

In this lesson, you learned the basics of working with functions, and you learned how to use Excel's Function Wizard to quickly enter functions. You also learned how to quickly total a series of numbers with the AutoSum tool. In the next lesson, you learn how to create and work with charts.

Creating Charts

In this lesson, you learn to create
graphical representations (charts) of workbook data.

Understanding Charting Terminology

Before you start creating charts, you should familiarize yourself with the
following terminology:

- **Data Series**—The bars, pie wedges, lines, or other elements that represent
  plotted values in a chart. For example, a chart might show a set of similar
  bars that reflects a series of values for the same item. The bars in the same
  data series would all have the same pattern. If you have more than one
  pattern of bars, each pattern would represent a separate data series. For
  instance, charting the sales for Territory 1 versus Territory 2 would require
  two data series—one for each territory. Often, data series correspond to
  rows of data in your worksheet.

- **Categories**—Categories reflect the number of elements in a series. You
  might have two data series that compare the sales of two different territo-
  ries and four categories that compare these sales over four quarters. Some
  charts have only one category, and others have several. Categories normally correspond to the columns in your worksheet, with the category
  labels coming from the column headings.

- **Axis**—One side of a chart. A two-dimensional chart has an x-axis (horizontal) and a y-axis (vertical). The x-axis contains the data series and categories in the chart. If you have more than one category, the x-axis often
  contains labels that define what each category represents. The y-axis
  reflects the values of the bars, lines, or plot points. In a three-dimensional
  chart, the z-axis represents the vertical plane, and the x-axis (distance) and
  y-axis (width) represent the two sides on the floor of the chart.

- **Legend**—Defines the separate series of a chart. For example, the legend for a pie chart will show what each piece of the pie represents.
- **Gridlines**—Typically, gridlines appear along the y—or value—axis, although they can emanate from the x-axis as well. Gridlines help you determine a point's exact value.

Working with Different Chart Types

With Excel, you can create many different types of charts. Some common chart types are shown in Figure 16.1. The chart type you choose depends on the kind of data you're trying to chart, and on how you want to present that data. These are the major chart types and their purposes:

- **Pie**—Use this chart type to show the relationship among parts of a whole.
- **Bar**—Use this chart type to compare values at a given point in time.
- **Column**—Similar to the bar chart; use this chart type to emphasize the difference between items.
- **Line**—Use this chart type to emphasize trends and the change of values over time.
- **Scatter**—Similar to a line chart; use this chart type to emphasize the difference between two sets of values.
- **Area**—Similar to the line chart; use this chart type to emphasize the amount of change in values over time.

Most of these basic chart types also come in three-dimensional varieties. In addition to looking more professional than the standard flat charts, 3D charts can often help your audience distinguish between different sets of data.

Creating and Saving a Chart

You can place your new chart on the same worksheet that contains the chart data (an embedded chart) or on a separate worksheet (a chart sheet). If you create an embedded chart, it is typically printed side-by-side with your worksheet data. Embedded charts are useful for showing the actual data and its graphic represen-tation side-by-side. If you create a chart on a separate worksheet, however, you can print it independently. Both types of charts are linked to the worksheet data that they represent, so when you change the data, the chart is automatically updated.

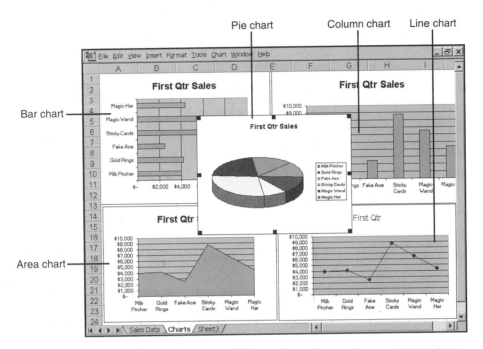

Pie chart   Column chart   Line chart

Bar chart

Area chart

.Figure 16.1 Excel chart types enable you to analyze and present your data.

The **Chart Wizard** button on the Standard toolbar enables you to quickly create a chart. To use the Chart Wizard, follow these steps:

1. Select the data you want to chart. If you typed column or row labels (such as Qtr 1, Qtr 2, and so on) that you want included in the chart, make sure you select them, too.

2. Click the **Chart Wizard** button on the Standard toolbar.

3. The **Chart Wizard Step 1 of 4** dialog box appears, as shown in Figure 16.2. Select a **Chart type** and a **Chart sub-type** (a variation on the selected chart type). Click **Next**.

4. Next you are asked if the selected range is correct. You can correct the range by typing a new range, or by clicking the **Collapse Dialog** button (located at the right end of the **Data range** text box) and selecting the range you want to use.

427

5. By default, Excel assumes that your different data series are stored in rows. You can change this to columns if necessary by clicking the **Series in Columns** option. When you're through, click **Next**.

6. Click the various tabs to change options for your chart (see Figure 16.3). For example, you can delete the legend by clicking the **Legend** tab and deselecting **Show Legend**. You can add a chart title on the **Titles** tab. Add data labels (labels which display the actual value being represented by each bar, line, and so on) by clicking the **Data Labels** tab. When you finish making changes, click **Next**.

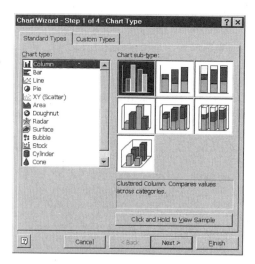

Figure 16.2   Choose the chart type using the Chart Wizard.

A preview of your chart appears here

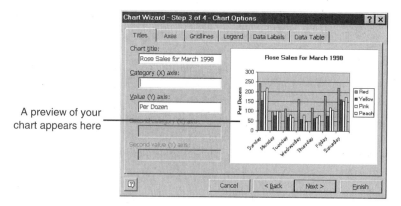

Figure 16.3   Select from various chart appearance options.

7. Finally, you're asked if you want to embed the chart (as an object) in the current worksheet (or any other existing worksheet in the workbook), or if you want to create a new worksheet for it. Make your selection and click the **Finish** button. Your completed chart appears.

 TIP   **Create a Chart Fast!**   To create a chart quickly, select the data you want to use and press F11. Excel creates a column chart (the default chart type) on its own sheet. You can then customize the chart as needed.

The charts you create are part of the current workbook. To save a chart, simply save the workbook that contains the chart.

Moving and Resizing a Chart

To move an embedded chart, click anywhere in the chart area and drag it to the new location. To change the size of a chart, select the chart, and then drag one of its handles (the black squares that border the chart). Drag a corner handle to change the height and width, or drag a side handle to change only one dimension. (Note that you can't really resize a chart that is on a sheet by itself.)

Printing a Chart

If a chart is an embedded chart, it will print when you print the worksheet that contains the chart. If you want to print just the embedded chart, click it to select it, and then open the **File** menu and select **Print**. Make sure that the **Selected Chart** option is turned on. Then click **OK** to print the chart.

If you created a chart on a separate worksheet, you can print the chart separately by printing only that worksheet. For more information about printing, refer to Lesson 12, "Printing Your Workbook."

In this lesson, you learned about the different chart types and how to create them. You also learned how to save and print charts. In the next lesson, you learn how to save and publish worksheets and workbooks to the Web.

Saving and Publishing Files to the Web

In this lesson, you learn how to prepare worksheets for use on the Internet.

Adding an FTP Site to Your Save In Box

An FTP site is a special computer attached to the Internet (or intranet) that handles only file transfers (file uploads and downloads). You can save your workbook to an FTP site on the Internet (or a local intranet), provided you have the permission to do so. The first step is to add the FTP site to the Save As dialog:

1. Open the **Save in** list and select **Add/Modify FTP Locations**. The Add/Modify FTP dialog box appears, as shown in Figure 17.1.

2. In the **Name of FTP site:** text box, enter the site's address, such as **ftp.microsoft.com**.

3. Select **Log on as**, either **Anonymous** or **User**, and enter a **password** if necessary.

4. Click **OK**.

5. After the site has been added to the Save As dialog box, you can select it from the FTP Locations folder in the Save in list.

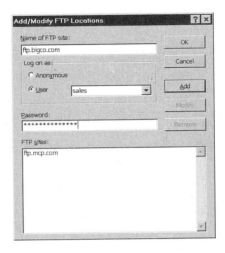

Figure 17.1 Add a new FTP site to your Save in List.

Saving a Workbook for the Web

You can save your Excel data to a Web site (or on your company's intranet) by converting your workbook to HTML format. When you save a workbook (or part of a workbook) in this way, it can be viewed through a Web browser.

HTML Short for HyperText Markup Language, HTML is the language in which data is presented on the World Wide Web. To display your Excel data on the Web, you must convert it to this format.

If you tried to use the HTML publishing feature in Excel 97 and gave up because it was too complex, now's the time to give it another try. In Excel 2000, the process is almost as simple as saving a workbook, as you'll soon see.

An entire workbook published to the Web can be viewed but it cannot be changed: the data is considered *static*. However, you can update the data yourself as needed by simply saving the workbook again. You can also publish part of a workbook, such as a worksheet, as static data.

If you want to make your data *interactive* so that a user can view it and change it, then you must publish only part of your workbook at a time. You can publish a worksheet, a chart, a PivotTable, or a selected range, to name a few possibilities.

431

Publishing Static Data

To publish data that cannot be changed, follow these steps:

1. If you're not publishing the entire workbook, select the item that you want to publish.

2. Open the **File** menu and select **Save as Web Page**. The Save As dialog box appears, as shown in Figure 17.2.

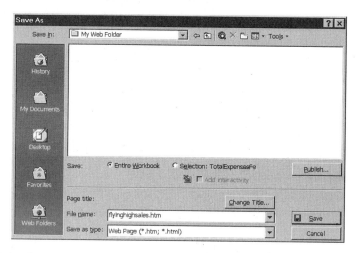

Figure 17.2 Select Save as Web Page to open the Save As dialog box.

3. In the Save in list, type (or select) the Internet or intranet location on which you want to save the workbook. You can also save the HTML file to a local hard drive.

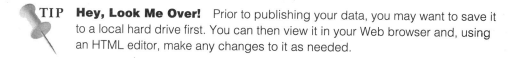

TIP **Hey, Look Me Over!** Prior to publishing your data, you may want to save it to a local hard drive first. You can then view it in your Web browser and, using an HTML editor, make any changes to it as needed.

4. Type a name for the HTML file in the File name text box.

5. If you want, click **Change Title** and then change the title for the Web page (the HTML file). (The title appears in the title bar of the users' Web browsers when they are viewing your page.)

6. Perform either of the following:

To save the entire workbook, select **Entire Workbook**, then click **Save**. (Skip the remaining steps.)

To save a part of the workbook (such as a worksheet or a chart), choose **Selection** and click **Publish**. The Publish as Web Page dialog box appears, as shown in Figure 17.3.

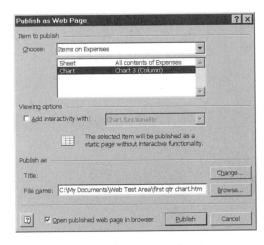

Figure 17.3 Access the Publish as Web Page dialog box to save part of a workbook.

7. Select the item you want to publish from the Choose list.

8. If you want, select **Open published web page in browser** to launch your Web browser so you can view the HTML file.

9. Click **Publish**.

Publishing Interactive Data

When you save part of a workbook, such as a worksheet or a chart, in interactive format, then users can both view and make changes to it. You might want to use this option if you're publishing group data to your company's intranet.

To publish interactive data:

1. Select the item to publish.

2. Open the **File** menu and select **Save as Web Page**. The Save As dialog box appears (see Figure 17.2).

3. In the Save in list, type (or select) the Internet or intranet location on which you want to save the workbook. You can also save the HTML file to a local hard drive.

4. Type a name for the HTML file in the File name text box.

5. If you want, click **Change Title** and then change the title for the Web page (the HTML file). (The title appears in the title bar of the users' Web browsers when they are viewing your page.)

6. Click **Publish**. The Publish as Web Page dialog box appears, as shown in Figure 17.4.

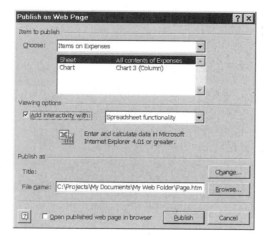

Figure 17.4 Access the Publish as Web Page dialog box to publish interactive data.

7. Select the item you want to publish from the Choose list.

8. Choose the **Add interactivity with** option, then select the type of interactivity:

   - Spreadsheet functionality—Allows users to enter, update, copy, move, delete, format, sort, or filter data.

   - PivotTable functionality—Allows users to change the layout of a PivotTable's data, or sort, filter, or change the data as well.

   - Chart functionality—Allows users to change the source data for a chart, which then updates the chart itself.

9. If you want, select **Open published web page in browser** to launch your Web browser so you can view the HTML file.

10. Click **Publish**.

Changing Interactive Data

When a user views your interactive data in his or her Web browser, it will look something like Figure 17.5.

Web Components toolbar

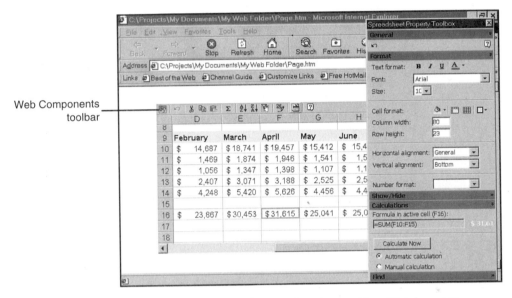

Figure 17.5 Your interactive data can be changed in a Web browser.

To change any of the data, just click in a cell, type the new data, and press **Enter** or use an arrow key to move to another cell. You can also use the buttons on the Web Components toolbar as needed (see Table 17.1). If you display the Property toolbox, you can change the format of a cell, show or hide data, locate data, change calculations, and control when calculations occur.

Table 17.1 Web Components Toolbar

Button	Name	Description
	Undo	Undo an action
	Cut	Cut data

continues

Table 17.1 Continued

Button	Name	Description
	Copy	Copy data
	Paste	Paste data
	AutoSum	Create a subtotal
	Sort Ascending	Sort data in ascending order
	Sort Descending	Sort data in descending order
	AutoFilter	Display only selected data
	Export to Excel	Export the data to Excel
	Property Toolbox	Display the Property toolbox
	Help	Display Help

Republishing Your Data

After your data has been published, follow these steps to update it:

1. Open the original workbook.
2. Make changes as needed.
3. Open the **File** menu and select **Save as Web Page**. The Save as Web Page dialog box appears.
4. If you saved the entire workbook before, then just click **Save**; otherwise, click **Publish**.
5. Select **Previously Published Items** from the Choose list.
6. Choose the item you want to republish from those listed.
7. Make any other changes as needed, then click **Publish**.

Adding Hyperlinks to a Worksheet

A hyperlink is a bit of text or a graphic that, when clicked, takes the user to a Web page, to a file on your hard disk, or to a file on a local network. You can also add a hyperlink to another sheet in the workbook if you like. To add a hyperlink, follow these steps:

1. Select the text or graphic you want to use for the link.

2. Click the **Insert Hyperlink** button on the Standard toolbar.

3. If asked, make sure you save your workbook. The Insert Hyperlink dialog box appears, as shown in Figure 17.6.

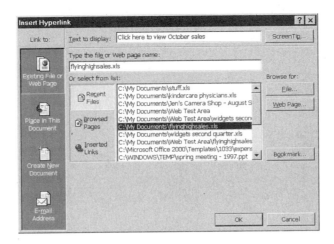

Figure 17.6 Insert a hyperlink in a workbook.

4. Perform one of the following:

   - **To link to a file or Web page**, enter the address of the Web page or file to which you want to link in the Type the file or Web page name text box, or click the **File** or **Web Page** button to select it from a dialog box. You can also click **Recent Files** or **Browsed Pages** to select it from a list. If you want to click to a bookmark within a Web page, select the page first, then click the **Bookmark** button, and select the bookmark you want to use.

   - **To link to a location within the workbook**, click the **Place in This Document** button in the Places Bar. Then enter the cell address in the Type the cell reference text box, or select it from the Or select a place in this document list.

- **To create a link to a new workbook**, click the Create New Document button in the Places Bar. Then type a name for the document in the Name of new document text box. To save the workbook in a directory other than the one shown, click the **Browse** button and select the directory you want to use.

- **To create a link to an e-mail address** (so that when clicked, the link will open your e-mail program, display a message window, and automatically address the e-mail message), click the EMail Address button in the Places Bar. Then type the e-mail address you want to link to in the E-mail address text box or select one from the Recently used e-mail addresses list. If you want to enter a subject for the message, type one in the Subject text box.

6. To display a ScreenTip when the mouse pointer rests on the hyperlink, click **ScreenTip**, and enter the description you want to display. Click **OK**.

7. Click **OK**. The text in the cell you selected becomes blue and underlined.

When you move the mouse pointer over this link, it changes to a hand. Next to the hand, you can see the address of the link. Click the link, and you're jumped to the appropriate worksheet, Web page, file, or email program. The text of the link changes to purple to indicate that you have used the link.

If you need to change the text for a link later on, or change the item that the link points to, right-click **link** and select **Hyperlink** from the shortcut menu. Then select **Edit Hyperlink**. The Edit Hyperlink dialog box appears. Make your changes and click **OK**. To delete the link, right-click, select **Hyperlink**, and then select **Remove Link** from the shortcut menu.

In this lesson, you learned how to save workbook files to an FTP site, how to publish your workbook data, and how to add hyperlinks. In the first lesson of the next part, you learn about Access databases.

Access

What Is a Database?

In this lesson, you learn some basic database concepts and find out how Microsoft Access handles them.

What Are Databases Good For?

Strictly speaking, a *database* is any collection of information. Your local telephone book, for example, is a database, as is your Rolodex file and the card catalog at your local library. With a computerized database in Microsoft Access, you can store information as described in the three examples in this lesson, but you can also do much more. For instance, if you keep a list of all your business customers in an Access database, you can

- Print a list of all customers who haven't bought anything in the last 60 days, along with their phone numbers, so you can call each one.
- Sort the customers by zip code and print out mailing labels in that order. (Some bulk-mailing services require that you presort by zip code to get the cheaper mailing rate.)
- Create a simple onscreen order entry form that even your most technically unskilled employee can use successfully.

These examples only scratch the surface. With Access, you can manipulate your data in almost any way you can dream up.

How Access Stores Your Data

In Access, you first need to create a database file. That file holds everything you create for that database—not only all the data, but also the customized forms, reports, and indexes. If you have two or more businesses, you might want to create two or more separate databases, one for each business.

Storing Data into Tables

The heart of each database is its tables. A table is a lot like a spreadsheet; the data is arranged in columns and rows. Figure 1.1 shows a data table (or just *table,* for short).

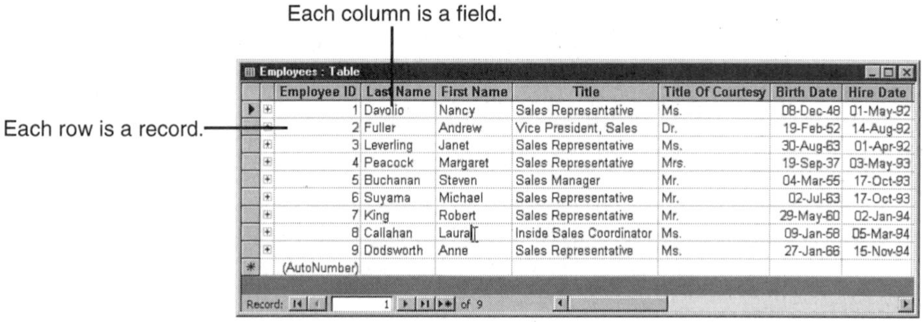

Each column is a field.

Each row is a record.

Figure 1.1 Access arranges data into columns and rows like a spreadsheet.

Access stores each database entry (for example, each employee or each inventory item) in its own row; this is a *record.* Each record is a collection of information about one thing—in this case, an employee. For example, all the information about Nancy Davolio, including Title, Birth Date, and Hire Date, forms a single record (refer to Figure 1.1).

Each type of detail is kept in its own column: a *field.* For example, Employee ID is one field and Last Name is another. All the last names in the entire table are collectively known as the Last Name field.

At the intersection of a field column and a record row is one individual piece of information for that particular record; this area is a *cell.* For example, in the cell where the Birth Date column and the Nancy Davolio record intersect, you'll find 08-Dec-48, Nancy's birth date.

You'll learn how to create tables in Lesson 5, "Creating a Table with the Table Wizard," and Lesson 6, "Creating a Table from Scratch." Each database file can have many tables. For instance, you might have one table that lists all your customers and another table that lists information about the products you sell. A third table might keep track of your salespeople and their performance.

Entering Data into Forms

All the data you enter into your database ends up in a table for storage. You can enter information directly into a table, but it's a little awkward to do so. Most people find it easier to create a special onscreen form in which to enter the data. A form resembles a fill-in-the-blanks sheet that you would complete by hand, such as a job application. You'll learn how to create a form in Lesson 12, "Creating a Simple Form."

Access links the form to the table and stores the information that you put into the form in the table. For instance, in Figure 1.2, Access stores the employee data I'm entering on this form in the table shown in Figure 1.1.

The form shown in Figure 1.2 has two tabs. To view and work with the fields on the second page, simply click its tab.

 TIP **Multitable Forms** You can use a single form to enter data into several tables at once, as you'll learn in later lessons.

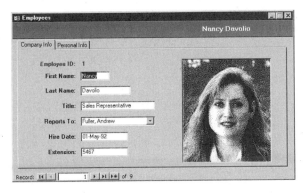

Figure 1.2 Forms make data entry more convenient.

Formatting Data into Reports

Although forms are designed to be used onscreen, reports are designed to be printed. Reports are specially formatted collections of data organized according to your specifications. For example, you might want to create a report of all your employees' sales performance (see Figure 1.3).

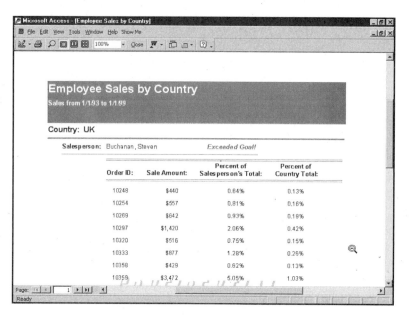

Figure 1.3   You can print this report and distribute it to your salespeople.

TIP   **Print Preview**   Although you create reports so that you can print them, you can also display them onscreen in Print Preview, as shown in Figure 1.3. You learn how to view and print reports in Lesson 19, "Creating a Simple Report."

Organizing Data by Using Queries

A *query* is a way of weeding out the information you don't want to see, so you can see the information you do need more clearly. You can think of it as a sieve you dump your data into; the data you don't want falls through the holes in the sieve, leaving only the data you're interested in.

Many people are afraid of queries because of the technical terms associated with them, such as *values*, *criteria*, and *masks*. But there's no need to be wary, as you learn in Lesson 17, "Creating a Simple Query," where you create and use a simple query.

How the Parts Fit Together

Although you create tables, reports, forms, and queries in separate steps, they're all related. As mentioned earlier, tables are the central focus of all activities—all the other objects do something to or with the table data. Reports summarize and organize the table data; forms help you enter information into the table; queries help you find information you want to use in the table. In later lessons, you see how each part relates to the whole database.

In this lesson, you learned some basics about databases and Access. In the next lesson, you learn some strategies for planning your database.

Planning Your Database

In this lesson, you learn some principles of good database design to help you plan your course of action.

Planning Is Important!

Access makes creating databases very straightforward and quite easy. However, when you do create a new database, you want to make sure that the database is designed from the very beginning to not only meet your data entry needs, but also to meet your needs for viewing and reporting the data that is held in the various database tables. Taking a little time to plan your database before you create it can save you from headaches down the road.

The list that follows can be used to help you plan your databases:

- Jot ideas down on paper and think through the database design; decide what tables, forms, and reports your database will most likely need. You can then build on this foundation.

- Set up the first table for the database. Make sure it provides all the information you will need for that particular category of data. If you design the table for customer data, make sure you include a column for zip code and phone number.

- Use forms for data entry. Forms enable you to concentrate on one record at a time and see each piece of information that needs to be input into the record. Incomplete records can be a real drag.

- Remember, Access is a relational database. Each table should contain information that meets the particular table's purpose. For instance, a customer table should hold information on customers, not on products. If you want product data listed, design another table for your products.

- Reports enable you to analyze your data. They present your data in a positive and clear format. Design them carefully. They are probably the only thing related to your database that other people will see.

Determining What Tables You'll Need

Technically, you need only one table—the minimum a database can function with. However, the biggest mistake most people make with Access is putting too much information in one table. Access is a relational database program; unlike simpler database programs, it's meant to handle many tables and create relationships among them. For example, in a database that keeps track of customer orders, you might have the following tables:

Customers	Customer Types
Orders	Shipping Methods
Payment Terms	Products
Salespeople	

TIP **Plan Tables Now!** You should plan your tables before you create your database, because changing a table's structure after it's filled with data is difficult (but not impossible).

Another big mistake people make is trying to make each table look like a standalone report. For instance, they might repeat a customer's name and address in all eight tables because they want that information readily available when it's required. This is a waste! You can easily create a report or a form that includes this information whenever you need it; it should appear in only one table.

Normalizing Your Database

When a database suffers from poor table organization, experts say it's not *normalized*. Rules govern how a relational database should store its tables; these are the rules of data normalization.

TERM **Data Normalization** Makes the tables as efficient and compact as possible to eliminate the possibility for confusion and error.

Five normalization rules exist, but the last three are fairly complicated and used mostly by database professionals. In this lesson, I'll explain the first two normalization rules, which are all a beginner really needs to understand to avoid major mistakes.

 TIP **Normalized Wizards** Luckily, database professionals had a hand in creating Access's Database Wizard, so any tables you create with this feature (see Lesson 4, "Creating a New Database") will be normalized.

1. Avoid Repeated Information

Suppose you want to keep contact information on your customers along with a record of each transaction they make. If you kept it all in one table, you would have to repeat the customer's full name, address, and phone number each time you entered a new transaction. It would also be a nightmare if the customer's address changed; you would have to change the address in every transaction record for that customer.

Customer Name	Customer Address	Customer Phone	Order Date	Order Total
ABC Plumbing	201 W. 44th St.	(317) 555-2394	2/5/96	$155.90
ABC Plumbing	201 W. 44th St.	(317) 555-2394	5/14/96	$90.24
ABC Plumbing	201 W. 44th St.	(317) 555-2394	7/9/96	$224.50
Jack's Emporium	1155 Conner Ave.	(317) 555-4501	6/6/95	$1,592.99
Jack's Emporium	1155 Conner Ave.	(317) 555-4501	7/26/96	$990.41
Millie's Pizza	108 Ponting St.	(317) 554-2349	8/29/96	$39.95

A better way is to assign each customer an ID number. Include that ID number in a table that contains names and addresses; then use the same ID number as a link in a separate table that contains transactions.

Customers Table

Customer ID	Customer Name	Customer Address	Customer Phone
1	ABC Plumbing	201 W. 44th St.	(317) 555-2394
2	Jack's Emporium	1155 Conner Ave.	(317) 555-4501
3	Millie's Pizza	108 Ponting St.	(317) 554-2349

Orders Table

Customer ID	Order Date	Order Total
1	2/5/96	$155.90
1	5/14/96	$90.24
1	7/9/96	$224.50
2	6/6/95	$1,592.99
2	7/26/96	$990.41
3	8/29/96	$39.95

2. Avoid Redundant Data

Suppose you want to keep track of which employees have attended certain training classes. Many employees and lots of classes are involved. One way would be to keep it all in a single Personnel table, such as this:

Employee Name	Employee Address	Employee Phone	Training Date	Class Taken	Credit Hours	Passed?
Phil Sharp	211 W. 16th St.	(317) 555-4321	5/5/96	Leadership Skills	3	Yes
Becky Rowan	40 Westfield Ct.	(317) 555-3905	5/5/96	Customer Service	2	Yes
Nick Gianti	559 Ponting St.	(317) 555-7683	6/15/96	Public Speaking	9	Yes
Martha Donato	720 E. Warren	(317) 555-2930	5/5/96	Public Speaking	9	No
Cynthia Hedges	108 Carroll St.	(317) 555-5990	6/15/96	Customer Service	2	Yes
Andrea Mayfair	3904 110th St.	(317) 555-0293	6/15/96	Leadership Skills	3	Yes

But what if an employee takes more than one class? You'd have to add a duplicate line in the table to list it, and then you have the problem described in the previous section—multiple records with virtually identical field entries. What if the only employee who has taken a certain class leaves the company? When you delete that employee's record, you delete the information about the class's credit hours, too.

A better way would be to create separate tables for Employees, Classes, and Training Done, like so:

Employee Table

Employee ID	Employee Name	Employee Address	Employee Phone
1	Phil Sharp	211 W. 16th St.	(317) 555-4321
2	Becky Rowan	40 Westfield Ct.	(317) 555-3905
3	Nick Gianti	559 Ponting St.	(317) 555-7683
4	Martha Donato	720 E. Warren	(317) 555-2930
5	Cynthia Hedges	108 Carroll St.	(317) 555-5990
6	Andrea Mayfair	3904 110th St.	(317) 555-0293

Class Table

Class ID	Class	Credits
C1	Leadership Skills	3
C2	Customer Service	2
C3	Public Speaking	9

Training Table

Employee ID	Date	Class	Passed?
1	5/5/96	C1	Yes
2	5/5/96	C2	Yes
3	6/16/96	C3	Yes
4	5/5/96	C3	No
5	6/15/96	C2	Yes
6	6/15/96	C1	Yes

Summary: Designing Your Tables

Don't be overwhelmed by all this information about database normalization. Good table organization boils down to a few simple principles:

- Each table should have a theme—for instance, Employee Contact Information or Customer Transactions. Don't try to have more than one theme per table.

- If you see that you might end up repeating data in a table in the future, such as storing the customer's phone number in every purchase transaction, plan now to split the information that will be repeated and place it into its own table.

- If you want to preserve a list of reference information (such as the names and credit hours for classes), put it in its own table.

- Wherever possible, use ID numbers; they'll help you link tables later and avoid typing errors that come from entering long text strings (such as names) over and over.

- If you already have unique customer numbers or employee Social Security numbers, you can use them; otherwise, use an AutoNumber field to automatically generate a unique number for each record.

Determining the Forms You Will Use

As explained in Lesson 1, "What Is a Database," forms are data-entry tools. You can arrange fields from several tables on a form and easily enter data into those fields on a single screen. For instance, a customer order form might include information from the Orders table and the Products table (see Figure 2.1).

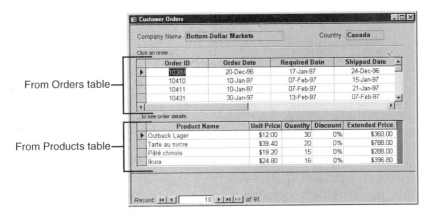

Figure 2.1 A form can be the link between several tables.

When you're thinking about what forms you'll need, the question is really about what actions you will perform. The following list describes some actions that might require a form:

- Hiring employees (and entering their information in the database)
- Selling goods or services
- Making purchases
- Collecting the names and contact information for volunteers
- Keeping track of inventory

I Can't Predict What Forms I'll Need! Although it's important to have effective forms, you can make changes to forms at any time fairly easily (unlike tables), so you don't have to know exactly what forms you want before you CAUTION start. You learn to create forms in Lesson 12, "Creating a Simple Form."

Determining What Reports You Will Want to Produce

A report satisfies your need for information about your data. It's usually printed (unlike tables and forms, which are usually used onscreen). For instance, you might want a report of all people who haven't paid their membership dues, or all accounts with a balance owed of more than $1,000. (You can find this information with a query, too, as you learn in Lesson 17, "Creating a Simple Query.")

A report is usually for the benefit of other people who aren't sitting with you at your computer. For instance, you might print a report to hand out to your board of directors to encourage them to keep you on as CEO. A report can pull data from many tables at once, perform calculations on the data (such as summing or averaging), and present you with neatly formatted results. The following are some things you can do with reports:

- Print a list of all your personal possessions with a replacement value over $50, for insurance purposes.
- Show a listing of all club members who haven't paid their dues.
- Calculate and show the current depreciated value of all capital equipment.
- List the commissions paid to each of your top 50 salespeople in the last quarter, compared with the companywide average.

You can create new reports at any time; you don't have to plan them before you create your database. However, if you know you will want a certain report, you might design your tables in the format that will be most effective for that report's use.

In this lesson, you planned your database tables, forms, and reports. In the next lesson, you learn how to start and exit Access.

Working in Access

In this lesson, you learn how to start and exit Microsoft Access.

Starting Access

You can start Access in several ways, depending on how you've installed it. One way is to use the Start menu button. Follow these steps:

1. Click the **Start** button. A menu appears.
2. Highlight or point to **Programs**. A list of your program groups appears, with a list of separate Microsoft applications under the groups.
3. Click **Microsoft Access** in the list of applications. Access starts.

 TIP   Moving Programs Around on the Start Menu   If you prefer to have Access in a different program group, open the **Start** menu and drag the Access item to another location of your choice.

Other Ways to Start Access

Some other ways to start Access require more knowledge of Windows and Microsoft Office. If you're confused by them, stick with the primary method explained in the preceding section.

- You can create a shortcut icon for Access to sit on your desktop; you can then start Access by double-clicking the icon. To create the shortcut icon, drag the Access item from the **Start** menu to the desktop.

- When you're browsing files in Windows Explorer, you can double-click any Access data file to start Access and open that data file. Access data files have an .mdb extension and a little icon next to them that resembles the icon next to Microsoft Access on the Programs menu.

- If you can't find Access, you can search for it. Click the **Start** button and select **Find**, select **Files or Folders**, and then type **msaccess.exe** in the **Named** text box. Open the **Look In** list and select **My Computer**. Then click **Find Now**. When the file appears on the list at the bottom of the Find window, double-click it to start Access, or right-click and drag it to the desktop to create an Access shortcut.

When you start Access, the first thing you'll see is a dialog box prompting you to create a new database or open an existing one (see Figure 3.1). For now, click **Cancel**. (We won't be working with any particular database in this lesson.)

Figure 3.1 This Microsoft Access dialog box appears each time you start Access.

Parts of the Screen

Access is much like any other Windows program: It contains menus, toolbars, a status bar, and so on. Figure 3.2 points out these landmarks. Notice that in Figure 3.2, many of the toolbar buttons are grayed out (which means you can't use them right now). In addition, nothing is in the work area because no database file is open. The Access screen becomes a much busier place in later lessons when you begin working with a database; the buttons become available, and your database appears in the work area.

Menu bar

Toolbar

Work area

Status bar

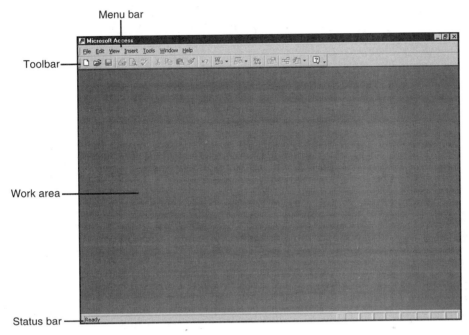

Figure 3.2 Access has the same interface landmarks as any Windows program.

Understanding Access Toolbars

If you've used Windows programs before, you're probably familiar with *toolbars*—rows of buttons that represent common commands you can issue. Toolbar buttons are often shortcuts for menu commands.

The Access toolbar changes, depending on which type of database object you're working with at the time (table, form, and so on) and what you're doing to it. More toolbars sometimes appear when you're doing special activities, such as drawing. To find out what a toolbar button does, put your mouse pointer over it; its name appears next to the pointer (see Figure 3.3). This feature is a *ToolTip* (or a *ScreenTip*); you can use ToolTips even when a button is unavailable (grayed out).

Close button

Button name

Figure 3.3 To find out what a toolbar button does, point at it.

TIP **Choose Your Toolbars** If you right-click any toolbar, a shortcut menu appears. You can select a toolbar for viewing from that list.

Exiting Access

When you finish working with Access, you should exit it to free up your computer's memory for other tasks. You can exit Access in several ways:

- Press **Alt+F4**.
- Select **File**, and then **Exit**.
- Click the Access window's **Close** (×) button (refer to Figure 3.3).

TERM **Alt+F4?** In this book I use a kind of shorthand to tell you what keys to press and which menu commands to select. When you see "press **Alt+F4**," it means hold down the **Alt** key on the keyboard while you press the **F4** key.

In this lesson, you learned how to start and exit Access, and you learned about the main parts of the screen, including the toolbar buttons. In the next lesson, you learn how to create, save, close, open, and work with your own databases.

Creating a New Database

In this lesson, you learn how to create a blank database. You also learn how to create a database with premade tables, reports, and forms with the Database Wizard. You also learn how to save your database, close it, reopen it, and how to find a misplaced database file.

Choosing the Right Way to Create Your Database

Before you create your database, you have an important decision to make: Should you create a blank database from scratch, and then manually create all the tables, reports, and forms you'll need, or should you use a Database Wizard, which does all that for you?

 TERM   **Database Wizard**   Access comes with several Database Wizards. These are miniprograms that interview you about your needs and then create a database structure that matches them. (You enter the actual data yourself.)

The answer depends on how well the available wizards match your needs. If a Database Wizard is close to what you want, it's quickest to use it to create your database and then modify the database as needed. (Of course, you won't know what wizards are available until you open the list of them, as you'll see later in this lesson.) If you're in a hurry, using a wizard can save you a lot of time.

On the other hand, if you want a special-purpose database that isn't similar to any of the wizards, or if you're creating the database primarily as a training exercise for yourself, you should create the blank database.

Creating a Blank Database

Creating a blank database is very simple because you're just creating an outer shell at this point, without any tables or forms. If you just started Access and the Microsoft Access dialog box is still displayed (see Figure 4.1), follow these steps:

1. Click **Blank Access Database**.

2. Click **OK**. The File New Database dialog box opens.

3. Type a name for the new file in the **File Name** text box, and then click **Create**. Access creates the new database.

Figure 4.1 When you first start Access, you can start a new database quickly from the Microsoft Access dialog box.

After you close the initial dialog box, you can't get it back until you exit and restart Access. But you don't need it to start a new database; at any time, you can follow these steps

1. Select **File**, and then **New**, or click the **New** button on the toolbar. The New dialog box appears (see Figure 4.2).

2. Make sure the **General** tab is on top by clicking it. Double-click the **Database** icon. The File New Database dialog box appears.

3. Type a name for your new database (preferably something descriptive) in the **File Name** text box. For example, I typed **Kennel Records**. Then click **Create**. Access creates the new database by default in the My Documents folder.

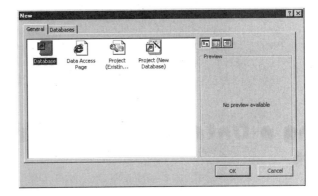

Figure 4.2 The New dialog box's different tabs give you options to create different kinds of databases.

Your database is completely blank at this point, and you see the database's window open to the Tables section (see Figure 4.3).

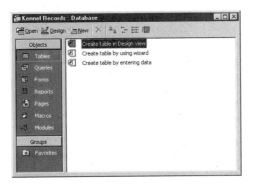

Figure 4.3 A new Database window opens to the Tables section.

Each item listed in the Objects section of Figure 4.3 represents a different kind of object you can create in a database. Later, you learn how to create tables (Lessons 5, "Creating a Table with the Table Wizard," and 6, "Creating a Table from Scratch"), forms (Lesson 12, "Creating a Simple Form"), queries (Lesson 17, "Creating a Simple Query"), and reports (Lesson 19, "Creating a Simple Report").

TIP **Object Shortcuts** The object shortcuts (such as Create Table in Design view) aren't necessary—you can create a new database object by clicking the **New** toolbar button. If you tire of these shortcuts and want to conserve list space for your own database objects, you can turn them off by choosing **Options** from the **Tools** menu, and then deselecting the **New Object Shortcuts** option.

Creating a Database with Database Wizards

A Database Wizard can create almost all the tables, forms, and reports you will ever need, automatically. The trick is to choose the right wizard to suit your purpose. Follow these steps:

1. If you just started Access and the Microsoft Access dialog box is still onscreen, click **Access Database Wizards, Pages and Projects**, and then click **OK**. Or, if you've already closed the dialog box, select **File**, and then click **New**. Either way, the New dialog box appears.

2. If it's not already on top, click the **Databases** tab to display the list of wizards.

3. Click one of the Database Wizards (the icons with the magic wands across them). For this example, I'll choose **Contact Management**.

4. When you've selected the wizard you want, click **OK**. The File New Database dialog box appears.

5. Type a name for the database, and then click **Create** to continue. The wizard starts, and some information appears explaining what the wizard does.

6. Click **Next** to continue. A list of the tables to be created appears (see Figure 4.4). The tables appear on the left, and the selected table's fields are on the right.

7. Click a table and examine its list of fields. Optional fields are in italic. To include an optional field, click it to place a check mark next to it. Click **Next** to continue.

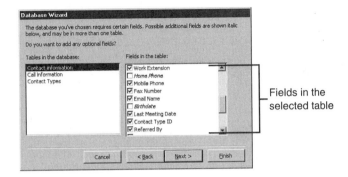

Fields in the
selected table

Figure 4.4 This wizard creates these tables and fields automatically for you.

CAUTION

I Don't Want These Tables and Fields! Sorry, that's the price you pay for going with a prefabricated wizard. You can't deselect any fields except the optional (italicized) ones. But you can delete the tables and fields you don't want later. See Lesson 7, "Editing Tables," to learn how to delete individual fields or an entire table. If the tables and fields appear totally inappropriate, perhaps you're using the wrong wizard for your needs; click **Cancel** and try another.

8. The wizard asks you what kind of screen display style you want. Click a display style in the list and examine the preview of the style that appears. After you decide on a style, click it, and then click **Next**.

9. The wizard asks you for a style for printed reports. Click a report style and examine the preview of it. When you decide on a style, click it, and then click **Next**.

CAUTION

Report Background The colored backgrounds used for some report styles look nice onscreen, but they don't print well on a black-and-white printer. Stick to plain backgrounds for the best report printouts.

10. The wizard asks what title you want for the database. This title appears on reports and can be different from the filename. Enter a title (see Figure 4.5).

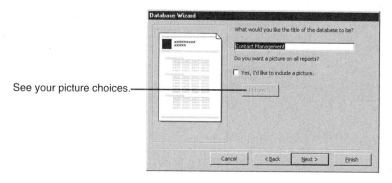

See your picture choices.

Figure 4.5 Enter a title for the database, and as an option, choose a graphic to use for a logo.

11. (Optional) To include a picture on your forms and reports (for example, your company's logo), click the **Yes, I'd Like to Include a Picture** check box. Then click the **Picture** button, choose a picture file (change the drive or folder if needed), and click **OK** to return to the wizard.

12. Click **Next** to continue. Then, at the Finish screen, click **Finish** to open the new database. The wizard goes to work creating your database. (It might take several minutes.)

When the database is done, the Main Switchboard window appears (see Figure 4.6). The Switchboard opens automatically whenever you open the database.

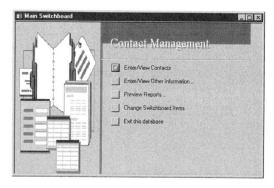

Figure 4.6 The Switchboard window is an extra bonus provided by the Database Wizards.

All the databases created by a Database Wizard include the Main Switchboard, which is nothing more than a fancy form with some programming built in.

It enables you to perform common tasks with the database by clicking a button. We won't be working with the Main Switchboard, so just click the Main Switchboard window's **Close** (×) button to get rid of it.

TIP   **I Hate That Switchboard!**   To prevent the Switchboard from opening when you open the database, choose **Tools**, and then **Startup**. Open the **Display Form** drop-down list and select **[None]**. Click **OK**.

After you close the Switchboard window, you see the Database window. If it's minimized, double-click its title bar (bottom-left corner of the screen) to reopen it. Click the **Tables** object type, and you see that several tables have been created for you. Click the other object types to see the other objects created, as well.

Although you might have all the tables, reports, and forms you need, you might still want to go through the lessons in this book in chronological order to learn about creating and modifying these objects. If you're in a hurry to enter data, though, skip to Lesson 8, "Entering Data into a Table," where you'll learn how to enter data into a table, or the end of Lesson 12, where you'll learn about data entry on a form.

Saving a Database

Before you close Access or turn off the computer, you need to save your work so that you don't lose anything you've typed .

When you created the database, you saved it by naming it. When you enter each record, Access automatically saves your work. (You learn how to enter records in Lesson 8.) You don't need to save your work until you're ready to close your database.

When you change the structure of a table, form, or other object, Access won't let you close that object or close the database without confirming whether you want to save your changes. You'll see a dialog box like the one in Figure 4.7; just click **Yes** to save your changes. If you have the Office Assistant enabled, the same question appears in a thought bubble over its head instead of in a dialog box. For more on the Office Assistant, see Appendix B, "Using the Office Help System."

Figure 4.7   When you change an object's structure, Access asks whether it should save your changes.

Notice that the Save and Save As commands on the File menu aren't even available most of the time; they're grayed out. When you have a particular object highlighted in the Database window, such as a table, the Save As/ Export command is available. You can use this command to save your table in a different format that another program (such as Excel) can read.

TIP   **Copy Tables to Other Programs by Using Copy and Paste Commands**   Highlight the table in the Database window and select **Edit**, and then **Copy**. Then open a different database or application and select **Edit**, and then **Paste**. A dialog box opens, which might give you the options of pasting the table structure only or the structure and its data. You can also choose to append the data to existing tables if the fields match up.

Closing a Database

When you finish working with a database, close it. When you finish using Access, just exit the program (see Lesson 3, "Working in Access"), and the database closes along with the program. If you want to close the database and then open another, however, do any of the following:

- Double-click the Control menu icon (in the top-left corner) for the database (see Figure 4.8).

- Click the Database window's **Close** (×) button (at the top-right corner).

- Click the Database window's **Open** button to close the current database and open a new one.

Can I Have More Than One Database Open?   Sure, you can. In fact, you might want several open so you can transfer data between them. However, if your computer is short on memory (less than 16MB), you'll find that Access runs faster when you close all files that you're not using.

CAUTION

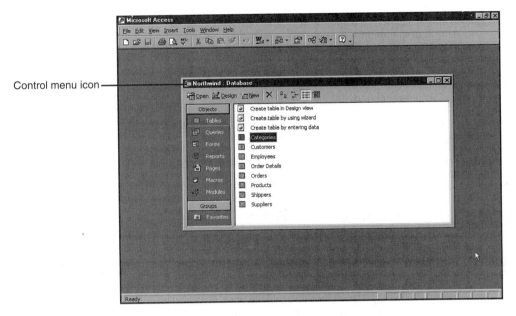

Control menu icon

Figure 4.8   You can close a database in several ways.

Opening a Database

When you start Access the next time you want to use your database, you won't create a new one from scratch, you'll open your existing one.

The easiest way to open a database you've recently used is to select it from the File menu. Follow these steps:

1. Open the **File** menu. You'll see up to nine databases you've recently used listed at the bottom of the menu.

2. Click the database you want to open.

TIP   **Want to See More Files?**   To increase the number of files displayed in this list, open the **Tools** menu and select **Options**. Then, from the **General** tab of the Options dialog box, select a number from 1 to 9 in the **Recently Used Files** drop-down list.

If the database you want to open isn't listed, you need to use the following procedure instead:

1. Select **File**, and then **Open**, or click the toolbar's **Open** button. The Open dialog box appears (see Figure 4.9).

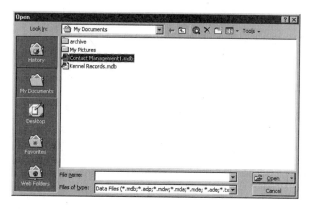

Figure 4.9 Open a different database file from within the Open dialog box.

2. If the file isn't in the currently displayed folder, browse drives and folders.

3. Double-click the file to open it.

TIP **New Feature** In Access 2000, the **Open** button in the Open dialog box has a drop-down list: **Open Read-Only** prevents changes from being saved to the database, **Open Exclusive** prevents another user from working on the database while you have it open, and **Open Exclusive Read-Only** does both. Any of these selections helps prevent inadvertent changes to a valuable database.

In this lesson, you learned how to create a database from scratch and how to use a Database Wizard. In addition, you learned how to save, close, and open a database. In the next lesson, you learn how to create a table by using the Table Wizard.

Creating a Table with the Table Wizard

In this lesson, you learn how to create a table by using the Table Wizard. To learn how to create a table from scratch, see the next lesson.

Why Create a Table?

Tables are the basis for the whole database. If you created an empty database in Lesson 4, "Creating a New Database," you'll need to create tables now, following the plan you developed in Lesson 2, "Planning Your Database." If you used a Database Wizard to create your tables, you can create new tables here to augment them, or you can skip to Lesson 7, "Editing Tables," where you'll learn to modify and customize the tables.

The Table Wizard can save you a lot of time by creating and formatting all the right fields for a certain purpose. Access comes with dozens of premade business and personal tables from which to choose. You can pick and choose among all the fields in all the premade tables, constructing a table that's right for your needs. Even if you can't find all the fields you need in premade tables, you might want to use the Table Wizard to save time, and then add the missing fields later (see Lesson 7).

How Can I Know Beforehand? You won't know exactly what premade fields Access offers until you start the Table Wizard and review the listings. If you find that no tables meet your needs, you can click **Cancel** at any time and start creating your own table (see Lesson 6, "Creating a Table from Scratch").

Creating a Table with the Table Wizard

If the fields you want to create are similar to any of Access's dozens of premade ones, the Table Wizard can save you a lot of time and effort. With the Table Wizard, you can copy fields from any of the dozens of sample tables.

To create a table using the Table Wizard, follow these steps:

1. In the Database window, click the **Tables** object and then double-click **Create Table by Using Wizard**.

TIP   Other Methods   Instead of following step 1, you can open the New Table dialog box (by either clicking the **New** button in the Database window or choosing **Insert**, and then **Table**). Then in the New Table dialog box, choose **Table Wizard** and click **OK**.

2. On the first Table Wizard dialog box (see Figure 5.1), click either **Business** or **Personal**. This determines the list of sample tables that appears.

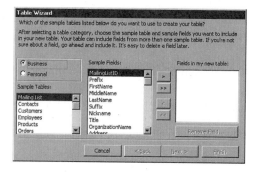

Figure 5.1   Choose your table's fields from those that come with any of the premade tables.

3. Choose a table from the **Sample Tables** list; its fields appear in the Sample Fields list.

4. Look at the **Sample Fields** list. If you see a field that you want to include in your new table, select it and then click the > button to move it to the **Fields in My New Table** list. To move the entire contents of the selected sample table to your list, click the >> button.

TIP **Name Change!** If you see a field that's close to what you want but you prefer a different name for it, first add it to your list (see steps 3 and 4). Then click the field name to select it; click the **Rename Field** button, type a new name, and click **OK**. This renames the field on your list only, not on the original.

5. Repeat steps 3 and 4 to select more fields from more sample tables until the list of fields in your new table is complete. You can remove a field from the list by clicking the < button. (You can also remove all the fields and start over by clicking the << button.) When you're finished adding fields, click **Next** to continue.

6. You're asked for a name for the table. Type a more descriptive name to replace the default one.

7. Click **Yes, Set a Primary Key for Me** to have the wizard choose your primary key field, or **No, I'll Set the Primary Key** to do it yourself. (If you choose Yes, skip to step 10.)

TERM **Primary Key** The designated field for which every record must have a unique entry. This is usually an ID number because most other fields could conceivably be the same for more than one record (for instance, two people might have the same first name).

8. Next, the wizard asks which field will be the primary key (see Figure 5.2). Open the drop-down list and select the field.

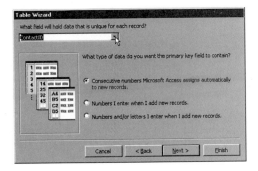

Figure 5.2 You can set your own primary key for the table.

469

9. Choose a data type for the primary key field:

- **Consecutive Numbers Microsoft Access Assigns Automatically to New Records**—Choose this if your primary key field is a simple record number—that is, if you want Access to number the records consecutively as you enter them.

- **Numbers I Enter When I Add New Records**—Pick this to enter your own numbers (Access won't let you enter any letters). This choice works well for unique ID numbers such as drivers' licenses.

- **Numbers and/or Letters I Enter When I Add New Records**—Pick this if you want to include both numbers and letters in the field. For instance, if your primary key field is a vehicle identification number for the cars in your fleet, you will need to enter both numbers and letters.

10. Click **Next** to continue.

11. If you already have at least one table in this database, a screen appears, offering to create relationships between tables. Just click **Next** to move past it for now; you'll learn about relationships in Lesson 11, "Creating Relationships Between Tables."

12. At the Finish screen, click one of the following options:

- **Modify the Table Design**—This takes you into Table Design view, the same as if you had created all those fields yourself. Choose this if you have some changes you want to make to the table before you use it.

- **Enter Data Directly into the Table**—This takes you to Table Datasheet view, where you can enter records into the rows of the table. Choose this if the table's design seems perfect to you as is.

- **Enter Data into the Table Using a Form the Wizard Creates for Me**—This jumps you ahead a bit in this book; it leads you right into the Form Wizard covered in Lesson 12, "Creating a Simple Form." Leave this one alone for now if you want to continue following along in order with the lessons in this book.

13. Click **Finish** to move where you indicated you wanted to go in step 12.

If you decide you don't want to work with this table right now (no matter what you selected in step 12), just click the **Close** (×) button for the window that appears.

Now you have a table. In the Database window, when you click the **Tables** icon, you can see your table on the list. Figure 5.3 shows two tables.

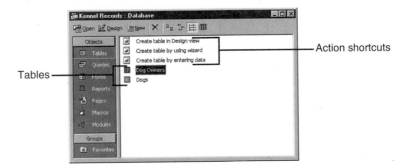

Figure 5.3   Now you have at least one table on your Tables list.

In this lesson, you learned how to create a new table by using the Table Wizard. In the next lesson, you learn how to create a table without the wizard.

Creating a Table from Scratch

In this lesson, you learn how to create a table in Table Design view.

Why Not Use a Wizard?

Access's wizards are very useful, but they don't offer as much flexibility as performing the equivalent tasks from scratch. For instance, if you want to create a table that contains special fields not available in a wizard, you are better off creating that table in Table Design view. You learn how in this lesson.

Creating a Table in Table Design View

To create a table in Table Design view, follow these steps:

1. In the Database window, double-click **Create Table in Design View**. Table Design view opens (see Figure 6.1).

 TIP   **Other Methods**   Instead of step 1, you can choose **Insert** and then **Table**, or click the **New** button in the Database window to open the New Table dialog box. Then click **Design View** and then **OK**.

2. Type a field name on the first empty line of the **Field Name** column. Then press **Tab** to move to the Data Type column.

3. When you move to the Data Type column, an arrow appears for a drop-down list. Open the **Data Type** drop-down list and select a field type. (If you don't make a choice, the field will be a text field by default.) See the section "Understanding Data Types and Formats" later in this lesson if you need help deciding which field type to use.

Start typing the first field name here.

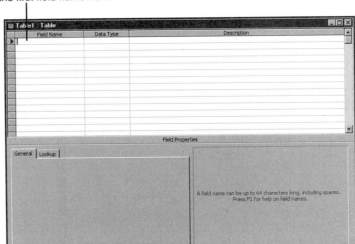

Figure 6.1 From Table Design view, you can control the entire table creation process.

CAUTION

Field Naming Rules Field names in Access can be up to 64 characters long and can contain spaces if you like, and any symbols except periods (.), exclamation marks (!), accent grave symbols (`), or square brackets ([]). Avoid punctuation marks (such as $, %, or #) in field names, because some of them have special meanings in Access code.

4. Press **Tab** to move to the Description column and type a description of the field. (This is optional; the table will work fine without it.)

5. In the bottom half of the dialog box, you see Field Properties for the field type you selected (see Figure 6.2). Make any changes to them that you want. See "Understanding Data Types and Formats" later in this lesson for help.

6. If you have more fields to enter, repeat steps 2 through 5.

7. Click the Table Design window's **Close** (×) button.

8. When you're asked if you want to save your changes to the table, click **Yes**. The Save As dialog box appears.

9. Type a name for the table in the **Table Name** text box, and then click **OK**.

473

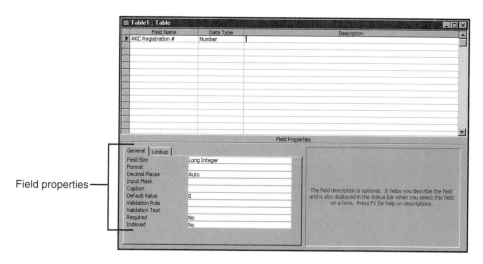

Field properties —

Figure 6.2 Field properties change depending on the field type.

 TIP **Switching Between Views** At any time after you enter the first field, you can switch to Datasheet view to see how your table will look. Just select **View**, and then **Datasheet**. You might be asked to save your work before you enter Datasheet view; if so, click **Yes**, enter a name, and then click **OK**.

 No Primary Key! When you close Table Design view, you might get a message that no primary key has been assigned. See the "Setting the Primary Key" section later in this lesson to learn about this.

CAUTION

Understanding Data Types and Formats

Each field must have a type so that Access will know how to handle its contents. Here are the types you can choose from:

Text	Plain, ordinary typing, which can include numbers, letters, and symbols. A Text field can contain up to 255 characters.
Memo	More plain, ordinary text, except you don't set a maximum field length, so you can type an almost infinite amount of text (64,000 characters).

Number	A plain, ordinary number (not currency or a date). Access won't allow any text.
Date/Time	Simply a date or a time.
Currency	A number formatted as an amount of money.
AutoNumber	Access automatically fills in a consecutive number for each record.
Yes/No	The answer to a true/false question. It can contain one of two values: Yes or No, True or False, On or Off.
OLE Object	A link to another database or file (see Appendix C, "Object Linking and Embedding").
Hyperlink	A link to a location on the Web.
Lookup Wizard	Lets you create a list to choose a value from another table or list of values in a combo box for each record. It's an advanced feature that you'll learn more about in Lesson 14, "Adding Controls to Forms."

In addition to a field type, each field has formatting options you can set. They appear in the bottom half of the dialog box, in the Field Properties area. The formatting options change depending on the field type; there are too many to list here, but following are some of the most important ones you'll encounter:

Field Size	The maximum number of characters a user can input in that field (applies only to Text fields).
Format	A drop-down list of the available formats for that field type. You can also create custom formats.
Decimal Places	For number fields, you can set the default number of decimal places a number shows.
Default Value	If a field is usually going to contain a certain value (for instance, a certain zip code for almost everyone), you can enter it here to save time. It will always appear in a new record, and you can type over it in the rare instances when it doesn't apply.
Required	Choose Yes or No to tell Access whether a user should be allowed to leave this field blank when entering a new record.

Setting the Primary Key

Every table should have at least one field that has a unique value for each record. For instance, in a table of the dogs your kennel owns, you might assign an ID number to each dog and have an ID number field in your table. Or you might choose to use each dog's AKC (American Kennel Club) registration number. This unique identifier field is known as the *primary key field*.

 Primary Key Field The designated field for which every record must have a unique entry is usually an ID number because most other fields could conceivably be the same for more than one record (for instance, two people might have the same first name).

You must tell Access which field you're going to use as the primary key so it can prevent you from accidentally entering the same value for more than one record in that field. To set a primary key, follow these steps:

1. In Table Design view, select the field that you want for the primary key.

 2. Select **Edit** and then **Primary Key**, or click the **Primary Key** button on the toolbar. A key symbol appears to the left of the field name, as shown in Figure 6.3.

Key symbol —

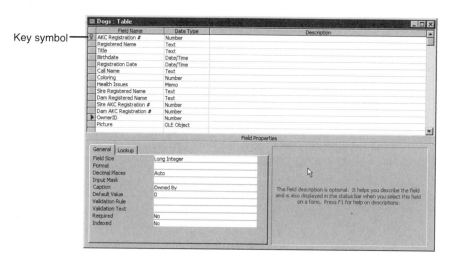

Figure 6.3 The primary key field is marked by a key symbol.

Switching Between Design and Datasheet Views

When you're working with tables, two views are available: Design and Datasheet. One easy way to switch between the views is by clicking the down arrow next to the **View** button on the toolbar (see Figure 6.4). Then select the view you want from the drop-down list that appears.

Figure 6.4 Choose the view you want from the View button's drop-down list.

Another way to switch between views is as follows:

1. Open the **View** menu.
2. Select **Table Design** or **Datasheet**, depending on which view you're now in.
3. If you're moving from Table Design to Datasheet view, you might be asked to save your work. If so, click **Yes**.
4. If you're asked for a name for the table, type one and click **OK**.

In this lesson, you learned to create a table without the help of a wizard. In the next lesson, you learn how to edit and enhance your table.

Editing Tables

In this lesson, you learn how to change your table by adding and removing fields and hiding columns.

Editing Fields and Their Properties

Now that you've created a table, you might be eager to begin entering records into it. You'll learn to do that in Lesson 8, "Entering Data into a Table." Before you begin, make certain that your table is structured exactly as you want it so you don't have to backtrack later. You also might want to work through Lesson 11, "Creating Relationships Between Tables," before you start your data entry.

No matter how you created your table (either with or without the Table Wizard), you can modify it by using Table Design view. If you created the table without the Table Wizard, Table Design view will look very familiar to you.

To enter Table Design view, do one of the following:

- From the Database window, click the **Table** object type, select the table you want to work with, and click the **Design** button or press **Alt+D**.
- If the table appears in Datasheet view, select **View**, and then **Design View**.
- From the Database window, right-click the table name and select **Design View** from the shortcut menu.

Don't forget that you can quickly change views with the **View** button at the far-left end of the Standard toolbar. (Refer to Figure 6.4 in the preceding lesson.) Click the down arrow next to the button and select a view from the list that appears.

When you're in Table Design view (see Figure 7.1), you can edit any field. Here is the general procedure:

1. Click any field name in the **Field Name** column.

2. If desired, click the field's **Data Type** area and select a new data type from the drop-down list.

3. In the **Field Properties** pane (the bottom half of the Table Design window), click any text box to change its value. Some text boxes have drop-down lists, which you can activate by clicking in the box.

4. Repeat steps 1 through 3 for each field you want to change.

Click here to list the
different data types.

Field properties

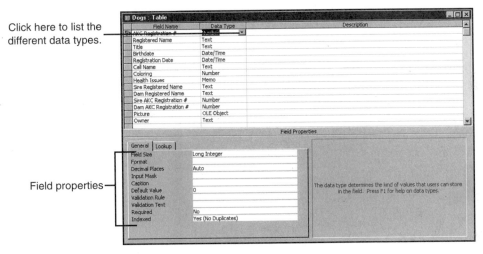

Figure 7.1 In Table Design view, you can modify the attributes of any field.

CAUTION

I Need More Help! If you created your table without a wizard, the preceding steps are self-explanatory. However, if you used the Table Wizard, you might be lost right now. Review Lesson 6, "Creating a Table from Scratch," to get up to speed.

Adding Fields

Before you enter data into your table (see Lesson 8), you should make very sure that you have included all the fields you'll need. Why? Because if you add a field later, you might have to go back and enter a value in that field for each record that you already entered. Also, if you change the field length, you risk truncating or invalidating data that has already been entered.

You can add a field in either Table Design or Datasheet view. Try it in Table Design view first because you're already there:

1. Click the record selector (the gray square to the left of the field name) to select the field before which you want the new field to appear (the entire row is now highlighted in black.

2. Press the **Insert** button on the keyboard, click the **Insert Rows** button on the toolbar, or select **Insert**, and then **Row**. A blank row appears in the Field Name list.

3. Enter a name, type, description, and so on for the new field.

Deleting Fields

If you realize that you don't need one or more fields that you created, now is the time to get rid of them. Otherwise, you'll needlessly enter information that you will never use into each record.

Don't Remove Important Fields! Be very careful about deleting fields after you start entering records in your table. When you delete a field, all the information stored for each record in that field is gone too. The best time to experiment with deleting fields is now, before you enter any records.

You can remove fields in either Table Design or Datasheet view. To delete a field in Table Design view, follow these steps:

1. Switch to Table Design view if you're not already there.

2. Select a field.

3. Do any of the following:

    • Press the **Delete** key on your keyboard.

     • Click the **Delete Rows** button on the toolbar.

    • Select **Edit**, and then **Delete Rows**.

The Delete Key Won't Work You can't delete a table column (field) in Datasheet view by using the **Delete** key—you must use the menu selection.

If you prefer, you can delete the field in Datasheet view. Unlike adding fields, where an advantage exists to using Table Design view, you can accomplish a field deletion easily in either view, and in Datasheet view you can see the data already entered into the field. Follow these steps to delete a field in Datasheet view.

1. Switch to Datasheet view if you're not already there.
2. Click the column heading to select the entire column for the field you want to delete.
3. Select **Edit**, and then **Delete Column**.

Hiding a Field

If you don't want to use a field at the moment but will want to later, you might want to hide it rather than delete it. Hiding a field has two advantages:

- If you've entered any records, you can preserve any data you entered into that field.
- The Field Properties you set when you created the field remain intact, so you don't have to reenter them later.

You must hide a field by using Datasheet view; you can't hide it using Table Design view. Follow these steps:

1. Switch to Datasheet view if you aren't there already.
2. Select the field(s) you want to hide.
3. Select **Format** and then **Hide Columns**, or right-click the columns and select **Hide Columns**. The columns disappear.

To unhide the column(s) later, follow these steps:

1. Select **Format**, and then **Unhide Columns**. The Unhide Columns dialog box appears (see Figure 7.2). Fields with a check mark next to them are unhidden; fields without a check mark are hidden.
2. Click the check box of any field that you want to change. Clicking the box switches between hidden and unhidden status.
3. Click **Close**.

481

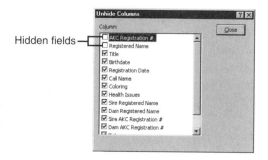

Figure 7.2 You can unhide or hide fields with the Unhide Columns dialog box.

Hidden fields are still very much a part of your database. As proof of that, you'll still see them in Table Design view, along with all other fields.

Deleting a Table

Now that you've created a table and worked with it a bit, you might discover that you made so many mistakes in creating it that it would be easier to start over. (Don't feel bad; that's what happened to me the first time.) Or you might have several tables by now and find that you don't need all of them. Whatever the reason, it's easy to delete a table. Follow these steps:

1. From the Database window, click the **Tables** object type.
2. Select the table you want to delete.
3. Select **Edit** and then **Delete**, or press the **Delete** key on your keyboard.
4. A message appears asking whether you're sure you want to do this. Click **Yes**.

Cut Versus Delete You can also cut a table. Cutting is different from deleting because the table isn't gone forever; it moves to the Clipboard. From there, you can paste it into a different database or into some other application.

In this lesson, you learned how to modify your table by adding and removing fields, hiding fields, and editing the information about each field. In the next lesson, you learn how to enter records, move around in a table, and how to print and close a table.

Entering Data into a Table

8

*In this lesson, you learn how to add
records to a table, print the table, and close it.*

Entering a Record

By now, you've created your table structure and fine-tuned it with the settings
you want. It's finally time to enter records! So open the table and start.

TIP **Other Ways to Enter Records** Entering records directly into a table,
which you learn how to do in this lesson, isn't always the best way to enter
records. If you have many records to enter, it's often more efficient in the long
run to take the time to create a form in which to do your data entry. You learn
how to create a form in Lesson 12, "Creating a Simple Form."

If you read Lessons 1, "What Is a Database?" and 2, "Planning Your Database,"
you know that a record is a row in your table. It contains information about a
specific person, place, event, or whatever. You enter a value for each record into
each field (column) in your table.

First, you must open the table. Remember, to open a table, you double-click it
in the Database window, or click it once and then click **Open**. Then follow these
steps to enter a record.

There's a Number in the First Column! If you've set up the first field to
be automatically entered (for instance, a sequentially numbered field with
AutoNumber), start with the second field instead.

CAUTION

1. Click the first empty cell in the first empty column.

Cell or Field? The intersection of a row and a column. It's where you enter the data for a field for a particular record. Sometimes, the word *field* is used to mean the entry in a field for an individual record, but *field* really refers to the entire column. *Cell* is the proper name for an individual block.

2. Type the value for that field.

3. Press **Tab** to move to the next field and type its value.

4. Continue pressing **Tab** until you get to the last field. When you press **Tab** in the last field, the insertion point moves to the first field in the next line, where you can start a new record.

Insertion Point When you click a field, you see a blinking vertical line, called an *insertion point*, which tells you that's where anything you type will appear.

5. Continue entering records until you've entered them all.

Using Data-Entry Tricks

You can enter all your data with nothing more than the Tab key and some typing, but here are a few keyboard tricks that make the job easier:

- To insert the current date, press **Ctrl+;** (semicolon). To insert the current time, press **Ctrl+:** (colon).
- To repeat the value from the same field in the previous record, press **Ctrl+'** (apostrophe).

Moving Around in a Table

In the earlier steps, you pressed Tab to move from field to field in the table, but you might find other ways to move around that are even more convenient. For instance, you can click in any field at any time to move the insertion point there. Table 8.1 summarizes the many keyboard shortcuts for moving around in a table.

Table 8.1 Table Movement Keys

To Move To...	Press
Next field	Tab
Previous field	Shift+Tab
Last field in the record	End
First field in the record	Home
Same field in the next record	↓
Same field in the previous record	↑
Same field in the last record	Ctrl+↓
Same field in the first record	Ctrl+↑
Last field in the last record	Ctrl+End
First field in the first record	Ctrl+Home

Printing a Table

Normally, you won't want to print a table—it won't look very pretty. A table is just a plain grid of rows and columns. Instead, you'll want to create and print a report that contains exactly the data you want (see Lesson 19, "Creating a Simple Report").

Sometimes, however, you might want a quick printout of the raw data in the table. In that case, follow these steps:

1. Open the table (by double-clicking it or by choosing it and clicking **Open**).

 2. Click the **Print** button on the toolbar. The table prints.

 TIP **More Printing Control** You can set some printing options before you print. Instead of clicking the **Print** toolbar button, choose **Print** from the **File** menu and select your printing options from the Print dialog box. Then click **OK** to print.

Closing a Table

By now you've probably discovered that a table is just another window; to close it, you simply click its **Close** button (×), press **Ctrl+F4**, or double-click its Control-menu box (see Figure 8.1).

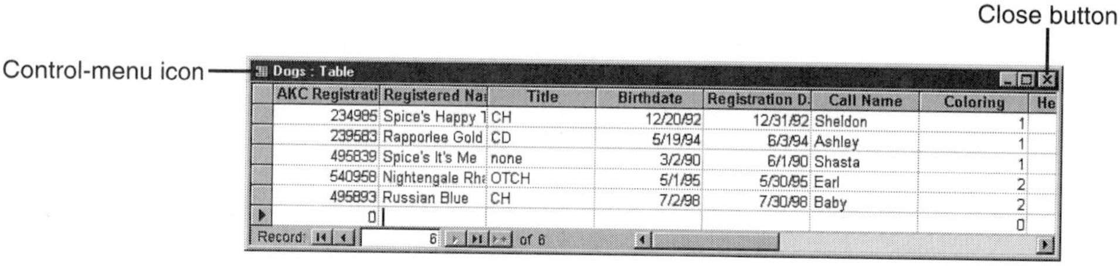

Figure 8.1   Close a table the same way you would close any window.

In this lesson, you learned how to enter records into a table, how to print the table, and how to close it. In the next lesson, you learn how to edit your table data.

To Move	Press
One word to the right	Ctrl+→
One word to the left	Ctrl+←
To the end of the line	End
To the end of the cell	Ctrl+End
To the beginning of the line	Home
To the beginning of the cell	Ctrl+Home

Selecting Records

In addition to editing individual cells in a record, you might want to work with an entire record. To do this, click the gray square to the left of the record (the record selection area). The entire record appears highlighted (white letters on black), as shown in Figure 9.3.

Record selection area

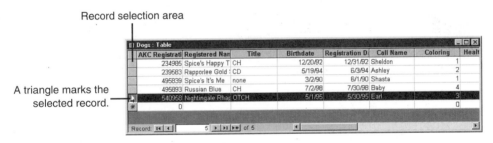

A triangle marks the selected record.

Figure 9.3 The highlighted, selected record.

You can select several records as a group (select the first one and hold down **Shift** while you select the others). You can select only contiguous groups of records; you can't pick them from all over the list.

 TIP **Selecting All Records** You can select all records at once in several ways. Click the blank box at the intersection of the row and column headings; select the **Edit** menu and click **Select All Records**; or press **Ctrl+A**.

Understanding Record Selection Symbols

When you select a record, a triangle appears in the record selection area (refer to Figure 9.3). You might see two other symbols in this area, too:

 Being entered or edited

 Empty line for next new record

CAUTION

Only One Triangle   If you select several records, only the first one you click will have the triangle symbol next to it. That doesn't matter, however; they're all equally selected.

Inserting New Records

New records are inserted automatically. When you start to type a record, a new line appears below it, waiting for another record, as you can see in Figure 9.3. You can't insert new records between existing ones; you must always insert new records at the end of the table.

TIP   **What If I Want the Records in a Different Order?**   It's easy to sort your records in any order you want. You learn how to sort in Lesson 16, "Sorting, Filtering, and Indexing Data."

Deleting Records

If you find that one or more records is out of date or doesn't belong in the table, you can easily delete it. You can even delete several records at a time. Follow these steps:

1. Select the record(s) you want to delete.

2. Do any of the following:

- Click the **Delete Records** button on the toolbar.
- Press the **Delete** key on the keyboard.
- Select the **Edit** menu and choose **Delete**.
- Select the **Edit** menu and choose **Delete Record**.
- Right-click the record(s) and choose **Delete Record**.

Delete Versus Delete Record If you select the entire record, no difference exists between these two commands. If you don't select the entire record, however, Delete removes only the selected text, whereas Delete Record removes the entire record. You can't undo a deletion, so be careful what you delete.

Moving and Copying Data

As with any Windows program, you can use the Cut, Copy, and Paste commands to copy and move data. Follow these steps:

1. Select the field(s), record(s), cell(s), or text that you want to move or copy.

2. Open the **Edit** menu and select **Cut** (to move) or **Copy** (to copy). Or press **Ctrl+X** to cut or **Ctrl+C** to copy.

3. Position the insertion point where you want to insert the cut or copied material.

4. Choose **Paste** from the **Edit** menu. Or, press **Ctrl+V** to paste.

    Toolbar Shortcuts—Cut, Copy, and Paste buttons can also be found on the toolbar.

You can move and copy entire objects, not only individual fields and records. From the Database window, select the table, report, query, and so on, that you want to move or copy; then use the **Cut** or **Copy** command. Move where you want the table to go (for example, in a different database) and execute the **Paste** command.

In this lesson, you learned how to edit data in a field, how to insert and delete fields, and how to copy and move data from place to place. In the next lesson, you learn how to format your table.

Making Tables Look Great

10

In this lesson, you learn how to improve the look of a table by adjusting the row and column sizes, changing the font, and choosing a different alignment.

Why Format a Table?

Most people don't spend a lot of time formatting Access tables simply because they don't have to look at or print their tables. They use data-entry forms to see the records onscreen, and reports to print their records. The tables are merely holding tanks for raw data.

However, creating forms and reports might be more work than you want to tackle right now. For instance, if your database is very simple—consisting of one small table—you might want to add enough formatting to your table to make it look fairly attractive; then you can use it for all your viewing and printing, forgoing the fancier forms and reports.

Even if you decide later to use a form or report, you might still want to add a bit of formatting to your table so it will be readable if you ever need to look at it.

Changing Column Width and Row Height

One common problem with a table is that you can't see the complete contents of the fields. Fields often hold more data than will fit across a column's width, so the data in your table appears cut off.

You can fix this problem in two ways: make the column wider, so it can display more data, or make the row taller, so it can display more than one line of data.

Changing Column Width

Access offers many ways to adjust column width in a table; you can choose the method you like best. One of the easiest ways to adjust column width is to simply drag the column headings. Follow these steps:

1. Position the mouse pointer between two field names (column headings) so that the pointer turns into a vertical line with left- and right-pointing arrows (see Figure 10.1). You'll be adjusting the column on the left; the column on the right will move to accommodate it.

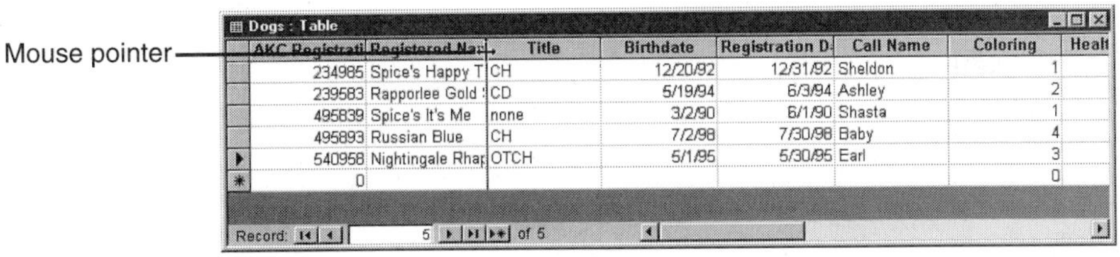

Mouse pointer
Dogs : Table
AKC Registrati Registered Nar Title Birthdate Registration D Call Name Coloring Healt
234985 Spice's Happy T CH 12/20/92 12/31/92 Sheldon 1
239583 Rapporlee Gold CD 5/19/94 6/3/94 Ashley 2
495839 Spice's It's Me none 3/2/90 6/1/90 Shasta 1
495893 Russian Blue CH 7/2/98 7/30/98 Baby 4
540958 Nightingale Rhap OTCH 5/1/95 5/30/95 Earl 3
0 0
Record: 5 of 5

Figure 10.1 Position the mouse pointer between two column headings.

2. Click and hold the mouse button and drag the edge of the column to the right or left to increase or decrease the width.
3. Release the mouse button when the column is the desired width.

Alternatively, you can double-click the column's vertical line when the double-headed arrow is showing, which automatically adjusts the width of the column on the left so its data just fits.

Another, more precise way to adjust column width is to use the Column Width dialog box. Follow these steps:

1. Select the column(s) for which you want to adjust the width.
2. From the **Format** menu choose **Column Width**, or right-click and choose **Column Width** from the shortcut menu. The Column Width dialog box appears (see Figure 10.2).

Column Width
Column Width: 26.5
Standard Width
OK
Cancel
Best Fit

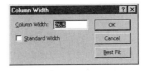

Figure 10.2 Adjust the column width precisely in the Column Width dialog box.

3. Do one of the following to set the column width:

- Adjust the column to exactly the width needed for the longest entry in it by clicking **Best Fit**.
- Set the width to a precise number of field characters by typing a value in the **Column Width** text box.
- Reset the column width to its default value by selecting the **Standard Width** check box.

4. Click **OK** to apply the changes.

Changing Row Height

If you don't want to make a column wider, but you still want to see more of its contents, you can make the rows taller.

 TIP **Which Rows Should I Adjust?** It doesn't matter which row you've selected; the height you set applies to all rows. You can't adjust the height of individual rows.

One way to make rows taller is to drag one—the same as you dragged a column in the preceding section. Position the mouse pointer between two rows in the row selection area, then drag up or down.

Another way is with the Row Height dialog box. It works the same as the Column Width dialog box, except that no Best Fit option is available. Right-click the column, select **Row Height**, and then enter a new height. Alternatively, from the **Format** menu choose **Row Height**, enter the new height, and click **OK**.

Changing the Font and Font Size

Unlike other Access views (such as Report and Form), you can't format individual fields or entries to be different from the rest. You can choose a different font for the display, but it automatically applies to all the text in the table, including the column headings.

Font changes you make in Datasheet view won't appear in your reports, queries, or forms; they're for Datasheet view only.

You might want to make the font smaller so you can see more of the field contents onscreen without bothering to adjust column width. Or you might make the font larger so you can see the table more clearly. You can change the default font used in Datasheet view by choosing **Tools**, and then **Options**, and making the change on the dialog box's Datasheet page.

To choose a different font from the table datasheet, follow these steps:

1. From the **Format** menu choose **Font**. The Font dialog box appears (see Figure 10.3).

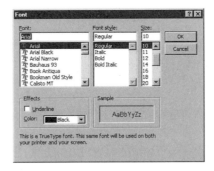

Figure 10.3   The Font dialog box enables you to set one font for the entire table.

2. Select a font from the **Font** list box.
3. Select a style from the **Font Style** list box.
4. Select a size from the **Size** list box.
5. Select a color from the **Color** drop-down list.
6. (Optional) Click the **Underline** check box if you want underlined text.
7. You can see a sample of your changes in the Sample area. When you're happy with the look of the sample text, click **OK**.

Another way you can change the look of your table is with the Datasheet Formatting dialog box (choose **Format**, and then **Datasheet**). You can change the cell special effects, background color, the color of the grid lines between each row and column, and whether the lines show.

In this lesson, you learned how to format a table. In the next lesson, you learn how to create relationships between tables so that you can work with them much as you would a single table.

Creating Relationships Between Tables

In this lesson, you learn how to link two or more tables
so that you can work with them much as you would a single table.

Why Create Relationships?

You've already learned (in Lesson 2, "Planning Your Database") that the best way to design a database is to create tables that hold discrete types of information. For example, one table may contain customer information, and another table may hold order information. By creating relationships between tables, you enable forms, queries, and reports to combine information from the tables to produce meaningful results.

Suppose that you have two tables in your database. One table, Customers, contains names and addresses; the other, Orders, contains orders the customers have placed. The two tables would have a common field: Customer ID. All records in the Orders table would correspond to a record in the Customers table. (This is called a one-to-many relationship because one customer could have many orders.)

As another example, in my kennel database, I have several tables describing my dogs and their activities. I have a table listing the different colorings a dog can have. I could create a relationship between the Dogs table and the Dog Coloring table, matching up each dog's coloring field with one of the accepted colors listed in the Dog Coloring table. This would ensure that I didn't record any dog's coloring as a type that's not allowed.

More Complicated I'm showing you only simple examples in this lesson. For more information on relationships, see your Access documentation or *Using Microsoft Access 2000*, also published by Que.

Creating a Relationship Between Tables

To create a relationship between tables, open the Relationships window and add relationships there. Follow these steps:

1. In the database, select **Tools** and then **Relationships**, or click the **Relationships** button on the toolbar to open the Relationships window.

2. If you haven't selected any tables yet, the Show Table dialog box appears automatically (see Figure 11.1). If it doesn't appear, choose **Relationships**, and then **Show Table**.

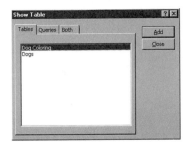

Figure 11.1 Add tables to your Relationships window with the Show Table dialog box.

3. Click a table that you want to use for a relationship, and then click the **Add** button.

4. Repeat step 3 to select all the tables you want, and then click **Close**. Each table appears in its own box on the Relationships window, as shown in Figure 11.2.

TIP **Make It Bigger** If you can't clearly see all the fields in a table's list, drag the table border to make it large enough to see everything. I've done that in Figure 11.2 to make the Dogs table completely visible.

497

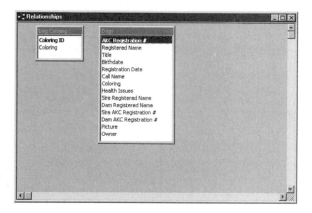

Figure 11.2 I've added two tables to my Relationships window for this example.

5. Click a field in one table that you want to link to another table. For instance, I'm going to link the Coloring field in my Dogs table to the Coloring ID field in my Dog Coloring table, so I'll click the **Coloring** field in the Dogs table.

CAUTION

Field Type Matters The fields to be linked must be of the same data type (date, number, text, and so on). The only exception is that you can link a field with an AutoNumber format to another field with a number format; AutoNumber fields are considered long integer number fields.

6. Hold down the mouse button and drag away from the selected field. Your mouse pointer turns into a little rectangle. Drop the little rectangle onto the destination field. For instance, I'm dragging to the Color ID field in the Coloring table. The Edit Relationships dialog box appears (see Figure 11.3).

Figure 11.3 The Edit Relationships dialog box asks you to define the relationship you're creating.

7. Choose any referential integrity options (see the following section), and then click **Create**. A relationship is created, and you'll see a line between the two fields in the Relationships window (see Figure 11.4).

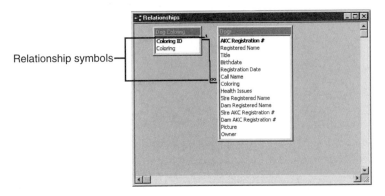

Relationship symbols—

Figure 11.4   The line represents a relationship between the two fields.

 TERM   **Relationship Symbols**   In Figure 11.4, notice that an infinity sign is next to the Dogs table, and the number 1 is next to the Dog Coloring table. These symbols appear in relationships where **Enforce Referential Integrity** is turned on. The infinity sign means *many*—which means that many records in this table can match a single record (hence the number 1) in the related Dog Coloring table.

 TIP   **Multitable Forms**   In Lesson 14, "Adding Controls to Forms," you learn how to use simple tables, such as the Dog Coloring one shown in this lesson, to create a list from which users can select when entering records into a form.

Enforcing Referential Integrity

Referential integrity keeps you from making data-entry mistakes. It means, essentially, that all the information in the two fields should match.

In the Coloring field in my Dogs database, for example, I have a number that matches the Color ID field in the Dog Coloring table. The Coloring table lists all the allowable colors for the breed of dog. I don't want my employees to be able to accidentally enter a number in the Dogs table that doesn't match any of the colors in the Coloring table, so I chose to Enforce Referential Integrity. Now Access won't let anyone enter anything in the Coloring field of the Dogs table (the "many" or infinity side) except one of the numbers contained in the Color ID field in the Coloring table (the 1 side).

What happens if someone tries? It depends on which of the other two check boxes shown in Figure 11.3 are marked.

Here is a summary of what happens with the check boxes:

- **Cascade Update Related Fields**—If this check box is marked, and if you make a change to the related table (in our example, the Dog Coloring table), the change is made in the other table, too (the Dogs table). For instance, if I decided to change a certain coloring number from 7 to 8, and I made the change in the Dog Coloring table (the 1 side), all the 7s in the Dog table (the many side) would change to 8s.
- **Cascade Delete Related Fields**—If this check box is marked, and you make a change to the 1 table (for instance, Dog Coloring) so that the entries in the related table aren't valid anymore, Access deletes the entries in the related table. If I deleted the record in the Dog Coloring table for Coloring ID number 3, all the dogs from my Dogs table that had coloring number 3 would also be deleted. (I would probably *not* want that!)
- **Neither check box is marked**—Access gives an error message that you need a related record in the **"[Table Name]"** and won't let you make the entry.

The best time to set up referential integrity is before you enter any data in the tables. However, you can set up relationships after data has been entered. For information about entering data in your tables, see Lesson 8, "Entering Data into a Table."

If you try to create a relationship with referential integrity after you've already entered some data into one or both of the tables, you might see an error message the first time you try. Perhaps one of the fields uses a data type of Text, for example, and the other uses Number. (It wouldn't matter that you had entered only numbers in the field with the Text data type.) Carefully read whatever error message appears, and troubleshoot by making changes to the table design.

Editing a Relationship

When a relationship is created, you can edit it by redisplaying the Relationships window (refer to Figure 11.2). To do so, double-click the relationship's line. From there, you can edit the relationship by using the same controls as when you created it.

Removing a Relationship

To delete a relationship, just click it in the Relationships window (the line between the tables turns bold to indicate selection), and then press **Delete**. Access asks for confirmation; click **Yes**, and the relationship disappears.

In this lesson, you learned how to create, edit, and delete relationships between tables. In the next lesson, you learn how to create forms using a help wizard or using tools to create forms from scratch.

Creating a
Simple Form

In this lesson, you learn how to create a form with and without the Form Wizard.

Why Create Forms?

As you saw in Lessons 8, "Entering Data into a Table," and 9, "Editing Data in a Table," you can do all your data entry and editing in a table, but that might not be the best way. One reason is that unless you set your column widths very wide, you probably can't see everything you type into a field. Also, if you have data you want to enter into several tables, you must open each table individually.

A better data-entry method is to create a form. With a form, you can allot as much space as needed for each field, and you can enter information into several tables at once. You can also avoid the headaches that occur when you try to figure out which record you're working with on a table; generally, each form shows only one record at a time.

You can create a form in three ways:

- AutoForms provide very quick, generic forms that contain all the fields in a single table.
- The Form Wizard helps you create a form by providing a series of dialog boxes in which you can choose the fields and style for the form.
- Creating a form from scratch provides a layout grid on which you place fields. It's the more difficult way, but it provides the most control.

Creating a Form with AutoForm

The easiest way to create a form is with AutoForm. AutoForm simply plunks the fields from a single table into a form; it's the least flexible way, but it's very convenient. Follow these steps:

1. From the Database window, click the **Forms** object type.

 2. Click the **New** button. The New Form dialog box appears (see Figure 12.1).

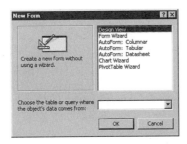

Figure 12.1 Choose how you want to create your form.

3. Click **AutoForm:Columnar** to create a columnar form (the most popular kind). This creates a form that contains your fields in a single column, from top to bottom. Click **AutoForm:Tabular** for a form that resembles a table or **AutoForm:Datasheet** for a form that resembles a datasheet.

4. Open the drop-down list at the bottom of the dialog box and choose the table or query to use as the source of the form's data.

5. Click **OK**. The form appears, ready for data entry.

The form you get with an AutoForm might not be very pretty. The field labels might be cut off, and the fields might be too close together to be attractive. If the form created by AutoForm isn't what you want, delete it and try again with the Form Wizard. To delete the form, close it, and then answer **No** when asked if you want to save your changes.

Creating a Form with the Form Wizard

The Form Wizard offers a good compromise between the automation of AutoForm and the control of creating a form from scratch. Follow these steps to use the Form Wizard:

1. From the Database window, click the **Forms** object type.

2. Double-click **Create Form by Using Wizard**. The Form Wizard opens (see Figure 12.2).

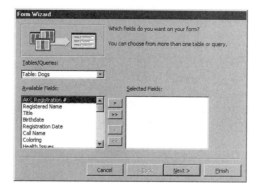

Figure 12.2 The Form Wizard enables you to choose which fields you want to include from as many different tables as you like.

3. From the **Tables/Queries** drop-down list, choose a table or query from which to select fields. (By default, the first table in alphabetical order is selected, which probably isn't what you want.)

4. Click a field in the **Available Fields** list that you want to include on the form, and then click the > button to move it to the Selected Fields list.

5. Repeat step 4 until you've selected all the fields you want to include from that table. If you want to include fields from another table or query, go back to step 3 and choose another table.

TIP **Selecting All Fields** You can quickly move all the fields from the Available Fields list to the Selected Fields list by clicking the **>>** button. If you make a mistake, you can remove a field from the Selected Fields list by clicking it and then clicking the **<** button.

6. Click **Next** to continue. You're asked to choose a layout: **Columnar**, **Tabular**, **Datasheet**, or **Justified**. Click each button to see a preview of that type (Columnar is the most common). Then click the one you want and click **Next**.

7. You're asked to choose a style. Click each style listed to see a preview of it; click **Next** when you've chosen the one you want.

8. Enter a title for the form in the text box at the top of the dialog box.

9. Click the **Finish** button. The form appears, ready for data entry (see Figure 12.3).

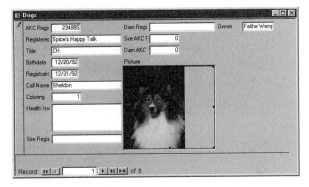

Figure 12.3   The Form Wizard has created this rough but usable form. The first record in the table appears in it.

If your form's field labels are cut off like the ones in Figure 12.3, you should edit the form to move the fields over so there's more room. You learn how to move fields around to improve the look in Lesson 13, "Modifying a Form."

Creating a Form from Scratch

The most powerful and difficult way to create a form is with Form Design view. In this view, you decide exactly where to place each field and how to format it.

The following steps introduce you to Form Design view; you'll learn more about this view in Lesson 13.

CAUTION

Don't Use the Shortcut Now You might be tempted to double-click the Create Form in Design View shortcut in the Forms list, but if you go this route rather than the route outlined in the following steps, you won't have the opportunity to select a table. You can select the table later from the form's RecordSource property, but that's rather advanced. If you're a beginner, it's best to stick with the steps here.

1. From the Database window, click the **Forms** object type.
2. Click the **New** button. The New Form dialog box appears. (You saw this previously in Figure 12.1.)
3. Click **Design View**.
4. Select a table or query from the drop-down list at the bottom of the dialog box. (You can change the table later on, if you need to, from the RecordSource property in the form's properties sheet.)
5. Click **OK**. A Form Design window appears (see Figure 12.4). You're ready to create your form.

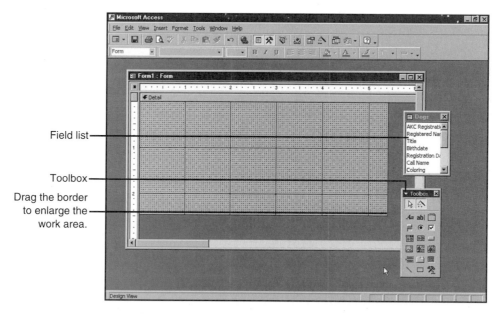

Field list

Toolbox

Drag the border to enlarge the work area.

Figure 12.4 Form Design view presents a blank canvas on which to design your form.

If you later need to add another table to the form's data source, click the **Build** button to the right of the RecordSource property to open the Query Designer. In the Query Designer, you can add a new table to the upper pane and, if necessary, set up a relationship to the original table. After closing the Query Designer, you should see the fields from both tables in the Field list.

 TIP **Toolbox and Field List** You'll want to use the Form Design toolbox and the Field list shown in Figure 12.4. If they're not visible, click the **Toolbox** button or the **Field List** button in the toolbar.

Adding Controls to a Form

The basic idea of the Form Design window is simple: It's similar to a light table or a paste-up board where you place the elements of your form. The fields you add to a form appear in the form's Detail area. The Detail area is the only area visible at first; you'll learn to add other areas in the next lesson.

 TERM **Controls and Fields** When you are working with a table, you work directly with *fields* of data; on forms and reports you work with *controls*, which are elements that display data from a field, hold informative text (such as titles and labels), or are purely decorative (such as lines and rectangles).

To add a control displaying a field to the form, follow these steps:

1. Display the Field list if it's not showing. Click the **Field List** button or choose **Field List** from the **View** menu to do so.

2. Drag a field from the Field list onto the Detail area of the form (see Figure 12.5). The mouse pointer changes to show a field is being placed.

3. Repeat step 2 to add as many fields as you like to the form. Don't worry about crowded labels; you'll fix that in the next lesson.

When you drag a field to a form from the Field list, it becomes a control that displays data from that field. You can drag more than one field to the form at once. In step 2, rather than clicking and dragging a single field, do one of the following before dragging:

- To select a block of fields, click the first one you want and hold down **Shift** while you click the last one.

507

- To select nonadjacent fields, hold down **Ctrl** as you click each one you want.

- To select all the fields on the list, double-click the **Field List** title bar.

The mouse pointer——

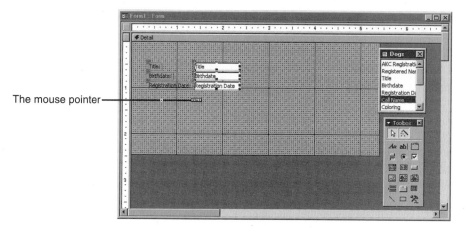

Figure 12.5   Drag fields from the Field list to the grid.

You can move objects around on a form after you initially place them; you'll learn how to do this in the next lesson. Don't worry if your form doesn't look very professional at this point; in the next several lessons, you see how to modify and improve your form.

TIP   **Using Snap to Grid**   If you find it hard to align the fields neatly, choose **Snap to Grid** from the **Format** menu to place a check mark next to that command. If you want to align the fields on your own, select it again to turn it off.

If you are satisfied with your form, go ahead and close it by clicking its **Close** (×) button. When asked if you want to save your changes, choose **Yes**. Type a name for the form in the text box provided, and then click **OK**. If, on the other hand, you want to make more modifications to your form, leave it open and skip to Lesson 13 now.

Entering Data in a Form

The point of creating a form is so that you can enter data more easily into your tables. The form acts as an attractive mask that shields you from the plainness of your table. When you create a form, follow these steps to enter data into it:

1. Open the form:
   - If your form appears in Form Design view, choose **View**, and then **Form View** to enter Form view, or select **Form View** from the **View** button.
   - If the form isn't open at all, click the **Form** tab in the Database window, and then double-click the form's name or click the **Open** button.

2. Click the field you want to begin with and type your data.

3. Press **Tab** to move to the next field. If you need to go back, you can press **Shift+Tab** to move to the previous field. When you reach the last field, pressing **Tab** moves you to the first field in a new, blank record.

   To move to the next record before you reach the bottom field or to move back to previous records, click the right and left arrow buttons on the left end of the navigation bar at the bottom of the window.

4. Repeat steps 2 and 3 to enter all the records you like. They're saved automatically as you enter them.

TIP **Data-Entry Shortcuts** See the "Using Data-Entry Tricks" section in Lesson 8, for some shortcut ideas. They work equally well in forms and tables.

In this lesson, you created a simple form and added data to it. In the next lesson, you learn how to modify and fine-tune your forms.

Modifying a Form

In this lesson, you learn to modify a form. You can use any
form created in any of the ways you learned in the previous lesson.

Cleaning Up Your Form: An Overview

The form you have onscreen now (from Lesson 12, "Creating a Simple Form")
might be functional, but it's probably not attractive. In this lesson, you learn
how to make it look better. Here's an overview of what you need to do to make
a more attractive form:

1. Move the controls as needed to create more space between them. See
the next section, "Moving Field Controls."

2. Adjust the spacing between each control and its label. See "Moving
Controls and Field Labels Independently."

3. Resize any controls or labels so they aren't truncated. See "Changing Field
Lengths."

4. Add any explanatory text. See "Adding Labels."

5. Add form headers and footers, if needed. See "Viewing Headers and
Footers."

6. Add text formatting to the text on your form (for example, make the text
in labels bold or a different font, or make the form header label text large).
See "Formatting Text on a Form."

Moving Field Controls

The most common change to a form is to move a control around. You might want to move several controls down so you can insert a new control, or you might want to rearrange how the controls appear.

 TIP **More Space** If you want to create extra space at the bottom of the controls so that you have more room to move them around, drag the Form Footer pane down so that more of the Detail area is visible. You can also drag the right side of the grid to make the form wider. If you need more space at the top of the form, highlight all the controls and move them down as a group.

Follow these steps:

1. If you aren't already in Form Design view, enter it, as you learned in Lesson 12.

2. Click a control's name to select it. Selection handles appear around it. You can select several controls by holding down **Shift** as you click each one.

3. Position the mouse pointer so that the pointer becomes a hand (see Figure 13.1). If you're moving more than one control, you can position the mouse pointer on any selected control.

Selection handles

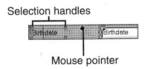

Mouse pointer

Figure 13.1 To move a control, first select it. Then drag it when the mouse pointer is a hand shape.

4. Click and hold down the left mouse button as you drag the control to a different location.

5. Release the mouse button when the control is at the desired new location. You can stretch a control vertically or horizontally from any side, or diagonally from any corner.

CAUTION

The Label Moved Without the Text Box Attached!   Be careful when you position the mouse pointer over the control to be moved. Make sure that the pointer changes to an open hand, as shown in Figure 13.1. If you see a pointing finger, move elsewhere. The pointing finger is used to move controls and labels independently, as you'll learn in the following section.

You can move many controls at once, maintaining the distances among them, by selecting all the controls first and then dragging. To select multiple controls, click each one you want while holding down the **Ctrl** key. Or drag an outline around all the controls you want to select.

Moving Controls and Field Labels Independently

Sometimes you might need to move a control or a field label independently of the other. For example, you might want to make a field's label box longer so that the field name doesn't appear cut off. (The next section shows how to change a control or field label length.) But to do that, you must first move the control to the right to make room for a longer label.

TIP   **Text Boxes: The Most Commonly Used Controls**   Text boxes and their attached labels are discussed in this lesson, but the same methods can be used with other controls that may have attached labels, such as combo boxes and images.

To move a text box or its attached label by itself, follow these steps:

1. Click the control that you want to move.
2. Position the mouse pointer over the selection handle at the top left so that it becomes a pointing finger (see Figure 13.2).
3. Drag the control to a new position.

TIP   **Deleting Labels**   If a certain control is self-explanatory (such as a picture), you might want to delete its attached label. To do so, select the label and press **Delete**.

Figure 13.2   Drag with a pointing-hand mouse cursor to move the control or label independently.

Changing Field Lengths

After you adjust the spacing between each text box and its label (as in the preceding section), follow these steps to change a field control's length:

1. Click the control to select it. Selection handles appear around it.

2. Position the mouse pointer at the right edge; the pointer turns into a double-headed arrow (see Figure 13.3).

3. Drag the control to its new length, and then release the mouse button.

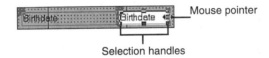

Mouse pointer

Selection handles

Figure 13.3   You can change the size of the control entry area by dragging it.

 TIP   **Multiline Labels**   If the text displayed in a text box or label control is too long to fit in the allotted space, consider making it multiline by dragging its bottom selection handle down. That way, its text can wrap to the next line, and it doesn't require so much space from side to side.

Viewing Headers and Footers

You've been working with the Detail area so far, but you can use other areas:

- Form Header and Form Footer—A place for text that should be repeated at the top or bottom of the form, such as a form title at the top or a copyright notice at the bottom.

- Page Header and Page Footer—A place for text that should be repeated at the top or bottom of every page of the form when you print the form. These aren't displayed by default; to display bars for them, choose **View**, and then **Page Header/Footer**.

When you create a form with the Form Wizard, the Form Header and Form Footer bars appear in Design view, but nothing is in them. And the Form Header bar is butted up against the Detail bar, so the header area has no height.

To make some room to work in the Form Header (see Figure 13.4), click the **Detail Header** bar to select it, position the mouse pointer between the bars, and drag down.

The Detail section contains controls whose data changes with every record. The Form Header contains text you want repeated on each onscreen form. After you display a header or a footer, you can add controls to these sections.

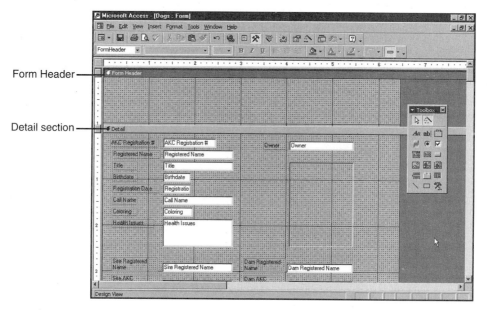

Figure 13.4 Drag the Detail bar down to create space to add text in the header.

Adding Labels

The next thing that most people want to do is add text to the form in the form of label controls to display titles, subtitles, explanatory text, and so on. Add titles and other general information to a header or a footer; add information specific to particular controls to the Detail area. Follow these steps:

1. If the toolbox isn't displayed, choose **Toolbox** from the **View** menu or click the **Toolbox** button on the toolbar.

2. Click the **Label** tool in the toolbox (the one with the italicized letters *Aa* on it). The mouse pointer changes to a capital A with a plus sign next to it (see Figure 13.5).

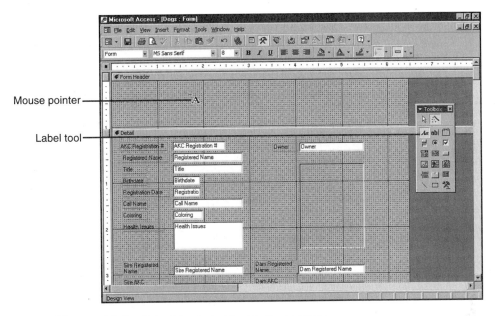

Figure 13.5 Select the Label tool in the toolbox.

3. Click anywhere on the form where you want to create the new text. A tiny box appears. (The box expands to hold the text as you type.)

4. Type the text.

You Must Type the Text Now! If you don't type anything before you go on to step 5, the box disappears as soon as you click away from it.

CAUTION

5. Click anywhere outside the control's area to finish, or press **Enter**.

Don't worry about positioning the label as you create it; you can move a label control in the same way that you move other controls. Just click it, position the mouse pointer so that the hand appears, and then drag it to where you want it to go.

Formatting Text on a Form

After you place all your information on the form (that is, the controls you want to include and labels to display any titles or explanatory text), the next step is to make the form look more appealing.

All the formatting tools you need are on the Formatting toolbar (the second toolbar from the top in Form Design view). Table 13.1 shows the tools. To format a control, just select it, and then click the appropriate formatting tool to apply the format to the control.

Table 13.1   Tools on the Formatting Toolbar

Tool	Purpose
B	Toggles bold on/off
I	Toggles italic on/off
U	Toggles underline on/off
	Left-aligns text
	Centers text
	Right-aligns text
	Fills the selected box with the selected color

Tool	Purpose
A	Colors the text in the selected box
(paint bucket icon)	Colors the outline of the selected box
(border icon) ▼	Adds a border to the selected box
(special effect icon)	Adds a special effect to the selected box

Some tools, such as the font and size tools, are drop-down lists. You click the down arrow next to the tool and then select from the list. Other tools are simple buttons for turning bold and italic on or off. Still other tools, such as the coloring and border tools, combine a button and a drop-down list. If you click the button, it applies the current value. You can click the down arrow next to the button to change the value.

You can change the color of the form background, too. Just click the header for the section you want to change (for instance, **Detail**) to select the entire section. Then right-click and choose **Fill/Back** color to change the color.

TIP **AutoFormat** Here's a shortcut for formatting your form. Choose **Format**, and then **AutoFormat**. You're asked to choose from among several premade color and formatting schemes. If you don't like the formatting after you apply it, press **Ctrl+Z** to undo.

Changing Tab Order

When you enter data on a form, press **Tab** to move from control to control in the order they're shown in the form. The progression from control to control is the *tab order*. When you first create a form, the tab order runs from top to bottom.

When you move and rearrange controls, the tab order doesn't change automatically. For instance, if you had 10 controls arranged in a column and you rearranged them so that the 10th one was at the beginning, the tab order would still show that control in 10th position, even though it's now at the top of the form. This makes it more difficult to fill in the form, so you'll want to adjust the tab order to reflect the new structure of the form.

TIP   **Tab Order Improvements**   To make data entry easier, you might want to change the tab order to be different from the obvious top-to-bottom structure. For instance, if 90% of the records you enter skip several controls, you might want to put those controls last in the tab order so that you can skip over them easily.

Follow these steps to adjust the tab order:

1. Choose **View**, and then **Tab Order**, or right-click the square in the form's upper-left corner and select **Tab Order** from the shortcut menu. The Tab Order dialog box appears (see Figure 13.6).

Figure 13.6   Use the Tab Order dialog box to decide what tab order to use on your form.

2. Choose the section for which you want to set tab order. The default is Detail.

3. The controls appear in their tab order. To change the order, click a control and then drag it up or down in the list.

4. To quickly set the tab order based on the controls' current positions in the form (top to bottom), click the **Auto Order** button.

5. Click **OK**.

In this lesson, you learned how to improve a form by moving controls, adding text, adding formatting, and adjusting the tab order. In the next lesson, you learn about some of the fancier controls you can add to a form.

Adding Controls to Forms

In this lesson, you learn about some special controls you can include on your forms.

Why Use Special Data-Entry Controls?

As you'll see in this lesson, it takes a little extra time to set up one of Access's special data-entry controls on a form. Here are some reasons why you should do it:

- Special data-entry controls make your form look more professional.
- They decrease the amount of typing you have to do when entering records.
- They decrease the possibility of typing errors, making for more reliable data.

Figure 14.1 shows the sample form you'll be working with in this lesson, with a list box, option group, and command buttons already created. You can see how these controls make the form much more attractive and easy to use!

Determining the Controls You Can Add

You can use several controls:

- **List box**—Presents a list from which you choose an item.
- **Combo group**—Like a list box, but you can type in other entries in addition to those on the list.
- **Option box**—Gives you options to choose from (but you can select only one). You can use option buttons, toggle buttons, or check boxes.

- **Command button**—Performs some function when you click it, such as starting another program, printing a report, saving the record, or anything else you specify.

- **Other controls**—In Access 2000, you can place ActiveX controls or any other kind of control or object on a form. For example, you can include a video clip for each record.

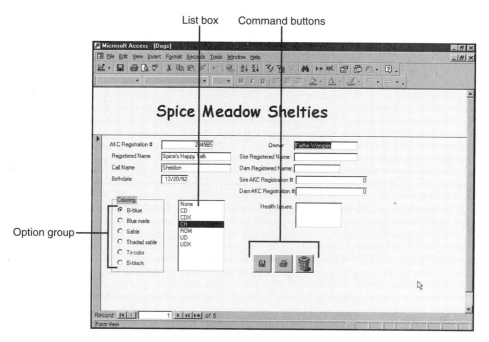

Figure 14.1   Special data-entry controls make the difference.

Access comes with a wizard for most of these control types, which makes it easy for you to use the controls.

For the benefit of advanced users, Access can create these controls with or without the wizards. To make sure that Access knows you want to use wizards, select the **Control Wizards** button in the toolbox (see Figure 14.2). Because creating custom controls without a wizard is rather difficult, this lesson focuses on the wizards.

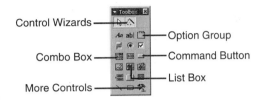

Control Wizards

Combo Box

More Controls

Option Group

Command Button

List Box

Figure 14.2   To use wizards, make sure that the Control Wizards button is selected.

Creating a List Box or Combo Box

A list box or a combo box can come in handy if you find yourself typing certain values repeatedly into a field. For example, if you have to enter the name of one of your 12 branch offices each time you use a form, you might find it easier to create a list box containing the branch office names, and then you can click to select from the list. With a list box, the person doing the data entry is limited to the pretyped choices that display.

A combo box is useful when a list box is appropriate, but it's possible that a different entry might occasionally be needed. For example, if most of your customers come from one of six states, but occasionally you get a new customer from another state, you might use a combo box. During data entry, you could choose the state from the list when appropriate and type a new state when it's not.

Follow these steps to create a list box or combo box from Form Design view:

1. Make sure that the **Control Wizards** button in the toolbox is selected.

2. Click the **List Box** or **Combo Box** button in the toolbox (refer to Figure 14.2). The mouse pointer changes to show the type of box you selected.

3. Drag your mouse to draw a box on the grid where you want the new element to be. When you release the mouse button, the wizard starts.

4. In the wizard's first dialog box, click the button labeled **I Will Type In the Values That I Want**. Then click **Next**.

TIP   **Another Way to Enter Values**   If you prefer, you can create a separate table beforehand containing the values you want to use in this field, and then select **I Want the List Box to Look Up the Values in a Table or Query**. Then choose the table or query rather than type in the values.

5. You're asked to type in the values that you want to appear in the list. Type them in (as shown in Figure 14.3), pressing the **Tab** key after each one. Then click **Next**.

Drag here to change the column width.

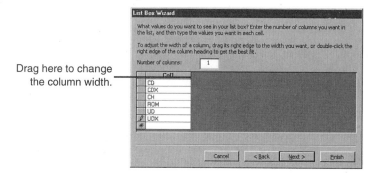

Figure 14.3   Type the values that you want to choose from in this list or combo box.

6. Select **Store That Value in This Field** and choose which field should receive the data. For example, I'm entering the various titles a dog can earn in dog shows, so I'll select the **Title** field here and click **Next**.

7. Type the title that you want to appear for the control (that is, the text of its attached label).

8. Click **Finish**. Your new box appears with the name of the field that you chose in step 6.

9. (Optional) If the list is self-explanatory and doesn't require a label, select the box's field label and press **Delete** to remove it.

CAUTION

Where Are My Values?   Don't be alarmed that the values you entered for the field don't appear in the box. You'll see them in Form view when you drop down the list. You can switch to Form view to see them now if you want to be sure; switch back to Form Design view after you finish looking.

CAUTION

I Picked the Wrong Type!   You can easily switch between a list box and a combo box, even after you create it. In Form Design view, right-click the control, click **Change To**, and select a new control type.

Creating an Option Group

An option group is helpful if you have a few choices for a field entry and never enter anything but those few choices. For instance, if you're recording the results of a multiple-choice quiz, the answer to question 5 is always A, B, C, or D—never anything else.

What About "Other" as a Quiz Answer? If you have a questionnaire in which the respondent can choose A, B, C, or D, or enter another response under Other, you're better off using a combo box on your form because a combo box allows for new entries.

CAUTION

An option group can include toggle buttons, option buttons, or check boxes. These are different styles, but they all do the same thing. You can select only one choice shown in an option group. When you select another, the one you originally selected is deselected.

If you want the look of an option group where you can check several check boxes at once, you can make several standalone check boxes and enclose them within a rectangle.

That's Not How Check Boxes Usually Work! You're right. In almost all Windows programs, check boxes are nonexclusive. You can select as many of them in a group as you like. But in this case, they aren't real check boxes; they're just option buttons that you can style to resemble check boxes or toggle buttons.

CAUTION

To create an option group, follow these steps:

1. Make sure that the **Control Wizards** button in the toolbox is selected.

2. Click the **Option Group** button in the toolbox (refer to Figure 14.2). Your mouse pointer changes to show the Option Group icon.

3. Drag your mouse pointer on your form to draw a box where you want the option group to appear. When you release the mouse button, the wizard starts.

4. The wizard prompts you to enter the values you want for each button (see Figure 14.4). Do so, pressing **Tab** after each one; then click **Next**.

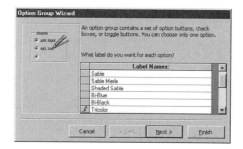

Figure 14.4 Enter the labels you want for each option here.

5. Choose **Yes** or **No** when asked whether you want a default choice. If you choose **Yes**, select the default choice from the drop-down list (this choice appears automatically when you use the form). Then click **Next**.

6. The wizard asks what value you want to assign to each option. Click **Next** to continue; you don't need to change the assigned default values.

7. Click **Store the Value in This Field** and choose which field should receive the data from the drop-down list. For instance, I'm entering the various colors a Shetland Sheepdog can be, so I'll select the Coloring field here and click **Next**.

8. Click to select a type of control (option button, check box, or toggle button) and a style for the controls; then click **Next**.

9. Enter a caption for the option group (for example, **Coloring**). Then click **Finish**. You've created your group.

CAUTION

They're All Marked! When you're in Form Design view, each option in an option group is selected, only to show that it can be. When you're actually using the form, however (in Form view), only one option in the group can be selected at a time. If you don't select a default option (step 5), all options will be gray (neither selected nor unselected) for a record until you choose one.

Adding Command Buttons

You're probably already familiar with command buttons. They're buttons in dialog boxes and elsewhere that you click to perform actions. For example, in Figure 14.1, the form has command buttons to **Save**, **Print**, and **Delete** the current record.

Access offers a wide variety of functions you can perform with command buttons:

- **Record navigation**—You can add command buttons that move users to the next, previous, first, or last record.
- **Record operations**—You can make buttons that delete, duplicate, print, save, or undo a record.
- **Form operations**—Command buttons can print a form, open a page (on a multipage form), close the form, and more.
- **Report operations**—Command buttons can print a report, send a report to a file, mail a report, or preview a report.
- **Application**—Command buttons can exit Access or run some other application.
- **Miscellaneous**—Command buttons can print a table, run a macro, run a query, or use the AutoDialer.

To place a command button on a form, follow these steps:

1. Make sure that the **Control Wizards** button in the toolbox is selected.
2. Click the **Command Button** in the toolbox (refer to Figure 14.2). Your mouse pointer changes to show the Command Button icon.
3. Click your form where you want the command button to appear. The Command Button Wizard opens.
4. Select an action category, and then an action (see Figure 14.5). Then click **Next**.

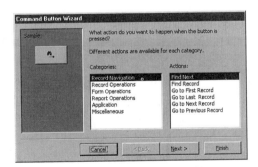

Figure 14.5 Choose what action you want the command button to execute.

5. Depending on your choice of action, another screen of options may be available to choose from. Fill in the extra information if prompted, and then click **Next**.

6. Choose **Text** or **Picture** for the button's face. If you choose **Text**, enter the text you want; if you choose **Picture**, select a picture from the list. Then click **Next**.

7. Type a name for the button.

8. Click **Finish**. The button appears on your form. You can move it around as with any other control.

In this lesson, you learned how to create list and combo boxes, option groups, command buttons, and other controls on your forms. In the next lesson, you learn the most basic ways to search for data in a database using the Find and Replace features.

Searching for Information in Your Database

In this lesson, you learn the most basic ways to search for data in a database using the Find and Replace features.

Using the Find Feature

The Find feature is useful for locating a particular record that you have previously entered. For instance, if you keep a database of customers, you might want to find a particular customer's record quickly when he is ready to make a purchase, so you can verify his address. Or, to continue the kennel example I've been using, you could quickly find the record for the dog with the call name of Sheldon to look up his birth date.

 TIP **Finding More Than One Record** If you need to find several records at once, Find is not the best tool because it finds only one record at a time. A better tool for finding multiple records is a filter, discussed in Lesson 16, "Sorting, Filtering, and Indexing Data."

To find a particular record, follow these steps:

1. Look at your table in Datasheet view or examine its content by using a form. Either view supports the Find feature.

2. Click in the field that contains the data you want to find, if you know which field it is.

3. Click the **Find** tool in the toolbar, select **Edit**, and then **Find**, or press **Ctrl+F**. The Find and Replace dialog box appears (see Figure 15.1) with the Find page on top.

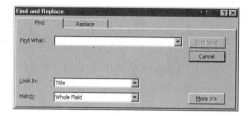

Figure 15.1 Use the Find and Replace dialog box to find data in a record.

4. Type the text or numbers that you want to find into the **Find What** text box.

5. The default value for Look In is the field you selected in step 2. If you want to search the entire table, drop down the **Look In** list and select the table's name.

6. From the **Match** drop-down list, select one of the following:

   - **Whole Field**—Select this to find fields where the specified text is the only thing in that field. For instance, "Smith" would not find "Smithsonian."

   - **Start of Field**—Select this to find fields that begin with the specified text. For instance, "Smith" would find "Smith" and "Smithsonian," but not "Joe Smith."

   - **Any Part of Field**—Select this to find fields that contain the specified text in any way. "Smith" would find "Smith," "Smithsonian," and "Joe Smith."

7. If you want to specify a search direction, search for a particular capitalization, or match formatting, click the **More** button to access additional controls (see Figure 15.2). If not, skip to step 11.

8. If you want to search forward only from the current record, open the **Search** drop-down list and select **Down**. If you want to search backward only, select **Up**. The default is **All**, which searches all records.

9. To limit the match to entries that are the same case (upper or lower), select the **Match Case** check box. Then "Smith" won't find "SMITH" or "smith."

10. To find only fields with the same formatting as the text you type, select **Search Fields As Formatted**. With this option on, "12/12/95" won't find

"12-12-95"—even though they are the same date—because they're formatted differently.

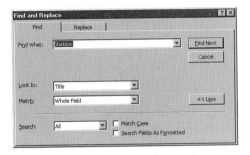

Figure 15.2 When you click **More**, these additional controls appear. Click Less to hide them again.

 TIP **Don't Slow Down** Because it makes your search go more slowly, don't use the **Search Fields As Formatted** option unless you specifically need it.

11. Click **Find Next** to find the first match for your search.

12. If needed, move the Find and Replace dialog box out of the way by dragging its title bar so that you can see the record it found. Access highlights the field entry containing the found text (see Figure 15.3).

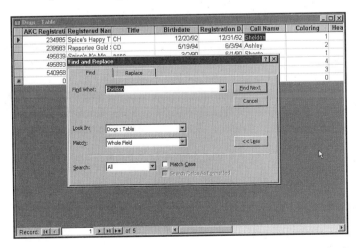

Figure 15.3 Access finds records, one instance at a time, that contain the selected text.

13. To find the next occurrence, click **Find Next**. If Access can't find any more occurrences, it tells you the search item was not found. Click **OK** to clear that message.

14. When you finish finding your data, click **Cancel** to close the Find and Replace dialog box.

Using the Replace Feature

Replacing is a lot like finding, except as an extra bonus, it replaces the found text with text that you specify. For instance, if you found that you misspelled a brand name in your inventory, you could replace the word with the correct spelling. Or, in our dog kennel example, you could find the dog named Sheldon and change his name to Sherman if his new owners changed his name.

To find and replace data, follow these steps:

1. Select **Edit**, and then **Replace**, or press **Ctrl+H**. The Find and Replace dialog box appears with the Replace controls displayed (see Figure 15.4).

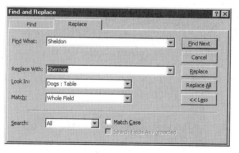

Figure 15.4   You can find specific text and replace it with different text.

TIP   **From Find to Replace**   If the Find and Replace dialog box is already open (from the preceding steps in this lesson), you can jump to the Replace controls by clicking the **Replace** tab.

2. Type the text you want to find in the **Find What** text box.

3. Type the text you want to replace it with in the **Replace With** text box.

4. Select any options you want, as you learned to do with the Find dialog box in the previous section.

5. Click **Find Next**. Access finds the first occurrence of the text.

6. If needed, drag the title bar of the Replace dialog box to move the box so you can see the text that was found.

7. Click the **Replace** button to replace the text.

8. Click **Find Next** to find other occurrences, if desired, and replace them by clicking the **Replace** button.

9. When you finish replacing, click **Cancel**.

If you are certain you want to replace every instance of the text in the entire table, choose **Replace All**. It's quicker than alternating repeatedly between **Find Next** and **Replace**. Be careful, though! You may not realize all the instances that might be changed—for instance, you wouldn't want to change "will" to "would" only to find that "willfully" has been changed to "wouldfully." Unlike Word's Find and Replace feature, no "Whole Word" option is available in the Access Find and Replace dialog box.

Other Ways to Find Data

The Find and Replace feature works well on individual records, but several more sophisticated ways of locating data in your database exist, as you'll learn in upcoming lessons. They include

- **Sorting**—Rearranging the data onscreen so that it's easier to skim through the list to find what you want. See Lesson 16.
- **Filtering**—Narrowing down the list to eliminate the data you know you don't want to see. See Lesson 16.
- **Indexing**—Defining other fields in addition to the primary key that you want Access to keep track of (that is, keep an index of). Indexing is optional, but in large databases it makes your searching and sorting faster. See Lesson 16.
- **Querying**—Creating a more formal filter with complex criteria that you can save and apply again and again. See Lesson 20, "Customizing a Report," and Lesson 21, "Taking Advantage of Database Relationships."
- **Reporting**—Creating a printed report containing only the records and fields that you're interested in. See Lessons 19, "Creating a Simple Report," and 20.

In this lesson, you learned how to find and replace data in a database. In the next lesson, you learn about other ways of locating the data you want: sorting, filtering, and indexing.

Sorting, Filtering, and Indexing Data

*In this lesson, you learn how to find data by sorting
and filtering and how to speed up searches with indexing.*

Finding and Organizing Your Data

Access has many ways of finding and organizing data, and each is good for a
certain situation. As you learned in previous lessons, Find and Replace are great
features when you're working with individual instances of a particular value—
for example, finding Mr. Smith's record quickly. This lesson explains other ways
of finding what you need.

Sorting Data

Even though you enter your records into the database in some sort of logical
order, at some point you'll want them in a different order. For instance, if you
entered the dogs into the kennel database according to registration number, you
might later want to look at the list according to the dogs' birth dates, from oldest
to youngest.

The Sort command is the perfect solution to this problem. With Sort, you can
rearrange the records according to any field you like. You can sort in either
ascending (A to Z, 1 to 10) or descending (Z to A, 10 to 1) order. The fastest
way to sort is to use either the **Sort Ascending** or **Sort Descending** button on
the Table toolbar.

TIP **Which View?** You can sort in either Form view or Datasheet view, but I prefer Datasheet view because it shows many records at once.

Follow these steps to sort records:

1. Place the mouse pointer on a particular field (such as the Birthdate field shown in Figure 16.1) and click to place the insertion point in that field (it can be placed in that field in any record).

2. To sort the records in the table by that field, click the **Sort Ascending** or **Sort Descending** button (to sort in either ascending or descending order, respectively). The records are sorted by the selected field, as shown in Figure 16.1, which sorts the records by the Birthdate field.

3. To place the records back in their presorted order, select the **Records** menu, then select **Remove Filter/Sort**.

	AKC Registrati	Registered Nar	Title	Birthdate	Registration D	Call Name	Coloring	He
▶	234520	Wempen's Best	none	8/18/85	8/25/85	Buddy	2	
	495839	Spice's It's Me	none	3/2/90	6/1/90	Shasta	1	
	493029	Spice's Never Mi	CH	4/9/90	4/9/90	Cindy	4	
	394821	Spice's Krazy 4	UDX	4/9/90	4/9/90	Betsy Mae	4	
	493492	Princess of the F	None	8/12/91	9/2/91	Bubbles	3	
	234985	Spice's Happy T	CH	12/20/92	12/31/92	Sheldon	1	
	495092	Happiglade Torn:	UD	2/3/94	4/5/94	Ruby	1	
	409385	King of the Hill	CD	2/3/94	4/5/94	Champ	2	
	239583	Rapporlee Gold :	CD	5/19/94	6/3/94	Ashley	2	
	540958	Nightingale Rhap	OTCH	5/1/95	5/30/95	Earl	3	
	209483	Carrolton Make :	CD	9/12/95	9/12/95	Boopsie	1	
	450981	Brazen Puppy G	None	3/3/96	5/6/96	Loudmouth	2	
	495893	Russian Blue	CH	7/2/98	7/30/98	Baby	4	
*	0						0	

Record: ◄◄ ◄ 1 ► ►► ►* of 13

Figure 16.1 The results of a sort using the Birthdate field and sorting the records in ascending order.

TERM **What Is Presorted Order?** If you defined a primary key field when you created your database (see Lesson 5, "Creating a Table with the Table Wizard"), by default the records appear sorted in ascending order according to that field. This is the order they revert to when you remove a sort (such as in step 3). If you save the datasheet or form without removing the sort, the sort order becomes part of that object.

You can also sort by two fields using the Sort buttons. The two fields that you want to sort by, however, must be adjacent in the table, and the fields must be in the order (from left to right) you want to sort by. For instance, if you wanted to sort a customer table by last name and then first name, the last name would have to be in the column that is directly to the left of the first name field. Just drag to select the two adjacent columns and then click either of the Sort buttons on the Table toolbar to perform your sort.

Filtering Data

Filtering is for those times when you want to get many of the records out of the way so that you can see the few that you're interested in. Filtering temporarily narrows down the number of records that appear according to criteria you select.

Filters Versus Queries   Queries also narrow down the records displayed, as you'll learn in Lesson 17, "Creating a Simple Query." A filter is easier and quicker to use than a query, but a filter can't be saved as a separate object for later use. (However, you can save a filter *as a query*, as you'll learn later in this lesson.)

You can apply a filter in three ways: Filter by Selection (or Filter Excluding Selection), Filter by Form, and Advanced Filter/Sort. The first two are the most common for casual users, so they are covered in the following sections. The third method is for advanced users only.

Neither of the filtering methods you learn in this lesson enables you to sort at the same time you filter. However, it's easy enough to sort the filtered records using the same sorting process you learned earlier in this lesson.

Filter by Selection

Filtering by selection is the easiest method of filtering, but before you can use it, you have to locate an instance of the value you want the filtered records to contain. For example, if you want to find all the dogs in your table that have earned the title of CD (Companion Dog), you must first locate a record meeting that criteria. You'll base the rest of the filter on that record.

To filter by selection, follow these steps:

1. In a field, find one instance of the value that you want all filtered records to contain.

2. Select the value:

- To find all records in which the field value is identical to the selected value, select the entire field entry.
- To find all records in which the field begins with the selected value, select part of the field entry beginning with the first character.
- To find all records in which the field contains the selected value at any point, select part of the field entry beginning after the first character.

 3. Click the **Filter by Selection** button on the toolbar, or select **Records**, then click **Filter**, and then choose **Filter by Selection**. The records that match the criteria you selected appear.

Figure 16.2 shows the Dogs table filtered to show only dogs that have earned the CD title.

Access filtered the table by this column.

Figure 16.2 The result of a filter; only the records that match the criteria appear.

With Filter by Selection, you can filter by only one criterion at a time. However, you can apply successive filters after the first one to further narrow the list of matching records.

You can also filter for records that *don't* contain the selected value. Follow the same steps as before, but choose **Records**, then click **Filter**, and choose **Filter Excluding Selection** in step 3.

 You can cancel a filter by clicking the **Toggle Filter** button, or by selecting **Records**, and then **Remove Filter/Sort**.

Filter by Form

Filtering by form is a more powerful filtering method than filtering by selection. With Filter by Form, you can filter by more than one criterion at a time. You can also set up "or" filters, which find records in which any one of several criteria is matched. You can even enter logical expressions (such as "greater than a certain value").

To filter by form, follow these steps:

1. In Datasheet or Form view, click the **Filter by Form** button on the toolbar, or select **Records**, then click **Filter**, and choose **Filter by Form**. A blank form appears, resembling an empty datasheet with a single record line.

2. Click in the field for which you want to set a criterion. A down arrow appears for a drop-down list. Click the arrow and select the value you want from the list. Or you can type the value directly into the field if you prefer.

3. Enter as many criteria as you like in various fields. Figure 16.3 shows two criteria, including one that uses a less than sign, a mathematical operator (explained in Lesson 17).

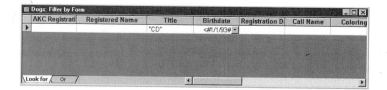

Figure 16.3 This query finds all dogs that were born before 1/1/93 and that have a CD (Companion Dog) title.

4. If you want to set up an "or" condition, click the **Or** tab at the bottom of the window and enter the alternative criteria. (Notice that another **Or** tab appears when you fill this one, so you can add multiple "or" conditions.)

5. After you enter your criteria, click the **Apply Filter** button on the toolbar. Your filtered data appears.

As with Filter by Selection, you can remove a filter by clicking the **Remove Filter** button again or by selecting **Records**, and then **Remove Filter/Sort**.

Saving Your Filtered Data as a Query

Filters are convenient alternatives to creating a simple query from scratch. You can save a filter as a query and use it as you would use a query; it even appears on your Queries list in the Database window. (You'll learn more about working with queries in Lesson 17.)

To save a filter as a query, follow these steps:

1. Display the filter in Filter by Form view.

2. Select **File**, and then **Save As Query**, or click the **Save as Query** button on the toolbar. Access asks for the name of the new query.

3. Type a name and click **OK**. Access saves the filter.

Indexing Data

Indexes speed up searches by cataloging the contents of a particular field. The primary key field is automatically indexed. If you frequently search, sort, or filter by using another field, you might want to create an index for that field.

Only Certain Field Types You can't index a field whose data type is Memo, Hyperlink, or OLE Object.

CAUTION

To index a field, follow these steps:

1. Open the table in Design view.

2. Select the field that you want to index.

3. On the General tab, click the **Indexed** field.

4. From the Indexed field's drop-down list, select either **Yes (Duplicates OK)** or **Yes (No Duplicates)**, depending on whether that field's content should be unique for each record (see Figure 16.4).

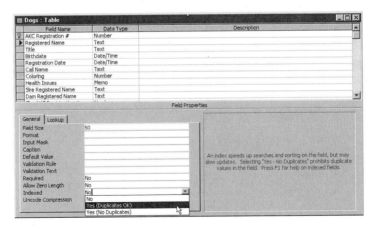

Figure 16.4 To index a field, set its Indexed value to one of the Yes choices.

5. Close the Design view of the table.

6. When asked whether you want to save your changes, click **Yes**.

You can't do anything special with an index; an index isn't an object in the same way that tables, databases, and queries are. An index works behind the scenes to speed up your searches but has no independent functions of its own.

In this lesson, you learned how to sort, filter, and index your database. In the next lesson, you begin learning about queries, a more sophisticated way of isolating and organizing information.

Creating a
Simple Query

In this lesson, you create a simple query.

What Is a Query?

As you learned in the previous lesson, Access offers many ways to help you narrow down the information you're looking at, including sorting and filtering. The most flexible way to sort and filter data, however, is the query. And the great thing about queries is that you can save queries and use them to create tables, to delete records, or to copy records to another table.

Queries enable you to specify

- Which fields you want to see
- In what order the fields should appear
- Filter criteria for each field (see Lesson 16, "Sorting, Filtering, and Indexing Data")
- The order in which you want each field sorted (see Lesson 16)

 **TIP**   **Saving a Filter**   When the primary purpose of the query is to filter, you might find it easier to create a filter and save it as a query. See Lesson 16 for details.

The purpose of this lesson is to show you how to create a simple query. In the next lesson, you learn how to modify your query to make it more powerful.

Creating a Query Using the Simple Query Wizard

The easiest way to create a query is with the Simple Query Wizard, which enables you to select the fields you want to display. You don't get to set criteria for including individual records or specifying a sort order. (You learn how to do those things in Lesson 18, "Creating Queries from Scratch.") This kind of simple query is useful when you want to weed out extraneous fields but still want to see every record.

 Select Query   The query that the Simple Query Wizard creates is a basic version of a Select Query, the most common query type. You can select records, sort them, filter them, and perform simple calculations on the results (such as counting and averaging).

 Query Wizard   A query wizard asks you questions and then creates a query based on your answers. Access has several query wizards available; you learn about others at the end of this lesson.

To create an easy Select Query with the Simple Query Wizard, follow these steps:

1. Open the database you want to work with and click the **Queries** tab.

2. Double-click **Create Query by Using Wizard**. The first dialog box of the Simple Query Wizard appears (see Figure 17.1). This dialog box might look familiar; it's similar to the first screen of the Form Wizard, described in Lesson 12, "Creating a Simple Form."

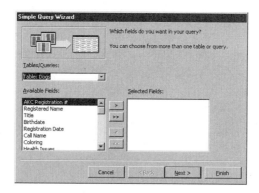

Figure 17.1   The Simple Query Wizard first asks what fields you want to include.

3. Choose the table from which you want to select fields from the Tables/ Queries drop-down list. For example, I'm going to use Dogs.

4. Click a field name in the Available Fields list; then click the > button to move it to the Selected Fields list. Repeat to move all the fields you want, or move them all at once with the >> button.

5. (Optional) Select another table or query from the Tables/Queries list and add some of its fields to the Selected Fields list, if you like. When you finish adding fields, click **Next**.

CAUTION

Relationships Required If you're going to use two or more tables in your query, they must be joined with a relationship. See Lesson 11, "Creating Relationships Between Tables," to learn how to create relationships between tables.

6. Enter a title for the query in the What Title Do You Want for Your Query? text box. I'm going to call mine Dog Names.

7. Click **Finish** to view the query results. Figure 17.2 shows my results.

Figure 17.2 Here are the results of my simple query.

But this query is too simple; it has limited usefulness and doesn't show off any of Access's powerful query features. You could get the same results by hiding certain columns in Datasheet view! Luckily, other means of creating a query are much more powerful than the Query Wizard makes it appear, as you'll see in the next lesson. But before you go there, take a look at a few basics that apply to any query.

541

Saving a Query

When you create a query, Access saves it automatically. You don't need to do anything special to save it. Just close the query window and look on the Queries tab of the Database window. You'll see the query on the list.

How Do I Close the Query? Close a query window the same way you close any window—by clicking its **Close** button (the × in the upper-right corner).

CAUTION

Rerunning a Query

At any time, you can rerun your query. If the data has changed since the last time you ran the query, the changes are represented.

To rerun a query, follow these steps:

1. Open the database containing the query.
2. Click the **Queries** tab in the Database window.
3. Double-click the query you want to rerun, or click it once and then click the **Open** button (see Figure 17.3).

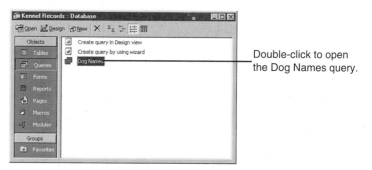

Double-click to open the Dog Names query.

Figure 17.3 Redisplay any query by opening it from the Queries tab.

Working with Query Results

Query results appear in Datasheet view, as shown in Figure 17.2. You can do anything to the records that you can do in a normal Datasheet view (see Lesson 9,

"Editing Data in a Table"), including copying and deleting records and changing field entries.

Suppose that you wanted to update a sales database to change the Last Contacted field (a date) to today for every record. From your Query Results window, you could make that change. Or perhaps you want to delete all records for customers who haven't made a purchase in the last two years. You could delete the records from the Query Results window, and they would disappear from the table, too.

Of course, with the latter example, it would be easier if the records were sorted according to the field in question, and then the Simple Query Wizard wouldn't let you sort. However, in Lesson 18 you learn about some other, more powerful Query Wizards that enable you to choose more options.

Printing Query Results

The Query Results window not only is edited similarly to a datasheet, but it also prints similarly to one. To print the query results, do the following:

1. Make sure the Query Results window is active.

2. Select **File**, and then **Print**, or press **Ctrl+P**. The Print dialog box appears.

3. Select any print options you want (refer to Lesson 8, "Entering Data into a Table"); then click **OK**.

 If you don't want to set any print options, you can just click the **Print** button on the toolbar, bypassing the Print dialog box.

Other Query Wizards

Access's query features are powerful; they can do amazingly complicated calculations and comparisons on many tables at once. You can create queries with their own dialog boxes for custom entry of special criteria, link a query to external databases (databases in other programs), and much more.

Unfortunately, the process for creating a lot of these powerful queries is quite complicated. It's enough to give casual users a headache. That's why in this book, we stick to the basic Select type of query, which does almost everything average users need to do.

Three other query wizards are available in Access. To run one of them, follow these steps:

1. In the Database window, click **Queries** to display the Queries list.

2. Click the **New** button to open the New Query dialog box (see Figure 17.4).

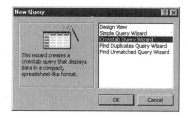

Figure 17.4   You can select another type of query wizard from the New Query dialog box.

3. Click the wizard you want to use.

4. Click **OK**.

5. Follow the wizard's prompts.

These are the other query types:

- **Crosstab Query Wizard**—This wizard displays summarized values, such as sums, counts, and averages, from one field. The values are grouped by one set of facts listed down the left side of the datasheet as row headings and by another set of facts listed across the top of the datasheet as column headings.

- **Find Duplicates Query Wizard**—The opposite of Find Unmatched, this wizard compares two tables and finds all records that appear in both.

- **Find Unmatched Query Wizard**—This wizard compares two tables and finds all records that don't appear in both tables (based on comparing certain fields).

In this lesson, you learned how to create a simple query and how to save, edit, and print query results. In the next lesson, you see how to modify the query you created.

Creating Queries from Scratch

In this lesson, you learn how to open a query in Design view, how to select fields to include in it, and how to specify criteria for filtering the records.

Introducing Query Design View

In Lesson 17, "Creating a Simple Query," you created a simple query by using the Simple Query Wizard, which selected and displayed fields from a table. You can do a lot more with your query when you enter Query Design view.

Query Design view is similar to Table Design and Form Design views, both of which you've encountered earlier in this book. In Query Design view, you can change the rules that govern your query results.

Opening a Query in Query Design View

To open an existing query in Query Design view, follow these steps:

1. Open the database that contains the query you want to edit.
2. Click the **Queries** tab.
3. Click the query you want to edit; then click the **Design** button.

Figure 18.1 shows the query created in Lesson 17 in Query Design view. You'll learn how to edit it in this lesson.

This query uses
only one table.

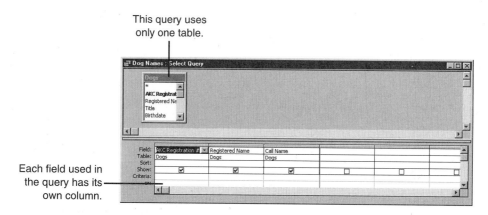

Each field used in
the query has its
own column.

Figure 18.1 In Query Design view, you can edit a query you've created.

Starting a New Query in Query Design View

Rather than using the Simple Query Wizard to begin your query, as you did in Lesson 17, you can begin a query from scratch in Query Design view. As you become more familiar with Access queries, you might find this method faster and easier than using a wizard.

To begin a new query in Query Design view, follow these steps:

1. Open the database in which you want the query.

2. Click the **Queries** tab in the Database window.

3. Double-click **Create Query in Design View**. The Show Table dialog box appears, listing all the tables in the database (see Figure 18.2).

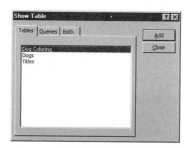

Figure 18.2 Choose which tables you want to include in the query.

4. Click a table you want to work with, then click the **Add** button. Repeat for each table you want to add. It's best to create a relationship between the tables in advance, using the Relationships window (see Lesson 11, "Creating Relationships Between Tables").

5. Click **Close** when you finish adding tables. The Query Design view window opens (refer to Figure 18.1), except that no fields are selected yet.

Adding Fields to a Query

If you created your query from scratch (as in the preceding steps), the first thing you need to do is add the fields you want to work with. You can also use this same procedure to add fields to an existing query.

 TIP **Adding More Tables** You can add tables to your query at any time. Just click the **Show Table** button on the toolbar, or select **Query** and then **Show Table**. Then select the table(s) you want and click **Add**. Click **Close** to return to your query design.

You can add a field to a query in three ways. All methods are easy; try them all to see which you prefer. Here's the first method:

1. Click in the **Table** row of the first blank column. A down-arrow button appears, indicating that a drop-down list is available.

2. Open the drop-down list and select a table. The tables available on the list are the same as the table windows that appear at the top of the Query Design window.

 TIP **Only One Table?** If you are using only one table in the query, you can skip the first two steps in this procedure.

3. Click in the **Field** row directly above the table name you just selected. A down-arrow button appears, indicating that a drop-down list is available.

4. Open the drop-down list and select a field. The fields listed come from the tables you selected for the query. The field's name appears in the Field row, in the column where you selected it.

Here's the second method of adding a field:

1. Scroll through the list of fields in the desired table window at the top of the Query Design box until you find the field you want to add.

2. Click the field name and drag it into the **Field** row of the first empty column. The field's name appears where you dragged it.

The third method is to double-click the field name in the field list. It moves to the first available slot in the query grid.

Deleting a Field

You can delete a field from your query in two ways:

- Click anywhere in the column and select **Edit**, then **Delete Columns**.
- Position the mouse pointer directly above the column so that the pointer turns into a down-pointing black arrow. Then click to select the entire column and press **Delete**, or click the **Cut** button on the toolbar.

TERM **Cut Versus Delete** If you cut the column rather than delete it, you can paste it back into the query. Just select the column where you want it and then click the **Paste** button, or choose **Edit** and then **Paste**. Be careful, however; the pasted column replaces the selected one—the selected column doesn't move over to make room for it. Select an empty column if you don't want to replace an existing one.

Adding Criteria

Criteria is familiar to you if you read Lesson 16, "Sorting, Filtering, and Indexing Data," which deals with filters. Criteria enable you to choose which records appear in your query results. For example, I could limit my list of dogs to those whose birth dates were before January 1, 1994.

TIP **Filters Versus Queries** If the primary reason for creating the query is to filter, you might want to create the filter part first by using one of the procedures described in Lesson 16, and then save the filter as a query. You can open that query in Query Design view and fine-tune it as needed.

To set criteria for a field that you've added to your query, follow these steps:

1. In Query Design view, click the **Criteria** row in the desired field's column.

2. Type the criteria you want to use (see Figure 18.3). Table 18.1 provides some examples you could have entered in Figure 18.3 and the subsequent results.

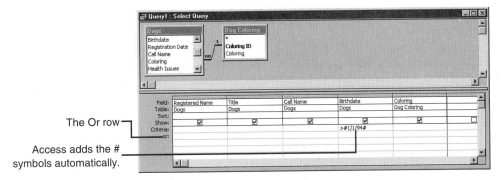

The Or row

Access adds the # symbols automatically.

Figure 18.3   Enter criteria into the Criteria row in the appropriate field's column.

In Figure 18.3, Access added # symbols because I was entering a date. For other types of criteria, Access adds other symbols, such as quotation marks around a text or number string.

Table 18.1   Sample Criteria for Queries

Enter This	To Get Records That Match This
1/1/93	Exactly 1/1/93
<1/1/93	Before 1/1/93
>1/1/93	After 1/1/93
>=1/1/93	1/1/93 or after
<=1/1/93	1/1/93 or before
Not <1/1/93	Not before 1/1/93
Not >1/1/93	Not after 1/1/93

You can also enter text as criteria. The < and > (before and after) operators apply to alphabetical order with text. For instance, <C finds text that begins with A or B.

Did you notice the Or row below the Criteria row in Figure 18.3? You can enter more criteria by using that line. The query finds records where any of the criteria is true. When you enter criteria into the Or row, another Or row appears so that you can enter more.

When you have two criteria that must both be true, you can put them together in a single Criteria row with the word And. For instance, you might want birth dates between 12/1/93 and 12/1/95. All the dates would appear in a single Criteria row, like this: >12/1/93 And <12/1/95.

Viewing Query Results

When you're ready to see the results of your query, click the **Run** button, or choose **Query** and then **Run**. Your results appear in a window that resembles a datasheet (see Figure 18.4).

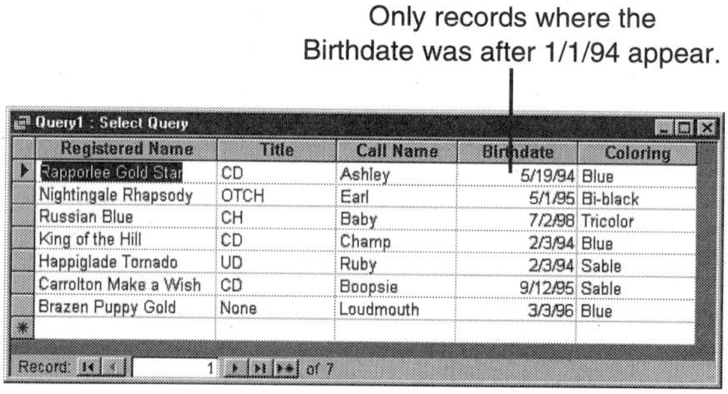

Only records where the
Birthdate was after 1/1/94 appear.

Figure 18.4 The results of a kennel query based on birth dates.

In this lesson, you learned how to choose the fields for a query and specify criteria. In the next lesson, you learn how to create reports in Access by using the AutoReport and Report Wizards.

Creating a
Simple Report

In this lesson, you learn how to create reports
in Access by using the AutoReport and Report Wizards.

Why Create Reports?

You've seen many ways to organize and view your data, but until now each method has focused on onscreen use. Forms help with data entry onscreen, and queries help you find information and display the results onscreen.

You can print any table, form, or query, but the results are less than professional-looking because those tools aren't designed to be printed. Reports, on the other hand, are designed specifically to be printed and shared with other people. With a report, you can generate professional results that you can be proud of, whether you're distributing them on paper or publishing them on the Internet.

You can create a report in several ways, ranging from easy, but limited (AutoReport) to difficult, but very flexible (Report Design view). The intermediate choice is the Report Wizard, which offers some flexibility along with a fairly easy procedure.

Using AutoReport to Create a Report

If you want a plain, no-frills report based on a single table or query, AutoReport is for you. You can go back and improve its appearance later, when you learn about customizing reports in Lesson 20, "Customizing a Report."

You can create a tabular or columnar report. A tabular report resembles a datasheet, and a columnar report resembles a form. They are equally easy to create.

To create a report with AutoReport, follow these steps:

1. Open the database containing the table or query on which you want to report.

2. Click the **Reports** tab in the Database window, and click the **New** button. The New Report dialog box appears (see Figure 19.1).

Figure 19.1   Choose one of the AutoReports from this window.

3. Select **AutoReport:Columnar** or **AutoReport:Tabular**.

4. In the drop-down list at the bottom of the dialog box, select the table or query on which you want to base the report.

CAUTION

Multiple Tables?   AutoReports can use only one table or query. If you want to create an AutoReport that uses several tables, first create a query based on those tables, and then base the AutoReport on the query.

5. Click **OK**. The report appears in Print Preview. See the "Viewing and Printing Reports in Print Preview" section later in this lesson to learn what to do next.

AutoReport's output isn't much better than a raw printout from a table or form, as you can see in Print Preview. If you want a better-looking report, try the Report Wizard.

Creating a Report with the Report Wizard

The Report Wizard offers a good compromise between ease-of-use and flexibility. With the Report Wizard, you can use multiple tables and queries and choose a layout and format for your report. Follow these steps to create a report with Report Wizard:

1. Open the database containing the table or query on which you want to report.

2. Click the **Reports** tab in the Database window.

3. Double-click **Create Report by Using Wizard** to start the Report Wizard (see Figure 19.2).

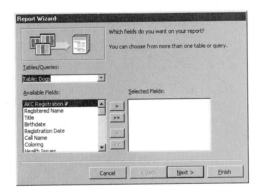

Figure 19.2 The first Report Wizard dialog box.

4. From the Tables/Queries drop-down list, select a table or query from which you want to include fields.

5. Click a field in the Available Fields list, and then click the > button to move it to the Selected Fields list. Repeat this step to select all the fields you want, or click >> to move all the fields over at once.

6. If desired, select another table or query from the Tables/Queries list and repeat step 5. The tables you choose should have relationships between them so that your data matches up on the report. When you finish selecting fields, click **Next**. The wizard's next dialog box appears (see Figure 19.3).

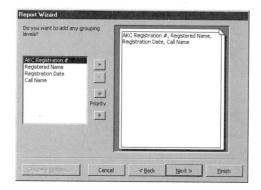

Figure 19.3   Set your report's grouping.

7. If you want the records grouped by any of the fields you selected, click the field, and then click the > button. You can select several grouping levels in the order you want them. Then click **Next** to move on.

CAUTION

Grouping?   By default, there are no groups. You have to select a field and click the > button to create a group. Grouping sets off each group on the report. If you use a field to group, the Grouping Options button becomes active, and you can click it to specify precise grouping settings.

8. The wizard asks what sort order you want to use (see Figure 19.4). If you want sorted records, open the top drop-down list and select a field by which to sort. Select up to four sorts from the drop-down lists, then click **Next**. By default, the sort is in ascending order (A–Z). Click the **AZ** button next to the box to change the sort order to descending (Z–A), if you like.

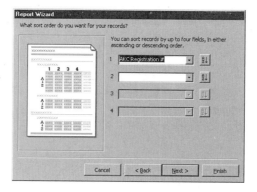

Figure 19.4   Set the sort order for your records.

9. In the next dialog box (see Figure 19.5), choose a layout option from the Layout section. When you click an option button, the sample in the box changes to show your selection.

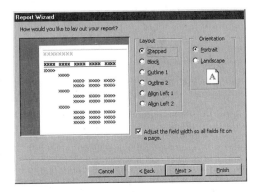

Figure 19.5 Choose the layout of your report.

CAUTION

Where Are All the Layouts? If you don't choose any groupings in your report, your layout choices are limited to three: Columnar, Tabular, and Justified. The layouts shown in Figure 19.5 are unique to grouped reports.

10. Choose the orientation for your printed report: **Portrait** (across the narrow edge of the paper) or **Landscape** (across the wide edge of the paper). Then click **Next** to continue.

11. In the next wizard dialog box, choose a report style. Several are listed; click one to see a sample of it, and then click **Next** when you're satisfied with your choice.

12. You're asked for a report title. Enter one in the Report text box, and click **Finish** to see your report in Print Preview (see Figure 19.6).

Viewing and Printing Reports in Print Preview

When you create a report with either the Report Wizard or AutoReport, the report appears in Print Preview (as shown in Figure 19.6). From here, you can print the report if you're happy with it, or go to Report Design view to make changes. (You'll learn more about this in Lesson 20.)

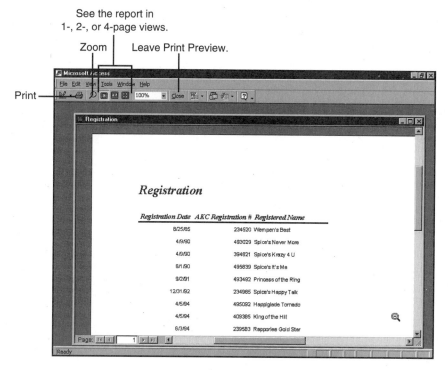

Figure 19.6 Here's a simple report with no grouping.

 If you want to print the report and specify any print options (such as the number of copies), choose **File**, and then **Print**. If you want a quick hard copy, click the toolbar's **Print** button. To go to Report Design view, choose **View**, and then **Design View**.

In this lesson, you learned how to create and print a simple report. In the next lesson, you learn how to work in Report Design view to customize your report.

Customizing
a Report

In this lesson, you learn how to use Report Design view to make your reports more attractive.

Entering Report Design View

When you finish previewing a report you've created, close Print Preview to close the report, or switch to Design view from the View menu. If you want to come back to Report Design view later, perform these steps from the Database window:

1. Click the **Reports** tab.
2. Click the report you want to modify.
3. Click the **Design** button. The report appears in Design view, as shown in Figure 20.1.

As you can see in Figure 20.1, the Report Header section shows the report title, whereas the Page Header shows the column labels for the report. The Detail area lists the fields that you chose to print under those columns. And the Page Footer contains a formula that prints the current date and time.

Report Design view might seem familiar to you; it looks similar to Form Design view. Almost everything you learned about editing forms in Lesson 13, "Modifying a Form," also applies to reports. Just as in Form Design view, Report Design view contains a toolbox of common editing tools that you can use to add all the special elements you learned about in Lesson 14, "Adding Controls to Forms."

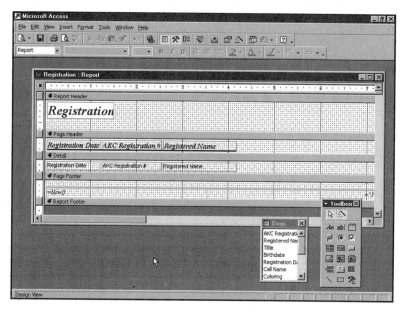

Figure 20.1 The report created in the previous lesson, in Report Design view.

 TIP **Command Button on a Report?** Access enables you to place any type of control on a report, even those that are frankly silly, such as command buttons or combo boxes. It's best, however, to stick to text boxes, labels, and graphics on reports.

Working with Controls on Your Report

Working with report controls in Report Design view is the same as working with controls in Form Design view. Turn back to Lesson 13 for the full story, or follow the brief review here:

- **Selecting controls**—The same as in Form Design view, you select a control on your report by clicking it. Selection handles (little squares in the corners) appear around it. See Lesson 13 for more details.

- **Moving objects**—To move a control, first select it. Next, position the mouse pointer over a border so that the pointer turns into an open black hand. Then, click and drag the control to a new location.

TIP **Moving Between Sections**   You can't drag an object to a different section, but you can cut and paste it. Select the object and press **Ctrl+X** to cut it. Then, click the title of the section where you want to move it, and press **Ctrl+V** to paste it into the newly selected section.

- **Resizing objects**—First, select the object. Then, position the mouse pointer over a selection handle and drag it to resize the object.
- **Formatting text objects**—Use the **Font** and **Font Size** drop-down lists on the toolbar to choose fonts; then use the **Bold**, **Italic**, and **Underline** toolbar buttons to set special attributes.

You can also add graphic lines and images to reports, just as you do with forms.

TIP **Access on the Web**   You can assign hyperlinks to objects on your forms and reports. Hyperlinks aren't much use on the printouts, of course, but if you save a report in Microsoft Word format, the hyperlinks can be activated when you open the document in Word.

Adding and Removing Controls

You can add more controls to your report at any time. Follow these steps:

1. If you don't see the Field list, choose **View**, and then **Field List**, or click the **Field List** button on the toolbar. A floating box appears, listing all the fields in the table you're using.
2. Drag any field from the field list into the report, where it becomes a control—by default, a text box. Place it anywhere you want in the Detail area.

Don't worry if the control isn't in the right place or overlaps another control; you'll learn how to fix that in the next section. To delete a control, select it by clicking it, and then press **Delete**. Deleting a control from the report doesn't delete the field from the table.

Arranging Your New Controls

When you add a control to your report, you're actually adding two things—a label and a text box. These two elements are bound together: The label describes the text box, and the text box represents the actual field that will be used (see Figure 20.2). You can change the text in the label without affecting the text box;

559

for instance, you could change the label on the Coloring field to Dog Color without affecting the contents. To change a label, just click it and retype.

Mouse pointer

Figure 20.2   Position the mouse pointer over the larger handle to move the object separately.

 By default, when you move the text box, the label follows. When you position the mouse over the border of the text box and the pointer changes to an open hand, it's your signal that the label will follow the text box when you drag it.

 However, you can also move the text box and the label separately. Notice that in the upper-left corner of each control is a selection handle (square) that's bigger than the others. When you position the mouse pointer over that handle, the cursor becomes a pointing hand. It's your signal that you can click and drag the object separately from the other.

Moving the label separately can come in handy when you don't want the label to appear in its default position (to the left of the text box). For instance, you might want the label to appear above the text box.

Adding Labels

 In the preceding section, you saw how to add a pair of controls—a text box and an attached label. But you can also add labels by themselves, with extra text in them that's not necessarily associated with a particular field—for instance, an informational note about the report in general. Click the **Label** button in the toolbox. Then, click anywhere on the report and start typing. When you finish, click anywhere outside the label.

Adding a Calculated Text Box

Text boxes most commonly display data from fields, as you've seen in this lesson. However, text boxes have another purpose—they can also hold calculations based on values in different fields.

Creating a text box is a bit complicated: First, you have to create an unbound text box (that is, one that's not associated with any particular field), and then you have to enter the calculation into the text box. Follow these steps:

1. Click the **Text Box** tool in the toolbox, and then click and drag on the report to create a text box.

2. Change the label to reflect what's going in the text box. For instance, if it's Sales Tax, change the label accordingly. Position the label where you want it.

3. Click in the text box and type the formula you want calculated. (See the following list for guidance.)

4. Click anywhere outside the text box when you finish.

The formulas you enter into your calculated text box use standard mathematical controls:

+	Add
–	Subtract
*	Multiply
/	Divide

All formulas begin with an equal sign (=), and all field names are in parentheses. Here are some examples:

- To calculate a total price by multiplying the value in the Quantity field by the value in the Price field, enter **=[Quantity]*[Price]**.
- To calculate a 25% discount off the value in the Cost field, enter **=[Cost]*.075**.
- To add the total of the values in three fields, enter **[Field1]+[Field2]+[Field3]**.

 TIP   **More Room**   If you run out of room in the text box when typing your formula, press **Shift+F2** to open a Zoom box, which gives you more room.

In this lesson, you learned how to customize your report by adding and removing objects, moving them around, and creating calculations. In the next lesson, you learn how to use related tables in forms, queries, and reports.

Taking Advantage of Database Relationships

In this chapter, you learn how to use related tables in forms, queries, and reports.

Introducing Related Tables

When you created your database in the beginning of this part of the book, I advised you to create relationships between tables. (You created the relationships in Lesson 11, "Creating Relationships Between Tables.") You might have wondered why you were doing this—what good it would do you. In this lesson, I'll show you some of the ways related tables help you manage your data.

A relationship links two tables by connecting matching fields. This makes it possible to break out repetitive or peripheral information into its own table, while still using that information in the main table.

For example, in Figure 21.1, the Titles and the Dog Coloring tables support the main table (Dogs) by providing lists of valid values for certain fields. The Titles table contains a list of all the titles a dog might have, and the Dog Coloring table contains a list of all the AKC-registerable colorings that a dog of the particular breed might have.

In more sophisticated databases, you might have many relationships among tables. See if you can trace and understand all the relationships in Figure 21.2, a Sales database.

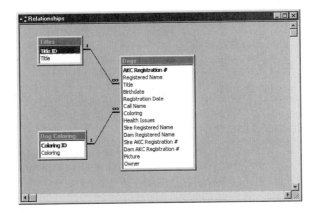

Figure 21.1 Open the Relationships window (# select the Tools menu, and then click Relationships) to view the current relationships.

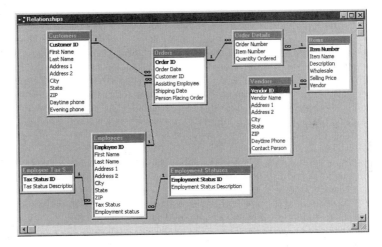

Figure 21.2 Businesses with customers, vendors, inventory, and employees can have a complex system of relationships.

Viewing Information Between Tables

When looking at a table in Datasheet view, you can quickly view information from a related table. (This is one of the many great new features in Access 2000.) Suppose that you are looking at the Titles table (from Figure 21.1) in Datasheet view. Plus signs appear next to each record. When you click a plus sign, a minitable appears, listing all the records from the related table with the same value (see Figure 21.3).

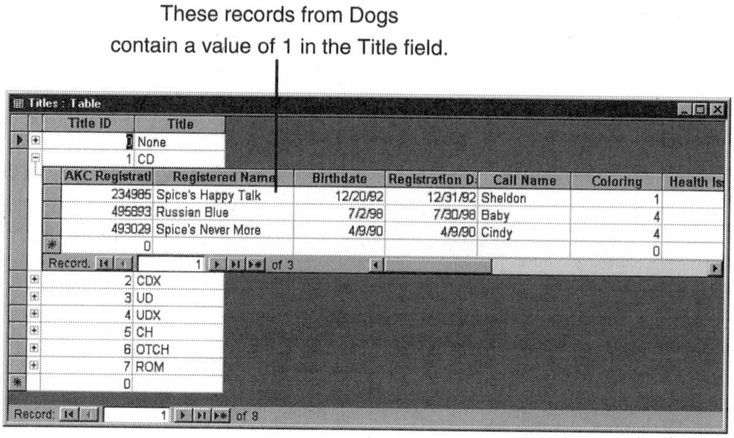

These records from Dogs
contain a value of 1 in the Title field.

Figure 21.3   Display related records in the linked table by clicking a plus sign next to a record.

When related records are displayed, the plus sign turns into a minus sign. Click that minus sign to hide the related records again.

Creating Multitable Queries

Multitable queries are very useful for pulling information from more than one table at the same time. You can then use that information in reports, forms, or other queries, or you can simply view the information in a tablelike Query Results window.

To create a multitable query, create a new query through Design view (refer to Lesson 18, "Creating Queries from Scratch"). In the Show Table dialog box, add more than one table before you click **Close**. You'll then have multiple tables from which to pull fields. Then proceed normally to finish the query, as you learned in Lesson 18.

When you join two tables, such as Titles and Dogs from Figure 21.1, you usually join them by number fields. In Figure 21.1, Title ID in the Titles table is joined to Title in the Dogs table. That means that a number, not a descriptive name, appears in the Dogs table for each dog's title. I don't have all the Title ID numbers memorized, so it's hard for me to tell what title a dog has. But I can create a query that includes all the fields in the Dogs table, except Title, and the Title field from the Titles table (which contains descriptive text). Then I can use that query's results instead of the Dogs table to create forms and reports.

Creating Multitable Forms

You learned in the preceding section how you can create a query that includes fields from more than one table—that's the easiest way to create a multitable form. Just create the query and then base the form on the query.

Another way is to create a form with an embedded subform. The subform can contain data from any related table. For example, on a Customers form, you could include a subform listing all the orders that customer has placed.

 TERM **Subform** A subform isn't another type of database object—it's just a form placed as an object on another form. You can make a form into a subform by dragging it to another form that's open in Design view.

To create a form with an embedded subform, follow these steps:

1. Start a new form by using the Form Wizard. To do so, from the Database window, click the **Forms** tab, and then double-click **Create Form by Using Wizard**.

2. In the Form Wizard's first dialog box, choose a table or query, and then select the fields you want to use from it. (You learned this in Lesson 12, "Creating a Simple Form.")

3. Rather than move on, choose the second table or query from the **Tables/Queries** drop-down list and select fields from it, too (see Figure 21.4).

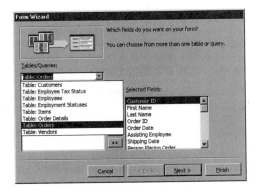

Figure 21.4 After selecting fields for one table, choose another one and select more fields before clicking Next.

4. Continue changing tables/queries and selecting more fields until you have all the fields you need. Then click **Next**.

5. The wizard asks how you want to view your data. Choose one table from the list to be the main form's data source; the other one will be the subform's data source (see Figure 21.5).

 TIP **Linked Forms** These steps show you how to create a form with a subform. If you prefer to have two separate forms to hold the data from the two tables or queries, click the **Linked Forms** button in the Wizard dialog box in Figure 21.5. Then complete the steps with the wizard normally, as you learned in Lesson 12.

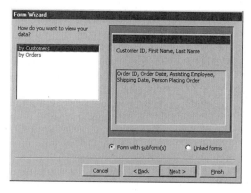

Figure 21.5 Choose how you want the tables to appear.

6. Click **Next**.

7. The wizard then asks about the format for the subform. Choose **Tabular** (similar to a table in Word) or **Datasheet** (similar to a spreadsheet in Excel) and click **Next**.

8. Choose a form style, and click **Next**.

9. Enter titles for your form and your subform. (They will be saved as separate forms in your database.) Then click **Finish**. Your form appears, as shown in Figure 21.6.

Creating Multitable Reports

Just as with forms, you can create reports that use multiple tables or queries. The process for doing so is almost the same as that for creating a single-table report, which you learned in Lesson 19, "Creating a Simple Report."

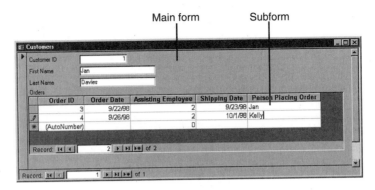

Figure 21.6 This form contains fields from one table in the main form and another table in the subform.

To create a report that uses multiple tables or queries, follow these steps:

1. Create the relationships between the tables. Refer to Lesson 11 if needed.

2. Start a new report by using the **Report Wizard**. (In the Database window, click the **Reports** tab, and then double-click **Create Report by Using Wizard**.)

3. Select the fields from the first table you want to use.

4. From the **Tables/Queries** drop-down list, select a different table or query. Then select fields from it. This is similar to what you did with forms back in Figure 21.4.

5. When you are finished, click **Next**.

6. When the wizard asks how you want to view your data, choose one of the tables. This is the same as the selection you made for forms back in Figure 21.5. Then click **Next**.

7. Continue with the wizard as usual, adding grouping, sorting, and so on. Refer to Lesson 19 if needed.

8. When you reach the end of the wizard's process, click **Finish** to create your report.

In this lesson, you learned how to create queries, forms, and reports based on more than one related table. In the next section, you learn how to start and work with Microsoft PowerPoint.

PowerPoint

Working in PowerPoint

In this lesson, you learn how to start and exit PowerPoint.
You also learn about the PowerPoint application and presentation
window and learn how to enter commands with shortcut menus and toolbars.

Starting PowerPoint

Before you start PowerPoint, you must have PowerPoint installed on your computer, and you should have a basic understanding of the Windows 95/98 or Windows NT operating systems. This book always refers to Windows 98, but keep in mind that in most cases, if you're using Windows 95 or NT, the information applies to you, too.

To start PowerPoint, follow these steps:

1. Click the **Start** button.

2. Move your mouse pointer to **Programs**. A menu of programs appears.

3. Move your mouse pointer to **Microsoft PowerPoint** and click it (see Figure 1.1). PowerPoint starts and displays the introductory screen shown in Figure 1.2.

The first thing you see when you start PowerPoint is a dialog box in which you choose whether you want to start a new presentation or open an existing one. You'll learn about this dialog box in Lesson 2, "Creating a New Presentation." For now, click **OK** to start a blank presentation. When the New Slide dialog box appears, click **OK** to start a new slide (you need some sort of presentation—even a blank one—on the screen to view the menus and toolbars discussed in the next sections).

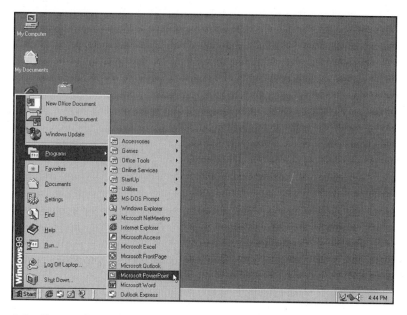

Figure 1.1   To start PowerPoint, move through the Start button's menu system to Microsoft PowerPoint.

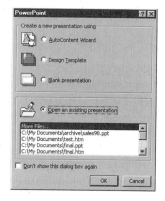

Figure 1.2   PowerPoint starts by first opening a dialog box.

PowerPoint Not on the Menu?   You may have specified a different menu when you installed PowerPoint, or you may not have installed PowerPoint yet.

There's a Paper Clip Talking to Me! The first time you start PowerPoint, one of the Microsoft Office Assistants opens a Help balloon to assist you in getting started. Click the **Start Using PowerPoint** option. (See Appendix B, "Using the Office 2000 Help System.")

CAUTION

Understanding the PowerPoint Window

Now that you have PowerPoint up and running, take a look at the PowerPoint window. The center area holds your presentation, and all around it are tools to help you issue commands and perform modifications.

Some of the controls are standard Windows ones, such as the title bar, the window control buttons (Minimize, Maximize, and Close), and the menu system. In addition, you see some toolbars and several other items that are unique to PowerPoint. You'll learn about these screen elements in this lesson and in upcoming ones.

Working with Menus

You are probably already familiar with menus; to open a menu, click its name on the menu bar, and then click the command you want to issue.

However, in Office 2000 programs such as PowerPoint, the menus have a special feature. When you open a menu, the entire menu does not display right away; only a select list of commands appears. If you pause a moment or click the down-pointing arrow at the bottom of the menu, the entire menu unfurls, showing the remaining commands. This is called a *personalized* menu because it adapts to the way you use the program. For example, in Figure 1.3, the menu on the left is the one that opens initially, and the one on the right is the full version that opens a few seconds later.

TIP **Which Comes First?** A core set of essential commands always appears on the initial menu. In addition, any command that you have recently used appears first. That way, over time, PowerPoint "learns" which commands you use most often, and displays them first.

Because a menu's commands vary depending on what actions you have taken, the figures in this book show the menus with the personalized feature turned off.

To turn off this feature yourself, open the **Tools** menu and choose **Customize**. Then on the **Options** tab, deselect the **Menus Show Recently Used Commands First** check box. (This is the same dialog box you use later in this lesson, in the section "Separating the Standard and Formatting Toolbars.")

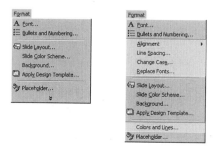

Figure 1.3   The most common or recently used commands appear first (left), and then the full menu appears a few seconds later (right).

Working with Toolbars

A *toolbar* is a collection of buttons that enables you to bypass the menu system. Instead of opening the **File** menu and selecting **Save**, for example, you can click the **Save** toolbar button to save your work. You learn more about toolbars later in this lesson.

PowerPoint displays three toolbars in Normal view: the Standard and Formatting toolbars below the menu bar and the Drawing toolbar at the bottom of the screen. In other views, or while certain features are active, you may see additional toolbars.

To select a button from the toolbar, click the button.

By default in PowerPoint 2000, the Standard and Formatting toolbars appear on the same line, and most of the buttons on the Standard toolbar are not visible. To view the undisplayed buttons, you must click the >> button at the right end of that toolbar to open a pop-up list of them, as shown in Figure 1.4.

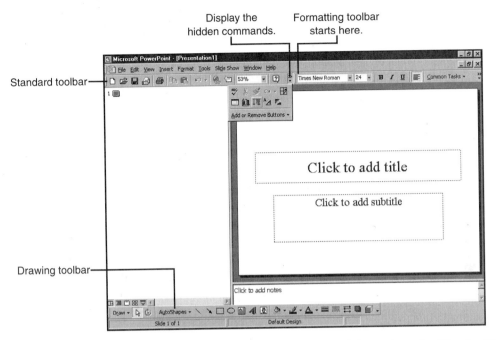

Figure 1.4 When both toolbars share a line, most of the tools on the Standard toolbar are hidden.

Separating the Standard and Formatting Toolbars

Many people prefer to move each toolbar to a separate line, as was the default in earlier versions of PowerPoint. To do so, follow these steps:

1. Open the **Tools** menu and choose **Customize**. The Customize dialog box appears.
2. Click the **Options** tab.
3. Click to remove the check mark in the **Standard and Formatting Toolbars Share One Row** check box.
4. Click **Close**. The toolbars appear on separate rows.

The remainder of the figures in this book use this two-row toolbar configuration because you can see the tools being referenced more easily.

Learning More About a Toolbar Button

To see the name of a button, move the mouse pointer over the button. PowerPoint displays a ScreenTip that provides the name of the button.

To learn more about a button, press **Shift+F1** or select **Help, What's This?** and then click the button for which you want more information.

Turning Toolbars On or Off

If you never use a particular toolbar, you can turn it off to free up some screen space. In addition, you can turn on other toolbars that come with PowerPoint but that don't appear automatically. To turn a toolbar on or off, do the following:

1. Right-click any toolbar. A shortcut menu appears (see Figure 1.5). A check mark appears next to each toolbar that is turned on.

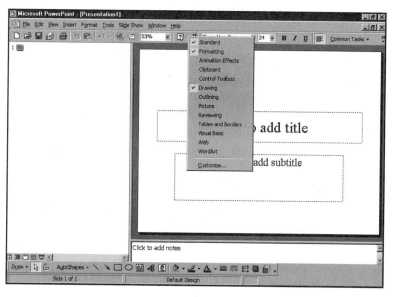

Figure 1.5 The shortcut menu for toolbars displays the names of all the toolbars.

2. Click the displayed toolbar you want to hide, or click a hidden toolbar that you want to display. Check marks appear next to displayed toolbars.

When you click a toolbar name on the menu, the menu disappears and that toolbar appears (if it was hidden) or the toolbar disappears (if it was displayed).

Using Shortcut Menus

Although you can enter all commands in PowerPoint using menus, PowerPoint offers a quicker way: context-sensitive shortcut menus like the ones in Windows. To use a shortcut menu, move the mouse pointer over the object you want the command to act on, and then click the right mouse button. A shortcut menu pops up, just as it did for the toolbars in Figure 1.5, offering commands that pertain to the selected object. Click the desired command. For example, Figure 1.6 shows the menu you get when you right-click some text on a slide.

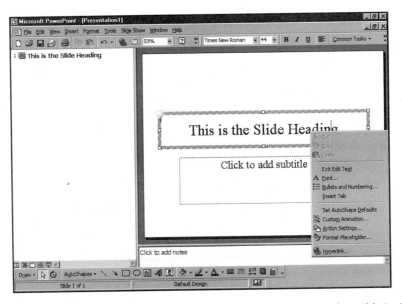

Figure 1.6 Display a shortcut menu by right-clicking an object, such as this text box.

Working with the Presentation Window

In the center of the PowerPoint window is your presentation. Its window contains one or more panes, depending on the view in use. Figure 1.7 shows Normal view, which contains three panes: Outline, Slide, and Notes. You'll learn more about this and other views in Lesson 3, "Working with Slides in Different Views."

TIP **Turning Off the Office Assistant** The Office Assistant (Clippit, the paper clip) provides help as you work. You can make it disappear: Right-click it and choose **Hide**. To make it reappear, select **Help**, and then **Show the Office Assistant**.

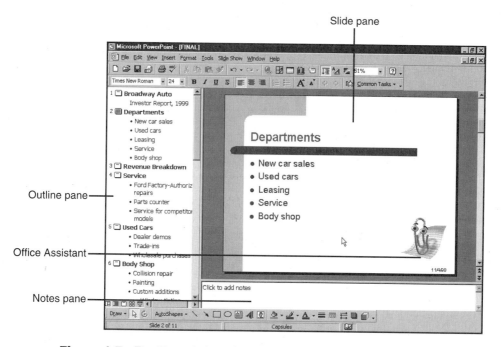

Figure 1.7 The Normal view of the presentation shows the Outline, Slide, and Notes panes.

As you will learn in Lesson 3, you can edit the presentation's text in either the Outline or the Slide pane. Changes in one pane affect the other. If you want to place a nontext object on a slide (such as a graphic), you do so in the Slide pane.

The Notes pane provides a space for entering your own notes, which are not visible to your audience.

Exiting PowerPoint

When you finish using PowerPoint, you should exit the program. Don't just turn off your computer, or you could create problems that could cause your PC to misbehave.

To exit PowerPoint:

1. If the PowerPoint dialog box is still onscreen, click the **Cancel** button to close it.

2. If this dialog box is not onscreen, do one of the following (see Figure 1.8):

- Click the PowerPoint window's **Close** (×) button.
- Double-click the **Control menu** icon in the left corner of the title bar, or click it once to open the **Control** menu and then select **Close**.
- Open the **File** menu and select **Exit**.
- Press **Alt+F4**.

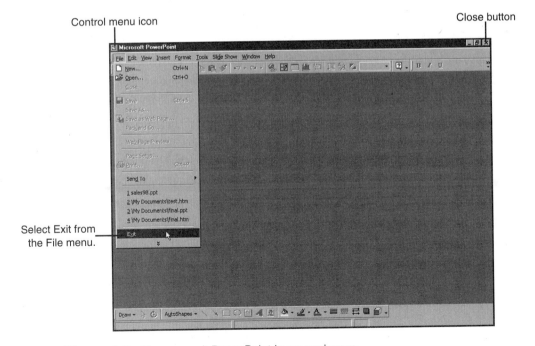

Figure 1.8 You can exit PowerPoint in several ways.

3. If you're asked if you want to save your changes, select **Yes** to save your changes. (If you choose Yes, see Lesson 2 to learn how to complete the Save As dialog box that appears.) Select **No** if you haven't created anything you want to save yet.

In this lesson, you learned how to start and exit PowerPoint. In addition, you learned about the PowerPoint application and presentation windows, and you learned how to enter commands with shortcut menus and toolbars. In the next lesson, you learn how to create a new presentation.

Creating a New Presentation

In this lesson, you learn several ways to create a presentation. You also learn how to save a presentation to disk, close a presentation, and open an existing presentation.

Three Choices for Starting a New Presentation

PowerPoint offers several ways to create a new presentation. Before you begin, decide on the method that's right for you:

- AutoContent Wizard offers the highest degree of help. It walks you through each step of creating the new presentation. When you're finished, you have a standardized group of slides, all with a similar look and feel, for a particular situation. Each template slide includes dummy text that you can replace with your own text.

- A design template provides a professionally designed color, background, and font scheme that applies to the slides you create yourself. It does not provide sample slides.

- You can choose to start from scratch and create a totally blank presentation. Building the presentation from the ground up is not recommended for beginners.

Wizards Wizards are a special feature that most Microsoft products offer. A wizard displays a series of dialog boxes that ask you design and content questions. Using your answers, the wizard creates something (in this case, a presentation) according to your instructions.

TERM **Design Template** A design template is a preformatted presentation file (without any slides in it). When you select a template, PowerPoint applies the color scheme and general layout of the template to each slide in the presentation.

A Word About the PowerPoint Dialog Box

If you have just started PowerPoint and the PowerPoint dialog box is displayed, you are ready to start a new presentation (see Figure 2.1). From here you can choose to create a new presentation using the AutoContent Wizard, a design template, or a blank presentation. Just click your choice, then click **OK** and follow along with the steps in the remainder of this lesson to complete the presentation.

Figure 2.1 Selecting from the PowerPoint opening dialog box is one way to create a new presentation.

Unfortunately, this dialog box is available only when you first start the program. Once you close the dialog box, you won't see it again until the next time you start the program. That's why the steps in the remainder of this lesson don't rely on it; instead, they show alternative methods for starting a presentation if this dialog box is not available.

Creating a New Presentation with the AutoContent Wizard

With the AutoContent Wizard, you select the type of presentation you want to create (such as strategy, sales, training, conveying bad news, or general), and PowerPoint creates an outline for the presentation.

TIP   **Quick Start**   You can click the **AutoContent Wizard** button in the PowerPoint dialog box shown in Figure 2.1, click **OK**, and then skip the first three steps in the following procedure.

Here's how you use the AutoContent Wizard:

1. Open the **File** menu and click **New**. The New Presentation dialog box appears.

2. Click the **General** tab if it's not already on top (see Figure 2.2).

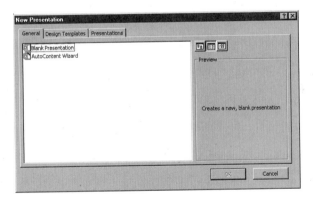

Figure 2.2 You can start a new presentation from here.

3. Double-click the **AutoContent Wizard** icon. The AutoContent Wizard starts.

Macro Warning   At step 3, you may get a warning message about macros possibly carrying viruses. Just click **Enable Macros** to continue.

CAUTION

4. Click the **Next** button to begin.

5. In the dialog box that appears (see Figure 2.3), click the button that best represents the type of presentation you want to create (for example, Sales/Marketing).

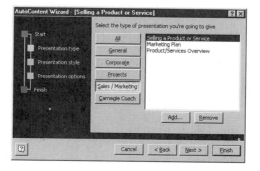

Figure 2.3 Just answer the AutoContent Wizard's questions and click Next.

6. Click a presentation on the list that further narrows your presentation's purpose (for example, Marketing Plan). Then click **Next**.

7. Choose the method that best describes how you will give the presentation:

- **Onscreen Presentation**—Choose this if you plan to use a computer and your PowerPoint file to present the show.

- **Web Presentation**—Choose this if you are planning to distribute the presentation as a self-running or user-interactive show.

- **Black-and-White Overheads**—Choose this if you plan to make black-and-white transparencies for your show.

- **Color Overheads**—Choose this if you plan to make color transparencies for your show.

- **35mm Slides**—Choose this if you plan to send your PowerPoint presentation to a service bureau to have 35mm slides made. (You probably don't have such expensive and specialized equipment in your own company.)

8. Click **Next** to continue.

9. Enter the presentation title in the field provided.

10. (Optional) If you want to include a footer (repeated text) on each slide, enter the text in the **Footer** text box.

11. (Optional) If you do not want a date and/or slide number on each slide, deselect the **Date Last Updated** and/or **Slide Number** check boxes.

12. Click **Finish**. The beginnings of your presentation, with dummy text in place, appear onscreen in Normal view. (You'll learn about Normal view, as well as other views, in Lesson 3, "Working with Slides in Different Views.")

TIP **Replacing Dummy Text** You can start personalizing your presentation right away by replacing the dummy text with your own text. Just select the existing text and type right over it.

Creating a New Presentation with a Design Template

A template is the middle ground between maximum hand-holding (the AutoContent Wizard) and no help at all (Blank Presentation).

Two kinds of templates are available: presentation templates and design templates. When you use the AutoContent Wizard, you use a presentation template. It contains not only formatting, but also sample slides. The other kind of template is a design template. It contains formatting only—no slides. If you want to use a presentation template, use the AutoContent Wizard, as explained in the preceding section.

To start a new presentation using a design template, follow these steps:

1. Open the **File** menu and select **New**. The New dialog box opens.

2. Click the **Design Templates** tab. A list of design templates appears.

3. Click a template. A preview of the template appears in the Preview area. Click each of the templates in turn to locate one you like.

Installing Templates On-the-Fly If you get a message that the template you have chosen is not installed, prompting you to install it, click **Yes** and let the Office 2000 installation program set up the template for you. You must have **CAUTION** the Office 2000 CD in your drive to do this.

4. After you select the template you want to use, click **OK**. PowerPoint creates the new presentation based on that template.

5. The New Slide dialog box appears, prompting you for the layout of the first slide (see Figure 2.4). Click the AutoLayout you want to use and click **OK**.

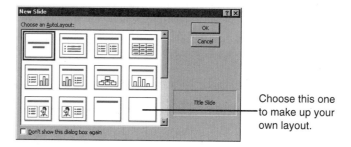

Choose this one to make up your own layout.

Figure 2.4   In the New Slide dialog box, you can choose a predesigned slide layout, or you can choose to design your own.

 TIP   **The Next Step?**   Add more slides by clicking the **New Slide** button on the toolbar, creating your presentation one slide at a time. (See Lesson 6, "Inserting, Deleting, and Copying Slides," for help.)

Creating a Blank Presentation

Are you sure you want to attempt a blank presentation on your first time out? A blank presentation has no preset color scheme or design and no dummy text to help you know what to write. To create a blank presentation, follow these steps:

1. Open the **File** menu and select **New**.

2. Click the **General** tab.

3. Double-click the **Blank Presentation** icon. The New Slide dialog box appears (refer to Figure 2.4).

4. Select the AutoLayout you want to use, click it, and click **OK**.

Saving a Presentation

Soon after creating a presentation, you should save it on disk to protect the work you have already done. To save a presentation for the first time, follow these steps:

1. Click **File**, then select **Save**, or just click the **Save** button on the Standard toolbar. The Save As dialog box appears.

2. In the **File Name** text box, type the name you want to assign to the presentation. You are not limited to the old 8-character filenames, as you were with PowerPoint versions designed for Windows 3.x. Your filenames can be as long as 255 characters and spaces. Do not type a file extension; PowerPoint automatically adds the extension .ppt (see Figure 2.5).

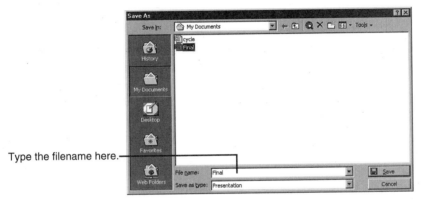

Type the filename here.

Figure 2.5 Type a name for your presentation in the Save As dialog box.

3. The Save In box shows which folder the file will be saved in. The default is My Documents. If you want to save to a different drive or folder, see the next section in this lesson. Otherwise, continue on to step 4.

4. Click **Save**.

Now that you have named the file and saved it to a disk, you can save any changes you make simply by pressing **Ctrl+S** or clicking the **Save** button on the Standard toolbar. Your data is saved under the filename you assigned.

To create a copy of a presentation under a different name (thus preserving your earlier saved version unchanged), select **File**, then click **Save As**. The Save As dialog box reappears, and you can follow steps 2 to 4 as before.

Saving to a Different Drive or Folder

The dialog boxes for opening and saving files in Office 2000 programs are different from the ones in Windows 95/98 in general. To change to a different drive (such as your company server or a floppy disk drive), you must open the **Save In** drop-down list (see Figure 2.6). From it, choose the drive on which you want to save the file.

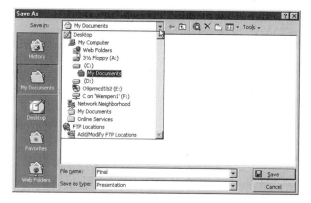

Figure 2.6 Use this drop-down list to save to a different drive.

Next, you must select the folder where you want to save the file. When you select the drive, a list of the folders on that drive appears. Double-click the folder you want to select.

Table 2.1 explains the buttons and other controls you see in the Save As dialog box.

Table 2.1 Buttons for Changing Drives and Folders in Windows 98 Dialog Boxes

Control	Name	Purpose
⬅	Back	Moves back to the preceding folder you looked at, if there is one. Otherwise, this button is unavailable.

Control	*Name*	*Purpose*
	Up One Level	Moves to the folder "above" the one shown in the Save In box (that is, the folder in which the current one resides).
	Search the Web	Opens Internet Explorer so you can search the Web for a file; seldom used.
	Delete	Deletes the selected file.
	Create New Folder	Creates a new folder.
	Views	Opens a list of viewing options for the file list (List, Details, Properties, and Preview).
Tools	Tools	Opens a menu of commands you can issue for the selected file (Delete, Rename, Print, and others).

In addition to the buttons across the top of the Save As and Open dialog boxes, shortcut icons are located along the left side. These point to folders that some people use to store files or shortcuts to files:

- **History**—Contains shortcuts for all the files you have used recently. This corresponds roughly to the Recently Used Documents list on the Start menu in Windows.

- **My Documents**—The default folder for storing PowerPoint presentations. Use this button to jump back there from some other folder you may have been browsing.

- **Desktop**—The folder that contains all the shortcuts on your Windows desktop. (You would seldom store a file there.)

- **Favorites**—A folder that contains shortcuts to all the files you have indicated you wanted there. You can add a shortcut to the Favorites folder by opening the Tools menu in the Save As or Open dialog box and choosing Add to Favorites.

- **Web Folders**—A special-purpose folder that holds any shortcuts to Web locations where you store files.

Closing a Presentation

You can close a presentation at any time. If you are working on multiple presentations, it's okay to keep them all open at once. The more presentations you have open, however, the slower PowerPoint's response time to your commands will be, so you should close any presentations that you are not working on.

Note that although this closes the presentation window, it does not exit PowerPoint. To close a presentation, follow these steps:

1. If more than one presentation is open, open the **Window** menu and select the one you want to close.

2. Choose **File** and then select **Close,** or click the presentation's **Close** (×) button. (If you see two × buttons, it's the lower of the two.) If you haven't saved the presentation, or if you haven't saved since you made changes, a dialog box appears asking if you want to save.

3. To save your changes, click **Yes.** If this is a new presentation, refer to the steps earlier in this lesson for saving a presentation. If you have saved the file previously, the presentation window closes.

Opening a Presentation

After you save a presentation to a disk, you can open the presentation and continue working on it at any time. Follow these steps:

1. Choose **File** and then select **Open,** or click the **Open** button on the Standard toolbar. The Open dialog box appears (see Figure 2.7).

2. If the file isn't in the currently displayed folder, select the **Look In** drop-down arrow to choose from a list of other drives and/or folders.

3. Double-click the file to open it.

In PowerPoint 2000, you can open files from some other presentation programs, such as Freelance.

 TIP **New Feature** In PowerPoint 2000, the Open button in the Open dialog box has a drop-down list. From it, you can choose Open Read-Only or Open as Copy. Open Read-Only prevents changes from being saved to the presentation; Open as Copy creates a copy to be saved under a different name. Both of these help prevent inadvertent changes to a valuable presentation.

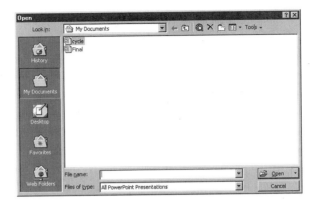

Figure 2.7   Select the presentation you want to open.

Finding a Presentation File

If you're having trouble locating your file, PowerPoint can help you look. Follow these steps to find a file:

1. Choose the **File** menu, then select **Open** (if the Open dialog box is not already open).

2. (Optional) If you know part of the name, use wildcards to indicate it. (See the following note.)

 TERM   **Wild Card**   If you don't have the entire name at your fingertips, insert a wildcard as part of the name. The asterisk (*) stands in for any one or more characters, and the question mark (?) stands in for any single character. For example, you could type **P*.ppt** to find all PowerPoint files that begin with the letter P.

3. (Optional) If you want to look for a certain type of file, choose the type from the **Files of Type** drop-down list.

4. Click the **Tools** button to open its menu and choose **Find**. The Find dialog box appears (see Figure 2.8).

5. In the **Look In** section at the bottom of the Find dialog box, narrow the search area as much as possible using these techniques:

- If you are sure the file is in a certain folder, type that folder's path (such as **C:\WINDOWS**) in the **Look In** box.
- If you are sure the file is on a certain drive, select that drive from the **Look In** drop-down list.
- If you don't know which drive contains the file, select **My Computer** from the **Look In** drop-down list.

6. Make sure the **Search Subfolders** check box is marked. If it isn't, click it.

7. If you want to specify any other properties, do so like this:

  a. Open the **Property** drop-down list and choose a property. For example, to find a file that contains a certain word, choose **Contents**.

  b. Open the **Condition** drop-down list and choose a condition. Your choices vary depending on the property you chose.

  c. Type a value to match in the **Value** text box. For example, to find a file containing the name John Smith, type **John Smith**.

  d. Click the **Add to List** button.

8. Click the **Find Now** button. The File Open dialog box reappears and displays the files that match your search criteria.

9. Double-click the desired file to open it.

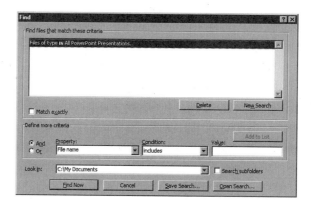

Figure 2.8   Use the Find dialog box to select the folders and drives you want to search.

Now that you've learned to create the basic shell of your presentation, you need to modify and customize it. If you're not in a hurry, read all the lessons, in order, so that you can learn PowerPoint fully. However, if you're in a hurry, refer to the following lessons:

- To change the view of the presentation so you can work with it more easily, see Lesson 3, "Working with Slides in Different Views."
- To apply a different design template or slide layout, see Lesson 5, "Changing a Presentation's Look."
- To add new slides, see Lesson 6, "Inserting, Deleting, and Copying Slides."
- To rearrange slides, see Lesson 7, "Rearranging Slides in a Presentation."
- To add and edit text, see Lesson 8, "Adding and Modifying Slide Text."

In this lesson, you learned how to create a new presentation. You also learned how to save, close, open, and find presentations. In the next lesson, you learn how to work with slides in different views.

Working with Slides in Different Views

In this lesson, you will learn how to display a presentation in different views and how to edit slides in Outline and Slide views.

Understanding PowerPoint's Tri-Pane View

PowerPoint can display your presentation in different views. Having the option of selecting a view makes it easier to perform certain tasks. For example, Normal view has Outline, Slide, and Notes panes, suitable for working on the text of each slide and for placing objects on a slide. Slide Sorter view enables you to quickly rearrange the slides. Figure 3.1 shows some of the different views.

To change views, open the **View** menu and choose the desired view: **Normal**, **Slide Sorter**, **Notes Page**, or **Slide Show**.

- **Normal** is the default, 3-pane view. Variations of it include Outline view and Slide view.
- **Slide Sorter** view shows all the slides as thumbnail sketches so that you can easily rearrange them.
- **Notes Page** view provides a large pane for creating notes for your speech. You can also type these notes in Normal view, but Notes Page view gives you more room.

- **Slide Show** is a specialized view that enables you to preview and present your show onscreen. You won't have much use for it until later, when your show is complete.

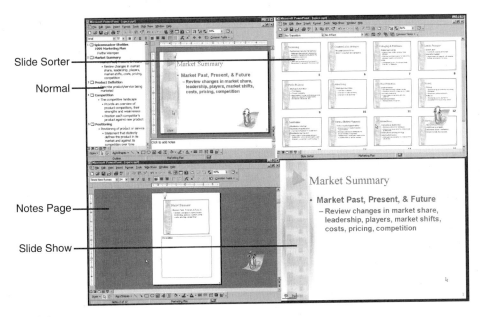

Figure 3.1 You can change views to make a task easier.

A quicker way to switch views is to click the button for the desired view at the bottom of the presentation window, as shown in Figure 3.2. Notes Page view is not available as a button; the buttons (from left to right) are Normal, Outline, Slide, Slide Sorter, and Slide Show.

Outline and Slide views are really nothing more than Normal view with the three panes resized to emphasize different things. Outline view scrunches up the Slide and Notes panes so the Outline pane is at maximum size. Similarly, Slide view scrunches up the Outline and Notes panes so that the slide is at maximum size. You can manually drag the dividers between the panes in any of these 3-pane views at any time. Figure 3.3 compares Normal, Slide, and Outline views.

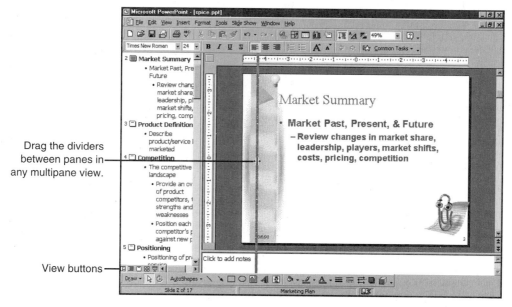

Drag the dividers between panes in any multipane view.

View buttons

Figure 3.2 Use View buttons to change views.

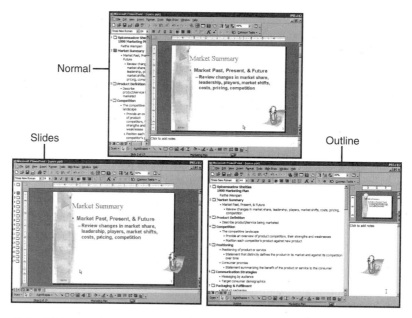

Normal

Slides

Outline

Figure 3.3 Slide and Outline views are simply variations of the 3-pane Normal view.

No Notes?   Notice that in Slide view, the Notes pane has been effectively "resized" out of existence, but the divider line is still there at the bottom of the Slide pane, and you can drag the divider up to reopen the Notes pane.

CAUTION

Moving from Slide to Slide

When you have more than one slide in your presentation, you will need to move from one slide to the next to work with a specific slide. The procedure for selecting a slide is determined by the view you are using:

- In any view that displays the Outline pane, scroll through the outline and click the text for the slide you want to see. The other panes will jump to display it.
- In any view except Slide Sorter, press **Page Up** or **Page Down** to move to the previous or next slide.
- In any view except Slide Sorter and Slide Show, click the **Previous Slide** or **Next Slide** button, just below the vertical scrollbar (as shown in Figure 3.4), or drag the box inside the scrollbar until the desired slide number is displayed.
- In Slide Sorter view, click the desired slide. A thick border appears around it.

Introduction to Slide Editing

If you created a presentation in Lesson 2, "Creating a New Presentation," using the AutoContent Wizard, you already have several slides, but they may not contain the text you want to use. If you created a blank presentation or based a new presentation on a design template, you have at least one slide on the screen that you can edit.

The following sections explain how to edit text. In later lessons, you will learn how to add and edit text objects, pictures, graphs, organizational charts, and other items.

TERM

Object   An object is any item on a slide, including text, graphics, and charts.

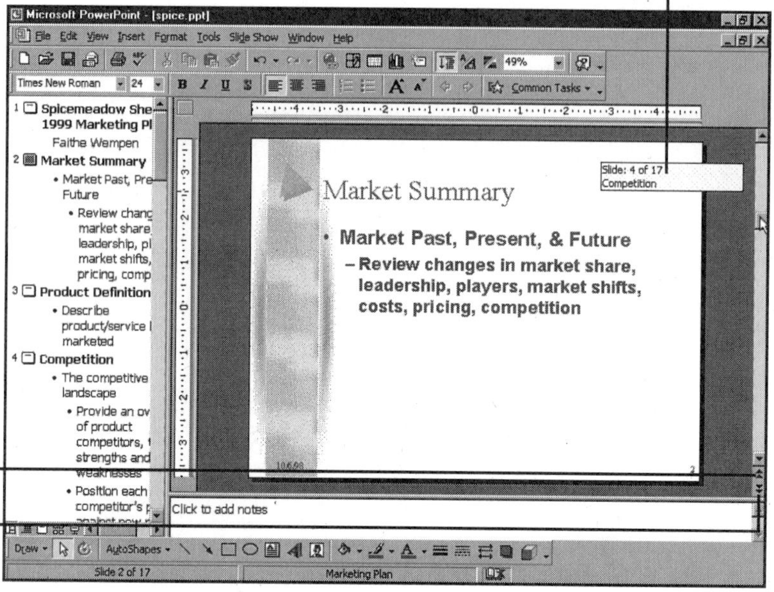

When you drag the scroll box, the slide
number shows where you're going.

Figure 3.4   Use the Previous Slide and Next Slide buttons to move between slides, or drag the scroll box.

Editing Text in the Outline Pane

The Outline pane provides the easiest way to edit text. You simply click to move the insertion point where you want it in the outline, and then type in your text. Press the **Del** key to delete characters to the right of the insertion point or the **Backspace** key to delete characters to the left.

TIP   **Larger Outline**   You may want to enlarge the Outline pane by dragging its divider to the right or by clicking the **Outline View** button. Outline view is shown in Figure 3.5.

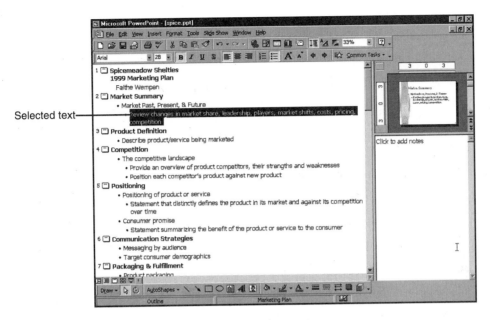

Selected text

Figure 3.5   You can edit your text in Outline view.

To select text, hold down the left mouse button and drag the mouse pointer over the desired text (see Figure 3.5). You can then press the **Del** or **Backspace** key to delete the text, or you can drag the text where you want to move it.

TIP   **Auto Word Select**   When you select text, PowerPoint selects whole words. If you want to select individual characters, open the **Tools** menu, select **Options**, click the **Edit** tab, and click the **When Selecting, Automatically Select Entire Word** check box to turn it off. Click **OK**.

Moving a Line in Outline View

As you work in Outline view, you may find that some slides need to be rearranged. One easy way is to drag a slide by its slide icon (next to its title on the outline) to a new position.

You can also turn on the Outlining toolbar and use its Move Up and Move Down buttons. To turn on the toolbar, right-click one of the other toolbars and choose **Outlining**. Then use these buttons, as shown in Figure 3.6:

• To move a paragraph up in the outline, select it and then click the **Move Up** button.

• To move a paragraph down in the outline, select it and then click the **Move Down** button.

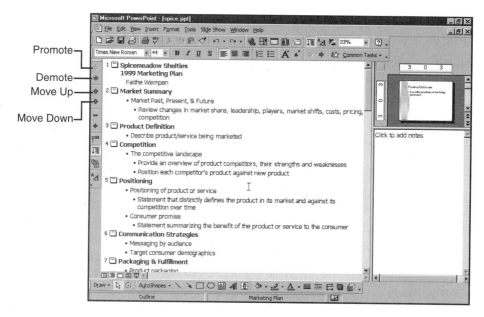

Promote

Demote

Move Up

Move Down

Figure 3.6 You can display an Outlining toolbar and use its buttons to alter the outline.

Changing the Text's Outline Level

As you can see from Figure 3.6, your presentation is organized in a multilevel outline format. The slides are at the top level of the outline, and each slide's contents are subordinate under that slide. Some slides have multiple levels of subordination (for example, a bulleted list within a bulleted list).

You can easily change an object's level in Outline view with the Tab key or the Outlining toolbar:

• **To demote a paragraph in the outline**—Click the text, then press the **Tab** key or click the **Demote** button on the Outlining toolbar.

• **To promote a paragraph in the outline**—Click the text, then press **Shift+Tab** or click the **Promote** button on the Outlining toolbar.

In most cases, subordinate items on a slide appear as items in a bulleted list. In Lesson 9, "Creating Columns and Lists," you will learn how to change the appearance of the bullet and the size and formatting of text for each entry, as well as how much the text is indented for each level.

 TIP **Dragging Paragraphs** You can quickly change the level of a paragraph by dragging it left or right.

Editing Text in the Slide Pane

Text appears on a slide in a text box. (All objects appear on a slide in their own boxes for easy manipulation.) As shown in Figure 3.7, to edit text on a slide, click the text box to select it and then click where you want the insertion point moved.

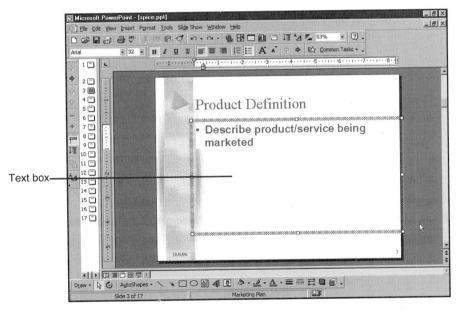

Figure 3.7 You can edit your text directly on the slide in the Slide pane.

When you work with the Slide pane, you may want to use Slide view or manually adjust the pane sizes. Figure 3.7 shows Slide view in use.

In Lesson 8, "Adding and Modifying Slide Text," you'll learn more about adding text to a slide, including creating your own text boxes on a slide. In Lessons 8 and 9, you'll learn how to fine-tune the look of your text for maximum impact.

You can also edit graphics on a slide in the Slide pane. Editing graphics is trickier than editing text. Lesson 10, "Adding Graphics to a Slide," discusses placing graphics on slides, and Lesson 12, "Working with PowerPoint Objects," covers manipulating graphics.

In this lesson, you learned how to change views for a presentation, move from slide to slide, and edit text. In the next lesson, you learn how to print your presentations, notes, and handouts.

Printing Presentations, Notes, and Handouts

In this lesson, you learn how to select a size and orientation for the slides in your presentation and how to print the slides, notes, and handouts you create.

 TIP **Notes and Handouts** Your audience handouts should be clear and concise and follow your presentation sequentially. Sometimes less is more—it helps the audience focus on you and your presentation.

Quick Printing—No Options

The quickest way to print is to use all the default settings. You don't get to make any decisions about your output, but you do get your printout without delay.

To print a quick copy, choose one of these methods:

- Click the **Print** button on the Standard toolbar.
- Choose the **File** menu, then choose **Print** and click **OK**.
- Press **Ctrl+P** and click **OK**.

When you use these methods for printing, you get a printout of your entire presentation in whatever view is onscreen and whatever pane is active. (To activate a pane, click it.) The following list describes what type of printout you can expect from each view:

- **Normal view, Slide pane active**—The entire presentation prints in Landscape orientation. Each slide fills an entire page.
- **Normal view, Outline pane active**—The entire outline prints in Portrait orientation.
- **Slide Sorter view**—The entire presentation prints in Portrait orientation with six slides per page.
- **Notes Pages view**—The entire presentation prints in Portrait orientation with one slide per page. Each slide prints with its notes beneath it.

 Orientation The orientation setting tells the printer which edge of the paper should be at the top of the printout. If the top is across the wide edge, it's Landscape; if the top is across the narrow edge, it's Portrait.

Changing the Slide Setup

If you didn't get the printouts you expected from the previous procedure, you can change the selected presentation's output, size, and orientation in the Page Setup dialog box. To customize your printouts, follow these steps:

1. Choose the **File** menu, then choose **Page Setup**. The Page Setup dialog box appears onscreen, as shown in Figure 4.1.

Figure 4.1 The Page Setup dialog box enables you to set the position and size of the slides on the page.

2. Perform one of the following procedures to set the slide size:
   - To use a standard size, select a size from the **Slides Sized For** drop-down list. For example, you can have slides sized for regular 8 1/2×11 paper, 35mm slides, or an onscreen slide show.
   - To create a custom size, enter the dimensions in the **Width** and **Height** text boxes.

Spin Boxes The arrows to the right of the Width and Height text boxes enable you to adjust the settings in those boxes. Click the up arrow to increase the setting by .1 inch or the down arrow to decrease it by .1 inch.

3. In the **Number Slides From** text box, type the number with which you want to start numbering slides. (This is usually 1, but you may want to start with a different number if the presentation is a continuation of another.)

4. Under the Slides heading, choose **Portrait** or **Landscape** orientation for your slides.

5. In the Notes, Handouts & Outline section, choose **Portrait** or **Landscape** for those items.

6. Click **OK**. If you changed the orientation of your slides, you may have to wait a moment while PowerPoint repositions the slides.

Choosing What and How to Print

If the default print options don't suit you, you can change them. Do you have more than one printer? If so, you can choose which printer to use. For example, you may want to use a color printer for overhead transparencies and a black-and-white printer for your handouts. You can also select options for printing multiple copies and for printing only specific slides.

To set your print options, follow these steps:

1. Choose the **File** menu, then choose **Print**. The Print dialog box appears, with the name of the currently selected printer in the Name box (see Figure 4.2).

2. If you want to use a different printer, open the **Name** drop-down list and select the printer you want.

 Printer Properties The **Properties** button enables you to adjust graphics quality, select paper size, and choose which paper tray to use, among other things.

3. Choose what to print in the Print Range section:

- Choose **All** to print all the slides in the presentation.
- Choose **Current Slide** to print only the currently displayed slide.
- Enter a range of slide numbers in the **Slides** text box—for example, **2-4** to print slides 2, 3, and 4.

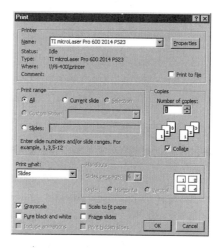

Figure 4.2 Choose your printing options in the Print dialog box.

4. Open the **Print What** drop-down list and choose what you want to print. You can print slides, handouts, notes, or outlines.

5. If you want more than one copy, enter the number of copies you want in the **Number of Copies** box.

6. Select or deselect any of these check boxes in the dialog box, as desired:

- **Print to File**—Select this option to send the output to a file rather than to your printer.
- **Collate**—If you are printing more than one copy, select this check box to collate (1, 2, 3, 1, 2, 3) each printed copy instead of printing all the copies of each page at once (1, 1, 2, 2, 3, 3).
- **Grayscale**—If you have a black-and-white printer, select this check box to make the color slides print more crisply. You also can select this check box to force a color printer to produce black-and-white output.

- **Pure Black & White**—This check box is like the preceding one except everything prints in solid black and plain white, with no gray shading. This makes all slides look like line drawings.

- **Scale to Fit Paper**—If the slide (or whatever you're printing) is too large to fit on the page, select this check box to decrease the size of the slide to make it fit on the page. Now you won't have to paste two pieces of paper together to see the whole slide.

- **Frame Slides**—Select this check box if you want to print a border around each slide.

- **Print Hidden Slides**—If you have any hidden slides, you can choose whether to print them. If you don't have any hidden slides, this check box will be unavailable. You'll learn about hidden slides in Lesson 7, "Rearranging Slides in a Presentation."

- **Include Animations**—If you have any animated elements on the slide, mark this check box and PowerPoint will do its best to approximate them in still form.

 TIP   Why Would I Print to File?   If you don't have the printer that you want to use hooked up to your computer, you can print to a file and then take that file to the computer where the printer is. The other computer does not need to have PowerPoint installed on it to print PowerPoint documents.

7. Click **OK** to print.

In this lesson, you learned how to print slides, outlines, and notes, and how to set options for your printouts. In the next lesson, you learn how to change the overall appearance of the slides in a presentation and work with AutoLayouts and the Slide Master.

Changing a Presentation's Look

In this lesson, you learn various ways to give your presentation a professional and consistent look.

Giving Your Slides a Professional Look

PowerPoint comes with dozens of professionally created designs you can apply to your presentations. These designs include background patterns, color choices, font choices, and more. When you apply a design template to your presentation, it applies its formatting to the Slide Master.

The Slide Master is not really a slide, but it looks like one. It is a design grid that you make changes to; these changes affect every slide in the presentation. When you apply a template, you are actually applying the template to the Slide Master, which in turn applies it to each slide.

There's another way to make global changes to an entire presentation: You can alter the Slide Master manually. For example, if you want a graphic to appear on every slide, you can place it on the Slide Master instead of pasting it onto each slide individually.

 TIP **Changing the Colors on a Single Slide** If you want to make some slides in the presentation look different from the others, check out Lessons 8, "Adding and Modifying Slide Text," and 10, "Adding Graphics to a Slide," to learn how to apply different colored fonts and graphics to individual slides.

Applying a Different Design Template

You can apply a different template to your presentation at any time, no matter how you originally created the presentation. To change the design template, follow these steps:

1. Choose the **Format** menu, then select **Apply Design Template**. The Apply Design Template dialog box appears (see Figure 5.1).

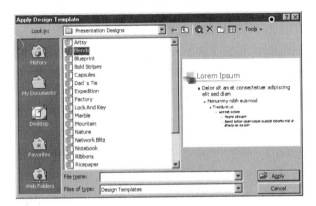

Figure 5.1 Choose a different template from the Apply Design Template dialog box.

2. Click the template name in the list. A sample of the template appears to the right of the list. If you do not see a sample area, click the **Views** button and select **Preview** until it appears.

3. When you find the template you want to use, click **Apply**.

You can also apply any of the designs from the presentation templates that come with PowerPoint (that is, the templates that also include sample text). "Borrowing" the design from one of these templates does not insert any sample text; to get the sample text, you must start a new presentation based on one of those templates.

To access the presentation templates, click the **Up One Level** button in the Apply Design Template dialog box, and then double-click the **1033** folder to see a list of them.

Using AutoLayouts

Templates enable you to change the color and design of the presentation, but AutoLayouts enable you to set the structure of a single slide. For example, if you want a graph and a picture on a slide, you can choose an AutoLayout that positions the two items for you.

If you prefer to place objects on your slide manually (without the placeholders provided by an AutoLayout), choose the **Blank AutoLayout** to create a blank slide with no placeholders. Then place objects manually on the slide, which you will learn to do in the upcoming lessons.

CAUTION

Individual Slides? PowerPoint applies AutoLayouts to individual slides, but the template you choose and the Slide Master modifications you make affect the AutoLayouts, too. This becomes more evident later in this lesson.

To use an AutoLayout, do the following:

1. In Normal, Outline, or Slide view, display the slide you want to change.

2. Choose the **Format** menu, then choose **Slide Layout**, or right-click the slide and choose **Slide Layout** from the shortcut menu. The Slide Layout dialog box appears (see Figure 5.2).

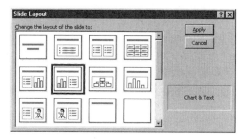

Figure 5.2 You can change an individual slide's layout with this dialog box.

3. Click the desired layout or use the arrow keys to move the selection border to it.

4. Click the **Apply** button. PowerPoint applies the selected layout to the current slide.

Editing the Slide Master

Every presentation has a Slide Master that controls the overall appearance and layout of each slide. The Slide Master contains all the formatting information that the template brings to the presentation, such as colors and background patterns, and it also marks where the elements you use from the AutoLayout feature (such as text boxes) will appear on the slide.

To make changes to the Slide Master for your presentation, follow these steps:

1. Choose the **View** menu, point at **Master**, then select **Slide Master**. Your Slide Master appears, as shown in Figure 5.3.

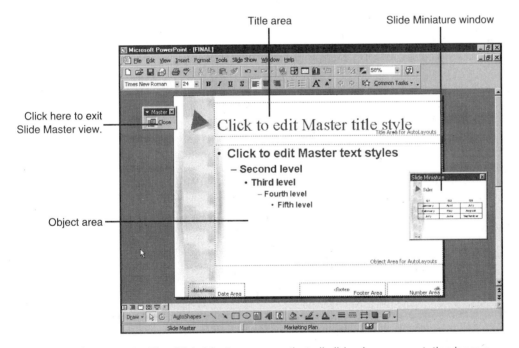

Figure 5.3 The Slide Master ensures that all slides in a presentation have a consistent look.

2. Make any changes to the Slide Master. (Anything you can do to a regular slide, you can do to a Slide Master.)
3. When you're finished working with the Slide Master, click the **Close** button (refer to Figure 5.3) to return to the view you started from.

The two most important elements on the Slide Master are the Title area and Object area for the AutoLayout objects. The Title area contains the formatting specifications for each slide's title; that is, it tells PowerPoint the type size, style, and color to use for the text in the title of each slide. The Object area contains the formatting specifications for all remaining text and AutoLayout objects on the slide.

 Slide Miniature The Slide Miniature window enables you to see what the actual slides will look like in the presentation. The Slide Miniature window appears not only when you are working with the Slide Master, but also in other views where the entire slide may not be visible, such as Notes Page view.

For most of PowerPoint's templates, the Object area sets up specifications for a bulleted list, including the type of bullet, as well as the type styles, sizes, and indents for each item in the list.

In addition to the Title and Object areas, the Slide Master can contain information about background colors, borders, page numbers, company logos, clip art objects, and any other elements you want to appear on every slide in the presentation.

In many ways, the Slide Master is like any other slide. In the following lessons, when you learn how to add text, graphics, borders, and other objects to a slide, keep in mind that you can add these objects on individual slides or on the Slide Master. When you add the object to the Slide Master, the object will appear on every slide.

In this lesson, you learned how to give your presentation a consistent look with templates and AutoLayouts. You also learned how to use the Slide Master to make global changes to your slides. In the next lesson, you learn how to insert, delete, and copy slides, and you learn to add slides from another presentation.

Inserting, Deleting, and Copying Slides

As you work on your presentation, you probably want to create new slides and remove others. In this lesson, you learn how to insert new slides, delete slides, and copy slides in a presentation.

Inserting a Slide

You can insert a slide into a presentation at any time and at any position in the presentation. To insert a slide, follow these steps:

1. Select the slide that appears just before the place where you want to insert the new slide. (You can select the slide in any view.)

2. Choose the **Insert** menu, then **New Slide**. The New Slide dialog box appears (see Figure 6.1).

> **TIP** **Inserting a New Slide Quickly** You can also insert a slide by clicking the **New Slide** button, or pressing **Ctrl+M**.

3. In the **Choose an AutoLayout** list, click a slide layout or use the arrow keys to highlight it.

4. Click the **OK** button. PowerPoint inserts a slide that has the specified layout (see Figure 6.2).

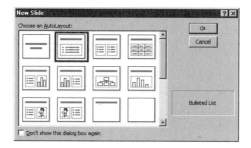

Figure 6.1 In the New Slide dialog box, you can choose a layout for the slide you're inserting.

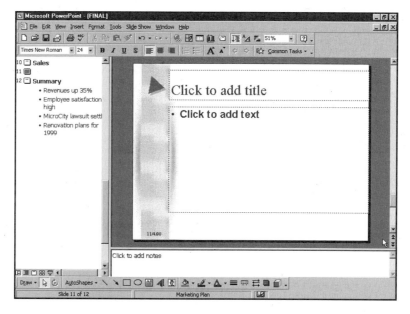

Figure 6.2 The new slide contains the blank structure you selected; you supply the content.

5. Follow the directions indicated on the slide layout to add text or other objects. For text boxes, you click an area to select it and then you type in your text. For other object placeholders, you double-click the placeholder.

TIP **Cloning a Slide** To create an exact replica of a slide (in any view), select the slide you want to duplicate. Click **Insert**, then select **Duplicate Slide**. The new slide is inserted after the original slide. You can move the slide anywhere you want, as you'll learn in Lesson 7, "Rearranging Slides in a Presentation."

Adding Slides from Another Presentation

If you want to insert some or all of the slides from another presentation into the current presentation, perform these steps:

1. Open the presentation into which you want to insert the slides.

2. Select the slide located before the position where you want to insert the slides.

3. Choose the **Insert** menu, then choose **Slides from Files**. The Slide Finder dialog box appears.

4. Click the **Browse** button to display the Browse dialog box.

5. Change the drive and folder if needed by clicking the **Look In** drop-down arrow.

6. Double-click the name of the presentation that contains the slides you want to insert into the open presentation.

7. Click the **Display** button. The slides from the presentation appear in the Slide Finder window (see Figure 6.3).

Click here to view the slides as a list with a preview window.

Use this scrollbar to move through the slides.

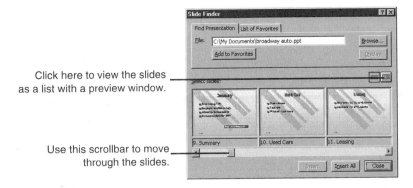

Figure 6.3 You can select any or all of the slides from the selected presentation to add to the open presentation.

TIP **View the Slides in a Different Way** You can click this button if you prefer to see a list of the slide titles instead of three slides at a time. When you click the button, the display changes to a list of titles on the left and a preview window on the right that displays the selected slide.

8. Click the slides you want to insert and then click the **Insert** button. If you want to insert all the slides, click the **Insert All** button.

9. When you are finished inserting slides, click the **Close** button. The inserted slides appear right after the slide that you selected in step 2.

TIP **Make a Favorites List** If you regularly insert slides from a specific presentation, add it to your Favorites List by clicking the **Add to Favorites** button in the Find Slides dialog box. The next time you want to insert slides from that presentation, click the **List of Favorites** tab in the Find Slides dialog box and select the presentation from the list.

Creating Slides from a Document Outline

If you have a word processing document with outline-style headings in it, PowerPoint can pull the headings from the document and use the headings to create slides with bulleted lists. To create slides from a document outline, follow these steps:

1. Choose the **Insert** menu, then choose **Slides from Outline**. The Insert Outline dialog box appears.

2. Use the Insert Outline dialog box to locate the document file you want to use. (Refer to Lesson 2, "Creating a New Presentation," if you need help locating the file.)

3. Double-click the name of the document file.

Selecting Slides

In the following sections, you learn to delete, copy, and move slides. However, before you can do anything with a slide, you have to select it. To select slides, follow these directions:

- To select a single slide, click it.
- To select two or more neighboring slides in the Outline pane, click the first slide, and then hold down the **Shift** key while you click on the last slide in the group.
- To select multiple contiguous slides in Slide Sorter view, click in front of the first slide and then hold down the mouse button and drag to the last slide. All slides that fall in between become selected (see Figure 6.4).

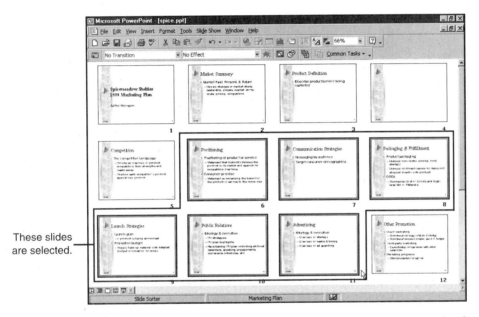

These slides are selected.

Figure 6.4   You can select a block of slides in Slide Sorter view by dragging from the first one to the last one.

Don't Drag the Slide   If you are trying to select multiple contiguous slides, drag from in front of the first slide. Don't start dragging while pointing directly at the first slide because it will move and fail to highlight the remaining slides that you wish to select.

CAUTION

- To select two or more non-neighboring slides (in Slide Sorter view only), hold down the **Ctrl** key while clicking on each slide. You cannot select non-neighboring slides in other views.

Deleting Slides

You can delete a slide from any view. To delete a slide, perform the following steps:

1. Select the slide you want to delete. You can delete multiple slides by displaying or selecting more than one slide.

2. Choose the **Edit** menu, then choose **Delete Slide**. The slide is removed from the presentation.

 TIP **Use the Delete Key** In Outline or Slide Sorter view, you can select the slides you want to delete and press the **Delete** key on the keyboard.

  Oops! If you deleted a slide by mistake, you can get it back. Select **Edit** and then choose **Undo**, or press **Ctrl+Z**.

CAUTION

Cutting, Copying, and Pasting Slides

In Lesson 7, you will learn how to rearrange slides in Slide Sorter and Outline views. However, you also can use the cut, copy, and paste features to copy and move slides either in the same presentation or into other presentations. To cut (or copy) a slide and paste it into a presentation, perform the following steps:

1. Change to Slide Sorter view, or display Normal view and work with the Outline pane.

2. Select the slide(s) you want to copy or cut.

 3. Open the **Edit** menu and select **Cut** or **Copy** to either move or copy the slide(s) to the Windows Clipboard, or use the **Copy** or **Cut** toolbar button.

 Windows Clipboard The Windows Clipboard is a temporary holding area for cut or copied items. You can cut or copy items to the Clipboard and then paste them on a slide, or cut or copy an entire slide or group of slides.

TIP   **Quick Cut or Copy**   To bypass the **Edit** menu, press **Ctrl+C** to copy or **Ctrl+X** to cut.

4. If you want to paste the slide(s) into a different presentation, open that presentation.

5. In Slide Sorter view, select the slide after which you want to place the cut or copied slide(s). Or on the Outline pane, move the insertion point to the end of the text in the slide after which you want to insert the cut or copied slide(s).

 6. Choose the **Edit** menu and then choose **Paste**, or click the **Paste** toolbar button. PowerPoint inserts the cut or copied slides.

 TIP   **Keyboard Shortcut**   You can also press **Ctrl+V** to paste an item that you cut or copied to the clipboard.

In this lesson, you learned how to insert, delete, cut, copy, and paste slides. In the next lesson, you learn how to rearrange the slides in your presentation.

Rearranging Slides in a Presentation

At times you will need to change the sequence of slides in a presentation. PowerPoint has the capability to reorder slides in either Slide Sorter view or on the Outline pane in Normal view. In this lesson, you will learn how to rearrange your slides.

Rearranging Slides in Slide Sorter View

Slide Sorter view shows miniature versions of the slides in your presentation. This enables you to view many of your slides at one time. To rearrange slides in Slide Sorter view, perform the following steps:

1. Switch to Slide Sorter view by selecting **View** and then choosing **Slide Sorter**, or click the **Slide Sorter** button on the toolbar.

2. Move the mouse pointer over the slide you want to move.

3. Hold down the left mouse button and drag the mouse pointer over the slide before or after which you want to insert the slide. As you drag the mouse pointer, the slide you pointed at becomes selected (dark border) and a line appears (as shown in Figure 7.1), showing where you are moving the slide.

CAUTION

Destination Not in View? If you have more than just a few slides in your presentation, you may not be able to see the slide's destination onscreen. Don't worry. Just drag the slide in the direction of the destination, and the display will scroll in that direction.

4. Release the mouse button. PowerPoint places the slide in its new position and shifts the surrounding slides to make room for the new slide.

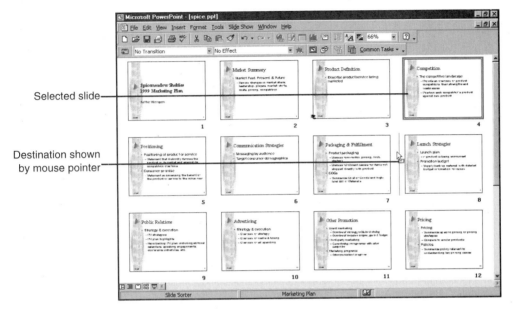

Figure 7.1   Move the slides by dragging them in Slide Sorter view.

You can copy a slide in Slide Sorter view as easily as you can move a slide. Simply hold down the **Ctrl** key while you drag the slide.

You can drag and drop slides to copy from one presentation to another. Open both presentations. (See Lesson 2, "Creating a New Presentation," for instructions on how to open presentations.) Select the **Window** menu, then choose **Arrange All**. The two windows appear side by side. Change to Slide Sorter view in each window. You can now drag and drop slides from one window to the other.

Rearranging Slides in the Outline Pane

In the Outline pane of Normal view (and also in Outline view, which, as you know, is a variation of Normal view), you see the titles and text on each slide. This gives you a clearer picture of the content and organization of your presentation than some of the other viewing options, so you may prefer to rearrange your slides from the Outline pane. Here's how you do it:

1. Switch to Normal or Outline view by choosing **View** and then selecting **Normal**, or by clicking the **Normal** or **Outline** view button on the toolbar.

2. Click the slide number or slide icon to the left of the slide you want to move. This action highlights the contents of the entire slide.

TIP **Moving the Contents of a Slide**   If you just want to insert some of the information from a slide into your presentation, you don't have to move the entire slide. Move only the slide's data—text and graphics—from one slide to another by selecting only what you want to move and dragging it to its new location.

3. Move the mouse pointer over the selected slide icon, hold down the mouse button, and drag the slide up or down in the outline, as shown in Figure 7.2, or click the **Move Up** or **Move Down** buttons on the Outlining toolbar.

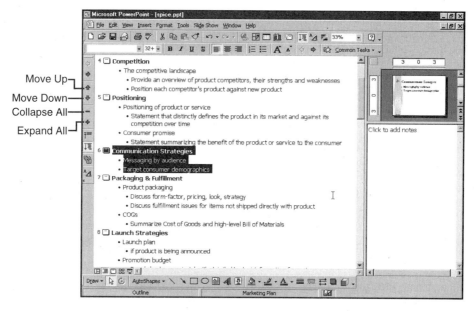

Figure 7.2 Drag the selected icon or click the Move Up or Move Down buttons.

4. Release the mouse button when the slide is at the desired new position. Be careful not to drop the slide in the middle of another slide! If you do, just choose the **Edit** menu, choose **Undo**, and then try again.

TIP   **Collapse the Outline**   You can collapse the outline to show only the slide titles. This enables you to view more slides at one time and to rearrange the slides more easily. Click the **Collapse All** button on the Outlining toolbar (refer to Figure 7.2). To restore the outline, click the **Expand All** button.

Hiding Slides

Before you give a presentation, you should try to anticipate any questions that your audience may have and be prepared to answer those questions. You might even want to create slides to support your answers to these questions and then keep the slides hidden until you need them. To hide one or more slides, perform the following steps:

1. Display or select the slide(s) you want to hide. (You can hide slides in any view except Notes Page or Slide Show.)
2. Choose the **Slide Show** menu, then select **Hide Slide**. If you are in Slide Sorter view, the hidden slide's number appears in a box with a line through it.
3. To unhide the slide(s), display or select the hidden slide(s), choose the **Slide Show** menu, then select **Hide Slide**—again.

 TIP   **Right-Click Shortcut**   To quickly hide a slide, you can right-click a slide and select **Hide** from the shortcut menu that appears.

In Lesson 4, "Printing Presentations, Notes, and Handouts," you learned about the Print Hidden Slides check box in the Print dialog box. Select this check box to print the hidden slides.

In this lesson, you learned how to rearrange the slides in a presentation in either the Slide Sorter or Outline view, and how to hide slides. In the next lesson, you learn how to add text to a slide and how to modify it.

Adding and Modifying Slide Text

In this lesson, you learn how to add text to a slide and change the text alignment and line spacing.

Creating a Text Box

As you have learned in previous lessons, you can put text on a slide by typing text in Outline view or filling in the placeholders on an AutoLayout (see Lesson 5, "Changing a Presenation's Look"). However, both of these methods provide fairly generic results. If you want to type additional text on a slide, you must first create a text box.

 TERM   **Text Box**   A text box acts as a receptacle for the text. Text boxes often contain bulleted lists, notes, and labels (used to point to important parts of illustrations).

To create a text box, perform the following steps:

1. Switch to the Normal or Slide view. (Select the **View** menu and then select the appropriate view.)

 TIP   **Adding the Text to a New Slide**   If you want the text box to appear on a new slide, insert a slide into the presentation. (Choose **Insert**, then **New Slide**; see Lesson 6, "Inserting, Deleting, and Copying Slides" for details.)

2. Click the **Text Box** button on the Drawing toolbar.

3. Click the slide where you want the text box to appear. A small text box appears (see Figure 8.1). (It will expand as needed as you type in it.)

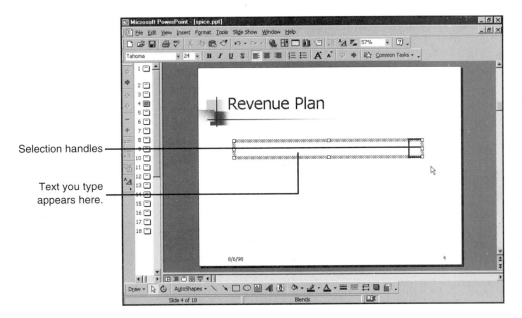

Selection handles

Text you type
appears here.

Figure 8.1   You can enter text in the text box.

4. Type the text that you want to appear in the text box. Press **Enter** to start a new paragraph. Don't worry if the text box becomes too wide; you can resize it after you are done typing.

5. When you are done, click anywhere outside the text box to see how the text will appear on the finished slide.

6. If desired, drag the text box's selection handles to resize it. If you make the box narrower, text within a paragraph may wrap to the next line to keep pace.

If the text does not align correctly in the text box, see "Changing the Text Alignment and Line Spacing" later in this lesson to learn how to change it.

Is That a Frame Around My Text Box? The border that appears around a text box when you create or select it does not appear on the printed slide.

Changing Font Attributes

You can enhance your text by using the Font dialog box or by using various tools on the Formatting toolbar. Use the Font dialog box if you want to add several enhancements to your text at one time. Use the Formatting toolbar to add one enhancement at a time.

Fonts, Styles, and Effects In PowerPoint, a *font* is a family of text that has the same design or typeface (for example, Arial or Courier). A *style* is a standard enhancement, such as bold or italic. An *effect* is a special enhancement, such as shadow or underline.

Using the Font Dialog Box

The font dialog box offers you control over all the attributes you can apply to text. Attributes such as strikethrough, superscript, subscript, and shadow are available as check boxes in this dialog box.

You can change the font of existing text or of text you are about to type by performing the following steps:

1. To change the font of existing text, select text by clicking and dragging the I-beam pointer over the text.

2. Choose the **Format** menu, then choose **Font**. The Font dialog box appears, as shown in Figure 8.2.

TIP **Right-Click Quick** You can right-click the text and select **Font** from the shortcut menu instead of performing steps 1 and 2.

3. From the **Font** list, select the font you want to use.

To Do This		Click This
Open a Format WordArt dialog box		Format WordArt
Change the WordArt shape		WordArt Shape
Rotate the WordArt object		Free Rotate
Make all the letters the same height		WordArt Same Letter Heights
Change between vertical and horizontal text orientation		WordArt Vertical Text
Change the text alignment		WordArt Alignment
Change the spacing between letters		WordArt Character Spacing

To edit the WordArt object, double-click it to display the WordArt toolbar and text entry box. Enter your changes, and then click outside the WordArt object. You can move the object by dragging its border or resize it by dragging a handle.

In this lesson, you learned how to add text to a slide, how to change the text alignment and spacing, and how to add WordArt objects. You also learned how to change the appearance of text by changing its font, size, style, and color. In addition, you learned how to copy text formats. In the next lesson, you learn how to use tables and tabs to create columns and lists.

Creating Columns and Lists

In this lesson, you learn how to use tabs to create columns of text, bulleted lists, numbered lists, and other types of lists.

Working in Multiple Columns

If you need multiple columns of text, you have several options:

- You can use separate text boxes. The easiest way is to use the two-column AutoLayout, which includes two automatic text boxes, but you can also create text boxes manually. (AutoLayouts are described in Lesson 5, "Changing a Presentation's Look," and manual text boxes in Lesson 8, "Adding and Modifying Slide Text.")
- You can place tab stops in a single text box and press Tab to create columns.
- You can use a table to create a grid.

In this lesson, you learn how to do all three of these things.

Creating Columns with an AutoLayout

The easiest way to create columns of text is to use an AutoLayout that contains one or more text boxes. The default AutoLayout is a single bulleted list, but you can change to a double-column list by changing the slide's AutoLayout as described in Lesson 5. (Choose **Format**, then select **Slide Layout**.)

When you use the two-column AutoLayout, the columns appear on the Outline pane as 1 and 2, as shown in Figure 9.1.

Figure 9.1   A two-column AutoLayout provides two panes in which to enter text.

Using Tabs to Create Columns

You can also create multiple columns using tab stops. To set the tabs for a multicolumn list, perform the following steps:

1. Open the presentation and view the slide you want to work with in Slide view.

2. Create a text box for the text if one does not already exist. (For instructions on how to create a text box, see Lesson 8.)

CAUTION

Disappearing Text Box   If you are creating a brand-new, manual text box in step 2, type a few characters in it to "anchor" it so it does not disappear when you click outside it. Then resize it to the final size you want by dragging its left and right selection handles. You should make the text box its final size before you set its tabs.

3. Click anywhere inside the text box for which you want to set the tabs.

637

4. If you already typed text inside the text box, select the text.

5. If the ruler is not onscreen, select the **View** menu, and then select **Ruler** to display the ruler.

6. Click the **Tab** button at the left end of the ruler until it represents the type of tab you want to set (see Table 9.1).

7. Click each place in the ruler where you want to set the selected type of tab stop, as shown in Figure 9.2.

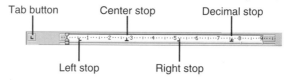

Figure 9.2   The ruler enables you to enter and change tab stop settings.

8. Repeat steps 6 and 7 if you want to set different types of tab stops at different positions.

9. To change the position of an existing tab stop setting, drag it on the ruler to the desired position. To delete an existing tab stop setting, drag it off the ruler.

10. (Optional) To turn off the ruler, select the **View** menu, then select **Ruler**.

Table 9.1   Tab Button Stop Types

Button Appearance	Tab Stop Type
⌞	Aligns the left end of the line against the tab stop.
⊥	Centers the text on the tab stop.
⌟	Aligns the right end of the line against the tab stop.
⫛	Aligns the tab stop on a period. This is called a decimal tab and is useful for aligning a column of numbers that uses decimal points.

TIP   **Don't Forget the Slide Master!**   Throughout this lesson, keep in mind that you can enter your changes on the Slide Master or on individual slides. If you change the Slide Master, the change affects all slides in the presentation. For details on displaying the Slide Master, see Lesson 5.

Creating a Table

The easiest way to create a table on a slide is to use the Table AutoLayout. Change the slide to AutoLayout (choose **Format**, then **Slide Layout**), and then double-click the table placeholder to create a table.

The other way to add a table is by using the Table command on the Insert menu. Follow these steps:

1. Display the slide on which you want to place the table.

2. Choose the **Insert** menu, and then choose **Table**. The Insert Table dialog box appears.

3. Enter the number of columns you want in the **Number of Columns** text box.

4. Enter the number of rows in the **Number of Rows** text box.

5. Click **OK**. The table appears, and the mouse pointer looks like a pencil.

6. Press **Esc**. The mouse pointer becomes normal again, and you are ready to work with the table (see Figure 9.3).

   After you have a table on a slide, you can work with it like this:

   - Click inside a table cell and type. You can move from cell to cell by pressing **Tab** to go forward or **Shift+Tab** to go back.
   - If you need to resize the table, drag a selection handle, just as you would with any object.
   - To adjust the row height or column width, position the mouse pointer on a line between two rows or columns and drag.
   - To change the borders around the cells, select the cells you want to work with and then use the buttons on the Drawing toolbar to adjust the thickness, color, and style of the table gridlines.

There is much more that you can do to format a table than I can tell you here. For more information, consult the PowerPoint Help system.

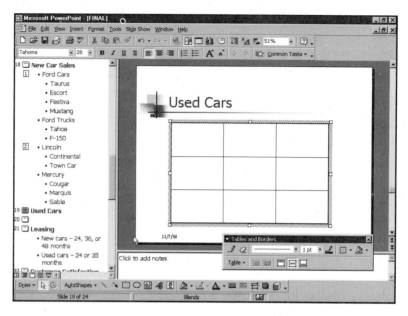

Figure 9.3 Type in the table cells, creating multiple columns.

To make a table appear to be multiple columns of untabular text, turn off all the gridlines in the table. To do so, select all the cells in the table; then right-click and choose **Borders and Fill**. In the Format Table dialog box that appears, click each of the border buttons to turn the border off for each side of each cell in the table. Click **OK** to finish up.

Making a Bulleted List

 When you enter new slides on the Outline pane, the default layout is a simple, bulleted list. If you've done this, you've already created a bulleted list. You can turn off the bullets in front of any paragraphs by selecting the paragraphs and clicking the **Bullets** button on the Formatting toolbar to toggle the bullet off.

When you create your own text boxes without relying on an AutoLayout, the text does not have bullets by default. You can add your own bullets by following these steps:

1. Click inside the paragraph you want to transform into a bulleted list or select one or more paragraphs.

2. Select the **Format** menu, then select **Bullets and Numbering**. The Bullets and Numbering dialog box appears.

TIP **Quick Bullets** To bypass the dialog box, click the **Bullets** button on the Formatting toolbar to insert a bullet, or right-click and select **Bullet** from the shortcut menu. You can click the **Bullets** button again to remove the bullet.

3. Select the bullet style you want (see Figure 9.4).

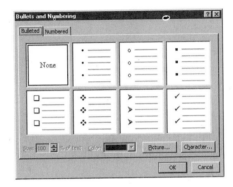

Figure 9.4 Choose the bullet character you want from the several samples provided.

4. Click **OK**. PowerPoint transforms the selected text into a bulleted list. (If you press **Enter** at the end of a bulleted paragraph, the next paragraph starts with a bullet.)

Other options are available for selecting a bullet design for your list. Click the **Character** button to select another character from any font to be used as your bullet, or click the **Picture** button to choose a picture as a bullet. You can also select a size and color for the bullet using the Size and Color controls in the Bullets and Numbering dialog box.

Working with Numbered Lists

 Numbered lists are just like bulleted ones, except they have sequential numbers instead of symbols. You can convert any paragraphs to a numbered list by selecting them and clicking the **Numbering** button on the Formatting toolbar. Select the paragraphs again and click the **Numbering** button again to toggle the numbering off.

You can also create numbered lists with the Bullets and Numbering dialog box, just as you did with bullets. Follow these steps:

1. Select the paragraphs that you want to convert to a numbered list.
2. Choose **Format**, then select **Bullets and Numbering**.
3. Click the **Numbered** tab. The numbered list styles appear (see Figure 9.5).

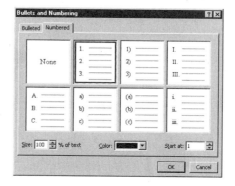

Figure 9.5 Choose the numbering style you want, or turn numbering off by choosing None.

4. Click the style you want for your list.
5. (Optional) Change the Size and/or Color of the numbers.
6. (Optional) If you want the list to start at a number other than 1, enter it in the **Start At** text box.
7. Click **OK**.

In this lesson, you learned how to create columns with AutoLayouts, tabs, and tables, and how to work with bulleted and numbered lists. In the next lesson, you learn how to add graphics to a slide and how to add clip art to the gallery.

Adding Graphics to a Slide

In this lesson, you learn how to add PowerPoint clip art to your presentations, as well as images from other sources.

Introducing the Clip Gallery

One of the major changes between Office 2000 and the previous version is the improved Clip Gallery. The Clip Gallery, shown in Figure 10.1, manages artwork, sounds, and videos (motion clips). In this lesson, you learn to use it for artwork; then in the following lesson we'll revisit it for sounds and videos.

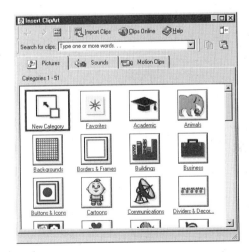

Figure 10.1 The Clip Gallery manages pictures, motion clips, and sounds, all in one convenient place.

Clip Art A collection of previously created images or pictures that you can place on a slide. Microsoft PowerPoint comes with clip art, and you also can buy more from other sources.

You can open the Clip Gallery in any of these ways:

- Click the **Clip Art** button on the Drawing toolbar.
- Select the **Insert** menu, point at **Picture**, and then choose **Clip Art**.
- Select the **Insert** menu, point at **Movies and Sounds**, and then choose **Sound from Gallery**.
- Select the **Insert** menu, point at **Movies and Sounds**, and then choose **Movie from Gallery**.

All of these methods open the Clip Gallery, but a different tab appears on top depending on which method you use. For example, if you select **Insert**, then **Picture**, and then **Clip Art**, the Pictures tab appears on top, as shown in Figure 10.1. Sometimes the dialog box title is different; for example, in Figure 10.1, it's Insert ClipArt. But it's the same old Clip Gallery any way you get there.

 TIP **PowerPoint on the Web** Click the Clips Online button in the Clip Gallery dialog box (refer to Figure 10.1) to connect to Microsoft's Web site and download additional clip art.

Inserting a Clip from the Gallery

To insert a piece of the clip art that comes with PowerPoint, follow these steps:

1. Open the Clip Gallery. (Select **Insert**, then choose **Picture** and select **Clip Art**.)
2. Click the category that represents the type of clip you want.
3. Click the clip you want to use. A pop-up menu of buttons appears.
4. Click the first button on the list, which is **Insert Clip** (see Figure 10.2).

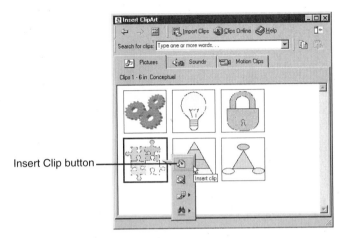

Insert Clip button

Figure 10.2 Insert a selected clip by clicking the Insert Clip button.

5. Close the Clip Gallery window. Your clip appears on the slide.

6. Resize and reposition the clip as needed. See Lesson 12, "Working with PowerPoint Objects," for help.

CAUTION

File Size Alert Artwork, movies, and sounds can really add a lot to a PowerPoint presentation on the Web, but they also add to the size of the file, and consequently, to the time it will take a reader to download it. For this reason, try to be judicious in your use of media on presentations designed for Web use.

Adding Art to the Gallery

You can place most types of images in the Clip Gallery for easy reference, even those that did not come with PowerPoint. To add some art to the Clip Gallery, follow these steps:

1. In the Clip Gallery, click the **Import Clips** button.

2. In the Add clip to Clip Gallery dialog box, locate and select the file you want to add (see Figure 10.3).

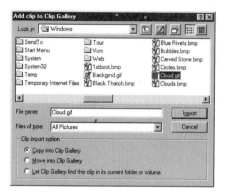

Figure 10.3 Choose the artwork that you want to be able to access through the Clip Gallery.

3. Choose one of the following option buttons:

- **Copy into Clip Gallery**—Choose this to make a copy of the graphic and place it in the same folder as the clip art images that come with PowerPoint. This is a good choice if the clip's original location is not always available (for example, on a network or a CD-ROM).

- **Move into Clip Gallery**—Choose this to move the graphic into the clip art folder.

- **Let Clip Gallery Find This Clip in Its Current Folder or Volume**— Choose this to create a shortcut to the file's original location in the Clip Gallery. This is usually the best choice, as it saves disk space.

4. Click **Import** to import the clip. The Clip Properties dialog box appears.

5. Type a description in the **Description of This Clip** field on the **Description** tab.

6. Click the **Categories** tab, and place a check mark next to each category to which you want to assign the clip (see Figure 10.4). You should assign it to at least one category. Create a new category if needed by clicking the **New Category** button.

7. (Optional) Click the **Keywords** tab. Then click the **New Keyword** button and enter a keyword that describes the clip. Click **OK** to accept that keyword. Repeat to add as many keywords as you like. You will be able to use these keywords later when searching for clips.

8. Click **OK**. The clip is added to the Clip Gallery.

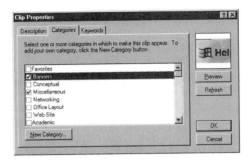

Figure 10.4 Categorize the graphic so it will appear in some of your Clip Gallery categories.

Inserting a Clip from a File

If you have an image stored on disk, you can quickly place it on a slide without using the Clip Gallery. You might want to do this, rather than adding the image to the Clip Gallery, if you are going to use the image only sporadically and don't need to keep it on file.

To place a graphic image from disk on a slide:

1. Select the slide on which the image should be placed.
2. Select the **Insert** menu, point at **Picture**, then select **From File**. The Insert Picture dialog box appears (see Figure 10.5).

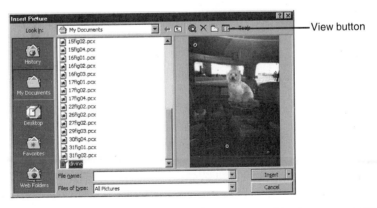

Figure 10.5 Use the Insert Picture dialog box to place any graphics image on a slide.

3. Select the picture you want to use. You can see a preview of the pictures in the Preview pane to the right of the file list. If the preview does not appear, click the **View** button (shown in Figure 10.5) until it comes into view.

4. Click **Insert** to place the image on the slide.

If the picture is too big or too small, you can drag the selection handles (the small squares) around the edge of the image to resize it. (Hold down **Shift** to proportionally resize.) See Lesson 12 for more details about resizing and cropping.

TIP   **Link It Up**   You can link a graphic to the presentation so that whenever the original changes, the version in the presentation changes too. Just open the drop-down list on the **Insert** button in the Insert Picture dialog box (refer to Figure 10.5) and choose **Link to File**.

In this lesson, you learned how to add clip art and other images to your slides. In the next lesson, you learn how to add sounds and videos and control when they play.

Adding Sounds and Movies to a Slide

In this lesson, you learn how to add sound and video clips to a PowerPoint presentation.

Four Ways to Include Sounds in a Presentation

You can use sounds in any of the following ways:

- You can insert a sound clip as an icon on a slide. When you click the icon, the sound plays. You can do this either from the Clip Gallery or from a file, just as you did with artwork in Lesson 10, "Adding Graphics to a Slide."
- You can assign a sound to another object on a slide so that when you click the object, the sound plays.
- You can assign a sound to an animated object on the slide so that when the object appears, the sound plays.
- You can assign a sound to a transition between two slides so that when the new slide appears, the sound plays.

In this lesson, we'll look at the first two methods, which both involve placing a sound clip directly on the slide.

Inserting a Sound on a Slide

To insert a sound clip as an object on a slide, you can either use the Clip Gallery or insert it from a file. The Clip Gallery may not have a very good selection of sound files unless you specifically import some, so you might have better luck with the "from file" method.

To insert a sound clip from a file:

1. Choose the **Insert** menu, point at **Movies and Sounds**, then choose **Sound from File**.

2. In the Insert Sound dialog box, navigate to the drive and folder containing the sound you want to use (see Figure 11.1).

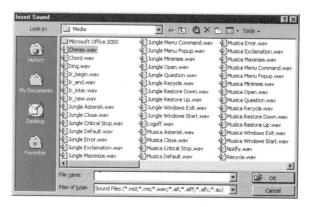

Figure 11.1 Choose the sound clip you want to include on your slide.

3. Select the sound clip, then click **OK**. If you need some sounds to practice with, try the Windows\Media folder on your hard disk.

To place a sound from the Clip Gallery, use these steps instead:

1. Choose the **Insert** menu, point at **Movies and Sounds**, then select **Sound from Gallery**.

2. Click one of the categories to view a group of available sounds.

3. Click the sound clip you want to use. A pop-up menu of buttons appears.

4. Click the top button on the list, which is **Insert Clip**.

5. Close the Clip Gallery window. Your sound clip's icon appears on the slide. It looks like a little speaker.

6. Resize and reposition the sound icon on the slide as needed.

Associating a Sound with Another Object on the Slide

If you want to avoid having a sound icon on your slide, you can associate the sound with some other object already on the slide, such as a graphic. To do so, follow these steps:

1. Right-click the object to which you want to assign the sound.

2. Choose **Action Settings** from the shortcut menu.

3. If you want the sound to play when the object is pointed at, click the **Mouse Over** tab. Otherwise, click the **Mouse Click** tab.

4. Mark the **Play Sound** check box. A drop-down list of sounds becomes available (see Figure 11.2).

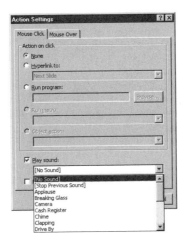

Figure 11.2 Choose a sound to be associated with the object.

5. Open the **Play Sound** drop-down list and choose the sound you want.

If the sound you want is not on the list, choose **Other Sound** and locate the sound using the Add Sound dialog box that appears. Select the sound from there and click **OK**.

6. When you have chosen the sound you want, click **OK** to close the Action Settings dialog box.

Now when you are giving the presentation, you can play the sound by clicking (or pointing at) the object. To test this, jump to Slide Show view (Select the **View** menu, then click **Slide Show**) and try it out. Press **Esc** to return to PowerPoint when finished testing.

Placing a Movie on a Slide

The procedure for placing a movie on a slide is very much the same as that for a sound. You can place a movie using the Clip Gallery or from a file. You will find that the Clip Gallery provides a number of movies that can be used to add interest to your slides. To insert a movie in a slide, follow these steps:

1. Choose the **Insert** menu, point at **Movies and Sounds**, then select **Movies from Gallery**.

2. Click one of the Categories to view a group of available clips.

3. Click the movie clip you want to use. A pop-up menu of button appears.

4. Click the first button on the list, which is **Insert Clip**.

5. Close the Clip Gallery window. Your movie clip appears as a static image on the slide.

 TIP   **Previewing the Movie**   If you want to preview the movie you are adding to the slide, click the movie in the Clip Gallery and then click the **Play Clip** button on the menu that appears.

Choosing When Movies and Sounds Should Play

Slides are static, for the most part. They appear and then they sit there. Movies and sounds, on the other hand, are dynamic—they are activated to play at certain times.

The default when you place a movie or sound on a slide is that the object does not activate until you click it. A slide may contain, for example, a recorded narration that explains a particular graph on the slide, but the narration will not play until the person giving the presentation clicks the sound icon to activate it.

CAUTION

When a Movie Isn't a Movie Most of the "motion clips" you get with PowerPoint, or that you download from the Microsoft Web site, are not true movie clips, but rather animated graphic files in the GIF format. These are not the same type of file as the AVI or MOV files that you create with real animation programs. PowerPoint sees them as graphics rather than as movies and does not allow you to change their play settings. If the steps that follow do not work for your video clip, it may be an animated GIF rather than a real movie.

You may want some sounds or movies to play automatically at certain times in the presentation. You can specify this if prompted when you initially place the clip on the slide, as mentioned in the previous section. Or you can change the setting later with the following procedure:

1. Click the object (the sound icon or movie image) on the slide.
2. Select the **Slide Show** menu, then select **Custom Animation**. The Custom Animation dialog box appears (see Figure 11.3).

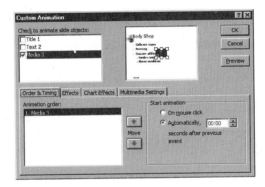

Figure 11.3 Use this dialog box to set when and how a sound or movie plays.

3. Click the **Order & Timing** tab.
4. In the Start Animation section, choose **On Mouse Click** or **Automatically**—your choice.
5. If you chose Automatically, enter the number of seconds that PowerPoint should pause after the previous event before playing the object.
6. Click **OK**.

TERM **Previous Event** If this is the only media clip on this slide, the previous event is the slide itself being displayed. If more than one media clip is on the slide, you can control in which order they activate by switching around their order in the Animation Order list, as shown in Figure 11.3.

7. Switch to Slide Show view to test the slide, making sure you have set up the sound or animation to play when you want it to.

You can set a sound or animation to loop continuously by clicking the **Multimedia Settings** tab in the Custom Animation dialog box, and then the **More Options** button. Select both the **Loop Until Stopped** and **Rewind Movie When Done Playing** check boxes.

In this lesson, you learned how to place sounds and movies in your presentation for great multimedia effects. In the next lesson, you learn how to select objects; work with object layers; and cut, copy, and paste objects, among other processes.

Working with PowerPoint Objects

As you may have already discovered, objects are the building blocks you use to create slides in PowerPoint. Objects are the shapes you draw, the graphs you create, the pictures you import, and the text you type. In this lesson, you learn how to manipulate objects on your slides to create impressive presentations.

Selecting Objects

Before you can copy, move, rotate, or resize an object, you must first select the object. Change to Normal or Slide view and perform one of the following steps to choose one or more objects:

- To select a single object, click it. (If you click text, a frame appears around the text. Click the frame to select the text object.)
- To select more than one object, hold down the **Shift** key while clicking each object. Handles appear around the selected objects, as shown in Figure 12.1.
- To deselect selected objects, click anywhere outside the selected objects.

TIP **Select Objects Tool** Use the Select Objects tool on the Drawing toolbar to drag a selection box around several objects you want to select. When you release the mouse button, PowerPoint selects all the objects inside the box.

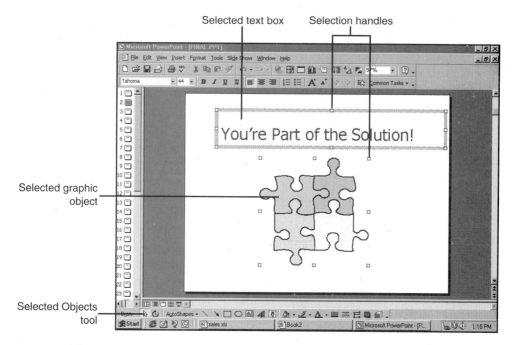

Figure 12.1   Handles indicate that objects are selected.

Working with Layers of Objects

As you place objects onscreen, they may start to overlap, making it difficult or impossible to select the objects in the lower layers. To move objects in layers, perform the following steps:

1. Click the object you want to move up or down in the stack.

2. Click the **Draw** button on the Drawing toolbar to open the Draw menu, and select **Order**, as shown in Figure 12.2.

3. Select one of the following options:

- **Bring to Front** brings the object to the top of the stack.
- **Send to Back** sends the object to the bottom of the stack.
- **Bring Forward** brings the object up one layer.
- **Send Backward** sends the object back one layer.

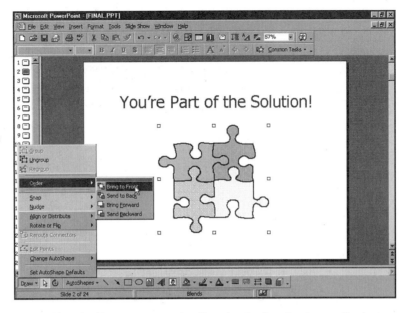

Figure 12.2 Use the Draw menu on the Drawing toolbar to change the layer on which a graphic appears on your slide.

Grouping and Ungrouping Objects

Each object you draw acts as an individual object. However, sometimes you want two or more objects to act as a group. For example, you may want to make the lines of several objects the same thickness, or group several objects together. If you want to treat two or more objects as a group, perform the following steps:

1. Select the objects you want to group. Remember, to select more than one object, hold down the **Shift** key as you click each one.

2. Click the **Draw** button on the Drawing toolbar to open the Draw menu, then select **Group**.

3. To ungroup the objects, select any object in the group and select **Draw**, then choose **Ungroup**.

Cutting, Copying, and Pasting Objects

You can cut, copy, and paste objects on a slide to rearrange the objects or to use the objects to create a picture. When you cut an object, PowerPoint removes the object from the slide and places it in a temporary holding area called the Windows Clipboard. When you copy an object, the original object remains on the slide, and PowerPoint places a copy of it on the Clipboard. In either case, you can then paste the object from the Clipboard onto the current slide or another slide. To cut or copy an object, perform the following steps:

1. Select the object(s) you want to cut, copy, or move.

2. Select the **Edit** menu, then choose **Cut** or **Copy**; or click the **Cut** or **Copy** button on the Standard toolbar.

TIP **Right-click Shortcut** Right-click the selection to choose **Cut** or **Copy** from the shortcut menu.

3. Display the slide on which you want to place the cut or copied object(s). (You can also open a different Windows program to paste it into, if you prefer.)

4. Select **Edit**, then choose **Paste**, or click the **Paste** button on the Standard toolbar. PowerPoint pastes the object(s) on the slide.

TIP **Keyboard Shortcuts** You can press **Ctrl+X** to cut, **Ctrl+C** to copy, and **Ctrl+V** to paste instead of using the toolbar buttons or the menu.

5. Move the mouse pointer over any of the pasted objects, hold down the mouse button, and drag the objects to where you want them.

6. Release the mouse button.

To remove an object without placing it on the Clipboard, select the object and then press the **Delete** key.

TERM **Drag and Drop** The quickest way to copy or move objects is to drag and drop them. Select the object you want to move. Point to it and hold down the mouse button. Then drag the object where you want it. To copy the object, hold down the **Ctrl** key while dragging.

Rotating an Object

The Rotate tools enable you to revolve an object around a center point. Not all pictures can be rotated; for example, bitmap images can't. If the selected picture can't, the Free Rotate tool will not be available.

To rotate an object to your own specifications using Free Rotate, do the following:

1. Click the object you want to rotate.

2. Click the **Free Rotate** tool on the Drawing toolbar. The selection handles on the centering line change to circles.

3. Hold down the mouse button and drag the circular handle until the object is in the position you want (see Figure 12.3).

Dotted outline shows new position.

Mouse pointer

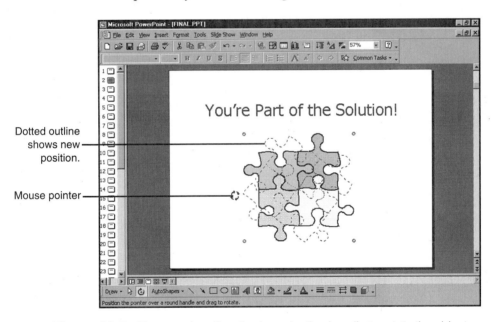

Figure 12.3   You can drag the circular selection handle to rotate the object.

4. Release the mouse button.

The Draw menu (on the Drawing toolbar) also contains a Rotate or Flip submenu that provides additional options for rotating objects. You can flip an object 90 degrees left or right, or flip the object over on the centering line to create a mirrored image of it.

Resizing Objects

At times, an object you create or import is not the right size for your slide presentation. You can resize the object by performing these steps:

1. Select the object to resize. Selection handles appear.

2. Drag one of the handles (the squares that surround the object) until the object is the desired size:

- Drag a corner handle to change both the height and width of an object. PowerPoint retains the object's relative dimensions.

- Drag a side, top, or bottom handle to change the height or width alone.

- Hold down the **Ctrl** key while dragging to resize from the center of the picture.

3. Release the mouse button, and PowerPoint resizes the object (see Figure 12.4).

Dotted outline shows how big object will be.

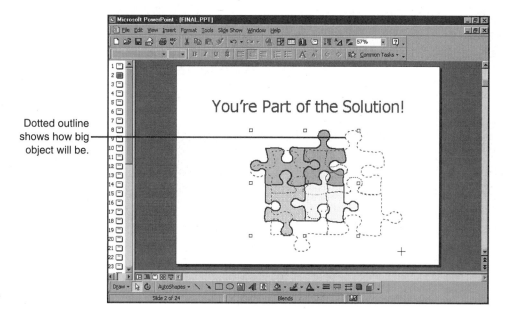

Figure 12.4   Drag a handle to resize an object.

Cropping a Picture

Besides resizing a picture, you can crop it—that is, you can trim a side or corner of the picture to remove an element from the picture or cut off some white space. Only true pictures can be cropped; AutoShapes cannot be.

To crop a picture, perform the following steps:

1. Click the picture you want to crop.

2. If the Picture toolbar isn't shown, right-click the picture and select **Show Picture Toolbar** from the menu.

 3. Click the **Crop** button on the Picture toolbar. The mouse pointer turns into a cropping tool (see Figure 12.5).

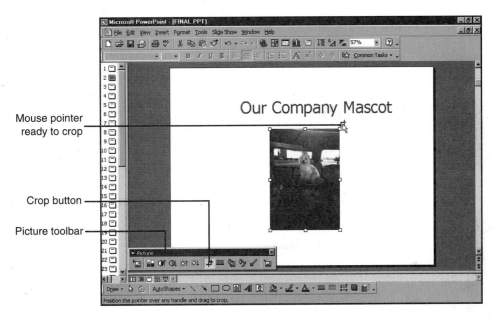

Figure 12.5 Use the cropping tool to chop off a section of the picture.

4. Move the mouse pointer over one of the handles. (Use a corner handle to crop two sides at once. Use a side, top, or bottom handle to crop only one side.)

5. Hold down the mouse button and drag the pointer until the crop lines are where you want them.

6. Release the mouse button. The cropped section disappears.

7. Resize or move the picture as needed for its new placement.

CAUTION

Stop that Crop!   To uncrop a picture immediately after cropping it, select **Edit**, then choose **Undo Crop Picture**, or click the **Undo** button on the toolbar. You can also uncrop at any time by performing the previous steps and dragging the selected handle in the opposite direction you dragged it for cropping.

In this lesson, you learned how to select, copy, move, rotate, and resize an object on a slide. In the next lesson, you learn how to present an onscreen slide show.

Presenting an Onscreen Slideshow

In this lesson, you learn how to view a slideshow onscreen, how to make basic movements within a presentation, and how to set show options. You also learn how to create a self-running show with timings and how to include a hyperlink on a slide by creating action buttons.

Viewing an Onscreen Slideshow

Before you show your presentation to an audience, you should run through it several times on your own computer, checking that all the slides are in the right order and that the timings and transitions between the slides work correctly. This also enables you to fine-tune the monologue you will give as you show the slides, making sure that what you are saying at any point in the presentation is synchronized with the slide that is being shown at that moment.

You can preview a slideshow at any time; follow these steps:

1. Open the presentation you want to view.

2. Choose the **Slide Show** menu, then choose **View Show**. The first slide in the presentation appears full screen (see Figure 13.1).

3. To display the next or the previous slide, do one of the following:
   - To display the next slide, click the left mouse button and press the **Page Down** key, or press the right-arrow or down-arrow key.
   - To display the previous slide, click the right mouse button and press the **Page Up** key, or press the left-arrow or up-arrow key.

4. When you have finished running the slideshow, press the **Esc** key.

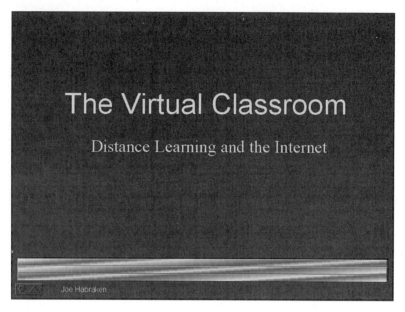

Figure 13.1   When you run your slideshow, the entire screen is used to display the sides.

 TIP   **Start the Show!**   You can also start a slideshow by clicking the **Slide Show** button in the bottom-left corner of the presentation window or by pressing **F5**.

Using the Slide Show Menu Tools

You will find that after you run the slideshow a few times, running through the slides in the presentation (even slides that include animation and interesting transitions) might not provide the impact that you want your overall presentation to have. Fortunately, PowerPoint provides several tools that you can use during the slideshow that enhance your interaction with the slideshow material itself and with your audience.

For example, you can turn the mouse pointer into a pen that allows you to actually draw on a particular slide, enabling you to quickly emphasize a particular point visually. A Meeting Minder feature enables you to take notes during the actual presentation—a great way to record audience questions or comments concerning the presentation.

These tools are found on a menu on the Slide Show screen. Figure 13.2 shows the menu. Three of the most useful tools are discussed in the following sections of this lesson.

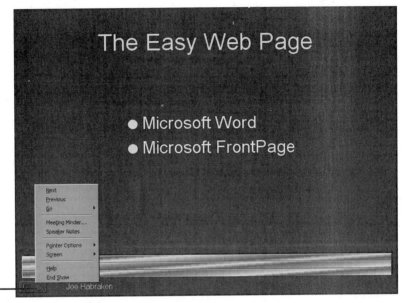

Click here to open the menu.

Figure 13.2 You can access the pen and other tools, such as your speaker notes, from the menu on the Slide Show screen.

Drawing with the Pen

An extremely useful tool is the pen, which allows you to draw on a particular slide. This is great for highlighting particular information on a slide to emphasize a particular point.

To use the pen during the slideshow, follow these steps:

1. With the slideshow running, right-click anywhere on the screen. The Slide Show menu appears.

2. Point at **Pointer Options** on the menu, then choose **Pen**. The mouse pointer becomes a·pen.

3. Press the left mouse button and draw on the slide as needed (see Figure 13.3).

665

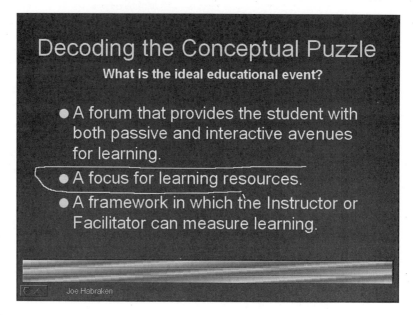

Figure 13.3   The pen provides you with an easy way to highlight a particular item on a slide.

4. After you've finished working with the pen, you can return to the arrow pointer. Right-click on the screen, point at **Pointer Options** on the menu, and then choose **Arrow**. You can now use the mouse to advance to the next slide.

You can also choose the pen color that you use to draw on the slides. This option is available on the Slide Show menu (point at **Pointer Options**, then point at **Pen Color**, and then select the pen color you want to use from the cascading menu). Pen color can also be set in the Set Up Show dialog box, which is discussed in this lesson in the section "Setting Slideshow Options."

Taking Notes with the Meeting Minder

Another useful tool that you can take advantage of while showing your slide presentation is the Meeting Minder. The Meeting Minder enables you to quickly take notes or create action related to the discussion or to audience comments made during your presentation.

To use the Meeting Minder, follow these steps:

1. With the slideshow running, right-click anywhere on the screen. The Slide Show menu appears.

2. Click **Meeting Minder**. The Meeting Minder dialog box opens (see Figure 13.4.)

Figure 13.4 The Meeting Minder makes it easy for you to record notes or a task related to your presentation.

3. Type your notes onto the **Meeting Minutes** tab of the dialog box.

4. If you want to create an action item, click the **Action Items** tab on the dialog box. Type a description in the **Description** box and the name of the person who will work on the item in the **Assigned To** box. After filling in this information, click the **Add** button to add the item to the Action item list on the tab.

5. When you have completed adding notes or creating action items related to the slide presentation, click the **OK** button to close the dialog box.

TIP **Schedule a Meeting Related to the Presentation** In a corporate setting, the actual presentation of your slideshow will no doubt lead to further discussion. You can quickly schedule a meeting using Outlook by clicking the **Schedule** button on the Meeting Minder dialog box. This opens an Outlook Meeting dialog box that you can use to schedule the proposed meeting. For more on using Outlook to schedule meetings, see Lesson 13, "Planning a Meeting," in the Outlook section of this book.

Finding a Particular Slide During the Show

As you reach the end of a presentation, you might be asked to reshow a particular slide or subset of slides that you included in your slideshow. The easiest way to go to a particular slide when you are in the Slide Show view is the Slide Navigator. The Slide Navigator lists all the slides in the current slideshow.

To use the Slide Navigator, follow these steps:

1. With the slideshow running, right-click anywhere on the screen. The Slide Show menu appears.
2. Point at **Go**, then click **Slide Navigator**. The Slide Navigator dialog box opens.
3. To move to a particular slide, click the slide's title in the Slide Navigator's slide list and then click **Go To**. You are taken to the selected slide.

Setting Up a Self-Running Show

In a self-running show, the slideshow runs itself. Each slide advances after a specified period of time, and the audience has no opportunity to control it. This differs from a user-interactive show, discussed later in this lesson, in which the audience can control which slides to see and how quickly to advance.

Setting Slide Timings

For a self-running show, you must set timings. You can set the same timing for all slides (for example, a 20-second delay between each slide), or you can set a separate timing for each slide individually.

First, configure the show to use timings by following these steps:

1. Open the presentation you want to view.
2. Choose **Slide Show** and then click **Set Up Show**. The Set Up Show dialog box appears.
3. Click the **Using Timings, If Present** option button.
4. Click **OK**.

Next, set the timings. The default timing for each slide is **None**, which means the speaker or audience must advance the slides manually. When you set timing for a transition between two slides, you are specifying the amount of time the first slide appears onscreen before the next slide moves in to take its place.

Follow these steps to set an automatic timing for a slide (or for all slides):

1. Switch to Slide Sorter view (click **View** and then choose **Slide Sorter**).

2. (Optional) If you want to set the timing for an individual slide or for a group of slides, select the slides you want to affect.

3. Choose **Slide Show** and then click **Slide Transition**. The Slide Transition dialog box appears, as shown in Figure 13.5.

4. In the **Advance** area, click to place a check mark in the **Automatically After** check box.

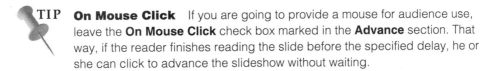

TIP **On Mouse Click** If you are going to provide a mouse for audience use, leave the **On Mouse Click** check box marked in the **Advance** section. That way, if the reader finishes reading the slide before the specified delay, he or she can click to advance the slideshow without waiting.

5. Enter an amount of time to wait. For example, to wait 20 seconds, enter **00:20** or click the up-arrow button next to the field until 00:20 is displayed there.

Figure 13.5 Enter the delay between this slide and the next one.

6. To apply the change to the selected slide(s), click **Apply**, or to apply it to all the slides in the presentation, click **Apply to All**.

You can now run the show and the slides change according to the timings that you set. If you want to continuously loop the show (so that it continues to run until you stop it), you can set this option in the Slide Show Options dialog box discussed later in this lesson.

Adding Action Buttons to User-Interactive Shows

In a user-interactive show, you provide the audience some means of controlling the show. You can simply provide access to a keyboard and/or mouse and let the user control the show in the same way you learned earlier in this lesson, or you can provide action buttons onscreen that make it easy to jump to specific slides.

Action buttons are like controls on an audio CD player—they enable you to jump to any slide quickly, to go backward, to go forward, or even to stop the presentation.

 TIP **The Same Controls on All Slides?** If you want to add the same action buttons to all slides in the presentation, add the action buttons to the Slide Master. To display the Slide Master, select **View**, and then click **Master** and choose **Slide Master**.

To add an action button to a slide, follow these steps:

1. Display the slide in Normal or Slide view.

2. Select **Slide Show**, and then click **Action Buttons** and pick a button from the palette that appears next to the command (see Figure 13.6). For instance, if you want to create a button that advances to the next slide, you might choose the button with the arrow pointing to the right.

 Which Button Should I Choose? Consider the action that you want the button to perform, and then pick a button picture that matches it well. To change the button picture, you must delete the button and create a new one.

CAUTION

3. Your mouse pointer turns into a crosshair. Drag to draw a box on the slide where you want the button to appear. (You can resize it later if you want.) PowerPoint draws the button on the slide and opens the Action Settings dialog box (see Figure 13.7).

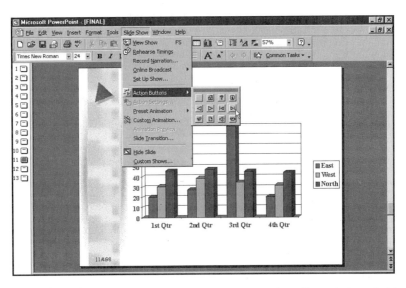

Figure 13.6 Choose the button that you think your reader will most strongly identify with the action assigned to it.

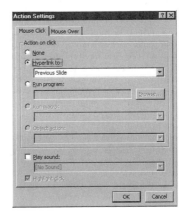

Figure 13.7 You can control the way one slide transitions to the next with the Action Settings dialog box.

4. Choose the type of action you want to happen when the user clicks the button. Most of the time, you will choose **Hyperlink To**, but your complete list of choices is

- **None**
- **Hyperlink To**—This can be a slide, an Internet hyperlink, a document on your computer—just about anything.

- **Run Program**—You can choose to have a program start when the user clicks the button.
- **Run Macro**—If you have recorded a macro, you can have the user run it from the button.
- **Object Action**—If you have embedded (OLE) objects in the presentation, you can activate one when the button is clicked.

5. Open the drop-down list for the type of action you chose and select the exact action (for instance, **Next Slide**). Or, if you chose **Run Program**, click the **Browse** button and locate the program to be run.

6. (Optional) If you want a sound to play when the user clicks the button, select the **Play Sound** check box and choose a sound from the drop-down list.

7. (Optional) If you want the button to look highlighted when the user clicks it (a nice little extra), leave the **Highlight Click** check box marked.

8. Click **OK**. Your button appears on the slide.

9. View the presentation (as you learned at the beginning of this lesson) to try out the button.

Figure 13.8 shows three buttons added to a slide. Actually, they were added to the Slide Master so that the same buttons appear on each slide in the presentation. This kind of consistency gives the reader a feeling of comfort and control.

CAUTION

No Controls on Slide 1   When you add action buttons to the Slide Master, they appear on every slide except the first one in the presentation. If you want action buttons on the first slide, you must add them specifically to that slide or to the Title Master.

TIP   **Make Your Own Buttons**   To create a custom action button with your own text on it, select the blank button and then type into it after you create it.

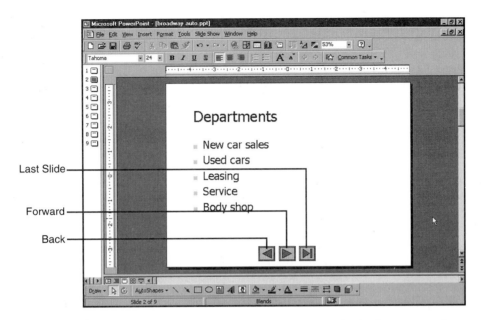

Figure 13.8 These control buttons display various slides in the presentation.

Setting Slideshow Options

Depending on the type of show you're presenting, you might find it useful to make some adjustments to the way the show runs, such as making it run in a window (the default is full screen) or showing only certain slides. You'll find these controls and more in the Set Up Show dialog box (see Figure 13.9). To open it, choose **Slide Show**, then select **Set Up Show**.

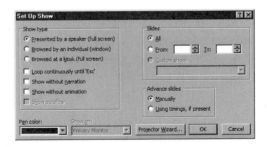

Figure 13.9 Use the Set Up Show dialog box to give PowerPoint some basic instructions about how to present your slideshow.

In this dialog box, you can choose from a number of options, including the following:

- Choose the medium for showing the presentation. Your choices are **Presented by a Speaker (Full Screen)**, **Browsed by an Individual (Window)**, and **Browsed at a Kiosk (Full Screen)**.

- Choose whether to loop the slideshow continuously or to show it only once. You might want to loop it continuously so that it operates unaided at a kiosk at a trade show, for instance.

- Show all the slides or a range of them (enter the range in the **From** and **To** boxes).

- Choose a custom show, if you have created one. (To create a custom show—for instance, one that contains a subset of the main show's slides—select **Slide Show**, then choose **Custom Show**.)

- Choose whether to advance slides manually or to use timings you set up.

- Choose a pen color. When you are giving a presentation, you can right-click and choose **Pointer Options**, and then choose **Pen** to turn your mouse pointer into a drawing tool.

In this lesson, you learned how to display a slide presentation onscreen, how to move between slides, and how to set slideshow options. You also learned how to set up a self-running slideshow and place action buttons on slideshows used in user-interactive slideshows. In the next lesson, you learn how to design a presentation that can be used on the World Wide Web; you learn how to add hyperlinks to the presentation as well as how to view the Web presentation in Internet Explorer 5.

Designing a Presentation for the Internet

In this lesson, you learn how PowerPoint makes it easy to publish your presentations on the World Wide Web or your corporate intranet.

What Is the World Wide Web?

The Internet is a global network of interconnected computer systems that provides several ways for users to communicate with each other. The World Wide Web is the most popular and graphical component of the Internet. Many businesses maintain Web sites containing information about their products and services for public reading. Still other businesses maintain an internal version of the Web that's strictly for employee use, and they use the company's local area network to make it available to its staff. These are called *intranets*.

The Web sites that you view on the Web are made up of linked documents created in HTML. Your Web browser is able to translate HTML into a format that is viewable (and usable) on your home or office computer.

 TERM   **HTML**   Hypertext Markup Language is the coding system used to create Web pages for the WWW.

Sooner or later, you may be asked to prepare a PowerPoint presentation for use on a Web site or an intranet. Don't panic! It's simpler than it sounds.

Special Considerations for Designing Web Shows

Creating a presentation for Web distribution is much like creating any other user-interactive presentation. However, consider these factors when dealing with the Web:

- For your viewers' convenience, keep the file size as small as possible. That means don't use gratuitous graphics, sounds, or movies.
- You should include action buttons on each slide that enable the user to jump to the previous and next slides, and possibly other action buttons, too.
- If you want the users to be able to jump from your presentation to other Web sites, make sure you include the appropriate hyperlinks. See the following section for details.
- If you convert the presentation to HTML (Web) format, anyone with a Web browser can view it on the Internet, but the presentation may not be the same as the PowerPoint version of it. Depending on the Web browser used to view it, sounds, movies, transitions, and other features may not play correctly.
- If you distribute the file in PowerPoint format, your audience must have PowerPoint installed on their PCs or must download a special PowerPoint Viewer (discussed later in this lesson).

Adding URL Hyperlinks

You can assign links to Web addresses (URLs) to a button. For instance, you might have a button that takes you to your company's home page (the top page at its Internet site) at the bottom of every slide.

A hyperlink can be attached to an action button (action buttons that move you from slide to slide are hyperlinks, too) or to some other graphic, or it can be attached to a string of text characters.

Assigning a Hyperlink to an Action Button or a Graphic

The following steps show you how to assign a hyperlink to an action button:

1. Choose the **Slide Show** menu, then choose **Action Buttons**. Select the button you want to place on the slide. For example, use the one that looks like a house to hyperlink to your company's home page.

2. When the Action Settings dialog box appears, click the **Hyperlink To** option button, and then choose **URL** from the **Hyperlink To** drop-down list (see Figure 14.1).

Figure 14.1   Choose URL from the Hyperlink To list.

3. Open the **Hyperlink To** drop-down list and choose **URL**. The Hyperlink to URL dialog box appears.

4. Enter the Web address in the **URL** text box (see Figure 14.2). Then click **OK**.

Figure 14.2   Enter the URL (the Web address) to which you want to hyperlink.

5. Click **OK** to close the Action Settings dialog box.

If you have already created an action button and you want to change its hyperlink, select the button and choose **Slide Show**, then select **Action Settings**. Then pick up the preceding steps at step 2. You can also assign a hyperlink to any graphic in this same way; select the graphic, then choose **Slide Show** and select **Action Settings**.

Creating a Text-Based Hyperlink

You can either insert a "bare" hyperlink, in which the text is the same as the URL, or you can assign a URL to some existing text. Follow these steps:

1. (Optional) To use existing text, select it.

2. Choose the **Insert** menu, then select **Hyperlink**. The Insert Hyperlink dialog box opens.

3. The text you selected in step 1 appears in the Text to Display box. If you want to change it, do so; or if you didn't type any text in step 1, type some now. For example, if the URL will take visitors to your home page, you might type **Click here to visit our home page**.

4. Click the **Existing File or Web Page** button.

5. Enter the Web page's URL in the **Type the File or Web Page Name** text box (see Figure 14.3).

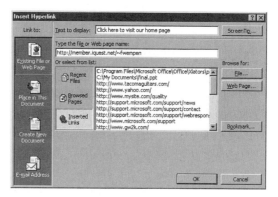

Figure 14.3 Enter the Web page address (its URL).

6. Click **OK**. The selected text appears underlined and in a different color, indicating that it is a hyperlink.

Can't Remember the Address? If you don't know the Web page's address, click the **Web Page** button to open your Web browser. Navigate to the page you want to link to, and then jump back to PowerPoint (by clicking the PowerPoint presentation's name on the Windows taskbar). The URL is automatically entered for you.

CAUTION

Testing the Hyperlink

To test your hyperlink, view the slide in Slide Show view and click the button with your mouse. Your Web browser should start and the selected URL should load in it. If it doesn't work, check to make sure you entered the URL correctly. If it is correct, check your Internet connection, or try again later. (Sometimes a Web page may be temporarily unavailable.)

Saving a Presentation in HTML Format

PowerPoint has the capability to save a presentation in HTML format so that it can be viewed using any Web browser. Because all World Wide Web users have Web browser programs, no one need miss out on your presentation.

The quality of the translation has improved considerably in PowerPoint 2000 over previous PowerPoint versions. PowerPoint 2000 saves in a Web format that enables your sounds, movies, animation, and other special effects to be seen just as you intended, provided the person viewing the presentation has a capable Web browser (Internet Explorer 4.0 or higher is best). With other Web browsers, not all special effects may appear, but at least the basic presentation (the slide text and graphics) will be shown.

To save a presentation in HTML format, follow these steps:

1. Choose the **File** menu, then choose **Save As Web Page**. The Save As dialog box appears (see Figure 14.4).

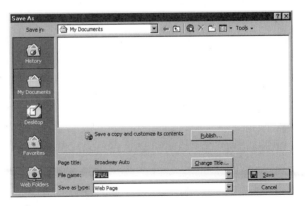

Figure 14.4 Choose a name for your saved Web presentation.

2. In the **File Name** text box, enter a filename for the first page of the presentation (the title slide). By default, this is the name of your presentation file.

3. (Optional) If you want the page title (the name in the title bar when the page is displayed in a Web browser) to be different than the one shown, click the **Change** button and enter a different title.

4. Click **Save**. Your presentation is saved.

Users of PowerPoint 97 may be wondering where all the special Web-saving options went that they used to be able to set. They're still there; they're just hidden.

Notice that in the Save As dialog box (refer to Figure 14.4), there is a **Publish** button. Click it to go to a Publish as Web Page dialog box in which you can set all kinds of options, including which Web browser your audience will likely use and which slides to include.

Within that Publish as Web Page dialog box, there is a **Web Options** button. Click it to open the Web Options dialog box, where you can choose even more special settings.

A saved HTML presentation is actually many files, not a single one. PowerPoint creates a home page (an entry point) with the same name as the original presentation. (This is the file you were naming when you chose a name in step 2 of the preceding list.) For example, if the presentation file was named Broadway.ppt, the home page would be named Broadway.htm. Then it creates a folder named {presentation name} Files (for example, Broadway Files) that contains all the other HTML, graphics, and other files needed to display the complete presentation. If you are transferring the HTML presentation to another PC (which is very likely, if you are going to make it available on the Internet through your company's server), you must transfer not only the lone HTML home page, but also the entire associated folder.

Viewing Your Presentation in Internet Explorer 5

As you work on a slide presentation that you plan on making part of a Web page (and have it viewed online), you can preview your presentation in Internet Explorer 5 to see how the slides look and operate in this Web browser. Viewing the presentation in Internet Explorer can really help you fine-tune the presentation for the Web before you actually place it on a Web server (as discussed in the next section).

To view your current presentation in Internet Explorer, follow these steps:

1. Choose the **File** menu, then choose **Web Page Preview**. The Internet Explorer Window will appear showing the first slide in your presentation (see Figure 14.5).

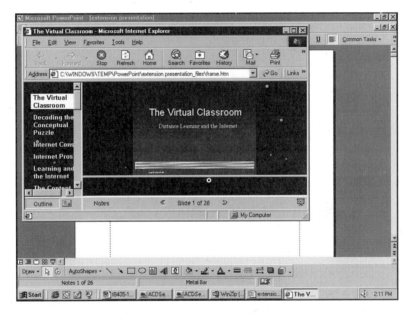

Figure 14.5   You can preview any of your presentations in Internet Explorer to see how it will look on the Web.

2. Use the navigation pane (on the left side of the Explorer window) to view each of the slides in the presentation.

3. When you have completed previewing the presentation in Internet Explorer, click the Internet Explorer **Close** button.

When you close the Internet Explorer window, you will be returned to the PowerPoint window. You can now fine-tune the presentation for the Web or save the presentation in the HTML format as discussed in the next section.

Transferring a Presentation Out to the Web

To make your Web presentation available to others on the Internet, you must copy it to your company's Web server or your Internet service provider's server. Find out from your system administrator the full path of the location where you should store your files.

One way to transfer the files is to use an FTP (file transfer protocol) program to upload the files to the appropriate directory on the server. This method is fairly easy, but if you do not have an FTP program, you must find and download one. A good one is WS_FTP, available from http://www.shareware.com.

You may also be able to save the presentation directly to the server through the Save As dialog box (refer to Figure 14.4). In the Save As Web Page dialog box, open the **Save In** drop-down list and choose **Add/Modify FTP Locations**; set up the location, and then choose that location to save to. This is a very efficient method, as it saves a few steps over saving and then transferring.

One final way to transfer your work to a Web server is the Web Publishing Wizard that comes with Windows 98. From the Start menu, point to **Programs**, then select **Internet Explorer** and choose **Web Publishing Wizard**. Follow the prompts to transfer a single file or a single folder at a time. You will have to run it twice—once for the starting file and once for the accompanying folder.

Preserving Your Special Effects on the Web

Instead of saving your work as a Web page, you can copy the PowerPoint presentation in its native .ppt format to the Web server and let the readers access it as a PowerPoint presentation. This is good because it preserves all your special effects, no matter what browser the audience is using; it does, however, require that all your readers have a copy of PowerPoint installed.

A partial solution for this situation is to provide your audience with a PowerPoint viewer program. This program is a "runtime" version of PowerPoint, containing just enough of the right stuff to view your presentation onscreen. The reader can't make any changes to the presentation; it's like being permanently in Slide Show view.

You can install the PowerPoint Viewer from the PowerPoint (or Office) setup program. Just pop the CD-ROM back in your drive, use Maintenance Mode's Add or Remove Features command to add components, and add the PowerPoint Viewer. (It's under Microsoft PowerPoint for Windows, and it's called PPT Files Viewer.)

The PowerPoint Viewer is free and freely distributed, so you can provide a copy to all your users on your intranet, or you can provide a link to the viewer on your company's Web site so that anyone who doesn't yet have the viewer can download it directly from Microsoft. After users have the PowerPoint Viewer and have downloaded your presentation file from the Web, they can run the viewer the same as any program and load the presentation file into it to view it. Figure 14.6 shows a presentation being loaded for viewing in the PowerPoint Viewer.

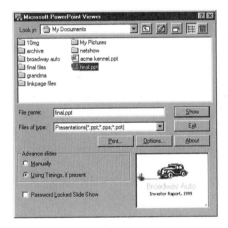

Figure 14.6   You can't give everyone a copy of PowerPoint, but it's perfectly legal to give everyone the PowerPoint Viewer.

In this lesson, you learned about PowerPoint's capabilities in helping you present your slides on the Web. In the next section, you learn about Outlook and how to better organize your communications, notes, and meetings for both the home and the office.

Outlook

Getting Started in Outlook

In this lesson, you learn to start and exit Outlook, identify parts of the Outlook window, and use the mouse to get around the program.

Starting Outlook

You start Outlook from the Windows desktop. After starting the program, you can leave it open, or you can minimize it to free up the desktop for other applications. Either way, you can access it at any time during your work day.

CAUTION

Outlook and System Performance If you leave Outlook open on your desktop, it still requires a certain amount of your system resources. This means that if you normally run multiple applications such as Word and Excel, you may see some loss of performance as you work. If this becomes a problem, close Outlook to free up your system's memory. Adding memory to your system, of course, also is an alternative for increasing performance.

To start Microsoft Outlook, follow these steps:

1. From the Windows Desktop, click the **Start** button, choose **Programs**, and then select **Microsoft Outlook**.

TIP **Shortcuts to Launching Office** You can also double-click the **Outlook** shortcut icon on the desktop to start Outlook, or you can click the **Outlook** icon on the Quick Launch toolbar on the Windows 98 taskbar. You can also launch Outlook from the Office toolbar if it is present on your desktop. Click the **Office** menu button to add the Outlook button to the Office toolbar.

2. If the Choose Profile dialog box appears, click **OK** to accept the default profile or choose your profile and open Microsoft Outlook. Figure 1.1 shows the Outlook screen that appears.

Profile The profile includes information about you and your communication services and is created automatically when you install Outlook. The profile includes your name, user ID, post office, and so on. Additional profiles enable you to set up Outlook for more than one user or communication service. For Outlook and Internet Mail Only and Corporate Email configurations, see Lesson 2, "Understanding the Outlook Configurations."

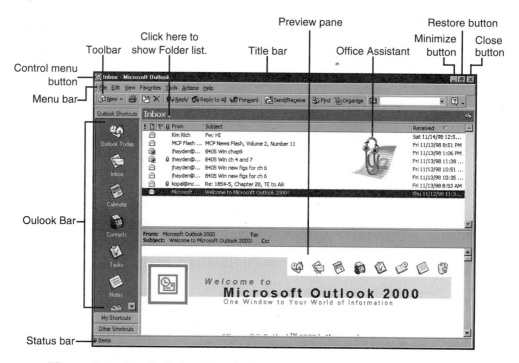

Figure 1.1 The Outlook window includes many icons and items used in your daily routine.

Understanding the Outlook Window

The Outlook window includes items you can use to navigate and operate the program. If you do not see some of the items listed in Figure 1.1 on your screen, open the **View** menu and select the command for the appropriate element (such as **Toolbars**, **Status Bar**, **Folder List**, or **Outlook Bar**). A check mark in front of an item means the item is currently showing. If you find the Preview Pane distracting when you first open the Outlook Window, click the **View** menu and click **Preview Pane** to close the Preview pane.

Table 1.1 describes the elements you see in the opening screen.

Table 1.1 Elements of the Outlook Window

Element	Description
Title bar	Includes the name of the application and current folder, plus the Minimize, Maximize, and Close buttons.
Control menu button	Opens the Control menu, which provides such commands as Move, Size, Minimize, and Close.
Minimize button	Reduces the Outlook window to a button on the taskbar; to restore the window to its original size, click the button on the taskbar.
Maximize button	Enlarges the Outlook window to cover the Windows 95 Desktop. When the window is maximized, the Maximize button changes to a Restore button you can click to return the window to its previous size.
Close (×) button	Closes the Outlook program window.
Menu bar	Contains menus of commands you can use to perform tasks in the program.
Toolbar	Includes icons that serve as shortcuts for common commands, such as creating a new message or printing a message.
Show Folder list	Displays the current folder. Click this to display a list of Personal Folders you can open.

continues

Table 1.1 Continued

Element	Description
Outlook Bar	Displays icons representing folders: Inbox, Calendar, Contacts, and so on. Click an icon to change to the folder it names. The Outlook, Mail, and Other buttons on the bar list specific groups of folders (for instance, the Mail button lists icons related to your mail, such as the Inbox and Sent items).
Status bar	Displays information about the items currently shown in the Information Viewer.
Preview pane	Displays a preview of the currently selected item in your Outlook Inbox or other selected folder.
Office Assistant	The Office Assistant provides you with the help you need to get the most out of Outlook. Click the Assistant when you need help.

TIP **Finding a Toolbar Button's Purpose** You can place the mouse pointer on any toolbar button to view a description of that tool's function.

Using the Mouse in Outlook

As with most Windows-based programs, you can use the mouse in Outlook to select items, open mail and folders, move items, and so on. In general, clicking selects an item, and double-clicking selects it and performs some action on it (for example, displaying its contents). In addition to clicking and double-clicking, there are some special mouse actions you can use in Outlook:

- **Drag**—To move an object to another position on the screen (to transfer a mail message to another folder, for example), you can drag the object with the mouse. To drag an object to a new location onscreen, point to the object and press and hold down the left mouse button. Move the mouse pointer to the new location, and then release the mouse button.

- **Right-Click**—You can display a shortcut menu by clicking the right mouse button when pointing to an item. For instance, you can right-click a folder in the Outlook bar or a piece of mail. A shortcut menu appears, which usually contains common commands relating to that particular item.

- **Multi-Select**—You can act upon multiple items at once by selecting them before issuing a command. To select multiple contiguous items, hold down the **Shift** key and click the first and last items you want to select. To select noncontiguous items (those that are not adjacent to each other), hold down the **Ctrl** key and click each item.

TIP   **Keyboard Shortcuts**   You can use the keyboard to move around Outlook and to access many, but not all, of its features. For example, to open a menu with the keyboard, press the **Alt** key and then press the underlined letter in the menu name (press **Alt+F** to open the File menu, for instance).

Exiting Outlook

When you're ready to exit Outlook, you may choose whether to leave the mail connection open or to disconnect:

- To remain connected to the mail program, choose **File**, then select **Exit**.
- To disconnect from the mail program, choose **File**, then select **Exit** and **Log Off**.

If you are connected to your email service through your corporate network, you really do not need to log off or close Outlook. This enables Outlook to periodically check the mail server for new mail. When you log off your corporate network and close down your computer, your connection to the mail server is also shut down. New email waits for you on the server and is downloaded the next time you log on to the network and start Outlook.

TIP   **Choose Your Weapon**   Microsoft gives you several additional ways of closing Outlook. You choose what's easiest for you: Double-click the **Control menu** button, press **Alt+F4**, or click the **Close** (×) button at the right end of Outlook's title bar.

If you send or receive your email through a mail server run by an Internet service provider, you connect through a dial-up connection. After you upload or download your email from the server using Outlook, you may want to disconnect from your provider to save on connection time or to free up your phone line. Figure 1.2 shows the connection box used for a dial-up service. To close the connection, click **Disconnect**.

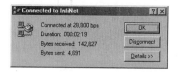

Figure 1.2   After downloading your email from your Internet service provider, you may want to close the connection.

In this lesson, you learned about the Outlook window, how to start and exit Outlook, and how to use the mouse to get around the program. In the next lesson, you learn about Outlook installation considerations, email account options, corporate email, and sharing information.

Understanding the Outlook Configurations

In this lesson, you learn how to set up Outlook for Internet only or corporate email and how to configure these two different options.

Choosing Your Outlook Installation

The choices that you make during Outlook's initial installation affects the functionality of the Outlook software and the features that are available to you. However, don't be overly concerned with the preceding statement; you can reinstall components of Outlook at any time or change your installation depending on your needs.

Outlook 2000 really comes in two forms: Internet Only and Corporate (or WorkGroup) email service (actually a third installation option enables you to install Outlook with no electronic mail support). Which configuration you choose depends upon whether you are connected to a corporate network or using Outlook as your Internet email client. Each installation also has certain ways of handling the sending and receiving of messages, the handling of faxes, and how collaboration with other users is conducted.

Installation Considerations

When you begin the Outlook 2000 installation, you should be aware that any previous version of Outlook is replaced. Another inescapable result of the Outlook 2000 installation is that Internet Explorer 5 (or later version) is installed replacing any previous versions of Microsoft Internet Explorer that you have on your computer. You don't have to use Internet Explorer 5 as your default

Web browser, but it must be installed on the computer for Outlook to have full functionality.

The only major installation decision that you must make is whether you want Internet Only email, Corporate or Workgroup email, or no email at all, as shown in Figure 2.1. The following sections look at the first two possibilities separately.

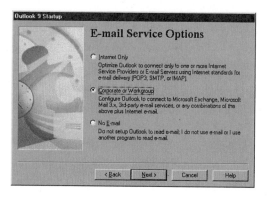

Figure 2.1   You must select the type of electronic mail you want to use with Outlook.

Internet Only Email

If you connect to the Internet using a modem and an Internet service provider (ISP), select Internet Only email. Your ISP has supplied you with a typical Internet email account that uses Internet communication protocols like POP3, IMAP, and SMTP. You use Outlook as your Internet email client to send and receive messages using your account.

The other reason that you might choose Internet Only email is in cases where you are physically connected to a network at your place of business, but your company does not operate a special network mail server with Microsoft Exchange Server software installed on it or another corporate email server software package installed on it. Therefore, your company uses Internet email for its corporate communications. Again, you are taking advantage of Outlook's ability to manage your email account and send and receive standard Internet email.

ISP (Internet Service Provider) A commercial, educational, or govern-ment institution providing individuals and companies access to the Internet.

POP3 (Post Office Protocol version 3) A set of rules used to download mail to your computer. Your ISP uses a POP3 host, or server, to transfer your mail to you.

SMTP (Simple Mail Transfer Protocol) A set of rules used to transfer Internet mail; your ISP goes through an SMTP host, or relay, server to get your mail to you.

IMAP (Internet Message Access Protocol) A set of software rules used by an email client to access email messages on a shared mail server as if the messages were stored locally.

The only features in Outlook that are affected by your selection of Internet Only email are your mail service and your fax service. The Calendar, Contacts, Notes, and Tasks features operate the same. However, the way that you share Calendar and Contacts information with other users is different than it is on a corporate network using Exchange Server.

One other point concerning the two different email configurations in Outlook is the different formats that are available to you for sending mail. The Internet Only configuration enables you to send messages as Text Only and Rich Text (HTML). The Rich Text (HTML) format for the Internet Only configuration is really just HTML, so do not be confused by the Rich Text reference. When you send HTML messages, you can use special fonts, bold, underline, and other font attributes. If the person receiving the message has an email client that can read HTML, that person sees your special formatting.

The Corporate configuration provides you with the Text Only format and the Rich Text (HTML) format and adds a third format, Rich Text Format (RTF). This Rich Text Format is normally used for messages sent locally on your corporate network. Local mail networks at a company usually employ the same email client, and so each user can take advantage of this RTF format. This RTF format differs from the RTF (HTML) format because it is particular to proprietary email packages such as Microsoft Mail and was not really designed to be used for messages sent over the Internet. The term *Rich Text* really refers (in both the HTML and Rich Text formats) to the fact that the text in the message can be formatted using special text attributes such as bold, underline, and italic.

Configuring an Internet Email Account

When you start Outlook for the first time after the installation in which you chose Internet Only, you are asked to configure your Internet email account. If your previous version of Outlook (or other Internet email client, such as Outlook Express) was configured for an Internet email account, this information is imported into Outlook 2000 during the installation process (a screen during preinstallation asks you to select the email client that you want to import the information from).

If no previous configuration exists, the Internet Connection Wizard walks you through the process of creating an Internet email account, as shown in Figure 2.2.

Figure 2.2   The Internet Connection Wizard helps you configure your Internet email account.

The Internet Connection Wizard asks you to provide your name, your Internet email account address (probably *yourname@company.com*), and the names of your POP3 or IMAP server (for incoming mail) and your SMTP server (for outgoing mail). You need to get this information from your ISP or network administrator.

You are also asked your POP account name and password. This information, again, must be provided to you by your ISP or network administrator.

The Internet Connection Wizard also asks you to provide a friendly name for the account you are creating. This is the name that appears in the Outlook Services box.

The final step in the Internet email configuration is to select the way that you connect to the Internet. You can connect using your phone line (Outlook helps you make the connection each time you send mail) or connect using your corporate network, as shown in Figure 2.3. A third choice is available if you want to manually connect to the Internet before attempting to send or receive mail using Outlook.

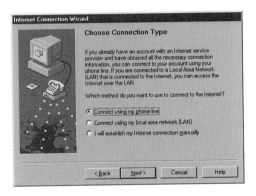

Figure 2.3 Choose how to connect to the Internet when you send and receive messages using your email account.

The final step in the process asks you to select an existing dial-up connection or create a new one to connect to the Internet (if you chose the Connect Using My Phone Line option in the previous step).

Dial-up connections dial the phone number of your service provider and connect you to their Internet server using your modem. If you configure a new dial-up connection, you must know your username, password, and the phone number for your ISP's Internet server.

Dial-Up Networking You must have the Windows 98/95 or NT Dial-Up Networking protocol installed to create new dial-up connections. See your operating system documentation to learn how to configure the Windows dial-up **CAUTION** adapter.

After you configure your Internet email account, you are ready to send and receive messages.

TIP   **Install It Any Time**   You can install your Internet email account at any time using the Internet Connection Wizard. Click **Tools**, **Accounts**. In the Accounts dialog box **Mail** tab, click **Add**, and then select **Mail**.

Configuring Internet Only Fax Support

Outlook also enables you to send and receive faxes. If you configure Outlook for Internet Only and choose to send and receive faxes, Semantics's WinFax Basic version is installed. WinFax can send faxes over your modem and answer your phone to receive incoming faxes.

The WinFax service is automatically installed during the initial installation of Outlook (if you choose Internet Only fax support during installation) and appears as one of the accounts in the Accounts dialog box. Sending and receiving faxes in Outlook is discussed in Lesson 23, "Managing Faxes with Outlook."

Sharing Information on the Internet

Even if you are not connected to a corporate network using Microsoft Exchange Server to share Outlook folder information, you can share your Calendar and Contacts information with others by means of the Internet. Outlook 2000 contains a feature called Net Folders. These special folders enable you to share information on the Internet with anyone to whom you can send Internet email. Net Folders are discussed in Lesson 24, "Outlook and the Internet."

Corporate Email

If you are using Outlook as a corporate email client over your company's network, you should select the Corporate email configuration for Outlook during the installation process. If your company has a Microsoft Exchange server on the network, you are using Outlook in an ideal environment. However, even if Exchange server is not used at your company, Outlook has been designed to work with other proprietary email systems, such as Lotus cc:Mail.

Configuring Your Email Account

If you use corporate email, your network administrator provides you with a mail account. You might or might not be allowed to choose your own user name and password for the account. Your corporate email account is configured as an account that appears in the Account dialog box. Using the Corporate email configuration enables you to take advantage of Outlook features such as the message recall, where you can recall a mail message that has not been opened by the recipient.

If you also desire to send and receive Internet email using the corporate configuration, you must also create an Internet email account. You can do this by adding Internet email as a service.

To add an Internet email account to the Corporate Outlook installation:

1. Select **Tools**, then **Services**.
2. In the Services dialog box, click the **Add** button. The Add Service to Profile dialog box appears.
3. Click **Internet Email** on the list of services and then click **OK**. The Mail Account Properties dialog box appears.
4. Provide the necessary account information and also provide the names of the POP3 and SMTP servers on the Server tab (these names are usually the same because most ISPs use one server to handle POP and SMTP).
5. Once you have provided all the necessary information, click the **OK** button. The new Internet email account is added to the list of services.
6. Click **OK** to close the Services dialog box. Outlook opens a message box to let you know that the new service is not available until you close Outlook and then restart it.

Sharing Information

Working on a corporate network that uses Exchange Server enables you to publish contact lists or calendars to a Microsoft Exchange Server public folder. Collaboration is made easy in the Exchange Server environment, and when you use Outlook to schedule a meeting, the availability of all the participants can be checked and routed to you immediately. A number of third-party collaboration applications also exist, making the Exchange Server environment ideal for employees using Outlook as their collaboration client.

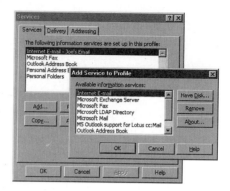

Figure 2.4   You can add an Internet email account to the Corporate Outlook configuration.

Using Outlook on an Exchange Server network enables a number of email features not available in the Internet Only email configuration. On a network, you can redirect replies, set message expirations, and even grant privileges to other users to monitor your email, Calendar, Contacts, and Tasks.

Working on a corporate network also enhances your ability to share information between users. Any folder on your computer can be set up as a shared resource. Shared folders can serve as discussion folders, where individuals on the corporate network can post and read messages (see Figure 2.5).

Another plus of working on a network is that you can stay connected to the network throughout the day. There need be no concern over connect time as there is with an Internet dial-in account. Being connected to the network constantly not only means that corporate email is downloaded to your computer periodically, but also that any incoming Internet email is also downloaded throughout the day.

TIP   **Using Net Folders on a Corporate Network**   If you are on a corporate network, you can still take advantage of Net Folders to share information with people over the Internet. Add Internet Folders as an Outlook service by selecting **Tools**, then **Services**.

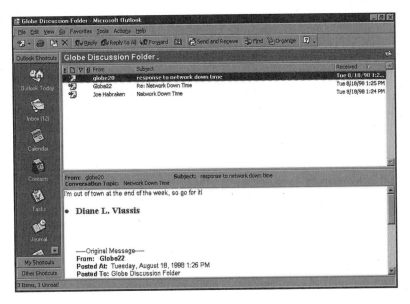

Figure 2.5 Shared folders can be created on the network and used for group discussions.

Making Your Installation Decision

While the choice of Outlook installation mainly is dictated by how you connect to electronic mail and other shared resources (Internet Only Email or Corporate installation), you do have the option of using either of the configurations even if you only plan to connect to the Internet and use Internet email.

While the Internet Email configuration is best suited for Internet connected users, you might find that you want to use the Corporate installation so that you can take advantage of the faxing capabilities of Microsoft Fax (remember, WinFax is installed with the Internet Only configuration and is not quite as flexible a fax tool as Microsoft Fax). Choosing the Corporate installation for a computer connecting to the Internet via a service provider would mean that you only want to set up the Internet E-mail service and forgo setting up any other electronic mail services such as Exchange Server or Microsoft Mail.

Whichever installation you adopt, remember that this gives a certain look and feel to the Outlook configuration. For instance, the Internet Only Email configuration does not have a Services command on the Tools menu. You also find that the Options dialog box (see Figure 2.6) has more tabs available than the Internet Only installation because of the additional Outlook functions provided by the Corporate installation. For more information on configuring Outlook, see Lesson 22, "Customizing Outlook."

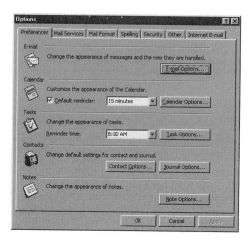

Figure 2.6 The customization options available to you in Outlook depend on the type of installation you chose when initially setting up Outlook on your computer.

Reconfiguring Your Mail Support

If you find that you've configured Outlook for one of the email configurations, such as Internet Only Email , and would like to switch to the other configuration (Corporate), you can reconfigure your mail support without reinstalling Outlook:

1. Select **Tools**, then **Options**. On the Options dialog box that appears, select the **Mail Services** tab.

2. Click the **Reconfigure Mail Support** button. The Outlook E-Mail Service Options screen opens. This is the same screen that appears the first time you start a new installation of Outlook (described in the "Installation Considerations" section of this lesson).

3. Select the type of email installation you wish to have and then follow the prompts to reconfigure your email setup for Outlook. You might need to place the Office 2000 or Outlook 2000 CD in your CD-ROM drive if prompted for installation files.

In this lesson, you learned about the Internet Only and the Corporate email configurations for Outlook 2000. In the next lesson, you learn the various Outlook tools such as the Outlook Bar.

Using Outlook's Tools

*In this lesson, you learn to change views
in Outlook, use the Outlook Bar, and use the Folder List.*

Using the Outlook Bar

Each Outlook organization tool has its own folder. You have a folder for email (Inbox), a folder for the calendar (Calendar), and so on. The Outlook Bar is a tool you can use to quickly change folders in Outlook. The icons in the Outlook Bar represent all of the folders available to you and provide shortcuts to getting to the contents of those folders. Figure 3.1 shows the Outlook Bar.

Three shortcut groups are located within the Outlook Bar: Outlook Shortcuts, My Shortcuts, and Other Shortcuts. Each group contains related folders in which you can work.

- **The Outlook Shortcuts group** contains folders for working with the different organizational tools in Outlook, such as the Inbox, Calendar, Tasks, and so on.
- **The My Shortcuts group** contains folders for organizing and managing your electronic mail and faxes.
- **The Other Shortcuts group** contains folders on your computer, such as My Computer, My Documents, and Favorites, which is a list of your favorite Web sites. You can use each of these folders to work with files and folders outside Outlook.

To switch from one group to another, click the **Outlook Shortcuts**, **My Shortcuts**, or **Other Shortcuts** button on the Outlook Bar. The Outlook shortcuts group is displayed by default, providing you with quick access to tools such as your Inbox, Calendar, and Contacts list.

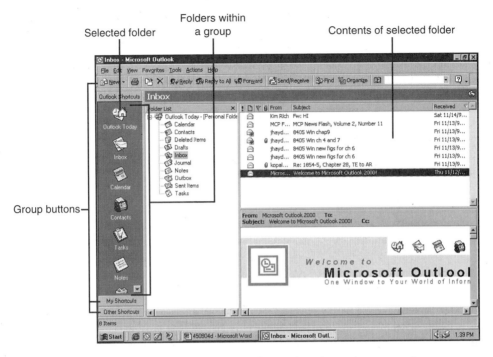

Selected folder

Folders within
a group

Contents of selected folder

Group buttons

Figure 3.1   Use the Outlook Bar to view various items in your work.

The Outlook Shortcuts Folders

The Outlook Shortcuts group's folder icons in the Outlook Bar enable you to access your work in Outlook. That includes your email messages, appointments, contact list, and so on. Table 3.1 describes each of the folders within the Outlook Shortcuts group.

Table 3.1   Outlook Shortcuts Group Folders

Folder	Description
Outlook Today	While not really a folder, the Outlook Today icon on the Outlook Bar provides a summary of Calendar events, tasks, and new messages for the current day (today).
Inbox	Includes messages you've sent and received by email and fax.
Calendar	Contains your appointments, events, scheduled meetings, and so on.

continues

Table 3.1   Continued

Folder	Description
Contacts	Lists names and addresses of the people with whom you communicate.
Tasks	Includes any tasks you have on your to-do list.
Journal	Contains all journal entries, such as phone logs, meeting notes, and so on.
Notes	Lists notes you write yourself or others.
Deleted Items	Includes any items you've deleted from other folders.

The My Shortcuts Group Folders

The My Shortcuts group folders provide a method of organizing your incoming and outgoing email messages (see Figure 3.2). Table 3.2 describes each folder in the Mail group.

Table 3.2   My Shortcuts Folders

Folder	Description
Draft	Contains messages you have started but not sent
Sent Items	Stores all messages you've sent
Outbox	Contains messages to be sent
Journal	Keeps track of your activities in Outlook

CAUTION

I See Other Folders in My Groups   You can add additional folders and folder icons very easily to Outlook. If you find folders other than the ones described here, folders have probably been added to your particular installation of Outlook.

The Other Shortcuts Folders

The Other Shortcuts group contains folders that are on your computer but not within Outlook: My Computer, My Documents, and Favorites. You can access a document or information in any of those areas so that you can attach it to a message, add notes to it, or otherwise use it in Outlook.

For example, with My Computer, you can view the contents of both hard and floppy disks, CD-ROM drives, and so on (see Figure 3.3). Double-click a drive in the window to view its folders and files. Double-click a folder to view its contents as well. Then you can attach files to messages or otherwise use the files on your hard drive with the Outlook features.

Figure 3.2 The My Shortcuts folder icons give you access to your email and fax messages that have been saved as drafts, sent, or are waiting to be sent.

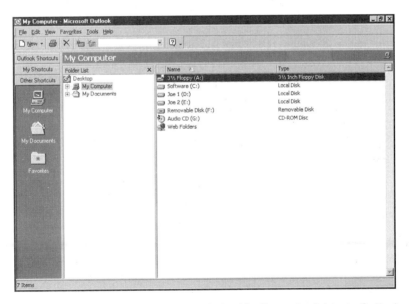

Figure 3.3 View your entire system through the My Computer folder in Outlook.

TIP **Moving On Up** Use the **Up One Level** button on the Advanced toolbar to return to a folder or drive after you've double-clicked to expand it and view its contents.

Using the Folder List

Outlook provides another method of viewing the folders within Outlook and your system: the Folder List. The Folder List displays the folders within any of the three groups (Outlook Shortcuts, My Shortcuts, or Other Shortcuts). From the list, you can select the folder you want to view.

To use the Folder List, first select the group (such as Outlook Shortcuts or Other Shortcuts) that contains the folders you want to view, and then select a particular folder (using the appropriate shortcut) from the Outlook Bar to display the list (see Figure 3.4).

Click here to display the Folder List.

Figure 3.4 The Folder List shows all folders in the group you selected.

TIP **Pinning Down the Folder List** When you open the Folder List button on a particular folder's name, the Folder List floats on top of the current folder window. Click the **push pin** button in the upper corner of the Folder List to "pin down" the list in the Outlook window. If you want to close the "pinned" Folder List, click its **Close** (×) button.

Choose any folder from the list, and the Information Viewer changes to reflect your selection. If you want to display another folder in the Information screen, double-click the folder to display its contents.

Changing Views

In Outlook, you are provided with different views that enable you to look at the information in your various folders from a particular perspective. Each view presents the information in a different format and organizational structure.

The easiest way to select the different views provided for each of your Outlook folders is a View box that is present on the Advanced toolbar for each folder type (Inbox, Calendar, Contacts, and so on). To open the Advanced toolbar for any Outlook folder, follow these steps:

1. Point to the Standard toolbar for an Outlook folder (such as the Inbox) and click the right mouse button.

2. A shortcut menu appears, as shown in Figure 3.5. Click **Advanced**. The Advanced toolbar appears.

3. You might want to close the Standard toolbar after you've opened the Advanced toolbar. Right-click either toolbar and then click **Standard** to remove the check mark. The Standard toolbar closes.

TIP **You Only Have to Open the Advanced Toolbar Once** After you've opened the Advanced toolbar for a folder, such as the Calendar or Inbox, it will be available for all the other Outlook folders.

Figure 3.5 Right-click the Standard toolbar to access the Outlook Advanced toolbar for any folder.

Each folder—Inbox, Calendar, Contacts, and so on—will have a different set of buttons on the Standard and Advanced toolbars. This is because the commands and features that you access on a toolbar will be particular to the folder that you currently have selected.

After you have the Advanced toolbar open, you can change the current view by clicking the **Current View** drop-down box, as shown in Figure 3.6. Each Current View box contains views that are appropriate for the currently selected folder on the Outlook Bar.

As you can see in Figure 3.6, you can change your view of the Inbox so that you can see all messages (Messages), messages and their first three lines of text (Messages with AutoPreview), messages that have been tagged with a follow-up flag (By Follow-Up Flag), messages from the last seven days (Last Seven Days), messages tagged with a flag for the next seven days (Flagged for Next Seven Days), messages organized by topic (By Conversation Topic), messages organized by sender (By Sender), unread messages only (Unread Messages), messages by recipient (Sent To), and messages arranged in a timeline (Message Timeline).

Similarly, the Calendar folder—which is arranged in the Day/Week/Month view type by default—enables you to view your appointments and events by active appointments, Day/Week/Month with AutoPreview, events, recurring appointments, and several other view types.

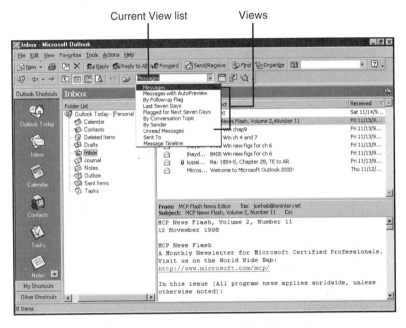

Figure 3.6   Select a view to change the format of the information.

You can also change the view type for any of your folders by selecting the **Edit** menu and then pointing at **Current View**. The View list appears as a submenu of Edit.

As you work your way through this part of the book, you'll see examples of each view type. When you change folders in Outlook, take a quick look at the available views in the **Current View** drop-down list.

Creating Custom Views

You can also create custom views of the information in your Outlook folders. To create a custom view for one of your Outlook folders, follow these steps:

1. Click the **View** menu, and then point at **Current View**. Select **Define Views**. A Define Views dialog box for the currently selected folder opens.

711

2. Click the **New** button in the Define Views box. The Create a New View dialog box appears, as shown in Figure 3.7.

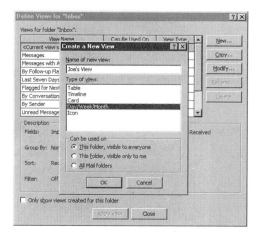

Figure 3.7   You can create custom views for your Outlook folders.

3. Enter a name for your new view and select a view type from the list in the Type of View box.

   You can select different view types for a custom view:

   - **Table view**—Presents items in a grid of sorts—in rows and columns. Use this view type to view mail messages, tasks, and details about any item.
   - **Timeline view**—Displays items as icons arranged in chronological order from left to right on a time scale. Use this to view journal entries and other items in this type of view.
   - **Day/Week/Month view**—Displays items in a calendar view in blocks of time. Use this type for meetings and scheduled tasks.
   - **Card view**—Presents items like cards in a card file. Use this to view contacts.
   - **Icon view**—Provides graphic icons to represent tasks, notes, calendars, and so on.

4. After you've selected the type of view you want to create, click the **OK** button. A View Settings dialog box appears. In this box you determine which fields you want to have in the view and the fonts and other view settings you want to use.

5. After you've selected the fields and view settings, click **Apply View**. The items in the current folder appear in the new view.

Fields A specific type of information that you want to appear in your custom view. For a custom Inbox view using the Timeline view type, the fields would include Received (when the message was received), Created (when the message was created), and Sent (when the message was sent).

Your new view appears on the Current View list on the Advanced toolbar. You can select it by clicking the list's drop-down arrow and then clicking the custom view's name.

Should I Design My Own Views? Designing your own views can prove to be complicated. Outlook provides several views for each of the folders on the Outlook Bar. You might want to explore all these possibilities before you begin to create your own views.

Using Outlook Today

A great way to get a snapshot view of your day is Outlook Today. This feature provides you with a window that lists all your messages, appointments, and tasks associated with the current day.

To open the Outlook Today window, click the **Go** menu, then select **Outlook Today**. Icons for your Calendar, Messages, and Tasks appear in the Outlook Today window, as shown in Figure 3.8. Items for the current day are listed below the icons.

You can click any of the listed items (a particular appointment or task) to open the appropriate folder and view the details associated with the items. You can even update the items.

The Outlook Today window also provides you with a Find a Contact box that you can use to find people in your Contacts folder. Type a name in the Person text box and then click the **Go** button. A Contact window appears for the person. You can edit the person's information or close the Contact box by clicking the **Close** button.

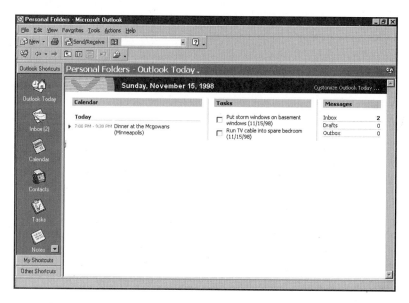

Figure 3.8   Outlook Today provides you with a list of all the items associated with the current day.

After you have viewed the items in the Outlook Today window, you can return to any of your folders by clicking their icons on the Outlook Bar. Outlook Today is an excellent way to get a handle on what your day has in store for you.

In this lesson, you learned to use the Outlook Bar, change and create views in Outlook, use the Folder List, and take advantage of the Outlook Today feature. In the next lesson, you learn to create and send mail in Outlook.

Creating Mail

In this lesson, you learn to compose a message, format text, check your spelling, and send mail. You also learn to use different email formats such as text-only and HTML mail.

Composing a Message

You can send a message to anyone for whom you have an address, whether his or her address is in your address book, your list of contacts, or scribbled on a Post-It note. In addition to sending a message to one or more recipients, you can send copies of a message to other people you have an email address for or to those whom are listed on your various address lists.

 TIP **Compose Your Messages Offline** If you connect to an Internet service provider and don't want to waste precious connect time while you compose email messages, you can create new messages in Outlook without being connected to the Internet. New messages you send are placed in your Outbox until you connect to the Internet and actually send them on to their final destination.

Entering an Address in a Message

You can either use the address book to choose the names of recipients to whom you want to send new messages or have the email address automatically placed in the To box when you forward messages or send a reply. Using the address book also makes sending carbon copies and blind carbon copies easy.

 Blind Carbon Copy A blind carbon copy (Bcc) of a message is a copy sent to someone in secret; the other recipients have no way of knowing that you are sending the message to someone as a blind carbon copy.

To address a message, follow these steps:

1. Choose **Compose**, then select **New Mail Message** from the Outlook Inbox window, or click the **New Message** button on the toolbar. A new message window appears (see Figure 4.1).

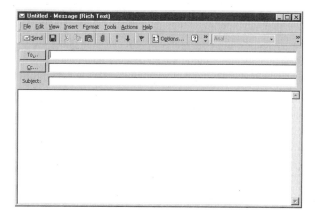

Figure 4.1   Compose a new message in the Untitled Message window.

2. In the Message window, click the **To** button to display the Select Names dialog box. If you have not added any names to the Address book or Contact's list, no names are available; follow the next tip to add an address or simply type the email address in the To text box. If you choose to type the email address directly in the To text box, you can then skip steps 3 through 7 (for more information on adding people to your Address book or Contact's list see Lessons 10 and 11).

 TIP   **Adding People to Your Address or Contact's List**   If your Contact's or Address list is currently empty, you can still quickly add a new address to either list and then use it for the To address on the current new message. When the Select Names dialog box appears, select the list to which you want to add the new name from the Show Names drop-down box at the top of the dialog box. Then click the **New** button. Enter the recipient's name in the Display Name box and then enter their email address in the Email Address box and click **OK**. The person's Display Name is placed in the message's To box, addressing the message for you.

3. Click the **address book** drop-down list box at the top right of the dialog box and choose the **Postoffice Address List**, **Contacts List**, **Global Address List**, or the **Personal Address Book** as appropriate. This enables you to view names in a particular address book.

4. From the list of addresses that appears on the left, choose the name of the intended recipient and select the **To** button. Outlook copies the name to the Message Recipients list. (You can add multiple names if you want.)

5. (Optional) Select the names of anyone to whom you want to send a carbon copy, and click the **Cc** button to transfer those names to the Message Recipients list.

6. (Optional) Select the names of anyone to whom you want to send a blind carbon copy and click the **Bcc** button. Figure 4.2 shows a distribution group listing as the To recipient of a message.

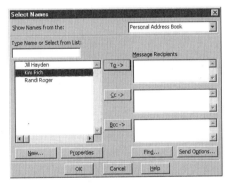

Figure 4.2 Address messages quickly with the Select Names dialog box.

7. Click **OK** to return to the Message window.

You can also easily send email to any people whose addresses you keep in your Contacts folder. How to use and maintain the Contacts folder is covered in Lesson 10, "Using the Contact and Personal Address Books."

8. Click in the text area, and then enter the text of the message. You do not have to press the Enter key at the end of a line; Outlook automatically wraps the text at the end of a line for you. You can use the Delete and Backspace keys to edit the text you enter.

9. When you finish typing the message, you can send the message to your OutBox (see "Sending Mail" later in this lesson), or you can check the spelling and formatting as described in the following sections.

No Address!   If you try to send a message without entering an address, Outlook displays a message that there must be at least one email address in the To box. Type in an address or select an address from your Contact's list or Address Book.

CAUTION

Formatting Text

You can change the format of the text in your message to make it more attractive, to make it easier to read, or to add emphasis. Any formatting you do transfers to the recipient with the message if the recipient has Outlook or another email client that can work with Outlook Rich Text (formerly known as Microsoft Exchange Rich Text) or HTML messages. However, if the recipient doesn't have an email package that can handle these special message formats, formatting may not transfer. Many Internet email clients do not offer this capability. Most corporate email clients, such as Lotus Notes and Novell GroupWise, do enable the sending and receiving of messages in Rich Text Format. You should keep in mind that if you send a Rich Text or HTML message to a person who has an email client that cannot handle special formatting, they receive the message in plain text.

TERM   **Outlook Rich Text (Exchange Rich Text)**   A special email format developed by Microsoft for use with Microsoft mail systems. Outlook 2000 can send and receive messages in the Exchange Rich Text format. This enables you to send and receive messages with special formatting such as bold, italic, fonts, and other special characters and graphics.

TERM   **HTML**   Hypertext Markup Language is used to design Web pages for the World Wide Web. Outlook 2000 can send messages in this format, providing you with a number of formatting options.

You format text in two ways. You can format the text after you type it by selecting it and then choosing a font, size, or other attribute; or you can select the font, size, or other attribute to toggle it on, and then enter the text.

To format the text in your message, first make sure the Formatting toolbar is showing. Choose **View**, then select **Toolbars** and click **Formatting**. Figure 4.3 shows a message with the Formatting toolbar displayed. Table 4.1 explains the buttons on this toolbar.

CAUTION

Formatting Toolbar Buttons Unavailable! Only messages sent in Microsoft Exchange Rich Text format or HTML format can be formatted. See the section in this lesson "Sending HTML Messages" for more information. If you have installed Outlook for Internet email only, you also find that when you select the Format command, only Plain Text and Rich Text (HTML) are available as choices.

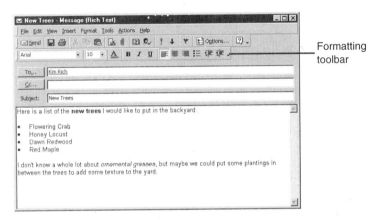

Figure 4.3 Use the Formatting toolbar to modify your message text.

Table 4.1 Formatting Toolbar Buttons

Button	Name
A	Font Color
B	Bold
I	Italic
U	Underline
≣	Align Left

continues

Table 4.1 Continued

Button	Name
	Center
	Align Right
	Bullets
	Numbering
	Decrease Indent
	Increase Indent

CAUTION

My Toolbars Look Completely Different!   If you've chosen to use Microsoft Word as your email editor, the toolbars that are present in the new message window reflect those you have selected in your Word installation. The Word and Outlook toolbars have many of the same buttons.

1. To apply a font to text, click the **down arrow** in the Font box on the Formatting toolbar. Scroll through the font list, if necessary, to view all fonts on the system, and click the font you want to apply to the text. You can also apply a style to selected text in the message. Click the **Style** drop-down arrow on the Formatting toolbar. The styles available range from a set of predefined heading styles to special styles such as Directory List and Menu List.

2. Assign a size by clicking the **down arrow** beside the **Font Size** drop-down list and choosing the size; alternatively, you can enter a size in the Font Size text box.

3. To choose a color, click the **Color** button and select a color from the palette box that appears.

4. Choose a type style to apply to text by clicking the **Bold, Italic,** and/or **Underline** buttons on the Formatting toolbar.

5. Choose an alignment by selecting the **Align Left, Center,** or **Align Right** button from the Formatting toolbar.

6. Add bullets to a list by clicking the **Bullet** button on the Formatting toolbar. If you prefer a numbered list, click the **Numbering** button.

7. Create text indents or remove indents in half-inch increments by clicking the **Increase Indent** or **Decrease Indent** buttons. (Each time you click the Indent button, the indent changes by half an inch.)

Yuck, No Thanks! If you assign formatting to your text and don't particularly like it, click **Edit,** and select **Undo** to remove the last formatting that you did.

CAUTION

Sending HTML Messages

Another alternative for sending messages with formatted text is the HTML format. HTML stands for Hypertext Markup Language and is the language used to design Web pages for the World Wide Web. You can choose to send your email messages in this format by following these steps:

1. Click **Tools,** then **Options.** The Options dialog box appears.

2. Click the **Mail Format** tab (see Figure 4.4).

TIP **Include Hyperlinks** If you send HTML or Rich Text Format messages, you can include hyperlinks. Hyperlinks are Web addresses and email addresses that can be accessed by clicking them in the message. Just type the Web address or email address, and the hyperlink is created automatically.

3. To select the message format, click the **Send in This Message Format** drop-down box. Select **HTML, Outlook Rich Text,** or **Plain Text.** If you want to use Microsoft Word as your email editor, click the **Use Microsoft Word to edit email messages** check box.

4. Click **OK** to close the dialog box.

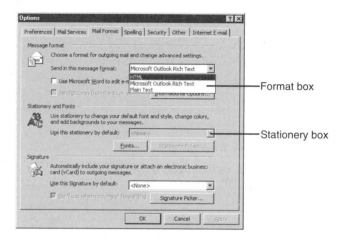

Figure 4.4   You can select to send your messages in HTML, Outlook Rich Text, or Plain Text Formats.

If you choose to use the HTML format in the Options box, you can also select special stationery to send your messages on. Click the **Use This Stationery by Default** drop-down box. Outlook provides a number of HTML stationery types. To see a preview of the stationery types listed, click the **Stationery Picker** button.

Using the HTML format for your messages provides you with the greatest number of possibilities as far as formatting and graphics in email messages. Remember, however, that you can only take advantage of the HTML format if the receiver of your message is using Outlook or another email client that can read a message in HTML.

CAUTION

But I Don't Know HTML Coding   When you select the HTML format for your email messages, this doesn't mean that you have to actually write HTML code to format the various elements in the message. All you have to do is select heading and other styles (that will use HTML formatting automatically) by clicking **Format** and then **Style**.

Sending Text-Only Messages

If you send most of your messages to recipients who do not use Outlook 2000 or another email client that can take advantage of Rich Text or HTML-formatted messages, you may want to set your default message type to text only. This sends all your messages in plain text that can be read by all email clients.

To select Plain Text as your message format, follow these steps:

1. Click **Tools**, then **Options**. The Options dialog box appears.
2. Click the **Mail Format** tab.
3. Click the **Send in This Message Format** drop-down box, and select **Plain Text**.
4. Click **OK** to close the dialog box.

Checking Spelling

To make a good impression and to maintain your professional image, you should check the spelling in your mail messages before you send them. Outlook includes a spelling checker you can use for that purpose. Your grammar is automatically checked, as well.

To check the spelling in a message, follow these steps:

1. In the open message, choose **Tools**, then select **Spelling and Grammar**, or press **F7**. If the spelling checker finds a word whose spelling it questions, it displays the Spelling dialog box (shown in Figure 4.5). (If no words are misspelled, a dialog box appears saying the spelling and grammar check is complete; choose **OK** to close the dialog box.)

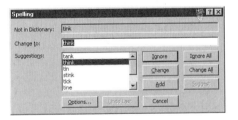

Figure 4.5 Check your spelling before sending a message.

2. Your response to the word Outlook questions in the Spelling dialog box will vary. If you recognize that Outlook has correctly flagged a misspelled word, choose one of the following:
   - **Suggestions**—Select the correct spelling in this text box, and it automatically appears in the Change To text box.
   - **Change**—Click this button to change this particular occurrence of the word in question to the spelling in the Change To text box.

723

- **Change All**—Click this button to change the word in question to the spelling listed in the Change To text box every time the spelling checker finds the word in this message.

If Outlook checks a word that you know is already spelled correctly (such as a proper name), choose one of the following:

- **Not in Dictionary**—Enter the correct spelling in this text box.
- **Ignore**—Click this button to continue the spelling check without changing this occurrence of the selected word.
- **Ignore All**—Click this button to continue the spelling check without changing any occurrence of the word in question throughout this message.
- **Add**—Click this button to add the current spelling of the word in question to the dictionary so that Outlook will not question future occurrences of this spelling.

Undo that Correction   Click the **Undo** button to reverse the last spelling change you made, thus returning the word to its original spelling.

CAUTION

3. Continue until the spelling check is complete (or click **Cancel** to quit the spelling check).

4. Outlook displays a message box telling you it's done. Click **OK** to close the dialog box.

TIP   **Set Your Spelling Options**   Click the **Options** button in the Spelling dialog box to set options that tell Outlook to do such things as ignore words with numbers, ignore original message text in forwarded messages or replies, always check spelling before sending, and so on.

Add a Signature

You can automatically add a signature file that includes text and images to your email messages:

1. Choose **Tools**, then select **Options** to open the Options dialog box and then select the Mail Format tab.

2. Click the **Signature Picker** button at the bottom of the dialog box. The Signature Picker dialog box opens.

3. Click the **New** button and follow the steps provided on the Create New signature screens.

Once you've created a signature, you can quickly add it to any message by choosing **Insert**, then **Signature**; all the signatures that you have created appear on the menu. Select the signature from the list you want to use in the message you are currently composing.

Sending Mail

When you're ready to send your mail message, Choose **File**, then select **Send**, or just press **Ctrl+Enter**.

 TIP   **Using Windows NT 4.0?**   You'll need to check your rights and permissions in relation to sending email within your network. Ask your system administrator for more information.

Recalling a Message

If you configured Outlook for corporate email, you can recall messages that you send over your corporate network and over the Internet. You can only recall messages that have not been opened or moved to another folder. If you want to recall a message on your corporate network, the individual from whom you are recalling the message must be logged on.

To recall a sent message, follow these steps:

1. Click the **My Shortcuts** button on the Outlook Bar, and then select the **Sent Items** Folder.

2. Double-click to open the message that you want to recall.

3. In the Message window, click the **Tools** menu, then click **Recall This Message**. The Recall This Message dialog box opens.

4. To recall the message click the **Delete Unread Copies of This Message** option button, and then click **OK**. A notice appears in the Message window (upper-left corner) informing you that you are attempting to recall this message.

5. Click **File**, and then **Save** to save the message with the recall option. Close the message.

6. You eventually receive a notification in your Inbox (as new mail) notifying you whether or not the recall was successful.

In this lesson, you learned to compose a message, format text, check your spelling, and send mail. You also learned how to select different email formats such as HTML and Plain Text. You also learned how to recall a message. In the next lesson, you learn to work with received mail.

Working with Received Mail

In this lesson, you learn to read your mail,
save an attachment, answer mail, and close a message.

Reading Mail

When you log on to Outlook, your Inbox folder appears, and any new messages you've received are downloaded from your company's mail server. If you use Internet Mail, you have to connect to your Internet service provider to download your mail using Outlook. Any new mail is placed in your Inbox (see Figure 5.1). If you watch closely, when you connect to your network or Internet service provider a downloading mail icon appears in the lower right of the Outlook window, showing you that new mail is being received.

CAUTION

My Outlook Doesn't Open to the Inbox   If Outlook opens to Outlook Today, click the **Inbox** folder on the Outlook Bar or click the **Messages** link in Outlook Today. Either of these alternatives will take you to your Inbox.

As you can see in Figure 5.1, the Inbox provides important information about each message. For example, one message has been labeled as high priority, one is low priority, and one message has an attachment. Messages that have already been replied to are marked with a curved reply arrow. You'll learn about priorities and attachments in Lesson 9, "Setting Mail Options." In addition, the status bar at the bottom of the Inbox window indicates how many items the Inbox folder contains and how many of those items are unread.

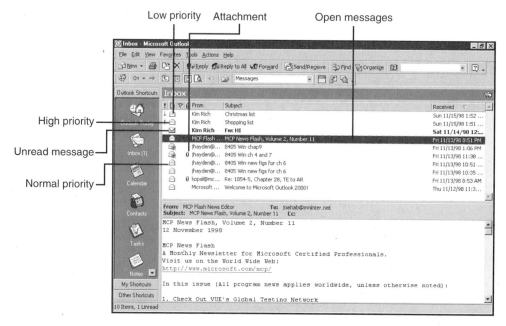

Figure 5.1 The Inbox provides information related to your received messages: the sender, subject, date received, and priority and attachment icons.

To read a message, you can click it, and its contents appear in the Outlook Preview pane. You can also open a message in its own window; double-click a mail message to open it. Figure 5.2 shows an open message.

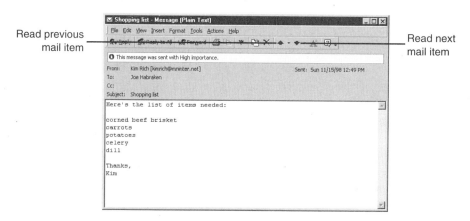

Figure 5.2 The Message window displays the message and some tools for handling this message or moving on to another.

To read the next or previous mail message in the Inbox, click the **Previous Item** or the **Next Item** button on the toolbar. Or you can open the **View** menu, choose **Previous** or **Next**, and choose **Item**.

Item Outlook uses the word *item* to describe a mail message, an attached file, an appointment or meeting, a task, and so on. *Item* is a generic term in Outlook that describes the currently selected element.

You can mark messages as read or unread by choosing **Edit**, then selecting either **Mark as Read** or **Mark as Unread**. Outlook automatically marks messages as read when you open them. But you might want to mark messages yourself once in a while (as a reminder, for example). Additionally, you can mark all of the messages in the Inbox as read at one time by choosing **Edit**, then **Mark All as Read**. You might want to mark mail messages as read so you don't read them again; you might want to mark important mail as unread so you'll be sure to open it and read it again.

No Mail? If you don't see any new mail in your Inbox, click the **Send and Receive** button on the toolbar, or choose **Tools**, then select **Check for New Mail**, and Outlook updates your mail for you.

CAUTION

Saving an Attachment

You often receive messages that have files or other items attached. In the Inbox list of messages, an attachment is represented by a paper clip icon beside the message. Save any attachments sent to you so you can open, modify, print, or otherwise use the document. Messages can contain multiple attachments.

What About Viruses? There is a (slight) chance that an attachment to a message can be infected with a virus. Computer viruses can really wreak havoc on your computer system. When you receive an email message from someone you don't know and that message has an attachment, the best thing to do is delete the message without opening it or the attachment. In cases where you save an attachment to your computer, you might want to check the file with an antivirus program before you actually open the file.

CAUTION

To save an attachment, follow these steps:

1. Open the message containing an attachment by double-clicking the message. The attachment appears as an icon in the message text (see Figure 5.3).

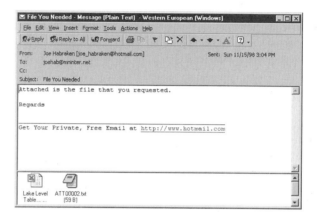

Figure 5.3 An icon represents the attached file.

2. (Optional) You can open the attachment from within the message by double-clicking the icon. The application in which the document was created—Word or Excel, for example—opens and displays the document in the window, ready for you to read. Close the application by choosing **File**, then **Exit**.

3. In the message, select the attachment you want to save and choose **File**, then **Save Attachments**. The Save Attachment dialog box appears (see Figure 5.4).

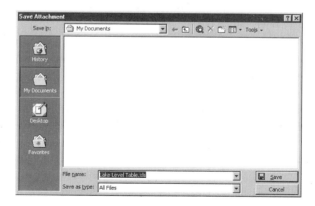

Figure 5.4 Save the attachment to a convenient folder.

4. Choose the folder in which you want to save the attachment, and click **Save**. You can change the name of the file, if you want. You can open the attachment at any time from the application in which it was created. The dialog box closes and returns to the Message window.

TIP **Use the Right Mouse Button** You can also quickly save an attachment by right-clicking the attachment icon. On the shortcut menu that appears, click **Save As**, and then save the attachment to an appropriate folder.

Answering Mail

You might want to reply to a message after you read it. The Message window enables you to answer a message immediately, or at a later time if you prefer. To reply to any given message, follow these steps:

1. Select the message in the Inbox window and then click the **Reply** button on the Inbox toolbar.

   If you have the message open, choose **Compose**, and then select **Reply**, or you can click the **Reply** button in the message window. The Reply Message window appears, with the original message in the message text area and the sender of the message already filled in for you (see Figure 5.5).

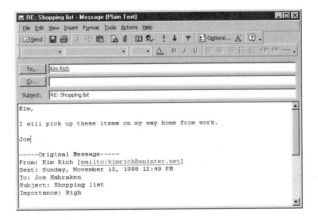

Figure 5.5 You can reply to a message quickly and easily.

TIP   **Reply to All**   If you receive a message that has also been sent to others—as either a message or a carbon copy (Cc)—you can click the **Reply to All** button to send your reply to each person who received the message.

2. The insertion point is in the message text area, ready for you to enter your reply. Enter the text.

 3. When you finish your reply, choose **File**, then select **Send** or you might click the **Send** button. Outlook sends the message.

If you are using Outlook as your Internet mail program, clicking the **Send** button only places the reply message in your Outlook Outbox. You must click the **Send and Receive** button on the Outlook toolbar to empty the Outbox and send your messages on to their respective recipients. You can also configure Outlook to send messages immediately. See Lesson 22, "Customizing Outlook," for information on customizing Outlook.

The next time you open a message to which you've replied, there is a reminder at the top of the Message tab telling you the date and time you sent your reply. And don't forget that the purple arrow next to a message in the Inbox window shows that the message has been replied to.

Printing Mail

You can print mail messages whether they're open or not. To print an unopened message, select the message in the message list of the Inbox or other folder and choose **File**, then select **Print**. If the message is already open, you can follow these steps:

1. Open the message in Outlook.

2. Choose **File**, then select **Print**, or press **Ctrl+P** to view the Print dialog box.

3. In the Print dialog box, click **OK** to print one copy of the entire message using the printer's default settings. See Lesson 17, "Printing in Outlook," for detailed information about configuring pages and setting up the printer.

TIP **Toolbar Shortcut** Click the **Print** button on the toolbar to print using defaults.

Closing a Message

When you finish a message, choose **File**, then select **Close** or just press **Alt+F4**.

 TIP **Alternate Methods of Closing** Choose what's easiest for you. Click the **Control-menu** button and click **Close** or click the **Close** (×) button in the title bar of the Message window.

In this lesson, you learned to read your mail, save an attachment, answer mail, and close a message. In the next lesson, you learn to manage your mail messages.

Managing Mail

6

In this lesson, you learn to delete and undelete messages, forward messages, and organize messages by saving them to folders. You also work with the Outlook Rules Wizard and the Organize tool, which provide a way to automate certain mail management tasks.

Deleting Mail

While you may want to store certain important messages, for the most part, you'll definitely want to delete much of the mail that you receive after reading it. You can easily delete messages in Outlook when you're finished with them.

To delete a mail message that is open, choose **File**, then select **Delete**, or press **Ctrl+D**.

 TIP **Toolbar Has a Delete Button, Too**   Click the **Delete** button on the toolbar.

If you have modified the message in any way, a confirmation message appears from the Office Assistant or as a message dialog box. Otherwise, the message is deleted without warning.

If you're in the Inbox and you want to delete one or more messages from the message list, select the single message to delete (or hold down the **Ctrl** key and click each message). Finally, press the **Delete** key.

Undeleting Items

If you change your mind and want to get back items you've deleted, you can usually retrieve them from the Deleted Items folder. By default, when you delete an item, it doesn't disappear from your system; it merely moves to the Deleted Items folder. Items stay in the Deleted Items folder until you delete them from that folder—at which point they are unrecoverable. To retrieve a deleted item from the Deleted Items folder click the **Undo Delete** icon in the Advanced toolbar. Or if multiple messages have to be undeleted, follow these steps:

1. Click the **scroll down** arrow on the Outlook Bar to locate the Deleted Items folder.

2. Click the **Deleted Items** icon in the Outlook Bar to open the folder.

3. Select the items you want to retrieve, and drag them to the folder containing the same type of items on the Outlook Bar. Alternatively, you can choose **Edit**, then **Move to Folder** and choose the folder to which you want to move the selected items.

Emptying the Deleted Items Folder

If you're sure you want to delete the items in the Deleted Items folder, you can erase them from your system. To delete items in the Deleted Items folder, follow these steps:

1. In the Outlook Bar, choose the **Outlook Shortcuts** or **My Shortcuts** group and then select the **Deleted Items** folder. All deleted items in that folder appear in the message list, as shown in Figure 6.1.

2. To permanently delete an item, select it in the Deleted Items folder. You also can choose more than one item at a time by holding down the **Shift** or **Ctrl** key as you click each item.

3. Click the **Delete** button or choose **Edit**, then select **Delete**. Outlook displays a confirmation dialog box asking if you're sure you want to permanently delete the message. Choose **Yes** to delete the selected item.

4. To switch back to the Inbox or another folder, select the folder from either the Outlook Bar or the Folders List.

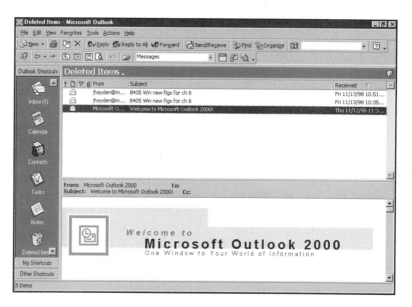

Figure 6.1 Deleted messages remain in the Deleted Items folder until you permanently delete them.

 TIP **Automatic Permanent Delete**   You can set Outlook to permanently delete the contents of the Deleted Items folder every time you exit the program. To do so, choose **Tools**, and click **OK**.

Forwarding Mail

Suppose you want to forward mail you receive from a coworker to another person who has an interest in the message. You can forward any message you receive, and you can even add comments to the message if you want.

 TERM **Forward Mail**   When you forward mail, you send a message you received to another person on the network; you can add your own comments to the forwarded mail, if you want.

You forward an open message or a message selected in the message list in the Inbox in the same way. To forward mail, follow these steps:

1. Select or open the message you want to forward. Choose **Actions**, and then select **Forward**, or just click the **Forward** button. The FW Message window appears (see Figure 6.2).

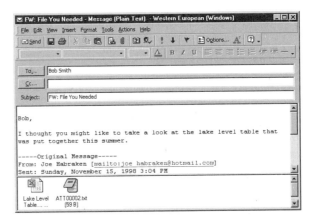

Figure 6.2   When you forward a message, the original message appears at the bottom of the message window.

2. In the To text box, enter the names of the people to whom you want to forward the mail. (If you want to choose a person's name from a list, click the **To** button to display the Select Names dialog box, and then select the person's name.) Lesson 10, "Using the Contact and Personal Address Books," explains more about using the Address Book. If you enter multiple names in the To box, separate the names with a semicolon and a space.

3. (Optional) In the Cc text box, enter the names of anyone to whom you want to forward copies of the message (or click the **Cc** button and choose the name from the list that appears).

4. In the message area of the window, enter any message you want to send with the forwarded text. The text you type is a different color.

 Attachments   If the message that you forward contains attached files, the attachments are also forwarded.

CAUTION

 5. Choose **File**, and select **Send**, or just click the **Send** button.

Saving Mail to a Folder

Although you delete some mail after you read and respond to it, you want to save other messages for future reference. You can save a message to any folder you want, but you should use a logical filing system to ensure that you can find each message again later. Outlook offers several methods for organizing your mail.

The easiest method of saving mail to a folder is to move it to one of Outlook's built-in Mail folders. You can use any of the folders to store your mail, or you can create new folders. Lesson 8, "Organizing Messages," describes how to create your own folders within Outlook.

To move messages to an existing folder, follow these steps:

1. Select one message (by clicking it) or select multiple messages by holding the **Ctrl** key while you click each message. To select an entire series of messages, click the first message and then hold the **Shift** key as you click the last message.

 TIP   Making Backup Copies   You can also copy a message to another folder as a backup. To do so, choose **Edit**, then select **Copy to Folder**.

 2. Choose **Edit**, then select **Move to Folder** or click the **Move to Folder** button on the toolbar. The Move Items dialog box appears (see Figure 6.3).

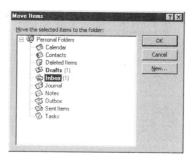

Figure 6.3   Choose the folder to which you want to move the selected message(s).

3. Select the folder to which you want to move the item and click **OK**. Outlook moves the item to the folder for you.

TIP **Quickly Creating Contacts or Tasks From Email** When you select the **Move to Folder** button on the toolbar, you are provided with choices for Contacts and Tasks on the drop-down menu that appears. Select either of these choices to quickly create a new contact or task from the selected email message or messages. For more information on creating contacts or tasks from messages see Lesson 19, "Using Outlook Integration, Forms, and Templates."

To view the message(s) you've moved, choose the folder from the Outlook Bar or the Folders List. Then click the item you want to view.

Attachments Move with Messages When you move messages to a folder other than the Inbox, any attachments to the message move to the new folder with the message. Attachments are really part of a message just as the **CAUTION** text of the message is.

Using the Organize Tool

Outlook 98 provides an easy-to-use tool that can help you move, delete, or color-code received and sent mail, called the Organize tool. The Organize tool can even help you deal with annoying junk email that you receive. The Organize feature centers on the email address of the sender of the particular message you select and uses it to find all the messages in the Inbox sent by this person.

The Organize tool provides you with two different possibilities: the Move message command and the Create a Rule command. Each of these avenues for moving messages to a particular Outlook folder have their own area and set of command buttons in the Organize pane.

If you want to manually move the selected message to a new location, you can use Move message. However, if you receive additional messages from this individual at a later time, you have to again manually move the messages to the new location.

To manage future messages from an individual, use the Create a Rule command. This creates a rule that moves new messages from the individual to the new location automatically. That way, you can find all the messages from a particular person in the same place when you need them (both the messages you move manually and the messages moved by the rule end up in the same folder).

Rules Rules are a set of conditions (such as a particular email address or message content) that you identify to move, delete, or manage incoming email messages.

CAUTION

Rules and Attachments The rules you create to organize your messages can look at the sender, receiver, message subject, and message text. Attachments to a message are not governed by the rules that you create, and so the content of file attachments to a message do not govern how they are handled by the Organize tool or rules.

To use the Organize tool to manage messages from a particular sender, follow these steps:

1. Select a message from the person in your Inbox.

 2. Click the **Tools** menu, and then click **Organize**; or click the **Organize** button on the toolbar. The Organize window appears (see Figure 6.4).

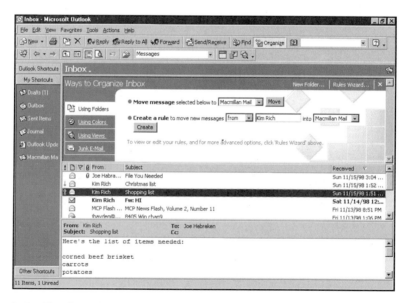

Figure 6.4 The Organize tool helps you manage messages using folders, colors, and views.

The Organize tool helps you manage and organize your messages using these methods:

- **Folders**—This method is used to move or delete messages.
- **Colors**—Color-codes the messages according to the rule you create.
- **Views**—Uses the rule to categorize messages by their view (Flagged, By Sender, and so on).

A special category is also provided for dealing with junk email.

To manually move the currently selected message in your Inbox, follow these steps:

1. Click **Using folders**. The email address of the person who sent you the selected email appears in the From box.
2. In the Move message selected below to box, click the **drop-down arrow** and select the **Outlook** folder to which you would like to move the message.
3. Click the **Move** button and the message is moved to the new location.
4. If you want to move other messages, select the message in the Message pane and then repeat steps 2 and 3.

As already mentioned, you can manage any new messages you receive from a particular individual by creating a rule that automatically moves these new messages to a folder of your choice. To create a new rule for the sender of the currently selected message in your Inbox, follow these steps:

1. Click **Using folders**. The email address of the person who sent you the selected email appears in the From box.
2. In the Create a Rule to Move new messages drop-down box, make sure **From** is selected.
3. In the **into** box, click the drop-down arrow and select the name of the folder to which you want to move the messages. If you want to move the messages to a folder that is not listed on the drop-down list, click **Other** folder.
4. When you have selected the folder that the messages are placed in by the rule, click **Create**.

A short message appears in the Organize window that says "Done." Now new messages from the individual are moved to the new location because of the rule that you created.

The Organize tool also provides you with an automatic strategy for dealing with annoying junk mail. Click **Junk E-mail** in the Organize window. The Organize tool enables you to either color-code junk mail and adult content email or move these kinds of email to a folder of your choice. In most situations, junk email and other unwanted email can be moved directly to the Deleted Items folder, which can then be easily discarded. Outlook automatically identifies these types of mail messages as you receive them by using a list of keywords as identifiers.

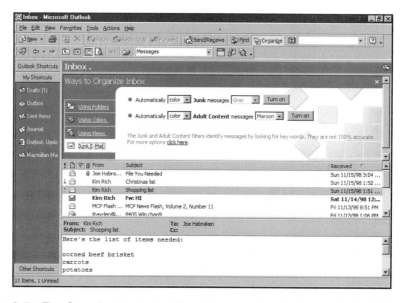

Figure 6.5   The Organize tool's Junk E-mail manager can help you deal with incoming junk mail.

To color-code junk messages or adult content messages make sure the Automatically drop-down box for each junk mail type contains the choice color. Then use the appropriate color drop-down box to select the color you want to use to code these messages as they are received. After you have selected the color, click the **Turn on** button to begin color coding all new messages that are identified as Junk mail or Adult Content mail by Outlook.

To send junk messages or adult content messages directly to a specific folder, select **move** in the Automatically drop-down box for either type of message. In the messages to drop-down box for either message type select **Junk Mail** or **Deleted**

Items to send mail messages directly to either of these folders. You can also send these messages directly to an alternative folder of your choice by clicking **Other Folder**. Once you have selected the folder you want to send these messages to, click the **Turn on** button. Messages identified as Junk mail or Adult Content mail by Outlook are sent directly to the folder you specified.

You can also click the **For more options click here** selection at the bottom of the Organize pane to access additional options related to Junk mail and Adult Content. Links are provided so that you can access the list of email addresses that you have identified as sources of Junk mail or Adult Content. Any email address on these lists is used to identify incoming email that should be color coded or moved to a specific folder by the Organize tool. After you have completed your selections in the Organize window, click its **Close** button.

You can quickly add email addresses to the Junk mail or Adult Content list by right-clicking on any message in your Inbox. A shortcut menu appears; point at Junk E-mail on the menu, and then select either **Add to Junk Senders list** or **Add to Adult Content Senders list** from the cascading menu that opens. This adds this email to the list marking it as a source of Junk mail or Adult Content messages.

Creating Advanced Rules with the Wizard

If the Organize tool isn't able to manage your email to the degree you desire, you can create more advanced rules for managing messages using the Outlook Rules Wizard. The Rules Wizard enables you to create pretty sophisticated rules using simple sentences.

To open the Rules Wizard, follow these steps:

1. Click **Tools**, then **Rules Wizard**. The Rules Wizard dialog box appears (see Figure 6.6).

All the rules previously created using the Organize tool appear in the Rules Description box. You can copy, modify, rename, or delete a rule in this dialog box. You can also change a rule's priority by selecting a rule and then moving it up or down using the Move up or Move down buttons.

Figure 6.6   The Rules Wizard helps you create rules for managing mail messages.

2. To create a new rule, click the **New** button. The Rules Wizard walks you through the rule creation process. The first screen asks you to select the type of rule you want to create, such as Check messages when they arrive, or Notify me when important messages arrive (see Figure 6.7).

3. Select the type of rule you want to create, and then click **Next**.

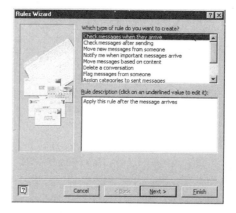

Figure 6.7   In the Rules Wizard, you select the type of rule you want to create.

4. The next screen asks you to select conditions that are to be used by the new rule. These conditions range from messages sent directly to you, to where your name appears in the message address (To, CC, and so on), to specific words in the body of the message, to email addresses that you have placed

on your junk email list. Use the check boxes provided to select the condition or conditions for your new rule. Click **Next** to continue.

 TIP **Conditions That Require Input from You** Some conditions such as "with specific words in the body," or "from people or distribution list" require that you provide a list of words or people for the condition to use. Conditions requiring additional information have an underlined selection for you to click.

5. The next screen asks you to decide what the rule should do to a message that meets the rules criteria. Several choices are provided, such as move it to the specified folder, or delete it (see Figure 6.8). Make your selections in the check boxes provided. Click **Next** to continue.

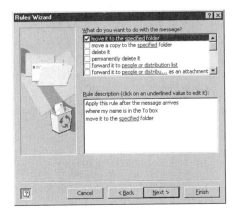

Figure 6.8 You determine the type of action you want Outlook to take when it finds a message that meets the rule's criteria.

6. The next screen provides you with the opportunity to add any exceptions to the rule. These exceptions can include "except if sent only to me" or "except where my name is not in the To or Cc box." You add them by clicking the check box next to a particular exception. You can select multiple exceptions or choose to have no exceptions to the rules. Then click **Next** to continue.

7. The Rules Wizard's final screen asks you to type a name for your new rule. After you've done that, click **Finish**. The new rule appears in the Rules Wizard dialog box. You can create more new rules or click **OK** to close the dialog box.

When you use the Rules Wizard for the first time, you may want to create a simple rule or two that handle messages that you do not consider extremely important. A poorly designed rule could delete important messages that you receive. A good rule of thumb is to use the Organize tool first and let it create simple rules, and if you need more advanced message management help, use the Rules Wizard.

In this lesson, you learned to forward messages, delete messages, and organize messages by saving them to folders. You also learned how to use the Organize tool and the Rules Wizard to help you manage your email messages. In the next lesson, you learn to attach files and items to a message.

Attaching Files and Items to a Message

In this lesson, you learn how to attach a file and Outlook items to a message.
You also learn how to insert an object in the other Outlook items, such as the calendar.

Attaching a File

You can attach any type of file to an Outlook message, which makes for a convenient way of sending your files over the network to your co-workers or sending family pictures (that have been scanned) or other files to people using your Internet email. You might send Word documents, Excel spreadsheets, a PowerPoint presentation, or any other document you create with your Windows 98/NT applications. If you can get the file on your computer, you can attach it to an email message.

HTML Becomes Text If you send a message to someone who uses an email client that cannot read HTML messages, the message appears as text. You must attach any pictures or other items to the message as an attachment if you want the user on the receiving end to view them.

CAUTION

When you send an attached file, it appears as an icon in a special attachment pane at the bottom of the message window. When the recipient gets the file, he or she can open it by double-clicking or save it for later use. However, the recipient must have the source program that you used to create the file on his or her computer. For instance, if you send a colleague a Microsoft Word file, he must have Microsoft Word to view the file he receives. Microsoft also supplies viewers for Microsoft Word and PowerPoint documents. These programs can be used to view Word and PowerPoint documents without having the full software installed.

CAUTION

How You Retrieve an Attachment Depends on the Email Package If you send messages with attachments to users who do not have Outlook or Microsoft's Outlook Express, how they retrieve the file attachment varies. Some email packages do not show the attachment as an icon, but save the attachment directly to a file after the email message is downloaded.

To attach a file to a message, follow these steps:

1. In the Message window, choose **Insert** and then select **File,** or click the **Insert File** button on the toolbar. The Insert File dialog box appears (see Figure 7.1).

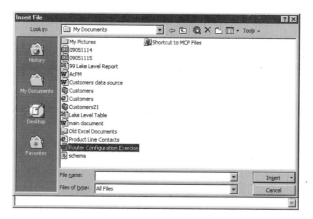

Figure 7.1 Select the file you want to attach to a message.

2. From the **Look In** drop-down list, choose the drive and folder that contain the file you want to attach.

3. Using the **Files of Type** drop-down list, choose the file type, such as Excel or Word.

4. Select the file you want to attach.

5. Click **OK** to insert the file into the message.

Figure 7.2 shows a file inserted as an attachment.

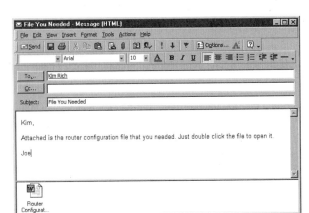

Figure 7.2 The recipient can double-click the icon to open the file.

Large Files Take Time Sending an extremely large file can take a great deal of time, depending on your connection speed. You might want to compress large files using products like WinZip or PKZip. These compression tools enable you to compress the size of attachments. However, the receivers of your messages will also need these tools if they are going to uncompress your attachments.

CAUTION

Understanding Attachment Format Types

When you attach a file to an email message, it is coded in a special way so that the information remains intact when sent as part of the email message. Two of the most popular coding systems for attachments are *MIME* (Multipurpose Internet Mail Extension) and *UUEncoding*.

TERM

MIME This coding scheme places a header in the email message just before the information contained in the attached file. This enables the recipient's email client to recognize which part of the sent message is the message text and which part is the attachment. Some online services and email packages have a problem decoding MIME attached files.

UUEncoding   One of the most popular coding schemes. Most email packages can recognize and decode UUEncoded messages.

Check with Online Service Providers   Some online services, such as America Online, have restrictions on the size of an email that their mail servers will accept. You should check with AOL or other service users before you send them files with large attachments to see if they have any special requirements.

Outlook enables you to select either MIME or UUEncoding as your default attachment format. To select the attachment coding system, follow these steps:

1. Click **Tools**, then select **Options**; the Options dialog box appears.
2. Click the **Internet Email** tab. Select either the **MIME** or **UUENCODE** option button. UUENCODE is embraced by most email clients and should be your choice unless you know that you are specifically sending to individuals who use a client that embraces the MIME format.
3. After making your selection, click **OK**.

Attaching Outlook Items

In addition to attaching files from other programs, you can also attach an Outlook item to a message. An Outlook item can be any document saved in one of your personal folders, including a calendar, contacts, journal, notes, tasks, and so on. You can attach an Outlook item in the same manner you attach a file.

Follow these steps to attach an Outlook item:

1. In the Message window, choose **Insert**, then select **Item**. The Insert Item dialog box appears (see Figure 7.3).
2. From the **Look In** list, choose the folder containing the item you want to include in the message.
3. Select from the items that appear in the **Items** list. To select multiple adjacent items, hold down the **Shift** key and click the first and last desired items; to select multiple nonadjacent items, hold down the **Ctrl** key and click the items.

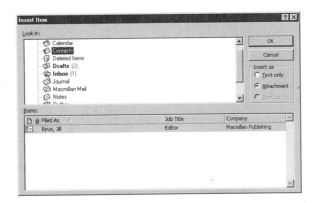

Figure 7.3   Select items from any folder in Outlook, such as a contact's information from the Contact folder.

4. In the Insert As area, choose from the following option buttons:

Text Only—Inserts the file as text into the message; if your file is not saved as an ASCII or other text-only file, do not use this option.

Attachment—Inserts an icon representing the document. The actual file follows the message to the recipient; the recipient saves it as his or her own copy.

Shortcut—Inserts a Windows 98/NT shortcut icon into the text. This option can be used only if the file is stored on a network drive from which the recipient can easily access it through a shortcut.

5. Click **OK**, and Outlook inserts the selected items in your message.

Text Only Is Only for Text!   If you try to insert a file from Word, Excel, or another application as Text Only, you'll end up with a lot of "garbage" characters in the text. That's because these programs' files contain special formatting codes. The only time you will use Text Only is when you export the data from its native program into a text-only file first.

CAUTION

It Doesn't Work Without Outlook   If the recipient doesn't have Outlook on her computer, she will not be able to view the attached item. If you know the recipient doesn't have the program, you'll need to cut and paste the data into the message or simply retype it.

CAUTION

751

Inserting an Object

Just as you can insert an object—a spreadsheet, chart, drawing, presentation, media clip, clip art, WordArt, and so on—in any Windows application that supports OLE, you can also insert an object into your Outlook items, such as your calendar or task list. Inserting a file in a message, as discussed earlier, is the equivalent of inserting an object into one of the other Outlook items.

 TERM **OLE (Object Linking and Embedding)** A method of exchanging and sharing data between applications; OLE is supported by most Windows applications and all Microsoft programs.

You can insert an existing object into an Outlook item, or you can create an object within a message using the source application. For example, you could create an Excel chart within your message using Excel's features through OLE.

When you send a message with an attached object, the object travels with the message to the recipient. If the recipient has the application on his computer (or applicable viewer), he can open the object and view it.

For more information about OLE, see Lesson 20, "Sharing Data with Office Applications."

To attach an existing object to an appointment or task in the calendar, follow these steps:

1. Click the **Calendar** icon in the Outlook Bar. Double-click an appointment or task on the task list. Position the insertion point in the appointment or task text box and choose **Insert**, then select **Object**. The Insert Object dialog box appears.
2. Choose the **Create from File** option (see Figure 7.4).
3. In the **File** text box, enter the path and the name of the file you want to insert. (You can use the **Browse** button and the resulting dialog box to find the file, if needed.)
4. Click **OK**. Outlook inserts the object into the Outlook item.

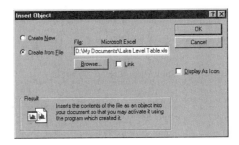

Figure 7.4 Insert an object to send with a message.

To edit an object, double-click within the frame, and the source application opens from within Outlook. Note that you'll still see your Outlook item and Outlook toolbars; however, you'll also see tools associated with the object's source application, which you can use to edit the object. Figure 7.5 shows an Excel spreadsheet object within a Calendar appointment. Notice the Excel toolbar and icons appear at the top of the Outlook window because the OLE object you have double-clicked is an Excel object and requires Excel's capabilities for editing.

Toolbar added for Excel —

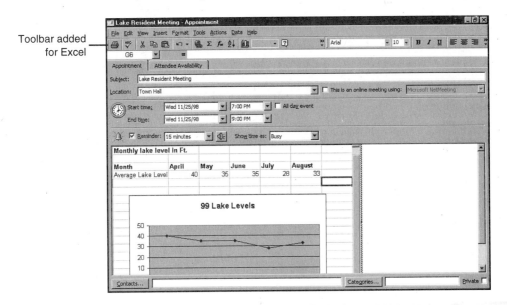

Figure 7.5 Edit the object from within your Outlook message.

When you double-click an object that is embedded in an Outlook item, you can resize the object to suit your needs. First select it, and a frame appears with eight small black boxes (called *handles*) on the corners and along the sides. To resize the object, position the mouse pointer over one of the black handles; the mouse pointer becomes a two-headed arrow. Click and drag the handle to resize the object.

For more information about working with the calendar and appointments, see Lesson 12, "Using the Calendar."

In this lesson, you learned how to attach a file and other items to a message. You also learned how to insert an object in an Outlook item. In the next lesson, you learn to organize messages.

Organizing Messages

*In this lesson, you learn to save a draft, view
sent items, create folders, and move items to the new folder.*

Saving a Draft

Suppose you start a message, but you are called away or need to do something
else before you can finish it. You don't have to cancel the message and start over
again later; you can save the message in the Draft folder and then open it later to
complete it.

To save a draft, follow these steps:

1. In the Message window, click the **Close** button. A dialog box appears
asking if you want to save changes, as shown in Figure 8.1.

Figure 8.1 Click Yes to save the message in the Drafts folder for later completion.

2. Click **Yes**. Outlook places the current message in the Drafts Folder.

To open the message and continue working on it at another time, follow these
steps:

1. Click the Drafts folder icon in the My Shortcuts group on the Outlook Bar,
or choose **Drafts** from the Folders list.

2. Double-click the message to open it. At the top of the Message tab, you'll see a reminder that This message has not been sent.

3. Continue your work on the message. If you need to store it again before you're finished, choose **File**, then select **Close** or click the **Close** button. The message remains in the Drafts folder until you move it or send it.

4. When you're finished, click the **Send** button to send the message.

TIP **Create an Outlook Bar Icon for Drafts** If you want to place a Drafts folder icon on the Outlook Bar when you are in the Outlook Shortcuts group, open the Folders list, pin the Folders list down, and then right-click the Draft folder. On the shortcut menu that appears, select **Add to Outlook Bar**. An icon appears on the Outlook Bar for the Drafts folder.

Viewing Sent Items and Changing Defaults

By default, Outlook saves a copy of all mail messages you send. It keeps these copies in the Sent Items folder, which is part of the Mail group of the Outlook Bar. You can view a list of sent items at any time, and you can open any message in that list to review its contents.

Viewing Sent Items

To view sent items, follow these steps:

1. In the Outlook Bar, choose the **My Shortcuts** group.

TIP **Save Time** You can select the Sent Items folder from the Folder list instead of following steps 1–3.

2. If necessary, scroll to the Sent Items folder.

3. Click the **Sent Items** icon, and Outlook displays a list of the contents of that folder. Figure 8.2 shows the Sent Items list. All messages you send remain in the Sent Items folder until you delete or move them.

4. (Optional) To view a sent item, double-click it to open it. When you finish with it, click the **Close** (×) button.

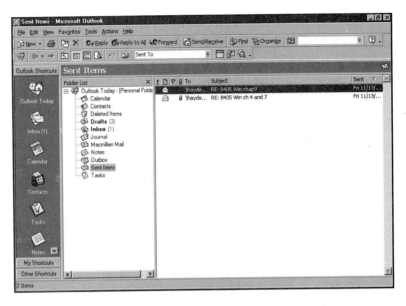

Figure 8.2 You can open any sent message by double-clicking it.

Changing Defaults for Sent Items

You can control whether or not Outlook saves copies of your sent messages (this is also true for unsent messages). To change the default setting for the Sent Items folder, follow these steps:

1. Choose **Tools**, and then select **Options**, and the Options dialog box appears.

2. Make sure the Preferences tab is selected on the dialog box.

3. Click the **E-mail Options** button. The E-mail Options dialog box appears (see Figure 8.3). This dialog box allows you to toggle several email-related features on and off:

   - **Close Original Message on Reply or Forward**—When this is checked, the message you currently have open will be closed when you reply to it or forward it. If this setting is unchecked, Outlook leaves the message window open.

   - **Save Copies of Messages in "Sent Items" Folder**—When this is checked, Outlook saves copies of all sent messages to the specified folder. (When the check box is empty, no copies of messages are saved automatically.)

757

- **Automatically Save Unsent Messages**—When this is checked, Outlook saves your unfinished messages every three minutes, placing them in the Drafts folder. If you remove the check mark from this feature, drafts are not automatically saved.

- **Close Original Message on Reply or Forward**—When this is checked, the message you currently have open will be closed when you reply to it or forward it. If this setting is unchecked, Outlook leaves the message window open.

- **Display a Notification Message When New E-mail Arrives**—When this is checked, a message appears in the Outlook window that new mail has arrived.

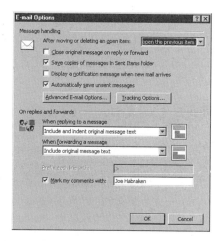

Figure 8.3 The E-mail Options dialog box gives you control over a number of features related to sending and receiving email messages.

The E-mail Options dialog box also gives you control over several other features related to the management of your email.

- **Advanced E-mail Options button**—This button opens the Advanced E-mail Options dialog box. Most of the feature controls in the Advanced E-mail Options dialog box take the form of either check boxes or drop-down boxes. This dialog box allows you to control:

  - The folder that unsent messages are sent to.

  - How often to save unsent messages.

– Whether or not to save forwarded messages.

– The default importance and sensitivity for outgoing messages.

- **Tracking Options button**—This button opens the Tracking Options dialog box where you can toggle on and off the following features:

    – Tell me when all messages have been delivered.

    – Tell me when all messages have been read.

    – Delete receipts and blank responses after processing.

To close the E-Mail Options dialog box, click **OK**.

CAUTION

Too Much Mail! If you save all the mail you receive and send, you may run the risk of running out of disk space. You can and should periodically delete mail from the Sent Items folder by selecting the mail and pressing the **Delete** key; you'll also need to remove the deleted mail from the Deleted Items folder. See Lesson 6, "Managing Mail," and Lesson 21, "Archiving Items."

Creating Folders

You'll probably want to organize your mail in various folders to make storing and finding items more efficient. You can create folders within Outlook that make it easier to manage your mail and other items in Outlook.

To create a folder, follow these steps:

1. Choose **File**, select **New**, and then **Folder**. The Create New Folder dialog box appears (see Figure 8.4).

2. In the **Name** text box, enter a name for the folder.

3. Click the **Folder Contains** drop-down arrow, and choose the type of items the folder will store: Mail, Appointments, Contact, Journal, Note, or Task.

4. Double-click the folder in which you want to create the new folder. You can, for example, make the new folder a subfolder of Personal Folders so that it appears in lists with all the Outlook folders. Or you might want to make it a subfolder of Sent Mail.

5. Click **OK** to close the dialog box. A message box appears asking if you want a shortcut icon created for the new folder on the Outlook Bar. Click **Yes** if you want the shortcut.

The new folder appears on the Outlook Bar and in the Folder List.

Figure 8.4   Create folders to organize your mail and other items.

TIP   **Add Folder Later**   Even if you choose not to add the folder to the Outlook Bar when you create the folder, you can add it later. Just right-click the folder in the folder list and select **Add to Outlook Bar** from the shortcut menu that appears.

CAUTION

I Want to Delete a Folder!   If you added a folder by accident or you change your mind about a folder you've added, you can delete it from Outlook. To delete a folder, select it and then choose **File**, select **Folder**, and click **Delete** *foldername*.

Moving Items to Another Folder

You can move items from one folder in Outlook to another; for example, you can create a folder to store all messages pertaining to a specific account or report. You can easily move those messages to the new folder and open them later for reference purposes. You also can forward, reply, copy, delete, and archive any items you move from one folder to another.

To move an item to another folder, follow these steps:

1. From the Inbox, or any Outlook folder, open the message you want to move.

2. Choose **Edit**, then select **Move to Folder**. The Move Items dialog box appears (see Figure 8.5).

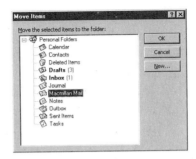

Figure 8.5 Choose the folder in which you want to store the message or messages.

3. In the list of folders, select the folder to which you want to move the message.

4. Choose **OK**. When you close the message, Outlook stores it in the designated folder.

TIP **Drag and Drop** You can quickly move an unopened message by dragging it from the open folder in which it resides to any folder icon in the Outlook Bar.

You can open the message at any time by opening the folder from the Outlook Bar and double-clicking the message. After opening it, you can forward, send, print, or otherwise manipulate the message as you would any message.

You can also copy messages from one folder to another. Copying a message works much like moving a message. To start the copy process, select the messages you want to copy and then choose **Edit**, then select **Copy to Folder**. Select the folder to which you want to copy in the Copy Items dialog box.

In this lesson, you learned to save a draft, view sent items, create folders, and move items to a folder. In the next lesson, you learn to set various Outlook mail options.

Setting Mail Options

In this lesson, you learn to set options for messages
in general, delivery of messages, and tracking of messages.

Customizing Outlook

Outlook provides options that enable you to mark any message with priority status so that the recipient knows you need a quick response, or with a sensitivity rating so that your words cannot be changed by anyone after the message is sent. With other options, you can enable the recipients of your message to vote on an issue by including voting buttons in your message and having the replies sent to a specific location.

You also can set delivery options. For example, you can schedule the delivery of a message for a specified delivery time or date if you don't want to send it right now.

CAUTION

Recognizing Priority Flags   Not all email packages will recognize the priority flags you place on messages you send. These priority flags work ideally in a network situation, where Outlook is the email client for all users (this works particularly well for networks using Microsoft Exchange Server as the email service).

To set message options, open a new Untitled - Message window and click the **Options** button on the toolbar. As you can see in Figure 9.1, the Message

Options dialog box is separated into four areas. The next four subsections discuss each group of options in detail.

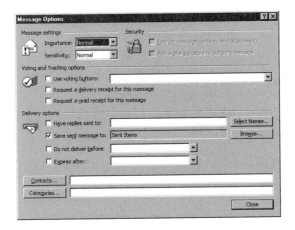

Figure 9.1 Use the Message Options settings to govern how your message is sent.

Message Settings

In the Message Settings area, set any of the following options for your message:

- Click the **Importance** drop-down arrow and choose a priority level of Low, Normal, or High from the list. (Alternatively, you could click the Importance High or Importance Low button on the message's toolbar when you compose the message.) When importance isn't specified, the message is given Normal Importance.

- Click the **Sensitivity** drop-down arrow and choose one of the following options:

   Normal—Use this option to indicate that the message contents are standard, or customary.

   Personal—Use this option to suggest that the message contents are of a personal nature.

   Private—Use this option to prevent the message from being edited (text changes, copy, paste, and so on) after you send it.

   Confidential—Use this option to indicate that the message contents are restricted or private.

763

TIP   **Mark All Messages As Private**   You can mark all your new messages as private automatically. Choose **Tools**, then select **Options** and then click the **E-mail Options** button. On the E-mail Options dialog box, click the **Advanced E-mail Options** button. Use the **Sensitivity** drop-down box at the bottom of the Advance E-mail Options dialog box to set the default sensitivity for all your new email messages.

Outlook also supplies you with two security options. You can choose to encrypt the contents and attachments of a message: Click the **Encrypt Contents and Attachments** check box next to the Security icon. You can also add a digital signature to the message that verifies you are the sender: Click the **Add Digital Signature to Outgoing Message** check box.

Encryption   Messages are coded so that they remain secure until the recipient opens them. The recipient is able to decode the message because he or she is identified by Digital ID.

Digital Signature   A Digital ID that is electronically stamped on messages that you send.

Before you can use the encryption and digital signature features in Outlook 2000, you must obtain a Digital ID, which is also often referred to as a certificate. Digital IDs are issued by an independent certifying authority. Microsoft's certifying authority of choice is VeriSign Digital ID. You can obtain, download, and install your Digital ID from VeriSign by following the steps on their Web page at http://digitalid.verisign.com/.

Voting and Tracking Options

The Voting and Tracking Options allow you to control special features like voting buttons (these allow recipients of the message to reply with a click of the mouse) and supply you with the means to track the receipt of your message. You must be using the corporate email installation to take advantage of Voting buttons (see Lesson 2, "Understanding the Outlook Configurations," for more information on the differences between the two different Outlook installations).

- Select the **Use Voting Buttons** check box to add the default choices (Approve and Reject) to your message. You can also add Yes and No choices or Yes, No, and Maybe choices. If you want to provide other choices, enter your own text in the text box.
- Select **Tell Me When This Message Has Been Delivered** to receive an email notification that the message has been received by the recipient.
- Select **Tell Me When This Message Has Been Read** to receive email confirmation that the message has been opened by the recipient.

Delivery Options

In addition to voting and tracking options, you can set certain delivery options, such as having replies sent to individuals you select. You can also choose a folder where a copy of the message is saved, or schedule the time of the delivery. In the Delivery Options area of the Message Options dialog box, choose any of the following check boxes:

- Choose the **Have Replies Sent To** check box and specify in the text box the person to whom you want the replies sent. You can use the **Select Names** button to view the Address Book and choose a name if you want.
- Select the **Save Sent Message To** check box to save your message to the Sent Items folder by default. Or specify another folder to save the message in, using the **Browse** button and the resulting dialog box if necessary to locate the folder.
- Select the **Do Not Deliver Before** option to specify a delivery date. Click the down arrow in the text box beside the option to display a calendar on which you can select the day.
- Select the **Expires After** check box to include a day, date, and time of expiration. You can click the down arrow in the text box to display a calendar from which you can choose a date, or you can enter the date and time yourself.

Categories

Outlook enables you to assign messages to certain categories—such as Business, Goals, Hot Contacts, Phone Calls, and so on. You set the category for a message in the Categories dialog box.

TERM   **Categories**   Categories offer a way of organizing messages to make them easier to find, sort, print, and manage. To find all of the items in one category, choose **Tools**, then select **Find Items**. Click the **More Choices** tab, choose **Categories**, and check the category for which you're searching.

To assign a category, follow these steps:

1. In the Message Options dialog box, click the **Categories** button. The Categories dialog box appears (see Figure 9.2).

Figure 9.2   Organize your messages with categories.

2. To assign an existing category, select the category or categories that best suit your message from the **Available Categories** list. To assign a new category, enter a new category in the **Item(s) belong to these categories** text box, and then click the **Add to list** button.

3. Click **OK** to close the Categories dialog box and return to the Message Options dialog box.

When you have set all the options for the current message, click the **Close** button to close the Message Options box and return to the message window.

Using Message Flags

A message flag enables you to mark a message as important, either as a reminder for yourself or as a signal to the message's recipient. When you send a message flag, a red flag icon appears in the recipient's message list, and Outlook adds text at the top of the message telling which type of flag you are sending. In addition, you can add a due date to the flag, and that date appears at the top of the message.

The following list outlines the types of flags you can send in Outlook:

Call	No Response Necessary
Do not Forward	Read
Follow Up	Reply
For Your Information	Reply to All
Forward	Review

To use a message flag, follow these steps:

1. In the Message window, click **Actions**, then select **Flag For Follow Up**. The Flag for Follow Up dialog box appears (see Figure 9.3).

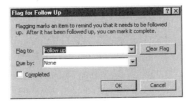

Figure 9.3 Flag a message to show its importance.

2. Click the **Flag To** drop-down arrow and choose the flag text you want to add to the message.

3. Click the **Reminder** drop-down arrow and enter a date in the text box.

4. Click **OK** to return to the Message window.

Figure 9.4 shows the Inbox and with a few flagged messages.

You can view just the header of a message to allow you more message text room if you want to hide the Cc, Bcc, and Subject lines. Choose **View**, then select **Message Header** to show only the To text box and any flag text; select **View**, then **Message Header** again to redisplay the Cc, Bcc, and Subject fields.

Marking messages with the Follow Up flag is a great way to remind yourself that you need to attend to a particular issue. Flagging messages for your email recipients helps them prioritize responses, so you receive the needed reply within a particular time frame.

When you double-click a flagged message and open it in a message window, the flag type appears at the top of the message, just above the From box.

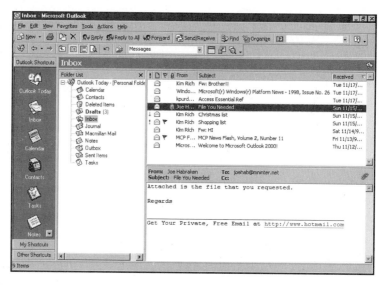

Figure 9.4 To view the type of flag attached, open the message.

Viewing the flag type on the message provides you with a quick reminder as to what your next action will be regarding the particular message (see Figure 9.5).

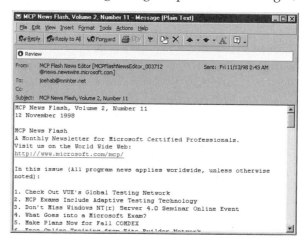

Figure 9.5 The message flag provides you with a quick reminder of what action you want to take in relation to the currently selected message.

In this lesson, you learned to set options for messages and delivery, and for tracking messages. In the next lesson, you learn to use the contact and personal address books.

Using
the Contact
and Personal
Address Books

In this lesson, you learn to use Outlook's Contact lists and address books with your email.

Using the Postoffice Address List

If you use Outlook as your email client on a corporate mail server (meaning you have installed Outlook using the corporate mail configuration), many of the messages you send will be to coworkers on that same network. The email addresses for these people are determined by your network administrator. Even if you use Outlook as a corporate client, you can set it up to also serve as your Internet email program (see Lesson 2, "Understanding the Outlook Configurations," for more information on the setup options).

 TIP   **Internet email**   Internet email is sent over the Internet by means of a modem or your corporate network. Internet email addresses usually take the form of *username@company.com.*

If you use corporate email, such as Microsoft Mail, or connect to Microsoft Exchange Server to communicate with your coworkers, all the email names within your organization usually appear on the Postoffice Address List created by your system's mail administrator. Whenever you want to send or forward an email, you can select the recipients from that list instead of typing in their names manually (or entering them in one of the other Outlook address books or contact lists).

Whether you have access to the Postoffice Address List depends on your permissions and rights on the network to which you are connected. If you have a question, see your network administrator.

If you've installed Outlook for Internet Only email, you will not have a Postoffice Address List as one of the possibilities in the drop-down list when you open the Address Book dialog box.

 Post Office   A directory, usually located on the network server, that contains a mailbox for each email user. When someone sends a message, that message is filed in the recipient's mailbox until the recipient receives the mail and copies, moves, or deletes it.

 Postoffice Address List   A list of everyone who has a mailbox in the post office; it's controlled by the mail administrator.

 Mail Administrator   The person who manages the email post office. (This person might also be the network administrator, but it doesn't necessarily have to be the same person.)

 To use the Postoffice Address List, choose **Tools**, and then **Address Book** or click the **Address Book** button on the toolbar. The Address book dialog box appears, as shown in Figure 10.1.

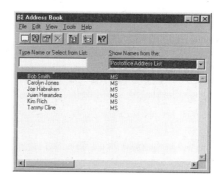

Figure 10.1   You can view the Postoffice Address List.

The following list outlines some of the ways in which you might use the Address List:

- To view more details about any entry in the Address Book dialog box (which contains the Postoffice Address List), double-click the person's name or click the **Properties** button on the toolbar. The person's Properties dialog box appears, with his or her name, address type, Postoffice name, and network type listed on the Address (1) tab. Click **OK** to close this dialog box and return to the Address Book dialog box.

- Click the **Properties** button on the toolbar and choose the **Business** tab in the person's Properties dialog box to view his or her phone number, office, or department, and any notes or comments that have been added to the description. Click **OK** to close this dialog box and return to the Address Book dialog box.

- To send a message to someone listed in the address book, select the name from the Address List and choose **File**, then select **New Message**.

- If you cannot find a particular name in the list, you can search for it. Choose **Tools**, then select **Find** or click the **Find** button, and then enter the name for which you're searching in the **Find Name** text box. Click **OK** to start the search.

If your corporation or organization uses Microsoft Exchange Server as its mail server, you can use Outlook as the email client, as you can for other email systems like Microsoft Mail or Internet mail. If you are connected to a Microsoft Exchange Server (the mail component of Microsoft NT Server), an additional list for mail addresses appears in the Address Book drop-down list. You will have access to a list called *Global Address List*. This list, like the Post Office Address list described earlier for Microsoft Mail Postoffice groups, is controlled and maintained by your Network Administrator.

Using the Personal Address Book

The Personal Address Book contains the names and email addresses of people you contact frequently. You may want to include coworkers from your department, or even people from outside your office (whom you contact by using Internet addresses).

The Contacts Book   You may notice contacts in the list of address books; this book contains entries you create in your Contacts list. For more information about the Contacts list, see Lesson 11.

 No Personal Address Book Is listed?   If you do not see a Personal Address Book in the Address Book dialog box, you can easily add it to your resources. Close the address book and choose **Tools**, then select **Services**. In the Services tab of the dialog box, choose the **Add** button, and from the list, choose the **Personal Address Book**; then choose **OK**. Close the Services dialog box and open the address book again; you'll see the Personal Address Book in the list.

To add names to the Personal Address Book, follow these steps:

1. Choose **Tools**, then select **Address Book**, or click the **Address Book** button on the toolbar. The Address Book dialog box appears (refer to Figure 10.1).

2. To add name(s) from the Postoffice Address List, select the name(s) and choose **File**, then select **Add to Personal Address Book**, or click the **Add to Personal Address Book** button on the toolbar. The name(s) remains on the Postoffice Address List, but Outlook copies it to your Personal Address Book as well. You can also add names from the Contacts list to the Personal Address Book in this manner.

3. To view your Personal Address Book, select the **Show Names from the** drop-down list and choose **Personal Address Book**. The list changes to display those names you've added to your personal address list, but the dialog box looks the same.

4. To add a completely new address to your Personal Address Book, click the **New Entry** button or choose **File**, then select **New Entry**. The New Entry dialog box appears (see Figure 10.2).

5. In the **Select the Entry Type** list, choose from the available options. The options you see will depend on the information systems installed on your network; for example, Microsoft Mail, Internet Mail, or some other service (such as Microsoft Fax) may be available. You can add an address entry that corresponds with one of the available information systems.

Figure 10.2 Choose a source for your new entry.

Additionally, you can choose to add one of the following two items:

- **Personal Distribution List**—Use this to create one address entry for a group of recipients. When you send mail to the list name, everyone on the list receives the message. You might use this option for grouping department heads, for example.

- **Other Address**—Choose this option to add one new recipient at a time. You can enter a name, email address, and email type for each entry. In addition, you can enter business addresses and phone numbers, and you can add notes and comments to the entry. Use this entry for Internet addresses, for example.

6. When you're done working in your Personal Address Book, close the window by choosing **File**, then **Close**. You return to the Outlook Inbox.

Importing Address Books and Contact Lists

If you are migrating from another personal information manager or email client and want to import your address book or Contacts list, Outlook contains a number of different conversion filters for this purpose. Outlook even provides you with an Import/Export Wizard that walks you through the steps of importing address lists and address books from these other software packages.

To start the Outlook Import/Export Wizard, follow these steps:

1. Click **File**, then select **Import and Export**. The Outlook Import and Export Wizard opens (see Figure 10.3).

2. On the first wizard screen, click **Import from another program or file**, then click **Next**. Conversion filters are available for popular personal

information managers like Lotus Organizer and Sidekick. You can also import information from Microsoft Access and Microsoft Schedule Plus among others. Also any program that can save your former address book as a delimited file allows you to import the information into Outlook.

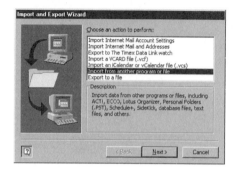

Figure 10.3 The Import and Export Wizard walks you through the process of importing your old address books.

 TERM **Delimited file** Most database programs and personal information managers can save address books in a delimited format. This means that spaces or tabs are placed between the different fields of information. Saving an address book as a delimited file makes it possible to import the information into a number of different software packages that do not share the same file format as the software you are importing from.

3. Choose the program or file type that you want to use to import the address book, and then click **Next**.

4. The next wizard screen asks you to type in the name of the file you are importing or to locate the file on your computer using the **Browse** button. After you have selected the file, you can select one of the following option buttons:

- Replace duplicates with items imported
- Allow duplicates to be created
- Do not import duplicate items

5. After making your selection, click **Next**.

6. The next screen asks you to select the folder in which you want to place the new information. Because you are importing an address book, you will want to place the imported data into your Contacts folder. Click **Next** to continue.

7. The last screen asks you to match up the fields in the imported data with fields available in a typical Contacts form, such as Name, Address, Phone Number, Fax, and so on. Click the **Map Custom Fields** button and the Map Custom Fields dialog box appears.

8. Drag a field from the import file box to the Outlook Contact box. Match fields that contain the same kind of data. For example, if the import file contains a field for Phone, and you want this information to appear in the Contact Business phone field, drag the Phone field from the import box and place it next to the Business phone field in the Contacts box (see Figure 10.4).

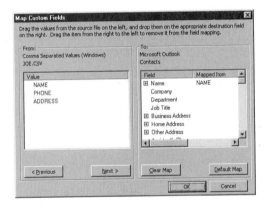

Figure 10.4   Match the fields in the import file with the fields in contacts.

When you have completed matching the fields, click **OK**. You return to the final wizard screen. Click **Finish**. The contact information from the import file is placed in your Outlook Contact folder.

In this lesson, you learned to use the address book with your email and import address books from other software programs. In the next lesson, you learn to create a Contacts list.

Creating a
Contacts List

*In this lesson, you learn to create and view a Contacts list,
and to send mail to someone on your Contacts list.*

Creating a New Contact

You use the Contacts folder to create, store, and access your Contacts list.
You can enter any or all of the following information about each contact:

- Name
- Job title
- Company name
- Address (Street, City, State, ZIP, and Country)
- Phone (business, home, business fax, mobile)
- Email address
- Web page address
- Comments, notes, or descriptions
- Categories

 Contact In Outlook, a contact is any person or company for which you've
entered a name, address, phone number, or other information. You can
communicate with a contact in Outlook by sending an email message,
scheduling a meeting, sending a letter, and so on.

You also can edit the information at any time, add new contacts, or delete contacts from the list. To open the Contacts folder and create a new contact, follow these steps:

1. To open the Contacts folder, click the **Contacts** shortcut on the Outlook Bar. The Contacts folder opens.

2. To create a new contact, select **Actions**, then choose **New Contact**, or click the **New Contact** button on the Standard toolbar. The Contact dialog box appears, with the General tab displayed (see Figure 11.1).

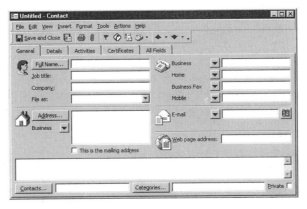

Figure 11.1 You can enter as much or as little information about each contact as you need.

3. Enter the contact's name in the Name text box. If you want to add more detailed information for the name, click the **Full Name** button to display the Check Full Name dialog box, and then enter the contact's title and full name (including first, middle, and last names) and any suffix you want to include. Click **OK** to close the Check Full Name dialog box and return to the Contact dialog box.

4. Press the **Tab** key and then enter the client's company name and job title. This information is optional.

5. In the **File As** drop-down box, enter or select the method by which you want to file your contact's names. You can choose last name first or first name first, or you can enter your own filing system, such as by company or state.

Keep It Simple The default filing method for contacts is last name first, which makes it easy to quickly find the contact when you need it.

6. Enter the address in the Address box and choose whether the address is **Business, Home**, or **Other**. Alternatively, you can click the **Address** button to enter the street, city, state, ZIP code, and country in specified areas instead of all within the text block. You can add a second address (say, the Home address) if you want. Address information is optional.

7. In the **Phone** drop-down lists, choose the type of phone number—Business, Callback, Car, Home Fax, ISDN, Pager, and so on—and then enter the number. You can enter up to 19 numbers in each of the four drop-down boxes in the Phone area of the dialog box.

8. You can enter up to three email addresses in the **E-mail** text box; in **the Web Page Address** text box, enter the address for the company or contact's URL on the World Wide Web.

If you have more than one email address for a contact, the first number or address in the list serves as the default. For example, when emailing a contact, the first email address in the list serves as the default and is placed in the To box on the new message. If you want to use a different email address for the contact, double-click the contact's name in the Message To box, and select one of the other email addresses in the contact's Properties box. When you want to call a contact for whom you have multiple numbers, a drop-down list appears in the New Call dialog box that enables you to choose the appropriate number.

URL Stands for Uniform Resource Locator, and means the address for a Web page on the World Wide Web. A typical URL would be written `http://www.companyname.com`, such as `http://www.mcp.com`.

9. In the comment text box, enter any descriptions, comments, or other pertinent information. Then select or enter a category to classify the contact.

10. After you have completed entering the new contact information, click the **Save and Close** button to return to the Contacts folder. You can also save the new contact by opening the **File** menu and choosing one of the following commands:

- **Save**—Saves the record and closes the Contact dialog box.
- **Save and New**—Saves the record and clears the Contact dialog box so that you can enter a new contact.

You can edit the information about a contact at any time by double-clicking the contact's name in the Contacts list; this displays the contact's information window. Alternatively, you can click within the information listed below a contact's name (such as the phone number or address) to position the insertion point in the text, and then delete or enter text. Press **Enter** to complete the modifications you've made and move to the next contact in the list.

Viewing the Contacts List

By default, you see the contacts in an Address Cards view. The information you see displays the contact's name and other data such as addresses and phone numbers. The contact's company name, job title, and comments, however, are not displayed by default. Figure 11.2 shows the Contacts list in the default Address Cards view.

Quickly find
a contact using
the index.

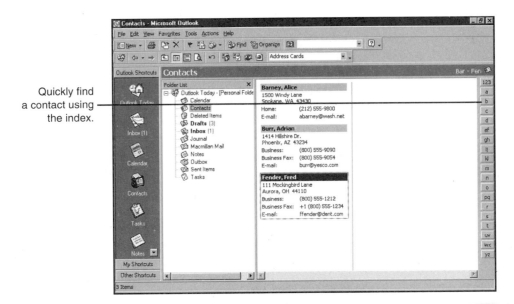

Figure 11.2 View your contacts in Address Cards view.

You can use the horizontal scrollbar to view more contacts, or you can click a letter in the index to display contacts beginning with that letter in the first column of the list.

Do I Save View Settings?   If you choose to save the current settings, Outlook lets you name the view and adds that view to the Current View list. If you choose to discard the current settings, your modifications to the view will be lost. If you choose to update the view, your modifications are saved with that view.

You can change how you view the contacts in the list by choosing one of these options from the Current View drop-down list on the Standard toolbar:

- **Address Cards**—Displays File As names (last name first, first name last, and so on), addresses, and phone numbers of the contacts, depending on the amount of information you've entered in a card format.

- **Detailed Address Cards**—Displays File As name, full name, job title, company, addresses, phone numbers, email addresses, categories, and comments in a card format.

- **Phone List**—Displays full name, job title, company, File As name, department, phone numbers, and categories in a table, organizing each entry horizontally in rows and columns.

- **By Category**—Displays contacts in rows by categories. The information displayed is the same as what's displayed in a phone list.

- **By Company**—Displays contacts in rows, grouped by their company. The information displayed is the same as what's displayed in a phone list.

- **By Location**—Displays contacts grouped by country. The information displayed is the same as what's displayed in a phone list.

- **By Follow Up Flag**—Displays contacts grouped by follow-up flags. The view also displays the due date for the follow-up that you specified when you marked the contact with a flag.

TIP   **Use the Letter Tabs to View Contacts Alphabetically**   If you have a large number of contacts in your contact list, you can quickly jump to just the contacts who have a last name that begins with a letter or letter range of the alphabet. Click the appropriate letter tab on the right side of the Contact list to view particular contacts.

Communicating with a Contact

You can send messages to any of your contacts, arrange meetings, assign tasks, or even send a letter to a contact from within Outlook. To communicate with a contact, make sure you're in the Contacts folder. You do not need to open the specific contact's information window to perform any of the following procedures.

Sending Messages

To send a message to a contact, you must make sure you've entered an email address in the General tab of the Contact dialog box for that particular contact. If Outlook cannot locate the mailing address, it displays a message dialog box (see Figure 11.3).

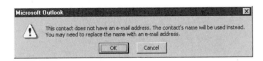

Figure 11.3 Outlook cannot send the email until you place the needed address in the To box of the New Message dialog box.

To send a message from the Contacts folder, select the contact and choose **Actions**, then select **New Message to Contact**. In the Untitled - Message dialog box, enter the subject and message and set any options you want. When you're ready to send the message, click the **Send** button. For more information about sending mail, see Lesson 4, "Creating Mail."

Scheduling a Meeting with a Contact

To schedule a meeting with a contact, the contact must have a valid email address. If no address is listed for the contact, Outlook notifies you with a message box and enables you to enter an address within the message dialog box. If the listed address is not found, Outlook responds with the Check Names dialog box, as described in the previous section.

To schedule a meeting with a contact, select the contact and choose **Actions**, then select **New Meeting with Contact**. The Untitled - Meeting dialog box appears. Enter the subject, location, time and date, and other information you need to schedule the meeting, and then notify the contact by sending an invitation. For more information about scheduling meetings, see Lesson 13, "Planning a Meeting."

Assigning a Task to a Contact

Tasks are assigned through email. Therefore, you must enter a valid email address for the contact before you can assign him or her a task.

To assign a task to a contact, select the contact and choose **Actions**, then **select New Task for Contact**. The Task dialog box appears. Enter the subject, due date, status, and other information, and then send the task to the contact. For detailed information about assigning tasks, see Lesson 14, "Creating a Task List."

Sending a Letter to a Contact

Outlook uses the Microsoft Word Letter Wizard to help you create a letter to send to a contact. Within the Word Wizard, you follow directions as they appear onscreen to complete the text of the letter.

To send a letter to the contact, select the contact in the Contacts folder and choose **Actions**, then select **New Letter to Contact**. Word opens the Letter Wizard onscreen. The Letter Wizard helps you format and complete the letter (see Figure 11.4). You can click the **Office Assistant** button if you need additional help. All you have to do is follow the directions and make your choices.

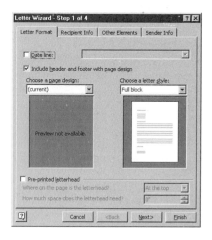

Figure 11.4 Use Word's Letter Wizard to create a letter to a contact.

Calling a Contact

Another obvious way to communicate with a contact is over the telephone. Outlook makes it easy for you to make a phone call to a contact by dialing the phone number for you.

For Outlook to dial the phone call for you, you must have a modem hooked to your computer that can dial out for you. On a network, if you have access to a network modem pool, you can also dial out using your computer, if the line you dial out on can also be accessed by your telephone.

To initiate a phone call to a contact, select the contact in the Contact list and follow these steps:

1. Select **Actions**, then select **Call Contact**, and then select the appropriate phone number from the cascading menu that appears (all the phone numbers including business, home, and fax for the selected contact appear). You can also click the **Autodialer** button on the Standard toolbar and select the appropriate phone number from the drop-down list. The New Call dialog box appears (see Figure 11.5).

Figure 11.5 You can quickly make a call to a contact using the Autodialer.

2. Click the **Start Call** button to allow Outlook to dial the contact's phone number using your modem.

3. The Call Status dialog box appears. Pick up your phone and click the **Talk** button in the Call Status dialog box. This engages the phone and you can speak to your contact when they answer the call.

Viewing a Map of a Contact's Address

A useful feature offered by Outlook is the ability to view an area Map based on the address of a particular contact. This can be incredibly useful when you aren't sure where a particular contact is located.

To view a map of a contact's address, double-click the contact in the Contact list. The contact's record opens in the Contact dialog box.

Click the **Display Map of Address** button on the Contact toolbar. Microsoft Internet Explorer opens to the Microsoft Expedia Web site and displays a map based on the contact's address as shown in Figure 11.6.

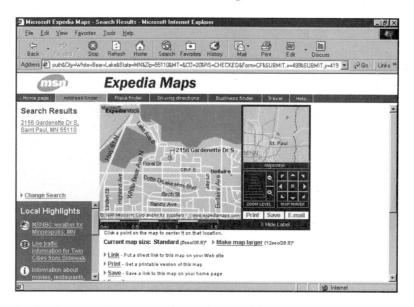

Figure 11.6   You can view a map of a contact's address.

You can zoom in and out on the map and you can print a hard copy. When you are done viewing the map, close the Internet Explorer window and you will be returned to the Contact dialog box and Outlook. For more information on using Outlook with Web tools like Internet Explorer see Lesson 24, "Outlook to the Internet."

In this lesson, you learned to create a Contacts list, view the list, and send mail to someone on your Contacts list. You also learned to view a map of a contact's address. In the next lesson, you learn to navigate the Calendar, create an appointment, and plan events using Outlook.

Using the Calendar

*In this lesson, you learn to navigate the Calendar,
create appointments, and save appointments.*

Navigating the Calendar

You can use Outlook's Calendar to schedule appointments and create a to-do list;
if necessary, Outlook can also remind you of appointments and daily or weekly
tasks. You can schedule appointments months in advance, move appointments,
cancel appointments, and so on. And the Calendar makes it easy
to identify the days on which you have appointments.

 To open the Outlook Calendar, click the **Calendar** icon in the Outlook Bar, or
select the **Calendar** folder from the Folder list. Figure 12.1 shows the Calendar in
Outlook.

Outlook provides multiple ways for you to move around in the Calendar and
view specific dates:

- Scroll through the Appointment pane to view the time of an appointment.
- In the monthly calendar pane, click the left and right arrows next to the
  names of the months to go backward and forward one month at a time.

 TIP **Changing Calendar Views** You can change to different views of the
Calendar by clicking the **Current View** drop-down arrow on the Advanced
Toolbar. Views including Active Appointments, Recurring Appointments, and By
Category are available.

- In the monthly calendar pane, click a date to display that date in the schedule pane.

- To switch to a different month in the schedule pane, click the current month in the monthly calendar pane, and select the name of the month from the shortcut list.

- To view a week or selected days in the schedule pane, select the days in the monthly calendar pane.

- To add a task to the Task list, click where you see **Click here to add a new Task**.

- Use the scrollbars for the Task list pane to view additional tasks, if necessary.

Monthly calendar pane

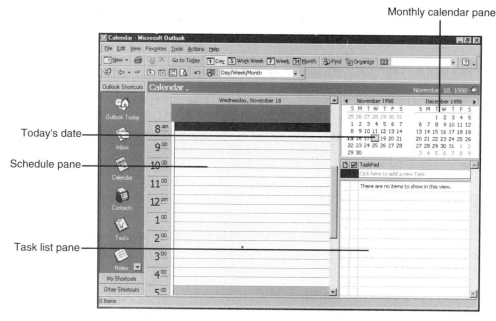

Today's date

Schedule pane

Task list pane

Figure 12.1 You can view all appointments and tasks at a glance.

TIP **Change the Date Quickly** To quickly go to today's date or to a specific date without searching through the monthly calendar pane, right-click in the schedule pane and choose either **Go To Today** or **Go To Date**.

Creating an Appointment

You can create an appointment on any day well past the year 2000 using the Outlook Calendar. When you create an appointment, you can add the subject, location, starting time, category, and even an alarm to remind you ahead of time.

Follow these steps to create an appointment:

1. In the monthly calendar pane, select the month and the date for which you want to create an appointment.

2. In the schedule pane, double-click next to the time at which the appointment is scheduled to begin. The Untitled - Appointment dialog box appears, with the Appointment tab displayed (see Figure 12.2).

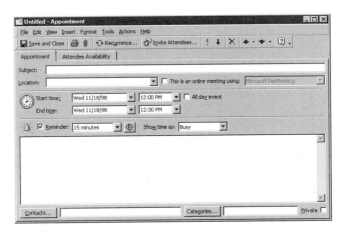

Figure 12.2 Enter all the details you need when scheduling an appointment.

3. Enter the subject of the appointment in the **Subject** text box (you can use a person's name, a topic, or other information).

4. In the **Location** text box, enter the meeting place or other text that will help you identify the meeting when you see it in your calendar.

5. Enter dates and times in the **Start Time** and **End Time** boxes (or click the drop-down arrows and select the dates and times).

TIP   **Autodate It!**   You can use Outlook's Autodate feature: Enter a text phrase such as "next Friday" or "noon" in the date box, and then press **Enter**; Outlook figures out the date for you and places it in the date box.

6. Select the **Reminder** check box and enter the amount of time before the appointment that you want to be notified. If you want to set an audio alarm, click the **Alarm bell** button and select a specific sound for Outlook to play as your reminder.

7. From the **Show Time As** drop-down list, choose how you want to display the scheduled time on your calendar.

8. In the large text box near the bottom of the Appointment tab, enter any text that you want to include, such as text to identify the appointment, reminders for materials to take, and so on.

9. Click the **Categories** button and assign a category (or categories) to the appointment.

10. Click the **Save and Close** button to return to the calendar.

The Attendee Availability tab enables you to schedule a meeting with coworkers and enter the meeting on your Calendar. See Lesson 13, "Planning a Meeting," for more information.

Scheduling a Recurring Appointment

Suppose you have an appointment that comes around every week or month, or that otherwise occurs on a regular basis. Instead of scheduling every individual occurrence of the appointment, you can schedule that appointment in your calendar as a recurring appointment.

To schedule a recurring appointment, follow these steps:

1. In the Calendar folder, choose the **Actions** menu, then **New Recurring Appointment**. The Appointment dialog box appears, and then the Appointment Recurrence dialog box appears on top of the Appointment dialog box (as shown in Figure 12.3).

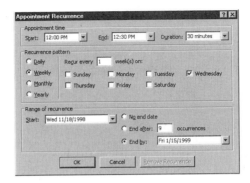

Figure 12.3 Schedule a recurring appointment once, and Outlook fills in the appointment for you throughout the Calendar.

2. In the Appointment Time area, enter the **Start**, **End**, and **Duration** times for the appointment.

3. In the Recurrence Pattern area, indicate the frequency of the appointment: **Daily**, **Weekly**, **Monthly**, or **Yearly**. After you select one of these options, the rest of the Recurrence Pattern area changes.

4. Enter the day and month, as well as any other options in the Recurrence Pattern area that are specific to your selection in step 3.

5. In the Range of Recurrence area, enter appropriate time limits according to these guidelines:

   - **Start**—Choose the date on which the recurring appointments will begin.

   - **No End Date**—Choose this option if the recurring appointments are not on a limited schedule.

   - **End After**—Choose this option and enter the number of appointments if there is a specific limit to the recurring appointments.

   - **End By**—Choose this option and enter an ending date to limit the number of recurring appointments.

6. Click **OK** to close the Appointment Recurrence dialog box. The Appointment dialog box appears.

7. Fill in the Appointment dialog box as described previously in this lesson. When you finish, click the **Save and Close** button to return to the Calendar. The recurring appointment appears in your calendar on the specified date and time. A recurring appointment contains a double-arrow icon to indicate that it is recurring.

 TIP   **Recurring Meetings**   You can schedule a recurring meeting by clicking the **Actions** menu and then selecting **New Recurring Meeting**. The Appointment dialog box and Recurrence dialog box will both be opened by this Calendar menu selection. Meetings are covered in Lesson 13.

Planning Events

In the Outlook Calendar, an *event* is any activity that lasts at least 24 hours, such as a trade show or a conference. You can plan an event in the Calendar program to block off larger time slots than you would for normal appointments. In addition, you can schedule recurring events.

To schedule an event, choose **Actions**, then select **New All Day Event**. The Event dialog box appears (see Figure 12.4; it looks much like the New Appointment dialog box). Fill in the **Subject**, **Location**, **Start Time**, and **End Time** text boxes. Make sure the **All Day Event** check box is checked (that's the only difference between an Event and an Appointment). Click the **Save and Close** button to return to the Outlook Calendar. The appointment appears in gray at the beginning of the day for which you scheduled the event.

To schedule a recurring event, open a New All Day Event window and fill in the information as described earlier. To make the event recurring, click the **Recurrence** button in the Event window. The Event Recurrence dialog box opens; fill in the appropriate information and click **OK**. Complete the information in the Event window, and then click the **Save and Close** button.

To edit an event or a recurring event, double-click the event in your Calendar. As with a mail message or appointment, Outlook opens the event window so you can change times, dates, or other details of the event.

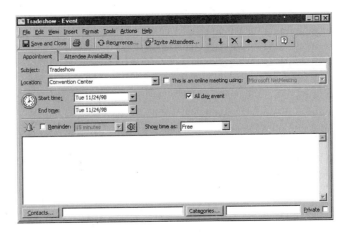

Figure 12.4 You can block out an entire day on the Calendar by scheduling an All Day Event.

In this lesson, you learned to navigate the Calendar, create appointments, and save appointments. In the next lesson, you learn to plan and schedule a meeting.

Planning a Meeting

In this lesson, you learn to schedule a meeting, enter attendees for a planned meeting, set the meeting date and time, and invite others to the meeting.

Scheduling a Meeting

Outlook provides you with the ability to plan the time and date of a meeting, identify the subject and location of the meeting, invite others to attend the meeting, and identify resources that will be needed for the meeting. You use the Calendar folder to plan and schedule meetings.

Meeting   In Outlook, a meeting is an appointment to which you invite people and resources.

Attendees   The people who will be attending your meeting.

Resources   Any equipment you use in your meeting, such as a computer, slide projector, or even the room itself.

To plan a meeting, follow these steps:

1. Click the icon for the Calendar folder on the Outlook bar, then choose **Actions**, and select **Plan a Meeting**. The Plan a Meeting dialog box appears (see Figure 13.1).

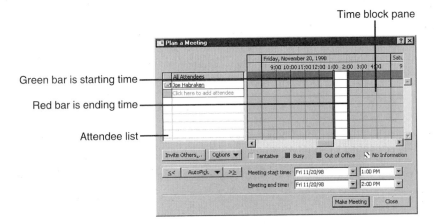

Figure 13.1 Choose the date and time of your meeting as well as the attendees.

2. To enter the names of the attendees, click in the **All Attendees** list where it says Type Attendee Name Here. You can type a name in the box and then press Enter. Continue adding new names as necessary. A better way to invite attendees to your meeting is to click the **Invite Others** button and choose the attendees from your Personal Address Book or the Outlook Address Book. This makes it easier to email invitations to those whom you want to attend.

3. To set a date for the meeting, open the **Meeting Start Time** drop-down list and select the date from the calendar, or just type the date in the text box. The ending date (in the **Meeting End Time** drop-down list) automatically shows the same date you set in the Meeting Start Time date box; you can change the End Time date if you want.

4. To set a start time for the meeting, do one of the following:

- Open the **Meeting Start Time** drop-down list, and select the time.
- Type a time in the text box.
- Drag the green bar in the time block pane of the dialog box to set the start time.

5. To set an end time for the meeting, do one of the following:

- Open the **Meeting End Time** drop-down list, and select the end time.
- Type a time in the text box.
- Drag the red bar in the time block pane of the dialog box to change the ending time of the meeting.

After you select the date and time for the meeting, you will notice that the time grid to the right of each attendee name shows the currently scheduled appointments that they have on the day of the meeting. The times blocked out in each attendee's grid are based on appointments and meetings in their Outlook Calendar. Outlook is able to check your corporate network and check attendee availability by using their calendars. If you have a conflict between your meeting time and an attendee's appointment, you can adjust the time of your meeting and avoid availability conflicts.

6. When you finish planning the meeting, click the **Make Meeting** button. The Meeting window appears (see Figure 13.2), from which you can refine the meeting details, as described in the next section.

 TIP   **Use AutoPick to Shift Meeting Time Frame**   You can click the **AutoPick** decrease or increase buttons to shift the meeting time (including the beginning and ending) to a half hour earlier or later, respectively. Each time you click AutoPick, the meeting shifts another half hour.

Working Out Meeting Details

After you plan a meeting, Outlook enables you to send invitations, identify the subject of the meeting, and specify the meeting's location. You enter these details in the Meeting dialog box.

When you schedule a meeting, you finish by clicking the **Make Meeting** button in the Plan a Meeting dialog box. When you do that, Outlook displays the Meeting dialog box with the Appointment tab in front (see Figure 13.2).

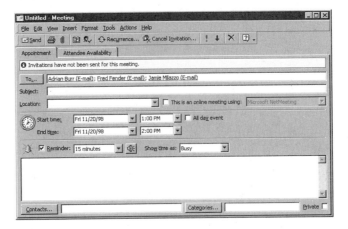

Figure 13.2 Specify the details related to the meeting in the Appointment tab of the Meeting dialog box.

Follow these steps to specify meeting details for a meeting you've already scheduled:

1. If you did not list the attendees in the Plan a Meeting dialog box, either click in the **To** text box and enter the names of the people you want to attend the meeting, or click the **To** button to select the attendees from an address book or Contact list.

2. In the **Subject** text box, enter a subject for the meeting.

3. In the **Location** text box, enter a location for the meeting.

4. (Optional) You can change the starting and ending dates and/or times in the Appointment tab. You also can choose the Attendee Availability tab to view the meeting in a format similar to that of the Plan A Meeting dialog box; make any changes to attendees, time, dates, and so on in the Attendee Availability tab.

5. (Optional) Select the **Reminder** check box, and enter a time for Outlook to sound an alarm to remind you of the meeting.

6. (Optional) Enter any special text you want to send the attendees in the text box provided.

If you plan on holding your meeting online using Microsoft NetMeeting, select the **This is an online meeting** check box on the Appointment tab of the Meeting dialog box. Scheduling an online meeting is really no different than scheduling a face-to-face meeting; you follow the same scheduling steps outlined in this lesson. An online meeting, however, requires that you specify a Directory Server (this will appear as a drop-down box when you select the online meeting check box) that will be used to connect the participants. Using NetMeeting is covered in Lesson 24, "Outlook and the Internet."

7. When you're ready to send the invitations to the meeting, click the **Send** button. Close the Meeting window by choosing **File**, then **Close**.

When you send an invitation, you're sending an email that requests the presence of the recipient at the meeting. The recipient can reply to your message, save your message, and forward or delete the message, just as he can with any other email message. If you want the recipient to reply, choose **Appointment**, then select **Request Responses**, and the recipients will be prompted to reply to your invitation.

An Invitation Mistake   To cancel an invitation after you've sent it, choose **Appointment**, then select **Cancel Invitation**.

CAUTION

Inviting Others to the Meeting

If you need to add names to your attendees list—either while you're planning the meeting or at some later date—you can use your personal address book, the Outlook address book, and/or your Contact list to find the names of the people you want to invite. Additionally, you can choose whether to make the meeting required or optional for each person you invite.

To invite others to the meeting, follow these steps:

1. In either the Plan a Meeting dialog box or the Attendee Availability tab of the Meeting dialog box, click the **Invite Others** button. The Select Attendees and Resources dialog box appears, as shown in Figure 13.3.

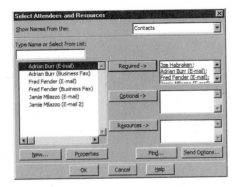

Figure 13.3 Use the address books to specify attendees to your meeting.

2. Open the **Show Names From The** drop-down list, and choose either **Personal Address Book** or **Contacts.**

3. To add a new name to a list, click the **New** button, and then enter the name, email address, phone numbers, and other pertinent information about the name you're adding to the list.

4. Select any name in the list on the left side of the dialog box and click the **Required** or **Optional** button to specify attendance requirements.

5. Click the **New** button to add resources to the list; then remember to notify the person who is in charge of those resources of your meeting.

6. Click **OK** to close the dialog box and add any attendees to your list.

Editing a Meeting

You can edit the details about a meeting, invite additional people, or change the date and time of the meeting at any time by opening the Meeting dialog box.

To open the Meeting dialog box and edit the meeting, follow these steps:

1. In the Calendar folder, choose the meeting date in the monthly calendar pane. The date appears in the schedule pane, and the meeting is blocked out for the time period you specified, as shown in Figure 13.4.

797

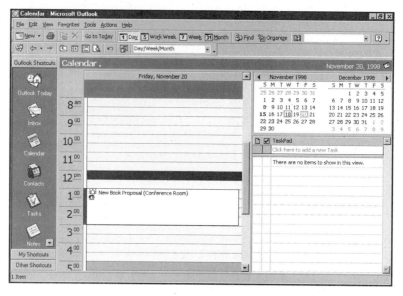

Figure 13.4 Select the meeting you want to edit from within the Calendar.

2. Double-click the meeting block to display the Meeting dialog box. You can edit anything in the Appointment or Meeting Planner tabs.

TIP **Any Responses?** Choose the **Show Attendee Status** option in the Attendee Availability tab of the Meeting dialog box to see if the people you invited to the meeting have responded to your invitation.

3. When you're done, choose **File,** then select **Close** to close the Meeting dialog box. If you've made changes to the meeting specifics, you should also send a message to your attendees to notify them of the change.

In this lesson, you learned to schedule a meeting, enter attendees for a planned meeting, set the meeting time, and invite others to the meeting. In the next lesson, you learn to create a Task list.

Creating
a Task List

In this lesson, you learn to enter a task and record statistics about the task.

Entering a Task

You can use the Tasks folder to create and manage your task list. You can list due dates, statuses, and priorities, and even set reminder alarms so you don't forget to perform certain tasks. To enter the Tasks folder, click the Task shortcut in the Outlook Bar.

 TERM **Task List**   A task list is a list of things you must do to complete your work, such as plan for a meeting, arrange an event, and so on. Various tasks might include making a phone call, writing a letter, printing a spreadsheet, or making airline reservations.

To enter a task, follow these steps:

1. In the Tasks folder, choose **Actions**, then select **New Task** or click the **New Task** button on the toolbar. The Untitled - Task dialog box appears (see Figure 14.1).

 TIP **Double-click to Start New Task**   Double-click in any space on the Task window and a new task will open. You can also use this technique with other Outlook items such as appointments and contacts when you are in the appropriate folder.

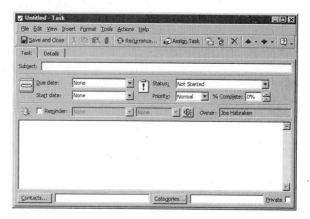

Figure 14.1 Enter data such as the subject of the task, due dates, and the task's priority.

2. In the Task tab, enter the subject of the task in the **Subject** box.

3. Enter a date on which the task should be complete, or click the down arrow to open the **Due date** drop-down calendar, and then choose a due date.

4. Enter a start date, or click the down arrow to open the **Start date** drop-down calendar, and then choose a starting date.

5. From the **Status** drop-down list, choose the current status of the project: Not Started, In Progress, Completed, Waiting on Someone Else, or Deferred.

6. In the **Priority** drop-down list, choose Normal, Low, or High priority.

7. In the % **Complete** text box, type a percentage or use the spinner arrows to enter one.

8. (Optional) To set an alarm to remind you to start the task or complete the task, select the **Reminder** check box and enter a date and a time in the associated text boxes.

9. Enter any comments, descriptions, or other information related to the task in the comments text box.

10. Click the **Categories** button and choose a category, or enter your own category in the text box.

TIP   **Access Denied**   If you are using Outlook on a corporate network where your folders are kept on the Corporate server, select the **Private** check box if you don't want others to see information about your task.

11. Click the **Save and Close** button when you're done.

Viewing Tasks

As in any Outlook folder, you can change how you view tasks in the list using the Current View drop-down list in the Standard toolbar. By default, the Tasks folder displays tasks in a Simple List view. Following is a description of the views you can use to display the Tasks folder:

- **Simple List**—Lists the tasks, completed check box, subject, and due date.
- **Detailed List**—Displays the tasks, priority, subject, status, percent complete, and categories.
- **Active Tasks**—Displays the same information as the detailed list but doesn't show any completed tasks.
- **Next Seven Days**—Displays only those tasks you've scheduled for the next seven days, including completed tasks.
- **Overdue Tasks**—Shows a list of tasks that are past due.
- **By Category**—Displays tasks by category; click the button representing the category you want to view.
- **Assignment**—Lists tasks assigned to you by others.
- **By Person Responsible**—Lists tasks grouped by the person who assigned the tasks.
- **Completed Tasks**—Lists only those tasks completed, along with their due dates and completion dates.
- **Task Timeline**—Uses the timeline view to display tasks by day, week, or month. Figure 14.2 shows the tasks assigned within one week.

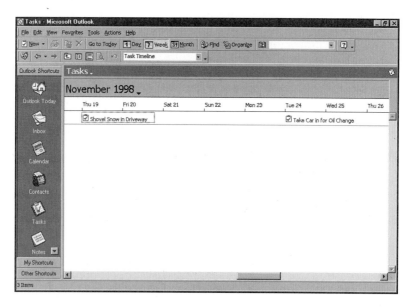

Figure 14.2 Double-click a task in timeline view to edit it.

Save What Settings? Depending on the changes you make to a view, Outlook might display the Save View Settings dialog box asking if you want to save the view settings before you switch to a different view. Generally, you'll want to discard the current view settings and leave everything the way you found it.

CAUTION

Managing Tasks

When working with a task list, you can add and delete tasks, mark tasks as completed, and arrange the tasks within the list. You also can perform any of these procedures in most of the task views described in the previous section. For information about printing a task list, see Lesson 17, "Printing in Outlook."

Figure 14.3 shows the Tasks folder; the following list describes how to manage certain tasks in the list.

Using the Journal

In this lesson, you learn to create Journal entries manually and automatically and to change views in the Journal.

Creating a Journal Entry

You can create a record of various items and documents so that you can track your work, communications, reports, and so on. In the Journal, you can manually record any activities, items, or tasks you want. You also can automatically record email messages, faxes, meeting requests, meeting responses, task requests, and task responses. Additionally, you can automatically record documents created in the other Office applications: Access, Excel, Office Binder, PowerPoint, and Word.

The Journal is especially useful for recording phone calls to and from contacts. That allows you to not only record the call as a Journal entry, but it also allows you to time the conversation and enter its duration. For information about calling a contact see Lesson 11, "Creating and Using a Contacts List."

 Journal A folder within Outlook that you can use to record interactions, phone calls, message responses, and other activities important to your work.

 Item An article or object in Outlook, such as a task, appointment, or contact.

You can automatically or manually record items in your Journal. You can, for example, choose to automatically record your email messages, meeting requests, task responses, and so on.

The first time you click the Journal folder to open it (in the Folder list or the Outlook bar), a message appears asking if you want to turn the Journal feature on. Click **Yes**. The Journal Options dialog box appears. In this dialog box you can specify what type of events you want to have automatically recorded in the Journal. Check boxes are provided to include email messages, meeting requests, and other events that are received from people in your Contacts folder (you click the check box for the specific contact). You can also choose to have files opened in Access, Excel, PowerPoint, and Word by checking the appropriate check box.

When you have completed your selections, click the **OK** button. The Journal opens. It is now ready to automatically record the items that you chose in the Journal Options dialog box (for more information on the Journal Options dialog box see the section "Automatically Recording Entries" later in this lesson).

You can also record items in the Journal manually. For example, you might add an email message to the Journal that is not normally recorded (because you didn't select messages from that particular contact as something you want automatically recorded in the Journal).

Recording an Entry Manually

To create a Journal entry manually, follow these steps:

1. In the Inbox folder (or any other folder in Outlook), select the item you want to record in the Journal and drag it onto the Journal folder in the Outlook Bar. The Journal Entry dialog box appears (see Figure 15.1).

2. The information in the Subject, Entry Type, Contact, and Company boxes and some other information is entered for you from the selected task, contact, or other selected item. However, you can change any of the statistics you want by entering new information in the following text boxes:

   - **Subject**—Displays the title or name of the item.
   - **Entry Type**—Describes the item based on its point of origin, such as a Word document, Meeting or Appointment, and so on.
   - **Contact**—Lists the name(s) of any attendees, contacts, or other people involved with the selected item.

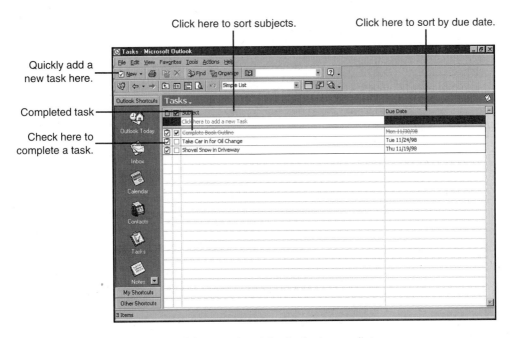

Click here to sort subjects.

Click here to sort by due date.

Quickly add a new task here.

Completed task

Check here to complete a task.

Figure 14.3 Add, delete, and sort the tasks in your list.

- To quickly add a task, click the top row of the task list where it says "Click Here to Add a New Task" and enter the subject and date.
- To edit a task, double-click the task in the list. The Task dialog box appears.
- To mark a task as completed, click the check box in the second column from the left, or right-click the task and choose **Mark Complete** from the shortcut menu. Outlook places a line through the task.
- To delete a task, right-click the task and choose **Delete** from the shortcut menu.
- To assign a task to someone else, right-click the task and choose **Assign Task** from the shortcut menu. Fill in the name of the person to whom you want to assign the task, and click the **Send** button to email him or her the task request.
- To assign a new task to someone else, choose **Tasks**, then select **New Task Request**. Create the task as you normally would, but send the task as an email by clicking the **Send** button.

TIP   **Get Rid of the Default Task**   If you don't want to leave the Start Up Microsoft Outlook task on your list, you can right-click the task and choose **Delete**.

Recording Statistics About a Task

You can record statistics about a task, such as time spent completing the task, billable time, contacts, and so on, for your own records or for reference when sharing tasks with your coworkers. This feature is particularly helpful when you assign tasks to others; you can keep track of assigned tasks and find out when they're completed.

To enter statistics about a task, open any task in the task list and click the **Details** tab. Figure 14.4 shows a completed Details tab for a sample task.

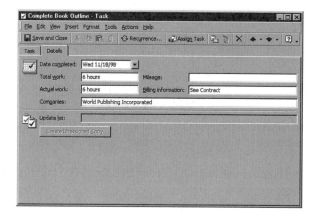

Figure 14.4   Fill in the status of the task so that you can share it with others and keep personal records.

You can export task lists and other Outlook information to a variety of applications, such as Microsoft Excel. Click **File**, then **Import and Export**. A wizard walks you through the steps so that you can place the appropriate task information in the cells of a spreadsheet or in a document in a word processor.

The following list describes the text boxes in the Details tab and the types of information you can enter:

- **Date Completed**—Enter the date the task was completed, or click the arrow to display the calendar and choose the date.
- **Total Work**—Enter the amount of time you expect the task to take. When you complete the job, Outlook calculates the actual time spent and enters it in this text box.
- **Actual Work**—Enter the amount of time it actually took to complete the job.
- **Mileage**—Enter the number of miles you traveled to complete the task.
- **Billing Information**—Enter any specific billing information, such as hours billed, resources used, charges for equipment, and so on.
- **Companies**—Enter the names of any companies associated with the contacts or with the project in general. Use semicolons to separate multiple names.
- **Update List**—Automatically lists the people whose task lists are updated when you make a change to your task. This is only available in situations in which you are on a Corporate network and using the Corporate installation of Outlook so that your Task folder is available on the local network.
- **Create Unassigned Copy**—Copies the task so that it can be reassigned; use the button to send a task to someone other than an original recipient. If the task is not sent to someone else, the button is unavailable.

To track tasks you've assigned to others and to receive status reports, follow these steps:

1. On the **Tools** menu, click **Options**; the Options dialog box appears. Click the **Other** tab, and then click **Advanced Options**.
2. In the Advanced Options dialog box, click **Delegated Tasks**. The Delegated Tasks dialog box opens.
3. To automatically track the progress of new tasks you assign to others, select the **Keep updated copies of assigned tasks on my task list** check box.

4. To automatically receive notification when an assigned task is complete, select the **Send status reports when assigned tasks are completed** check box.

5. After you've made your selections, click **OK** in each of the three open dialog boxes to return to the Outlook window.

 TIP   **Color Your Task List**   You can also set color options for overdue and completed tasks. Click the **Tools** menu, then select **Options**, and from the Preferences tab, click the **Task Options** button.

In this lesson, you learned to enter a task and record statistics about the task. In the next lesson, you learn to use the Journal.

Using the Journal

*In this lesson, you learn to create Journal entries
manually and automatically and to change views in the Journal.*

Creating a Journal Entry

You can create a record of various items and documents so that you can track
your work, communications, reports, and so on. In the Journal, you can manually
record any activities, items, or tasks you want. You also can automatically record
email messages, faxes, meeting requests, meeting responses, task requests, and
task responses. Additionally, you can automatically record documents created in
the other Office applications: Access, Excel, Office Binder, PowerPoint, and Word.

The Journal is especially useful for recording phone calls to and from contacts.
That allows you to not only record the call as a Journal entry, but it also allows
you to time the conversation and enter its duration. For information about
calling a contact see Lesson 11, "Creating and Using a Contacts List."

 Journal   A folder within Outlook that you can use to record interactions,
phone calls, message responses, and other activities important to your work.

 Item   An article or object in Outlook, such as a task, appointment, or contact.

You can automatically or manually record items in your Journal. You can, for example, choose to automatically record your email messages, meeting requests, task responses, and so on.

The first time you click the Journal folder to open it (in the Folder list or the Outlook bar), a message appears asking if you want to turn the Journal feature on. Click **Yes**. The Journal Options dialog box appears. In this dialog box you can specify what type of events you want to have automatically recorded in the Journal. Check boxes are provided to include email messages, meeting requests, and other events that are received from people in your Contacts folder (you click the check box for the specific contact). You can also choose to have files opened in Access, Excel, PowerPoint, and Word by checking the appropriate check box.

When you have completed your selections, click the **OK** button. The Journal opens. It is now ready to automatically record the items that you chose in the Journal Options dialog box (for more information on the Journal Options dialog box see the section "Automatically Recording Entries" later in this lesson).

You can also record items in the Journal manually. For example, you might add an email message to the Journal that is not normally recorded (because you didn't select messages from that particular contact as something you want automatically recorded in the Journal).

Recording an Entry Manually

To create a Journal entry manually, follow these steps:

1. In the Inbox folder (or any other folder in Outlook), select the item you want to record in the Journal and drag it onto the Journal folder in the Outlook Bar. The Journal Entry dialog box appears (see Figure 15.1).

2. The information in the Subject, Entry Type, Contact, and Company boxes and some other information is entered for you from the selected task, contact, or other selected item. However, you can change any of the statistics you want by entering new information in the following text boxes:

   - **Subject**—Displays the title or name of the item.
   - **Entry Type**—Describes the item based on its point of origin, such as a Word document, Meeting or Appointment, and so on.
   - **Contact**—Lists the name(s) of any attendees, contacts, or other people involved with the selected item.

- **Company**—Lists the company or companies associated with the contacts.
- **Start Time**—Displays the date and time of the meeting, appointment, or other item.
- **Start Timer**—Like a stop watch, the timer records the time that passes until you click the Pause Timer button.
- **Pause Timer**—Stops the timer.
- **Duration**—Enter the amount of time for completing the item.
- **Text box**—Displays a shortcut to the item itself, such as the Calendar appointment, Contact, or Message, that you originally dragged onto the Journal folder. You can open the item by double-clicking the shortcut icon.
- **Categories**—Enter or select a category in which to place the item.

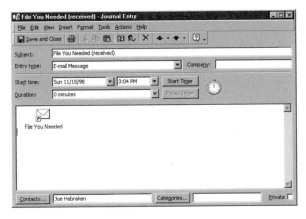

Figure 15.1 Drag any item from a folder onto the Journal icon in the Outlook Bar to add the item to the Journal.

3. Click **Save and Close** to complete the Journal entry.

 TIP **Time Your Calls** When making phone calls or meeting with clients, create a Journal entry to record the event, and use the Start Timer and Pause Timer buttons to record billable time. When you start the Timer, you will notice that the duration of the Journal entry is recorded in the Duration box. This is updated each minute. When you complete the Journal entry, the total time is reflected in the Duration box.

If you want to create a new Journal entry, but you don't have a contact, task, email, or other item that you want to use to create the entry, you can manually record a Journal entry by following these steps:

1. Change to the Journal folder.

2. Choose **Actions**, then select **New Journal Entry** or click the **New Journal Entry** button on the Standard or Advanced toolbar. The Journal Entry dialog box appears.

3. Enter the subject, entry type, contact, time, and any other information you want to record.

4. When you finish, click the **Save and Close** button.

Automatically Recording Entries

You can set options to automatically record items and their related contacts and/ or statistics about Microsoft Office documents you create. Suppose, for example, that you want to keep a record of all memos you send to your boss. You can record them in your Journal. When you first open the Journal, you are given the option of setting automatic entries in the Journal Options dialog box. You can also change your settings or add additional items to the automatically recorded list.

To set the options to automatically record Journal entries, follow these steps:

1. In the Journal folder, choose **Tools**, then select **Options**. The Options dialog box appears. Click the **Preferences** tab if necessary, then click the **Journal Options** button. The Journal Options dialog box appears, as shown in Figure 15.2.

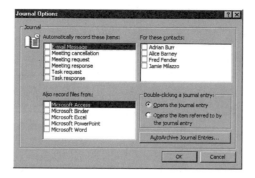

Figure 15.2 The Journal Options dialog box is where you set the options for automatically recording items in your Journal.

2. In the **Automatically Record These Items** list, check those items you want Outlook to automatically record in your Journal. (The items recorded correspond with the people selected in the list of contacts in step 3.)

3. In the **For These Contacts** list, check any contacts you want automatically recorded in the Journal. Outlook records any items checked in step 2 that apply to the selected contacts.

4. In the **Also Record Files From** list, check the applications for which you want to record Journal entries. Outlook records the date and time you create or modify files in the selected program.

You can also choose to have your Journal entries AutoArchived. Click the **AutoArchive Journal Entries** button and then choose a folder on your computer where you want to have the Journal Archive file stored. Then click **OK** to complete the process. For more information about the AutoArchive feature, see Lesson 21.

 TIP **Automatic and Easy** When you're creating a new contact in Outlook, you can set items to be automatically recorded in the Journal by choosing the **Journal** tab in the Contact dialog box and checking the **Automatically Record Journal Entries for This Contact** check box.

Viewing Journal Entries

By default, the Journal folder displays information in the Timeline view and By Type, as shown in Figure 15.3. However, you can display the entries in various views, as described in the following list. To select a particular view, click the **Current View** drop-down button on the Advanced toolbar.

 Save Settings? As in other views, Outlook might display the Save View Settings dialog box to ask if you want to save the view settings before you switch to a different view. You're probably getting used to this dialog box **CAUTION** by now.

- **By Type**—In Timeline view, this option groups Journal entries by type, such as email messages, meetings, Word documents, and so on. Double-click a type to display its contents, and then position the mouse pointer over an entry to view its contents or name. When you switch to the Journal in the Type view, a Journal Options dialog box appears. This dialog box allows you to specify which email messages will be recorded in the Journal based on the contact they are received from. This dialog box also allows you to select which application use will also be recorded in the Journal, such as Excel, Word, or Access.

- **By Contact**—In Timeline view, this displays the name of each contact that you selected in the Options dialog box. Double-click any contact's name to view recorded entries.

- **By Category**—If you've assigned categories to your Journal entries and other items, you can display your Journal entries by category in the timeline view.

- **Entry List**—Displays entries in a table with columns labeled Entry Type, Subject, Start, Duration, Contact, and Categories.

- **Last Seven Days**—Displays entries in an entry list, but includes only those entries dated within the last seven days.

- **Phone Calls**—Lists all entries that are phone calls.

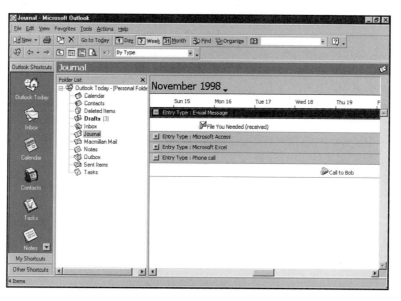

Figure 15.3   View the Journal entries by type.

TIP **Sort Journal Entries** You can click the heading bar—Subject, Start, or Duration—in any Entry list view to sort the items in that column in ascending or descending order.

In this lesson, you learned to create Journal entries manually and automatically and to change views in the Journal. In the next lesson, you learn to create notes.

Using Outlook Notes

In this lesson, you learn to create, sort, and view notes.

Creating Notes

If you've ever used a paper sticky note to remind yourself of tasks, ideas, or other brief annotations, Outlook's Notes are for you. Notes are similar to paper sticky notes. You can use Notes to write down reminders, names, phone numbers, directions, or anything else you need to remember. In Outlook, all notes are kept in the Notes folder. You'll have to remember to look at the folder so you can view your notes.

 TIP **The Long and Short of It** You can enter pages and pages of text if you want. As you type, the page scrolls for you; use the arrow keys and the Page Up/Page Down keys to move through the note text. Keep in mind, however, that the purpose of the note is a quick reminder, or information that you will eventually transfer to one of the other Outlook items, such as an appointment or task.

To create a note, click the Notes folder on the Outlook Bar and then follow these steps:

1. In the Notes folder, choose **Actions**, then select **New Note** or click the **New Note** button on the Standard or Advanced toolbar. A note appears, ready for you to type your text.
2. Enter the text for your note (see Figure 16.1).

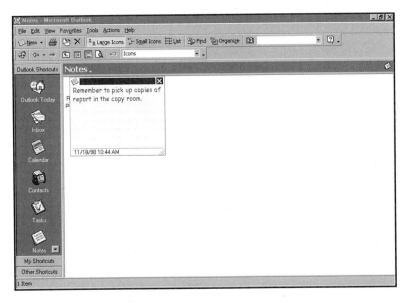

Figure 16.1 A note automatically includes the date and time it was created.

3. When you finish, click the **Close** (×) button to close the note. You can reopen a note and edit the text as you need to.

If you press Enter after entering text in the note, you create a line break and you create a title, of sorts, at the same time. Only the text before the hard return displays when the note is closed. If you do not add a hard return, but enter the note text so that it automatically wraps from line to line, the entire note text appears below the note in Icons view.

Setting Note Options

You can change the default color and size of your notes. You also can change the default font used for your notes. To set note options, follow these steps:

1. In the Notes folder (or any of the Outlook folders), choose **Tools**, then select **Options**. The Options dialog box appears. On the Preferences tab, click **Note Options**; the Notes Options dialog box appears (see Figure 16.2).

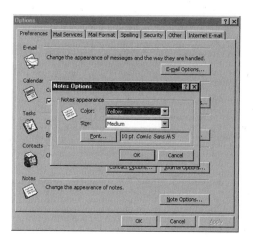

Figure 16.2   You can customize your notes.

2. The Notes Options dialog box allows you to change the color, size, and font for your notes. Using the **Color** drop-down box, you can change the color to yellow, blue, green, pink, or white. The default is yellow.

3. Open the **Size** drop-down list and choose **Small, Medium,** or **Large** for the size of the notes. The default is Medium.

4. To change the font, click the **Font** button. The Font dialog box appears. Change the font, font style, size, color, and other options, and then click **OK**.

Managing Individual Notes

To open an existing note, double-click it in the Notes folder. You can edit the text in an open note as you would edit any text. To move a note, drag its title bar. You can delete, forward, or print notes; you can change the color of individual notes; and you can specify categories for your notes. You can also drag the notes to the Windows Desktop and arrange them there.

Click an open note's Control-menu button to display a menu with the following commands:

- **New Note**—Creates a new note but leaves the first note open.
- **Save As**—Enables you to save the note and its contents.
- **Delete**—Deletes a note and its contents. (You also can delete a note by selecting it in the Notes list and pressing the **Delete** key.)

- **Forward**—Enables you to send the note as an attachment in an email message.
- **Cut, Copy, Paste**—Enables you to select text from the note and cut or copy it to the Clipboard. The Paste command enables you to paste items on the Clipboard at the insertion point in the note.
- **Color**—Choose another color for the individual note.
- **Categories**—Enter or choose a category.
- **Print**—Print the contents of the note.
- **Close**—Closes the note. (You can also click the **Close** (×) button in the note's title bar.) A closed note appears in the Notes folder.

Viewing Notes

The Notes folder provides various views for organizing and viewing your notes. You can also sort notes in any entry list view by right-clicking the heading bar—Subject, Created, Categories, and so on—and selecting the sort method.

The default view is Icons, but you can change the view using the Current View drop-down list in the Standard toolbar. Figure 16.3 shows the Notes folder in the default view.

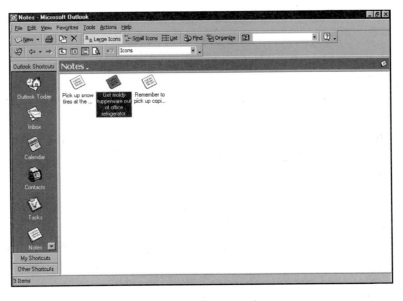

Figure 16.3 This view displays the notes in Icons view.

You can choose to display your Notes folder in any of the following views:

- **Icons**—Displays the notes as note icons with the message (or a portion of the message) displayed below the icon.
- **Notes List**—Displays the notes in a list, showing the title and note contents in the Subject column, the creation date and time, and the categories.
- **Last Seven Days**—Displays all notes written in the last seven days, by subject, creation date, and categories.
- **By Category**—Displays the categories; double-click a category to show its contents.
- **By Color**—Displays notes by their color. Double-click a color to display the notes.

In this lesson, you learned to create, sort, and view notes. In the next lesson, you learn to print in Outlook.

Printing in Outlook

In this lesson, you learn to print items in Outlook, change the page setup, preview an item before printing it, and change printer properties.

Choosing Page Setup

In Outlook, before you print, you choose the print style you want to use. Each folder—Inbox, Calendar, Contacts, and so on—offers various print styles, and each style displays the data on the page in a different way.

Page   In Outlook, this is the area of the paper that will actually be printed on. You might, for example, print two or four pages on a single sheet of paper.

Print Style   The combination of paper and page settings that control printed output.

You can choose from Outlook's built-in print styles, modify the default print styles, or create your own print styles. These lists show the default print styles available for each folder. To access the print styles for a particular item, select **File**, then choose **Print**. The Inbox, Contacts, and Tasks use the Table style and the Memo style; the Journal and Notes use only the Memo style.

• **Table Style**—Displays data in columns and rows on an 8 1/2 × 11 sheet, portrait orientation, 1/2-inch margins.

 • **Memo Style**—Displays data with a header of information about the message and then straight text on an 8 1/2 × 11 sheet, portrait orientation, 1/2-inch margins.

The Calendar folder provides the Memo style, plus the following styles:

 • **Daily Style**—Displays one day's appointments on one page on an 8 1/2 × 11 sheet, portrait orientation, 1/2-inch margins.

 • **Weekly Style**—Displays one week's appointments per page on an 8 1/2 × 11 sheet, portrait orientation, 1/2-inch margins.

 • **Monthly Style**—Displays one month's appointments per page on an 8 1/2 × 11 sheet, landscape orientation, 1/2-inch margins.

 • **Tri-fold Style**—Displays the daily calendar, task list, and weekly calendar on an 8 1/2 × 11 sheet, landscape orientation, 1/2-inch margins.

 • **Calendar Details Style**—Shows the currently displayed Calendar items and the body text of each item (such as an appointment) in a list format.

The Contacts folder provides the Memo style, plus the following styles:

 • **Card Style**—Two columns and headings on an 8 1/2 × 11 sheet, portrait orientation, 1/2-inch margins.

 • **Small Booklet Style**—One-column pages that print the contacts in a format similar to mailing labels by placing multiple contacts on a page. This style can be printed in Portrait or Landscape mode.

 • **Medium Booklet Style**—One column that equals 1/4 of a sheet of paper. Four pages are on one 8 1/2 × 11 sheet of paper, portrait orientation with 1/2-inch margins.

 • **Phone Directory Style**—One column, 8 1/2 × 11 sheet of paper, portrait orientation with 1/2-inch margins.

Will Page Setup Change My View? No matter how you set up your pages, it will not affect your view of tasks, calendars, or other Outlook items onscreen. Page setup only applies to a print job.

CAUTION

You can view, modify, and create new page setups in Outlook. To view or edit a page setup, follow these steps:

1. Change to the folder for which you're setting the page.

2. Choose **File**, then point at **Page Setup**. A secondary menu appears that lists the available print types.

3. Select the print type you want to view or edit, and the Page Setup dialog box appears (see Figure 17.1).

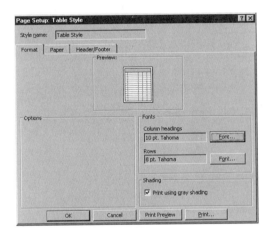

Figure 17.1 Customize the print style to suit yourself.

4. Click the **Format** tab to view and/or edit the page type, to choose options (in some cases), and to change fonts.

5. Click the **Paper** tab to view and/or edit paper size, page size, margins, and orientation.

6. Click the **Header/Footer** tab to view and/or edit headers for your pages.

Previewing Before Printing

You can choose to preview an item before printing it so that you're sure it looks the way you want it to look. If you do not like the way an item looks in preview, you can change the page setup.

Before you display an item in print preview, you must change to the folder containing the item you want to print. Then you can choose to preview the item in any of the following ways:

- Click the **Print Preview** button in the Page Setup dialog box.
- Choose **File**, and then select **Print Preview**.
- Click the **Print Preview** button on the Advanced Toolbar.
- Click the **Preview** button in the Print dialog box.

Figure 17.2 shows a calendar and task list in Print Preview. You can change the page setup by clicking the **Page Setup** button; the Page Setup dialog box appears. Click the **Print** button to send the job to the printer. Click the **Close** button to exit Print Preview and return to the Outlook folder.

Mouse pointer changes to a magnifying glass

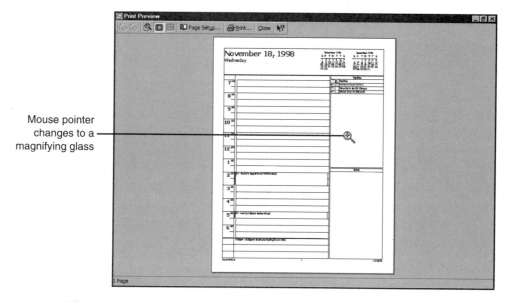

Figure 17.2 Preview the item before printing it.

 TIP **Enlarge the View** When the mouse pointer looks like a magnifying glass with a plus sign in it, you can click to enlarge the page. When the mouse pointer looks like a magnifying glass with a minus sign in it, you can click to reduce the view again.

Printing Items

After you choose the print style and preview an item to make sure it's what you want, you can print the item. You can indicate the number of copies you want to print, select a printer, change the print style or page setup, and set a print range.

When you're ready to print an item, follow these steps:

1. Choose **File**, and then select **Print** or click the **Print** button on the Standard toolbar. The Print dialog box appears, as shown in Figure 17.3.

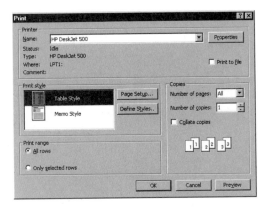

Figure 17.3 Set the printing options before printing the item.

2. In the Printer area of the dialog box, choose a different printer from the **Name** drop-down list if necessary.

3. In the Print Style area, choose a print style from the list. You also can edit the page setup (with the **Page Setup** button) or edit or create a new style (with the **Define Styles** button).

4. In the Copies area of the dialog box, choose **All**, **Even**, or **Odd** in **Number of Pages** and enter the number of copies you want to print.
   Click the **Collate Copies** check box if you want Outlook to automatically assemble multiple copies.

5. Set the print range with the options in that area. (The Print Range options vary depending on the type of item you're printing.)

6. Click **OK** to print the item.

Printing Labels and Envelopes

A handy Outlook feature is the capability to print mailing labels and envelopes from your Contacts list. To take advantage of this feature, you will also need to have Word 2000 installed on your computer. Creating form letters, mailing labels, or envelopes is called a *mail merge*. Basically, you create some type of main document (such as mailing labels, envelopes, and so on) in Word that will hold field codes which relate to the information you keep on each contact, such as name or address. To actually start the merge process, open your Contacts folder and select **Tools** and then **Mail Merge**. The Mail Merge Contacts dialog box allows you to specify the contacts for the merge and specify the Word document into which the contact information will be merged. You may read more about Mail Merge in the Word section of this book.

Setting Printer Properties

Whether you're printing to a printer connected directly to your computer or to a printer on the network, you can set printer properties. The properties you set apply to all print jobs you send to the printer until you change the properties again.

Printer Properties   Configurations specific to a printer connected to your computer or to the network. Printer properties include paper orientation, paper source, graphics settings, fonts, and print quality.

Access Denied?   If you cannot change the printer properties to a network printer, it's probably because the network administrator has set the printer's configuration and you're not allowed access to the settings. If you need to change printer properties and cannot access the printer's Properties dialog box, talk to your network administrator.

To set printer properties, open the Print dialog box (by choosing **File**, then **Print**). In the Printer area, select a printer from the Name drop-down list, and then click the **Properties** button. The printers' Properties dialog boxes differ depending on the make and model of printer.

Most likely, you'll be able to set paper size, page orientation, and paper source using options on a Paper tab in the dialog box. In addition, you might see a Graphics tab, in which you can set the resolution, intensity, and graphics mode of your printer. A Fonts tab enables you to set options on TrueType fonts, font cartridges, and so on. You might also find a Device Options tab, in which you can set print quality and other options. For more information about your printer, read the documentation that came with it.

In this lesson, you learned to print items in Outlook, change the page setup, preview an item before printing it, and change printer properties. In the next lesson, you learn to manage your files and Outlook items.

Saving, Opening, and Finding Outlook Items

In this lesson, you learn to save, open, and find items in Outlook.

Saving, Opening, and Using Items

Generally, when you finish adding a new task, appointment, meeting, contact, or other item, Outlook automatically saves that item for you or you're prompted to save the item yourself. You can also save most items in Outlook for use in other applications by using the Save As command. After you save an item by naming it, you can open that same item and edit, print, or otherwise use the saved file in Windows applications that support the file type. You might save an item—a journal entry or appointment page, for example—so you can refer to it later, edit the original, or keep it as a record.

 Save As   When you save an item using the File, Save As command, you can designate a drive, directory, and new filename for that item, as well as a file type.

 File Type   A file type is the same thing as a file format. When you save a file, you specify a file type that identifies the file as one that can be opened in specific applications. For example, the file extension .DOC identifies a file type that you can open in Word, and the extension .TXT represents a text-only format you can open in nearly any word processor or other application.

TERM **Save and Close** This command choice is available when you create new contacts, appointments, and tasks. It saves the current item and closes the item's dialog box, returning you to the currently selected folder, such as the Contacts folder or the task list.

To save an item, follow these steps:

1. In the folder containing the item you want to save, choose **File**, then select **Save As**. The Save As dialog box appears (see Figure 18.1).

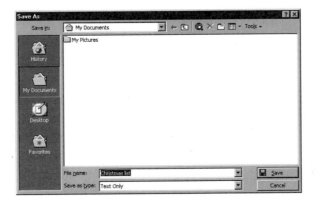

Figure 18.1 Save items as files for use in other programs, as copies of the originals, or for later use.

 TERM **Why Is Save As Dimmed?** When the Save As command is dimmed, you must first select an item—an appointment, meeting, task, note, and so on—before you can save it.

2. From the **Save In** drop-down list, choose the drive to which you want to save the file. From the folders on that drive, select the one you want to save to. The Folder icons on the left of the dialog box give you quick access to your History, My Documents, Desktop, and Favorite folders.

3. In the **Save As Type** drop-down list, choose a file type. You can save the file in Text Only, RTF Text Format, Outlook Template, and Message Format.

4. After you choose the type, enter a name for the item in the **File Name** text box, or accept the default.

5. Click the **Save** button. Outlook not only lets you save items in different formats, but it also allows you to open certain file formats and use the files in Outlook.

The following discussion explains several file formats, including how you would save to the particular file type in Outlook and how you would open a file in this format in Outlook:

- **Text Only**—Saves in ASCII format, which you can use in other applications, such as Word, Notepad, and so on. Save Outlook items in ASCII when you want to send them to someone who does not have Outlook and text-only format will suffice. Any special formatting in the item will be lost when you save in this format. You can also open text-only items in Outlook. Choose **File**, select **Open**, and then in the Open dialog box, choose **Text Only**. Select the text file, and then click **Open**. Information in text-only files can be converted into Messages, Tasks, or Contacts.

- **RTF Text Format**—Saves in rich text format. You can also use this format in Word, Outlook, or Lotus Notes, for example. This format allows you to save items for use in other applications and maintains the text formatting such as bold, underline, and other font attributes.

  To open an RTF file in Outlook or another Windows application, choose **File**, and then select **Open**. In the Open dialog box, click in the **Files of Type** drop-down list and choose **Rich Text Format** (or **RTF Text Format**). The saved files appear in the file list. Select the file and click the **Open** button.

  Figure 18.2 shows an email message from Outlook saved as an RTF file and opened in Word. After opening a file, you can format it, cut or copy items to it, insert objects, print, edit, and otherwise manipulate the file. Additionally, you can open the attachment to the email message from within the saved RTF file and read it.

CAUTION

RTF Isn't Listed?   If RTF isn't listed in the application's Files of Type list box, see if Text Only is listed. You can also save Outlook items as Text Only. And if you are using Word as your email editor, you also have the option of saving the mail message in a Word document format.

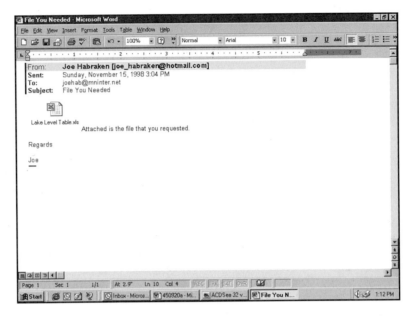

Figure 18.2 Exchanging data between applications makes your work easier.

- **Outlook Template**—Saves as a template (or style sheet) that you can use as a basis for other items. You can open an Outlook template when you are in any of the Outlook folders. Templates supply you with ready-made formatting for your Outlook items.

- **Message Format**—Saves in a format you can use in your email messages. After you save an item as a message text file, you can insert the item into an email message to send. Suppose you saved a contact's information or an especially long note that you want to share with someone else; you can insert the file as an object into a message and send the email as you normally would. Then the recipient can open the message and the message file.

To insert a message file into a message, open the message and choose **Insert**, and then select **Object**. In the Insert Object dialog box, choose **Create from File**. Enter the path and filename, and click **OK**. Figure 18.3 shows a message file in the text of an email.

829

If you haven't saved the message as a file, you can also insert it as an item into the current message that you are composing. Choose **Insert**, and then select **Item**. The Insert Item dialog box appears. Choose the folder that the item (such as a mail message) resides in using the appropriate folder icon in the top of the Insert Item dialog box. Then select the actual item in the list that appears at the bottom of the dialog box. After you have made your selection, click **OK**.

TIP **Files As Objects** As described in Lesson 7, "Attaching Items to a Message," you can insert any existing file as an object. Therefore, you can insert an RTF, text-only, or message file into a Word document, Excel spreadsheet, mail message, or any other Windows document that supports OLE.

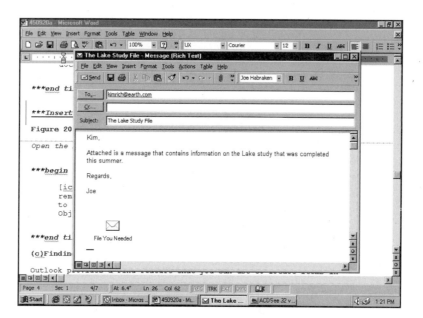

Figure 18.3 Open the MSG file by double-clicking its icon.

Can't Remember the Path? If you don't remember the location and filename of the object you want to insert in your message, use the **Browse** button in the Object dialog box to locate the file.

Finding Items

Outlook provides a Find feature that you can use to locate items in your various Outlook folders. You can search for messages, files, journal entries, notes, tasks, contacts, appointments, and so on, depending on which folder you are currently in. When you use the Find feature, it opens in its own pane at the top of the current folder window. You type in a key word or phrase, and the Find feature searches all the items in the current folder for your search word or words. When it finds items that match the search phrase, it lists them in the current folder window. Items not matching the search criteria are hidden.

To find an item in an Outlook folder, follow these steps:

1. Select the folder that you want to search for the item. Choose **Tools**, then select **Find** or click the **Find** button on the Standard toolbar. The Find pane appears, as shown in Figure 18.4.

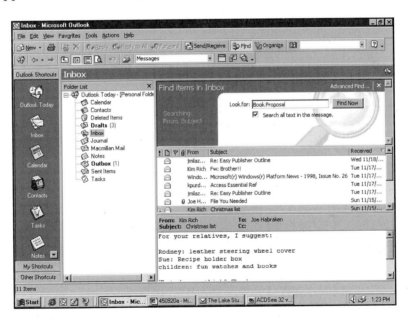

Figure 18.4 Use the Find pane to search for items in the current folder.

2. Type your search criteria in the **Look For** box.
3. When you are ready to run the search, click **Find Now**.

831

4. The items that match your search word or phrase appear in the Folder list (if no matches were found, the message `Did you find it? if not, try` will appear followed by a link to the Advanced find feature or Clear Search).

5. You can perform a new search by clicking the **Clear Search** button; enter a new search phrase in the **Look For** box and then click **Find Now**. When you have completed your search, you can close the Find pane by clicking its **Close** button.

Using the Advanced Find Feature

The Find pane includes an Advanced Find button in the upper-right corner. You can use Advanced Find to perform more detailed searches than you can with the Find feature. In the Advanced dialog box, you can set multiple search criteria such as a category, from, sent to, and subject (when searching for mail messages, additional search criteria exist for each of the other items found in Outlook).

To use the Advanced Find feature, follow these steps:

1. Open the Find dialog box by choosing **Tools**, and then selecting **Find Items**.

2. Click the **Advanced Find** button in the upper-right corner of the Find pane.

3. In the Advanced Find dialog box, set the criteria for your search using the criteria boxes found on the various tabs that appear. For instance, the Message Advanced Find dialog box includes a tab for Messages, More Choices, and Advanced. Each tab provides you with more advanced methods for conducting the search.

4. Set your search conditions on the various tabs. The More Choices tab is the same for each Outlook item and lets you search for items that have not been read or items that have an attachment.

5. When you've finished setting your criteria, click the **Find Now** button. A box opens at the bottom of the Advanced dialog box that lists the items that have met the search criteria. To open an item, double-click it.

Figure 18.5 shows the Advanced dialog box with the tabs that are used for searching the Inbox or other message folders. A drop-down list at the top left of the dialog box allows you to change the type of item that you are searching.

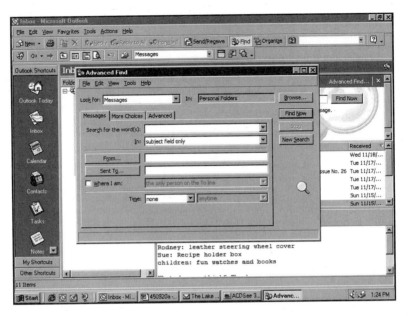

Figure 18.5 Set advanced criteria in the Advanced Find dialog box to find specific items.

In this lesson, you learned to save items, open items, and find items in Outlook. In the next lesson, you learn to integrate items between Outlook folders.

Using Outlook Integration, Forms, and Templates

In this lesson, you learn to use various items in Outlook together (to create a task or an appointment from a mail message and to create a document within Outlook, for example). You are also introduced to the Outlook templates.

Creating a Task from a Mail Message

You can use a mail message to create a task easily in Outlook. Instead of printing the message and then opening your Task List to add the information, you can create the task by using drag-and-drop copying. For more information about using the Tasks folder, see Lesson 14, "Creating a Task List."

Will I Lose the Message? When you use a message to create another item, Outlook copies the message so that the original message remains in the Inbox.

CAUTION

To create a task from a mail message, follow these steps:

1. Open the Inbox folder.
2. Click and drag the unopened mail message from the Inbox window to the Tasks icon on the Outlook Bar. The Task dialog box opens (see Figure 19.1).

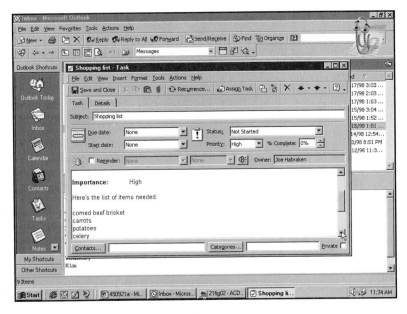

Figure 19.1   Create a task from an email message.

3. Change the subject or other data if you want, and then set any options for the task (such as due date, priority, reminders, categories, and so on).

4. Click the **Save and Close** button, and Outlook adds the task to your list.

Creating an Appointment from a Mail Message

In addition to creating tasks from messages, you can create an appointment from a mail message. When you create the appointment, you can set a time and date, invite attendees, create a meeting, and otherwise set options for the appointment. For more information about creating appointments, see Lesson 12, "Using the Calendar."

To create an appointment from a mail message, follow these steps:

1. Open the Inbox and locate the mail message you want to use.

2. Drag the unopened message from the Inbox window to the Calendar folder on the Outlook Bar. The Appointment dialog box opens with some information automatically filled in (see Figure 19.2).

The Subject is automatically filled in.

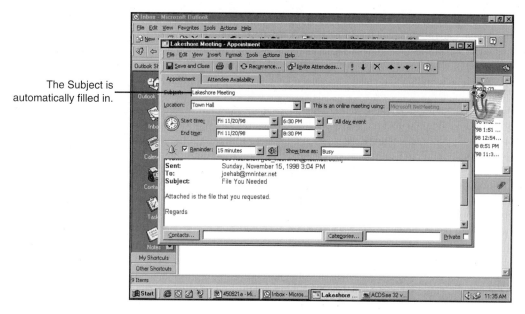

Figure 19.2   Create an appointment using the data in a mail message.

3. Add the location to the appointment and make any desired changes in the **Subject**, **Start Time**, or **End Time** boxes, or in any other of the options.

4. Click the **Save and Close** button to complete the appointment.

Create a Note from Any Item

Just as you can create tasks and appointments from a mail message, you can also create a note from any item in Outlook. Suppose someone emailed you information about a product or service that you want to add to a report; you can create a note with the information on it. Or suppose you want to call someone at a certain time later in the day. You can create a note from your contact entry so that you won't forget.

You can create a note from a mail message, appointment or meeting, contact, task, or journal entry. After you create the note, you can edit the text in the note without affecting the original item.

To create a note from any Outlook item, drag the item into the Notes folder in the Outlook Bar. Outlook creates and displays the note, and you can edit the text if you want. For more information about notes, see Lesson 16, "Using Outlook Notes."

Using Outlook Forms and Templates

As you already know, Outlook provides you with a number of different forms that you can use to create items for your various Outlook folders: an Appointment form, a Contact form, a Journal entry form, and so on. In most cases, you choose a particular form when you are in a particular folder; for instance, when you are in the Calendar folder, you open a new Appointment form.

You can also open the various forms that Outlook provides from the File menu, no matter which folder you are currently in. You can be in the Inbox folder, but you can still quickly open a new appointment form. To open any of Outlook's available forms, select **File**, then point at **New**, then select **Choose Form**. The Choose Form dialog box appears. Select the form you want to use from the list provided in the dialog box, and then click the **Open** button.

Outlook also includes a number of form templates on which you can base new messages. You can access these templates by using the Choose Form dialog box. The templates offer you alternative layouts and special features such as decorative fonts and graphics to add pizzazz to a new message.

To use an Outlook template for a message, follow these steps:

1. Open the **Choose Form** dialog box (choose **File**, then select **New**, and click **Choose Form**).
2. In the Choose Form dialog box, click the **Look In** drop-down box arrow and select one of the form libraries listed. The available forms appear in the Choose Form dialog box (see Figure 19.3). These forms can be default forms in the Standard Forms Library, or special forms that you have created (appearing in the Personal Forms Library or some other location on your computer or on your company's network).

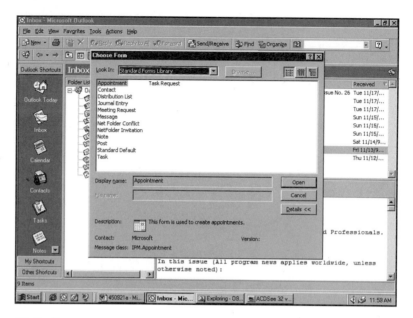

Figure 19.3   Base your new message on a specific form in Outlook.

3. Select the form you want to use and click **OK**. Outlook displays the message window in which you can create your item.

When you use templates for messages, the person who receives the message must have an email client that can view the special graphics and text formatting options offered to you by the template. If you send messages to people who have a text-only email package, you may want to forgo using the templates. Templates, however, are a good way to dress up your other Outlook items, such as tasks or appointments (see Lesson 4, "Creating Mail," for more information on using special mail types, such as HTML).

In this lesson, you learned to use various items in Outlook together—to create a task and an appointment from a mail message and to create a document within Outlook. In the next lesson, you learn to share data with other Office applications.

Sharing Data with Office Applications

In this lesson, you learn to share data between Outlook and other Office applications.

Creating a New Office Document

You can create a new Office document from within Outlook; for example, you can write a letter, write a report, create a spreadsheet, and so on using any of the other members Office 2000. To create the document, you work in the actual Office application, such as Word, using that application's tools and features. When you save the document, a shortcut saves to Outlook so that you can easily open the document at any time.

CAUTION **Outlook 2000 and Older Versions of Office** Outlook 2000 has been designed to fully integrate with the applications in Microsoft Office 2000. You may lose functionality and have problems with the integration features if you use Outlook 2000 with an earlier version of Office.

To create a new Office document, follow these steps:

1. In the Outlook window, choose **File**, then select **New**, and click **Office Document**. The New Office Document dialog box appears, as shown in Figure 20.1.

CAUTION

I Don't See the New Office Document Dialog Box For this dialog box to appear, Office must be installed and you must have at least one Office template located in the Microsoft Office Templates folder.

Figure 20.1 Select the template that you will base your new Office document on.

2. Select the template for an Excel worksheet or chart, a Word document, or a PowerPoint presentation, and click **OK**. In the dialog box that opens, select one of the options:

   - **Post the document in this folder**—If you want to save the item.
   - **Send this document to someone**—Makes it part of a new email message.

3. Click **OK**. The template opens in a document window. Enter and format the text. Use the menus to check spelling, create pictures, and otherwise manage the document as you would in a word processor (or spreadsheet or presentation software package).

4. To print the document, choose **File**, **Print**.

5. To save the document, choose **File**, and then select **Save As**. The Save As dialog box appears.

6. Enter a filename and file type, and choose a location for the file.

7. Choose **File**, and then select **Close** to close the document and the document window. The document is added to the Outlook item you were in when you created it.

To open the document for editing, printing, or other manipulation, double-click it.

Creating an Outlook Item from an Office File

You can create an appointment from a Word document, a mail message from an Excel document, or one of many other items by dragging a file to an Outlook item. This capability is great for when you want to include data in a mail message or record items in your journal. Sharing data between Office applications makes your work easier and more efficient.

To create an Outlook item from an Office file, follow these steps:

1. Open the Windows Explorer window and the Outlook window so that you can see both onscreen at the same time (see Figure 20.2).

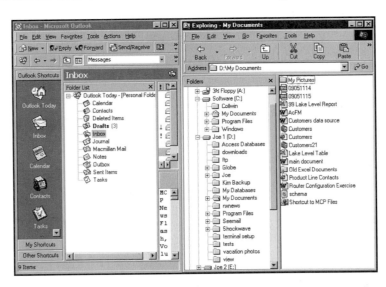

Figure 20.2 Arrange the two windows onscreen so you can drag from one to the other.

2. In the Explorer window, select the file from which you want to create an Outlook item, and then drag it to the folder in the Outlook Bar. For example, drag a worksheet to the Task Folder to create a task.

3. The New Item dialog box opens, with the Office file represented as an icon in the item. Enter any details, such as subject, dates, and so on, and then save the item as usual.

> **TIP** **Shortcut** Drag an Outlook item onto the Windows desktop to create a copy of the item that you can open quickly.

Importing and Exporting Files

You can import files to Outlook for the other Office applications and export files from Outlook to other Office applications, such as Word and Excel. When you import, you're opening another Office application's file in a format that Outlook can read, so you can use the file's contents in Outlook. When you export, you're saving Outlook data in a format that one of the other Office applications can use.

Importing

You might import files from Access, FoxPro, dBASE, Schedule+, Excel, or some other application for use in Outlook.

To import data, follow these steps:

1. In Outlook, choose **File**, and then select **Import and Export**. The Import and Export Wizard appears (see Figure 20.3).

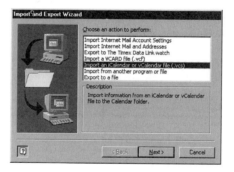

Figure 20.3 Import or export files with the help of a wizard.

Wizard In Microsoft Office products, a wizard is a series of dialog boxes containing instructions and options. A wizard helps you complete a task.

2. Choose **Import from Schedule+ or Another Program or File** and click the **Next** button. The second wizard dialog box appears.

3. Scroll through the list using the vertical scrollbar if necessary, and choose the type of file you want to import from the list. Click the **Next** button.

CAUTION

Word's Not There!   You won't see Microsoft Word on the list, but you can still import a Word file. Select **the Comma Separated Values (Windows)** option to import a Word file that you've converted to text-only; first you'll have to use Word to save the Word file in Text Only format.

4. In the third wizard dialog box, enter the path and the filename in the **File to Import** text box, or click the **Browse** button and select the file from the Browse dialog box. Set any options in the Options area of the dialog box, and click the **Next** button.

5. In the fourth wizard dialog box, select the folder in which you want to import the file, and click **Next**.

You may wonder why you should go through the import process when you can drag a Word or Excel file into any of the Outlook items. Importing a file translates the imported information into a format that Outlook can use directly. For instance, information imported into a Contact or Task becomes the same as information you entered directly into the Contact or Task. When you drag files onto Outlook items, you are embedding the file in the Outlook item, but you are not converting it. An Excel workbook dragged into the Task Folder is embedded, which means a copy of the workbook becomes a part of the Outlook item. When you double-click an embedded object, such as an Excel Workbook, the Outlook menus and toolbars change to those found in Excel, enabling you to use Excel's features as you work with the embedded object (for more information about Object Linking and Embedding, see the next section in this lesson).

Exporting

You can export Outlook files to Access, Excel, Word, and so on for use with other applications. For example, you might export an email message to Word as a memo, or you might export data from your journal into an Excel worksheet. When you export a file, you're saving the file's contents in a format another application can open and use.

To export a file, follow these steps:

1. Select the item you want to export as a file, choose **File**, and then select **Import and Export**. The Import and Export Wizard appears.
2. Choose **Export to a File** and click **Next**.
3. In the second wizard dialog box, select the folder to export from and click **Next**.
4. In the third wizard dialog box, select the file type, and click **Next**.
5. In the fourth wizard dialog box, enter the path and name of the file to be exported, and then click **Next**.

Linking and Embedding Objects

You can use Windows OLE to share data between Office applications. Object Linking and Embedding is a feature that most Windows applications support. OLE enables you to share data between a source application and a destination application, ensuring that all documents are updated automatically and in a timely fashion. For example, you can link an Excel worksheet to a mail message to ensure that the data you send with the message is up-to-date and accurate. You can also embed objects into mail messages in Outlook.

One of the biggest advantages of using OLE is that you can edit an object by double-clicking it. When you do, the file is updated in both the source and the destination applications with the changes you've made. You can use existing files or create new files for both linking and embedding.

Linking   Creating a bridge between two applications so that the data in one application is copied exactly into the second application and updated automatically whenever changes are made.

Embedding   Using one application to create an object within another application.

Source   The application or document in which the object was created.

Destination The application or document into which the object is copied or embedded.

Object The Word document, Excel worksheet, Outlook Note, or other item that is linked or embedded.

Linking Objects

Outlook enables you to link data between two or more applications when you want to ensure that all data is kept up-to-date automatically. If, for example, you link an Excel worksheet to an Outlook message, each time you make a change to the numbers in the worksheet, those numbers also change in the linked data in the message.

To link an object between Outlook and another application, follow these steps:

1. In Outlook, create a new mail message or reply, and then place the insertion point in the body of the message.

2. Choose **Insert, Object**. The Insert Object dialog box appears.

3. Choose **Create from File**. The Insert Object dialog box changes to look like the one shown in Figure 20.4.

4. Enter the path and filename of the object you want to link in the **File** text box, or click the **Browse** button and select the file.

5. Select the **Link** check box and click **OK**. Outlook inserts a copy of the object in the message text. The link remains—guaranteeing updated information—until you send the message.

Linked Files Cannot Be Moved When you create a link between a file, such as an Excel workbook and an Outlook item, the link remains in force only as long as the Excel workbook remains in the same location on your computer. For example, if the Excel Workbook is in an Excel folder on your computer's C: drive, the file must remain in this location if the link with the Outlook item is going to work.

845

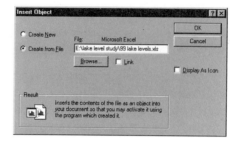

Figure 20.4 Create a link to an existing object.

Embedding Objects

You might want to embed a new or existing file, such as a Word table and text, into an email message to send to someone in your company. When you embed the data, the recipient can just double-click the embedded object to open, read, edit, and/or print the file's contents. Note, however, that embedded data (unlike linked data) isn't updated when a source file changes.

To embed an object in Outlook, follow these steps:

1. In Outlook, create a new mail message or reply, and then place the insertion point in the body of the message.

2. Choose **Insert**, and then select **Object**. The Insert Object dialog box appears.

3. Choose **Create New**, and a list of available Object Types appears in the dialog box.

4. Select the object type you want and click **OK**. Windows inserts a window into the message, from which you can create a document, spreadsheet, chart, or other object.

For example, if you choose to insert a spreadsheet, Windows creates a window within the message that looks like an Excel worksheet. In addition, the Outlook message window changes temporarily to look similar to Excel's, as shown in Figure 20.5.

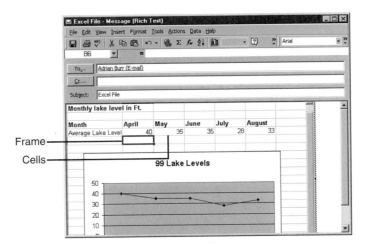

Frame —
Cells —

Figure 20.5 Create a worksheet from within an Outlook message using Excel toolbar buttons and Excel commands on the menus.

When you finish entering data, click outside the frame to return to Outlook. At any time, you can double-click anywhere in the frame to edit the data.

CAUTION

You Get the Entire Excel Workbook If you create an object from an existing Excel workbook, Outlook inserts the whole workbook into the item. You can display only one worksheet at a time, however. Double-click the Excel object to choose a different worksheet.

In this lesson, you learned to share data between Outlook and other Office applications. In the next lesson, you learn to archive items.

Archiving Items

In this lesson, you learn to use AutoArchive and to archive files, retrieve archived files, and delete archived files manually.

Using AutoArchive

You can set an option in Outlook to automatically archive your mail messages periodically into files. The AutoArchive feature cleans your Inbox for you but saves the specified messages in an archive file. AutoArchiving is similar to the backup procedure you use to compress and save files on your computer in case your computer crashes and you have to resort to disaster recovery. Mail messages are compressed and saved in a file that can then be transferred to a storage device like a floppy disk or other removable drive (such as an Iomega Zip drive or Imation Superdisk) for safekeeping.

 Archive To save items to a file that you can open at any time and print, view, or otherwise use. You might, for example, want to archive some of your mail messages to keep for your records instead of leaving those messages in your Inbox. Archived items are removed from the folder and copied to an archive file.

To use AutoArchive, follow these steps:

1. Choose **Tools**, then select **Options**. The Options dialog box appears.
2. Click the **Other** tab.
3. Click the **AutoArchive** button to display the AutoArchive options (see Figure 21.1).

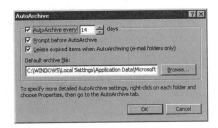

Figure 21.1 Specify options for automatically archiving items into files.

4. Choose from the following check box options:

- **AutoArchive Every x Days**—Enter a number for how often (in days) you want Outlook to automatically archive items. If you enter 14, for example, when you start Outlook on the fourteenth day, it automatically archives the contents of your folders into an archive file.

- **Prompt Before AutoArchive**—If you check this, Outlook displays a dialog box each time it is about to perform the AutoArchive; you can click **OK** or **Cancel** to continue or stop the operation.

- **Delete Expired Items When AutoArchiving**—(Email Folders Only) Check this box to have Outlook delete messages from the Inbox after archiving them.

5. In the Default Archive File text box, enter a path to where you want to save the file, and name it (if you don't want to use the default).

6. Click **OK** to close the AutoArchive dialog box. Click **OK** to close the Options dialog box.

In addition to setting the AutoArchive options in the AutoArchive dialog box, you can set additional AutoArchive options for each folder—Inbox, Tasks, Calendar, and so on. To set an individual folder's AutoArchive options, follow these steps:

1. Right-click the folder in the Outlook Bar to display the shortcut menu.

2. Choose **Properties**. The item's Properties dialog box appears.

3. Choose the **AutoArchive** tab. Figure 21.2 shows the Inbox's Auto-Archive tab.

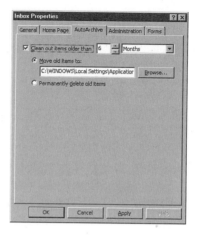

Figure 21.2 Set AutoArchive options for individual folders.

4. Set the options you want in the dialog box. You can change the length of time you want the archived files to be saved before they're deleted or saved to another file, and you can enter a path and filename for the second save.

5. Click **OK** to close the dialog box.

Archiving Manually

You can choose to archive one or two folders or all folders manually whenever you're ready to create an archive file. If you choose to do it yourself, you control exactly how and when archives are created.

To create an archive, follow these steps:

1. Choose **File**, then select **Archive**. The **Archive** dialog box appears (see Figure 21.3).

2. Choose one of the following options:

- **Archive All Folders According to Their AutoArchive Settings**—Use this option to save archives of each folder, using the settings you select in the AutoArchive tab of the folder's Properties dialog box.

- **Archive This Folder and All Subfolders**—Select this option to archive the selected folder.

Figure 21.3   Enter settings for manual archiving.

3. Enter a date in the Archive Items Older Than text box, or select a date from the drop-down calendar.

4. In the Archive File text box, enter a path and filename with which to save the file.

5. Click **OK** to archive the selected folder(s).

Retrieving Archived Files

You can retrieve an archived file by importing it. When you retrieve an archived file, it becomes a part of your Outlook folder just as it was before you archived it. Outlook Archived files (.pst files) are saved in a special format and can only be opened using Outlook.

To retrieve an archived file, follow these steps:

1. Choose **File**, then select **Import and Export**. The Import and Export Wizard dialog box appears.

2. Choose **Import from Another File or Program** and then click **Next**.

3. On the Import a File screen, select **Personal Folders File (*.PST)** and click the **Next** button.

4. In the Import Personal Folders dialog box, enter the path and the filename of the archived file. Select any one of the following options, and then click the **Next** button:

   - **Replace Duplicates with Items Imported**—To overwrite any copies of the data with imported items.

   - **Allow Duplicates to Be Created**—To create duplicates of the items instead of overwriting them.

   - **Do Not Import Duplicates**—To preserve the originals in the folder instead of overwriting them with items from the archived file.

5. In the Choose Folders dialog box of the Import/Export Wizard, choose the folder into which you want to import. (The default is to import the archived item to the Personal Folders area; you may have created subfolders into which you want to import.)

6. Click the **Finish** button, and Outlook imports the archived files.

Deleting Archived Files

The easiest way to delete archived files is by using Windows Explorer. However, you can also delete files from the Find Files and Folders dialog box or from My Computer (both part of Windows).

To delete an archived file, follow these steps:

1. Open Windows Explorer and locate the files. Archived files are saved with a .PST extension in the My Documents folder (by default) or any other folder you designate.

2. Open the folder containing the files and select the file(s) you want to delete.

3. Press the **Delete** key, or drag the file(s) to the Recycle Bin.

4. Empty the Recycle Bin by right-clicking the Bin and choosing **Empty Recycle Bin**.

5. Close the Explorer by clicking the **Close** (×) button.

In this lesson, you learned to use AutoArchive and to manually archive files, retrieve archived files, and delete archived files. In the next lesson, you learn to customize Outlook.

Customizing Outlook

In this lesson, you learn to set email, calendar, and other options in Outlook.

Setting Outlook Options

You can set all of Outlook's options by using the Options dialog box. (To open the Options dialog box, select **Tools**, then choose **Options**.) The number of tabs on this dialog box depends on the installation option that you chose when you installed Outlook (Internet E-mail Only or Corporate Installation). The Options dialog box for the Corporate configuration can have eight tabs: Preferences, Mail Services, Mail Format, Spelling, Security, Other, Delegates, and Internet E-mail (depending on the services you have set up). Each of the tabs controls a specific category of Outlook's settings. For example, the Options tab, shown in Figure 22.1, controls options such as the Deleted Items Folder, AutoArchive, and Preview Pane options.

You will find that the tabs available on the Options dialog box for the Internet Only installation of Outlook reflect the fact that only one kind of email service is available: Internet email. Also because you work with accounts rather than services in the Internet Only installation, the Mail delivery tab allows you to quickly access the Accounts Manager (see Figure 22.2).

Each tab on the Options dialog box has some obvious settings that you can control with option buttons or check boxes. Each tab, however, also contains buttons that allow you to set more specific options.

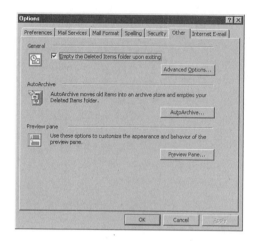

Figure 22.1 The Options dialog box gives you control over all the various features of Outlook 2000.

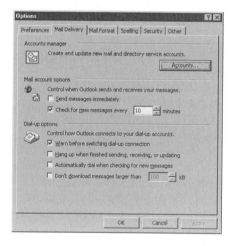

Figure 22.2 The Options dialog box tabs will be different for Outlook when you use the Internet E-Mail Only configuration.

Setting Email Options

Email, Calendar, Tasks, Journal, and Notes options are set on the Preferences tab of the Options dialog box. To open a more specific dialog box related to the features of each of the Outlook item types, click the appropriate button on the Preferences tab (see Figure 22.3).

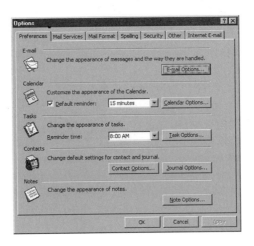

Figure 22.3 Customize E-mail, Calendar, Tasks, Journal, and Notes options on the Preferences tab.

To set email options, click the **E-mail Options** button. The E-mail Options dialog box appears. This dialog box allows you to set items using check boxes and drop-down menus; there are also buttons for Advanced E-mail Options and Tracking Options.

In the Message Handling box of the E-mail Options dialog box, check the boxes of the options you want to activate, such as **Close Original Message on Reply**, **Forward**, and **Save Copies of Messages in Sent Items Folder**.

Two drop-down boxes in the On Replies and Forwards section provide you with options for replying to and forwarding messages. You can choose whether you want to include the original message text with replies and forwards, or attach the original message as an attached file.

You can also set Advanced E-mail options and Tracking options in this dialog box. When you click the **Advanced E-mail Options** button, the Advanced E-mail Options dialog box appears. This dialog box allows you to control how unsent messages are handled, what happens when new mail arrives, and the importance level of new messages that you send. When you've completed setting options in this dialog box, click **OK**.

The Tracking Options button in the E-mail Options dialog box opens the Tracking Options dialog box. In this box you can set options that notify you when email you send is received and when that email is read. After setting options in this dialog box, click **OK**. Click **OK** again, to close the E-mail Options dialog box.

Setting Calendar Options

If you work during unusual days or hours, you can change your default Calendar workweek in the Calendar Options dialog box. Suppose your workweek runs from Tuesday through Saturday, and your workday is from 4 a.m. to 12 noon. You can make changes to the Calendar so that it reflects your actual workweek. You can also set your time zone and add holidays to your calendar. To make changes to the Calendar Options, open the Calendar Options dialog box: Click the **Calendar Options** button on the Preferences tab of the Options dialog box (see Figure 22.4).

In the Calendar Working Week area, set your starting and ending time (the default is 8 a.m. to 5 p.m.).

To set the time zone for your area, click the **Time Zone** button, and then choose the zone that describes your location.

To add holidays to your calendar, click the **Add Holidays** button. Then check the box representing your country (US is the default) and click **OK**. Outlook imports the U.S. holidays to the calendar.

When you finish setting the options in this dialog box, return to the Preferences tab by clicking **OK**.

Figure 22.4   Calendar options are set in the Calendar Options dialog box.

The Preferences tab also allows you to set options for your other Outlook items, such as Tasks, the Journal, and Notes.

Setting Mail Services and Mail Format Options

The Mail Services tab allows you to set options that govern which Outlook Profile is loaded when Outlook starts and which of your installed mail services is checked for mail. Click the appropriate check boxes for the services you want checked when new messages, such as faxes and email, are downloaded to your Inbox.

If you installed Outlook for Internet Only, Outlook does not need a profile to load the services that you install such as your Internet email account and Outlook Fax. For more information on the Internet Only and Corporate email installations, see Lesson 2, "Understanding the Outlook Configurations."

 Profile A group of settings that control how your mail is delivered, received, and stored in Outlook and the software used to transfer your mail, such as Microsoft Mail, Microsoft Exchange, or Lotus Notes.

 TIP **Check for New Mail?** The mail types listed in the Check for New Mail On list box are added when you add a new profile to Outlook. You add a profile by choosing **Tools**, then **Services**.

The Mail Format tab in the Options dialog box allows you to choose your Message format, such as HTML, Plain Text, Microsoft Word, and Microsoft Exchange Rich Text. The Mail format that you use dictates the special fonts and WordMail templates that are available to you. Remember, however, that special fonts and templates are of no use to you if those receiving your messages do not have email software that can take advantage of the fonts and formatting. To always send plain text to certain individuals, open their Properties dialog box in the Address book and click the **Send E-mail Using Plain Text only** check box.

 TIP **Applying Your Changes** When you make changes on the tabs of the Options dialog box, you can apply these new options to Outlook by clicking the **Apply** button. The Options dialog box remains open, so you can configure other options.

Other Options Dialog Box Tabs

The Options dialog box also contains additional tabs that control other features associated with Outlook. Each of the tabs is listed here with a description of the settings available:

- The Spelling tab enables you to change settings associated with Outlook's spell checker. You can choose (using check boxes) to have the speller always suggest replacements for misspelled words, always check spelling before sending, and ignore words in uppercase. A drop-down box also allows you to pick the language of the dictionary you want to use to spell check your Outlook items.

- The Internet E-mail tab enables you to set the coding scheme for Internet email attachments. Settings are also available that have Outlook check your network periodically for new email messages. This tab only appears when you use the Outlook Corporate E-Mail configuration.

- The Security tab enables you to set options regarding whether outgoing messages should be encrypted or have digital signatures attached to them. There is also an option that allows you to get a digital ID to use for your outgoing messages.

When you have completed all the changes you want to make to the various Outlook options, click **OK** to close the Options dialog box.

In this lesson, you learned to set email, calendar, and other options in Outlook. In the next lesson, you learn to send and receive faxes using Outlook.

Managing Faxes with Outlook

In this lesson, you learn how to set up and use the Windows Fax and Semantics WinFax services in Outlook to send, receive, and manage faxes.

Setting Up the Fax Service

Microsoft Outlook can be used to send and receive faxes using Microsoft Fax. To use Microsoft Fax when you are in Outlook, you must configure its features so that your computer can send or receive faxes over a modem or a network that uses a network fax server.

Microsoft Fax is only available if you are using the Corporate installation of Microsoft Outlook. If you are using the Internet Only configuration of Outlook, you can send and receive faxes using Symantec's WinFax Starter Edition, which is installed when you install Outlook for Internet Only. For more about this alternative method of sending and receiving faxes, see "Using WinFax" later in this lesson.

Microsoft Fax is not a standard communication component of Windows 98 as it was in Windows 95 (where it was an installation option). After you install Windows 98, you have to manually install the Microsoft Fax software to your computer. Make sure the Windows 98 CD is in your CD-ROM drive. Click the **Start** button and then choose **Run**. In the Run dialog box, type **E:\tools\oldwin95\message\us\awfax** (E: would be the letter of your CD-ROM drive). Then click **OK**. The Microsoft Fax software is installed on your computer.

CAUTION

Installing Microsoft Fax in Windows 98 Make sure you install the Microsoft Fax software before you install Outlook.

Adding the Microsoft Fax Service to Outlook is straightforward if you installed Outlook in the Corporate configuration. New services such as Microsoft Fax are added via the Outlook Tools menu.

1. In the Outlook Window, select the **Tools** menu, and then choose **Services**.

2. The Outlook Services dialog box opens (see Figure 23.1). This dialog box allows you to control the services that are set for the Outlook User Profile currently in use. Click the **Add** button to add a new service.

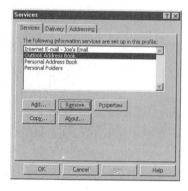

Figure 23.1 Add, remove, and control the properties of the services included in your Outlook User Profile.

3. The Add Service to Profile dialog box appears. All the available services such as Microsoft Fax will be listed in this box.

4. To add Microsoft Fax to the Outlook services, select **Microsoft Fax**, and then click **OK**.

CAUTION

No Fax Service If the Microsoft Fax Service is not available in the Services dialog box, you have installed Outlook in the Internet Only configuration. Uninstall Outlook using the Add/Remove Programs icon in the Windows Control Panel and then reinstall Outlook in the Corporate configuration.

5. A Microsoft Fax message box appears letting you know that you must provide certain information (such as your name, fax number, and modem type) before you can send and receive faxes in Outlook. Click **Yes** to continue.

6. The Microsoft Fax Properties dialog box appears (see Figure 23.2). This dialog box is where you supply the information that Outlook needs to send and receive faxes via Microsoft Fax.

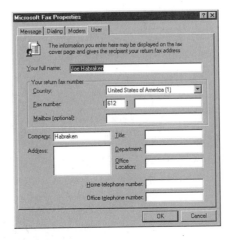

Figure 23.2 Supply Outlook with the information that it needs to send and receive faxes using Microsoft Fax.

The following list describes the tabs on the Microsoft Fax Properties dialog box:

- **User**—Provide information about yourself here. This information includes your name, return fax number, and information regarding the company you work for. Much of the information is optional; however, you must provide your name and a return fax number on this tab.

- **Modem**—The Modem tab provides you with a list of the modems currently installed on your PC. Select the modem you want to use to send and receive your faxes.

- **Dialing**—The Dialing tab allows you to set the number of retries the modem will make when dialing a fax number. This tab also gives you access to other dialing properties, such as dialing to access an outside line or using a calling card when dialing.

- **Message**—The Message tab is where you select the time to send the fax, the type of cover page to use when sending, and the page format used for the message.

You must at least fill out the information on the **User** tab and select a modem to send and receive your faxes on the **Modem** tab. After you have done this, click **OK**. The Microsoft Fax service appears in your Services dialog box. Click **OK** to close it.

You might get a message that the new service you added (Microsoft Fax) will not operate until the next time you start Outlook. If this is the case, close Outlook and restart the program so that the Fax service is available.

TIP **Re-open Properties** If you closed the Microsoft Fax Properties box after you added the Fax service to Outlook, you can re-open the properties box: Select **Tools**, **Microsoft Fax Tools**, and **Options**.

Sending Faxes

After you've configured Microsoft Fax, you are ready to send faxes using Microsoft Outlook. New faxes are launched via the Outlook Compose menu. To create and send a new fax, follow these steps:

1. Select the **Actions** menu, and then choose **New Fax**. The Compose New Fax Wizard appears.

2. You must specify your dialing location (which is usually the default setting unless you are using a portable computer) using the drop-down box in the wizard window. Then click **Next** to continue.

3. Enter the information that pertains to the person (or persons) you want to send the fax to; type the person's name in the **To** box. Select the country that you are sending the fax to using the **Country** drop-down box. Type the fax number in the **Fax #** box (see Figure 23.3).

TIP **Use your Outlook Address Book or Contacts List** Make sure the person's address book entry includes a fax number. Click the **Address Book** button and then double-click to choose the name or names to add to the list.

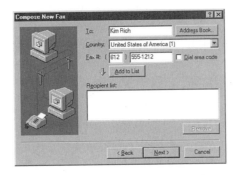

Figure 23.3   Enter the name and fax number of the recipient and then click
Add to List.

4. After completing the entries, click **Add to List**. The person's name is added
   to the Recipient List box. Repeat the procedure for any others you want to
   send the fax to, and then click **Next**.

5. Select a cover page style for your fax; click the appropriate option button
   to select your fax cover page style. If you don't want a fax cover page, click
   the **No Option** button.

6. On the next screen, type the subject of your fax in the **Subject** box. If you
   want to include a note on the cover sheet, type it in the **Note** box.

7. After you've completed your note, click the **Next** button to continue. The
   next screen is where you designate the body of your fax message. You can
   attach a document, spreadsheet, or other file type to a fax in Outlook. The
   added file will serve as the pages of the fax and be included with your fax
   cover page.

8. Click **Add File** to browse your hard drive and select the file. Click **Open** to
   add the file to the fax and return to the Fax Wizard. Click **Next** to continue.

9. You've completed the fax composition and are ready to send the fax; click
   Finish. The Microsoft Fax Status box appears.

10. The fax is formatted to be sent and the phone number you specified is
    dialed. After a connection is made, your fax is sent and the Fax Status
    window appears, keeping you apprised of the status of the sending fax.
    When the fax is sent, the Status window will disappear.

CAUTION

If Your Fax Is Aborted   Microsoft Fax may not be accessing the modem correctly. Select **Help** and **Microsoft Help Topics**. Under **Contents**, double-click the **Troubleshooting** icon. The help system walks you through your fax and modem setup to try and help you fix any problems.

Receiving and Processing Faxes

The faxes that you receive will eventually be available in the Outlook Inbox. How Microsoft Fax answers the call for an incoming fax depends on whether you are using a modem with its own line or if you share one line between your phone and modem.

If your modem has its own line, you can set it to automatically answer incoming fax calls:

1. Click **Tools**, then point at **Microsoft Fax Tools**; click **Options** to open to Microsoft Fax Properties box. Select the **Modem** tab.

2. To set the fax properties of the modem, click **Properties**. The Fax Modem Properties box appears.

3. To set the answer mode to automatic, click the **Answer After** option button and then use the arrows to set the actual number of rings that will take place before the modem answers the call.

4. You can also set the modem speaker volume in this box by dragging the speaker volume switch. After setting your answer options and speaker volume, click **OK**. You are returned to the Microsoft Fax Options box. Click **OK** to close it.

To receive a fax manually, you need to know that the incoming call on your phone line is a fax rather than voice call. You should verify with the sender of the fax when they plan on sending the fax to you, so you can manually answer the fax call using Microsoft Fax.

When you open Microsoft Outlook, a fax machine icon is placed on the right side of the Windows taskbar. This icon supplies you with the tool to answer your fax calls.

1. Click the fax machine icon on the taskbar. The Microsoft Fax Status box opens.

2. When your telephone rings, click the **Answer Now** button on the Microsoft Fax Status box.

3. Microsoft Fax directs your modem to answer the incoming call. The Idle designator on the Microsoft Fax Status box changes to "Answering Call."

4. After the connection is established, the Status box displays the status of each page of the fax as it is received.

5. When the fax transmission is complete, the Fax Status box returns to "idle." Click the **Close** button to close the Status window.

After you've received a fax, either by having your modem answer the call automatically, or by answering the call manually, you need to download the received fax to Microsoft Outlook. After the fax is in the Outlook Inbox, you can read it, print it, or move it to another Inbox folder.

To download the new fax to the Outlook inbox, select the Outlook **Tools** menu, then select **Send and Receive**. New faxes and email are downloaded into your Inbox.

Reading Faxes

Opening a new fax in the Outlook Inbox is handled in the same way that you read the other items that appear in your Inbox, such as your new email messages. In the Outlook Inbox, double-click the fax message you want to read. A fax viewer window opens, displaying the fax, as shown in Figure 23.4.

The Fax Viewer enables you to zoom in (or out) on the fax to get a better view. Click the **Zoom In** button on the viewer toolbar. Zoom in on the fax until you can easily read the text.

If you want a hard copy of your fax, click the **Print** button. The file version of the fax will be formatted into a facsimile of the original sent document by the Viewer and your printer.

When you have completed viewing or printing your fax, close the Fax Viewer. You are returned to the Outlook Inbox.

You can delete, move, or copy faxes in your Inbox just as you would email messages.

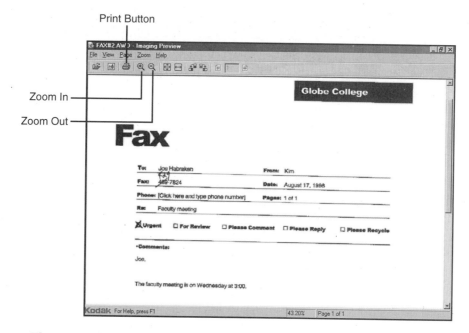

Print Button

Zoom In

Zoom Out

Figure 23.4 The Fax Viewer enables you to read the faxes that you receive.

Using WinFax

When you install Outlook using the Internet E-mail Only option, you can still send and receive faxes using WinFax. This fax utility is installed as one of the Internet accounts found in the Accounts dialog box.

To view the WinFax account, select the **Tools** menu, and then select **Accounts**. Your current email account and the WinFax account appear in the Internet Accounts dialog box, as shown in Figure 23.5.

You should not tamper with any of the Properties settings for the WinFax account; these are set for you during the Outlook installation. Click the **Close** button to close the Internet Accounts dialog box.

To set the options for the WinFax account, open the **Tools** menu, and then choose **Options**. Select the **Fax** tab in the Options dialog box (see Figure 23.6). The Fax tab allows you to set your fax number, select a cover page for the faxes you send using WinFax, and select the modem you will use to send and receive your faxes.

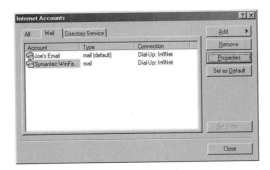

Figure 23.5 Set the parameters for the WinFax service.

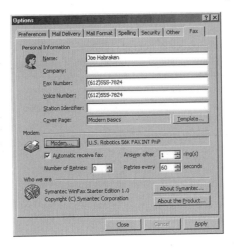

Figure 23.6 Set the options for your WinFax account on the Fax tab of the Options dialog box.

If a modem does not appear in the Modem box on the Fax tab, you need to click the **Modem** button. The Modem Properties dialog box appears. If a modem is available in this dialog box, click the modem and select **Properties**. The WinFax Wizard sets up your modem for the WinFax account. If a modem does not appear in the Modem Properties dialog box, select **Add** and a search is made to find your modem. After the modem is found, click the **Properties** button and the WinFax Wizard sets up your modem for use with the fax account.

Before closing the Fax options, you may want to click the **Automatic Receive Fax** check box on the dialog box. This sets WinFax to automatically answer your phone using the modem after the number of rings you specify. After you have set the options for the fax account, click the **OK** button.

Sending a fax with the WinFax account is a little different from sending a fax with Microsoft Fax. To send a fax using WinFax, follow these steps:

1. Select **File**, point at **New**, and then select **Fax Message**. The new Fax message appears in a message window (see Figure 23.7).

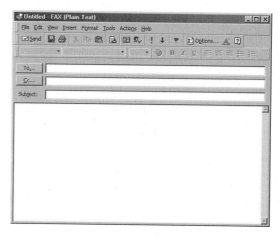

Figure 23.7 The blank fax message appears.

2. Select a recipient for the fax by clicking the **To** button and then selecting the recipient from your Address Book or Contact folder. The selected contact must have a fax number entered in the contact information, so WinFax knows the appropriate fax number for the recipient.

3. After selecting the recipient, enter the Subject and text for the fax.

4. Click the **Send** button and your fax is sent to the recipient.

You will find that WinFax does not have the number of bells and whistles that Microsoft Fax possesses. So when your fax is sent, it appears that you are sending typical email. A separate Fax Status window will not appear on the Windows desktop.

In this lesson, you learned how to set up the Outlook Fax service and send and receive faxes using Microsoft Fax and WinFax. In the next lesson, you learn how to take advantage of Internet services like newsgroups from within Outlook.

Outlook and the Internet

24

In this lesson, you learn about Outlook and its connection to the Internet, using Outlook Express Newsreader, Microsoft Internet Explorer, and Microsoft NetMeeting. You also learn how to use Net Folders.

Using Newsgroups

Microsoft Outlook not only provides all the tools you need to manage your messages, contacts, and calendar, it also provides you with an easy connection to Internet services, such as newsgroups and the World Wide Web. Outlook even provides you with the ability to conduct real-time meetings over the Internet.

Newsgroups are a large collection of discussion groups held on news servers around the world. A particular newsgroup is much like a bulletin board; you can read messages posted there and post your own. Newsgroups cover information from current events to software, hobbies, pets, and other personal interests.

 Newsgroup An Internet online bulletin board that allows users to post and read messages. Newsgroups are part of Usenet, which is a consortium of Internet news servers that enable users (such as yourself) to download and post messages.

To access Internet newsgroups and read or reply to the postings there, you need a newsreader. When you install Microsoft Outlook, the Microsoft Outlook Express newsreader software is also installed.

Setting Up the Newsreader

You can access newsgroups from Outlook by starting the Outlook Express newsreader. First make sure that you are connected to the Internet through your corporate network or by your dial-up connection to your Internet service provider. After you've connected, take the following steps to start the Outlook Express Newsreader and download newsgroup postings.

1. In the Outlook window, click the **Go** menu, and then click **News**. The Outlook Express Newsreader opens.

2. The first time you use the Newsreader, it runs the Internet Connection Wizard, which leads you through the process of setting up your news server and creating a newsgroup account for yourself. The first screen asks you to type the name you will use when you post messages to your news server. After typing a name, click **Next**.

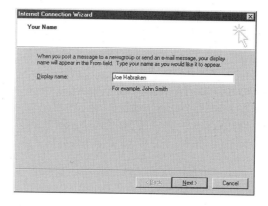

Figure 24.1   The Internet Connection Wizard walks you through setting up your news server.

3. The next screen asks you to provide your email address. Click **Next** after doing so.

4. You must provide the name of your news server. This name should be provided to you by your network administrator or Internet service provider. Click **Next** after entering the server name (it will be something like news.company.com).

5. Type a friendly name for the new account. The friendly name that you choose for your new account appears on your Outlook Express folder list and can be used to open the newsgroups that you subscribe to. This account name differs from the name that you must choose in step 2, which actually

identifies the postings that you place on the news server. This name is seen by everyone who looks at the posts in the newsgroup. You should choose your newsgroup posting name carefully, so you don't inadvertently offend anyone when you post or have your posts be taken less seriously than you intended. Type a name and then click **Next**.

6. Select the type of connection you will use to access the Internet: your phone line, Local Area Network, or a manual connection. Select the connection type, and then click **Next**.

7. The last screen appears, letting you know you've completed the process. Click **Finish**.

When you complete the account creation process, a message box appears telling you that the newsgroups available on your news server will be downloaded. After the newsgroups are downloaded, the Newsgroup Subscriptions dialog box for the news account appears (see Figure 24.2). The Newsgroup Subscriptions dialog box allows you to "subscribe" to a particular newsgroup by clicking the newsgroup name. Then click the **Subscribe** button. This places the newsgroup on the Subscribed tab of the Subscription Manager, making it easier for you to find and access a particular newsgroup.

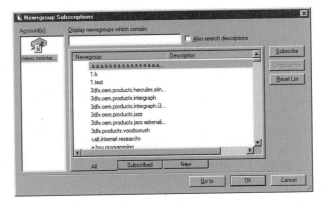

Figure 24.2 Subscribe to the newsgroups using the Subscriptions dialog box.

 TIP **Find Your Newsgroups** The Find box at the top of the Subscription Manager dialog box allows you to quickly find newsgroups that contain a particular keyword. Type the word in the **Find** box and then click **Find** to search for all the newsgroups that contain your search word in their name.

After subscribing to the newsgroups you want to read, click the **OK** button. You return to the Outlook Express window (see Figure 24.3). A list of the groups you subscribed to appears in the News window on the right side of the Outlook Express Window.

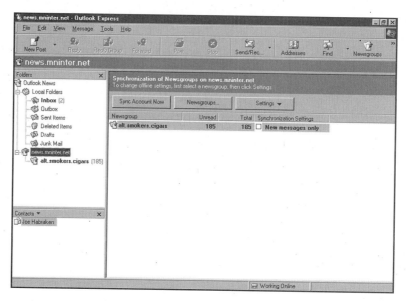

Figure 24.3   Read and post messages in Internet newsgroups.

Reading Newsgroup Postings

After you have set up an account and downloaded and subscribed to newsgroups, you are ready to read and post messages. If you have just subscribed to your newsgroups for the first time and have closed the Newsgroup Subscriptions dialog box, just double-click any of your subscribed groups to read the postings.

In the future when you enter the Outlook Express window (via Outlook and the View menu) click **Read News** on the main Outlook Express window in the Newsgroups area of the window. Your newsgroups will appear as shown in Figure 24.3. Double-click any of your subscribed newsgroups to download and view the postings. Messages in the newsgroup appear in the Message pane. To read a particular message, click the message. The message text appears in the preview pane. You can also open a separate message window by double-clicking a particular posting (see Figure 24.4).

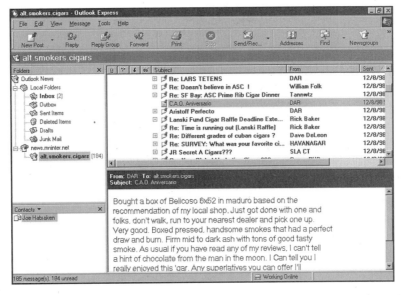

Figure 24.4 Select a message in the Newsgroup window to read it in the preview pane.

Posting to Newsgroups

To post your own message to a newsgroup, follow a procedure that is similar to sending new email messages using Outlook itself:

1. In the Outlook Express window, select the newsgroup to which you want to post.

2. Click the **New Post** button on the Outlook Express toolbar. A new message window opens. Type a subject for the message in the **Subject** box. Type the message itself in the message pane of the new message window. After you've completed your message, click the **Post** button.

3. A message window appears telling you that your new message has been posted but may not immediately appear with the messages already in the newsgroup.

When you have completed reading and sending newsgroup messages, you can close the Outlook Express Newsreader. Click the Outlook Express **Close** (×) button. You are returned to the Outlook 98 window.

When you do find a post that you want to respond to, or you want to send email to the individual who made the post, select the post message in the Outlook Express message window. Then either click the **Reply to Group** button (this sends a post in response to the selected post), or the **Reply to Author** button to send email to the author of the post.

Posting Etiquette

When you post to newsgroups, you should follow the same rules of politeness that you use when you converse with someone in person or send email to colleagues and friends. Do not type in all caps; this is considered shouting. Remember that humor and sarcasm are not always apparent in written communication. Be as straightforward and clear as you can in your postings. An extremely annoying post can lead to *flaming*, or a barrage of angry and unsolicited email.

Unsubscribing from Newsgroups

If you want to unsubscribe from a newsgroup, click the **Newsgroup** button on the Outlook Express toolbar. In the Newsgroup Subscriptions dialog box select the **Subscribed** tab. To remove a group from your subscription list, select the newsgroup and then click the **Unsubscribe** button.

Launching Internet Explorer

You can also launch Microsoft Internet Explorer 5 from the Outlook window. This enables you to quickly browse the World Wide Web. Again, before launching Internet Explorer, you must be connected to the Internet either by your company network or by a dial-up connection to your Internet service provider.

CAUTION

Launching Other Web Browsers If you use another Web browser, such as Netscape Navigator, you will not be able to launch it directly from Outlook. Create a shortcut for your browser on the desktop so that you can launch it quickly when you need it.

1. To start Internet Explorer, click the **Go** menu, and then click **Web Browser**. The Internet Explorer window opens (see Figure 24.5).

2. You can browse the Web using all the features of Internet Explorer. Use links on your home page to move to other Web pages, or click the **Search** button to find other sites of interest.

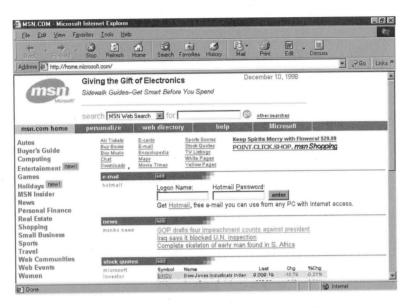

Figure 24.5 Internet Explorer provides you with all the capabilities you need to take advantage of the World Wide Web.

TIP **Launching Internet Explorer from Outlook Messages** You can also launch Internet Explorer from Outlook messages that contain Web page references. Click the Web address in the message (such as `http://www.mcp.com`), to open the designated Web page.

When you have completed your use of Internet Explorer, click the **Close** (×) button in the Explorer window. You are returned to the Outlook 98 window.

Launching Microsoft NetMeeting

Another software package that takes advantage of communication on the Internet and that can be launched from Outlook is Microsoft NetMeeting. Microsoft NetMeeting allows real-time voice and video communication over the Internet. This allows you to conduct "live" meetings without leaving your office.

To start NetMeeting from Outlook, follow these steps:

1. Click **Go**, and then point at **Internet Call**; click **From Address Book** or **Start NetMeeting**.

2. If you chose the Address Book option, double-click the name of the person you want to hold the meeting with in the Address Book window. NetMeeting starts and connects you to the other participant (skip to step 4). If you clicked Start NetMeeting, you have to select the other participant from the list of users currently logged in to the NetMeeting server, as shown in Figure 24.6.

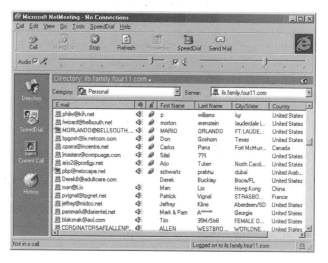

Figure 24.6 The NetMeeting server listing provides a list of all individuals currently logged in to the various Microsoft NetMeeting communication servers.

To Launch a NetMeeting from Outlook Make sure you have entered the contact's email address in the appropriate field. NetMeeting uses the email address to find the person on the NetMeeting Server that the contact is **CAUTION** connected to.

3. Double-click the name of the person you want to meet with in the NetMeeting directory server list.

4. Regardless of which route you used to start the new meeting, the Current Call window opens. At this point you are connected to the other individual and can hold your meeting using audio and video (if the appropriate

hardware is available on both users' computers). NetMeeting also provides a Chat window that the participants can use to communicate by typing (see Figure 24.7).

5. When you have completed your meeting, close the Current Call window, and then close the NetMeeting window. You are returned to the Outlook 98 window.

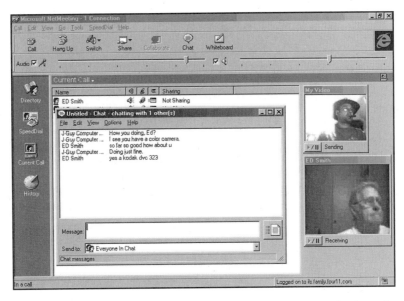

Figure 24.7 Communicate with others using audio, video, or your keyboard.

 TIP **To Launch a NetMeeting from the Contacts Folder** Open a Contact form for a particular contact. Click the **Actions** menu, and then click **Call Using NetMeeting**. NetMeeting launches, and you are connected to the appropriate meeting server and then to your contact.

Working with Net Folders

Outlook provides a great deal of team computing power when you use it in a corporate environment. You can share folders and create new folders that are available to everyone who has an account and the appropriate rights on a network. Outlook provides a great deal of flexibility for sharing information when you use it in the Corporate installation option and connect to a network using Microsoft Exchange Server.

Outlook does not leave users out in the cold that use the Internet E-mail installation configuration and connect to the Internet using a service provider, however. You can share Contact and Calendar information and create shared folders that can be accessed over the Internet by other users. These folders are called Net Folders.

You can publish a Net Folder or subscribe to a Net Folder that has been published by someone else. Net Folders can be based on any of the folders in Outlook except for your Inbox or Outbox.

To create a Net Folder based on an Outlook item such as your Calendar, follow these steps:

1. Select the **File** menu, and then select **Share**. Choose **Calendar** on the cascading menu that appears (or any of the other items listed).

2. The Net Folder Wizard appears. The opening screen reads "Sharing Your Calendar" (or names any other folder item you selected to share). To begin the sharing process, click the **Next** button.

3. Select contacts from your personal address book or Outlook Contacts list that you will share the file with. Select a name on the left side of the dialog box and then click the **To** button to include that person in the Subscriber Database.

4. When you have completed your selection of subscribers, click **OK**. The next Net Folder Wizard screen shows a list of the subscribers for the Net Folder. Click **Next** to continue.

5. Enter a description for the shared folder, such as "This is Joe's Calendar" or some other name that will easily identify the shared folder. Click **Next** to move to the final screen in the Net Folder creation process and then click **Finish**.

You now have a shared folder that appears in your Outlook folder list. When you complete the Net Folder creation process using the Net Folder Wizard, invitations are automatically sent out to all the email addresses that appeared in the Subscribers list you created. If a subscriber accepts the invitation to share your new Net Folder, the new folder will also appear on their list of Outlook folders.

You can also share Net Folders created by others by accepting an invitation to share a Net Folder; you receive the invitation as an email message in your Inbox. Click the **Accept** button at the bottom of the invitation and a copy of the Net Folder is placed in your folder list.

In this lesson, you learned how to read newsgroup postings using the Microsoft Outlook Express newsreader. You learned to launch Internet Explorer from the Outlook window and to launch meetings on the Internet using Microsoft NetMeeting. You also learned how to create and share a Net Folder. In the next lesson, you learn to start Microsoft Publisher and become familiar with the Publisher application window.

Publisher

Getting Started with Publisher

In this lesson, you learn how to start Publisher, and you learn how to use common tools such as the menus, toolbars, and dialog boxes. You also become familiar with the process of planning a new publication and preview the three options for creating a publication.

Starting Publisher

Publisher makes it easy for you to create a variety of publication types. These publications can range from business cards to tri-fold brochures to World Wide Web pages. However, before you can take advantage of Publisher's sophisticated but easy-to-use tools for creating great-looking publications, you need to open the Publisher application window.

To start the Publisher program, follow these steps:

1. From the Windows Desktop, click **Start**, then point at **Programs**. The Programs menu appears (see Figure 1.1).

2. Select **Publisher**. The Publisher program window appears on the desktop.

You will find that the Publisher window looks and feels like other Office applications such as Microsoft Word or Excel. These applications usually present you with a blank workspace, such as a blank document or blank worksheet, to begin working in; however, Publisher opens the Publisher Catalog, which provides you with three ways of creating new publications: Publications by Wizard, Publications by Design, and Blank Publications. These three avenues to creating your publications are discussed in the next section of this lesson.

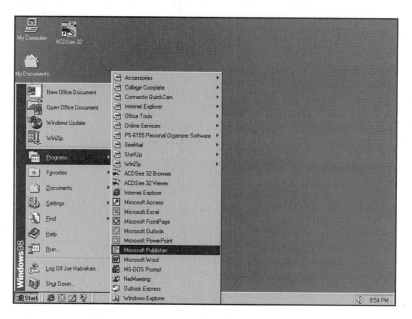

Figure 1.1 Open the Programs menu and select Publisher to start the application.

Whichever route you take to create your new publication, you will eventually find yourself in the Publisher application window. For the moment, you might want to close the Catalog (click the **Close** (×) button in the upper-right corner of the Catalog window) and take a look at the geography of the Publisher window itself. This window is where your publication appears. Figure 1.2 shows the various parts of the Publisher window, which currently holds a blank publication.

You will notice that the largest area of the window is devoted to your publication. All the other areas, such as the menu bar, the toolbars, the Quick Publication Wizard, and the status bar, either provide a fast way to access the various commands and features that you use in Publisher, or they supply you with information concerning your publication, such as what page you are on and where the mouse pointer is currently located on the publication page.

Table 1.1 describes the elements you see in the Publisher application window.

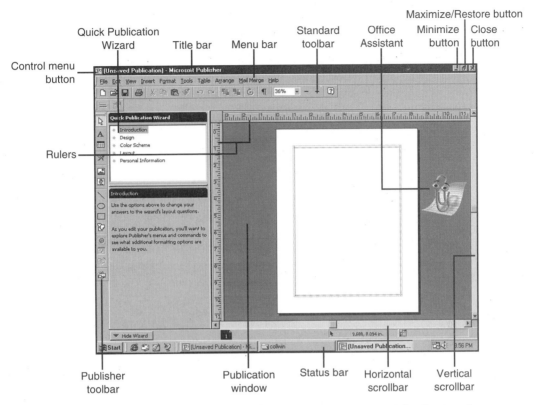

Figure 1.2   The Publisher window is where you create your publications and access Publisher's tools and commands.

Table 1.1   Elements of the Publisher Window

Element	Description
Title bar	Includes the name of the application and current document, and the Minimize, Maximize/Restore, and Close buttons.
Control menu button	Opens the Control menu, which provides such commands as Move, Size, Minimize, and Close.
Minimize button	Reduces the Publisher window to a button on the taskbar; to restore the window to its original size, click the button on the taskbar.

continues

Table 1.1   Continued

Element	Description
Maximize/Restore button	Enlarges the Publisher window to cover the Windows desktop. When the window is maximized, the Maximize button changes to a Restore button that you can click to return the window to its previous size.
Close (×) button	Closes the Publisher program.
Menu bar	Contains menus of commands you can use to perform tasks in the program.
Standard toolbar	Includes icons that serve as shortcuts for common commands, such as Save, Print, and Spelling.
Publisher toolbar	Contains icons that can be used to draw objects and add pictures and text frames to your publications.
Status bar	Displays information about the current page number and the mouse pointer's position on the horizontal and vertical ruler. Information is also provided on the status bar concerning the height and width of an object that you draw on the publication page.
Publication window	This is where you create and enhance your publication.
Scrollbars	The horizontal scrollbar is used to scroll your view of the current document from left to right or vice versa. The vertical scrollbar is used to scroll up and down through the current document.
Quick Publication Wizard	Makes it easy for you to change major properties of the current publication, such as the design, color scheme, or page size and layout.
Office Assistant	The Office Assistant provides you with the help you need to get the most out of Publisher. Click the Assistant when you need help.

Deciding How to Create a New Publication

As previously mentioned, when you first open the Publisher window, the Publisher Catalog appears (see Figure 1.3). The Catalog window provides you with three tabs that supply you with three ways to create a new publication:

- **Publications by Wizard**—The Publication Wizard provides you with a step-by-step process to creating a new publication. The wizard asks you questions and the new publication is built based on your answers. A large number of wizard-based publications are available in a series of publication categories. For instance, when you click **Invitations** in the Wizards pane of the Catalog window, you are provided with thumbnail previews of several invitation types. You select the particular invitation type that you wish to create and then click the **Start Wizard** button to begin the publication creation process. Creating a publication using a wizard is discussed in detail in Lesson 2, "Creating a New Publication."

- **Publications by Design**—Design sets enable you to create a family of publications that have the same look. Each master design set uses a particular set of design elements and colors that are consistent across all the publications in the set. For instance, you might want to create letterhead, business cards, and invoices that all have the same design look for your small business. You can create these publications by choosing a particular design set in the Design Sets pane and then selecting the particular publication (such as the business cards) in the Master Sets window. After you select a particular publication type, you then start the publication creation process by clicking the **Start Wizard** button. Using and understanding design sets is discussed in Lesson 3, "Using Design Sets and Templates."

- **Blank Publications**—A third possibility for creating your new publication is to create your new publication from scratch. However, you will find that Publisher doesn't totally abandon you when you take this approach. The Blank Publications tab actually provides a number of blank templates that help you with the initial layout and page orientation of the new publication. For instance, if you wish to create a side-fold card, you can select the side-fold card template on the Blank Publications tab. After you select a particular template, you then click the **Create** button. The techniques used to create blank publications are discussed in many of the lessons in this book. These techniques also apply to editing existing publications.

 TIP   **Use the File Menu to Open the Catalog**   If you inadvertently close the Catalog, select the **File** menu, then select **New** to reopen it.

As far as selecting a route for creating your new publication, that will depend on your experience with Publisher and the particular design aspects of your publication. The Publication Wizard and the design sets provide you with a lot of help as you initially design your publication; in both cases, this help is provided by a wizard. Wizard-based publications not only help you select the layout and color aspects of your publication, they also create placeholder objects in your new publication that you can replace with your own pictures or design elements.

For the new user, the wizards offer a quick and easy way to create a new publication. However, if you find that you want to create a publication in which you select all the aspects of the publication design, you might find that creating a publication from scratch is easier than creating a publication using a wizard, and then modifying that wizard-based publication to meet your needs. However, you might not find that creating publications from scratch is very useful until you have a good understanding of all the Publisher tools and some basic design principles.

How you create your publication will also relate to the plan you have formulated regarding a particular publication or set of publications. For some tips on planning your publications, see Lesson 2.

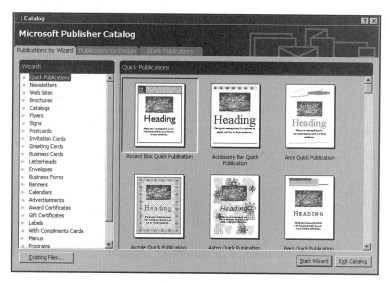

Figure 1.3 The Publisher Catalog window provides you with three ways to create your new publication.

Using Menus and Toolbars

After you've begun a publication using either the Publication Wizard, the design sets, or by starting your new publication from scratch, you work with the various commands and features that enable you to edit and enhance the publication. Publisher provides you with several ways to access the commands and features you use as you work on your publications. You can access these commands using the menus on the menu bar and the buttons on the toolbars that Publisher supplies.

You can also access a number of Publisher commands using shortcut menus. These menus are accessed by right-clicking a particular document element. The shortcut menu appears with a list of commands related to the item you are currently working on, such as a word or paragraph.

The Publisher Menu Bar

The Publisher menu bar gives you access to all the commands and features that Publisher provides. Like all Windows applications, Publisher's menus are found below the title bar and are activated by clicking a particular menu choice. The menu then opens, providing you with a set of command choices.

Publisher 2000 (and the other Office 2000 applications) has adopted a new menu system that provides the capability to quickly access the commands that you use most often. When you first choose a particular menu, you will find a short list of menu commands, with the most recently used commands listed first. As you use commands, Publisher adds them to the menu list.

To access a particular menu, follow these steps:

1. Select the menu by clicking its title (such as **Insert**), as shown in Figure 1.4. The most recently used commands appear; wait just a moment for all the commands on a particular menu to appear.
2. Select the command on the menu that invokes a particular feature (such as **Object**, as shown in Figure 1.4).

 TIP **Full Menus at Once**   If you want to view all the commands available for the menu system, click the **Tools** menu, click **Options**, and then click the **General** tab on the Options dialog box. To show all the commands on the menus, clear the **Menus Show Recently Used Commands First** check box. This book covers the various features of Publisher with the Personalized menus turned off.

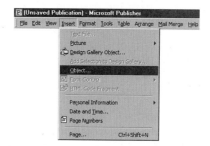

Figure 1.4   Select a menu to view, and then select a Publisher command from the menu.

You will find that a number of the commands found on the menu are followed by an ellipsis (…). When one of these commands is selected, a dialog box opens that requires you to provide Publisher with additional information before the particular feature or command can be used. More information about working with dialog boxes is found later in this lesson.

Some of the menus also contain a submenu or cascading menu that you use to make your choices. The menu commands that produce a submenu are indicated by an arrow to the right of the menu choice. In cases where a submenu is present, you point at the command (marked with the arrow) on the main menu to open the submenu.

The menu system itself provides you with a logical grouping of the Publisher commands and features. For instance, commands related to files, such as opening, saving, and printing, are all found on the File menu.

 TIP   **Activating Menus with the Keyboard**   You can also activate a particular menu by holding down the **Alt** key and then pressing the keyboard key that matches the underscored letter in the menu's name. This underscored letter is called the hotkey. For instance, to activate the File menu in Publisher, you would press **Alt+F**.

Shortcut Menus

A fast way to access commands that are related to a particular document element is to hover the mouse pointer over a particular publication object, and then right-click. This opens a shortcut menu that contains commands related to the particular object you are working with.

Publisher Object Any element found in a publication, such as text, a graphic, a hyperlink, or other inserted item. Objects residing in frames are discussed in Lesson 7, "Enhancing Frames with Borders and Colors."

If you select an object such as clip art, for instance, or a drawn object such as a circle, right-clicking the selected object (see Figure 1.5) opens a shortcut menu with commands such as Cut, Copy, Paste, and other commands related to that particular object.

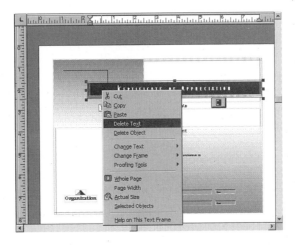

Figure 1.5 Right-click to quickly access Publisher commands using shortcut menus.

Publisher Toolbars

The Publisher toolbars provide you with a very quick and straightforward way of accessing commands and features. After you start a new publication, you are provided with Standard, Formatting, and Publisher toolbars. The Standard and Formatting toolbars reside under the Publisher menu bar. These toolbars provide you with easy access to commands such as Save and Open, or access to formatting features such as bold, underline, and centering.

Where Is the Formatting Toolbar? In Publisher, the Formatting toolbar only appears when you have an object in your publication selected. In addition, the actual Formatting buttons available on the toolbar depend on the type of object selected. For more about objects, see Lessons 9–11.

To access a particular command using a Standard or Formatting toolbar button, click the button. Depending on the command, you see an immediate result in your publication (such as the bolding or centering of a selected text object) or a dialog box appears, requesting additional information from you.

The Publisher toolbar, which provides quick access to drawing tools and other object-related commands, resides along the left edge of the Publication window. Many of the tools on this toolbar are covered in Lesson 11, "Drawing Objects in Publisher."

 TIP   **Finding a Toolbar Button's Purpose**   You can place the mouse pointer on any toolbar button to view a description of that tool's function.

The Publisher toolbars provide you with a quick fix whenever you need to fire off a particular command. Buttons exist for all the commands that are available on the Publisher menu system.

Understanding Dialog Boxes

When you are working with the various commands and features found in Publisher, you will invariably come up against dialog boxes. Dialog boxes are used when Publisher needs more information from you before it can complete a particular command or take advantage of a special feature. Dialog boxes always appear when you select a menu command that is followed by an ellipsis. Dialog boxes also appear when you invoke the same command using the appropriate toolbar button.

The way you provide information in the dialog box can vary. Some dialog boxes require that you type a text entry in a text box. Other dialog boxes provide you with a list of choices on a drop-down menu, but others enable you to make your selection by clicking a particular option button.

Figure 1.6 shows the Font dialog box. This dialog box enables you to make selections using check boxes, drop-down lists, and radio buttons. Some dialog boxes also contain text boxes in which you set an option by typing a particular parameter or value into a box.

Drop-down list

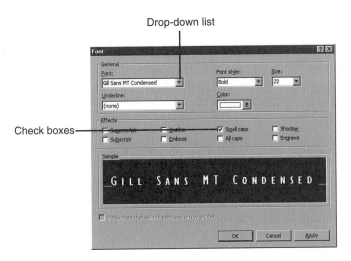

Figure 1.6   Dialog boxes ask you for additional information regarding a particular Publisher command or feature.

Dialog boxes vary, however, and each might use a different way to get you to supply the needed information for a particular Publisher feature. In most cases, when you complete your selections in a dialog box, you click the **OK** button to close the box and complete the command that you originally started with a menu choice or toolbar button.

Exiting Publisher

After you have completed your initial survey of the Publisher application window, or whenever you have completed a particular publication, you will want to exit the software. More than one way exists to close the Publisher window, which is the same as exiting the program.

You can exit Publisher by selecting the **File** menu, then **Exit**. Or you can close Publisher with one click of the mouse by clicking the Publisher **Close** (×) button in the upper-right corner of the application window.

When you do close Publisher, you might be prompted to save any work that you have done in the application window. If you were just experimenting as you read through this lesson, you can click **No**. The current document will not be saved and the Publisher application window closes. All the ins and outs of actually saving your publications are covered in Lesson 2.

In this lesson, you learned how to start Publisher and explore the various parts of the Publisher window. You also learned how to work with the menu system, toolbars, and dialog boxes. Finally, you also learned how to exit the Publisher program. In the next lesson, you learn how to create a new document and save your work.

Creating a New Publication

*In this lesson, you learn how to plan and create a new
publication using the Publication Wizards. You become familiar
with selecting publication color schemes and other attributes and learn
how to use personal information sets to automatically place information into your publications.*

Planning Your Publication

You will find that Publisher makes it very easy for you to create professional-looking publications without a massive amount of effort. However, even though Publisher does a great deal of hand holding during the publication creation process, you might want to take a little time to plan your publication before you invest the effort to create it.

Planning your publication can be as simple as asking a few questions that enable you to get a good feel for the type of publication you actually want to create. The following list provides some of the questions you might ask yourself before you actually dive into the publication creation process.

- **What is the purpose of my publication?**—Is this publication a greeting card for a friend or a publication such as business cards that will help define your small company to your clients? Obviously, the look and feel of the publication will vary a great deal depending on its purpose.

- **Do I have any examples of publications that I really like?**—You've probably had the opportunity to examine a brochure or you've been given a business card that you found eye-catching and unique. Adapting layouts and designs that you like can help you create great-looking publications. You don't have to "reinvent the wheel" every time you start a new publication.

- **Is this publication going to be part of a family of publications?**—Are you creating the first of many publications for your home business or small company? You might want to take advantage of Publisher's design sets to create an entire family of publications (such as business cards, envelopes, and letterhead) that have the same look and feel.

- **Does my publication involve special papers?**—If you are using special papers to create brochures, business cards, or another publication type, make sure that the color scheme and design elements that you choose work well with any pre-existing design elements or colors on the special paper.

- **How will I print the completed publication?**—Printing a publication on an inkjet printer that supplies 300 dots per inch gives you decidedly different results than a publication printed by a service bureau or a print house (a professional printer that prints your publication on high-end printing equipment). You should gauge your use of colors and overlapping design elements based on the quality you will get during the printing process. If you have access only to a grayscale laser printer, designing a publication extremely rich in color would be a waste of your time.

If you at least take the time to consider some of these questions, you might find that your completed publication will better suit your means and needs.

Using the Publication Wizards

A straightforward method of creating a new publication that also provides you with a lot of help is using one of the Publication Wizards. Taking advantage of a wizard not only makes sure that your publication layout and orientation are appropriate for any special papers you are using (such as brochure or business-card paper), but the various wizards also help you with the color schemes and design elements in your publication.

When you first start Publisher, the Publisher Catalog appears. You can immediately start your new publication using a wizard by selecting the **Publications by Wizard** tab.

If you have already been working in Publisher, you can open the Publisher Catalog by following these steps:

1. In the Publisher window, click the **File** menu, then click **New**.

2. If you are asked to save changes to any current publication, click **Yes** to save the changes, or click **No** to clear the publication from the Publisher window. The Publisher Catalog appears.

3. Click the **Publications by Wizard** tab if necessary. The Wizards pane and the publication Preview window appears, as shown in Figure 2.1.

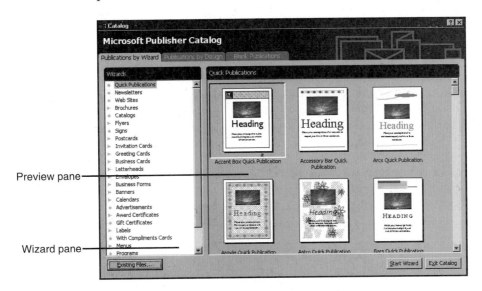

Figure 2.1 The Publications by Wizard tab provides you with access to all the Publication Wizards that Publisher has to offer.

Selecting a Publication Category

After you have access to the Wizards pane, you are provided with a list of different publication types, ranging from Quick Publications (which consist of one-page flyers) to Origami (yes, Publisher can help you design an Origami boat or crane, as well as others). When you click a particular category, a set of thumbnail previews is provided in the Preview window.

It's at this stage of the publication creation process where you select your publication type (in the Wizards pane) and a particular layout in the Preview pane. After you've made your choices, you can actually start the particular wizard that will help you create the chosen publication.

To choose your Publication category and particular publication layout, follow these steps:

1. Select a publication category in the Wizards pane.
2. Select a publication in the Preview window (see Figure 2.2).

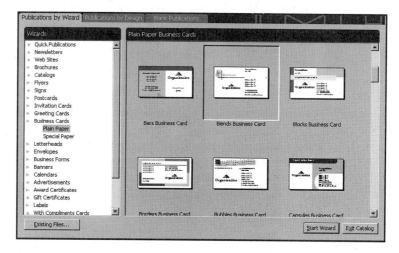

Figure 2.2   Select a publication category, and then select a specific publication to create.

3. After you've picked the publication you wish to create, click the **Start Wizard** button on the lower-right corner of the Preview window.

 TIP   **Double-Click to Start Your New Publication**   You can also select a publication in the Preview window and start its associated wizard by double-clicking the publication preview itself.

The wizard you have started will create the new publication, which appears in the Publication window. Next, the wizard walks you through the publication creation process.

Selecting a Publication Color Scheme

After you've selected a particular publication, the next series of steps are controlled by the specific publication wizard. The wizard poses its question in a pane on the left side of the Publisher window. The changes that you make to the publication appear in the Publication window on the right side of the Publisher application window.

 TIP **The Wizard Comes First** When you choose to use a wizard to create your new publication, you will find that, if you click anywhere else in the Publisher window (on the menus or the publication itself), you get a message that the wizard is available to help you design your publication. You can quickly bypass the wizard questions, if you want, by clicking the **Finish** button in the Wizards pane.

The first time you use one of the Publication Wizards to create a publication, the publication you create will have little or no text entries present in it. This is because information related to you and your company is held in a profile file used by the wizard to fill in certain "blanks" on the publication (such as your name, phone number, and company name). One of the wizard steps is to either create or modify this profile. Supplying profile information is covered in the "Creating a Personal Profile" section later in this lesson.

The first of the publication attributes you are asked to choose is the color scheme for the publication. You have the option of going with the default (that was provided when you selected a particular publication for creation), or you can choose your own scheme.

To begin using the wizard and select a color scheme, follow these steps:

1. The first wizard screen explains how to use the wizard. When you are ready to begin, click the **Next** button.

2. The next wizard screen lists the color schemes available for your publication. You can preview a particular color scheme by clicking it. The scheme takes effect on the current publication (see Figure 2.3).

3. When you have decided on a color scheme, make sure that it is selected and then click **Next** to continue.

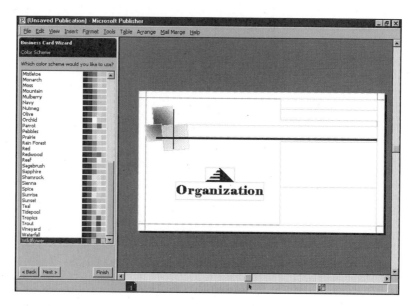

Figure 2.3   Glance through the various color schemes until you find the one you want to use for the current publication.

Selecting Page Orientation

The next step provided by the wizard is where you select the orientation for your new publication. You can choose to create the publication in Portrait (the publication is orientated on paper from top to bottom, and the height of the paper is greater than the width) or you can select Landscape (the height of the paper is less than the width), where the paper has been rotated ninety degrees.

 Portrait or Landscape   If you are dealing with a regular 8 1/2 by 11-inch sheet of paper, Portrait orientation means that the height is 11 inches and the width is 8 1/2 inches. If you use Landscape orientation, the paper is turned on its side, and the height is 8 1/2 inches and the width is 11 inches.

Depending on the type of publication you are creating, the default page orientation usually provides the best layout for the particular publication. For instance, business cards are typically printed on card in a landscape orientation.

To select the orientation for your publication, click either the **Portrait** or the **Landscape** button. When you have completed your selection, click the **Next** button to continue with the publication creation.

Understanding Placeholders

Depending on the type of document you are creating, in the next step the wizard might ask you if you wish to include various placeholders on your publication. These placeholders can be for company logos, pictures, or other graphical elements. For instance, in the case of business cards, the wizard asks you if you want to include a logo placeholder on the business card publication that you are creating (if you have a scanned image or a graphic of your company logo, you replace the placeholder with your image after completing the wizard steps).

When the wizard asks if you want to include a particular type of placeholder in your publication, select **Yes** to include the placeholder, or **No** to remove the placeholder from the publication. If you are asked what type of content you want in the publication, such as pictures and text, choose from the list provided. Then click **Next** to continue.

CAUTION

Wizard Steps Might Vary Depending on the type of publication you are creating, the number of steps provided by the wizard might vary. Read each of the wizard screens carefully as you work with the various publication types.

Creating a Personal Profile

Depending on the type of publication you are creating, the wizard might prompt you to create a personal profile. This profile contains information such as your name, company name, phone number, and other information. For business forms, business cards, and letterhead, you are prompted to create a new personal profile or edit the existing profile during the wizard-based publication creation. Figure 2.4 shows a Business Card Wizard that has created a blank business card because no information is available in the personal profile.

The best thing about the personal profile is that you enter the information once and it can be used again and again as you create your various publications.

To create or edit the personal profile, follow these steps:

1. Click the **Update** button in the Wizard pane. The Personal Information dialog box appears.
2. Use the **Choose a Personal Information Set to Edit** list box to choose the type of profile you want to edit or create (**Primary Business, Secondary Business**, and so on).

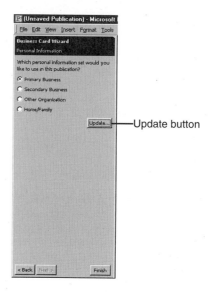

—Update button

Figure 2.4   Business forms and publications such as business cards derive information automatically from your personal profile.

3. After you've selected the information set, fill in the various text boxes (see Figure 2.5).

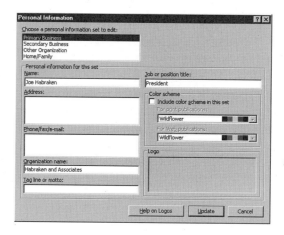

Figure 2.5   Fill in the text boxes in the Personal Information dialog box to create a personal information profile.

4. After supplying the information, you can click another profile set in the information set box and fill in the information by following the above steps. When you have completed your various information sets, click **Update**.

The information that you provided in the information set is placed in the publication. Typically, supplying the information profile for the publication is the last step in the wizard-based publication creation. You can click **Finish** to close the wizard and complete the publication.

Saving Your Publication

After you complete the wizard steps, you will want to save your publication. This enables you to take a breather before you begin the editing or enhancement process.

To save your new publication, follow these steps:

1. Select the **File** menu, then select **Save**. The Save As dialog box appears.
2. Type a filename in the **File Name** box.
3. Click the **Save In** drop-down box and select the drive in which you want to save the publication.
4. Folders on the selected drive appear in the **Save as Type** box. Double-click the folder where the publication will reside.
5. When you have provided a filename and a location for your new publication, click the **Save** button.

The publication is saved to your computer.

In this lesson, you learned how to create a new publication using the Publication Wizards. You also learned how to select color schemes and create a personal information profile. In the next lesson, you learn how to create publications using design sets and from scratch.

Using Design Sets and Templates

3

In this lesson, you learn how to create new publications as part of a design set. You also learn how to create publications from scratch.

Understanding the Publication Design Sets

Publisher provides you with a way to create sets of publications that share the same color and design attributes. This makes it easy for you to create small-business publications such as business cards, envelopes, brochures, and letter-heads that share the same look.

The great thing about using the design sets is that not only do you end up with a group of publications that share the same basic design and color elements, but when you create each of the individual publications in the set, you are walked through the creation process by a wizard (in the same manner as in Lesson 2, "Creating a New Publication," when you create individual publications using a wizard).

Selecting the Design Set

You select the design set for your new publication from the Publisher Catalog, which appears when you start Publisher, or when you start a new publication from the File menu. To select a design set for a new publication, follow these steps:

1. Start Publisher using the **Start** menu, or if you are already in the Publisher window, click the **File** menu, then click **New**.

2. If you are asked to save changes to any current publication, click **Yes** to save the changes, or click **No** to clear the publication from the Publisher window. The Publisher Catalog appears.

3. Click the **Publications by Design** tab. The Design Sets pane and the Master Sets preview window appear, as shown in Figure 3.1.

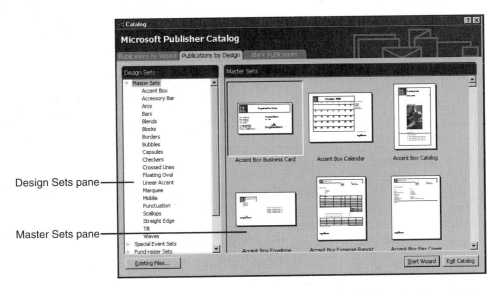

Figure 3.1 The Publications by Design tab of the Publisher Catalog enables you to create publications with a unified design.

4. The design sets are listed in the Design Sets pane on the left side of the Publisher window. A master design set exists for business publications, and specialty design sets include Special Event and Holiday Sets. To expand one of the set categories (such as Master Sets or Special Event Sets), click the set category. The design sets under that particular category appear.

5. To view the publications included in a particular design set, click the set in the Design Sets pane. A preview of the publications in the set appears in the Master Sets window (see Figure 3.2).

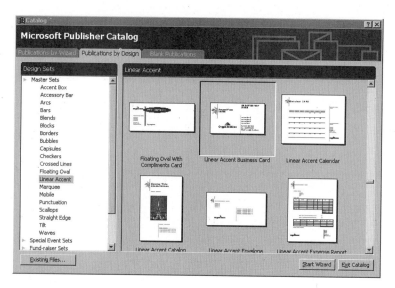

Figure 3.2   Each design set contains several publication masters that embrace the same design elements.

6. After you've previewed the various design sets that include the type of publication you want to create (such as a brochure or business cards), select the design set in the Design Sets list.

TIP   **Use the Scrollbar to Peruse the Design List**   To view all the design sets in the Design Sets pane, click the down scroll arrow on the vertical scrollbar.

Selecting a Design Master

After you've selected a particular design set, you can choose the actual publication that you will create using the design elements of that particular set. The publications available for the set are previewed in the right pane of the Catalog window (the title of the pane changes to the design set that you chose in the left pane).

To select your design master and begin the publication creation process, follow these steps:

1. Click a publication master in the Publication pane of the Catalog window (see Figure 3.3).

2. After you've picked the publication you want to create, click the **Start Wizard** button on the lower-right corner of the Publication window.

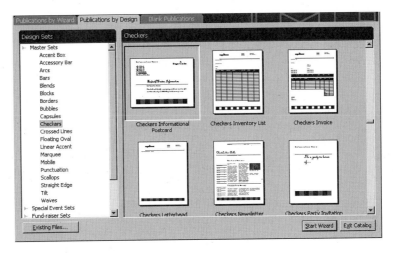

Figure 3.3   Select a publication category, and then select a specific publication to create.

The wizard you have started creates the new publication, which will appear in the Publication window. Next, the wizard walks you through the publication creation process.

Completing the Publication

Completing the publication merely requires that you answer each question that is posed by the specific Publication Wizard, which appears in the left pane of the Publisher window. Your publication, using the design set you chose on the Design Sets pane, appears in the Publication window.

Complete each wizard step as you would for any wizard-created publication (for more about the Publication Wizards, see Lesson 2). However, when you are given the option of changing the color scheme for the particular publication, you should accept the default for this step. Remember that your strategy in using the Design Sets pane was to create a group of publications that embraced the same color scheme and design elements. If you change the color scheme for this

particular publication, it will no longer match other publications you have
created or will create using the design set.

 When you have completed the various steps provided by the wizard (you
complete these steps when you click **Finish**), be sure to save your new publication. You can quickly open the Save As dialog box and assign a name to the new
publication using the **Save** button on the Publisher Standard toolbar. When you
have assigned a name and a location to the new publication, click the **Save**
button in the Save As dialog box.

Adding Your Own Design and Color Schemes

If you want, you can also create a publication from scratch. This means that all
design elements and color schemes have to be added to the publication manually. Publisher does provide you with a set of templates, however, that help set
up the page size and orientation for blank publications. You can use templates
to create business cards, Web pages, tent cards, and other publication types from
scratch.

To start the process of creating a new publication from scratch, follow these
steps:

1. With the Publisher Catalog open (the Catalog opens either when you start
   Publisher or when you click the **File** menu, then click **New**), click the
   Blank Publications tab. The Blank Publications pane appears on the left
   side of the Catalog and the Blank Publications preview window appears on
   the right, as shown in Figure 3.4.

2. You can select the template you wish to use for your blank publication
   either by clicking a choice in the Blank Publications list (in the left Catalog
   pane) or by clicking one of the publication previews in the Preview
   window.

3. When you have selected your publication, click the **Create** button.

The blank publication appears in the Publication window. On the left side of the
Publisher window, the Quick Publication Wizard pane appears. You can select
any of the headings available in the Quick Publication Wizard to edit the design
parameters of your blank publication.

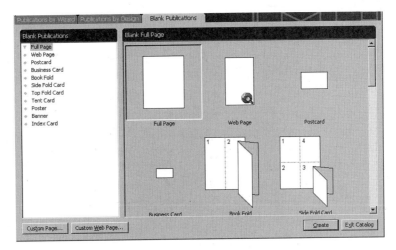

Figure 3.4 You can base your blank publication on several templates provided by Publisher.

For instance, if you want to assign a color scheme to the blank publication, click the Color Scheme heading. The Color Scheme pane appears (see Figure 3.5). Use the scrollbar to scroll through the Color Scheme list; when you find the color scheme you want to use, click it.

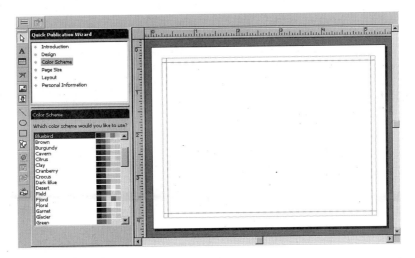

Figure 3.5 The Quick Publication Wizard makes it easy for you to assign a color scheme and other design parameters to your blank publication.

You can also select a design (a set of design elements are added to your publication), a page size (portrait or landscape), and a layout for your blank publication. Selecting a layout that includes text and pictures also enables you to have information in your profile automatically placed in the publication. Figure 3.6 shows a blank publication that has been customized with a color scheme, design, and layout.

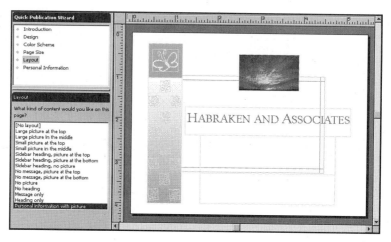

Figure 3.6   Blank publications can be enhanced to look as well-designed as those created by using a wizard or one of the design sets.

As you can see, even creating a publication from scratch in Publisher is very straightforward; Publisher offers a great deal of help in setting the design parameters for the publication. When you have completed setting the design parameters for your from scratch publication using the Quick Publication Wizard, make sure you save the publication.

TIP   **You Can Close the Quick Publication Wizard**   After you've set the various design parameters for your blank publication, you can close the Quick Publication Wizard by clicking the **Hide Wizard** button at the bottom of the Wizard pane.

In this lesson, you learned how to create a new publication using the design sets. You also learned how to create a new publication from scratch. In the next lesson, you learn how to change the view of your publication and how to zoom in and out on the pages.

Viewing Your Publications

In this lesson, you learn the different options for viewing your
publication, including the Zoom feature. You also learn how to
work with positioning tools such as the ruler and guides.

Changing the Publication Display

When you create publications in the Publisher window, the default view is
the Whole Page view. This enables you to see the entire current page from a
bird's-eye view that is excellent for determining the overall layout of the page
and the positioning of the various text frames, picture frames, and other objects.

As you work with your publications, you will find that it's convenient to be able
to change the view from a single page to a two-page spread and to have the
capability to zoom in and out on a particular page. The following sections
describe the three basic views that are available to you.

Whole Page

The default view is Whole Page. It shows the entire current page and shows the
margins for the page. Figure 4.1 shows a publication in the Whole Page view.

If you are in any other view and want to return to the Whole Page view, select
the **View** menu, then point at **Zoom**. Select **Whole Page** from the cascading
menu.

 TIP **Go to Whole Page View Using the Keyboard** You can quickly go to
the Whole Page view by pressing **Ctrl+Shift+L** on the keyboard.

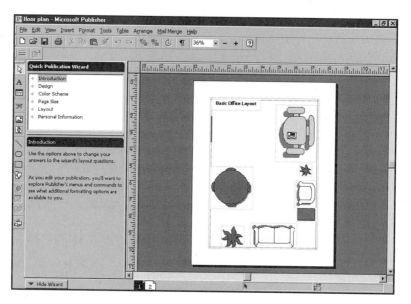

Figure 4.1 The Whole Page view enables you to view the spatial relations of all the items that you've placed on a particular page.

Page Width

Another useful view is the Page Width view. This enables you to zoom in on the publication page but still see the left and right margins. The Page Width view provides a view that is slightly larger than zooming to 50% (58%). Because this view maintains the total width of the page and enables you to see the left and right margins, you can then easily scroll up and down on the page using the vertical scrollbar. Figure 4.2 shows the page depicted in Figure 4.1 (the Whole Page view) in the Page Width view.

To place the current publication page in the Page Width view, select the **View** menu, then point at **Zoom**. Select **Page Width** from the cascading menu.

Two-Page Spread

Another useful view is the Two-Page Spread. This enables you to examine facing pages in a publication. This is particularly useful when you want to make sure that the frames and objects on these two pages are balanced and arranged appropriately. Any publication that opens (for example, a greeting card or brochure) has facing pages inside it.

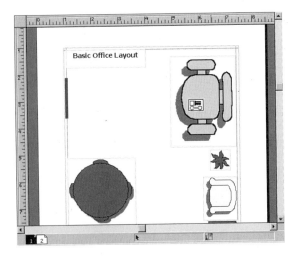

Figure 4.2 The Page Width view enables you to zoom in on your publication page, but it still shows the left and right margins for reference.

Figure 4.3 shows a three-page publication with the facing pages (pages 2 and 3) in the Two-Page Spread view. To view a publication in the Two-Page Spread view, select the **View** menu, then select **Two-Page Spread**. A check mark appears next to the Two-Page Spread selection on the View menu.

When you want to return to the single-page view, select the **View** menu and click **Two-Page Spread** to remove the check mark.

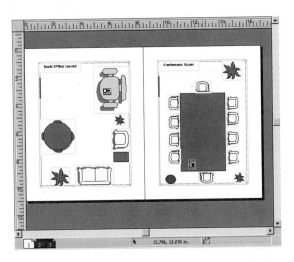

Figure 4.3 The Two-Page Spread view enables you to look at facing pages in your publication.

CAUTION

First Pages Don't Have Facing Pages The very first page of your publication is considered a "cover" page. If you think about greeting cards and other booklet-type publications, the first page is visible when the publication is closed. The first inside page is page 2 (on the left of the open card), with page 3 as its right-facing page.

Using the Zoom Feature

Because your publication pages will consist of various frames containing text and other items such as pictures, you will often need to edit or otherwise fine-tune these items. When you are trying to concentrate on a particular item on the page, you want to be able to zoom in on that item. Publisher provides you with the capability to zoom in and out on your publication pages using a range from 10% to 400% (the larger the percentage, the more you've zoomed in on your publication).

To zoom in or out on the current page, follow these steps:

1. Select the **View** menu, then point at **Zoom**.

2. Select your Zoom percentage from the cascading menu (such as **75%**). Figure 4.4 shows a page zoomed at 75%.

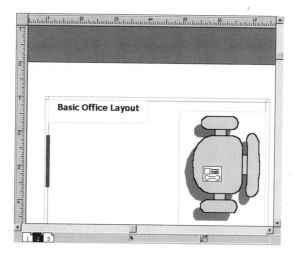

Figure 4.4 Use the Zoom feature to zoom in and out on your publication pages.

TIP **Zoom In and Out Quickly Using the Toolbar** You can also zoom in and out on your publication pages using the **Zoom** drop-down box on the Standard toolbar. Click it and select the zoom percentage.

Scrolling in the Publication

When you zoom in on your publication, you may need to adjust your point of view up or down or to the left or right to see a particular part of the page or focus on a particular item. The vertical and horizontal scrollbars provide you with the capability to do this.

To move up or down on the publication page, click the up or down arrow on the vertical scrollbar. To scroll to the right or left, click the right or left scroll arrow on the horizontal scrollbar.

You can also use the scroll boxes on either of the scrollbars to scroll to a particular position in the document. For instance, if you want to scroll halfway down a page, you can drag the vertical scroll box to the middle of the vertical scrollbar (see Figure 4.5).

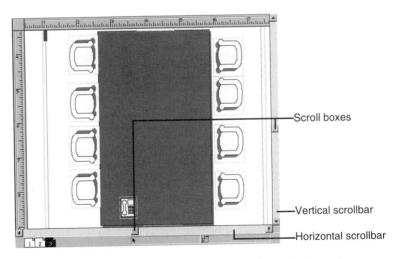

Scroll boxes

Vertical scrollbar

Horizontal scrollbar

Figure 4.5 The scrollbars enable you to scroll vertically and horizontally through a document page.

Working with Rulers and Guide Lines

Another visual aspect of working on your publications is the use of the rulers and guides. A vertical ruler and a horizontal ruler are supplied in the Publication window to help you place items on the page. *Guides* are really extensions of the ruler and appear as guide lines (both vertical and horizontal) that you can drag onto the document page (from either ruler) to help you appropriately place text and pictures on the page.

Guide A layout guide is a nonprinting vertical or horizontal line that you place on the publication page to help you align the various elements that the publication contains. Guides appear on the document page in green.

Where Are My Rulers? If you don't see the rulers in the Publication window, select the **View** menu, and then select **Rulers**.

Using the Ruler

When you move the mouse on the page, you will notice that the vertical and horizontal positions of the mouse pointer are tracked by a tick mark (a line) on each of the rulers. The actual position (horizontal and vertical) of the mouse pointer is also displayed on the Publisher taskbar (see Figure 4.6).

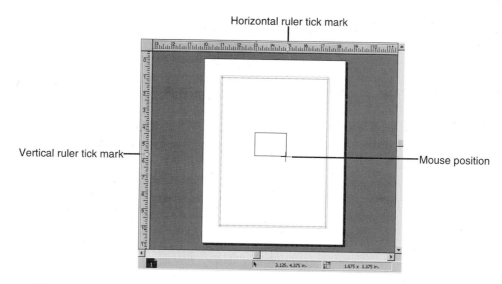

Horizontal ruler tick mark

Vertical ruler tick mark

Mouse position

Figure 4.6 The rulers show you the position of the mouse pointer on the page.

Being able to see the position of the mouse pointer on the rulers and in the taskbar enables you to position object frames on the page with precision. For instance, to place a picture frame two inches down from the top of a page, you drag the object by its top (because you want the top at the two-inch mark) and watch until the vertical ruler tick mark reaches the two-inch mark. Then you release the object. For more information about inserting and moving frames on a publication page, see Lesson 6, "Working with Publication Frames."

Using Layout Guides

Another tool that you can use to precisely position frames and other items on your Publisher page is the layout guide. These guides, as already mentioned, are nonprinting vertical and horizontal lines that you place on a publication page. The great thing about using layout guides is that they help you maintain the overall layout design on publications that run a number of pages (you set up the same layout guides on each page).

Placing guides on the page enables you to actually place a frame on the guide. This is called *snap to guide*. When you move the frame near the guide, the frame "snaps" onto the guide, positioning the item.

 TIP   **Turning On Snap to Guides** If you are going to use guides in your publications to help you place items on the page, you should turn on the Snap to Guide feature. Select the **Tools** menu, then select **Snap to Guides**.

Guides are created and positioned on your pages using the mouse. Follow these steps to create guides on a publication page:

1. To create a vertical layout guide, place the mouse pointer on the vertical ruler.
2. Hold down the **Shift** key and drag the mouse onto the page. A vertical guideline appears (see Figure 4.7).

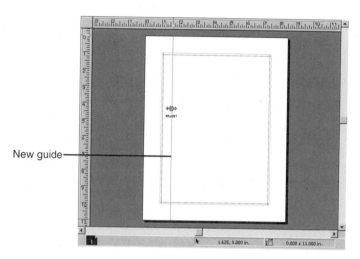

New guide

Figure 4.7 Position guides on your pages to help you align text and picture frames.

3. Position the guideline at the appropriate position on the page and release the mouse button.

4. To create a horizontal layout guide, repeats steps 1–3, but drag a guide down from the horizontal ruler.

Where Are My Guides? If you attempt to create guides and they don't appear in the Publication window, select the **View** menu, and then select **Show Boundaries and Guides**.

CAUTION

You can place as many guides as you need on your pages. If you find that you like using guides but don't like creating and positioning them with the mouse, you can also choose to have a series of horizontal and vertical guides created for you automatically. This forms a grid pattern on the publication, providing you with a sort of topography that you can use to appropriately align your publication items.

To create a grid system for a page, follow these steps:

1. Select the **Arrange** menu, then select **Layout Guides**. The Layout Guides dialog box appears (see Figure 4.8).

2. To set guides, use the **Columns** and **Rows** click boxes in the **Grid Guides** area of the dialog box to set the number of vertical (column) and horizontal (row) guides you want to place on the page.

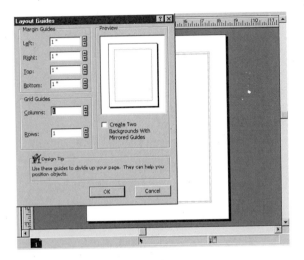

Figure 4.8 You can quickly set up an entire grid of guides in the Layout Guides dialog box.

3. After you have specified the number of columns and rows you want for the guides, click **OK**. The new guides appear on your publication page.

TIP **Set Margins Here, Too** The Layout uides dialog box also enables you to set the margins for a particular publication page. Setting publication margins is covered in Lesson 14, "Formatting Publication Pages."

In this lesson, you learned how to change the view of your publication and use the Zoom feature. You also learned how to use the ruler and place guidelines on a publication page. In the next lesson, you learn how to work with and enhance existing publications.

Working with Existing Publications

In this lesson, you learn how to open, close, and save an existing publication, add pages to the publication, and save the publication under a new filename. You also learn how to complete wizard-based publications including text frames and placeholders.

Opening an Existing Publication

You will probably find that you end up with a library of saved publications that you use on a fairly regular basis. Items such as certificates, invitation cards, and various business forms can be created and saved to your computer and then used when needed.

 TIP **Saving Is Not Just for Finished Publications** If you've worked on a publication and don't really have its design or colors the way that you want it, you can, of course, save the file and then work on it again at your earliest convenience.

The great thing about recycling publications in this way is that you take the time to design them well once, and then you can open them and edit them to fit your particular need. To open an existing publication, follow these steps:

1. In the Publisher window, select the **File** menu, then select **Open**. The Open Publication dialog box appears (see Figure 5.1).

920

TIP **Use the Open Button** To quickly open a publication, click the **Open** button on the Publisher Standard toolbar.

2. In the Open Publication dialog box, click the **Look In** drop-down box to select the drive on which your file is located.

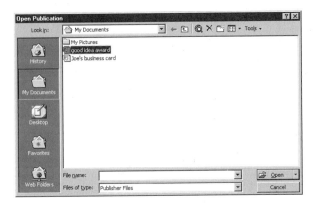

Figure 5.1 Select a location on your computer to open a specific file.

3. After you select a drive, double-click the appropriate folder in the folder list that appears.
4. Select the file you want to open, and then click **Open**. The publication opens in the Publisher window.

 TIP **Saving the Previous Publication** Publisher allows you to work on only one publication at a time. If you try to open or start a different publication and have not saved the current publication, you will be asked to save the current publication when you click the **Open** button in the Open Publication dialog box.

Completing a Wizard-Based Publication

When you create publications using a wizard, it's impossible for the wizard to fill in all the information needed in the publication. Of course, a great deal of information is added automatically from the personal information set that you use for the publication. However, in a publication such as a certificate or an invitation, you still have to fill in the recipient's name or the time and place of the event. So, after opening a previously saved publication, you must edit the content to meet your current needs.

Editing Text in a Publication

When you work with text in Publisher, the text is held inside a frame called a *text frame*. You learn more about creating and working with text frames in Lesson 8, "Changing How Text Looks."

 Frame The container that is created to hold a picture, text, or other object in a publication. A frame, by default, does not have a border around it that prints, but it can be customized with borders, colors, and other attributes. See Lesson 6, "Working with Publication Frames."

To modify or complete text entries in a publication, follow these steps:

1. To modify the contents of a text frame, click the text frame to select it (click anywhere on the frame around the text).

 TIP **Zoom In When Working on Text** When you need to edit text in a text frame, you might want to zoom in on the publication for a closer look. Select the **View** menu, point at **Zoom**, then select the zoom percentage from the cascading menu.

2. Double-click the text in the text frame to select all the text (see Figure 5.2). To select a portion of the text, use click-and-drag.

3. Type the appropriate text into the text frame. The selected text is deleted and replaced by the new text.

Filling a Picture Placeholder

Not all the additions that you need to make to a wizard-based publication are text, however. In some cases you need to fill placeholders (such as for a company logo or a picture of the chairperson of the board) with the appropriate graphic. These graphics are held in a frame the same as text and are often referred to as *picture frames*. See Lesson 9, "Working with Graphics," for more information on working with picture frames.

To fill a picture placeholder with a new picture, follow these steps:

1. Click the placeholder picture frame in the publication (see Figure 5.3) to select it (it will be a picture frame or some other type of object frame).

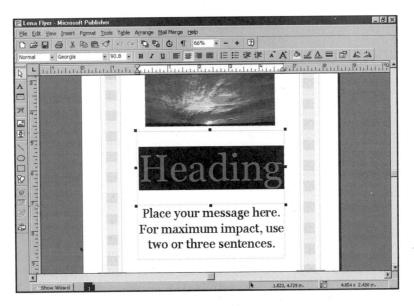

Figure 5.2 Select the text that you want to modify.

Figure 5.3 Select any picture placeholders and insert a picture in its place.

2. Select the **Insert** menu, then point at **Picture**. From the cascading menu select one of the following:

Clip Art—You can select a new picture from the Clip Art Catalog.

From File—You can select a picture that you have stored on your computer.

From Scanner or Camera—If you have either of these devices hooked to your computer, you can create a new image and place it immediately into Publisher.

New Drawing—You can draw your own image to replace the placeholder item.

Depending on your choice above, you work either with the Clip Art Catalog, the Insert File dialog box, your scanner or camera, or the Publisher Drawing tool, respectively. Figure 5.4 shows a picture selected for insertion into a publication using the **From File** option. For more information on working with and manipulating pictures, see Lesson 9.

Figure 5.4 You can replace placeholders with Publisher clip art or other pictures that you have stored on your computer.

After you replace a placeholder item with a picture or graphic of your own, you can continue to edit the text and graphic items in the publication. The number of text frames and placeholder items that you need to edit to complete a particular publication depends on the publication itself. Typically, the more complex the publication, the more items you have to personalize.

Adding Pages to a Publication

You might find after you complete a particular publication that you need to add additional pages to it. This can be a common need when you build publications from scratch.

To add pages to the current publication, follow these steps:

1. Select the **Insert** menu, then select **Page**. The Insert Page dialog box appears (see Figure 5.5).

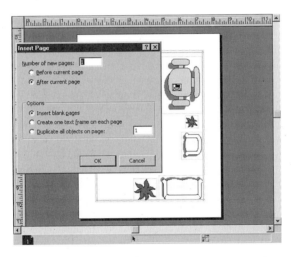

Figure 5.5 You can insert new pages into a publication before or after the current page.

2. Type the number of new pages you want to insert in the **Number of New Pages** box.

3. Click either the **Before Current Page** or **After Current Page** button to select the appropriate option.

4. In the Options area, select the appropriate option for your blank pages:

Insert Blank Pages—The pages are inserted into the publication with no frames.

Create One Text Frame on Each Page—A text frame is placed on each of the new pages.

Duplicate All Objects on Page—Copies the objects on the designated page (type the number in the page box) and places them on the new page or pages inserted.

After you make your selections, click **OK**; the new page or pages are inserted into your document.

> **TIP**   **Save Your Work**   When you make changes, such as adding pages to your publications, remember to save your work. Publisher prompts you every so often to save your work if you've been remiss. To save your publication changes, just click **Yes** in the dialog box that appears.

Saving a Revised Document Under a New Name

When you work with publications that you use again and again, such as award certificates or invitations, you might want to keep your original publication incomplete (with award recipient names not filled in or other items left blank until the publication is made ready for printing) under a particular filename. For instance, you might create an award certificate and leave the recipient name blank. Then, when you are ready to create an award for a particular person, you open the award publication and edit the text frame that contains the recipient name.

You might also want to save the completed publication (the one with the recipient name or other information) under a different filename. This can be done using the Save As command.

To save a publication under a different filename, follow these steps:

1. Select the **File** menu, then select **Save As**. The Save As dialog box appears.
2. Type a new name for the publication in the **File Name** box.
3. Use the **Save In** drop-down box to designate the drive to which you will save the file. Also, make sure to select a folder on that drive by double-clicking the folder.
4. Click **Save** to save the file.

You have now saved any changes that you made to your original publication under a new filename. This means that the original file under the original filename still exists, and it can be used whenever you need it to create personalized publications that can then be saved under a different filename.

Closing a Publication

After you have saved a particular publication and are finished working with it, you will want to close the publication. To close the current publication, select the **File** menu, then select **Close**. The publication closes and Publisher opens a new blank publication in the Publisher window.

In this lesson, you learned how to open an existing publication, modify the publication, and use the Save As command to change the name of the publication. In the next lesson, you learn the basics of working with frames.

Working with Publication Frames

In this lesson, you learn the basics of working with frames: You learn how to insert, copy, delete, and manipulate frames on your publication pages.

Inserting a Frame

When you place an item such as text, a picture, or another object on a publication page, you are actually inserting a *frame* that contains the particular item. Being able to insert, delete, or move frames and manage their border and color attributes provides you with the capability to give your publication pages a customized look as you control the overall layout of individual pages.

 TERM   **Frame**   The bordered space that holds your text, picture, or other item.

When you insert a new frame onto a page, you are actually selecting a particular object to insert onto the page, such as text, a picture, or a drawn object such as a line or circle.

To insert a frame onto your page, follow these steps:

1. Click a frame tool on the Publisher toolbar (such as the Text Frame tool).

2. Place the mouse pointer on the page where you want to place the new frame. The mouse pointer becomes a crosshair.

3. Click and drag to create the frame, as shown in Figure 6.1 (you determine the height and width of the frame).

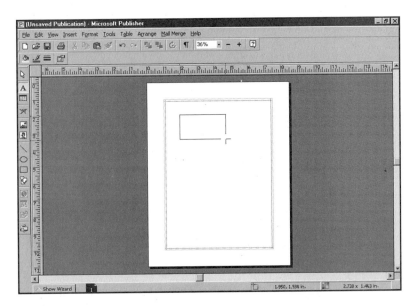

Figure 6.1 Click and drag to place the new frame on your publication page.

The new frame appears on your page. Your next action depends on the type of frame you created. If you used the Text Frame tool to create the frame, you now type the text you want to place in a frame (for more about working with text, see Lesson 8, "Changing How Text Looks"). If you used the Picture Frame tool, the Insert Clip Art dialog box appears, enabling you to insert your choice of pictures (for more about working with pictures and clip art in Publisher, see Lesson 9, "Working with Graphics").

After you have the frame on the page, a number of options are available to you. You can size the frame, move the frame, delete the frame, or group the frame with other frames on the page. These frame manipulations are covered in the balance of this lesson.

Removing a frame from a publication page is very straightforward. Select the frame that you want to delete and then press the **Delete** key on the keyboard. This removes the frame from the publication.

Undoing the Placement of a New Frame If you place a frame on a page and want to quickly remove it, click the **Undo** button on the Standard toolbar.

CAUTION

Sizing a Frame

You can change the width and height (or both) of a frame that is located either on a publication page or in the background of your publication (see Lesson 14, "Formatting Publication Pages"). Changing the size of a frame is accomplished using the sizing handles that appear on the selected frame.

Select the frame by clicking the object that is contained in the frame. Sizing handles appear on the border of the frame (see Figure 6.2). To change the frame size, select one of the options discussed in the following list:

- **Change the Width**—To change the width of the frame, place the mouse pointer on one of the sizing handles on either the left or right vertical border of the frame. The mouse pointer changes to a Resize pointer. Drag to change the width of the frame.

- **Change the Height**—To change the height of the frame, place the mouse pointer on one of the sizing handles on either the top or bottom horizontal border of the frame. Drag to change the height of the frame using the **Resize** pointer.

- **Change the Width and Height**—To change the width and height of the frame simultaneously and maintain the current width and height ratio, place the mouse pointer on any of the diagonal sizing handles (handles positioned where the vertical and horizontal border meet in a corner) and drag to change the overall size of the frame (see Figure 6.3).

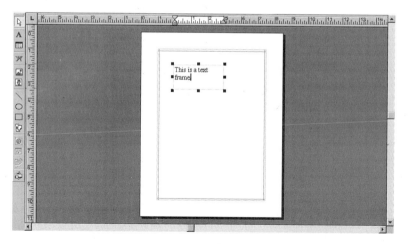

Figure 6.2 The sizing handles provide you with a way to change the height or width of a selected frame.

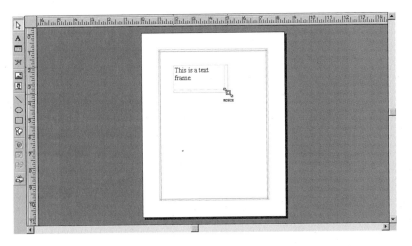

Figure 6.3 Drag any of the sizing handles to change the size of the frame.

 TIP **Zoom Out When Sizing a Frame** If you have zoomed in on a frame to place text or some other object in it, you might want to zoom out to the Whole Page view when you size your frame. Select **View**, and point at **Zoom**, and then select **Whole Page** to switch to the Whole Page view. Now you can size the frame in relation to other frames on the page.

If you require more exacting measurements for the height and width of a particular frame than you can attain with the mouse, you can also specify these measurements in the Size and Position dialog box. Follow these steps to specify an exact set of measurements for a frame:

1. Click anywhere on a frame to select it.

2. Select the **Format** menu, then select **Size and Position**. The Size and Position dialog box appears (see Figure 6.4).

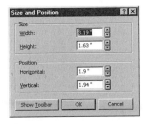

Figure 6.4 Use the Size and Position dialog box to control the size of your selected frame.

3. Use the click arrows or type a new width in the **Width** box.

4. Use the click arrows or enter a new height in the **Height** box.

5. Click **OK** to resize the frame and close the dialog box.

Your frame is resized using the width and height values you entered.

TIP   **Use the Measurements Toolbar to Control Frame Size**   You can also control the size and position of a frame using the Measurements toolbar. Select **View**, then point at **Toolbars**, and select **Measurements** from the toolbar list. The second set of measurement boxes (from the left) on the Measurements toolbar controls the width and height of the selected frame.

Moving a Frame

Publisher also provides you with the capability to move your frames on your publication pages. Any selected frame can be moved using the mouse or the Size and Position dialog box.

Follow these steps to move a frame:

1. Click anywhere on a frame to select it.

2. Place the mouse pointer on any of the border edges surrounding the frame (do not place the mouse pointer on the sizing handles). A Move pointer appears.

3. Drag the frame to a new position on the page.

You can also place a frame in a particular position on the page using the Size and Position dialog box; follow these steps:

1. Select **Format**, then select **Size and Position** to open the dialog box.

2. Use the **Horizontal Position** box to select the horizontal position for the frame, and use the **Vertical Position** box to set the vertical position.

3. When you have entered your position settings, click the **OK** button.

TIP   **Snapping Frames to Grid and Ruler Guides**   Another way you can position frames with more accuracy is to turn on the Snap to Grid feature (select **Tools**, then **Snap to Grids**). Frames then snap to the nearest grid line. For more about guides, see Lesson 5, "Working with Existing Publications."

You might find that you want to fine-tune the position of a frame in reference to other frames and objects on a page. This can be done using the Nudge feature.

1. Click anywhere on a frame to select it.

2. Select the **Arrange** menu, then select **Nudge**. The Nudge dialog box appears (see Figure 6.5).

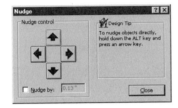

Figure 6.5   Use the Nudge dialog box to move a frame slightly in any direction.

3. Click the appropriate arrow button in the Nudge dialog box to nudge the frame in that direction.

4. To nudge the frame by a specific measurement, click the **Nudge By** check box and enter a number in the accompanying text box. When you click the arrow buttons on the Nudge dialog box, the frame moves in that direction (by the increment specified).

5. When you have finished nudging the object (you can drag the dialog box out of the way to view the frame), click the **Close** button to close the Nudge dialog box.

Copying a Frame

You can also copy frames and place multiple occurrences of the same frame on a page or copy a frame to another page in your publication. This enables you to easily place repeating design elements on a page or within an entire publication.

To copy a frame, follow these steps:

1. Click a frame to select it.

2. Select the **Edit** menu, then select **Copy**.

3. Select the page from the status bar on which you want to place the copy of the frame, or remain on the current page.

4. Select the **Edit** menu, then select **Paste**.

If you want to move the frame from the current page to another page in the publication, select the **Edit** menu and select **Cut**, then proceed with steps 3 and 4.

 TIP 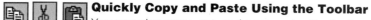 **Quickly Copy and Paste Using the Toolbar**
You can also copy, cut, and paste using the toolbar. Click the **Copy** or the **Cut** button, then select the **Paste** button after moving to the appropriate page.

Grouping Frames

After you have frames placed on a page, you might want to adjust the overall positioning of all the frames in relation to the top or bottom of the page or some other special element on the page (such as a large banner heading). Moving each of the frames individually can be time consuming and frustrating, especially if you have the frames currently positioned exactly where you would like them to be in relation to each other.

The solution to this problem is to group the frames and then move them together as one unit. This enables you to fine-tune the layout of the page without moving each frame individually.

To group frames, follow these steps:

1. Select the first frame that will be in the group by clicking it.
2. Hold down the **Shift** key and select additional frames. A selection box appears around all the selected frames, as shown in Figure 6.6. A Group Objects icon also appears on the selection box.

You can now move the entire group of frames by placing the mouse on the group frame and dragging it to a new position. You could also delete all the selected frames at once, or copy the frames and then paste them on another page in your publication.

When you have finished manipulating the grouped frames, click anywhere outside the group to make the group frame disappear.

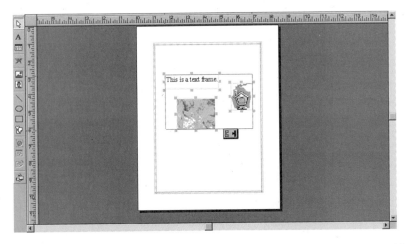

Figure 6.6 Group several frames and then move them together to a new position on the page.

If you want to group the objects on a more permanent basis (to keep them together as a group), select the frames to be part of the group and then select **Arrange**, then **Group Objects**. Even when you click outside of these grouped frames to deselect them, the group remains intact. Click any frame in the group and all the frames are selected within the group frame. Selecting the **Ungroup Objects** command on the **Arrange** menu ungroups the frames in a selected group.

TIP **Arrange Frame Groups Using the Align Objects Command** You can also align an entire group of objects (or just one object) using the Align Objects command. Select a group of objects, select the **Arrange** menu, and then select **Align Objects**. In the Align Objects dialog box, use the appropriate option buttons to align the frames left-to-right or top-to-bottom.

Arranging Frames in Layers

You might find occasion to layer several frames on top of each other in a stack. For instance, you might decide to place a text frame on top of a picture to produce an eye-catching heading for a publication. You can layer a number of objects and their frames using the layering commands on the Arrange menu.

To layer frames, follow these steps:

1. Drag a frame onto another frame to form a layer. For instance, drag a text frame onto a picture frame.

2. The text in the text frame seems to disappear. With the Text frame still selected, click the **Arrange** menu, then click **Bring to Front**. The text frame is placed on top of the Picture frame, as shown in Figure 6.7.

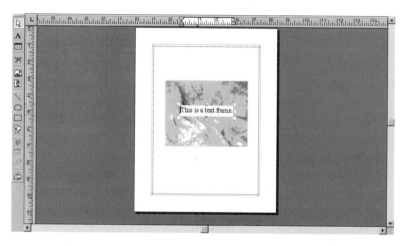

Figure 6.7   Layer frames on your pages to add interest to your publications.

With some practice, you can layer several frames into complex arrangements on your publication pages. Understanding the layering commands on the Arrange menu will help you work with the frames that you have layered.

- **Bring to Front**—This moves the currently selected frame to the top of the stack of frames you have layered.

- **Send to Back**—This moves the currently selected frame to the bottom of the stack.

- **Bring Forward**—This moves the currently selected frame up one position in the stack. For instance, if the frame is the second frame in the layer of the stacks, this moves the frame to the first position, or the top of the stack.

- **Send Backward**—This moves the currently selected frame down one position in the stack. For instance, a frame in the second layer of the stack would be moved to the third layer.

TIP **Make Your Frame Stack One Group** After you have layered several frames and have them positioned and stacked appropriately, make the frames a permanent group (select **Arrange**, then **Group Objects**). This prevents you from inadvertently disturbing the stack when you are working on the other elements on the publication page.

In this lesson, you learned how to insert, size, move, and work with frames on your publication pages. In the next lesson, you learn how to enhance your frames with borders and colors.

Enhancing Frames with Borders and Colors

In this lesson, you learn to create borders and add colors and shading to the frames on your publication pages.

Adding Borders to Frames

When you place a frame on a publication page, the frame is transparent and does not have a border. And you can really discern only the size and shape of the frame when you select the object (for instance, the text or picture) that the frame contains. You can add borders to your frames and also place shading and background colors on any frame you've created.

Adding borders to your frames is very straightforward. You have control over the line thickness, style, and color.

To add borders to a frame, follow these steps:

1. Click the frame you want to place the border around.
2. Select the **Format** menu, then point at **Line/Border Style**.
3. Select a **Line Style** on the cascading menu that appears. A border appears around your frame.

You don't always have to place a box around a selected frame. You can select certain borders of the frame (such as the left vertical border or the bottom horizontal border) and just add a border line to this area of the frame. This is done in the Border Style dialog box.

Follow these steps to add selected borders to a frame:

1. Select **Format**, then **Line/Border Style**, then **More Styles**. The Border Style dialog box appears.

2. Use the **Select a Side** box in the dialog box to select certain sides of the frame for formatting (see Figure 7.1). For instance, click the top of the frame in the **Select a Side** box, and the border indicator triangles for the rest of the border disappear.

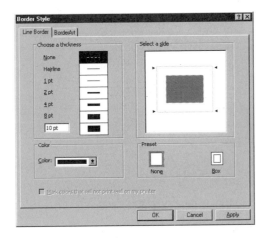

Figure 7.1 In the Border Style dialog box, select the sides on which you want to place a border.

3. Hold down the **Shift** key and click any of the other frame sides on which you also want to place a border.

4. Choose a border thickness on the left side of the dialog box.

5. Click **OK** to add the border to your frame.

Changing Border Attributes

After you have a border around a particular frame, it is very easy to change the attributes for that border, such as the border color or line style. In fact, when you have a frame, selected buttons related to border attributes appear on the Publisher Formatting toolbar. Table 7.1 provides a thumbnail sketch of each frame formatting button.

Table 7.1 The Formatting Toolbar Makes It Easy for You to Edit Border Attributes

Toolbar Button	Frame Attributes
	Fill Color
	Border Color
	Line/Border Style

Changing Border Color

After you've assigned a border to a frame, you can change the color of that border. By following these steps:

1. Select the frame.

2. Click the **Border Color** button on the Formatting toolbar (see Figure 7.2).

3. Click a color on the **Border Color** box.

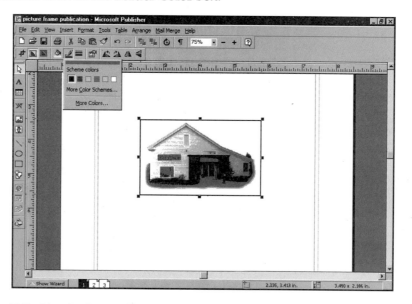

Figure 7.2 Use the Border Color button to assign a new color to your frame's border.

The border around your frame is assigned the selected color. If you want to choose from more colors than provided by the Color drop-down box, click the **More Colors** button on the drop-down list. The Colors dialog box appears. Click the **Color Spectrum** box to select a new color for your frame borders. Then click **OK** to return to the Border Style dialog box.

Using Fill Colors

You can also fill a particular frame with a selected color. This is a great way to add interest to your publications, particularly those that you print in color. When you add color to the frame, be advised, however, that it can obscure the object that resides inside the frame. When you color a text frame, you might have to change the text color so that it can still be read after a fill color has been selected (for instance, a blue fill color might require a yellow text color so that the text is readable; for more about working with text in frames, see Lesson 8, "Changing How Text Looks," in this section of the book).

In the case of picture frames, the fill color fills only the part of the frame (the interior) that is not occupied by the picture itself. The color, in effect, becomes a background for the picture.

To add a fill color to a frame, follow these steps:

1. Select the frame to which you want to add a fill color.

2. Click the **Fill Color** button on the Formatting toolbar.

3. Select a fill color from the color box that appears. The fill color appears in the selected frame.

If you want to choose from more colors than those provided by the Fill Color button, click the **More Colors** selection on the color box. The Colors dialog box appears. Click the **Color Spectrum** box to select a new color for your frame borders. Then click **OK** to place that color in the frame as the fill color.

Using Fill Effects

When you work with fill colors in your frames, you can actually manipulate these colors with tints, patterns, and gradients that really add visual interest to your frames. You work with the various fill effects in the Fill Effects dialog box.

To add effects to a frame's fill color, follow these steps:

941

1. Select the frame to which you want to add fill effects.

2. Click the **Fill Color** button on the Formatting toolbar.

3. Click **Fill Effects** on the drop-down box that appears. The Fill Effects dialog box opens (see Figure 7.3).

Figure 7.3 You can add effects to a frame's fill color in the Fill Effects dialog box.

4. To select a type of fill effect, select one of the option buttons at the top of the dialog box:

   - **Tints/Shades**—Select this option button if you want to apply a special tint/shade for the current fill color. You can then select a tint of the color that ranges from white through all the shades of the color up to black.

   - **Patterns**—Select this option button to select from a number of patterns based on the current fill color (including lines, crosshatching, and so on).

   - **Gradients**—Select this option button to apply a particular gradient (swirling and patterned gradations of the current fill color) from a range of supplied gradient effects.

5. After you select a fill effect category, then select an effect in the **Style** scroll box located directly beneath the Effects option buttons. The effect that you select is previewed in the Sample box.

6. When you have selected an effect that you want to apply to your frame's fill, click **OK**.

The chosen effect formats the fill area of your frame.

Applying Shading

You can also place a shadow on your frame border. This shading on the bottom and right sides of the frame adds depth to the frame. Shadows particularly enhance text frames and picture frames where you have placed a border around a particular frame. The shadow lifts the frame away from the publication page, giving it a three-dimensional feel.

To add shading to a frame, follow these steps:

1. Click the frame on which you want to place the shadow.
2. Select the **Format** menu, then choose **Shadow**.

Shading appears on the right and the bottom of the frame, as shown in Figure 7.4.

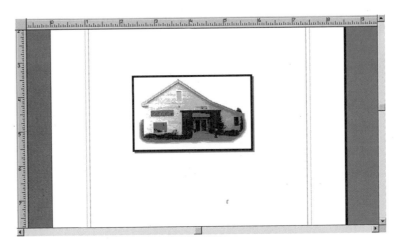

Figure 7.4 Shading gives your frames depth.

You will find that shadows work best when a border has been placed around a particular frame. The shadow adds depth and definition to an otherwise flat border and frame.

In this lesson, you learned how to place borders around frames and how to change the color and other attributes of those borders. You also worked with frame fill colors and placed a shadow around a frame. In the next lesson, you learn how to change the way text looks in text frames and how to add special text objects to publications such as mastheads.

Changing How Text Looks

8

In this lesson, you learn how to add text to your publications and change formatting options related to text, such as font selection text alignment, and text color. You also learn how to add text banners to your pages and connect text frames.

Adding Text to Your Publications

Text is added to your publication in text frames using the Text Frame tool on the Publisher toolbar. You will find that Publisher provides you with complete control over the look and formatting of text in a frame, including the font style, font size, font attributes (such as bold and italic), and the color of your font. Any or all of these font parameters can be edited on a particular text frame.

To add a text frame to a publication page, follow these steps:

1. Click the **Text Frame** tool on the Publisher toolbar.

2. Place the mouse pointer on the page and drag to create the text frame.

3. The insertion point appears in the text frame. Type the text that you want to place in the frame.

 TIP **Zoom In to Concentrate on Your Text** If you are in the Whole Page view when you place your text frames on your page, you might want to zoom in on the text before you type the text or attempt to edit it. Click the **Zoom** drop-down box on the Standard toolbar and select a zoom percentage that zooms you in on your page.

Inserting Text

You can also easily add additional text to a text frame. To add text to a frame that already contains text, follow these steps:

1. Place the mouse pointer on the text in the text frame. The pointer becomes an I-beam.

2. Click the I-beam on the text where you want to place the insertion point.

3. Type the text you want to insert into the text box (see Figure 8.1).

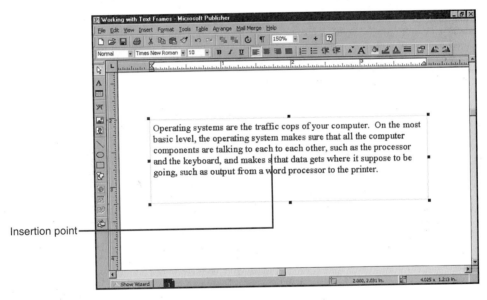

Insertion point—

Figure 8.1 Place the insertion point in a text box and then use the keyboard to add text.

Selecting and Deleting Text

You can also easily delete text in a text frame. Select the text you want to delete and press the **Delete** key on the keyboard. You will find that the mouse provides the easiest method for selecting text in the text frame. Table 8.1 provides a list of ways to use the mouse to select text.

Table 8.1   Use the Mouse to Quickly Select Text in the Document

Text Selection	Mouse Action
Selects the word	Double-click a word.
Selects a text block	Click and drag, or click at the beginning of text and then hold down the Shift key and click at the end of text block.
Selects all the text	Triple-click in the text frame.

You will find that these selection techniques are also useful when you want to change the format (or color) of text in a text frame (as discussed in subsequent sections of this lesson).

 TIP   **Copy, Cut, and Paste Text**   You can also copy or cut selected text in a text box and then paste it into another text frame or in another position in the current text box. Use the **Copy** button, the **Cut** button, and the **Paste** button on the Standard toolbar, respectively.

Working with Fonts

The text that you type in a new frame is created in the default Publisher font, which is Times New Roman, 10 point. Each available font has a particular style or typeface.

A variety of font types exists, such as Arial, Courier, Times New Roman, CG Times, Bookman Old Style, and so on; the fonts you have to choose from depend on the fonts that have been installed on your computer (Windows 98 and 95 provide most of the font families that applications such as Publisher use). Publisher also installs several font types when you install it from the Microsoft Office or Publisher 2000 CD-ROM (see the introduction in this book for some installation considerations for Publisher).

The size of the font is measured in points. A point is 1/72 of an inch, and the standard point size for business letters and other documents is 12 points. The higher the number of points (such as 18) the larger the font size.

You can change the font for existing text in a text frame by following these steps:

1. Select the text in the text frame (using the mouse) that you want to change to a different font type.

2. Click the **Font** drop-down box on the Formatting toolbar and select a new font from the list (see Figure 8.2).

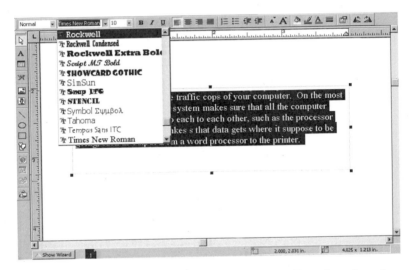

Figure 8.2   Choose a new font for selected text using the Font drop-down box.

If you have finished working with a particular text frame, click outside the frame to deselect the frame itself.

If you create a new text frame, you can change the font that you use for the text that you place in the frame before you actually type any text. This, in effect, changes the default font for that particular text frame. To change to a different font, click the **Font** drop-down box and select a new font.

You can change the font size of text in a text frame in much the same way. Select the text in the text frame to which you would like to assign a new font size. Then click the **Font Size** drop-down box on the Formatting toolbar and select a new font size.

Changing Font Attributes

You also have control over other font attributes associated with the text in your text frames. You can quickly change the style of the font to bold, italic, or underline. These font styles are readily available on the Formatting toolbar (see Table 8.2). A number of other font attributes can also be selected in the Font dialog box.

Table 8.2   Use the Appropriate Button on the Formatting Toolbar to Change the Style of Selected Text

Formatting Toolbar Button	Style
B	Bold
I	Italic
U	Underline

To change the font attributes for text in a text frame, follow these steps:

1. Select the text in the text frame for which you want to change the font attributes (for example, changing the text style to bold).
2. Click the appropriate button on the Formatting toolbar.

You can also change font attributes for selected text in a frame using the Font dialog box. Select the **Format** menu, then select **Font**.

The Font dialog box enables you to change the font, the font style, the font size, and a number of other font attributes (such as superscript, subscript, small caps, and so on), as shown in Figure 8.3.

To select any of the font attributes in the Effects area of the dialog box, click the appropriate check box. A preview of the particular effect (and other attribute changes that you have made) appears in the Sample box. When you have completed making your font changes, click the **OK** button to return to your publication.

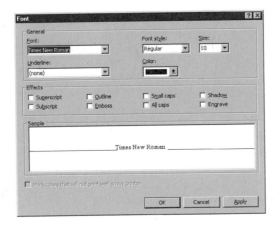

Figure 8.3   The Font dialog box gives you control over a number of font attributes.

Changing Font Colors

You can also change the color of the text in a text frame. Changing font color enables you to emphasize certain text and can add interest to your publication pages.

To change the font color for text in a text frame, follow these steps:

1. Select the text in the text frame that you will change to a different font color.
2. Click the **Font Color** button on the Formatting toolbar.
3. Select a new color from the color box that appears (if you don't see a color you like, continue with step 4).
4. If you want to select from additional colors, click the **More Colors** selection in the color box. The Colors dialog box appears (see Figure 8.4).
5. Click anywhere in the color palette to select a new color range for the text.
6. In the color *luminescence* box to the right of the color palette, drag the slider to select the depth of the color you will use for your text.
7. After you've selected your new color, click **OK** to return to your publication.

Luminescence slider box

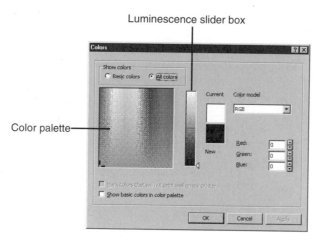

Color palette

Figure 8.4   The Colors dialog box offers you all the colors of the spectrum for your text.

Luminescence   In Publisher, luminescence is the tone or degrees of light and dark you find in a particular color. The luminescence slider bar enables you to select the tone for the currently selected palette color.

Aligning Text in a Frame

You also have control over the alignment of the text in the frame. You can center the text (in relation to the frame itself), right-align the text, left-align the text, or use different alignments on different text lines or paragraphs in a text box. For lines or paragraphs to be treated separately, place a line break (press **Enter**) between the line and the next line in the text frame.

The alignments align the text to the left and right borders of the frame. Table 8.3 gives you a summary of the alignment buttons available on the Formatting toolbar.

Table 8.3 Use the Alignment Buttons on the Formatting Toolbar to Change Selected Text Alignment in the Frame

Formatting Toolbar Button	*Alignment*
	Left
	Center
	Right
	Justify (straight margins on the left and right)

To align text in a frame, follow these steps:

1. Place the insertion point in the paragraph (any line or lines of text followed by a line break) that you want to align.

2. Click the appropriate button on the Formatting toolbar (as detailed in Table 8.3).

Your text is aligned according to the button you selected on the Formatting toolbar.

 TIP **Align Multiple Paragraphs** If you have a text box with more than one paragraph of information in it, you can select all or some of the paragraphs and then click an alignment button to change the alignment of several paragraphs at once.

Adding Text Mastheads

Publisher does not limit you to text frames for the text items that you place on your publication pages. You can also add special text banners using the Publisher Design Gallery. These text banners are called mastheads in Publisher; they are predesigned elements that offer color and other design items that really help dress up text entries so that they look great on your publications. Mastheads work well as the heading text for your publication pages.

To add a masthead from the Design Gallery, follow these steps:

1. Click the **Design Gallery** button on the Publisher toolbar. The Design Gallery appears.

2. Make sure that **Mastheads** is selected in the Categories pane of the Design Gallery (see Figure 8.5).

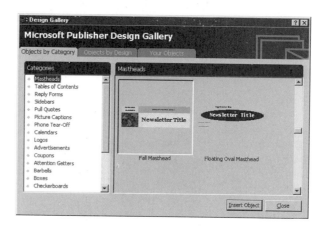

Figure 8.5   You can add mastheads to your publications as page headings.

3. Scroll through the mastheads available in the Mastheads pane of the Design Gallery and select a particular masthead for your page.

4. Click the **Insert Object** button to add the selected masthead to your page.

CAUTION

Mastheads Are Made Up of Multiple Frames   Mastheads can be made up of several text frames that have been formatted differently and then grouped together. This means that in any one masthead, you might have to edit several grouped text frames to replace all the placeholder text in the masthead. Just select each individual placeholder text entry and then type in your text. For more about grouping frames, see Lesson 6, "Working with Publication Frames."

When the masthead is placed on the page, it contains generic placeholder text. You can edit this text by selecting the text as you would any text frame; then type your new text to replace it. The text you replace the placeholder text with takes on the font and other font attributes of the replaced placeholder.

Connecting Text Frames

You might find that you want to place a large amount of text onto one publication page, but don't want to place the text in only one text frame (a lot of text stuck in one frame can be overwhelming to the eye and diminish your message). Instead, you can break up the text into more "bite-sized" pieces of information by enabling the text to flow between several text frames as a story. The amount of text in each frame is then determined by the frame size. A story can be placed in several text frames on one page, or the story can flow to text frames that are on different pages of the same publication.

 Story Text that flows between several text frames.

To create a story in multiple text frames, follow these steps:

1. Click the **Text Frame** tool on the Publisher toolbar and place a text frame on your publication page. Make the text box big enough to hold all the text in the story.

2. Type all the text that will be included in your story into the current text box.

3. Size the text frame (place the mouse on the border of the frame and drag it) so that it shows only the text that you want to appear in this particular frame (other text will be moved to other text frames).

4. When you reduce the size of the text frame, the text you typed exceeds the size of the current text box and an Overflow indicator appears at the bottom of the frame (see Figure 8.6). This means that text not shown in the text frame is held in an overflow area.

5. Create the other text frames that will hold the overflow portion of the story that was typed into the first text frame.

6. Click the text frame that holds the text.

7. Select the **Tools** menu, and then select **Connect Text Frames**.

8. A Connect Text Frames button appears on the Standard toolbar. Click the **Connect Text Frames** button.

9. The mouse pointer becomes a pitcher of text, as shown in Figure 8.7. Place the Pitcher pointer on the first empty text frame into which you want the story text to flow. Click the left mouse button.

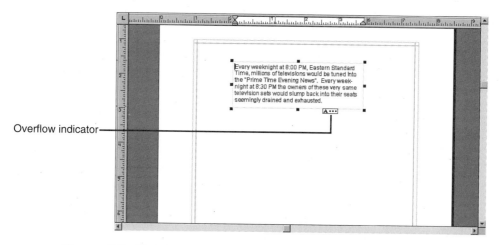

Overflow indicator

Figure 8.6 Text that exceeds the size of a text frame is held in an overflow area, and an Overflow indicator appears on the text frame.

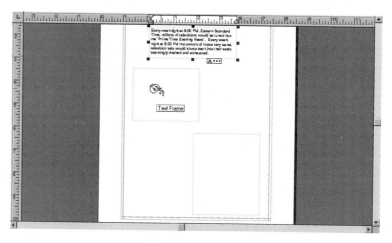

Figure 8.7 Select all the text frames that will hold the story text.

10. Story text flows into the text frame, and the text frame becomes the selected text frame (sizing handles and a border appear around the text frame). An Overflow indicator might (depending on the amount of text left) also appear on this text box.

11. Click the **Connect Text Frames** button on the toolbar again and use the Pitcher pointer to flow text into the next text frame you have on the page.

When all the text in the original story has been placed in the text frames, you will find that the last text frame does not have an Overflow indicator on its border (this assures you that all the story text appears in the text frames included in the set). You will want to spell check large stories; for information on using the spell checker, see Lesson 15, "Fine-Tuning Publisher Publications."

In this lesson, you learned to change the look of text in a text frame by changing the font type, the font size, the font color, and other font attributes such as font style (bold, italic, and so on). You also learned to insert mastheads from the Publisher Design Gallery and create text stories that flow to multiple text frames. In the next lesson, you learn to insert and modify pictures and graphics in your publications.

Working with Graphics

In this lesson, you learn how to add pictures and clip art to your publications. You also learn how to scale, crop, and change the color of graphical objects such as pictures and clip art.

Inserting a Picture

Publisher provides you with a lot of flexibility as to the type of objects that you can add to your publication pages. You can add a picture file to a page, or you can choose to add a clip-art image from the extensive Clip Gallery that comes with Microsoft Publisher.

Pictures can come in a variety of file types, and pictures can consist of files you have on disk, items you copy from the World Wide Web, or pictures that you create using a scanner or a digital camera (for more about inserting pictures from scanners and other sources, see Lesson 10, "Adding Special Objects to Your Publications").

Publisher supports a wide variety of picture file formats that you can insert into a publication. Table 9.1 lists some of the most common picture file types.

Table 9.1 Publisher Can Use Pictures Created in a Variety of File Formats

File Type	Extension
Windows Bitmap (Windows Paint)	.bmp
CorelDRAW!	.cdr
Encapsulated PostScript (QuarkXPress)	.eps

Table 9.1 Continued

File Type	Extension
Graphics Interchange Format (CompuServe format)	.gif
Joint Photographics Expert Group (commonly used on the World Wide Web)	.jpeg or .jpg
Kodak PhotoCD and Pro PhotoCD	.pcd
PC Paintbrush	.pcx
TIFF, Tagged Image File Format (PhotoDraw)	.tif
Windows Metafile (Microsoft Word Clip Art)	.wmf
WordPerfect Graphics	.wpg

To insert a picture onto a publication page, follow these steps:

1. Click the **Picture Frame** tool on the Publisher toolbar.

2. Place the mouse pointer on the page and drag to create the picture frame.

3. With the picture frame selected, select the **Insert** menu, then point at **Picture**. Then select **From File** on the cascading menu.

4. The Insert Picture dialog box appears. Use the **Look In** drop-down arrow to select the drive on which the picture resides.

5. Double-click the appropriate folder that holds the file.

6. Click the picture filename in the dialog box. A preview of the picture appears (see Figure 9.1).

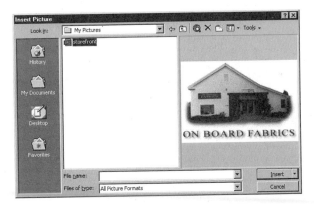

Figure 9.1 Use the Insert Picture dialog box to locate the picture file that you will place in your picture frame.

957

7. Click the **Insert** button. The picture is placed in the picture frame on the publication page.

TIP **Open the Insert Picture Dialog Box with a Double-Click** You can also insert a picture file into a picture frame by double-clicking the empty picture frame. The Insert Picture dialog box appears.

Using Clip Art

An alternative to placing picture files into your publications is to use clip art. Clip art is a library of ready-made images that are arranged in categories (such as animals or business) to make it easy for you to find the right type of graphic image.

You will find that the Publisher Clip Art Gallery is quite extensive and has clip art that will serve in nearly every situation. To insert clip art onto a publication page, follow these steps:

1. Click the **Clip Art Gallery** tool on the Publisher toolbar.

2. Place the mouse pointer on the page and drag to create the Clip Art frame. The Clip Art Gallery window appears.

3. The Clip Art Gallery has three tabs: Pictures, Sounds, and Motion Clips. Make sure the **Pictures** tab is selected. The available categories of clip art appear in the Gallery window (see Figure 9.2).

TIP **Maximize the Gallery Window** You will find it easier to view and navigate the categories in the Clip Art Gallery if you maximize the Gallery window by clicking the **Maximize** button in the upper-right corner.

4. Click a category (such as Animals) to see the clip art available in that particular category.

5. To insert a particular clip-art image, click the image. A toolbar appears next to the image (see Figure 9.3).

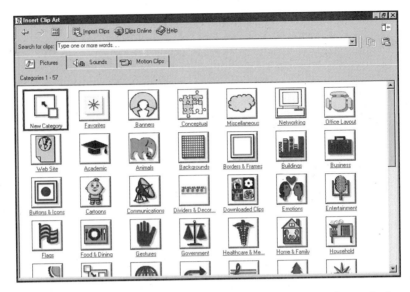

Figure 9.2 The Clip-Art Gallery provides you with clip-art categories so that you can choose images by theme.

Insert Clip button ——

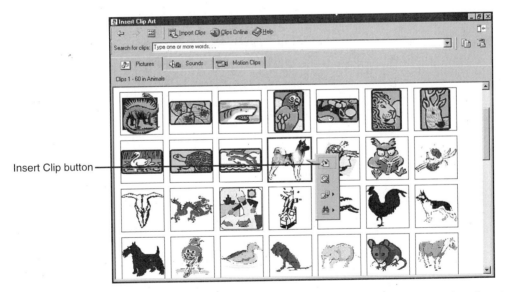

Figure 9.3 Click the Insert Clip button on the image toolbar to insert the clip art.

6. Click the **Insert Clip** button and the image is inserted into your publication.

7. When you have finished working with the Clip Art Gallery, click its **Close** (×) button to return to your publication.

Search for Clips   You can also do a search for clip art by keywords. The clips that satisfy the search parameters appear in the Gallery window. Click in the **Search for Clips** box at the top of the Gallery window. Type in your search word and then press **Enter**.

Clip art reacts to changes in the frame size the same way that pictures do. Increase the size of the frame and the clip art inside the frame is enlarged.

The Clip Art Gallery also provides you with sound and animated video clips you can place in publications that are viewed online, such as a Web page. See Lesson 10 for more information.

Scaling Pictures

After you have a picture in a picture frame or a clip-art image in a clip-art frame, you can easily scale the image using the mouse. Select the frame and then use the sizing handles that appear to size the image.

To increase or decrease the size of an image, drag the image frame (see Figure 9.4).

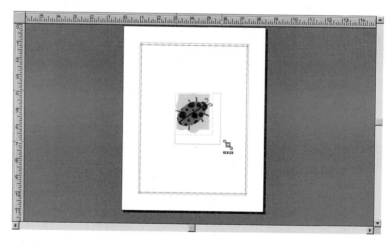

Figure 9.4 Drag a sizing handle to scale the image in a particular frame.

CAUTION

Don't Distort Your Pictures   When scaling your pictures, however, you usually want to maintain the height/width ratio of the picture. Otherwise, images appear elongated or squashed if you only change their scale in one direction (such as just dragging one of the vertical borders to change the width).

You can also scale an image based on a percentage of the original size of the image. When you insert the image, it fills the frame that you created for the image. The frame constitutes a particular width and height for the image. The final size of the inserted image might be less than that of the original image you used (the size at which it was originally created and then saved as a file)—less than 100%—or it might be greater than the original image size if you used a particularly large frame—greater than 100%.

Your overall image size is based on two measurements: height and width. You can adjust both of these by a percentage if you want, using the Scale Picture dialog box.

Follow these steps to scale the picture using percentages for width and height:

1. Select the frame that holds the image you want to scale.
2. Select **Format**, then select **Scale Picture**. The Scale Picture dialog box appears.
3. Click in the **Scale Height** box and enter a percentage for the height of the image.
4. Click in the **Scale Width** box and enter a percentage for the width of the image.
5. Click **OK** to close the dialog box.

The image is scaled according to the percentages that you entered. This will also, in effect, scale the frame where the picture resides.

Cropping Pictures

You might run across a situation where you want to trim the edges off a particular image. For instance, you have a clip art image that contains a picture surrounded by a border, and you want to crop the border and just keep the picture itself in the frame. Or you might have an image that contains several items, such as a picture of several people, and you want to crop the image so that only one person appears in the frame.

961

You can easily crop an image using the Publisher cropping tool. To crop
a picture or clip-art image, follow these steps:

1. Select the picture or clip-art frame that holds the image you want to crop.
2. Select **Format**, then select **Crop Picture**.
3. The mouse pointer becomes a cropping tool (see Figure 9.5).
4. Place the cropping tool on any of the sizing handles on the picture's frame
   and drag to crop the picture, as shown in Figure 9.5.

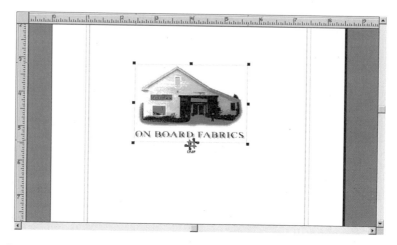

Figure 9.5   Use the cropping tool to crop an image in a picture or clip-art frame.

5. When you have completed cropping the picture, click anywhere on the
   page to deselect the image frame.

TIP   **Crop in More Than One Direction**   After you invoke the cropping tool, you
can crop the image in more than one direction (such as cropping it on the right
and then cropping it on the top) in the same cropping session. The cropping tool
disappears only when you clip outside the picture frame and deselect it.

Changing Picture Colors

You can also change the color of an image in a picture or clip-art frame. Changing
the color of a picture means that you change all the current colors to one selected
color. Changing picture colors works well with images that are only one or two
colors. You will find, however, that images that are multicolored do not look very

good when changed to only one color. Coloring images is not without its place, however; you can get some nice visual effects coloring certain images in your publications.

To change the color of an image, follow these steps:

1. Select the frame that holds the picture or clip art you want to recolor.

2. Click **Format**, than click **Recolor Picture**. The Recolor Picture dialog box appears (see Figure 9.6).

3. Click the **Color** drop-down box to select a new color (if you find a color you want to use on the color box that appears, you can skip step 4).

Figure 9.6   The Recolor Picture dialog box enables you to select one color for the selected picture.

4. If you want to select from additional colors, click the **More Colors** selection in the color box. The Color dialog box appears. Click any color on the palette, and then click **OK** to return to the Recolor Picture dialog box.

5. Click a color on the **Color** drop-down box and then click **OK** to close the Recolor picture dialog box.

The new color is applied to your picture. Because you are creating a mono-chrome picture (a picture of one color), you might find that you have to experi-ment a little to find a color that gives you a satisfactory image.

In this lesson, you learned how to insert pictures and clip art into your publica-tions. You also learned how to scale, crop, and color an image. In the next lesson, you learn how to add special objects such as banners and other design elements to your publications.

Adding Special Objects to Your Publications

In this lesson, you learn how to add special objects using the Design Gallery, how to import objects from other applications, and how to insert video, audio, and pictures from scanners and cameras.

Using the Design Gallery

Publisher makes it easy for you to add a variety of special objects to your publications. The Design Gallery provides a set of wizards that create *smart objects* (such as logos, mastheads, calendars, and other special objects). These objects are called smart objects because they can be edited at any time using the appropriate wizard, which makes them very different from the typical static object, such as a picture or clip art, that you add to your pages.

To insert a Design Gallery object onto a publication page, follow these steps:

1. Click the **Design Gallery Object** tool on the Publisher toolbar.

2. In the Design Gallery window, click an Object category in the **Categories** pane (such as Calendar).

3. In the **Object** pane, click the object you wish to insert on the page (see Figure 10.1).

4. Click the **Insert Object** button to insert the object onto the page.

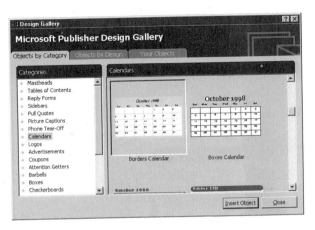

Figure 10.1 Insert special objects using the Design Gallery.

TIP **Dealing with Oversized Objects** Some of the smart objects created using the Design Gallery will be inserted onto your page at a size that cannot be accommodated by a typical page size. You will have to size the new object to fit within the boundaries of your page.

Editing Design Gallery Objects

When you add a smart object to your publication using the Design Gallery, Publisher makes it very easy for you to change the formatting of any of these special items. A wizard is associated with each of the smart objects and can be consulted to make changes to a particular object. Suppose, for instance, you create a calendar, such as the one that is shown in Figure 10.2, and you want to change the look of the calendar.

To edit a Design Gallery object, follow these steps:

1. Click the smart object to select it.

2. Click the **Wizard** button that appears on the smart object's border (it contains a magic wand). The wizard associated with the object opens (such as the Calendar Creation Wizard shown in Figure 10.2).

3. Click a design element category in the top pane of the wizard (in this case, Design has been selected in the Calendar Creation Wizard).

965

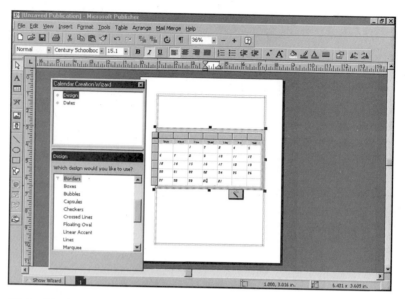

Figure 10.2   Each Design Gallery object can be quickly edited using its own wizard.

4. Select a new design (such as Borders in Figure 10.2) in the lower pane of the current wizard. You can preview as many designs as you wish by selecting them in the lower wizard pane.

5. When you have finished working with the wizard for a particular smart object, you can close the wizard to give you more working room in the Publisher window. Click the **Close** button in the upper-right corner of the wizard window.

The number of attributes you can change for a particular Design Gallery object depends on the object itself. For instance, a calendar enables you to change the overall design and the way dates are displayed. Logos enables you to change the picture associated with the logo, the number of lines in the logo, and the overall design of the logo.

Inserting Objects from Other Applications

You can also place objects created in other applications into your publication. For instance, you can place an Excel worksheet and a chart into a publication. Or you can place a PowerPoint slide on the page of a publication. These types of objects are often referred to as Object Linking and Embedding (OLE) objects.

To insert an OLE object onto a publication page, follow these steps:

1. Create an object in any Windows application, such as a worksheet and chart in Microsoft Excel (see Figure 10.3). Save the item as a file. Then close the application.

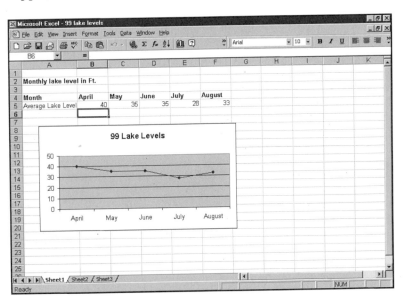

Figure 10.3 Any file you create in a Windows application, such as Microsoft Excel, can be inserted into Publisher.

2. In Publisher, click the **Insert** menu, then click **Object**.
3. In the Insert Object dialog box, click the **Create from File** option button (see Figure 10.4).

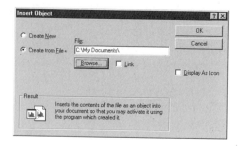

Figure 10.4   The Insert Object dialog enables you to insert a new object or an existing object.

4. Click the **Browse** button to open the Browse dialog box.

5. Locate the file you wish to insert as an object and then select it in the Browse dialog box.

6. Click **Insert** to close the Browse dialog box and return to the Insert Object dialog box.

7. Click **OK** to insert the object into Publisher.

TIP   **Creating an OLE Object On-the-Fly**   You can also choose to create your OLE object from scratch during the process of inserting the object into Publisher. From the Insert Object dialog box, choose **Create New,** then select an application from the **Object Type** list and click **OK**. Place the new object in the appropriate place on the page. Double-click the object to edit it.

After you place OLE objects on your publication pages, you can actually edit them using the features of the application that you created them in (such as Excel). Double-clicking an OLE object in Publisher changes the Publisher menu system and toolbars to provide the features that are available in the server application.

TERM   **Server Application**   The application used to create the file that has been inserted into Publisher as an object.

To edit an object, double-click the object. Figure 10.5 shows an Excel worksheet that has been inserted as an object. After the object is activated (by the double-click), you can edit it as if you were in the server application in which the file was created (in this case, Excel).

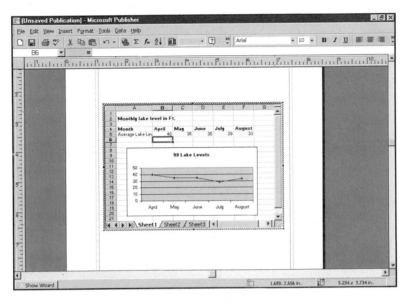

Figure 10.5 Double-click an OLE object to edit it.

Inserting Video and Audio

If you are creating a publication that will be viewed on your computer or online (such as a Web site; see Lesson 19, "Creating a Publisher Web Site," for information on using Publisher to build a Web site), you can add video and sound to the publication. This provides you with the capability to add some very interesting visual and sound effects to any publication.

Publisher actually provides a library of video animation and sounds that can be inserted into your publications. Both these media types can be found in Publisher's Clip Art Gallery.

If you have a sound card and a microphone, you can record your own audio and place it in your publications. Use the Windows sound recorder application to create audio files. You can also insert your own video files if you have video capabilities (a connection for your camcorder or a digital video camera) on your computer.

In addition, a number of Web sites have audio and video clips you can use in your own publications and on your own Web site. Use any of the Web search engines (such as WebCrawler) and search for audio and/or video clips.

CAUTION

Check the Copyright Make sure that clips you use are not copyrighted and that you have permission to use them. Not everything on the Web is in the public domain.

To insert an audio or video clip from the Clip Art Gallery, follow these steps:

1. To insert an audio or video clip into a presentation, click the **Insert** menu, point at **Picture**, and then click **Clip Art**.
2. In the Clip Art window, click the **Audio** or **Video** tab.
3. Select a category of sounds or videos (such as **Animals** on the Video tab) from the selected tab (the categories available depend on the tab you select).

Sample the Clip If you want to play a video or sound clip before you place it in your publication, click the video or sound clip in the Clip Art Gallery and then select **Play Video** or **Play Sound** from the shortcut bar that appears.

4. Click a sound or video in the window and click the **Insert** button to place it on the publication page (see Figure 10.6).

Insert —

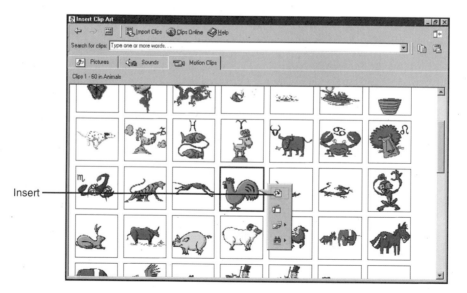

Figure 10.6 Insert audio or video clips from the Publisher Clip Art Gallery.

5. Click the **Close** button on the upper-right corner of the Clip Art window to close it.

After you have a video or audio clip on the publication page, you can test it by double-clicking. Audio clips play automatically (you hear them immediately) and video clips (depending on the source) open a player application (usually Windows Media Player) that plays the clip. Be advised, however, that the animated clips that you place in your publications from the Clip Art Gallery work only in publications that have been created as a Web page. The clip plays when you view the publication in a Web browser such as Microsoft Internet Explorer (for more about Web pages, see Lesson 19).

Acquiring Images from Scanners and Other Sources

You can also place images into your publications that do not currently exist as a picture or clip art file. You can actually attach to a particular input device and then have it scan an image or take a picture on–the-fly that is then inserted into your publication.

Input Device Any device, such as a scanner or a digital camera, that is attached to your computer and can be used to acquire a picture.

Publisher enables you to acquire images from an attached scanner, digital camera, or other device such as a video camera. Set up the device so that it works on your computer, and Publisher will have no problem using it to capture a particular image.

To capture an image from an attached device, follow these steps:

1. Click the **Picture Frame** tool on the Publisher toolbar.

2. Place the mouse pointer on the page and drag it to create the picture frame.

3. With the picture frame selected, select the **Insert** menu, then point at **Picture**. Then point at **Acquire Image** on the cascading menu. The image currently on your digital camera or on your scanner appears in the Capture dialog box (see Figure 10.7).

Figure 10.7   Images can be acquired from any scanner or camera you have attached to your computer.

4. Click **Capture** to place the image in the picture frame.

You can size the image the same as you would any other frame in your publication. You can also add borders or change the color of the image (for more about enhancing frames, see Lesson 7, "Enhancing Frames with Borders and Colors").

In this lesson, you learned how to insert special objects using the Design Gallery. You also learned how to insert an object from another application and how to insert video, audio, and pictures from scanners and cameras into your publications. In the next lesson, you learn how to draw your own objects using the Publisher drawing tools.

Drawing Objects in Publisher

In this lesson, you learn how to draw objects for your publications using the Publisher drawing tools. You also work with Microsoft Draw to add drawn objects to your publication pages.

Using the Drawing Tools

Although you can insert different kinds of objects using the Design Gallery or insert objects created in other applications (see Lesson 10, "Adding Special Objects to Your Publications," for more about the Design Gallery), you can also choose to draw your own objects. Publisher provides you with drawing tools that make it easy to draw circles, rectangles, lines, and other shapes. Drawn objects function much the same as any objects you insert into your publications. You can change their fill colors, resize them, and move them on the page.

Publisher provides you with several drawing tools, which are found on the Publisher toolbar. Table 11.1 shows these tools and lists the objects they help you create.

Table 11.1   The Publisher Drawing Tools

Tool	Object
 Line tool	Line
Oval tool	Oval
Rectangle tool	Rectangle
Custom Shapes tool	Custom Shapes

The Line, Oval, and Rectangle tools all function in the same way. You click the appropriate tool and then drag to create the object. The Custom Shapes tool provides a palette of different shapes. Select a particular shape and then drag to create it on the page.

Drawing a Line

Publisher makes it easy for you to create a vertical, horizontal, or otherwise-oriented line. Lines that you create using the Line tool on the Publisher toolbar can also include arrowheads and be designed with different line weights and colors.

1. Click the **Line** tool and place the mouse pointer on the page.

2. Drag on the publication page to create the line (either dragging vertically or horizontally to create the appropriate orientation), as shown in Figure 11.1.

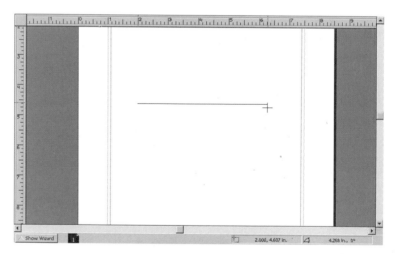

Figure 11.1 Drag to create a line on the publication page.

3. Release the left mouse button and the line appears on the page.

 TIP **Drawing a Straight Line** To draw a perfectly straight horizontal or vertical line, hold down the **Shift** key as you drag to create the line.

To format a line that you've drawn, double-click the line. The Line dialog box appears. In this dialog box, you can control the line thickness, whether the line has arrowheads, and the color of the line.

When you change the formatting options for a particular line, the changes can be viewed in the Sample box of the Line dialog box (see Figure 11.2). After you've made all your line formatting selections for the selected line, click **OK** to close the dialog box.

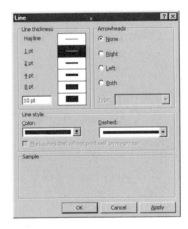

Figure 11.2 The Line dialog box enables you to control the formatting for the selected line.

Drawing an Oval or a Rectangle

The Oval and Rectangle tools function similarly. You drag in two directions (down and then to the right, for instance) to create the two dimensions of the object (height and width).

TIP **Getting Your Dragging Technique Down** When you create a new drawing object such as a circle or rectangle, drag the mouse downward on the page to create the height for the object, and then drag to the right to create the width for the object. This gives you greater control over the final size of the object. But don't let go of the left mouse button until you have the object sized appropriately.

To create an oval or a rectangle, follow these steps:

1. Click either the **Oval** or the **Rectangle** tool on the Publisher toolbar.

2. Drag on the publication page to create the drawn object (such as a circle).

3. Release the left mouse button, and your new drawn object appears on the page.

 TIP   **Drawing a Perfect Circle or Square**   If you want to draw a perfect circle or square using the Oval or Rectangle tool, hold down the **Shift** key as you drag to create your new object.

Drawing a Custom Shape

Publisher also provides you with the capability to draw a number of custom shapes. These shapes range from triangles to stars to sunbursts.

To draw a custom shape, follow these steps:

1. Click the **Custom Shapes** tool on the Publisher toolbar.

2. Select a custom shape from the shape palette that appears (see Figure 11.3).

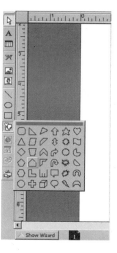

Figure 11.3   Select from a number of custom shapes.

3. Drag on the publication page to create the drawn object.

4. Release the left mouse button, and your new drawn object appears on the page.

Custom shapes can be formatted the same as circles or rectangles that are created using the drawing tools. The next section discusses formatting the borders and the interior color of a drawn object.

 TIP **Layering Objects** You can layer drawn objects using the commands on the Arrange menu. Use the same techniques discussed in Lesson 6, "Working with Publication Frames," under the heading "Arranging Frames in Layers."

Formatting Drawing Objects

You can change the outside border color and the interior fill color of any drawn object. Both of these color attributes can easily be changed on a selected object by using the Line Color and Fill Color buttons on the Formatting toolbar.

To change the border color of a drawn object, follow these steps:

1. Click the drawn object for which you want to change the line color.

 2. Click the **Line Color** button on the Formatting toolbar.

3. Select a color on the color palette that appears.

Changing the fill color is a similar operation. Follow these steps:

1. Select the object for which you wish to select a fill color.

 2. Click the **Fill Color** button on the Formatting toolbar.

3. Click a fill color on the color palette that appears. If you want to choose from more colors than provided by the Fill Color menu, click the **More Colors** button on the color palette. The Colors dialog box appears. Click a color box to select a new color for your fill color. Then click **OK** to close the dialog box. You are returned to the color palette and you can make your selection.

977

Rotating an Object

You can easily rotate and flip objects that you create on your publication pages. Rotating an object enables you to reorient an object to the right or to the left. For instance, if you want to make a horizontal line a vertical line, you can rotate the line to the right.

To rotate an object, follow these steps:

1. Click the object you want to rotate to select it.

2. Click the **Rotate Right** (or **Rotate Left**) button on the Standard toolbar to rotate the object in that direction. The object rotates.

The Rotate Right and Rotate Left commands rotate an object 90 degrees in either the right or left direction. If you want to custom rotate an object, select the object and then click the **Custom Rotate** button on the Standard toolbar. In the Custom Rotate dialog box that appears, click either the **Rotate Left** or **Rotate Right** buttons to increase the rotation angle in that direction.

You can also change the orientation of an object by flipping it. For instance, you might have a right-pointing object (such as a clip-art arrow) that you would like to orient so that it points to the left. You can flip the image to the left to get a mirror image of its original orientation.

To flip an object, follow these steps:

1. Click the object that you want to flip to select it.

2. Click the **Flip Horizontal** button to reverse the horizontal orientation of the object (or click the **Flip Vertical** button to flip the object vertically).

Drawing with Microsoft Draw

You can also choose to draw your own images using Microsoft Draw. Microsoft Draw is an add-in application that comes with Publisher 2000 and Microsoft Office 2000. It provides an assortment of drawing tools that you can use to create your own images.

The tools operate much like the Line, Oval, and Rectangle tools on the Publisher toolbar. The difference between the Publisher drawing tools and Microsoft Draw is that the Publisher drawing tools create individual objects, whereas your Microsoft Draw image (made up of a number of drawn elements) is treated as a single object. Table 11.2 shows and describes a number of the available tools.

Table 11.2 The Microsoft Draw Tools

Tool	Object
	Line
	Arrow
	Rectangle
	Oval
	Text Box
	Fill Color
	Line Color
	Font Color

When you start Microsoft Draw, the application actually takes over the Publisher window. You will notice that all the toolbars and commands that are normally found in the Publisher window are replaced by toolbars for Microsoft Draw. When you click outside the Drawing frame, you are returned to Publisher and its toolbars.

1. Click the **Insert** menu, then point at **Picture**. Then click **New Drawing** on the cascading menu. The Draw toolbar appears.

2. Click a tool on the Draw toolbar (such as the **Rectangle**) and drag to create an item in the Draw frame.

3. Use other tools on the Drawing toolbar as needed to complete your drawing (see Figure 11.4).

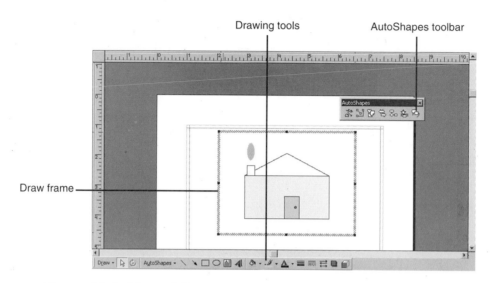

Drawing tools   AutoShapes toolbar

Draw frame

Figure 11.4 Microsoft Draw provides a number of tools that you can use to create your own objects.

4. Click outside the Draw frame to return to Publisher.

Microsoft Draw provides a number of object shapes and special objects (such as callouts) that enable you to draw some fairly sophisticated objects. Remember that Draw objects are treated as a single object in Publisher, no matter how many individual shapes were used to create the object itself.

 TIP **Microsoft Draw Provides More Tools** You will find that Microsoft Draw offers a greater number of tools and shapes than those found on the Publisher toolbar. Custom shapes such as flow chart shapes, block arrows, and star and banner shapes can be quickly drawn using the AutoShapes toolbar that appears in the Draw window.

In this lesson, you learned how to draw and format objects using the Publisher drawing tools. You also worked with Microsoft Draw to create a drawn object. In the next lesson, you learn how to work with line spacing, tabs, indents, and numbered and bulleted lists.

Working with Line Spacing, Indents, and Lists

In this lesson, you learn how to change line spacing, indent text, and format lists with bullets or numbers.

Setting Line Spacing in a Text Frame

Text is added to your publications in text frames (as discussed in Lesson 8, "Changing How Text Looks"). Each text frame can be formatted differently in respect to line spacing, text indents, tab settings, and how lists are formatted (bulleted or numbered). In fact, every paragraph in a text frame can be set up with different attributes.

Publisher considers any text line or lines followed by a line break (created when you press the **Enter** key) a separate paragraph. Therefore, every block of text followed by a line break can potentially have different line spacing.

To change the line spacing for text in a frame, follow these steps:

1. Place the insertion point in the paragraph for which you want to change the line spacing.
2. Click **Format**, then **Line Spacing**. The Line Spacing dialog box appears (see Figure 12.1).

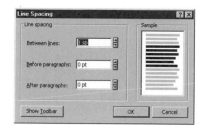

Figure 12.1   The Line Spacing dialog box gives you control over the line spacing in a text frame.

3. Type in the new line spacing in the **Between Lines** box (or use the click arrows to select a new spacing).

4. Click **OK** to close the dialog box and apply the new line spacing.

 TIP   **Setting Line Spacing Before and After Paragraphs**   The Line Spacing dialog box also provides you with the capability to add additional spacing before and after paragraphs that appear in a text frame. This makes it easy to offset paragraphs of information from each other or from other text elements such as headings.

After you set the line spacing for a particular paragraph, you can then move to the next paragraph and set a different spacing. In cases where you have several separate paragraphs in the same text frame and want to assign the same line spacing to them, select all the paragraphs and then follow the steps outlined above.

Indenting Text

 You can offset text lines from other text in a text frame by using the indent buttons on the Formatting toolbar. Each time you click the **Increase Indent** button, your text is indented 1/2 inch from the left edge of the text frame.

Indents work nicely for lists that are grouped under a particular heading. To indent text in a text frame, follow these steps:

1. Place the insertion point in the text line or paragraph you want to indent.

 2. Click the **Increase Indent** button on the Formatting toolbar.

You can also increase the indent that you've placed on a paragraph or particular line of text. Place the insertion point in the line or paragraph and click the **Increase Indent** button.

To indent lines of text that are not part of the same paragraph (lines or blocks of text separated by a line return), select the lines and then click the **Increase Indent** button.

Setting Tabs

Another way to indent and align text in a text frame is by using tabs. Tabs are set every 1/2 inch by default. Every time you press the Tab key on the keyboard, you offset the text line from the left margin of your text frame one tab stop. Setting tabs is done by clicking the horizontal ruler to place a particular tab type at a particular point on the ruler.

You can set different tab types by clicking the Tab selector (located where the two rulers join in the upper-left corner).

- Left Tab—Aligns the beginning of the text line at the tab stop.

- Center Tab—Centers the text line at the tab stop.

- Right Tab—Right justifies the text line at the tab stop.

- Decimal Tab—Lines up numerical entries at their decimal point.

Setting a series of tabs on the ruler can enable you to line up text in columns in a text frame. Each tab stop designates the start of a particular column of text. This is useful when you want to place text in rows of information (for another way to arrange text in rows and columns, see Lesson 13, "Adding Tables to Your Publications").

To set a tab on the ruler, follow these steps:

1. Click the **Tab** selector to select the type of tab you want to place.
2. Click the horizontal ruler at the position where you want to place the new tab.

3. Repeat steps 1 and 2 to place other tabs on the ruler.

4. Press the **Tab** key on the keyboard and type the text you want to align at the tab stop (see Figure 12.2).

5. Press the **Tab** key as needed to align the new text at the tab stops.

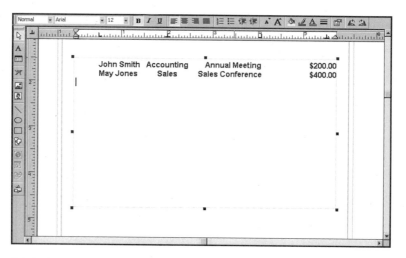

Figure 12.2   Tabs can be used to align text in a text frame.

Working with Numbered Lists

You can easily create a numbered list in a Publisher text frame. You have the choice of creating the list and then assigning the numbers, or turning on the automatic numbering and then creating the list from scratch.

The great thing about using Publisher's automatic numbering is that if you add or delete a line in the numbered list, all the numbering changes to accommodate the addition or deletion.

1. Select the text list you want to number.

 2. Click the **Numbers** button on the toolbar. The list is numbered (see Figure 12.3).

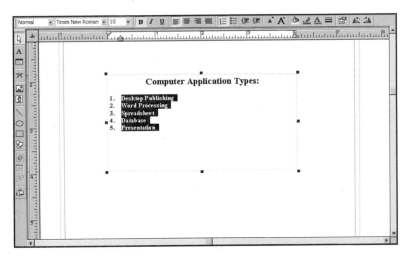

Figure 12.3 Lists can easily be numbered using automatic numbering.

3. Click anywhere on the page to deselect the list.

You also have control over the format of the numbering for the list. You can choose the style of the numbering and where the numbers in the list begin (the start value).

To change the number format for a list, follow these steps:

1. Select the numbered list.

2. Select the **Format** menu, then click **Indents and Lists**. The Indents and Lists dialog box opens (see Figure 12.4).

3. Use the **Format** drop-down list to select a new numbering format for the selected list.

4. If you want to change the starting number in the list, type a new value in the **Start At** box.

5. When you have completed your choices, click **OK** to close the dialog box.

If you find that you would rather center or otherwise align the list (rather than using the default indent), click the **Alignment** drop-down box in the Indents and Lists dialog box and select a new alignment.

Figure 12.4   Change the numbering style for the list using the Indents and Lists dialog box.

Adding Bullets to Your Text Lists

You can also quickly add bullets to a text list. Bullets help to delineate items in a list from other text in the text frame. You can add bullets to existing lists or turn on the bulleting and then type a new list.

To add bullets to an existing list, follow these steps:

1. Select the text list to which you want to add bullets.

2. Click the **Bullets** button on the toolbar.

3. Click anywhere to deselect the list.

Bulleted lists can also be formatted using the Indents and Lists dialog box. Select the bulleted list and choose **Format**, then select **Indents and Lists**.

In the Indents and Lists dialog box (see Figure 12.5), click to select a new bullet type for your list. After you've made your choice, click **OK** to close the dialog box.

If you don't see a bullet style that you want to use for your list in the Indents and Lists dialog box, click the **New Bullet** button. The New Bullet dialog box appears, and you can choose from different symbols to use as bullets.

Figure 12.5 Several bullet types are provided for your bulleted lists.

In this lesson, you learned how to set line spacing for text and how to use indents and tabs to align text in a text frame. You also learned how to add numbers and bullets automatically to lists. In the next lesson, you learn how to insert and format tables onto your publication pages.

Adding Tables to Your Publications

13

In this lesson, you learn how to insert a table onto a page. You also learn how to move, size, and format the table.

Inserting a Table

Another way to present information in a publication is to use a table. A table enables you to place information into rows and columns, making it easy to arrange information in a highly accessible format. The intersection of a row and a column is called a cell; the cells are where you place your data. Publisher gives you complete control over the number of rows and columns in your table and their size.

Tables are added to a publication page much the same as any object (such as a text frame or a picture frame). You use the Table tool on the Publisher toolbar.

To insert a table onto a page, follow these steps:

1. Click the **Table** tool on the Publisher toolbar.

2. Click and drag to create the table on the page.

3. In the Create Table dialog box, type the number of rows and columns for the table (see Figure 13.1).

4. Click **OK**. The table appears on the publication page.

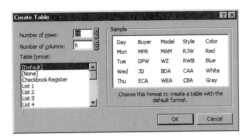

Figure 13.1 The Create Table dialog box enables you to select the number of rows and columns for the table.

TIP **Selecting a Format for the Table** You can select an autoformat for your table in the Create Table dialog box by using the Table Format list. For more about autoformatting, see "Formatting the Table Automatically," later in this lesson.

In cases where you want to place information side-by-side on the page, you will find that tables make it a simple task. Tables provide you with much more control over the placement of information as compared to trying to align items with indents or tabs.

Sizing and Moving Tables

You can resize a table at any time. When you change the table's width (making it larger), this also makes all the column widths larger. If you change the table's height, this changes all the row heights in the table.

To size your table, follow these steps:

1. Click the table to select it.
2. Place the mouse on the appropriate sizing handle and drag to increase or decrease the size (see Figure 13.2).
3. Release the left mouse button when the table is the appropriate size.

TIP **Maintaining the Table's Height/Width Ratio** If you want to maintain the table's overall height/width ratio when you increase or decrease the size of the table, be sure to drag by one of the table's corners, and drag on the diagonal.

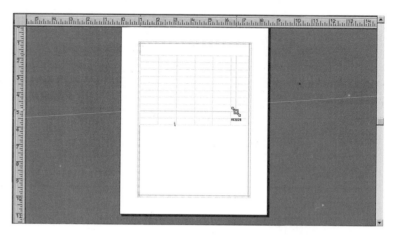

Figure 13.2 Size the table the same as you would any object frame.

Because tables are contained in a frame—the same as the other objects that you've worked with in Publisher—you can also easily move them to a new location on the page. You drag them using the mouse.

To change the location of a table, follow these steps:

1. Place the mouse pointer on the edge of the table frame.
2. When the Move icon appears, drag the table to a new location.
3. When the table is in the correct position, release the mouse button.

 TIP **Paste from One Page to Another** You can also copy or cut the table and then paste it on a different page in the publication.

Sizing Table Columns and Rows

When you change the width of the table, you've already seen that it changes the relative width of all the columns in the table. You can also control the individual width of each column in the table to better accommodate text entries that you place in a particular column. This is also true for row heights. You use the mouse to drag a row divider and increase or decrease a row height as needed.

To change a column width or row height, follow these steps:

1. Click the table to select it.

2. Place the mouse pointer on a column divider to the right of the column you want to size (or on a row divider below the row you want to size). The Adjust icon appears.

3. Drag to increase or decrease the width of the column, as shown in Figure 13.3 (or drag to change the row height, if applicable).

4. Release the mouse button. The column or row is sized accordingly.

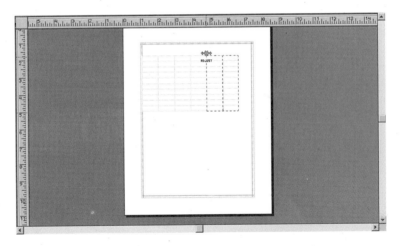

Figure 13.3 You can individually size columns and rows.

TIP **Keeping the Table's Size the Same When Widening Columns**
If you hold down the **Shift** key while dragging the column width tool, the table stays the same size, and only the column is widened.

TIP **Using Grow to Fit Text** If you are changing row heights in anticipation of typing several lines of text into a row's cell, don't bother. Just make sure that the **Grow to Fit Text** command is selected on the **Table** menu. Then the row's height becomes greater, as needed, when you type in the text.

Adding Columns and Rows to the Table

If you find that you need additional columns or rows in the table, you can easily add them. You can add one column or row or add multiple columns and rows.

To add a column or row to a table, follow these steps:

1. Click the table to select it.

2. Click a column or row selector to select it. To add multiple columns or rows, drag to select the appropriate number of column or row selectors (see Figure 13.4).

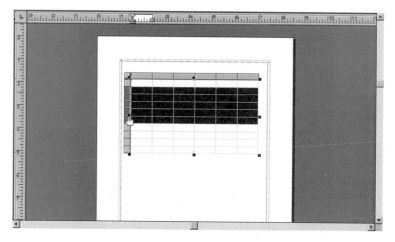

Figure 13.4   You can add columns and rows to your table by selecting existing columns or rows.

3. Select the **Table** menu, then select **Insert Columns** or **Insert Rows**.

The new columns are inserted to the right of the selected columns or rows are inserted below the selected rows.

   TIP   **Resizing the Table After Adding Columns or Rows**   Adding columns or rows to a table makes the table and its frame larger as well. You might have to resize tables to which you add additional columns.

You can also use this same technique to delete columns or rows in a table. Select the columns or rows that you want to delete and then select the **Table** menu. Then choose either **Delete Columns** or **Delete Rows,** as needed.

Using Special Cell Formats

You also have control over the formatting of the individual cells in your tables. For instance, you can merge several cells (a whole row of cells) and use the merged cells as a place to add a heading for the table.

You can also insert a diagonal line in cells in a Publisher table. This enables you to divide the cell into two areas. This is often used on calendars to divide a cell (a certain day of the week) that then holds two dates (such as the 24th and the 31st).

Merging Cells

You might find that you want to take several cells in the same row and make them one continuous cell. The Merge Cells command removes the column dividers between the cells and merges the cell into one continuous cell.

To merge cells in a table, follow these steps:

1. Click the table to select it.
2. Drag to select the cells that you want to merge.
3. Select the **Table** menu, then select **Merge Cells**.

The cells are merged into one cell.

 Merging the cells in the first row of a table makes an excellent place to type a heading for the table. Because the entire row is one cell, you can then center the heading text using the **Center** button on the Formatting toolbar.

Inserting a Diagonal in a Cell

You can divide a cell on the diagonal, making the cell in effect, two cells that can contain different information. To divide a cell diagonally, follow these steps:

1. Click the table to select it.
2. Drag to select a cell or cells that will be split on the diagonal.
3. Select the **Table** menu, then select **Cell Diagonals**.
4. In the Cell Diagonals dialog box (see Figure 13.5), select **Divide Down** or **Divide Up**.

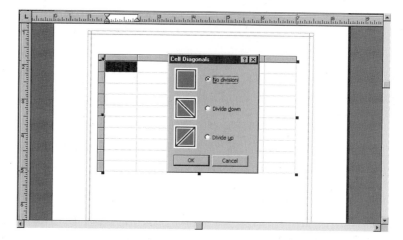

Figure 13.5 You divide a selected cell on the diagonal using the Cell Diagonals dialog box.

5. Click **OK** to close the dialog box. The cell is divided by a diagonal line.

To enter text in a cell divided on the diagonal, click below the line and then enter text at the insertion point. You can then click above the diagonal line and enter text in that area as well.

Filling Your Table with Information

After you've created a new table, you can quickly enter text into the table cells. When you've entered your text, you can format the text using any of the text attribute tools discussed in Lesson 8, "Changing How Text Looks."

To enter the text in the table, follow these steps:

1. Click in the first table cell in which you want to enter text.

2. Type the text for the first cell.

3. Press the **Tab** key to move to the next cell.

4. Enter the text for this cell (see Figure 13.6).

As you type in the table, you can quickly move forward a cell by pressing **Tab**. Press **Shift+Tab** to move back a cell. The up- and down-arrow keys move you quickly up or down a cell.

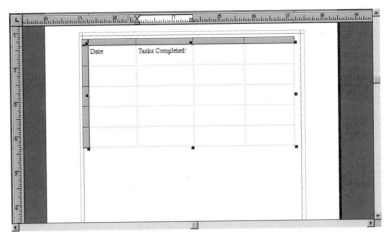

Figure 13.6 Enter text in the table cells the same as you would text in any text frame.

Formatting the Table Automatically

You can format a table quickly by using one of the AutoFormats provided by Publisher. These AutoFormats provide you with text formatting, cell color formatting, and several other formatting attributes. The AutoFormat feature is a great way to create eye-catching tables for your publications.

To autoformat your table, follow these steps:

1. Click the table to select it.
2. Select the **Table** menu, then select **Table AutoFormat**. The Table AutoFormat dialog box appears (see Figure 13.7).
3. Select a format for the table from the list provided.
4. Click **OK**. The table is formatted.

If you find that you don't like the autoformat that you chose, repeat the steps to select a different table format. All the previous formatting will be changed to the new autoformat.

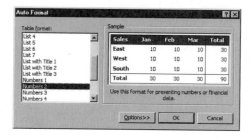

Figure 13.7   Select an autoformat to format the entire table.

Formatting the Table Manually

If you would rather format the table border and fill colors manually, you can use the **Line Color** and **Fill Color** buttons on the Formatting toolbar to selectively format the table.

 For instance, if you want to add a fill color to certain cells in the table, select those cells (see Figure 13.8) and then click the **Fill Color** button and choose a fill color. You can then add a different fill color to other cells in the table.

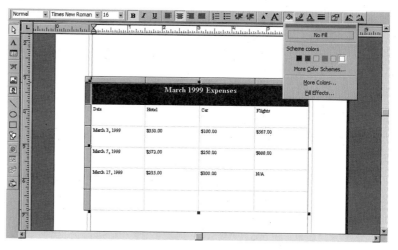

Figure 13.8   Select the cells to which you want to add a fill color.

Adding border colors to the entire table is even easier. With the entire table selected, choose any of the border colors provided on the Line Color palette.

Formatting tables and cells is like formatting frames. Adding borders to your table or adding borders and fill colors to cells uses the same techniques that you use to enhance frames with borders and colors. See Lesson 7, "Enhancing Frames with Borders and Colors," for more information on working with borders and fill colors.

In this lesson, you learned how to insert and format a table. You also learned how to autoformat the table and add text to the table. In the next lesson, you learn how to format publication pages, including their margins, page attributes, and objects placed in the background, such as page numbers.

Formatting Publication Pages

In this lesson, you learn how to change the margins on your publication pages. You also learn how to add a border to a page, add page numbers to pages, and work in the publication background to insert headers and footers.

Changing Page Margins

When you start a new publication (particularly one that you create from scratch), you might want to change the margins for the publication pages. Publisher enables you to shift the margin guides (the blue and pink lines that surround the page) in the Layout Guides dialog box. You can adjust the top, bottom, left, and right margins.

To change the margins for the current page, follow these steps:

1. Select the **Arrange** menu, then select **Layout Guides**. The Layout Guides dialog box appears (see Figure 14.1).
2. Use the appropriate click arrows to increase (or decrease) the left, right, top, or bottom margins, as needed.
3. Click **OK**; the new margins appear on your page.

CAUTION

Don't Change Wizard-Created Publications If you created your publication with a wizard, it's a good idea to leave the margins alone. The wizard placed objects on your pages and set up the margins to accommodate the objects and the layout of the publication. Changing the margins might wreak havoc on your page layout.

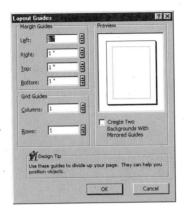

Figure 14.1 You can adjust your page margins using the Layout Guides dialog box.

You can also manually drag the margins on a page to a new location with the mouse. However, you must be in the background of the page to manipulate the margins. Select **View**, then **Go to Background**. Then hold down the **Shift** key and drag any margin to a new location. Working in the background of a page is discussed in the section "Working in the Publication Background" later in this lesson.

Adding Page Borders

You can place borders around the edges of your pages. This gives you a design element that helps emphasize the objects that are placed within these borders.

When you create a new publication using a wizard or a design set (see Lessons 1, "Getting Started with Publisher," and 2, "Creating a New Publication," for more information on wizard-created publications and design set publications), the page border for the publication might be part of the design that you select for that particular publication. However, if you want to place a border around pages in a publication you created from a blank publication template, you can use the Quick Publication Wizard.

To place a border around your publication pages, follow these steps:

1. If the wizard pane is not open in the Publisher application window, click the **Show Wizard** button.
2. Click **Design** in the top pane of the wizard (see Figure 14.2).

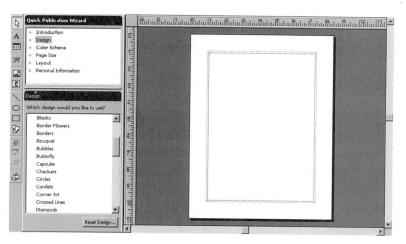

Figure 14.2   Borders are found in the Design category provided by each wizard.

3. Click to select one of the borders in the design list in the bottom pane of the wizard pane.

You can try out as many of the border designs as you want. Figure 14.3 shows a publication page with a border around the page. When you have decided on a particular border, be sure to save your publication.

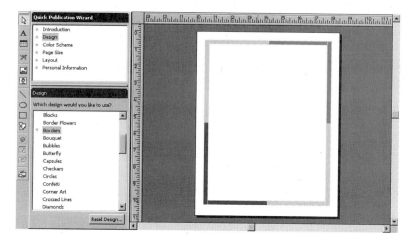

Figure 14.3   Borders can add visual interest to the pages of your publications.

CAUTION

Inserting Blank Publication Pages Negates the Current Wizard
If you insert a blank page or pages into a publication that was created using one of the wizards (even a blank publication is created using the Quick Publication Wizard), you won't be able to add a border to these new pages. They are "wizardless" pages. To ensure that the same border is placed around inserted pages, select the **Duplicate All Objects on Page** option button in the Insert Page dialog box before inserting the new page. You can delete any duplicated objects from the page that you don't need.

Working in the Publication Background

When you place the various objects on your publication pages, you are working in the publication foreground. You are placing objects on top of the page. You can also work in the publication background.

Working in the background enables you to easily place repeating elements onto every page of a publication. For instance, you might want to number the pages in the publication. You place the page numbering code (discussed in the next section) in the background of the publication, and it shows the appropriate page number on the page.

To go to the publication background, choose the **View** menu, and then choose **Go to Background**. You will find that all the objects that were on the current page (when you were in the foreground) have disappeared. That is because you are working in a different layer (the background) of the publication.

In the background, you can insert a text frame or other object that you want to repeat on each of the pages of the publication (as discussed in the next two sections of this lesson). However, you must make sure that objects placed in the background are not obscured by objects that exist in the foreground. For instance, if you place a text frame in the background that holds the current date, it will not show on the publication pages if items in the foreground overlay it.

Figure 14.4 shows a two-page spread of a publication (showing the foreground) where a header text frame has been placed in the background. Notice that the header appears on both pages. Notice also that guides (that were placed on the background) have been used to make sure the header text frame is not obscured by an object on either of the pages (for more about guides, see Lesson 3, "Using Design Sets and Templates").

Background header

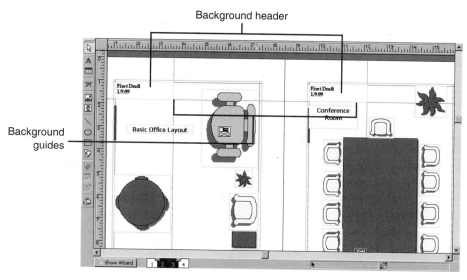

Background guides

Figure 14.4   Placing objects in the background enables you to place repeating elements on your pages.

When you have finished working in the background of your publication, select the **View** menu, and then select **Go to Foreground** to return to the foreground of the current page.

Creating Page Numbers in the Background

When you create publications that contain multiple pages, you might want to number the pages. Page numbers are placed in the background of the publication in a text frame. The great thing about using the page number feature is that even if you insert or delete pages in the publication, the appropriate page number always appears on your pages because Publisher places a page numbering code in the text frame.

To create a page number frame in the background, follow these steps:

1. In the background of a publication page, click the **Text Frame** tool on the Publisher toolbar.

2. Drag the mouse to create the text frame that will hold the page number code.

3. Select the **Insert** menu, then **Page Numbers**. A page number code is placed in the text frame (see Figure 14.5).

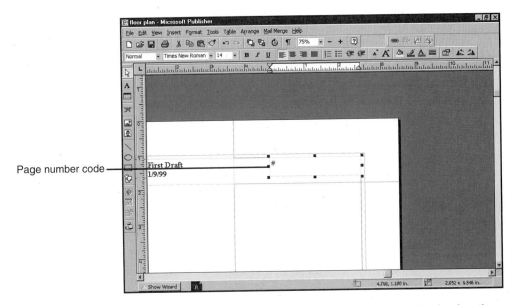

Page number code ──

Figure 14.5 Place the page number code in the background to number the pages in the publication.

If you want to have page numbers that read Page 1 and so on, you can click the mouse just in front of the Page Number code (#) and add the text—**Page** in this example—that you want to appear on every page with the page number.

Inserting the Date into a Text Frame

Another useful feature is the capability to automatically insert the date into a text frame. When you place the text frame in the background, you can conveniently place the current date on all the pages of your publication.

To place the date in the background, follow these steps:

1. In the background of a publication page, click the **Text Frame** tool on the Publisher toolbar.

2. Drag the mouse to create the text frame that will hold the page number code.

3. Select the **Insert** menu, then **Date and Time**.

1003

4. Click the date format you want to place in the text frame.

5. Click **OK** to place the date in the text frame.

TIP **Updating the Date Automatically** If you want to have the date refreshed (the current date placed into the text frame that you placed the date
code into) in your publication whenever you open the saved publication, click
the **Update Automatically** check box in the Date and Time dialog box.

In this lesson, you learned how to change the page margins and add a border
to your pages. You also learned how to work in the background and add a page
number and date code to a text frame in the publication background. In the next
lesson, you learn how to fine-tune your publications with the Spell Checker, the
Design Checker, and the AutoCorrect features.

Fine-Tuning Publisher Publications

In this lesson, you learn how to use the Spelling feature, control hyphenation in a text box, check your publication design with the Design Checker, and set up the AutoCorrect feature.

Using the Spell Checker

After you spend a lot of time designing a publication, you will want to print a hard copy of the final product or prepare the material for printing by a commercial printing service (Lesson 16, "Printing and Outputting Publisher Publications," covers outputting your publications). Publisher offers several tools that enable you to fine-tune your publication.

The Spelling feature checks your documents for misspellings and typos, and it displays each suspect word in the Spelling dialog box. You can choose to replace the word with a suggested correct spelling, ignore the word, or correct the misspelling yourself.

To use the Speller, follow these steps:

1. Select a text frame that you want to spell check.
2. Select **Tools**, point at **Spelling,** and then choose **Check Spelling**.

3. The Check Spelling dialog box appears (see Figure 15.1). The first suspect word (a word considered misspelled) appears in the Not in Dictionary box. To correct the word, choose one of the following:

- Select the correct spelling in the **Suggestions** box and then click **Change**.

- To change all occurrences of the word to the new spelling, click **Change All**.

- To ignore the word (in cases where the word is correctly spelled), click **Ignore** (click **Ignore All** to ignore all occurrences of the word).

- If you want to add the word to the dictionary file so that it will not be flagged as misspelled in the future, click **Add**.

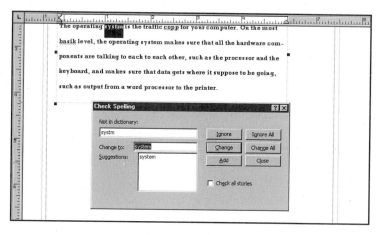

Figure 15.1 The Check Spelling dialog box offers you several options for a flagged word.

4. After you make your selection, the next flagged word is shown in the Not in Dictionary box. Correct other suspected misspellings as needed. When the current text frame is completed, the Speller moves on to the next text box. In situations where you have created more than one story that flows throughout a series of text boxes, a dialog box appears asking if you want to continue checking the publication. Click **Yes** to correct the rest of the publication or **No** to stop spell checking with the currently selected text frame.

TIP **Check All the Text Frames at Once** If you want to automatically check all the text in the publication (all text frames), click the **Check All Stories** check box in the Check Spelling dialog box.

As you might have noticed, Publisher actually flags suspected misspellings as you type. A red, wavy line is placed under the flagged word. You can choose to correct a flagged misspelling without running the Spell Checker. Right-click the word and select a correct spelling from the list provided on the shortcut menu that appears.

Controlling Hyphenation in Text Frames

Another element of fine-tuning a publication is determining where words are hyphenated in your text frames. You can have Publisher automatically hyphenate the text in your text frames (which means it determines where to break words with a hyphen and continue the remaining portion of the word on the next line).

When you choose to use the automatic hyphenation feature, hyphens are only placed as needed. The great thing about the feature is that if you edit the text, unnecessary hyphens are removed (automatically) and new hyphens are placed as needed.

To hyphenate a text frame automatically, follow these steps:

1. Click the text box that you want to automatically hyphenate.
2. Select the **Tools** menu, then point at **Language**, then select **Hyphenation**. The Hyphenation dialog box appears (see Figure 15.2).

Figure 15.2 You can automatically hyphenate text in a text frame.

3. Click the **Automatically Hyphenate This Story** check box in the Hyphenation dialog box.
4. Click **OK** to exit the dialog box and hyphenate the text.

You can also choose to hyphenate the text manually. To do this, click the **Manual** button in the Hyphenation dialog box. A Hyphenate dialog box appears, displaying the first word in the text frame that needs to be hyphenated (see Figure 15.3).

Figure 15.3   Manual hyphenation enables you to select the words that are hyphenated.

To use the hyphenation shown in the Hyphenate box, click **Yes**. If you don't want to hyphenate the word, click **No**. The next word to be hyphenated is displayed, and you are given the same choices as already described. Continue through the text until all the words have either been hyphenated or rejected (by you) and not hyphenated.

CAUTION

Auto-Hyphenation Might Be On by Default   Depending on your Publisher settings, the automatic hyphenation feature might already be turned on in the Hyphenation dialog box. You can turn it off by clearing the **Automatically Hyphenate This Story** check box.

Using the Design Checker

The Design Checker is another great tool for helping you fine-tune your publication. The Design Checker actually looks at the design elements and objects in your publication and helps you find empty frames, improperly proportioned pictures, font problems (such as too many fonts), and other design problems. The Design Checker also offers you help when it identifies a potential design problem.

To use the Design Checker, follow these steps:

1. Select the **Tools** menu, then select **Design Checker**. The Design Checker dialog box appears.

2. In the Design Checker dialog box, specify the number of pages you want to check, and then click **OK** to start checking the publication (see Figure 15.4).

Figure 15.4   Use the Design Checker to check your publication for design flaws.

3. When the Design Checker finds a potential design error, you are offered several options (see Figure 15.5):

- If you want to ignore the flagged design error and move on to the next potential error, click **Ignore** (click **Ignore All** to ignore all suspected errors similar to the currently flagged error).

- To have the Design Checker fix the flagged error (this option is not available in all cases), click **Change**.

- If the flagged error is an empty text frame, click **Delete Frame** to remove it.

- If you're not sure why the Design Checker has flagged the current item, you can get additional help from the Publisher help system related to the problem; click **Explain**.

- To move to the next design problem without acting on the currently flagged item (when you run the Design Checker again, this problem will be flagged again), click **Continue**.

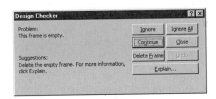

Figure 15.5   You are provided with several options when checking your publication design with the Design Checker.

4. When you have checked the entire publication (and you've either ignored or fixed the flagged design problems), the Publisher dialog box appears; click **OK** to close it.

In many cases the Design Checker will not be able to fix a specific problem for you (as the Spell Checker can), but it explains what it thinks the potential design flaw is. You can then close the Design Checker and fix the problem. To continue checking the publication, restart the **Design Checker** from the **Tools** menu.

Setting Up AutoCorrect

When you add text to your publications, it's nice to have misspellings and typos corrected automatically. The Publisher AutoCorrect feature does this for you. You can set the various AutoCorrect options and add your own common misspellings and typos to the AutoCorrect list.

To set up AutoCorrect, follow these steps:

1. Select the **Tools** menu, then select **AutoCorrect**. The AutoCorrect dialog box appears (see Figure 15.6).

Figure 15.6 You can set the options for AutoCorrect in the AutoCorrect dialog box.

2. To add a common misspelling or typo, type the misspelling in the **Replace** box and the correct spelling in the **With** box.

3. Click **Add** to add the items to the AutoCorrect list.

4. To remove an item from the AutoCorrect list, click the item and then click the **Delete** button.

5. Click **OK** when you have finished working in the AutoCorrect dialog box.

The AutoCorrect dialog box also controls some automatic formatting options. To view these options, click the **AutoFormat as You Type** tab (see Figure 15.7).

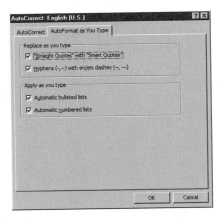

Figure 15.7 The AutoFormat as You Type tab controls automatic numbered lists and other formatting options.

This tab controls several formatting options, including the automatic numbering of items in a list when you start the list with a number. It also automatically applies bullets to items in a list when you add an asterisk to the beginning of the list (Publisher converts the asterisk to the default bullet type).

All the options on the **AutoFormat as You Type** tab are on (selected) by default. If you do not want to use any of the options, clear the appropriate check box.

In this lesson, you learned how to spell check your publication. You learned how to hyphenate text in text frames, and you checked your publication design with the Design Checker. You also worked with the AutoCorrect feature. In the next lesson, you learn how to print your publication and prepare it for printing by a printing service.

Printing and Outputting Publisher Publications

In this lesson, you learn how to print your publications and prepare them for output by a commercial printing service.

Previewing the Publication

When you are working in Publisher, you are, in effect, always previewing the publication as it will print. Publisher is a What You See Is What You Get (WYSIWYG) environment. This means that the placement of objects, frames, and other items appears in the Publisher window as it will appear on the printed page.

CAUTION

Web Publications Are the Exception Web pages created in Publisher are meant to be viewed in a Web browser. You will find that Web pages viewed in the Publisher window and in the Internet Explorer window do differ slightly on the placement of objects and other items.

The best strategy for previewing your publication is to go from the general to the specific. Zoom in and make sure that individual objects are correctly set up and that text boxes do not contain typos. When you zoom out on the publication, you can check placement of objects, the overall design of the publication, and the use of color (for more about using the different views in Publisher, see Lesson 4, "Viewing Your Publications").

Printing the Publication

No matter how hard you work on the color and design parameters of your publication, the final judge of your skills will be how the publication appears on the printed page. Publisher actually does a good job printing both full-color and black-and-white (grayscale) publications. If you turn on color matching, as discussed in the next section of this lesson, you also greatly increase the matching of colors between your monitor and printer.

To print your publication, follow these steps:

1. Select the **File** menu, then select **Print**. The Print dialog box appears (see Figure 16.1).

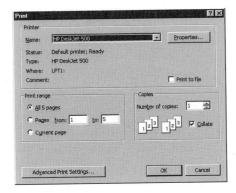

Figure 16.1 Select the page range to print in the Print dialog box.

2. If necessary, click the **Name** drop-down box and select the printer to which you want to send the print job.

3. Set the page range of the printout, if necessary.

4. Use the **Number of Copies** click box to specify the number of copies.

5. Click **OK** to send the print job to the selected printer.

TIP   **Print Quickly with the Print Button** You can send your publication directly to the printer and bypass the Print dialog box. Click the **Print** button on the toolbar.

Your publication will be printed. If you have problems with the printout, or if you don't like the way it looks, you can work with the various print options (discussed in the next section) to enhance the final printout. If you still have problems with the print job, you can use the Print Troubleshooter (see the section "Troubleshooting Printing Problems" in this lesson) to try to solve any printing problems.

Working with Print Options

You can also set a number of print options before sending the print job to the printer. These options range from settings such as the paper type that is used for the printout and the orientation of the printout (Portrait or Landscape) to more advanced settings such as color matching. Unfortunately, not all these settings are contained in one specific dialog box, so you have to hunt around a little before you find all the available print options.

Setting Paper Type and Orientation

The paper type and the orientation for the printout are set in the Print Setup dialog box. This dialog box looks very much like the Print dialog box. However, even after you set options in the Print Setup dialog box, you still have to return to the Print dialog box to actually print out the publication.

To set options in the Print Setup dialog box, follow these steps:

1. Select the **File** menu, then select **Print Setup**. The Print Setup dialog box appears (see Figure 16.2).

Figure 16.2 Set paper type and page orientation for the publication in the Print Setup dialog box.

2. If necessary, click the **Name** drop-down box and select the printer to which you want to send the print job.

3. Click the **Paper Size** drop-down box to select any special paper types you are using.

4. Click either the **Portrait** or **Landscape** option button to select the orientation for the printout.

5. Click **OK** to close the dialog box.

CAUTION

Wizard-Created Publications Have Their Own Print Setup Options
If you create a publication using one of the wizards, options such as page orientation and special paper type are set automatically. In most cases, you should not change the Print Setup options for a wizard-created publication.

After you've selected the various options in the Print Setup dialog box, you can then print the publication.

Matching Monitor and Printer Colors

As you ready a publication for printing, you want to make sure that the colors that are actually printed by the printer are the same (or at least very close) to the colors that you see on your monitor as you design the publication. To aid the printer in matching the colors on the computer monitor, you can turn on the Color Matching feature.

To set up the Color Matching feature, follow these steps:

1. Select the **File** Menu and then select **Print**.

2. In the Print dialog box, click **Advanced Print Settings**. The Print Settings dialog box appears (see Figure 16.3).

3. Click the **Improve Screen and Printer Color Matching** check box.

4. Click **OK** to close the dialog box.

5. You can send the publication to the printer by clicking **OK,** or click **Cancel** to close the Print dialog box without printing.

Even if you do turn on the color-matching feature, you may find that some colors still do not print the same as they appear on your monitor. You can have Publisher mark these colors for you in the color palette so that you can avoid using them in future publications (colors that do not match are typically the result of your printer's inability to properly create that color).

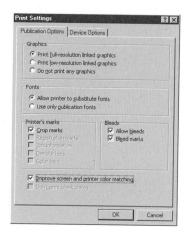

Figure 16.3   Color matching can help you get the colors you see on the screen onto the printed page.

Select any object on the page, then select **Format**, point to **Fill Color**, and then click **More Colors**. Click the **Mark Colors That Will Not Print Well on My Printer** check box.

Colors that do not print well are now displayed with an X in the color palette. For instance, on a black-and-white printer, all the colors on the palette, except for white and black, are marked with an X.

Troubleshooting Printing Problems

Although Publisher makes it fairly simple for you to print your publications to a printer attached to your computer, you may find, on occasion, that you have a problem. Your text may not look right, a portion of a picture may be cut off, or the printer won't print the publication at all. When you run into printing problems, you can call on the Print Troubleshooter, which provides you with advice on how you might overcome a particular printing problem.

To use the Print Troubleshooter, follow these steps:

1. Select the **Help** menu, and then select **Print Troubleshooter**.
2. The Help window appears on the desktop (see Figure 16.4). Click one of the print troubleshooting topics in the Help window (for example, click **My Text or Fonts Do Not Look Right**).

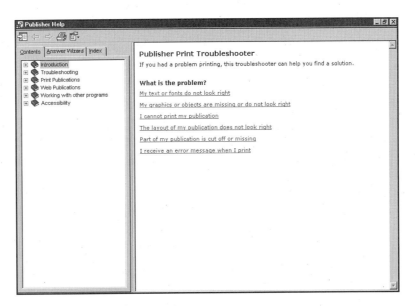

Figure 16.4 The Print Troubleshooter can help you fix printing problems.

3. A second, more specific, level of help topics associated with your last selection appears. Click a selection to view the help associated with it (such as **My Text Does Not Wrap Correctly**).

4. Help is provided to specifically remedy the problem you selected. After you are done reading the remedy for the problem, click the **Close** button to close the Help window.

If a particular solution provided by the Print Troubleshooter does not alleviate your current problem, you may want to open the Troubleshooter again and try a different solution. If you can't print at all, make sure your printer is turned on, plugged in, and securely attached to your computer via a printer cable. Physical connections are often the culprit when you cannot print at all.

Working with an Outside Print Service

In some cases, you may design a publication that you won't print on your own printer. For instance, you create a flyer or a business card and you want to have the publication placed on special papers using high-quality inks that only a commercial printer can provide. You can use the commercial printing tools in Publisher to prepare any publication for printing by a professional printer.

Two of the most important aspects of preparing a publication for outside printing are to select the appropriate color scheme (so that it matches the one used by the printer) and to save embedded pictures and graphics as separate files that are linked to your publication (this is a necessity if you use a professional printer).

Setting the Color Scheme

The color scheme that you select for your publication will be determined by the printing service. All you have to do is use the Color Printing dialog box to specify the particular color scheme.

To set the color scheme for your publication, follow these steps:

1. Select the **Tools** menu on the Publisher toolbar, point at **Commercial Printing Tools**, and then click **Color Printing**. The Color Printing dialog box appears (see Figure 16.5).

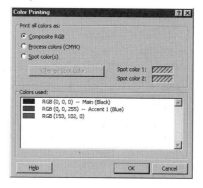

Figure 16.5   Select the color system that will be used by your printing service.

2. In the Color Printing dialog box, click the option button for the color scheme specified by the printing service that you will use:
   - **Composite RGB**—This is the default color system and is used by most color printers you use at home or in the office. This is the setting to use if you will print the publication yourself.
   - **Process Colors (CMYK)**—CMYK is a color system used by most commercial printers. It works particularly well on publications where color photos are included.

- **Spot Color(s)**—For black-and-white publications that use only one or two additional colors to emphasize items on the pages, select **Spot Color(s)**.

3. If you select Spot Color(s), click the **Change Spot Color** button to edit the spot color (the color other than black and white that will appear in the publication).

4. In the Choose Spot Color dialog box, use the drop-down lists to choose **Spot Color 1** and **Spot Color 2** (if one exists) that will be used in the publication.

5. Click **OK** to return to the Color Printing dialog box.

6. After you've selected your color scheme, click **OK** to close the dialog box.

Linking Graphics to the Publication

When you place your pictures and clip art on a publication page, you are making that image part of the page. When you have a publication printed by a commercial service, you typically have to provide the pictures and clip-art images as separate files that are linked to the publication rather than placed in it. The Commercial Printing Tools provides a Graphic Manager that enables you to convert your publication objects to linked objects before you take the publication to a printing service. (For a general discussion of object linking and embedding (OLE), see Appendix C, "Object Linking and Embedding.")

To create separate graphic files for your publication, follow these steps:

1. Select the **Tools** menu on the Publisher toolbar, point at **Commercial Printing Tools**, and then click **Graphics Manager**. The Graphics Manager dialog box opens.

2. In the Graphics Manager, click the first picture or clip-art item in your publication (see Figure 16.6), and then click **Create Link**. The Create Link dialog box appears.

3. In the Create Link dialog box, click the **Create a File** option button.

4. Click **OK** to create the linked file. The Save As dialog box appears.

5. In the Save As dialog box, click **Save**, and the linked file is created (you can go with the default filename for the object).

6. Repeat the above steps to create other links as needed for your graphic files.

7. When you have created files for all the graphics, click the **Close** button.

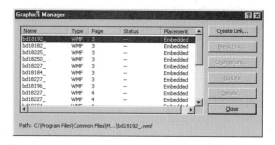

Figure 16.6 Select the first graphic that will be saved as a separate file.

Using Pack and Go

You will find that a publication jam-packed with pictures, text frames, and various design elements constitutes a file that is a pretty good size. In many cases, the publication may be too large to fit on a floppy disk. However, you can compress your publications using Pack and Go. This makes it easy for you to take your publication to another computer or take it to a commercial printer.

To pack a presentation, follow these steps:

1. Select the **File** menu, point at **Pack and Go**, and then click **Take to Another Computer**. The Pack and Go Wizard appears.

2. Click **Next** to start the Pack and Go Wizard.

3. To pack the publication to a floppy disk, click **Next** (or specify another drive on your computer and then click **Next**).

4. To embed the fonts and pictures in the publication in the Pack and Go file, click the appropriate check boxes (see Figure 16.7), and then click **Next**.

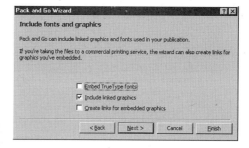

Figure 16.7 Select the items that should be included in the Pack and Go file.

5. Click **Finish** to pack the publication onto a disk.

If the packed publication will not fit on one floppy disk, the Pack and Go Wizard prompts you to place additional floppy disks in your floppy disk drive.

A copy of Unpack.exe is also placed on the floppy disk (or floppy disks) that hold your packed presentation. You can use this program to unpack your publication onto another computer.

To unpack a packed file, place the floppy disk in the other computer and then click **Start**, then **Run**. In the Run box, type **a:\unpack.exe**. You are prompted for a destination folder for the unpacking of your publication; specify the folder and then click **OK**.

In this lesson you learned how to print your publications. You also learned to set print options and prepare your publication for printing by a printing service. In the next lesson, you learn how to create publications for mass mailings using the Publisher merge feature.

Mass Mailing Publications

*In this lesson, you learn how to create a mailing list
in Publisher and then merge the list with a publication for mass mailings.*

Understanding the Mail Merge Feature

The Publisher merge feature actually helps walk you through the process of creating a publication, such as envelopes or mailing labels, that can be churned out in large quantities for mass mailings. The merge process uses the publication and a data source to create a personalized version of the publication for each individual in the data source.

Data Source   A file that contains names and addresses that will be merged with another publication. Data sources in Publisher are really mini-database files. Publisher makes it easy for you to create a data source using the Publisher Address List feature.

To complete a merge, you have to create only two items: a mailing list that contains the names and addresses of the people who will receive the publication, and a publication such as an envelope, mailing label, or other publication (create the publication using a particular wizard or a blank design template). After you have these two items, you can start the merge process and insert *merge codes* (derived from the fields in the mailing list) into the publication (the envelope or mailing label) as placeholders.

After the merge is completed, you can send the merged publications to your printer. The process is really that straightforward. And you can use any type of publication with the merge feature.

Merge Codes The names of the various fields of information that you place in the mailing list. Publisher automatically sets up field names (merge codes) for you, such as First Name, Last Name, and so on.

Building a Mailing List

The first step in creating a merge is to build a mailing list for the publication that will be mass mailed. After the mailing list has been created, it's easy to use the merge feature to personalize the publication for each person on the list.

To create a Publisher Mailing List, follow these steps:

1. Select **Mail Merge**, then select **Create Publisher Address List**. The New Address List dialog box appears. The dialog box provides blank address fields (see Figure 17.1).

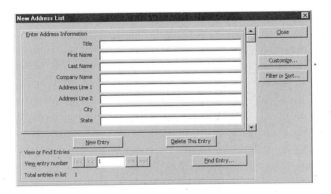

Figure 17.1 Fill in the blanks in the New Address List dialog box to build a mailing list.

2. Type the appropriate information for your first addressee in each of the fields in the New Address List dialog box (press the **Tab** key to move to the next field).

3. When you have completed entering the information, click **New Entry** to enter the next person.

4. Repeat steps 2 and 3 as necessary. Click **Close** when you have entered all the names and addresses.

1023

When you close the New Address List dialog box, you are asked to save your new mailing list (see Figure 17.2). Follow these steps to save the file:

1. Type a name for your mailing list file in the **File Name** box.
2. Select the drive and folder where you want to save the file.
3. Click the **Save** button.

Figure 17.2   Type a name and specify a location for your mailing list file.

 TIP   Use Other Data Sources   If you use Microsoft Access and have already created a table of names and addresses for your contacts, you can use it as your mailing list for merges with Publisher publications. Publisher actually saves its mailing list in the Access (.mdb) file format.

After you create the mailing list, you can use it over and over again with any number of publications.

You can also edit your mailing list as needed. Select the **Mail Merge** menu, then select **Edit Publisher Address List**. Open your mailing list in the Open dialog box. You can then edit entries, add entries, or delete entries from the file.

Starting the Merge and Inserting Merge Codes

After you've created a mailing list, you then need to place the merge codes into the publication. As previously discussed, these codes are placeholders for information that will be pulled from the mailing list file. For instance, to place the first name of a person in the merged publication, you need to enter the First Name code into the publication before you actually perform the merge.

To have access to the appropriate merge codes, you start the merge process and identify the mailing list from which the codes will be derived.

To begin the merge process and insert the merge codes, follow these steps:

1. Open the publication (such as a mailing label or envelope) and create a text frame to hold the merge codes (see Figure 17.3).

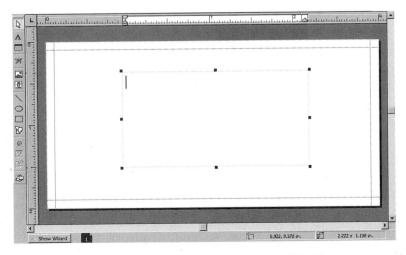

Figure 17.3   In the publication, create a text frame that will hold the merge codes.

2. Select **Mail Merge**, then select **Open Data Source**. The Open Data Source dialog box appears.

3. Click **Merge Information from Another Type of File** to open the Open Data Source dialog box (see Figure 17.4).

Figure 17.4   Specify your mailing list file in the Open Data Source dialog box.

4. Select your mailing list file and click **OK**.

After you open the data source, an Insert Fields dialog box appears. It lists all the fields that were contained in the mailing list form that you filled out for each of your recipients.

5. Select a merge code in the Insert Fields dialog box (see Figure 17.5).

Figure 17.5   Select the field in the dialog box and then click Insert.

6. Click **Insert** to insert the appropriate merge code.

7. If you need to place a space after the current merge code before you insert the next merge code, drag the dialog box out of the way and click in the text frame. Type a space or other punctuation mark as needed.

8. Insert the next merge code, as described in steps 5 and 6. If the next merge code needs to go on a new line, click in the text frame at the end of the first line and press **Enter**.

9. Insert all your merge codes as required. When you have completed inserting the various fields, click **Close**.

Figure 17.6 shows a text frame on an envelope that contains merge codes.

Completing the Merge

After you've inserted the merge codes into a specific publication (in a text frame), you are ready to perform the merge. As you perform the merge, you are given an opportunity to preview the results. You can then send the merged publication to the printer connected to your computer (or on your computer network), and a personalized publication is printed out for each individual in the mailing list.

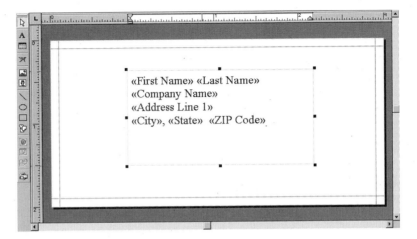

Figure 17.6   Insert the necessary merge codes into the text frame.

To complete the merge, follow these steps:

1. Select the **Mail Merge** menu, then select **Merge**. The data from the first record in your mailing list appears on the publication in place of the merge codes (see Figure 17.7).

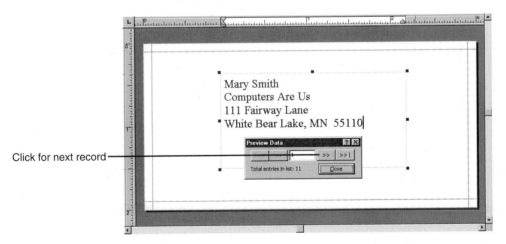

Figure 17.7   A preview is given of each record in the mailing list.

2. Click the **Next Record** button on the Preview Data dialog box to view the next record.

3. Click **Close** when you are done previewing the merge.

4. To print the merge, select **File**, and then select **Print Merge**.

5. Click **OK**. The merged publications are sent to the printer.

Stop the Merge!   If you find a problem with the merge when you preview your entries, click **Mail Merge**, then **Cancel Merge**. You can then edit the mailing list or publication and try the merge again.

CAUTION

In this lesson, you learned how to create a mailing list and how to insert merge field codes into a text frame in a publication. You also learned how to run a merge and print out the merged publications. In the next lesson, you learn how to create publications that require special paper, such as business cards, envelopes, and mailing labels.

Creating Publications on Special Paper

In this lesson, you learn how to create publications that require special papers, such as tri-fold brochures, business cards, envelopes, or mailing labels.

Creating Tri-Fold Brochures

Publisher gives you the capability to create publications that use special papers. These special papers can take the form of scored brochure paper (scored to fold), perforated business card papers, various mailing label sheets, and different envelope sizes.

Although many folding publications, such as brochures and greeting cards, can be created on regular printer paper, special papers provide added design elements and ease–of-use features (such as scoring or fold lines) that regular paper cannot provide. Special papers are provided by a number of companies, such as Paper Direct, Avery (the label company), and others.

Tri-fold brochures can normally be one of the most complicated publications to tackle because you must visualize how the paper will fold and then place the text and objects on the correct panel of the brochure. Publisher, however, makes it easy for you to create brochures, and Publisher also takes into account that special paper types exist for your use in creating brochures.

To create a brochure using a special paper, follow these steps:

1. Select the **File** menu, then select **New**. The Publisher Catalog appears.
2. Click **Brochures** in the Wizards pane of the Catalog.

3. To view the special paper brochures, click **Special Paper Informational**.

4. To view the different special paper brochures, scroll through the brochures in the Special Paper Informational Brochures pane of the Catalog (see Figure 18.1)

Special paper logos

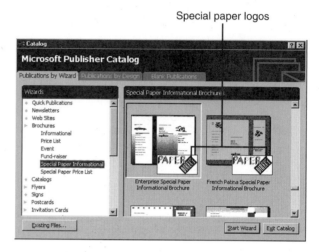

Figure 18.1   Special paper brochures use papers that already contain design elements and colors.

5. Special paper brochures are marked by the logo of the paper manufacturer (such as Paper Direct). The special paper name (such as Aristocrat Special Paper) is also noted on each brochure. Click the brochure that you want to create.

6. Click **Start Wizard** to create the brochure and use the wizard that enables you to make design and color decisions related to the brochure.

After you have created the brochure and are ready to print it, you can load your printer with the special paper. Be sure to read any information that came with the paper that gives you tips on how the paper should be oriented and loaded into your specific printer.

Design Decisions Are Limited   When you use a special paper, the wizard does not provide as many color and design decisions as with some plain paper publications. This is because the overall design and layout of the brochure is closely tied to the special paper on which you will print the brochure.

Special Papers Can Give Mixed Results   When you use high-gloss special papers, you may find that your inkjet printer does not give you the same quality of print that you get on regular paper. In some cases, you may need to buy special papers that are designed for color inkjet printers because the paper must let the spray of ink penetrate the paper surface easily.

Creating Business Cards

Business cards are another publication where using special papers can provide you with a much better result than using regular card stock. A number of companies make business card paper that is of a card stock quality and that comes in 8 1/2- × 11-inch perforated sheets that fit into most printers.

Using a wizard is your easiest route to creating business cards that take advantage of a special paper. To create the business card, follow these steps:

1. Select the **File** menu, then select **New**. The Publisher Catalog appears.
2. Click **Business Cards** in the Wizards pane of the Catalog.
3. To view the special paper brochures, click **Special Paper**.
4. Select any of the special paper business cards in the Special Paper Business Cards pane of the Catalog, and then click **Start Wizard** to begin the business-card creation process.

Figure 18.2 shows a business card created using the Paper Direct Influential business card paper. The advantage of using special paper for business cards is that the sheet is perforated so that each individual card can be pulled from the main sheet and have fairly straight edges. This enables you to create business cards that can look practically as good as commercially printed cards.

Figure 18.2   Special papers enable you to create professional-looking publications.

A number of companies make special papers for your printers (including Hewlett-Packard, which makes many kinds of printers). If the special paper you purchased isn't listed, do a little experimenting. Try to match up to one of the special papers listed for the type of publication you want to create. Then create the publication and print a test page. If the paper works, you can mass-produce your work. If it doesn't work, fine-tune the publication until you get an adequate printout.

Creating Envelopes

Creating envelopes isn't really an issue of special paper as much as having the right envelope size selected. You can create envelopes using a wizard (and special papers are available for envelopes), following the same sequence of steps described for special paper brochures and business cards.

If you want to quickly print an address or create an envelope for a mail merge (as discussed in Lesson 17, "Mass Mailing Publications"), you can open a blank publication and then change the page size in the Page Setup dialog box.

To create an envelope from a blank publication, follow these steps:

1. Click the **New** button on the Standard toolbar. A blank publication opens in the Publisher window.

2. Select the **File** menu, then select **Page Setup**. The Page Setup dialog box appears.

3. In the dialog box, click the **Envelopes** option button (see Figure 18.3).

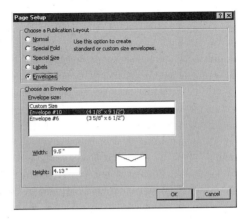

Figure 18.3   Select the envelope size in the Page Setup dialog box.

4. Choose the envelope size in the **Envelope size** box.

5. Click **OK** to return to the publication.

The publication is now an envelope. Place text frames on the envelope as needed to place an address, or place field merge codes on the envelope for a mail merge.

When you create an envelope using a wizard or selecting an envelope from a design set, the envelope size is set for you in the Page Setup dialog box.

Creating Mailing Labels

Mailing labels are another special publication type that deserve some discussion. Many companies make mailing labels for printers. Avery mailing labels are considered the standard, however, and both the wizards and the Page Setup dialog box use Avery label numbers to configure the size and number of labels that come on the label sheet you place in your printer.

If you want to use labels made by a company other than Avery, many manufacturers supply the equivalent Avery number for their label. Look for this information on the label packaging. Or you can measure and count the labels on the sheets that you purchased and try to match them up with the specifications for one of the listed Avery label types.

You can create labels using a wizard or by formatting a blank publication as a label using the Page Setup dialog box. If you use a wizard, as discussed for brochures and business cards, select the publication wizard that uses the Avery number of the labels you plan on using in your printer.

If you want to quickly set up a label publication with no frills for a mail merge, follow these steps:

1. Click the **New** button on the Standard toolbar. A blank publication opens in the Publisher window.

2. Select the **File** menu, then select **Page Setup**. The Page Setup dialog box appears.

3. In the dialog box, click the **Labels** option button in the Layout area.

4. To select your label type, scroll through the labels listed in the Choose a Label box (see Figure 18.4).

5. When you've located your label number, click the label and then click **OK** to exit the dialog box.

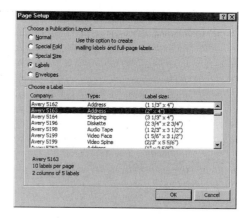

Figure 18.4 Select a label number in the Page Setup dialog box.

Your new label is now available in the Publisher window. You can add text to it by placing a text frame on the label.

In this lesson, you learned about special papers, and you learned how to create brochures, business cards, envelopes, and mailing labels. In the next lesson, you learn how to create your own Web site using Publisher.

Creating a Publisher Web Site

In this lesson, you learn how to create a Web site for the World Wide Web.

What Is the World Wide Web?

The Internet is a global network of interconnected computer systems that provides several ways for users to communicate with each other. There is electronic mail (email), Internet Relay Chat, and—more important—the World Wide Web (WWW). The Web is actually the newest onramp to the Internet, and it enables you to quickly move from computer to computer (no matter the distance between the computers) by hopping from Web page to Web page using a Web browser (such as Microsoft Internet Explorer).

The Web sites that you view on the Web are made up of linked documents created in the HTML programming language. Your Web browser is able to translate HTML into a format that is viewable (and usable) on your home or office computer.

 TERM   **HTML**   Hypertext Markup Language is the coding system used to create Web pages for the WWW.

Publisher makes it easy for you to create your own Web site without worrying about HTML coding. You create the Web site in Publisher, and it makes sure that the publication ends up in the correct format. Publisher also enables you to preview your site as you work on it.

Creating a Web Site Using the Web Site Wizard

Publisher can walk you through the entire Web site creation process. The Web Site Wizard helps you select the various design elements for your new Web site as well as a page layout. After you create your basic Web site with the wizard, you can then modify it using any of Publisher's tools for creating new objects.

To create a Web site using the Web Site Wizard, follow these steps:

1. Select the **File** menu, then select **New**. The Publisher Catalog appears.
2. Click **Web Sites** in the Wizards pane of the Catalog.
3. Scroll through the layouts available in the Web Sites pane and select a layout for your Web site (see Figure 19.1).

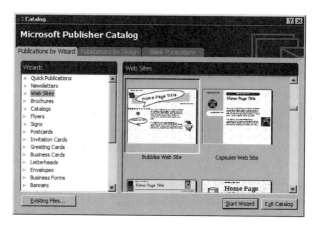

Figure 19.1 Select a layout for your Web site in the Publisher Catalog.

4. Click **Start Wizard** after making your selection. The Web site appears in the publication window and the wizard appears in the Wizard pane (on the left side of the screen).

5. To start the selection of design elements with the help of the wizard, click **Next** in the Wizard pane.

6. The first choice offered by the Web Site Wizard is the color scheme for the Web site. Select a color scheme (see Figure 19.2) and then click **Next** to continue.

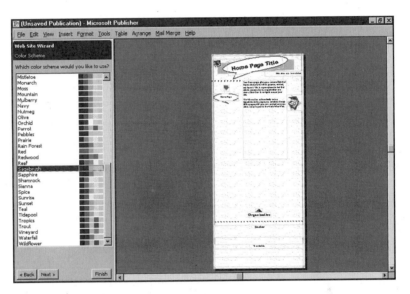

Figure 19.2 Select a color scheme for the Web site in the Wizard pane.

7. The next wizard screen provides you with the options of including additional pages in your Web site. You can include a Story page, a Calendar page, an Event page, and others. You can select some or all of the options. Click the check boxes for the additional pages you want to include.

8. After selecting the additional pages, click **Next** to continue.

9. The next wizard screen asks if you would like to add a form to the Web site. Forms are used to gather information from Web users who visit your site. You can select from the following option button options: **Order Form**, **Response Form**, **Sign-up Form**, or **None** (see Figure 19.3). Click your selection.

Figure 19.3 You can add user response forms to the Web site.

10. Click **Next** to continue.

11. The next wizard screen offers you choices related to the navigation bar used on the Web site to link other pages to the site. The navigation bar can be set up with the following choices: both a vertical and a horizontal bar, only a vertical bar, or none. Click the appropriate option button.

12. Click **Next** to continue.

13. The next wizard screen asks if you want to have a sound played when your Web site is opened. Click either **Yes** or **No**, and then click **Next** to continue.

14. The next wizard screen enables you to choose whether a texture (a background pattern) is applied to your Web site pages. Select **Yes** or **No**, and then click **Next** to continue.

15. The final wizard screen asks you to select the personal information set that will be used to replace certain placeholder text on the Web site. Select the information set (see Figure 19.4) by clicking the appropriate option button.

16. Click **Finish** to complete the Web site.

After you've finished working with the wizard, you can edit the Web site pages the same as you would the pages of any other publication. You can add text (see Lesson 8, "Changing How Text Looks," for help with text), pictures, and other objects (see Lesson 9, "Working with Graphics," for help in adding graphics and Lesson 10, "Adding Special Objects to Your Publications," for help in adding special objects). Clip art motion clips are an excellent addition to Web site pages because they provide animated events that add interest to the Web page itself.

Figure 19.4 Choose the personal information set that will supply information for the Web site.

Converting an Existing Publication to a Web Site

If you prefer to build your Web site using the various Publisher features but without the help of a wizard, feel free; you can place text frames, place picture frames, and add pages as needed. Publisher can then help you convert your pages to the HTML format.

To convert an existing publication to the Web site format, follow these steps:

1. Open the publication you want to convert.
2. Select the **File** menu, then select **Create Web Site from Current Publication**.

3. You are asked if you want to run the Design Checker, as shown in Figure 19.5 (see Lesson 15, "Fine-Tuning Publisher Publications," for information on using the Design Checker). Click **No** to continue (you can always run the Design Checker after the file has been converted).

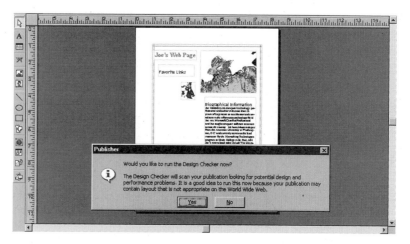

Figure 19.5   During the conversion of a publication to a Web site, you are asked to run the Design Checker.

4. After the conversion, you need to save the converted publication. Select the **File** menu, then select **Save**.

5. Type a name for the new Web site and select a drive and folder for the file. Click **Save** to complete the process.

After the publication has been converted to a Web site, you can preview it in Internet Explorer and save it as a Web site (see "Publishing Your Web Site" later in this lesson) for uploading to a Web server.

Adding and Removing Hyperlinks

Web pages are typically linked to other Web pages by hyperlinks.

Hyperlink   A link to another Web site or another page on your own Web site. Hyperlinks can take the form of text entries or pictures. Click them and you are taken to a new location.

Publisher makes it easy for you to insert hyperlinks into your Web site publications. These links become active when you preview your Web site using Microsoft Internet Explorer. Hyperlinks are a great way for you to link multiple pages for your own Web site or to create links to some of your favorite sites on the Web.

To insert a hyperlink into your publication, follow these steps:

1. Select text in a text frame or another object on the Web page (such as a picture) that will serve as the hyperlink (see Figure 19.6).

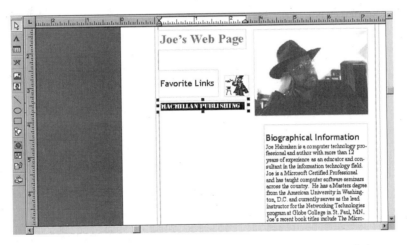

Figure 19.6 Select the text or other object that will serve as the hyperlink.

2. Select **Insert**, then select **Hyperlink**. The Hyperlink dialog box appears. You can create hyperlinks to different items using the option buttons at the top of the dialog box.

- **A Web Site or File on the Internet**—Select to create links to other Web sites.

- **Another Page in Your Web Site**—Select to create links to other pages in your own Web site publication.

- **An Internet E-mail Address**—Select to create a link that automatically sends an email to the specified address when a user clicks the link.

- **A File on Your Hard Disk**—Select to create links that enable a user to download a particular file that you specify.

3. To create a link to another Web site, type the address of the Web site for which you want to create the link in the Internet Address of the Web Site or File box (see Figure 19.7).

Figure 19.7   Specify the Web address for the hyperlink.

4. Click **OK**. This closes the dialog box and creates the hyperlink in the publication.

TIP   Add Hyperlinks from Your Favorites List   If you've added Web sites to your Favorites list when using the Internet Explorer Web browser, you can add these sites as hyperlinks by clicking the **Favorites** button in the Hyperlink dialog box. You don't have to type the Web site address into the Hyperlink dialog box.

You can also remove a hyperlink from a text entry or a picture on your Web page. This doesn't remove the object, but does take away its linking capabilities.

To remove a hyperlink, follow these steps:

1. Select the text in a text frame or another object on the Web page that contains the hyperlink.

2. Select **Insert**, then select **Hyperlink**. The Hyperlink dialog box appears.

3. Click the **Remove** button.

Viewing Your Web Site

After you've set up your Web site publication, you can preview it in the Microsoft Internet Explorer Web browser. This enables you to make sure that your overall design looks good and that items such as hyperlinks work correctly.

To preview your Web site, follow these steps:

1. Select **File**, then select **Web Page Preview**. Internet Explorer opens, showing your Web site (see Figure 19.8).

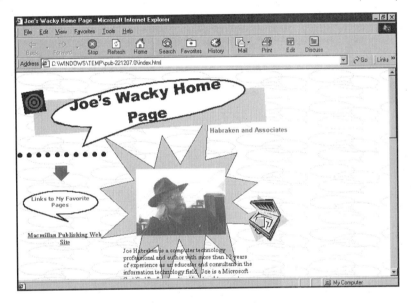

Figure 19.8 Preview your Web site in Internet Explorer.

2. After previewing your Web site, click the **Close** button to close Internet Explorer.

After previewing the site, you are returned to the Publisher window. You can make changes to the site, if needed, and then preview the site again to see how the changes work.

Publishing Your Web Site

Web sites that you view on the World Wide Web actually consist of text objects, pictures, and other items that exist as separate elements. The Web page itself is just a way for you (using your Web browser) to link to the different items that you click.

When you create a Web site in Publisher, all the items (the pictures, text, and so on) are saved a part of the publication. For your site to work on the Web, the publication has to be broken down into all its elements and saved to a folder. The files in the folder can then be placed on a Web server that enables people on the Web to access your site.

 TERM   **Web Server**   A computer connected to the Internet that provides access to your Web site.

To publish your Web site, follow these steps:

1. Select **File**, then select **Save as Web Page**. The Save as Web Page dialog box appears.
2. Specify a folder on your computer for the files to be saved in (see Figure 19.9).
3. Click **OK** and the Web site is saved to the folder as several component files.

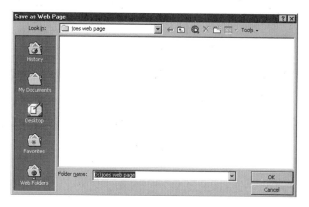

Figure 19.9   Specify a folder for the Web site files.

For your Web site to be available on the World Wide Web, it must be placed on a Web server—a computer that "serves up" Web pages to people using a Web browser. Contact your Internet service provider for information on uploading your Web page to a Web server.

After you save your Web site to a folder, it is ready to be placed on a Web server and accessed via the World Wide Web. If you decide you want to edit a particular part of the Web site, you must edit the original Publisher file and then publish the file to a folder, as discussed previously. This replaces the original file with the revised file.

In this lesson, you learned how to create your own Web site using Publisher. You also learned how to insert and remove hyperlinks from your Web site publication and how to publish your Web site for use on the World Wide Web.

FrontPage/
PhotoDraw

Getting Familiar with FrontPage

In this lesson, you learn to start Microsoft FrontPage and navigate the FrontPage window. You also learn to use common tools like the menus, toolbars, and dialog boxes.

Starting FrontPage

Microsoft FrontPage 2000 is a full-featured Web design application that provides you with all the tools you need to create your own *Web page* or *Web site* and get it onto the Web. Wizards and templates are provided that make it easy for you to create simple, personal Web sites or complex Web sites for your business. FrontPage not only makes it easy for you to create your own Web pages and sites, it also gives you the ability to test and troubleshoot the site before publishing it to the World Wide Web.

Web pages and sites must be created in the HTML (Hypertext Markup Language) programming language for them to function when viewed in a Web browser such as Microsoft Internet Explorer (for more about Explorer, see Lessons 10 through 13 in the Windows 98 section of this book). FrontPage helps you create sophisticated Web pages and sites without having to learn HTML.

 Web Page   A single page containing text and graphics that has been labeled with the appropriate HTML coding for the Web.

 Web Site   A collection of linked Web pages containing various content that can easily be navigated using a Web browser.

Before you can take advantage of FrontPage's capabilities, you need to open its application window. To start the FrontPage program, follow these steps:

1. From the Windows Desktop, click **Start** and select **Programs**. The Programs Start menu appears (see Figure 1.1).

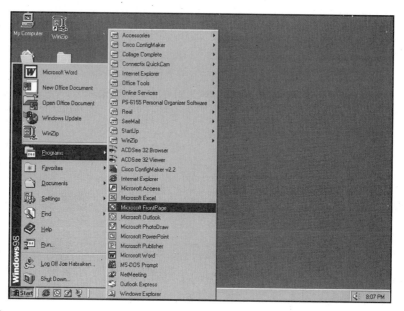

Figure 1.1   Open the Programs Start menu and click the FrontPage icon to start FrontPage.

2. To start FrontPage, click the **FrontPage** icon. The FrontPage application window opens.

 TIP   **Use the Office Toolbar**   If you installed the Office toolbar during the Office installation, it should appear on your Windows Desktop. Click the **FrontPage** icon on the toolbar to quickly start FrontPage.

Understanding the FrontPage Environment

When you start FrontPage, the FrontPage application window opens (see Figure 1.2). The overall geography of the FrontPage window is very close to that of other Microsoft Office applications, such as Excel and Word. In fact, you will find that, when you create and edit Web pages and Web sites in the FrontPage window, you use many of the techniques and tools you use in a word processing application such as Microsoft Word.

FrontPage does have an area of its window that is distinct from other Office applications. The Views bar on the left side of the FrontPage window (see Figure 1.2) allows you to quickly switch between different views associated with the currently open Web site. For instance, the Page view allows you to view and edit the current Web page. Another of the views, the Navigation view, allows you to view all the pages in the current Web site and see how they are linked together to form a complete site (for more about the views available on the Views bar, see Lesson 2, "Creating a New Web Site").

CAUTION

Don't Confuse the Views Bar with the View Tabs   FrontPage actually uses the term *view* in two different contexts. The Views bar allows you to change your view of your Web site by changing the entire View pane to a Page view, a Navigation view, and so on. Within Page view, the View tabs allow you to change the view for the current Web page between a regular view, an HTML code view, and a preview (for more about the View tabs, see Lesson 3, "Working with Web Pages and Themes").

You might notice that the largest area of the window is currently blank; a new, blank Web page appears in the FrontPage window when you start the application (serving the same function as a blank document window in Word). You can build a new Web page from scratch, using a blank Web page such as the one that appears when you start FrontPage, or use one of the templates that FrontPage offers (for more about creating individual Web pages and the use of templates, see Lesson 3).

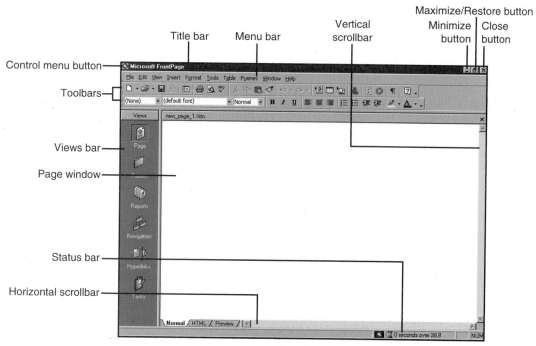

Figure 1.2   The FrontPage window is where you create your Web pages and Web sites.

Table 1.1 describes the elements you see in the FrontPage application window.

Table 1.1   Elements of the FrontPage Window

Element	Description
Title bar	Includes the name of the application (FrontPage) plus the Minimize, Maximize, and Close buttons.
Control menu button	Opens the Control menu, which provides such commands as Move, Size, Minimize, and Close.
Minimize button	Reduces the FrontPage window to a button on the taskbar; to restore the window to its original size, click the button on the taskbar.
Maximize/Restore button	Enlarges the FrontPage window to cover the Windows Desktop. When the window is maximized, the Maximize button changes to a Restore button that you can click to return the window to its previous size.

Element	Description
Close (×) button	Closes the FrontPage program window.
Menu bar	Contains menus of commands you can use to perform tasks in the program.
Toolbar	Includes icons that serve as shortcuts for common commands, such as Save, Print, and Spelling.
Status bar	Contains the Page View tabs and also provides information such as the time the current page would take to load in a Web browser window at a particular speed.
Page window	This is where you create and edit the current Web page.
Scrollbars	The Horizontal scrollbar is used to scroll your view of the current page from left to right, or vice versa. The Vertical scrollbar is used to scroll up and down through the current page.
Views bar	Provides quick access of the different views associated with the current Web site.

Using Menus and Toolbars

FrontPage provides several different ways to access the commands and features used to create your Web pages. You can access these commands using the menus on the menu bar and using the buttons on the various toolbars that FrontPage supplies.

You can also access a number of FrontPage commands using shortcut menus. These menus are accessed by right-clicking on a particular page element. The shortcut menu appears with a list of commands related to the item that you are currently working on, such as text or a picture.

The FrontPage Menu Bar

The FrontPage menu bar gives you access to all the commands and features FrontPage provides. Like all Windows applications, FrontPage's menus are found below the title bar and activated by selecting a particular menu choice. The menu then opens, providing you with a set of command choices.

FrontPage 2000 (and the other Office 2000 applications) has adopted a new menu system that provides you with the ability to quickly access the commands you use most often. When you first choose a particular menu, you find a short list of menu commands. As you use commands, FrontPage adds them to the menu list.

This personalized menu system allows you to quickly access the commands you use the most. To access a particular menu, follow these steps:

1. Select the menu by clicking its title (such as Format, as shown in Figure 1.3). The most recently used commands appear; wait just a moment for all the commands on a particular menu to appear.

2. Select the command on the menu that invokes a particular feature (such as Font).

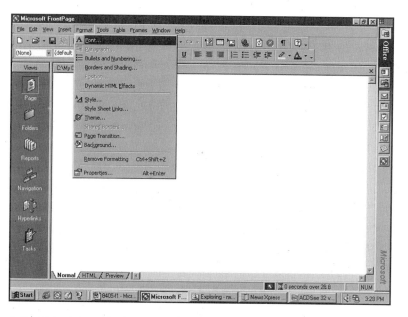

Figure 1.3   Select a particular menu and then point to a FrontPage command.

You might find that a number of the commands found on the menu are followed by an ellipsis (...). These commands, when selected, open a dialog box that requires you to provide FrontPage with additional information before the particular feature or command can be used (more information on working with dialog boxes appears later in this lesson).

Some of the menus also contain a submenu or cascading menu that you can use to make your choices. The menu commands that produce a submenu are indicated by an arrow to the right of the menu choice. In cases where a submenu is present, you point at the command (marked with the arrow) on the main menu to open the submenu.

TIP **Activating Menus with the Keyboard** You can also activate a particular menu by holding down the **Alt** key and then pressing the keyboard key that matches the underscored letter—also called a hotkey—in the menu's name. For instance, to activate the File menu in FrontPage, you press **Alt+F**.

If you would rather have access to all the menu commands (rather than just those you've used recently), you can turn off the personalized menu system. To do this, follow these steps:

1. Click the **Tools** menu, then click **Customize**.
2. In the Customize dialog box, click the **Options** tab.
3. To show all the commands on the menus, clear the **Menus show recently Used Commands First** check box.
4. Click **OK** to close the dialog box.

Shortcut Menus

A fast way to access commands that are related to a particular document element is to select a particular page object and right-click. This opens a shortcut menu that contains commands related to the particular object you are working with.

TERM **Object** Any element found on a page, such as text, a graphic, a hyperlink, or other inserted item.

For instance, if you select a line of text on a Web page, right-clicking on the selected text (see Figure 1.4) opens a shortcut menu with commands such as **Cut**, **Copy**, and **Paste**.

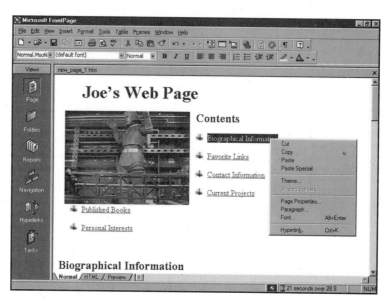

Figure 1.4   You can quickly access FrontPage commands using shortcut menus.

FrontPage Toolbars

The FrontPage toolbars provide you with a very quick and straightforward way of accessing commands and features. When you first start FrontPage, you are provided with the Standard and Formatting toolbars, each of which resides on a separate line directly below the menu bar.

To access a particular command using a toolbar button, click the button. Depending on the command, you see an immediate result in your document (such as the removal of selected text, when you click the Cut button), or a dialog box appears requesting additional information from you.

TIP   **Finding a Toolbar Button's Purpose**   You can place the mouse pointer on any toolbar button to view a description of that tool's function.

FrontPage also offers several other toolbars, many of them containing buttons for a specific group of tasks. For example, the Table toolbar provides you with buttons that help you format a table that you've placed on your Web page.

The Table toolbar appears when you draw the table on the page (for more about adding tables to your Web pages, see Lesson 6, "Inserting Special FrontPage Components").

Other toolbars, like the Picture toolbar (covered in Lesson 7, "Working with Hyperlinks"), can be added to the FrontPage window and then used to quickly access commands related to pictures that have been placed on the Web page. To add a toolbar, right-click on any toolbar currently shown and select from the list that appears. You will find that there are specific toolbars for working with tables, pictures, styles, and a number of other elements related to Web pages.

Missing Toolbar Buttons? If the Standard and Formatting toolbars have been configured to share one row, you might not be able to see a particular toolbar button. To find a hidden button, click the **More Buttons** button on either toolbar.

CAUTION

Understanding Dialog Boxes

When you are working with the various commands and features found in FrontPage, you will invariably come up against dialog boxes. Dialog boxes are used when FrontPage needs more information from you before it can complete a particular command or take advantage of a special feature. Dialog boxes always appear when you select a menu command that is followed by an ellipsis. Dialog boxes also appear when you invoke this same command using the appropriate toolbar button.

Figure 1.5 shows the Font dialog box. This dialog box allows you to make selections using check boxes and drop-down lists. Other dialog boxes use radio buttons, click boxes, and other methods of allowing you to quickly make selections in a particular box.

In most cases, when you complete your selections in a dialog box, you click the OK button to close the box and complete the command, which was originally started with a menu choice or toolbar button.

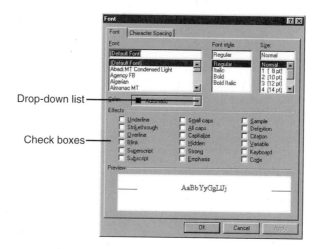

Drop-down list

Check boxes

Figure 1.5   Dialog boxes ask you for additional information regarding a particular FrontPage command or feature.

Exiting FrontPage

When you have completed your initial survey of the FrontPage application window or whenever you have completed your work in the program, you will want to exit the software. You can exit FrontPage by selecting the **File** menu, then **Exit**. Or you can close FrontPage with one click of the mouse by clicking the FrontPage **Close** (×) button in the upper-right corner of the application window.

When you close FrontPage, you might be prompted to save any work that you have done in the application window. If you were just experimenting as you read through this lesson, you can click **No**. The current Web page is not saved, and the FrontPage application window closes. All the ins and outs of actually saving your documents are covered in Lesson 2.

In this lesson, you learned how to start FrontPage and explored the various parts of the FrontPage window. You also learned how to work with the menu system, toolbars, and dialog boxes. Finally, you learned how to exit the FrontPage program. In the next lesson, you learn how to create a new Web site.

Creating a
New Web Site

In this lesson, you learn to create a new Web site using the FrontPage Web Wizards. You also become familiar with the different Web views provided on the FrontPage Views bar.

Using the Web Site Wizards

FrontPage provides several wizards you can use to create your own Web site (in FrontPage, a Web site is referred to as a *web*). These wizards can create different kinds of sites ranging from the personal to business or can help you add certain types of functions to your current Web site (such as a discussion page or a page for project management).

Table 2.1 lists the Web Wizards that are available and the type of web they help you create.

Table 2.1   Selecting a Web Wizard for Your New Web Site

Web Wizard	Site Created
One Page web	A web consisting of a single blank page (the home page).
Corporate Presence	A multipage web with pages for products and services and links for email messages to the company.
Customer Support	A web that provides a FAQ (frequently asked questions) page, suggestion page, download page, and a search page to help support customers using the site.
Discussion web	A web consisting of a discussion page that allows visitors to your site to post and read discussion messages.

continues

Table 2.1   Continued

Web Wizard	Site Created
Empty web	A web consisting of no pages.
Import web	A web based on imported files from a Web site created in another program or directly from the World Wide Web.
Personal web	A multipage web consisting of interests, photo, and links pages.
Project web	A multipage web used to manage a particular project. A schedule page, discussion page, and other project management pages are created. This type of site would typically be used on an intranet (a corporation's private web).

When you work with the various wizards, you will find that they provide you with blank pages, partially completed pages, or pages containing text, links, and picture placeholders. In all cases, you have to add and edit material in the site to complete your Web before it can be published to the World Wide Web and accessed.

Remember that when you provide a name for the web you are going to create using the wizard, you are actually creating a folder on your computer where the web will reside. Webs do not consist of a single file like an Excel worksheet or Word document. Webs consist of a number of page files, picture files, and other elements. When you specify the name for the web, you are making a place for FrontPage to store all the files that make your web look the way it does.

Creating a New Web

The various Web Wizards walk you through web creation, and the level of sophistication of your new web depends on the wizard you select. Although the wizards act in similar ways, the more complex the site, the more questions you have to answer and the more steps you have to complete to create the site. For instance, the Personal Web Wizard provides a fast and easy avenue to a simple Web site for your own use, whereas the Corporate Web Wizard helps you create a complex web that contains a great deal of information (which you provide) on the company that the site is for.

CAUTION

Close the Open Blank Page Before Creating a New Web   When you start FrontPage, it automatically opens a new blank Web page for you and displays it in the Page view (discussed later in this lesson). When you create your new web using a wizard, this page does not become part of the actual web but it still takes the theme and attributes of the web you create. You might want to close this blank page (click the **Close** button in the upper-right corner of the page) before you build your site. This can prevent confusion caused by a page that appears in the Page view, but is not really part of the web you have created.

To create a site using one of the wizards, follow these steps:

1. With the FrontPage application running on the Windows desktop, select the **File** menu, point at **New**, and then select **Web** from the cascading menu. The New dialog box opens showing the Web Site Wizards (see Figure 2.1).

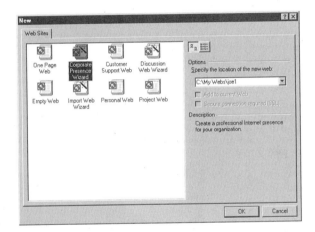

Figure 2.1   The New dialog box is where you select the wizard you want to use to build your new web.

2. Select one of the wizard icons in the dialog box, such as **Corporate Presence Wizard**.

3. Specify a name for the new web in the **Specify the Location of the New Web** text box on the right side of the dialog box (the default main folder for FrontPage webs is My Web).

4. Click **OK** to begin the web creation process.

5. Depending on the wizard you selected, your next action either begins editing and enhancing the Web pages that are created by the wizard, or you must answer some questions posed by the wizard before pages can be created. For instance, in the case of the Corporate Presence Web (and other business-related webs such as the Customer Support site), a wizard screen appears, as shown in Figure 2.2. Click **Next** to continue.

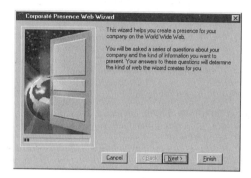

Figure 2.2   Some of the Web Wizards ask you a series of questions when building your new Web site.

6. Answer the questions on each of the wizard screens and click **Next** to continue. Figure 2.3 shows a screen from the Corporate Presence Web Wizard in which it asks you to determine the topic areas that should appear on the new web's home page.

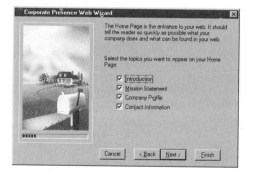

Figure 2.3   The wizard screens let you determine the pages in the web as well as topic areas and items found on individual pages.

7. Depending on the wizard that you chose to create your new web, you might be asked to select a theme for your new site. FrontPage themes provide design elements and color schemes that can really help you create eye-catching webs. Themes are discussed in Lesson 6, "Inserting Special FrontPage Components." After you have completed all the questions posed by the wizard, the final wizard screen provides a Finish button. Click **Finish** to end the web creation process.

Understanding the Web Views

When you complete your new web, you are taken to the Navigation view of the web, which shows all the pages that were created for your new site and their relationship to other pages in the site. The site consists of a home page and several other pages that branch from the home page (and are subordinate to it). Figure 2.4 shows the Navigation view of a web created using the Personal Web Wizard. Each wizard creates a different number of pages for the site and arranges them in a manner that depends on the purpose of the web.

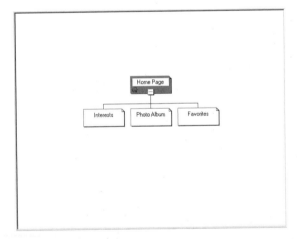

Figure 2.4   The various wizards end the creation process by showing your new web in the Navigation view.

CAUTION

Some Wizards Dump You in the Task View The Corporate Presence Wizard provides an option on the second-to-last wizard screen to take you to the Task view rather than the Navigation view. If you do not deselect the check box for Task view, you will end up there upon completion of the web. The different views available to you in FrontPage are covered in the remainder of this lesson.

The key to completing a web that has been created using a web wizard is understanding how the various views on the FrontPage Views bar are used as you edit and enhance the new web. Each view provides you with a different information set that shows you how the overall construction of the web is progressing. These views are defined in the sections that follow. You also use these views in the subsequent lessons that discuss FrontPage.

The Navigation View

The Navigation view (refer to Figure 2.4) allows you to see all the pages in the web in a flowchart format, which gives you the hierarchy for the site (this view is usually the default view for a site created using one of the wizards). The home page for the site is at the top of the hierarchy, and all pages that branch from the home page are shown below the home page with a connecting line. The pages that are below the home page in the web are called *child pages* by FrontPage.

Child pages are not limited to the home page, however, and any page in the Web site can have child pages. A page that has child pages is called a *parent page*.

You can drag and drop pages in the Navigation view to change their location in the web structure. New pages created for a site are inserted into the web in this manner (see Lesson 3, "Working with Web Pages and Themes" for more about inserting new pages into a Web site in the Navigation view).

To move to the Navigation view from any other FrontPage view, click the **Navigation** icon on the Views bar.

The Page View

The Page view is used to view and edit a particular page in your web. You use the Page view when you add text, pictures, or other objects to the individual Web pages in the site. The Page view is similar to an Excel worksheet window or a Word document window. It provides a workspace.

To enter the Page view for a specific page in the Web, follow these steps:

1. Go to the Navigation view by clicking the **Navigation** icon on the Views bar.

2. Double-click on a particular page in the Navigation view. The page opens in the Page view (as shown in Figure 2.5). The look of the page depends on the theme that you chose.

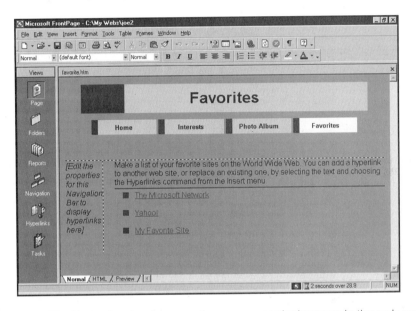

Figure 2.5   The Page view is where you focus on a particular page in the web and edit and enhance it.

When you are in the Page view, you can edit the current page as needed (which is discussed in detail in Lesson 3.

TIP   **Quickly Return to the Previously Opened Page**   If you open a particular page in the Page view by double-clicking it in the Navigation view (or Folders view) and then move to a different view (such as returning to the Navigation view), you can quickly return to the previously opened page by clicking the **PageView** icon on the Views bar.

The Folders View

The Folders view shows the folders and files in the current web. When you create a web using one of the wizards, several folders and files are created (the files created depend on the wizard that you used).

Click the **Folders** icon in the Views bar to view the folders and files in the web. Figure 2.6 shows the folders and files that are created when you use the Personal Web Wizard to create a new web.

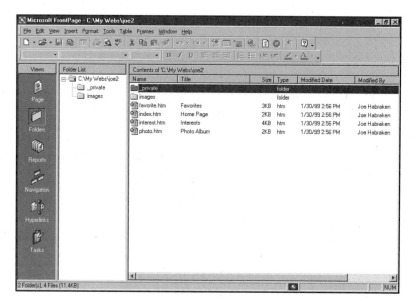

Figure 2.6 The Folders view allows you to view the folders and files contained in the current web.

The folders created for any of your new webs (no matter what wizard you use) consist of the following:

- **Web folder**—This is designated by the name that you provided for the web's location in the Specify the Location of the New Web box in the New dialog box.
- **_private folder**—This folder is created to hold any data that is input into special forms or other data input objects that you place on a page or pages in your Web site. Because the folder is private, there is no way for a visitor to your Web site to gain access to the information that it holds.

- **images folder**—This folder provides a place to save pictures and clip art that are part of the Web site. Any images placed in the web by the wizard are contained in this folder.

Files that are contained in the web can also be seen in the Folders view. Each web typically contains an index.htm file that serves as the home page for the web; the other pages in the web depend on the wizard that was used (each with the .htm extension, which means the page is an HTML document).

You can delete files from the web in the Folders view (select the file and then press the Delete key). You can also open pages in the Folders view by double-clicking them. They open in the Page view.

The Reports View

The Reports view allows you to view statistics and other information related to your web. These statistical reports are created automatically when you create the web, and they are updated as you work on the web. To view the statistics for your site, click the **Reports View** icon on the Views bar.

Figure 2.7 shows the Reports view for a personal web. Statistics such as the number of files and pictures in the web are reported as *mini-reports*. Other data provided include unverified links in the web (these usually consist of links to other Web sites on the World Wide Web that have not yet been verified by going online with your web).

A Reports toolbar allows you to change the statistics displayed in the Reports window. The default list for the Reports view is the Site Summary (refer to Figure 2.7), which shows all the statistics. If you want to view a certain statistic, such as unlinked files (in the web), click the drop-down box on the Reports toolbar and select the statistic—in this example, **Unlinked Files**—from the list. These files are listed. Any of the views found in the Site Summary view can be viewed alone by selecting the appropriate report title from the toolbar drop-down list.

The Hyperlinks View

The Hyperlinks view allows you to view the hyperlinks from a particular page in the site to other pages in the site and to other Web sites on the World Wide Web. Figure 2.8 shows the Hyperlinks view for the Favorites page in a Personal Web site. The page has internal links to the other pages in the web (so that you can quickly go to those pages). It also contains external links that allow you to jump to other sites found on the World Wide Web.

1067

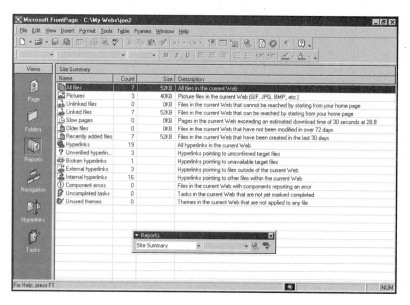

Figure 2.7 The Reports view provides you with important statistics related to your web.

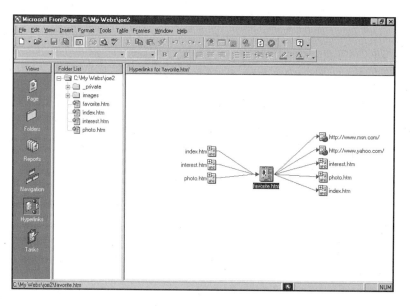

Figure 2.8 The Hyperlinks view shows you the internal and external hyperlinks on a specific page in the web.

To go to the Hyperlinks view for a page in your web, make sure that you first select the page in the Folders view or the Navigation view. Then click the **Hyperlinks View** icon on the Views bar. The page and its hyperlinks are displayed. Creating and managing hyperlinks is discussed in Lesson 7, "Working with Hyperlinks."

The Tasks View

The Tasks view allows you to see tasks that are used to help you in completing various aspects of your Web site. You can create tasks related to specific pages in the web or items on a Web page such as a picture or other item. When you start a task that appears on your tasks list, the task automatically opens the page or goes to the item on the page that the task was created for. Some of the wizards, such as the Corporate Presence Wizard, automatically create a list of tasks that is used to make sure all aspects of the new web are addressed before the web is placed on the World Wide Web for viewing. Tasks are covered in more detail in Lesson 10, "Completing and Publishing Your Web Site."

To go to the Tasks view, click the **Tasks View** icon on the Views bar. Figure 2.9 shows the tasks that were created when the Corporate Presence Wizard was used to create a new web.

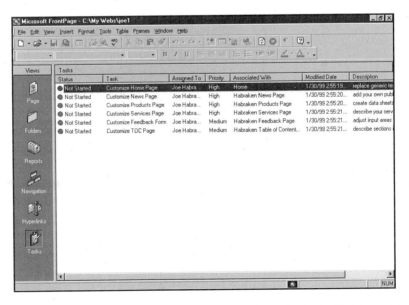

Figure 2.9   The Tasks view allows you to create and monitor tasks that are related to the completion of your web.

You might find that you use different views provided by the Views bar as you create or fine-tune your webs. These views are visited and revisited in the other lessons found in this part of the book.

In this lesson, you learned how to create a web using the FrontPage web wizards. You also learned how to navigate the views provided on the FrontPage Views bar and how each view gives you different information about your Web site. In the next lesson, you learn how to create new pages for your web and insert them into the Web site hierarchy.

Working with Web Pages and Themes

In this lesson, you learn to create new Web pages using the FrontPage templates, delete pages, and import pages created in other applications. You also learn to enhance the look of your Web pages with FrontPage themes.

Creating a New Web Page

FrontPage makes it easy for you to create new Web pages and place them in your web. You can create blank pages or pages that use a FrontPage template. These templates provide you with pages that can add functionality to your Web site. For instance, templates are available for creating different input forms on the web, search pages for your web, and even Guest Book pages. Creating form pages for your web is covered in Lesson 8, "Creating Special Forms for Your Web."

To create a new page in a web, follow these steps:

1. To open the web where you want to place the new page, select the **File** menu and point at **Recent Webs**; from the cascading menu that appears, select the web you want to open.

2. With the appropriate web open, you can now create a new page for the web. First, click the **Page View** icon to go to the Page view.

3. Select the **File** menu, point at **New**, and then select **Page** from the cascading menu. The New dialog box opens (see Figure 3.1).

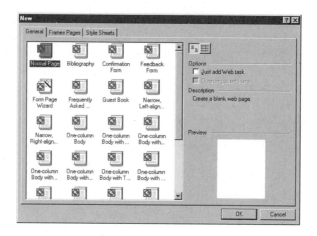

Figure 3.1   The General tab of the New dialog box is where you select the template for your new page.

4. The new page templates are available on the General tab of the New dialog box. Click the template that you want to use for your new page. Then click **OK** to create the new page.

The new page appears in the FrontPage Page view. Figure 3.2 shows a two-column page that was created using the Two-Column Body template. The templates create pages that contain placeholder text and other items that you can modify (working with text on your pages is covered in Lesson 4, "Working with Text in FrontPage").

You will also find that the new page (even though it's not included in the navigational structure of your web yet) embraces the theme that you assigned to the current web (FrontPage themes are covered later in this lesson).

Now that you have the new page, you need to save it. Follow these steps:

1. Click the **Save** button on the FrontPage toolbar. The Save As dialog box opens.
2. Type a filename for your new page in the **File Name** box.
3. You also should change the page title for the new page. This title appears in the Web browser when you view the particular page on the World Wide Web. To change the page title, click the **Change** button. The Set Page Title dialog box opens (see Figure 3.3).

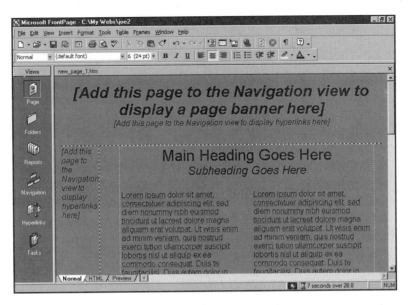

Figure 3.2 The new page appears in the FrontPage editing window in the Page view.

Figure 3.3 Type the page title that you want to appear in the Web browser when the page is viewed on the World Wide Web.

4. Type the new page title, and then click **OK**. You are returned to the Save As dialog box. Click **Save** to complete the process.

Inserting the Page into the Web

After you've created and saved the new page, you need to make the page part of the current web. You might think creating the page when the current web is open in FrontPage should have taken care of that, but it doesn't.

You add the page to the current web by linking the page to your site's home page. In most cases, the home page has the name index.htm (.htm because it's an HTML file).

To add the new page to the navigational structure of your web, follow
these steps:

1. Click the **Navigation** icon on the Views bar. The current navigational
   structure of your page appears.

2. To the left of the Navigation view, a Folder list should appear. If you don't
   see a list of all the pages available in the web (in the Folder list), click the
   Folder List button on the toolbar.

3. To add the new page to the structure of the web, locate the file in the
   Folder list, then drag the file onto the Navigation view, placing the box
   that represents the file underneath your home page. (Figure 3.4 shows a
   page named latestnews.htm being added to the web structure.)

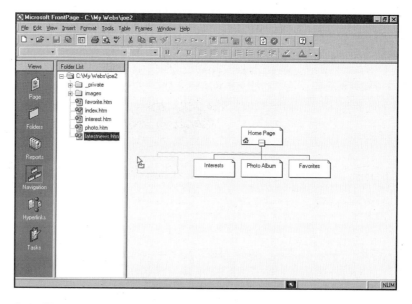

Figure 3.4   The Navigation view makes it easy for you to add new pages to your web.

Deleting a page from the web is best done in the Navigation view. This not only
allows you to quickly delete the page from the navigational structure of the web,
but it also removes the appropriate HTML document from the Folder list at the
same time.

To delete a page from your web, follow these steps:

1. Click the **Navigation** icon on the Views bar to go to the Navigation view.

2. Click the page that you want to remove from the web (in the Navigation window).

3. Press the **Delete** key on the keyboard. The Delete Page dialog box appears.

4. You have the choice of removing the page from the navigational structure of the web (this does not delete the page file) or deleting the page from the web (this removes it from the structure and deletes the file). Select the appropriate option button in the Delete Page dialog box, as shown in Figure 3.5.

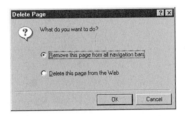

Figure 3.5 You can easily remove a page from the web in the Navigation view.

5. Click **OK**. The page is removed from the structure. (The file is deleted if Delete This Page from the Web was selected in the dialog box.)

Importing Files from Other Applications

You can also import page files into your web that you create in other applications. For instance, let's say that you designed a Web page in Microsoft Word and saved the document as an HTML file. You can easily import that particular file into the current web (for more about using Word to create Web pages, see Lesson 22 in the Word part of this book, "Word and the World Wide Web").

To import a file into the current web, follow these steps:

1. Select the **File** menu, then select **Import**. The Import dialog box appears.

2. Click the **Add File** button. The Add File to Import List dialog box appears.

3. Use the **Look In** drop-down box to locate the drive that holds the file you want to import. Also select the folder where the file resides (see Figure 3.6). After selecting the file, click the **OK** button.

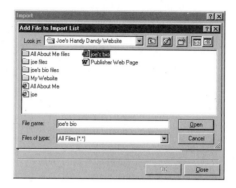

Figure 3.6   Locate the file you want to import into the current web.

4. The filename appears in the Import dialog box (see Figure 3.7). Repeat steps 2 and 3 if you want to add more files to the import list.

5. When you have added all the files to the import list that you want to import into the current web, click the **OK** button.

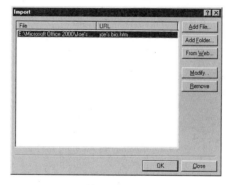

Figure 3.7   You can import one or a number of files into the current web.

The file (or files) is imported into the current web. You can find the files listed in the Folder list of your web. The files then must be made part of the web's navigational structure. Go to the Navigation view and drag the file or files from the Folder list and add them to the Navigation window as subordinates to your home page for the web (see the section "Inserting the Page into the Web" in this lesson for more details).

Using the FrontPage Themes

Although the page templates available in FrontPage for creating new pages control the overall layout of function of the page, the FrontPage themes control things like the look, design, and color scheme of the page. When you create a new web using some of the wizards (such as the Corporate Presence Wizard), you are asked to choose a theme during the web creation process. You can, however, select a theme for the pages that are inserted into an empty web or created with one of the wizards (such as the Personal Web Wizard) that use the default theme (Straight Edge theme) for the newly created web.

To choose a theme for your Web pages, follow these steps:

1. Go to the Page view by clicking the **Page** icon on the Views bar.
2. Select the **Format** menu, then select **Theme**. The Themes dialog box appears (see Figure 3.8).

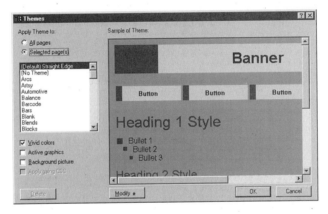

Figure 3.8   The Themes dialog box gives you access to all the FrontPage themes.

3. You can apply the theme to the currently open Web page (the page that was shown in the Page view) or apply the theme to all the pages in the web. Click either the **Selected Page(s)** or **All Pages** option button, respectively.
4. To choose your theme, scroll down through the themes in the **Theme** scroll box. Select a particular theme to see a preview of the theme in the Sample of Theme box in the dialog box.
5. When you have found the theme you want to use for your page or pages, select it and then click the **OK** button.

The theme is applied to the page (or pages) in your Web. Figure 3.9 shows a page that the Kids theme has been applied to.

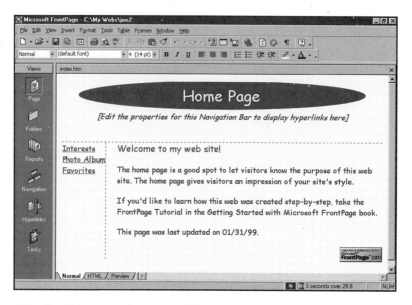

Figure 3.9 Each theme embraces a different color scheme and design elements.

Themes can help set the tone for a Web site and can also add a great deal of visual interest to a web. You will find that you do have control over some aspects of the theme's design.

When you are in the Themes dialog box, click the **Modify** button located near the bottom center of the dialog box. Three buttons appear just above the Modify button: Color, Graphics, and Text. Click the **Color** button to select a new color scheme for the theme. To change the background graphic used in the theme, click the **Graphics** button and then use the drop-down box to select a new graphic file. (The background graphic is similar to the wallpaper that you place on your Windows 98 Desktop; see Lesson 6 in the Windows part of the book, "Customizing the Appearance of Windows 98.") To modify the font used in the theme, click the **Text** button and make a font selection using the **Font** scroll box that appears.

In this lesson, you learned how to create new pages for your web; you also learned to delete unwanted pages from your web. You learned to import files from other applications and enhance your Web pages with FrontPage themes. In the next lesson, you learn how to work with text in FrontPage.

Working with Text in FrontPage

In this lesson, you learn to add, edit, and format text on your Web pages including the creation of your own styles. You also learn to change the page names for pages in your web.

Inserting and Modifying Text

Working with text in FrontPage is very similar to working with text in any word processor, particularly Microsoft Word. Many of the text commands and features that you find in Word are also available in FrontPage (for more about working with text in Word, see Lesson 3, "Editing Documents," in the Word part of this book).

If you create your Web pages using a wizard or create a new page using a template, you will see placeholder text on the pages or page. A great deal of the text work you do in FrontPage is replacing placeholder text with your own text. When you replace placeholder text with your own text, the formatting (font, text size, color, and so on) that was present on the placeholder text is also applied to the text you enter.

If you create a blank page, any text that is inserted onto the page has to be formatted with an appropriate font, color, or other text attribute. FrontPage also provides you with the ability to align text (as does Word).

Replacing Placeholder Text

Replacing the placeholder text that the wizards and templates place on your text pages is just a matter of selecting the text and then typing your new text.

To replace placeholder text, follow these steps:

1. Open the page you want to edit in the Page view.

2. Select the placeholder text you want to replace on the page (see Figure 4.1).

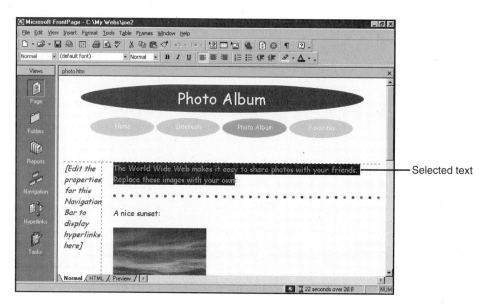

Figure 4.1 Select the placeholder text and then type your own text to replace it.

3. Type the text that replaces the placeholder text.

4. After you change the text on a particular page, make sure you save the changes; click the **Save** button on the toolbar.

Inserting New Text

Inserting new text is just a matter of positioning the insertion point (the mouse I-beam) on the page and then typing your new text. When you add new text to the page, the text is formatted using the default text attributes for the page (determined by the theme assigned to the page). This includes text formatting such as the font, size, and color of the text.

If you insert text onto a new page that does not have a theme assigned to it, the text is inserted in a Times New Roman default font. You can then modify the look of the text as needed.

Copying, Moving, and Deleting Text

You can copy or cut text and then paste it to another location on the current page or switch to another page in the web and paste the text there. Follow these steps to copy and paste text:

1. Select the text you want to copy.
2. Select the **Edit** menu and then select **Copy**.
3. Place the insertion point on the page where you want to place a copy of the copied text.
4. Select the **Edit** menu and then select **Paste**. A copy of the text is inserted at the insertion point.

Moving text is very similar to copying the text—the only difference being the use of the Cut command rather than Copy:

1. Select the text you want to move.
2. Select the **Edit** menu and then select **Cut** to cut the text from the its current position.
3. Place the insertion point on the page where you want to move the text.
4. Select the **Edit** menu and then select **Paste**. The text is moved to the new location (defined by the insertion point).

 TIP **Drag and Drop Your Text** You can also use drag and drop to move text on a Web page. Select the text and then drag it to a new location.

To delete placeholder text or text that you've placed on a page, select the text and then press the **Delete** key on the keyboard.

Changing How the Text Looks

You have complete control over the formatting attributes of the text on the pages of your web. You can format text using the various buttons on the FrontPage Formatting toolbar, or you can take advantage of the text styles that are provided by the theme or template that you assign to your Web page or pages.

Using the Formatting Toolbar

The Formatting toolbar gives you the ability to change the font, text size, text attributes (such as bold and italic), and color of the font. In most cases, it's just a matter of selecting the text and then clicking the appropriate attribute button on the Formatting toolbar to change the look of the text. Bold, italic, and underline work in this manner.

Other attributes, such as the font, font size, or font color, require that you select the text and then select your formatting change from a list or palette. For instance, to change the font, you select the text and then select a new font using the Font drop-down box on the Formatting toolbar. Font size is also controlled by a drop-down box on the Formatting toolbar. Changing the color of selected text requires that you choose a new color from a color palette.

To change the color of the text on a page, follow these steps:

1. Select the word or other text you want to change the color of.

2. Click the **Font Color** drop-down button on the Formatting toolbar. The color palette appears (see Figure 4.2).

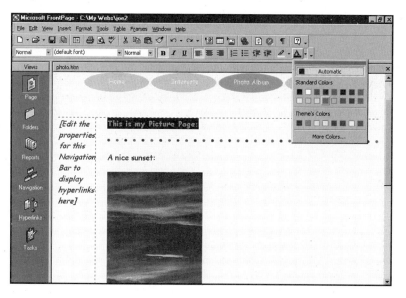

Figure 4.2 Changing text attributes like color requires that you select the text and then choose the new attribute on the Formatting toolbar.

3. Choose a font color from the palette. The text color changes.

4. Click anywhere on the page to deselect the text.

CAUTION

Text Attribute Changes Override Theme Styles   FrontPage relies heavily on styles to format the text on the pages in your web, especially if you've chosen a theme for your pages. When you select text and change the formatting using the buttons on the Formatting toolbar, these changes override the current style. In fact, even if you change the style of this modified text, the attributes provided by the new style also are overridden by your former formatting changes.

Using FrontPage Styles

A style is a grouping of formatting attributes identified by a style name. A style might include text-formatting attributes such as bold, a particular font color, and a particular font size. Styles can also contain text alignment attributes such as center or right align (for more information, see the next section, "Aligning Text").

FrontPage provides a number of built-in styles that you can take advantage of. There are a series of heading styles, styles for bulleted and numbered lists, and a number of others. To use styles, you need to understand how FrontPage views text on a Web page. Each line of text that is followed by a paragraph mark (placed at the end of the line or paragraph when you press the Enter key) is considered a separate paragraph. To assign a particular style to a text paragraph (be it a single line or several lines of text), all you have to do is place the insertion point somewhere in the text block.

To assign a built-in style to text on a page, follow these steps:

1. Place the insertion point in the paragraph you want to assign the style to.

2. Click the **Style** drop-down box on the Formatting toolbar.

3. Select a style from the drop-down list.

The style is assigned to your text paragraph.

You can also create your own text styles if you want. Follow these steps:

1. Select **Format** and then **Style**, and the Style dialog box appears (see Figure 4.3).

2. Click the **List** drop-down box under the currently listed styles and select **User-Defined Styles**.

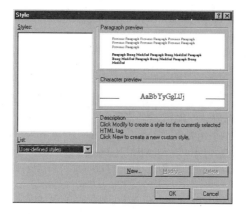

Figure 4.3   The Style dialog box is the starting place for creating, editing, and managing the styles for your pages.

3. To create the new style, click the **New** button. The New Style dialog box appears.

4. Type a name for your new style in the **Name** box.

5. Click the **Format** button on the bottom left of the New Style dialog box. Select **Font** to change the font attributes for style (the Font dialog box appears).

6. After completing your font attribute selections, click **OK** to return to the New Style dialog box. To include other attributes in the style, click the **Format** button again and select **Paragraph**, **Border** or other style attributes as required.

7. When you have completed the formatting choices for the style, click **OK** to close the New Style dialog box and return to the Style dialog box. Your new style appears in the style list.

8. Click **OK** again to return to your page.

You can assign your new style to text on the page just as you can any of the pre-made styles. Place the insertion point on the text and then click the **Style** drop-down box on the Formatting toolbar. Select your style (which appears at the end of the style list).

Styles Are Not Shared by Different Pages   When you create a
FrontPage style for a particular page, it is only good on that page. You can't
use it on any other pages—not even pages in the same web.

CAUTION

Aligning Text

Another aspect of formatting text is aligning text on the page. The default
alignment for new text on a Web page is left justified. This means it aligns
directly against the left margin of a page or against any shared borders that
have been placed on the left side of a page. (Shared borders are discussed in
Lesson 6, "Inserting Special FrontPage Components.")

The simplest way to align text on a page is using the alignment buttons on the
Formatting toolbar. First, place the insertion point in the text and then select one
of the following alignment possibilities:

- **Left Justified**—The default justification for normal text, aligned on the left.
  Click the **Align Left** button on the Formatting toolbar.

- **Right Justified**—Text is aligned at the right margin. A ragged left edge is
  present on text that is right aligned. Click the **Align Right** button on the
  Formatting toolbar.

- **Center**—The text is centered between the left and right margins of the
  page. Click the **Center** button on the Formatting toolbar.

Changing Page Names

When you create pages using the Web Wizards, default page names are
assigned to the pages in the web. Often, you want to customize these page
names to suit your own needs. Unfortunately, when you click on one of the
pre-made page banners placed at the top of the page, you will find that you
cannot edit the text as you would regular text on the page. The banner does
not allow you to select the text or place the insertion point on the banner.

For instance, if you create a new web using the Personal Web Wizard, four
pages are created for you: Home Page, Interests, Photo Album, and Favorites.
Page banners are automatically placed at the top of each page by the wizard.
(More about page banners is covered in Lesson 6.) If you want to change the text
in the banner, you must change the page name itself. For example, if you want
to change the Interests page's banner to read *Hobbies*, you have to change the
page's name.

To change the page name for a page in your web, follow these steps:

1. Click the **Navigation** icon on the Views bar to go to the Navigation view.

2. Right-click the page you want to rename and select **Rename** from the shortcut menu that appears (see Figure 4.4).

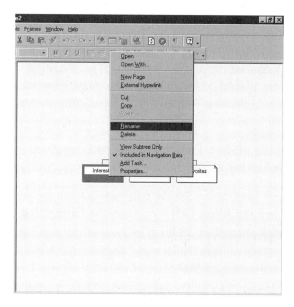

Figure 4.4   Change the page name of a page in the Navigation view.

3. Type the new name for the page.

4. Click any other page in the web to deselect the **Name** box for the page that was edited.

In this lesson, you learned how to add, edit, and format text on your Web pages including the creation of your own styles. You also learned to change the page names for pages in your web. In the next lesson, you learn how to work with graphics in FrontPage.

Working with Graphics in FrontPage

In this lesson, you learn to insert pictures, clip art, and motion clips onto your Web pages and save the graphic files as part of your web. You also learn how to preview pages in the web.

Inserting Pictures

FrontPage makes it easy for you to insert images, clip art, and special animated images into your Web pages. You can insert pictures that you download from the World Wide Web, scan with a scanner, or capture with a digital camera. You can also insert clip art and motion clips from the Clip Art Gallery.

You will find that FrontPage allows you to insert a number of different picture file formats into your Web pages:

- CompuServe GIF (.gif)
- Encapsulated Postscript (.eps)
- Various paint programs (.pcx)
- Tagged Image File Format (.tif)
- Windows bitmap (.bmp)
- JPEG File Interchange format (.jpg)

Inserting a picture onto a Web page is really just a matter of placing the insertion point at the appropriate position and then locating the picture file that you want to insert.

To insert a picture file, follow these steps:

1. Open the page (double-click it in the Navigation view) where you want to place the picture. You are in the Page view.

2. Place the insertion point where you want to place the graphic.

3. Select **Insert**, point at **Picture**, and select **From File** on the cascading menu. The Picture dialog box appears (see Figure 5.1).

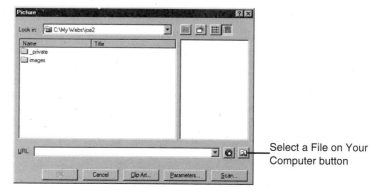

Select a File on Your Computer button

Figure 5.1 The Picture dialog box allows you to insert picture files into your Web pages.

4. The Picture dialog box shows you a list of the picture files that are already in the current web. To locate a picture stored on your computer, click the **Select a File on Your Computer** button in the lower-right corner of the dialog box. The Select File dialog box appears.

5. Use the **Look In** box to locate the drive that contains the picture file and double-click to open the folder that holds the file. After you locate the picture, click the file to select it.

6. Click **OK**, and the image is placed on your page (see Figure 5.2).

TIP **Move Your Pictures to Your Web Folder** To save yourself some time searching for pictures on your computer's hard drive, copy or move all the picture files for your Web site to the web folder that is created when you first create the new web in FrontPage. This way, all the pictures are immediately available when you open the Picture dialog box.

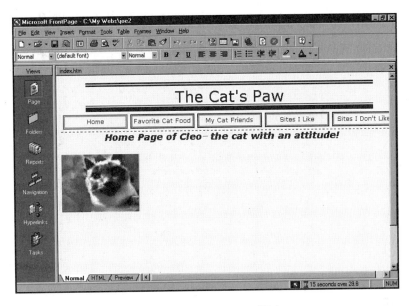

Figure 5.2 Pictures can add visual interest to your Web pages.

Inserting Clip Art

You can also insert any number of images from the Clip Art Gallery. Drawings of animals, computers, and even cartoons are available for you to use on your Web pages.

To insert clip art images, follow these steps:

1. Open the page (double-click it in the Navigation view) where you want to place the picture. You are in the Page view.
2. Place the insertion point where you want to place the clip art.
3. Select the **Insert** menu and point at **Picture**. Select **Clip Art** from the cascading menu. The Clip Art Gallery opens.
4. Click one of the clip art categories (such as Animals) to view a set of images (see Figure 5.3).
5. When you locate the image you want to use, click the image. A shortcut toolbar appears (see Figure 5.4).
6. Click the **Insert Clip** button on the shortcut toolbar to place the image on your page.

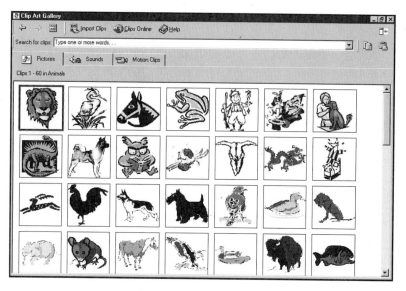

Figure 5.3   Each Clip Art Gallery category provides a set of related images.

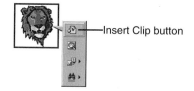

Insert Clip button

Figure 5.4   Select an image and click the Insert Clip button to place the image on the page.

TIP   **Search for Specific Clip Art**   You can search for specific clip art by doing a keyword search. Click in the Clip Art Gallery's **Search for Clips** box and type a word or words to search for. Press **Enter** when you are ready to do the search. A set of clip art related to your search terms appears in the Clip Art Gallery.

Inserting Clip Art Gallery Motion Clips

The Clip Art Gallery also provides you with a number of motion clips that you can place on your Web pages. These motion clips are actually animated clip art. These animated images are activated when someone visits a page on your web that contains the animation.

Motion clips can add interest and excitement to your site. To insert a motion clip, follow these steps:

1. Open the page (double-click it in the Navigation view) where you want to place the picture. You are in the Page view.

2. Place the insertion point where you want to place the clip art.

3. Select the **Insert** menu and then point at **Picture**. Select **Clip Art** from the cascading menu. The Clip Art Gallery opens.

4. Click the **Motion Clips** tab in the Clip Art Gallery window.

5. Click one of the categories (such as Entertainment) to view a set of motion clips.

Not All the Clip Categories Provide Motion Clips   When you are looking for motion clips in the various Clip Art Gallery categories, don't be alarmed if you find that a particular category does not provide any motion clips at all.

CAUTION

6. To preview a motion clip, click the clip and then click the **Play Clip** button on the shortcut toolbar. A preview box appears, and the animation plays (see Figure 5.5).

Figure 5.5   Motion clips can be previewed before you insert them on your Web pages.

7. When you have completed previewing the motion clip, click the **Close** button in the preview's upper-right corner.

8. To insert a motion clip, click the image and then click the **Insert Clip** button on the shortcut toolbar to place the image on your page.

The motion clip appears as a static image on your Web page. You have to preview the page to actually see the motion clip in action (see the section "Previewing Your Images" in this lesson for more information).

Saving the Image to Your Web

You might think that inserting a picture file, clip-art image, or motion clip onto a particular page makes that image part of your web—it is, after all, on one of the web's pages. Well, that's not the case. When you save the page where you inserted the image, you also have to save the image itself as a separate file that is placed with the other files held in the current Web folder.

Web pages can't have graphics that are embedded on the pages. So when you insert a graphic onto a FrontPage Web page, you are actually setting up a link between the page and the graphic that you inserted. When you view Web pages on the World Wide Web using your Web browser, the pictures you see are actually linked to the page that you open in your browser.

Another thing you should be aware of is that when the inserted image (picture, clip art, and so on) is saved to the web, it is saved in a file format that is best for viewing on Web pages. Files in any format other than .gif or .jpg are converted to .gif files when you save them to the web. .gif and .jpg files are typically used on Web pages because these two file formats provide good resolution and color in a fairly compact file size. (.gifs and .jpgs display a great-looking picture using a smaller file size than .bmps or .tifs, which require much larger files to show the same image.)

To save a page image as part of the web, follow these steps:

 1. With the page open in the Page view, click the **Save** button on the toolbar. The Save Embedded Files dialog box appears (see Figure 5.6).

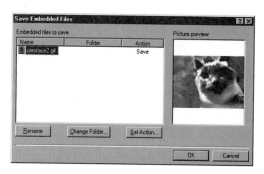

Figure 5.6   Embedded graphics must be saved as separate files in the Web folder.

2. A new name for the file is provided (based on the original filename of the image) and the image is saved as a .gif file (if it's not already a .jpg). Click **OK** to save the file.

The image file is now part of the web. The new file created in step 2 is placed in your Web folder.

CAUTION

The Save As Dialog Box Appears If the Page Hasn't Been Saved   When you click the Save button to save an embedded image on a page, the Save As dialog box appears if the page itself hasn't been saved before. Provide a name and save the page. Then the Save Embedded Files dialog box appears, and you can save the image file to the web.

Sizing the Image

You can size any image you place on a page. As you size an image you will find that it affects the text below the image. The larger you make the picture, the more the text is moved down the page.

To size an image, follow these steps:

1. Click the image to select it.

2. Place the mouse pointer on any of the sizing handles that appear around the image. The mouse pointer becomes a two-headed arrow.

3. Drag to increase or decrease the size of the image (see Figure 5.7). Release the mouse when you have finished sizing the image.

mouse pointer

Figure 5.7   Use the sizing handles to increase or decrease the size of your image.

TIP   **Maintain the Image's Height/Width Ratio**   Use the sizing handles on the corners of the image and drag diagonally to maintain the image's height/width ratio. This keeps the image from looking distorted.

Aligning the Image

 You can also align your images on the page. The simplest way to align a graphic is using the Alignment buttons on the Formatting toolbar. For instance, to place an image on the center of the page, click the **Center** button on the toolbar.

When you use the Formatting toolbar buttons, however, you are only changing the position of the image; you are not changing how text on the page wraps around the image. The default setting for how text relates to a picture is for text not to wrap around the image.

To change the position of an image in relation to surrounding text, you must use settings found in the Picture Properties dialog box.

To change image alignment and how text wraps around the image, follow these steps:

1. Right-click the image and select **Picture Properties** from the shortcut menu. The Picture Properties dialog box appears.

2. Click the **Appearance** tab on the Picture Properties dialog box. Picture alignment and text wraps around the picture are controlled by the **Alignment** drop-down box (see Figure 5.8).

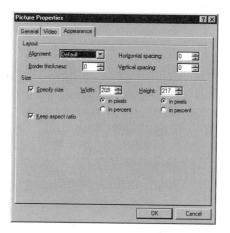

Figure 5.8   Use the Alignment box on the Appearance tab to control the alignment of a picture and how text wraps around it.

3. The first time you go to the Appearance tab, the setting in the Alignment box is Default. Default means that the picture is aligned where you inserted it (normally on the left side of the page, unless you changed its position using the Alignment buttons on the Formatting toolbar) and text does not wrap around the picture.

4. To change the position of the picture and how text wraps around the picture, click the Alignment drop-down box and make one of the following selections:

   - **Left**—This aligns the picture on the left of the page and allows text to wrap around the image on the right.
   - **Center**—This allows you to place text on both the left and right side of the image. (It does not center the image relative to the page, but places the image in the center of the text.)
   - **Right**—Places the image on the right of the page and allows text to wrap around the left side of the picture.

5. After you make your alignment selection, click the **OK** button to close the Picture Properties dialog box.

You are returned to your page. You can now insert text on the page so that it wraps around the picture (depending on which of the alignment options you chose).

If you want to place a border around a particular picture, open the Picture Properties dialog box for that picture and click the **Appearance** tab. Use the **Border Thickness** box to set a thickness for a border around the picture. Click **OK** to close the dialog box after you've set the border thickness.

CAUTION

Enhance Pictures Before You Post FrontPage does not provide tools for enhancing the pictures you place on your Web pages. You can edit and enhance images in PhotoDraw. Lessons 11 through 15 look at the tools PhotoDraw provides.

Previewing Your Images

When you work with pictures and graphics on a page, it's nice to be able to take a quick look at how they appear when your pages are viewed on the World Wide Web. This is particularly useful if you've placed motion clips on your pages and want to see how they look when the animations are playing.

When you are in Page view, you can quickly preview a particular page and the elements you have placed on that page. Click the **Preview** tab at the bottom of the page window. The page as it appears in a Web browser displays in the Preview mode (see Figure 5.9).

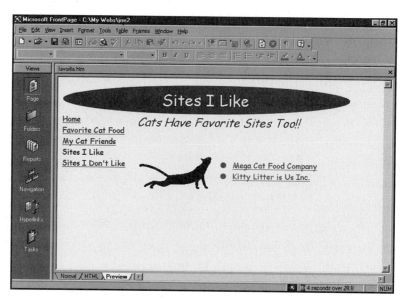

Figure 5.9   Previewing your pages allows you to see how graphics (especially motion clips) look on the World Wide Web.

To return to your page so that you can edit it, click the **Normal** tab.

The Preview mode provides a quick view of how things will appear on the World Wide Web. The test, however, is to view pages in a Web browser, which gives you a true picture of how the site will look.

In this lesson, you learned how to place picture files, clip art, and motion clips on your pages. You also learned how to save the pictures to the web and align the pictures on the page. In the next lesson, you learn how to insert special FrontPage components on your Web pages.

Inserting Special FrontPage Components

In this lesson, you learn to insert special FrontPage components like navigation bars, page banners, shared borders, and hit counters.

Understanding Special Components

FrontPage provides a number of special elements, called *components*, that you can place on your Web pages. These components are designed to take the place of sophisticated elements like navigation bars and hit counters that you would normally have to create using the HTML coding language.

A number of special components are available in FrontPage. Table 6.1 defines some of the commonly used components.

Table 6.1 FrontPage Special Components

Component	Purpose
Shared borders	A shared border is an area that is common to the pages in your Web. Any item placed in a shared border appears on all the pages of the Web.
Page banner	Displays the page name at the top of the page. Page banners use the text attributes and pictures of a theme assigned to that page. Page banners placed in shared borders display the page name of every page in the Web.
Navigation bar	A set of text or graphics that provides hyperlinks to the other pages in a Web site. A navigation bar placed in a shared border is displayed on all the pages in the Web.

continues

Table 6.1   Continued

Component	Purpose
Hit counters	A page component that appears as a numbered counter and keeps count of the number of visits (referred to as *hits*) to your Web site.

Normally, the creation of items like those mentioned in Table 6.1 require a good understanding of HTML programming and are usually the sign of a fairly sophisticated Web site. However, FrontPage allows you to place very complex components (complex in a programming sense) on your Web pages by taking advantage of the options available on the Insert menu.

Using Shared Borders

Shared borders allow you to create an area on the top, bottom, left, or right of a page that can be shared by all the pages in the Web site. Shared borders are similar to headers and footers used in Microsoft Word where you want information of some type to appear on all the pages of a document. In FrontPage, this allows you to put items like navigation bars or page banners in the shared border area so that they appear on all the pages. This means that you only have to insert the component (such as a navigation bar) in the shared border area on one of the pages in the Web, and the component appears on all the pages in the Web (in the shared border area).

If you've used any of the Web Wizards to create your Web, you've already seen the application of shared borders. For example, Webs created using the Personal Web Wizard automatically place shared borders on the left and top of the pages in the Web.

To insert shared borders on your Web pages or to modify the current shared borders, follow these steps:

1. Open one of the pages in your Web (double-click it in the Navigation view).

2. Select the **Format** menu and then select **Shared Borders**. The Shared Borders dialog box appears (see Figure 6.1).

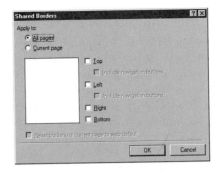

Figure 6.1   Set shared borders parameters in the Shared Borders dialog box.

3. Option buttons at the top of the dialog box allow you to place the shared borders on **All Pages** or **Current Page**. For a Web with consistent design, select the **All Pages** option button.

4. Click the appropriate check box for the location of the shared borders you want to place on the pages: **Top, Left, Right, Bottom**. You can check more than one box.

5. If you select Top or Left, you can also choose to have navigation buttons for the Web automatically placed in the shared border area. Click the **Include Navigation Buttons** check box as needed to include navigation buttons.

6. When you have completed your selections, click **OK**. A message box appears telling you that any content previously contained in shared borders can be overwritten by the selections that you made in the Shared Borders dialog box. Click **Yes** to close the box.

Your shared borders appear on the page or pages of your Web (depending on the selections you made in the Shared Borders dialog box). The shared border areas are excellent places to insert other special components, such as page banners, navigation bars, or even company logos or pictures. Any items you want to repeat on your Web pages can be placed in a shared border area. Figure 6.2 shows a Web page that has shared borders at the top and left of the page.

Figure 6.2 Shared borders allow you to place repeating elements on all the pages in your Web.

Creating Page Banners

Page banners provide a colorful heading for your pages that is consistent across the pages in a Web. Page banners can consist of text that uses the font and colors of the theme selected for the Web (if a theme was selected). Or, page banners can consist of a graphic with text that uses graphic elements, fonts, and colors from the current theme.

Page banners can be placed anywhere on the page (but are most useful at the top of the page as the main heading for that page). When a page banner is placed in a shared border area, it displays the appropriate page name for the current page and also appears on the other pages in the Web. (The page name is the name assigned to the page in the Navigation view.)

To insert a page banner, follow these steps:

1. Open the page (double-click it in the Navigation view) where you want to place the page banner. If you plan on placing the banner in a shared border area, you can open any page in the Web (displaying the shared border).

2. Place the insertion point where you want to place the banner. To place it in a shared border area, click within the shared border (placeholder text in the border area is selected).

3. Select **Insert** and then select **Page Banner**. The Page Banner Properties dialog box appears (see Figure 6.3).

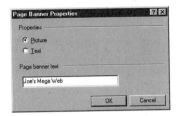

Figure 6.3 The Page Banner Properties dialog box allows you to insert a text or graphic banner on your Web page.

4. Select the **Picture** or **Text** option button to determine the type of banner you create.
5. If you want to change the page banner text, select the text in the **Page Banner Text** box and type the new banner heading.
6. Click **OK** and the banner is placed on your page (see Figure 6.4).

New banner

Figure 6.4 The new page banner appears on your Web page.

If you chose to place the page banner in a shared border, you will find that the new banner appears on each of the pages in the Web. If you want to modify a page banner, double-click the banner to open the Page Banner dialog box. You can remove a banner by selecting it and pressing the **Delete** key on the keyboard.

CAUTION

Changing the Banner Text Changes the Page Name If you decide to change the text for the banner in the Page Banner dialog box, you will find that this also changes the name of that particular page when you go to the Navigation view for the Web.

Inserting Navigation Bars

Making it easy for a visitor to your Web site to move between the pages in your Web is a necessity (or you aren't going to get very many visitors to stay and view your site). Navigation links must be available on each of the pages. Fortunately, FrontPage provides you with a way to quickly (and easily) place navigation links on your page in the form of navigation bars. Navigation bars are preprogrammed components that can be placed in the shared border area of your Web pages and provide navigation buttons that take you to the other pages in the Web.

To insert a navigation bar in your Web, follow these steps:

1. Open the page (double-click it in the Navigation view) where you want to place the navigation bar. If you plan on placing the navigation bar in a shared border area, you can open any page in the Web (displaying the shared border).

2. Place the insertion point where you want to place the banner. To place it in a shared border area, click within the shared border (placeholder text in the border area is selected).

3. Select **Insert** and then select **Navigation Bar**. The Navigation Bar Properties dialog box appears (see Figure 6.5).

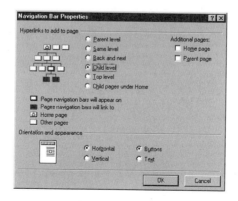

Figure 6.5 The Navigation Bar Properties dialog box allows you to determine the type of navigation structure created on the pages.

4. Option buttons are provided for you to choose the type of links (set up for you as hyperlinks) that can appear on the navigation bar. Select one of the buttons depending on the navigation links you want to create:

Parent Level—Provides a button or text link that takes you to the parent page of the current page.

Same Level—Provides links to other pages in the Web that are at the same level as the current page (when viewed in the Navigation view).

Back and Next—Provides links to take you to the previous and next page.

Child Level—Provides links to any child pages of the current page (pages shown below the current page in the Navigation view).

Top Level—Provides links to any pages (including the home page) that are on the home page's level in the navigational structure of the Web.

Child Pages Under Home—Provides links to pages under Home. This is useful if you've divided your Web into sections using section pages under Home in the navigational structure of the Web.

5. You can also choose to have links to your home page or parent page of the current page by selecting either the **Home Page** or **Parent Page** check box on the right of the dialog box. These links appear on the navigation bar in addition to the other links that you chose in step 4.

6. Use the option buttons at the bottom of the dialog box to determine the orientation of the links on the navigation bar: **Horizontal** or **Vertical**.

7. Select either the **Buttons** or **Text** option button to select the appearance of the links on the navigation bar.

8. After making all your selections, click **OK**.

The navigation bar appears on the current page. Figure 6.6 shows a navigation bar that uses the colors and design elements of the current theme for the Web (the Cactus theme). Buttons are chosen to show links to the home page of the Web (the current page shown) and child pages of the current page (the other pages currently in the Web).

If you want to edit the navigation bar, double-click it to open the Navigation Bar dialog box. If you want to delete the navigation bar, select it and press the **Delete** key.

Figure 6.6   A navigation bar provides links to the other pages in your Web.

Inserting Hit Counters

Another useful component that you might want to place on the home page of your Web is a hit counter. Hit counters show you and the visitors to your Web site how many hits (or visits) have been made to your site. It's fun for visitors to see their visit number, and it's also important to see what kind of traffic your Web site is experiencing. Creating a hit counter normally requires pretty good knowledge of HTML coding. Fortunately, FrontPage provides a number of ready-made hit counters that you can insert as components.

To insert a FrontPage hit counter, follow these steps:

1. Open the home page for your site in the Page view. (The hit counter is typically placed on the main page for your site.)
2. Place the insertion point where you want to place the hit counter. Most sites place them directly below any text or graphics found on the home page of the Web.
3. Select **Insert**, point at **Component**, and then select **Hit Counter**. The Hit Counter Properties dialog box appears (see Figure 6.7).
4. Select one of the hit counter styles from the dialog box.
5. Click **OK** to insert the selected hit counter onto your page.

Figure 6.7 The Hit Counter Properties dialog box provides you with several different hit counter styles.

The hit counter appears on your page as text (Hit Counter) enclosed in brackets. You cannot view the hit counter until you save the current Web and publish it to a Web server that contains the Office 2000 server extension files. (Discuss the server extensions with your Internet service provider; the extension files must be on the ISP's Web server for special components such as the hit counter to work. (Learn more about the server extensions in Lesson 10, "Completing and Publishing Your Web Site.") Figure 6.8 shows a hit counter on a Web that has been published to a Web server and is being viewed in Internet Explorer.

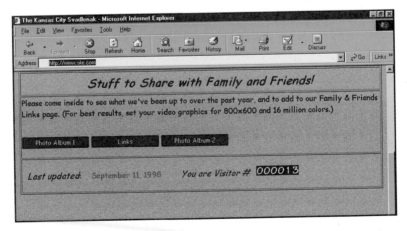

Figure 6.8 Hit counters allow you to see what kind of traffic your Web site is experiencing.

In this lesson, you learned how to place shared borders, page banners, navigation bars, and other special components such as hit counters on your Web pages. In the next lesson, you learn how to work with hyperlinks.

Working with Hyperlinks

In this lesson, you learn to insert and manage hyperlinks on your Web pages.

Understanding Hyperlinks

An important aspect of creating Web pages is being able to insert hyperlinks onto the pages of your Web site. A *hyperlink* references another Web page on your site or another Web site on the World Wide Web. Hyperlinks are the main tool for navigating the World Wide Web.

For instance, the navigation bars that you place on your Web pages so visitors can navigate your Web site really consist of a list of ready-made hyperlinks to the pages on your site. (For more about navigation bars, see Lesson 6, "Inserting Special FrontPage Components.") Hyperlinks can also be inserted into your site that allow you to access other Web sites on the Web or send email to a specific person.

Because FrontPage provides navigation bars that automatically provide hyperlinks to the pages in your Web, you might wonder why you would ever create your own hyperlinks. First of all, if you want to create links to other Web sites on the Web, you must use hyperlinks. Also, if you place your Web on a Web server that does not recognize the Office Web Server extensions, special FrontPage components like the navigation bars do not function correctly, so you have to insert your own hyperlinks for the navigation of the pages in your site. You can then build a working site and post it to any Web server.

Hyperlinks can take the form of text or graphics. For example, a text line referencing a particular Web site can be easily turned into a hyperlink that takes you to that site. If you would rather link to another site using a graphic (such as a company logo), it can also be set up as a hyperlink.

FrontPage also makes it easy for you to create hyperlinks to the pages in your own Web site using bookmarks. Bookmarks are discussed later in this lesson in "Using Bookmarks."

Creating Text Hyperlinks

Text hyperlinks are great for listing your favorite Web sites. You can create a list of text entries that describe the site that the hyperlink links to. These sights then allow you to create descriptive text. The descriptive text can be selected and then turned into a hyperlink for the described destination.

Another plus of using text for hyperlinks is that the text appears in a default color when viewed on the Web (blue, for instance, is the default in FrontPage). When the link has been used (to go to the destination of the hyperlink) and the text is viewed again, it appears in a different color (violet is the default color for used hyperlinks in FrontPage). This makes it easy to keep track of the hyperlinks that have been used and those that have not.

To place a text hyperlink on a Web page, follow these steps:

1. Open the page (double-click it in the Navigation view) where you want to place the hyperlink.
2. Type the text that will serve as the hyperlink. It can be the name of the site or any text you want.
3. Select the text you want to use as the hyperlink.
4. Select **Insert** and then select **Hyperlink**. The Create Hyperlink dialog box appears (see Figure 7.1).
5. To create a link to a Web site, type the address of the site in the **URL** box. This address typically takes the form www.*nameofsite*.com. You can also select the address for the link by using your Web browser. If you are connecting to the Internet, you can click the **Use Your Web Browser to Select a Page or File** button directly to the right of the URL box. Your Web browser opens. Go to the page you want to link to and then return to FrontPage. The address of the page appears in the URL box.

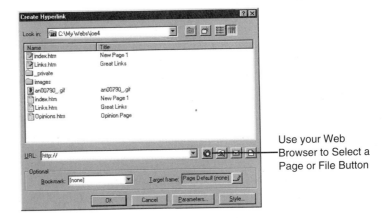

Use your Web
Browser to Select a
Page or File Button

Figure 7.1 The Create Hyperlink dialog box allows you to create hyperlinks on your Web pages.

6. After you have the address in the URL box, click the **OK** button.

7. Click anywhere on the page to deselect the hyperlink text.

The text that was selected for the hyperlink is now underlined and appears in the default hyperlink color (see Figure 7.2).

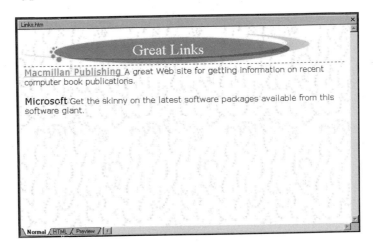

Figure 7.2 Your text hyperlink is underlined on the Web page.

TIP **How to Test External Hyperlinks** If you want to test a hyperlink you've created that points to another Web site, open the page that contains the hyperlink. Make sure that you are connected to the Internet and then click the **Preview in Browser** button. This opens the current page in your Web browser. Click the hyperlink, and you should be taken to the site the hyperlink points to.

Creating Graphic Hyperlinks

You can also make a graphic, such as a picture or clip art, a hyperlink to a page in your Web or to a page in another Web site. The process of creating image hyperlinks is very straightforward and similar to the process of creating text hyperlinks.

To place a graphic hyperlink on a Web page, follow these steps:

1. Open the page (double-click it in the Navigation view) where you want to place the hyperlink.
2. Insert the picture or clip art you want to use as the hyperlink.
3. Select the graphic you want to use as the hyperlink.
4. Select **Insert** and then select **Hyperlink**. The Hyperlink dialog box appears.
5. Type the address for the Web site you want to link to in the **URL** box. To select the site using your Web browser, click the **Use Your Web Browser to Select a Page or File** button. Locate the page in your Web browser and then return to the FrontPage window.
6. Click **OK** to return to the Web page.

The graphic is now a hyperlink to the address you provided in the Hyperlink dialog box. Save the page and then use your Web browser (click the **Preview in Browser** button) to test the link.

 TIP **Create Your Own Buttons Using PhotoDraw** You can create your own buttons in PhotoDraw and place them on your FrontPage pages. See Lesson 15, "Creating Web Graphics with PhotoDraw."

Using Bookmarks

If you want to create hyperlinks between pages on your own Web site or create links that jump to a particular position on a page (useful for long pages that a visitor normally has to scroll through to view all the information), you might want to take advantage of bookmarks. A bookmark is a particular place or text on a page that you have marked—that is, you have made that spot on the page a bookmark. You can then use the bookmark to create a hyperlink that takes you to that bookmark.

To place a bookmark on a page, follow these steps:

1. In Page view, position the insertion point where you want to create a bookmark, or select the text or a graphic to which you want to assign the bookmark (see Figure 7.3).

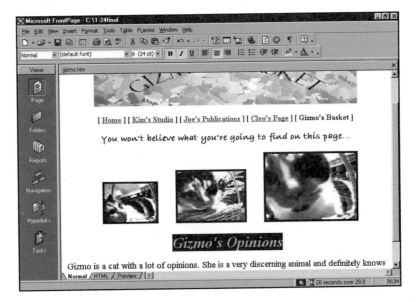

Figure 7.3 Place the insertion point on the page or select the text that will serve as the bookmark.

2. Select the **Insert** menu and then select **Bookmark**. The Bookmark dialog box opens (see Figure 7.4).

3. In the **Bookmark Name** box, type the name of the bookmark. If you selected text to serve as the bookmark, the selected text appears in the Bookmark Name box.

4. When you have finished naming your bookmark, click **OK**.

Figure 7.4 The Bookmark dialog box is where you name the new bookmark.

Selected text that has been designated a bookmark has a dashed-line under it. If you designate a particular place on a page as a bookmark by inserting the insertion point, a small flag is shown at that point on the page.

Now that you've got a bookmark, you can create a hyperlink using it. Follow these steps:

1. Go to the page where you want to place the hyperlink and select the text or graphic you will use as the hyperlink.

2. Select **Insert** and then select **Hyperlink**. The Create Hyperlink dialog box appears.

3. In the Optional box at the bottom of the Create Hyperlink dialog box, click the **Bookmark** drop-down arrow and select the bookmark that will serve as the destination for the hyperlink.

4. Click **OK** to return to the Web page.

Now when you test the hyperlink, you should find that it takes you to the page in your web where you placed the bookmark.

To delete a bookmark that you no longer want or need, follow these steps:

1. Select the **Insert** menu and then select **Bookmark**.
2. In the Bookmark dialog box, select the bookmark you want to remove and then click the **Clear** button.
3. Click **OK** to close the dialog box.

Editing or Deleting Hyperlinks

You can also edit or delete the hyperlinks you place on your pages. You might think that by deleting a graphic or text that has been assigned a hyperlink, you also delete the hyperlink; in fact, you do. But in most cases, you probably want to keep the text or graphic on your Web page and change the hyperlink URL address or remove just the hyperlink attached to the text or graphic. Both of these tasks are handled in the Hyperlink dialog box.

Follow these steps to edit or remove a hyperlink:

1. Right-click the graphic or text that has been assigned the hyperlink. A shortcut menu appears.
2. Select **Hyperlink Properties** on the shortcut menu. The Hyperlink dialog box opens.
3. To edit the hyperlink, select the address in the **URL** box and type a new address.
4. If you want to delete the hyperlink, delete the address currently shown in the **URL** box.
5. Click the **OK** button.

You will find that if the link was a text entry and you removed its hyperlinking capability, the text is no longer underlined. Edited hyperlinks can be tested by previewing the page in your Web browser.

In this lesson, you learned how to create and edit hyperlinks. You also learned to create bookmarks. In the next lesson, you will learn how to create input forms on your Web pages.

Creating Special Forms for Your Web

In this lesson, you learn how to create input forms on your Web pages.

Understanding Web Forms

Although you probably have a feel for how a FrontPage Web uses text and pictures to supply different kinds of information to visitors of your site, you might not know that you can design your site to request information from those visitors. FrontPage provides you with the ability to create various input forms that can be placed on your Web pages for use by your site visitors. This makes it easy for you to gather a variety of information. For example, on a personal Web, you can ask visitors to vote Yes or No on whether or not they like your site. On a corporate site, you can ask visitors interested in your products to provide their names and addresses so they can receive special offers or a catalog from your company.

The forms you create can be a combination of text boxes, radio buttons, check boxes, and drop-down lists that provide a set of choices for visitors to choose from. Before creating the form, however, you should first decide what kind of information you want to collect, which definitely affects how the form looks and the type of input fields (text boxes versus check boxes) you place on the form. Figure 8.1 shows some of the input field types you can place on a form.

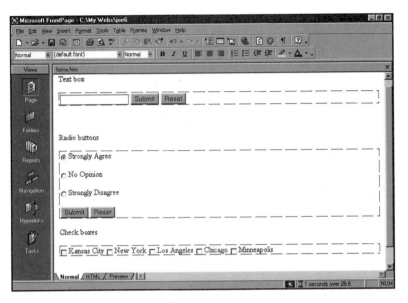

Figure 8.1 Your input forms can use different kinds of fields to gather information from visitors to your Web page.

Creating a Web Form

The forms you create can be as simple or as complex as your need dictates. You can create a form that consists of just one text box that requests visitors to provide their email addresses. Or, you can design a complex form that uses different field types such as check boxes or drop-down lists.

How you begin the form creation process depends on how complex you want to make the form. If you are planning on making a form with a number of different input fields, your best bet is to insert a form on a page and then insert the various input fields (such as radio buttons, text boxes and so on) as required.

To place a blank form on a Web page, follow these steps:

1. Open the page (double-click it in the Navigation view) where you want to place the form.
2. Place the insertion point where you want to create the form.
3. Select the **Insert** menu and then select **Form**. From the cascading menu, select **Form**. The blank form is placed on your page (see Figure 8.2).

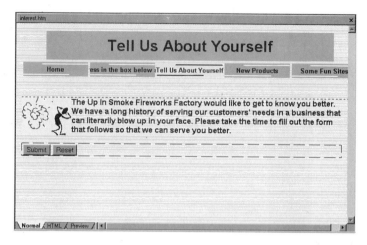

Figure 8.2   The blank form consists of a form box and Submit and Reset buttons.

The blank form provides Submit and Reset buttons and a workspace that you can use to insert the various form field types that receive input from visitors to your site. The next step in the process is to insert those input fields.

Inserting Form Fields

Form fields are the various text boxes, check boxes, or other items that you place on the form to gather information. FrontPage provides a number of different form field types. Table 8.1 lists the fields and what you might use them for in a form.

Table 8.1   Field Types for Your Forms

Field Type	Purpose
One-line text box	Use when requesting a single line of information such as an email address from a visitor.
Scrolling text box	Use when providing room for multiple lines of text in a scroll box format.
Check box	Use when providing a number of different options where one or more options may be applicable.
Radio button	Use when providing several choices and only one selection is required.
Drop-down menu	Use when providing choices where one selection from menu is needed and there are space restraints (a drop-down menu takes up less room than several check boxes or radio buttons).

To place an input field in your form, follow these steps:

1. Place the insertion point in the form where you want to add the new input field. (You also can make room for fields by pressing the **Enter** key several times to move the Submit and Reset buttons down in the blank form.)

2. If you need label text to describe the input field, type the text in the form box. (For instance, if you are going to place a text box in the form for email addresses, you might want to type **Email Address** in the blank form and then insert the field.)

3. To insert the field, select the **Insert** menu and then select **Form**. From the cascading menu, select the field you want to insert, such as **One-line Text Box**.

The field appears in your form at the insertion point. Figure 8.3 shows a form where text (First Name) was inserted in the form and then a one-line text box was inserted to the right of the text. This field can be used by a visitor to enter his first name. You can add fields to the form as needed using the steps discussed. If you place a field in the wrong place or decide you don't want to use a particular field type, select the field on the page and press the **Delete** key to remove it.

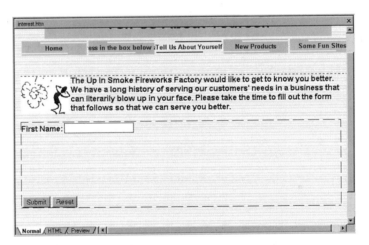

Figure 8.3   You can place descriptive text for the fields you insert in the form box.

As you can see, inserting the different field types into the form is very straightforward. The only field type that requires some extra work is the drop-down menu. After inserting it, you must provide the menu choices that appear on the menu. Follow these steps:

1. Insert a drop-down menu field onto your form.

2. Right-click the **Drop-Down Menu** field and select **Form Field Properties**. The Drop-Down Menu Properties dialog box appears.

3. To add menu choices to the current menu, click the **Add** button. The Add Choice dialog box appears (see Figure 8.4).

4. Type a menu choice into the **Choice** box and then click **OK**. You are returned to the Drop-Down Menu Properties dialog box, and your menu choice is listed. Add additional menu choices as needed.

5. When you have completed adding menu choices, click the **OK** button to close the Drop-Down Menu Properties dialog box.

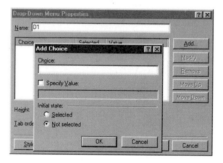

Figure 8.4 Use the Add Choice dialog box to add menu choices for your drop-down menu field.

Testing Your Forms

 After you create your form, you can quickly test the fields in the Preview mode. First, save the page by clicking the **Save** button on the toolbar. Then click the **Preview** tab at the bottom of the Page window. Your Web page and its form appear as they do on the World Wide Web.

You can fill in text boxes, make check box selections, and test drop-down menus. When you have finished taking a look at your form and its fields, click the **Normal** tab to return to the Page edit mode.

CAUTION

Click the Submit Button and Get an Error   When you create a form on a page and then publish that page and the rest of the Web to a Web server, FrontPage creates a submission page for the form. When you are in the Preview mode, this page does not exist (because the Web hasn't been published) and so you get an error.

You cannot fully test your form's capabilities until you publish the Web site to a Web server that contains the FrontPage Server Extensions. The form feature, like the theme and special component features, does not work correctly unless the Web server contains the appropriate server extensions.

Determining Where the Data Goes

Because the purpose of creating a Web form is to gather data, you probably want to select the format that all the collected information is placed in. FrontPage offers different file formats for the submitted data. You can have the data placed in a text file, you can have the data emailed to a particular email address, or you can have the data placed directly into a Microsoft Access database.

To select the format for the data collection, follow these steps:

1. Right-click the form and select **Form Properties**. The Form Properties dialog box appears (see Figure 8.5).

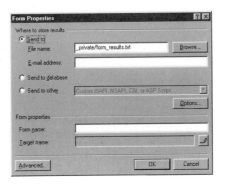

Figure 8.5   The Form Properties dialog box allows you to select how the results of your form are saved.

2. Three different possibilities are available for how the data gathered by the form can be handled:

- **Text file**—The default location for the results to be stored is a text file. The text file is stored on the Web server where you publish your web (the _private folder). You need access to the Web server so that you can open the text file and view the contents. Designate a name for that file in the **File Name** box.

- **Email Address**—An alternative to a text file is to have the form results sent to a particular email address. This is useful if you do not have easy access to the Web server where you publish your Web. Type an email address in the **E-mail Address** box. Then click the **Options** button. Click the **E-mail Results** tab on the Options for Saving Results of a Form dialog box. Enter the **Subject** line that you want placed on the email message that provides the results. Click **OK** to close the dialog box and return to the Form Properties dialog box.

- **Access Database**—If you want to have your data collected in an Access database (which you would then open in Microsoft Access), click the **Send to Database** radio button. Then click **Options**. The Options for Saving Results to Database dialog box opens. Click the **Create** button, and a new database is created to contain the data. A message box opens and provides the location of the new database (a folder in the current Web) and a data connection phrase such as **Interest**. Write this information down and then click **OK**. Click **OK** again to close the Options for Saving Results to Database dialog box.

3. After making one of the preceding selections, click the **OK** button to close the Form Properties dialog box.

After you publish your Web to a Web server and the form is used by visitors to your site, you can view the data in the text file contained in the _private folder, or you will receive the data in an email, depending on the choice you made in the Form Properties dialog box.

If you choose to have the results saved in a database, you can directly access the database file using Access. In Access, you have to create a new FTP location in the Open dialog box by clicking the **Look In** drop-down arrow and selecting **Add/Modify FTP Locations**. In the Add/Modify FTP Locations dialog box, enter the FTP address for your Web server (usually **FTP.***servername***.com**) and your username and password. After the FTP location has been created, you can use it to open the database.

An alternative to working in Access is to have the database results displayed on a Web page. The Web page should be held in the _private folder that is part of your Web (and is published to the Web server with the other folders and files in the Web) because only you have access to the files in the _private folder.

To create a database results page, follow these steps:

1. Go to the Folders view and open the _private folder. Then click the **New Page** button on the Standard toolbar. A new page is placed in the folder.

2. Type in a new name for the page, such as **results.htm** or something similar.

3. Double-click the page to open it in the Page view. Place the insertion point where you want to place the database results box.

4. Select the **Insert** menu, point at **Database**, and then select **Results**. The Database Results Wizard appears (see Figure 8.6).

Figure 8.6   Using the Database Results Wizard, you can create a results page that allows you to view the data input by visitors to your site.

5. Use the drop-down box to select the database connection for the database that was created when you chose Access database as the collection mode for the data (back in step 3 of the previous set of steps). If you've only created one database connection for the Web, it already appears in the drop-down box.

6. Click **Next** to continue. You are asked to select a record source from the database. (This is the table the data is placed in.) The default table for the new database appears in the Record Source box automatically.

7. Click **Next** to continue. The fields in the database table are displayed. (These are the fields found in the original form that you created.) Click **Next**.

8. The next wizard screen provides you with the option of displaying the date in one record per row or placing each record in a list. Use the drop-down box to make your selection and then click **Next**.

9. The last wizard screen appears; click **Finish** to create the results page.

The fields on the original form appear on the database results page. The page only displays results from the form when viewed using your Web browser. And, of course, the Web must also be published to the Web server and the Web server must have the FrontPage Server Extensions on it. After the Web is up and running and you get some input from visitors, you can then access the results page using your Web browser and view the data.

In this lesson, you learned how to create input forms on your Web pages. In the next lesson, you learn to work with tables and numbered and bulleted lists.

Working with Tables and Bulleted and Numbered Lists

9

In this lesson, you learn how add tables and bulleted and numbered lists to your Web pages.

Using Tables on Web Pages

Organizing information on your Web pages so that it's easy to read is a real necessity. FrontPage provides different ways to easily group information on your pages or place text elements in special lists that offset the information from other text on the page. Tables make it easy to place information in rows and columns on your Web pages, and text lists can be embellished by adding bullets or numbers (which are covered later in this lesson).

Tables provide an excellent way to group numerical information in columns and rows (even displaying a total that summarizes a row or column of information), or tables can be used as layout grids to help you align elements, such as text or graphics, on pages. So although you might typically think of tables as containing numerical data only, you can actually use tables as a nice design feature on your Web pages.

TIP **Insert an Office Spreadsheet** If you want to be able to include formulas in a table that you place on a Web page, an Office spreadsheet provides you with all the formulas and capabilities provided by Microsoft Excel. Select **Insert**, point at **Component**, and then click **Office Spreadsheet**. For help with adding formulas to the new spreadsheet table, see Lesson 15, "Performing Calculations with Functions" in Part III, "Excel."

For example, you can create several buttons that act as hyperlinks to other pages or sites. Or, you can place the button graphics in a table column and add descriptive text for each button in the next column of the table, making it easy to align the appropriate graphic with the appropriate descriptive text.

To insert a table onto the current Web page, follow these steps:

1. Open the page (double-click it in the Navigation view) where you want to place the table.

2. Place the insertion point where you want to place the table.

3. Click the **Insert Table** button on the toolbar. On the table grid that drops down, drag to select the number of rows and columns you want in the table. When you release the mouse button, the table appears on the page (see Figure 9.1).

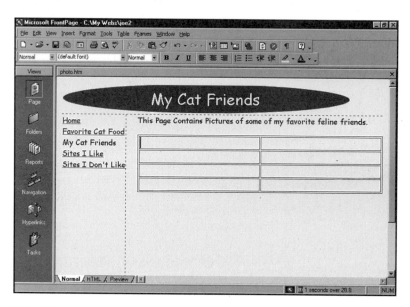

Figure 9.1   The new table allows you to arrange text and pictures in rows and columns on the page.

After the table is placed on a particular page, you can enter text or images into the cells of the table (a *cell* is the intersection of a row and column). Click the mouse pointer on a particular cell to place the insertion point within it. Then type your text or use the Insert menu to insert some other item. Figure 9.2 shows a table that contains images and text and is used to easily line up a particular text entry with a corresponding image.

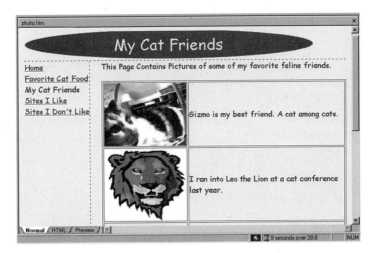

Figure 9.2 Tables can contain pictures and text.

Inserting and Deleting Rows and Columns

Inserting and deleting rows and columns is straightforward. To insert a row or column in the table, follow these steps:

1. Select the row or column that you want to insert a new row or column adjacent to.

2. Select **Table**, point at **Insert**, and select **Rows or Columns**. The Insert Rows or Columns dialog box appears (see Figure 9.3).

Figure 9.3 The Insert Rows or Columns dialog box allows you to insert one or more new rows or columns.

1125

3. Click either the **Rows** or **Columns** option button to select the item you want to insert.

4. Click the up- or down arrow or enter a number in the **Number Of** click box to indicate the number of rows or columns you want to insert.

5. In the **Location** area of the dialog box, choose either the **Above Selection** or **Below Selection** option button when you are inserting rows and either the **Left of Selection** or **Right of Selection** option button when inserting columns.

6. When you have made your various selections, click **OK** to insert the new rows or columns.

You can also easily delete columns or rows from your table. Select the rows or columns. Then select the **Table** menu. Click **Delete Cells**, and the selected columns or rows are removed from the table.

Changing the Way the Table Looks

You also have control over the way the table looks, such as the color and width of the table's borders and background and the alignment of the table on the page. Formatting and alignment of a table is controlled in the Table Properties dialog box. However, the look of the table (border and background color) might also be affected by the theme that is currently selected for the page the table resides on. The theme supplies the default background and border color for the table.

You can change the background color and border width for a table that has been assigned a theme; however, the border color cannot be changed and remains the theme default. The only way to override the theme color is to remove the theme from the page. (For more about themes, see Lesson 3, "Working with Web Pages and Themes.")

Follow these steps to change the table background color, border width and color, or the alignment of the table:

1. Right-click the table and select **Table Properties** from the shortcut menu. The Table Properties dialog box appears (see Figure 9.4).

2. To change the color for the table borders, click the **Color** drop-down box in the **Borders** area of the dialog box. Select a new color for the table border.

3. To change the background color of the table, click the **Color** drop-down box in the **Background** area of the dialog box.

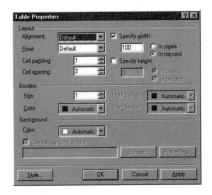

Figure 9.4 The Table Properties dialog box allows you to change a number of parameters related to the look of the table.

4. If you want to change the thickness of the table border, use the **Size** click box in the **Borders** area of the dialog box.

5. To change the alignment of the table (Left, Right, Center, or Justify), click the **Alignment** drop-down box and select the appropriate alignment. (This aligns the table on the page, not the text or items within the table cells.)

6. When you have completed setting the various parameters for the table, click the **OK** button to close the Table Properties dialog box and return to the table.

If you want to have a table with no borders (an invisible table), create a new table and then place your text and other items in the table. After you have completely finished placing items in the table, right-click the table and select **Table Properties** from the shortcut menu. Then use the **Borders Size** click box to make the border size **0** (zero) and click **OK**. The items in the table are still aligned (almost magically), but the table itself disappears because it has no visible borders.

Adding Bullets to Lists

Another way to make text on a Web page stand out is to assign bullets to the text. Bullets are great when you want to visually break out a text list from other text on the page. Bullets also help to make the page more interesting by adding additional design elements.

To add bullets to a text list, follow these steps:

1. Create a text list on the page.

2. Select the lines of text in the list.

3. Click the **Bullets** button on the Formatting toolbar. Bullets are placed at the beginning of each text line.

The style of the bullets assigned to your list is dictated by the current theme. If you change the theme, the color and style of the bullets also change. You can, however, use any graphic as a bullet, so you do have the option of replacing the current bullet style with a particular graphic. This can be a picture or actual bullets that you create yourself (using a tool like PhotoDraw, which is also covered in this part of the book).

The only requirement for the graphic that you use to replace the bullets is that the image is small (initially created to be the same relative size as a bullet).

To select a graphic to use as a bullet, follow these steps:

1. Right-click the list you assigned the bullets to and click **List Properties** on the shortcut menu that appears. The List Properties dialog box appears (see Figure 9.5).

2. In the List Properties dialog box, click the **Specify Picture** option button.

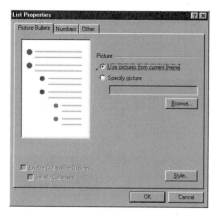

Figure 9.5   The List Properties dialog box allows you to select a picture to use as the bullet for the current list.

3. To select the picture to serve as the bullet for the list, click the **Browse** button. The Select Picture dialog box opens.

4. Click the **Select a File on Your Computer** button. The Select File dialog box appears. Use the Select File dialog box to select the picture file and then click **OK**.

5. The name of the picture file appears in the List Properties dialog box. Click **OK** to return to the Web page and assign the new bullet to the list.

The selected graphic replaces all occurrences of the bullet in your list. You can add some very nice effects to your Web pages by using special bullets.

Working with Numbered Lists

Another way to denote the relative importance of the lines in a text list or to put a sequential list together (such as a list of steps) is to add numbering to your text. FrontPage gives you control over the style of the numbers in the list and also gives you the ability to change the start number for the list.

To add numbers to a text list, follow these steps:

1. Create a text list on the page.

2. Select the lines of text in the list.

3. Click the **Numbering** button on the Formatting toolbar. Numbers (in order from top to bottom beginning with the number one) are placed at the beginning of each text line.

The font and color of the numbers placed on the list depend on the theme that is currently assigned to the page you are working on. You can change the number style (from Arabic to Roman or to letters of the alphabet), and you can change the start number for the list (to some number other than one).

Right-click the numbered list and select **List Properties** from the shortcut menu. The List Properties dialog box appears (see Figure 9.6) with the Numbers tab selected. To change the style of the number, select any of the styles provided (such as Roman, letters of the alphabet, and so on) by clicking one of the style boxes. If you want to change the start number, select a new start number using the **Start At** click box.

Figure 9.6   The List Properties dialog box provides a Numbers tab that can be used to select a different numbering style or start number.

When you have finished changing the number list properties, click **OK** to close the dialog box. Changes that you make to the style or start number in the list take effect immediately.

In this lesson, you learned how to create tables on your Web pages and assign bullets and numbers to text lists. In the next lesson, you learn to complete your Web site with the help of tasks, and you also learn how to publish your Web site.

Completing and Publishing Your Web Site

In this lesson, you learn how to complete a Web using tasks and how to publish your Web to the World Wide Web.

Using Tasks to Complete a Web

As you create and fine-tune a Web you want to place on the World Wide Web, you will find that there are lots of individual tasks you must complete before the site is ready to be published. You have to make sure that graphics or other images have been placed in the appropriate places and that hyperlinks correctly point to their particular destinations. Even the simplest of sites require you to make changes and improvements to pages in the Web, even if you created the Web with a wizard.

FrontPage offers a tool for helping you to stay organized as you create and complete a Web. FrontPage tasks provide a way to keep a running list of your Web duties as you work on the site. This task list can be viewed anytime in the Tasks view.

You will find that tasks are automatically created by some of the FrontPage wizards such as the Corporate Presence Wizard. Figure 10.1 shows a list of tasks associated with a new Web created using the Corporate Presence Wizard.

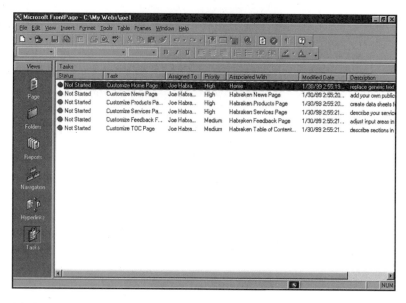

Figure 10.1   Tasks are automatically created by some of FrontPage's Web wizards.

Creating a New Task

You can create tasks and link them to an entire Web page or to items on that page, such as pictures or other objects. The easiest way to create a new task that is linked to a particular page is to create the task with the page in the Page view. For example, let's say you have a page that will contain hyperlinks to your favorite sites. You can create a task for this page to make sure you've placed all the appropriate hyperlinks (to your favorite sites) on the page before you publish the Web.

Follow these steps to create a new task:

1. Open the page (double-click it in the Navigation view) that you want to create a task for.

2. Select the **File** menu, point at **New**, and then select **Task** (or select **Edit**, then **Task**, and then **Add Task**). The New Task dialog box opens (see Figure 10.2).

3. Type a task name in the **Task Name** box. To assign a priority to the task (other than the default, which is Medium), click the appropriate option button in the **Priority** area.

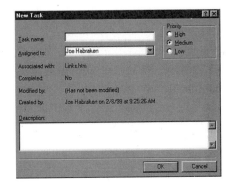

Figure 10.2   The New Task dialog box is where you name, set the priority for, and describe your new task.

4. Type a description for the task in the **Description** box.

5. Click **OK** to create the new task.

The new task is created and linked to the current page. To view the new task, click the **Tasks** button on the Views bar.

TIP   **Create Your Task List Up Front**   To help you plan the work flow on a new Web site, create the tasks for that Web as soon as you (or a wizard) create the pages for that Web. Staying organized assures that your site is complete before you place it on the World Wide Web.

Starting a Task

After you create the task (or several tasks), you can view the task in the Tasks view. This view is also where you start a task, mark a task as complete, or delete an unwanted task.

To start a particular task, follow these steps:

1. In the Tasks view, double-click the task you want to start. The Task Details dialog box opens (see Figure 10.3).

2. Click the **Start Task** button.

You are taken to the page or other object that the task was linked to. For instance, if your task is to create hyperlinks on a particular page, you are taken to that page where you can begin creating the needed hyperlinks.

1133

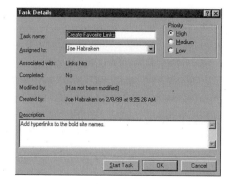

Figure 10.3   Start your task using the Task Details dialog box.

Completing a Task

After you finish a particular task, you can mark that task as completed. Saving the page that the task was assigned to does this. Follow these steps:

1. Click the **Save** button on the toolbar. A message box appears letting you know that this page was opened from the Tasks view.

2. To mark the task as completed, click **Yes** (if you haven't completed the task but want to save your changes, click **No**, and you can complete the task at a later time).

When you return to the Tasks view (click the **Tasks** icon on the Views bar), the task is marked as completed. You can also mark tasks as completed directly in the Tasks view. Right-click the task and select **Mark as Completed** on the shortcut menu that appears.

If you find that you end up with redundant tasks or create a task that doesn't end up fitting into your Web plan—for instance, you delete the page associated with the task—you can easily delete any task on the list. Right-click the task and select **Delete** on the shortcut menu. You are asked if you want to delete the current task. Click **Yes** to delete the task.

Check the Web Reports   Even if you use tasks to make sure that you cover all the details related to your Web, check the Reports view before publishing the site. Reports concerning unverified or broken hyperlinks or unlinked graphics (these reports are generated automatically by FrontPage) can help you avoid the embarrassment of publishing a Web site that doesn't work the way it is supposed to.

CAUTION

Publishing Your Web

After you have completed your site (check the Tasks view to decide if you are truly finished), you are ready to publish the Web. Publishing the Web means that you place all the folders and files in the Web onto a Web server. The Web server then serves up your site to visitors on the World Wide Web.

You have two different routes you can take to get your Web onto your Web server: You can use HTTP (Hypertext Transfer Protocol) to upload your Web to the server, or you can use FTP (File Transfer Protocol) to move the files.

If you use HTTP, the server you send your Web files to must have the FrontPage Server Extensions installed on it. You should check with your Internet service provider before you upload a FrontPage Web to the server to make sure the extensions are available.

If the server is not enabled with the FrontPage extensions, you can still upload to your Web server by using FTP. Be advised, however, that Web servers that do not support the FrontPage extensions preclude you from using special components on your Webs—for example, FrontPage hit counters and themes might not work correctly.

Specifying whether you are publishing your site using HTTP or FTP is hand led by how you enter the address for the Web server in the FrontPage Publish Web dialog box (covered in detail in the steps that follow). For example, let's say that your Web server on the World Wide Web is called joe.com. If you are using HTTP to upload your Web files, this server's address is specified as http://www.joe.com. If you are using FTP to upload the files, the address for this site is ftp.joe.com.

To publish your Web, follow these steps:

1. Connect to the Internet using your dial-up connection to your Internet service provider.

2. In FrontPage, select the **File** menu and then select **Publish Web**. The Publish Web dialog box appears (see Figure 10.4). Click the **Options** button to view the entire dialog box.

3. Enter the address of the server that you will upload your Web to in the **Specify the Location to Publish Your Web To** box (using either an HTTP or FTP address, as discussed earlier in this section).

1135

4. Specify whether you want to publish only pages that have changed or all pages by clicking the appropriate option button.

5. If the current Web contains hyperlinks to other Webs that you have created but not published (called subWebs), select the **Include SubWebs** check box to publish these along with the current Web.

6. Click the **Publish** button.

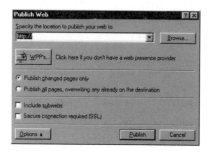

Figure 10.4   Set publishing options in the Publish Web dialog box.

You are kept apprised of the progress of the publishing of your Web while you wait. When the process has completed, click the **Done** button to close the notification box.

Your Web is now available on the World Wide Web. You can use your Web browser to visit your Web and make sure it is functioning correctly. In cases where you need to modify pages or update the Web, modify the original Web in FrontPage and then publish the Web to the server again, making sure that you check the option for changed pages to replace pages already on the server.

In this lesson, you learned how to create tasks to help you complete your Webs, and you learned how to publish your Web to a Web server. In the next lesson, you become familiar with the Microsoft PhotoDraw application window and learn how to open and exit PhotoDraw.

Introducing PhotoDraw

*In this lesson, you become familiar with Microsoft PhotoDraw
and learn about the different areas of the PhotoDraw application window.*

Starting PhotoDraw

PhotoDraw is an easy-to-use yet full-featured graphics studio you use to create your own images and modify and enhance nearly any existing image file. You can touch up photos, add special effects to a scanned image, or even create your own images using PhotoDraw's design tools and templates. PhotoDraw is particularly useful for editing images and creating banners and buttons for use in your FrontPage Web pages (see Lesson 15, "Creating Web Graphics with PhotoDraw," for more information).

To start PhotoDraw, follow these steps:

1. From the Windows Desktop, click **Start** and point at **Programs**.
2. On the Programs menu, click the **PhotoDraw** icon (see Figure 11.1).
3. When the PhotoDraw application window opens, you are greeted by the Microsoft PhotoDraw dialog box (see Figure 11.2). This dialog box provides several options:
   - **Blank Picture**—This allows you to choose from a number of blank templates (including envelopes and mailing labels) that can be used to create your own picture from scratch. The template opens in the PhotoDraw picture area.
   - **Design Template**—This option allows you to select from templates you use to create banners and buttons (typically used on Web pages).

- **Download from Digital Camera**—This option allows you to capture an image directly from a digital camera connected to your computer.
- **Scan Picture**—This option allows you to scan an image on your scanner directly into PhotoDraw.
- **Open an Existing Picture**—This option allows you to open an image already on your computer.

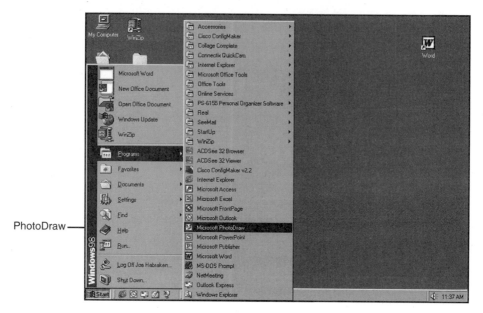

PhotoDraw—

Figure 11.1 Open the Programs menu and click the PhotoDraw icon to start PhotoDraw.

Many of these options are discussed in subsequent lessons; for now, make sure **Blank Picture** is selected and click **OK**. The New dialog box appears.

4. The New dialog box offers a number of blank picture templates that make it easy for you to create business cards, envelopes, and mailing labels. For now, make sure the **Default Picture** template is selected and click **OK**.

A new blank picture opens in the PhotoDraw workspace.

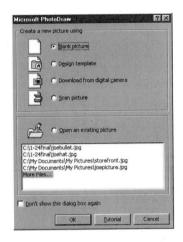

Figure 11.2 The PhotoDraw dialog box provides several options for starting or opening an image.

Understanding the PhotoDraw Workspace

Although PhotoDraw looks similar to other Microsoft Office applications, such as Word or FrontPage, and embraces typical application tools, such as menus and toolbars, you will find that the PhotoDraw window is designed to help you create and enhance pictures. You might notice some specialization in the workspace area not found in other Office applications (see Figure 11.3).

When you open a new picture or an existing picture, you have the occasion to use the *picture* and *scratch* areas as you edit existing images or combine elements to create a new image.

Picture Area The portion of the PhotoDraw workspace that contains the current image.

Scratch Area The gray area surrounding the picture area. The scratch area is used to hold additional images or items you draw that are not part of the current image, which resides in the picture area.

1139

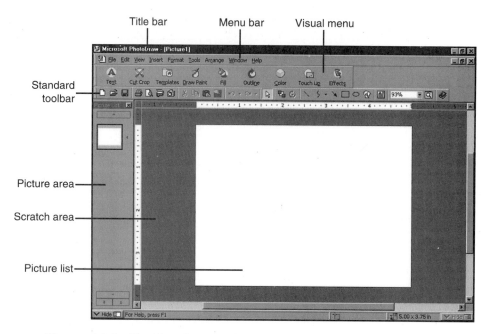

Figure 11.3   The PhotoDraw window is where you create new images or edit existing ones.

The PhotoDraw window also contains a *picture list* on the left side of the workspace that shows a *thumbnail* picture of all the images currently open in PhotoDraw. This list can be used to quickly go to a particular image by clicking its thumbnail.

 Thumbnail   A small version of a particular picture that resides on the picture list. Click a thumbnail to go to that particular picture.

Using the PhotoDraw Menus and Toolbars

PhotoDraw provides several different ways to access the commands and features that you use as you create or edit your images. You can access these commands using the menus on the menu bar and the buttons on the various toolbars that PhotoDraw supplies, such as the Standard and Formatting toolbars.

To use one of the menus, select the menu and then select the appropriate command on the menu. To use a toolbar button, click the button on the appropriate toolbar. PhotoDraw does not currently embrace the personalized menus and toolbars that you can work with in other Office applications, such as Microsoft Word or Excel. For example, when you click the Insert menu in PhotoDraw, you are given immediate access to all the commands on that menu. You are not shown only the most recently used commands as you are in other Office applications when the personalized menu system is turned on.

PhotoDraw has a special menu called the *visual menu* (see Figure 11.4). The visual menu provides access to the different design tools that you can use in PhotoDraw.

To use the visual menu, click any of its menu items (depending on the design tool you want to use). A menu opens, providing a number of choices related to that design tool. For example, if you click the **Draw Paint** button, a list of choices (Draw, Shapes, Paint) is provided (see Figure 11.4).

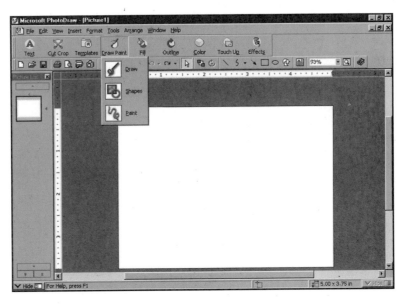

Figure 11.4 The visual menu makes it easy to use the various design tools provided by PhotoDraw.

After you select a tool, such as Draw on the Draw Paint menu, a workpane for the Drawing tools appears on the right side of the PhotoDraw window. The different effects and settings for a particular design tool, such as Draw, can be accessed in the workpane (see Figure 11.5). Most of the tools found on the visual menu use a workpane to give you access to the various options for that tool.

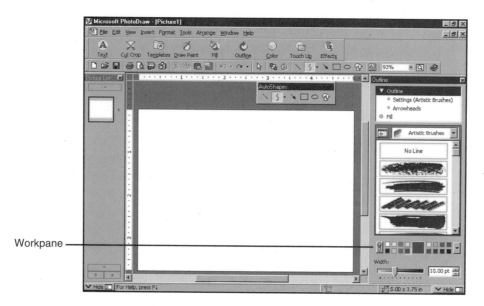

Figure 11.5   The workpane for the Drawing tools provides access to a number of different options.

You will become familiar with a number of the PhotoDraw design tools and the options available in their workpanes in the other PhotoDraw lessons found in this section.

Exiting PhotoDraw

When you have completed your initial survey of PhotoDraw, you should exit the software. There is more than one way to close the PhotoDraw window, which is the same as exiting the program.

You can exit PhotoDraw by selecting the **File** menu and then **Exit**; or you can close PhotoDraw with one click of the mouse by clicking the PhotoDraw **Close** (**x**) button in the upper-right corner of the application window.

When you close PhotoDraw, you might be prompted to save any work that you have done in the application window. If you were just experimenting as you read through this lesson, you can click **No**. The current image is not saved, and the PhotoDraw window closes.

In this lesson, you explored the PhotoDraw window and learned to start and exit the application. In the next lesson, you learn how to create your own images by using the PhotoDraw Drawing tools and new images by combining elements of existing images.

Creating Your
Own Images

In this lesson, you learn to use the Drawing tools available in PhotoDraw, and you learn how to combine existing images to create new images. You also learn how to save your PhotoDraw pictures.

Drawing in PhotoDraw

PhotoDraw provides a number of Drawing tools you can use to create your own design elements and pictures. For example, you can create your own background images for Web pages, or create page borders and a variety of other items. What you create is limited only by your imagination (and to a small degree to your artistic abilities). Table 12.1 lists a number of the Drawing tools you can access from the AutoShapes toolbar or the Standard toolbar.

Table 12.1   PhotoDraw Drawing Tools

Button icon	Name	Purpose
\	Line	Draws a straight line with any orientation
∫	Curve	Draws curves or closed shapes made of curves
↘	Arrow	Draws a line with an arrow head
▭	Rectangle	Draws squares or rectangles
○	Ellipse	Draws circles or other oval shapes
⊕	AutoShapes	Choose from a number of special shapes, including basic shapes, stars, and banners

The Line, Arrow, Rectangle, and Ellipse tools all function in the same way. You click the appropriate tool, and then drag to create the object. The Curve tool requires that you drag to create the initial curve, and then add additional curves as needed. You double-click to end the shape. The AutoShapes tool provides a palette of different shapes. Select a particular shape, and then drag to create it on the page.

To successfully create drawings in PhotoDraw, you also need to become familiar with the Draw workpane, which contains the settings, effects, textures, and colors you will use for your Drawing tools as you draw your new picture. Figure 12.1 shows the workpane for the Draw feature.

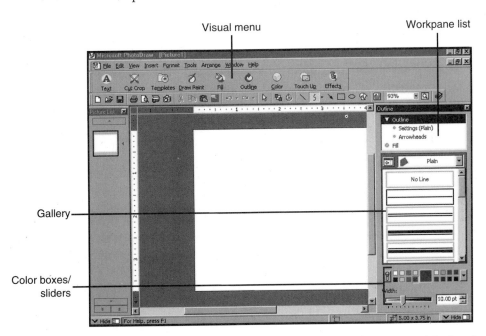

Figure 12.1 Each set of design tools provides you with a workpane full of options.

The various workpanes you work with vary depending on their function, but they contain any or all the items described here:

- The Workpane List—Enables you to switch to different sets of commands in a particular workpane. For instance, in the Draw workpane, the Outline choice provides the line styles available for drawing a new object such as a circle or rectangle. Other workpane choices such as Fill enable you to set the parameters for the fill color you use to fill a drawn object such as a circle or rectangle.

- The Gallery—Provides a drop-down list that enables you to choose between broad categories of settings. Below this category drop-down list is a scroll box that provides the settings available for the particular category you have chosen. For example, the Line/Brush Gallery in the Draw workpane provides a drop-down box that enables you to choose between plain brushes, artistic brushes, or photo brushes. Depending on which brush type you choose, the scroll box below the category drop-down list reflects a list of brush shapes and effects related to the chosen category.

- Color Boxes, Sliders, and so on—The bottom pane of the workpane (such as the Draw workpane; other workpanes do not contain these items) contains color boxes and sliders that allow you to control parameters like the color of a line or the width of the line.

 TIP **Almost Every Feature Has a Workpane** Nearly every type of tool you use in PhotoDraw, whether it's the Drawing tools, the Touch-up tools, or the Special Effects tools, has its various settings controlled in a workpane.

To explore the Drawing tools supplied by PhotoDraw, follow these steps:

1. Start PhotoDraw and choose **Blank Picture** on the Microsoft PhotoDraw dialog box. Then click **OK**. Select the **Default Picture** in the New dialog box and click **OK** to place a blank picture in the picture area. If you already have PhotoDraw open, click the **New** button on the toolbar to open a blank picture.

2. Click the **Draw Paint** button on the visual menu. Click **Draw** to open the Draw workpane. The workpane appears on the right side of the PhotoDraw window, and an AutoShapes toolbar appears in the scratch area (see Figure 12.2).

3. To draw a new object on the picture area, select a tool on the AutoShapes toolbar, such as the **Line** tool.

4. In the Line/Brush Gallery (refer to Figure 12.1), select the line type you want to use, such as Straight Line, Thin-Thin Line, and so on.

5. Drag the mouse on the picture to draw a new object.

AutoShapes toolbar   Workpane

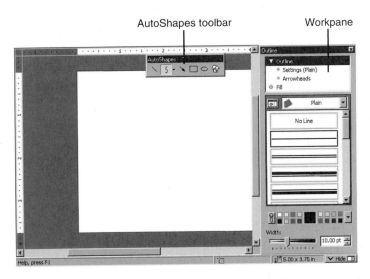

Figure 12.2 The workpane provides the design settings for the different shapes you use on the AutoShapes toolbar.

The object you have drawn appears on the picture area. Figure 12.3 shows several objects that have been drawn using some of the different drawing shapes on the AutoShapes toolbar and some of the different line settings in the Line/Brush Gallery. At this point, you can draw other items (first selecting their color or line weight in the workpane gallery). Or you can alter the current object using some of the Line/Brush Gallery options discussed in the next two sections.

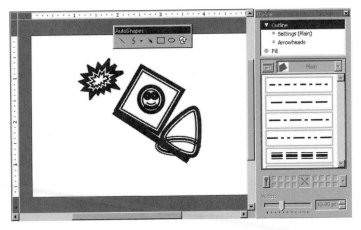

Figure 12.3 The AutoShapes toolbar provides different shapes you can draw by dragging the mouse.

New pictures are typically created by combining a number of different objects. For instance, you can use a combination of circles, lines, and rectangles to create a logo for your company (you also might want to place text on your new picture; see the section "Adding Text to an Image," in this lesson).

Using the Artistic Brushes

By default, Plain is selected in the Gallery drop-down box of the Draw workpane. The Plain option provides you with the ability to select line type and line color for the various Drawing tools on the AutoShapes toolbar. If you want to add an artistic and eye-catching flare to the objects you draw on the picture area, you might want to take advantage of the artistic brushes PhotoDraw provides for you to draw with.

To use the artistic brushes to draw objects, follow these steps:

1. In the Draw workpane, click the **Line/Brush Gallery** drop-down box and select **Artistic Brushes** (you might be asked to place the PhotoDraw CD in your CD-ROM drive). The gallery now provides a number of different brush styles, such as Charcoal and Watercolor.

2. Select one of the Drawing tools on the AutoShapes toolbar (such as the **Ellipse** tool), and then select a brush style in the gallery (such as **Stamp-Potato Imprint**). Draw an object using the brush style (see Figure 12.4).

The object appears in the picture area and is selected (sizing handles appear around the object). If you don't like the brush style you've used, select another brush style in the gallery, and the selected item converts to the newly chosen brush style. You can try out as many brush styles as you want using this technique.

TIP   **Rotating a Selected Object**   When an object is selected on the picture area, a small, green handle appears at the top of the object. This is the rotate handle. Drag this handle in either direction to rotate the selected item.

Using the Photo Brushes

The photo brushes enable you to create paint strokes that are made up of photographic elements. For instance, you can create a circle that is made up of rope images or draw a line that is an image of a snake. Using the different photo brushes provides a huge number of interesting effects you can add to any PhotoDraw picture.

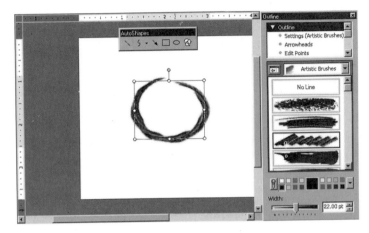

Figure 12.4 The artistic brushes enable you to apply painterly effects to your drawn objects.

To use the photo brushes to draw objects, follow these steps:

1. In the Draw workpane, click the **Line/Brush Gallery** drop-down box and select **Artistic Brushes** (you might be asked to place the PhotoDraw CD in your CD-ROM drive). The gallery now provides a number of different brush styles, such as Charcoal and Watercolor.

2. Select one of the Drawing tools on the AutoShapes toolbar (such as the **Rectangle** tool), and then select a photo brush style in the gallery (such as **Dice**). Draw an object using the brush style (see Figure 12.5, which shows a rectangle drawn with the Dice brush).

The photo brushes make it easy for you to create marquees that contain text (draw a rectangle using any photo brush style, and then place text in the rectangle as detailed in the next section) or many other interesting objects, particularly different design elements you can use to dress up your Web pages.

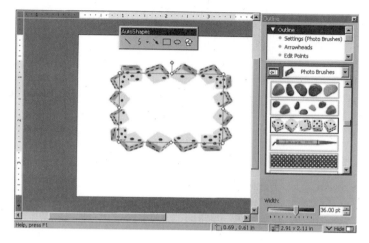

Figure 12.5   The photo brushes enable you to paint brush strokes that consist of photo images.

Adding Text to an Image

PhotoDraw makes it very easy for you to add text to an existing image or an image you are creating by using the various Drawing tools. After the text is placed on the picture area, you are provided with different formatting options.

To insert text into the picture area, follow these steps:

1. Click the **Text** button on the visual menu. Then click **Insert Text**. A text box appears in the picture area. A text workpane appears on the right of the PhotoDraw window.

2. The text **Your text here** appears in the text box on the picture area and in the middle pane of the text workpane. Make sure this placeholder text is selected in the workpane, and then type your own text.

3. After you've entered your text, you can change the font, font size, and font style by using the drop-down boxes in the bottom of the text workpane.

4. If you want to use designer text, click **Designer Text** in the workpane list (at the very top of the text workpane). A series of designer text effects appears in the gallery of the workpane.

5. Select a particular designer text effect for your text (such as Designer Text 8; see Figure 12.6).

6. If the designer text effect requires that you resize the text, use any of the round sizing handles on the text box to resize the text box as needed.

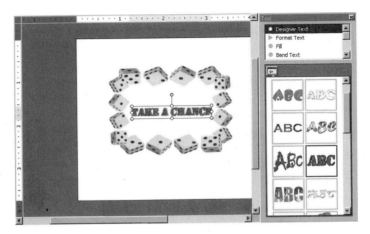

Figure 12.6 You can easily place text in your images.

 TIP **Closing a Workpane** When you have finished working with a particular workpane (Draw, Text, and so on), you can close the workpane by clicking its **Close** button in the upper-right corner of the workpane.

Combining and Arranging Existing Images

You can also create new images by combining several images together. For instance, you can draw a portion of an image using the Drawing tools, and then insert a clip art image or a photo to complete the new image. In fact, you can even create a collage of images (insert several photos or clip art images into the picture area), and then save it as a single image file.

To combine images on the picture area, follow these steps:

1. Select the **Insert** menu, and then select either **Clip Art** or **File** (depending on the type of image you want to add to the picture area).

2. If you choose to insert clip art, choose the clip art image from the Clip Gallery, and then insert it into the PhotoDraw picture area.

3. If you choose to insert a file (a scanned photo or other image), locate the file using the Insert dialog box, and then click **Open** to place the file in the PhotoDraw picture area.

4. Repeat either step 2 or 3, depending on the type of additional images you want to combine on the picture area.

Figure 12.7 shows a picture that is a combination of photos, clip art, and artistic and photo brush strokes.

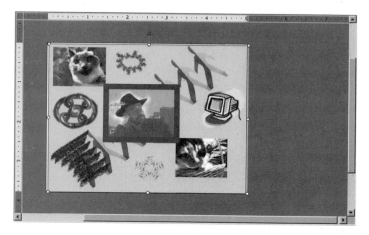

Figure 12.7 You can combine any number of pictures, clip art, or drawn objects to create a new PhotoDraw image.

As you add the different images to the picture area, you might find that you want to arrange the objects in layers. The Arrange menu provides you with all the commands you need to arrange your objects in the background or foreground of the new picture you are trying to complete.

To arrange items on the picture area, follow these steps:

1. Select a particular object or picture.

2. Select the **Arrange** menu, and then point at **Order**, and select one of the following choices from the cascading menu that appears:

   - **Bring to Front**—Bring the selected image to the top of the stacked images.

   - **Send to Back**—Places the selected image on the bottom of the stack.

- **Bring Forward**—Moves the selected image up one position in the stack of objects.

- **Send Backward**—Moves the selected image back one position in the stack of objects.

Getting your images in the proper order can take some time. If you find that you have chosen to send an image backward or forward in the stack and you do not like the results, select the **Edit** menu, and then select **Undo** to reverse that action.

TIP **Use the Object List to Arrange Images** Click the list arrow next to the thumbnail of the picture you are currently working on. An Object list appears showing thumbnails of all the objects in the current picture. To change the layering of the items, drag a particular object to a new position in the Object list.

Saving Your Images

After you create a new image, you should save it to a file. PhotoDraw enables you to save your files in a number of different file formats. If you are working on images you want to use on your Web pages, you need to save your images as either .gif or .jpg files. These are the two file formats used for Web pages (such as those you create in FrontPage).

To save your picture, follow these steps:

1. Select the **File** menu, and then select **Save**. The Save As dialog box appears.

2. Type a name for the new file in the **File Name** box.

3. If you want to save the file in a format other than the default (PhotoDraw), click the **Save as Type** drop-down arrow and select the file format you want to use.

4. Use the **Save In** drop-down box to specify the drive on your computer you want to use to store the file. Also, double-click on the appropriate folder to open it.

5. When you are ready to save the file, click **Save**. The file is saved to your computer.

In this lesson, you learned how to create your own images using the Drawing tools. You also learned how to use special brush types like the artistic and photo brushes. You learned how to combine images to create a new picture and how to save the pictures you create. In the next lesson, you learn how to touch up photos and crop and cut images in PhotoDraw.

Enhancing and Editing Images with PhotoDraw

In this lesson, you learn how to touch up photos in PhotoDraw and how to crop, cut, and size images.

Touching Up Photos in PhotoDraw

PhotoDraw provides a number of tools you can use to touch up photos you scan, download from the Internet, or capture using a digital camera. You can remove dust specks and spots from an image, remove scratches, and even smudge borders or clone areas of the photo to retouch certain areas.

These different photo Touch-up tools are very straightforward to use but will require that you become somewhat adept with using the mouse as a retouching tool. You can find the photo Touch-up tools on the Touch Up menu of the visual menu system. Table 13.1 lists the commands available on the Touch Up menu and what you can use them for.

Table 13.1 PhotoDraw Touch-Up Tools

Name	Purpose
Fix Red Eye	Removes red glare from eyes
Remove Dust and Spots	Cleans up specific dust specks or other spots on a scanned photo
Despeckle	Removes large amounts of dust or spots on a photo
Remove Scratch	Removes a scratch or scratches from a scanned photo

Name	Purpose
Clone	Copies an area of the photo and then uses it as a clone to cover another area of the photo
Smudge	Blends together colors and smears an area of the photo so that it is out of focus
Erase	Removes a portion of the photo

The various Touch-up tools also supply you with a workpane (as do other tools you have used in PhotoDraw). You can use these tools to set the various parameters for the Touch-up tool you are using, such as tool size (for example, the correction amount for that particular Touch-up tool). When you use these tools, specifically tools like Fix Red Eye or Clone, you might want to zoom in on your photograph so you can concentrate on the specific area of the photo you want to edit.

To use one of the Touch-up tools supplied by PhotoDraw, follow these steps:

1. To open the photo you want to edit or enhance, select the **File** menu, and then select **Open**. The Open dialog box appears (see Figure 13.1).

2. Use the **Look In** drop-down box to locate the drive that holds the photo. Then double-click on the appropriate folder.

3. Click on the file you want to open, and then click **Open**.

 **TIP** **Preview Your Images** Click the **Preview** button in the Open dialog box to get a preview of the images that reside in a particular folder or on a particular drive on your computer. Or when you want to open a file and preview it, select the **File** menu, and then select **Visual Open**. The Visual Open dialog box appears, supplying you with a preview of all the images in a particular folder.

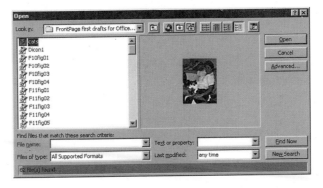

Figure 13.1 The Open dialog box enables you to locate the photo you want to open.

4. To use one of the Touch-up tools, click **Touch Up** on the visual menu to open the Touch Up menu, and then click a tool, such as **Fix Red Eye**. The workpane for the tool appears on the right side of the PhotoDraw window. A toolbar for the specific Touch-up tool also appears in the picture area.

5. Click the **Zoom** drop-down arrow and select a new zoom percentage that enables you to zoom in on the area of the photo you want to touch up.

6. To use a tool such as Fix Red Eye, click the **Red Eye** button on the Red Eye toolbar (this is the small toolbar that is specific for the Touch-up tool you are currently using). This turns the mouse pointer into a Red Eye selector (see Figure 13.2).

7. Click on the areas of the picture you want to touch up. In the case of the Fix Red Eye tool, click on the eyes of the subjects of the picture.

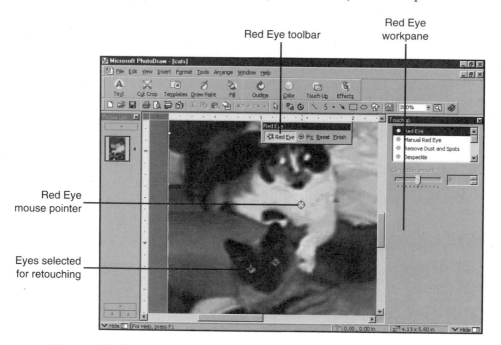

Figure 13.2 You can touch up your photos with tools like Fix Red Eye.

8. Use the **Correction Amount** slider (or other slider bar, depending on the tool selected) on the workpane to set the amount of correction for the current tool.

9. Click **Fix** on the Red Eye toolbar. Repeat steps 5 through 7 to retouch any other eyes found in the picture.

10. When you have completed your touch-up work with this particular tool, click the **Finish** button on the toolbar for the Touch-up tool you have used (in this case, the Red Eye toolbar).

After you click the **Finish** button, the photo is retouched based on the selections you have made on the picture and the settings you have chosen in the workpane.

Undo That Touch Up Most of the toolbars for the Touch-up tools have an **Undo** or **Undo Last** button that enables you to undo any touch-up you make to the image.

CAUTION

Each of the Touch-up tools operates in a slightly different manner. For instance, the Fix Red Eye and the Remove Scratch Touch-up tools require that you select an area of the picture, and then fix that area. The Clone tool requires that you first select an area to clone, and then clone it onto other areas of the picture. The Despeckle tool does not require that you select any part of the image because this tool attempts to retouch the entire photo. You only have control over the degree of despeckling that takes place.

When you have completed using a particular Touch-up tool, you might want to zoom out using the Zoom drop-down to inspect how your touch-up changes look when the image is viewed at a more normal view percentage (around 100 percent). This gives you a better idea of how the image will look when it's placed on a Web page or how it will look when it's printed.

Cropping Images

Another important aspect of working with images is being able to crop the image. Cropping enables you to remove areas of a photo that you don't need. For instance, you might have a group photo and want to cut out and save just a particular individual's picture. Or you have a fantastic art shot of the forest, but someone's hand is showing on one side of the frame. You can easily fix both these images using the Cropping tool.

To crop an image, follow these steps:

1. Open the image you want to crop.

2. Use the **Zoom** drop-down box to choose a zoom level that enables you to zoom in for cropping the image.

3. Click the **Cut Crop** button on the visual menu. Click **Crop** on the menu.

4. The Crop toolbar and Crop workpane appear in the PhotoDraw window. In the workpane, click one of the crop shapes in the gallery (such as the **Square**).

5. A crop shape appears on the image (it is the same shape as the crop shape you chose in the gallery).

6. Drag the sides of the crop shape so that it encloses the part of the picture you want to keep (see Figure 13.3). Everything outside the crop frame is cropped.

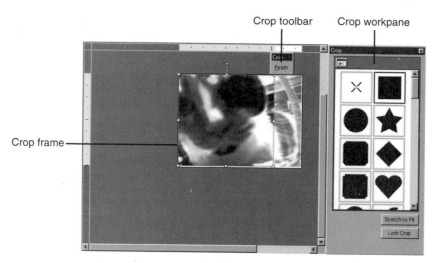

Figure 13.3 Select the area of the picture you want to keep; the rest is cropped.

7. When you have the frame positioned correctly, click the **Finish** button on the Crop toolbar. The picture is cropped.

After you crop your image, it no longer covers the entire picture area; white space shows. Select your picture. To trim the picture area so that it fits the newly cropped image, click the **View** menu, and then click **Fit Picture Area to Selection**.

Cutting Out an Image

The alternative to cropping an image is to cut out a part of the image. For instance, if you just want to use a cutout of a certain person or thing from the picture, you can use the Cut Out tool. The same shapes are available for the Cut Out tool that are available for the Crop tool. The major difference between these two tools is that cropping is meant to be used to trim the edges of an image, whereas the Cut Out tool lets you lift a portion of an image with a particular cut shape.

To cut out a portion of an image, follow these steps:

1. Open the picture you want to use the Cut Out tool on. Use the **Zoom** drop-down box as necessary.
2. Click the **Cut Crop** button on the visual menu. Click **Cut** on the menu.
3. The Cut workpane and Cut toolbar appear in the PhotoDraw window.
4. In the workpane, click one of the cut shapes in the gallery (such as the **Star**).
5. Drag the cut shape so that it encloses the area of the picture you want to cut out. Use the sizing handles to change the size of the cut shape as necessary.
6. When you have selected the area of the picture you want to cut out, click **Finish** on the Cut toolbar.

The item enclosed in the cut shape is cut from the picture and placed in the picture area of a new picture window. The original picture remains intact in its own window. You can switch between the cut image and the original image by clicking the appropriate image in the Picture list (see Figure 13.4).

Cutting out a portion of a picture using the Cut tool enables you to make pictures that come in all sorts of interesting shapes, including stars, hearts, and circles (to name a few).

Sizing Images

Sizing an image is just a matter of dragging the sizing handles on the image. You can make the image larger or smaller by dragging these small circular handles, which appear when the image is selected.

When you drag to size your image, you can use the rulers in the PhotoDraw window to determine the height and width of your image. If you increase the size of an image so it no longer fits on the picture area (which by default is 5 inches wide and 3.75 inches high), you can make the picture area expand to accommodate your picture. Select the **View** menu, and then select **Fit Picture Area to Selection**. You can also use the **Fit Picture Area to Selection** command when you make a picture smaller than the picture area.

Figure 13.4 You can quickly create a new image by cutting out a portion of an existing image with the Cut tool.

TIP **Saving a Picture with a New Filename** After you touch up, crop, or otherwise modify a particular picture, you might want to save it under a new filename. Select the **File** menu, and then select **Save As**. Type the new filename in the **File Name** box and click **Save**.

In this lesson, you learned how to touch up a photo with the Touch-up tools. You also learned how to crop, cut, and size an image. In the next lesson, you learn how to add special effects to your images.

Using PhotoDraw Color and Effect Tools

In this lesson, you learn how to use a number of color and special effect tools available in PhotoDraw.

Working with the Color Tools

PhotoDraw makes it easy for you to adjust a number of the color settings related to photos and images, such as brightness, contrast, tint, and color balance. You can even colorize a picture or image (color it with one color) or change a multi-color image to grayscale.

These different Color tools are available by clicking the Color button on the visual menu. Table 14.1 lists the Color tools and their particular purpose.

Table 14.1   PhotoDraw Color Tools

Name	Purpose
Brightness and Contrast	Sets the brightness and contrast of the image or picture
Tint	Adds a tinge of color to a picture
Hue and Saturation	Shifts a color along the color spectrum (hue) or change the color brightness (saturation)
Colorize	Makes a photo a monochrome picture by colorizing the image with a particular color
Color Balance	Increases or decrease the amount of a certain color in the picture

continues

Table 14.1 Continued

Name	Purpose
Negative	Changes the colors in the picture to their complementary colors
Grayscale	Changes a color image to a range of gray shades (making the image black and white)

The various Color tools supply you with a workpane where you will choose the settings related to that particular tool. Each tool uses one or more slider bars (which appear in the workpane) to actually change the settings and might also contain a color palette that enables you to choose a particular color. For example, the Colorize tool shown in Figure 14.1 contains an Amount slider bar that enables you to select the intensity of the color you colorize the photo with and a color palette where you choose the color.

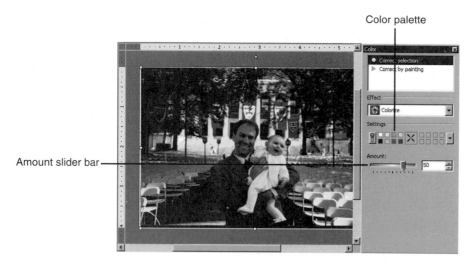

Figure 14.1 Color tools such as Colorize provide a workpane where you make the various selections related to that tool.

To use one of the Color tools supplied by PhotoDraw, follow these steps:

1. To open the photo you want to change the color settings for, select the **File** menu, and then select **Open**. The Open dialog box appears.

2. Use the **Look In** drop-down box to locate the drive that holds the photo. Then double-click the appropriate folder.

3. Click the file you want to open, and then click **Open**.

4. To use one of the Color tools, click **Color** on the visual menu, and then click a tool, such as **Brightness and Contrast**. The workpane for the tool appears on the right side of the PhotoDraw window.

TIP   **Use the Gallery Drop-Down Box to Switch Tools**   After you've opened a workpane for a particular Color tool, you can switch between the tools available by clicking the **Gallery** drop-down box and selecting a new tool by name.

5. Use the slider bars to increase or decrease the amount of a particular setting. For example, to increase the brightness of a photo in the Brightness and Contrast workpane, slide the **Brightness** slider to the right (see Figure 14.2).

Figure 14.2   You can improve a poorly lit photo by using the Brightness and Contrast tool.

6. When you have completed your work with this particular tool, close the tool's workpane by using the **Close** (×) button in the upper-right corner of the workpane.

 After you have completed working with the various Color tools to edit a photo or image, click the **Save** button to save your work.

The Color tools also enable you to adjust the settings for a part of an image or photo. Select **Correct by Painting** in the workpane list. Then edit the settings for the tool you are using (such as increasing or decreasing brightness or contrast).

Then use the mouse to paint on the area of the photo you want to change by using the current Color tool. Only that portion of the picture is changed by the settings you have chosen.

Working with the Effect Tools

PhotoDraw also provides you with a set of Effect tools you can use to enhance your PhotoDraw images. These tools can be used to enhance and edit scanned images or photos, and you can use these tools to enhance images you create in PhotoDraw by using the Draw tools. Table 14.2 lists the various Effect tools and their purposes.

Table 14.2   PhotoDraw Effect Tools

Name	Purpose
Shadow	Adds and positions a shadow for the selected object
Transparency	Makes an object or image transparent
Fade Out	Fades an object from opaque to transparent
Blur and Sharpen	Makes an object or image fuzzy or sharp
Distort	Distorts an image using a wide range of effects, including funhouse mirror and kaleidoscope effects
3-D	Adds depth and dimension to objects with a number of 3D effects
Designer Effects	Adds effects like Chalk and Charcoal or Wild Cave Painting to totally change the look and feel of objects and images

TIP   **Using Plug-Ins**   The Effects menu also provides a command for plug-ins. Plug-ins are third-party software tools you can add to PhotoDraw. In fact, PhotoDraw can use any plug-ins designed for Adobe Photoshop, a popular tool used to edit and enhance images. Plug-ins provide additional functionality and tools.

As with the other tools provided on the PhotoDraw visual menu, the Effects tools provide you with a workpane where you can make your choices regarding the settings for that particular effect. And while the workpanes vary for each tool, you primarily use slider bars and drop-down lists to make your various selections (as you do with other visual menu tools, such as the Color tools discussed in this lesson).

To use one of the Effects tools, follow these steps:

1. Open the image you want to add the effect to.

2. Click the **Effects** button on the visual menu. Then click a particular effect, such as **Designer Effects**. A workpane appears for that particular effect (see Figure 14.3).

Figure 14.3 A workpane appears for the effect you select on the Effects menu.

3. To choose a particular effect category in the Designer Effects workpane, click the effects gallery drop-down list. Click an effect category such as **Sketch**.

4. To select an effect in the Sketch category, use the scrollbar on the Effects scroll list to locate a particular effect, and then click that effect (such as **Graphic Pen**). The effect is applied to the selected object or image. Figure 14.4 shows the same photo that appeared without any effects in Figure 14.3 with the Graphic Pen effect selected.

Figure 14.4 You can add great effects to your images by using the PhotoDraw Designer effects.

TIP **Use Lock Effect to Combine Effects** If you want to combine several effects on one image or object, assign the first effect, and then click the **Lock Effect** button in the lower part of the workpane. This locks the effect on the image. Then select your next effect. You can lock as many effects as you want on the image or object.

The various effects provided by PhotoDraw require a fair amount of exploration by you before you understand what each of them can do to a photo or image. However, the Designer effects work best on scanned images or images from digital cameras. The Shadow and 3-D effects work best on items you have drawn by using the Draw tools provided in PhotoDraw. The other effects work equally well on photos and drawn items, depending on the particular effect you are trying to achieve.

In this lesson, you learned how to edit and enhance the colors in an image by using the Color tools and how to add effects to your images using the Effects tools. In the next lesson, you learn how to create buttons and banners for your Web pages.

Creating Web Graphics with PhotoDraw

In this lesson, you learn how to create Web graphics such as banners and buttons for your Web pages. You also learn how to save these items in an appropriate format for the Web.

Creating Web Page Banners

As you've already seen in this section of the book, PhotoDraw has a number of tools that make it easy for you to create, edit, and enhance images. All the tools discussed so far are excellent for getting your images ready to place on the Web pages you create by using Microsoft FrontPage or other Office applications such as Word or Publisher.

PhotoDraw also supplies a number of templates you can use to easily create different graphic types. In particular, you can create banners and buttons you can then use on your Web pages. PhotoDraw even supplies a wizard that helps you get these banner and button files into the appropriate file format to use on your Web pages.

Web page banners enable you to highlight the purpose or the name of a particular page. Page banners that use a frame or other graphical element add visual interest to a Web page.

A number of different page banner templates are available in PhotoDraw. When you use PhotoDraw templates to create an image, the Templates workpane actually walks you through the steps involved, much as a wizard does in some of the other Office applications.

To create a page banner, follow these steps:

1. Click the **New** button on the PhotoDraw Standard toolbar to open a blank image.

2. Click the **Templates** button on the visual menu. Then select **Web Graphics**. The workpane for the templates feature appears in the PhotoDraw window. The template type selected by default is Banners (see Figure 15.1). The banner templates available appear to the left of the workpane in what becomes the picture area after you select a particular banner.

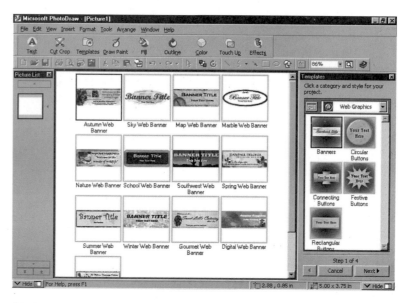

Figure 15.1   PhotoDraw makes it easy for you to select from a number of different banner templates.

3. Click the banner template you want to use to create your banner, and then click the **Next** button on the bottom right of the Templates workpane. The banner template you have chosen appears in the picture area.

4. The next step in the banner creation process gives you the option of replacing the picture provided for your banner with a picture file you have created or one you have scanned, downloaded from the Web, or taken with a digital camera. To locate the picture, use the **Browse** button in the workpane. To continue the banner creation process (using your picture or the picture provided by the template you have chosen), click the **Next** button in the workpane.

5. In the next step, you are asked to type the text for the banner title. Type the text in the workpane in the **Banner Title** text box. If you want to change the font, font size, or font style, use the appropriate drop-down box in the workpane (see Figure 15.2).

Figure 15.2 Enter the title text for your new banner in the Templates workpane.

6. After providing the text and other text attributes for the banner, click the other text box on the banner template (it currently contains the text **Your Text Here**). Type the text for this text box in the workpane text box and select the font, font size, and font style you want to use for this text. Click **Next** when you finish typing and formatting the text.

7. The final step in the banner creation process appears in the workpane. You are advised that after you click the Finish button, you can save your new banner as a PhotoDraw file (.mix), save the banner for use on a Web page, or print the banner. You should save the banner for use on a Web page (which is discussed in the last section of this lesson). Click **Finish** to conclude the creation process.

You can now use any of the PhotoDraw tools such as Draw, Color, or Effects to edit or enhance the banner you've created.

Creating Web Page Buttons

Another useful Web graphic is the button. You find buttons on nearly every Web page you view on the World Wide Web. Buttons can be used as links to other Web pages in your Web site or as links to other Web sites. After you create a button in PhotoDraw, you can place it on a Web page and then make it into a hyperlink that links to another Web location (for information on creating hyperlinks, see Lesson 7, "Working with Hyperlinks").

To create a button graphic in PhotoDraw, follow these steps:

1. Click the **New** button on the PhotoDraw Standard toolbar to open a blank image.

2. Click the **Templates** button on the visual menu. Then select **Web Graphics**. The workpane for the templates feature appears in the PhotoDraw window. Click one of the button type groups in the workpane: Circular Buttons, Connecting Buttons, Festive Buttons, or Rectangular Buttons. The buttons available in that group appear to the left of the workpane.

3. Click the button template you want to use to create your button, and then click the **Next** button on the bottom right of the Templates workpane. The button template you have chosen appears in the picture area (see Figure 15.3).

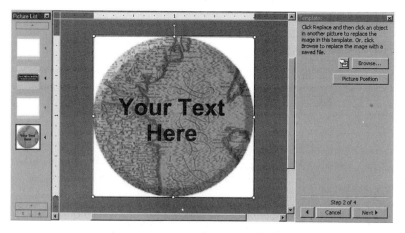

Figure 15.3   Select a button template for the new button you want to create.

4. The next step in the button creation process gives you the option of replacing the picture provided for your button with a picture file you have created or one that you have scanned, downloaded from the Web, or taken with a digital camera. To locate the picture, use the **Browse** button in the workpane. To continue the button creation process (using your picture or the picture provided by the template you have chosen), click the **Next** button in the workpane.

5. In the next step, you are asked to type the text for the button. Type the text in the workpane in the **Button** text box. If you want to change the font, font size, or font style, use the appropriate drop-down box in the workpane. Then click the **Next** button to continue.

6. The final step in the button creation process appears in the workpane, and you are advised that after you click the Finish button, you can save your new button as a PhotoDraw file (.mix), save the button for use on a Web page, or print the button. Click **Finish** to conclude the creation process.

Saving an Image for Use on the Web

After creating the banners and buttons you want to use on your Web pages, you should save those items so you can actually use them on a particular Web page. PhotoDraw can walk you through the steps to save any image you create in a file format appropriate for use on a Web page.

Follow these steps to save an image for use on a Web:

1. Select the **File** menu, and then select **Save for Use In**. The Save for Use In Wizard appears.

2. The first wizard screen asks you to select where you want to put your picture. Each option is represented by an option button (see Figure 15.4). For Web pages, select either **On the Web** (the default selection) or in cases where you want a small thumbnail image (in the case of buttons or other graphics you want to use as hyperlinks), click **On the Web as a Thumbnail**. After making your selection, click **Next**.

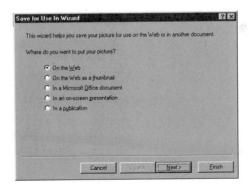

Figure 15.4 The wizard makes it easy for you to save your images for use on the Web.

3. The next wizard screen helps you select how transparent areas on the picture are handled. You can choose to have the Web page you place the graphic on show through the transparent areas of the image, or you can fill the transparent areas of the picture with a particular color (see Figure 15.5). Select the appropriate option button and click **Next**.

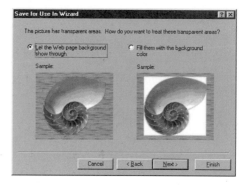

Figure 15.5 You can choose to have the Web page background show through the transparent areas of your image or you can fill the image with a color.

4. The next Wizard screen helps you avoid a halo around the image (when it is placed on the Web page) by allowing you to specify the type of background on your Web page. You can select either a solid background and the color of the solid background or select an option stating that the background on the Web page is a tiled image (the same image repeated over and over again). Select the appropriate option button (see Figure 15.6), and then click **Next**.

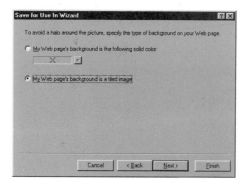

Figure 15.6 The wizard helps you avoid having a halo around your graphic when it is placed on the Web page.

5. The final wizard screen you the format for the graphic and other file details related to the choices you made on the other wizard screens. Web graphics are saved as .gif files, which is a format that provides fairly high resolution but keeps the file size relatively small. When you are ready to save the graphic, click **Save**. The Save for Use In dialog box appears.

6. Type in a name for the file and use the **Save In** drop-down box to choose the drive you want to store the file on. You also need to specify the folder to hold the file. When you have provided the location and name for the file, click **Save**. The file is saved to your computer.

After you save the file to your computer, you can open your Web page editor (such as FrontPage) and place the graphic on a particular Web page.

In this lesson, you learned how to create banners and buttons for your Web pages. You also learned how to save an image for use on a Web page. In Appendix A, you learn how to install Microsoft Office 2000.

Appendixes

Installing Microsoft Office 2000

In this appendix, you learn how to install Office 2000 on your computer.

What Office 2000 Edition Are You Installing?

Before you can begin to take advantage of all the great applications and features contained in Microsoft Office 2000, you need to install the software. The applications that are placed on your computer's hard drive during the installation process depend on which edition of the Office 2000 suite you have purchased.

Each edition contains a different grouping of Microsoft applications. The various editions available are detailed in Table A.1.

Table A.1   Office Applications Found in the Different Office Editions

Edition	Applications Included
Standard	Word, Excel, Outlook, PowerPoint, and Internet Explorer
Small Business	Word, Excel, Outlook, Publisher, Office Small Business Tools, and Internet Explorer
Professional	Word, Excel, Outlook, PowerPoint, Access, Publisher, Office Small Business Tools, and Internet Explorer
Premium	Word, Excel, Outlook, PowerPoint, Access, Publisher, Small Business Tools, FrontPage, PhotoDraw, and Internet Explorer

Installing Microsoft Office from the CD-ROM

Installing Microsoft Office from its CD-ROM (or CD-ROMs—some of the editions include multiple CDs) probably seems deceptively straightforward, especially because the CD autostarts when you place it in your CD-ROM drive. You might find, however, that Microsoft has put some new spin on the installation of the 2000 version, including a change in the installation interface and how and when programs are installed from the CD to the computer. Understanding the various changes made to the Office installation program helps you install the Office software so that you have access to the applications that you need to get your work done. To begin a new installation of Office 2000, place your CD-ROM in your CD-ROM drive. The CD autostarts, opening the Office Installation window.

CAUTION

My Office CD-ROM Did Not Autostart You can load the installation software manually. Click the Windows **Start** button and then click **Run**. In the Run box, type **D:\setup.exe**. Make sure that you designate the drive letter of your CD-ROM in the place of the "D" shown. Then click **OK** to load the Office installation program.

The Installation window welcomes you to the Office 2000 installation and asks you to provide your name, initials, organization, and—more importantly—the CD Key for your Office CD (see Figure A.1). The key is usually found on the back of the jewel case (on an orange label) that the Office CD came in.

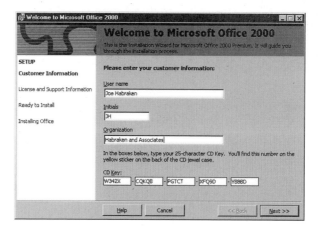

Figure A.1 Provide your name and CD Key to begin the Office installation.

After you've provided this information (only a name and the CD Key are actually required), click **Next** to continue with the installation.

The next screen in the installation process asks you to read the license agreement for the Office software that you have purchased. After you have read the agreement, click the **I Accept the Terms in the License Agreement** option button and then click **Next** to continue.

The next screen is the Microsoft Office 2000 Ready to Install window and it provides you with two different installation possibilities (see Figure A.2). You can select **Install Now** (this reads **Upgrade Now** if you have a previous version of Office on your computer), which installs the most commonly used Office 2000 components and Internet Explorer 5, or you can choose to customize your installation by selecting the **Customize** button.

You may want to customize the installation to place the Office files on a drive other than your C: drive or to select the Office components that are actually installed during the process. The best thing about customizing the installation is that you can make sure that all the Office components you use are installed during this initial process. Otherwise, when you attempt to use a particular feature, you may be instructed to insert the Office installation CD (while you are working on something) and wait until that particular component is installed.

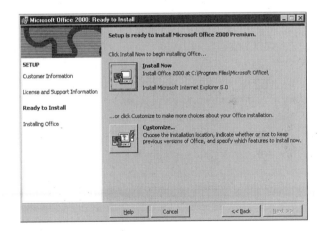

Figure A.2   You are provided with the option of a quick installation or you can take charge of the installation by selecting Customize.

Understanding the Typical Installation

When you select Install Now, you are basically leaving the installation up to the Office CD, which installs the applications and tools that are considered the common Office components (this includes all the Office core applications including Word, Excel, Access, PowerPoint, Outlook, and FrontPage). Internet Explorer 5, an integral part of Office 2000, is also installed during the typical installation.

The Install Now option requires no further input from you and you will not be prompted again until the typical Office components are installed on your C: drive. At the completion of the installation, a dialog box appears, letting you know that the installation was completed. You are then asked to restart your computer. Click **Yes** to automatically restart the computer.

When your computer restarts, you can run any of the Office applications. However, be aware that you will eventually experience Microsoft's new strategy for conserving your hard drive space during the Office installation—Installed on First Use.

Dealing with Installed-on-First-Use Components

Components that are not considered typical are not installed onto your hard drive during the Upgrade installation. These components include certain templates, converters, wizards, and other Office tools and items (a good example are the Web page themes provided in Microsoft Word; the full set is not installed during the Upgrade process). However, when you try to use one of these components for the first time in a particular application, they will be installed on-the-fly. This means that you must have the Office CD handy because this special installation (accomplished while you are using a particular application) needs the files on the CD that run the particular component. These components are labeled *Installed on First Use*, which simply means that when prompted, you must insert the CD and wait a moment for them to be installed after you start them with a particular menu selection or toolbar button.

After the component is installed, you can go ahead and use it without really skipping a beat (other than to wait for the installation to conclude). It's not necessary to shut down the Office application that you are using when the component is installed.

After you use one of these components and it is installed, you do not need to reinstall it the next time you need to use it. If you never use one of the components considered an installed-on-first-use component, it will never be installed on your machine.

A way around installed-on-first-use components is to do a Custom installation and change the status of installed-on-first-use components so that they are placed on your computer's hard drive during the installation process, as are the other more typical components. The section below describes how to take advantage of the Custom installation.

Selecting the Custom Installation

An alternative to the Upgrade installation is the Custom installation, which provides you much more control over where the Office components are installed and which components are installed.

To start the Custom Installation, select the **Customize** button. The next screen provides you with the options for selecting the folder and drive that the Office applications will be installed into (see Figure A.3)

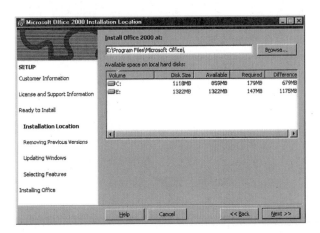

Figure A.3 In the Custom installation you can specify the folder and drive for the Office software.

The screen also provides you information on the free space available on each drive on your computer to aid you in your selection. To change the drive or folder for the installation, click the **Browse** button. Select the drive and/or folder in the Browse window and then return to the Installation window by clicking **OK**.

After you specify a location, the installation program actually creates the folder for you, if it doesn't already exist. To continue with the installation, click the **Next** button.

Removing Previous Versions of Office

The next step in the installation process is the detection of previous versions of Office software. If the installation software detects previous versions of Office components on your computer, it lists them on the installation screen. You are advised to remove these components (you can remove them by canceling the installation process, placing your CD-ROM for the older version of the software in your CD drive, and then using the Remove feature to remove the software from your computer).

After you have removed previous versions, place the Office 2000 CD-ROM into your CD and repeat the steps necessary to do a Custom installation.

Selecting Features for Installation

One of the biggest changes in the installation is how you select the various Office components that you want to install. Office provides you with a selection structure that resembles an outline. Each Office component is listed in the Select features interface window (such as Word, Excel, and so on). Each Office application has a plus (+) symbol to the left of the application name. When you click the plus (+) symbol, a tree structure opens up, revealing the various components of the application that you clicked on. Some components of an application also have a plus (+) symbol to the left of their names. Click this plus (+) symbol to further show the outline of the Office software (click the minus (–) symbol next to an application to collapse its component branches).

 Components that are automatically installed during your installation are marked with a small computer icon that stands for **Run from My Computer**. This means that the component will be installed on your hard drive.

 In the Select features interface, files can be marked in two other ways. Those files marked with a yellow one (1) in front of the computer icon are designated **Installed on First Use** and are installed on your computer the first time that you use them in a particular application (see "Dealing with Installed-on-First-Use Components," earlier in this lesson).

 Files marked with a CD-ROM icon can be run from the Office CD when they are required. They are marked as **Run from CD** (this means you have to keep the Office CD in your CD-ROM drive when you work with the various Office applications).

You can select a particular Office file or component and change how it is installed during the Custom installation. For instance, you can change a file's status from *installed on first use* to *run from my computer*. That way the component is placed on the hard drive during the installation and you don't have to deal with it being installed on-the-fly the first time you try to use it.

To change how files are installed, expand a particular application or component tree (by clicking the appropriate **plus** [+] symbol). Then click the file that you want to select the installation option for (see Figure A.4). From the drop-down menu that appears, select **Run from My Computer**, **Run from CD**, or **Installed on First Use**.

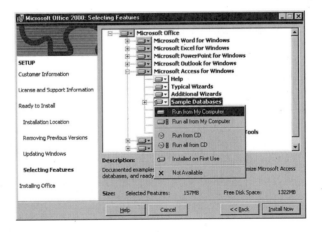

Figure A.4   Components can be marked as Run from My Computer, Run from CD, or Installed on First Use.

 TIP   **I Don't Want to Install All the Components**   You can flag a component you don't want to install by selecting it and then choosing the **Not Available** choice on the drop-down menu for that particular component. Items marked Not Available are not installed during the installation process.

Completing the Installation

After you have chosen the components you want to install and how you want to install them (running from your hard drive, the CD-ROM, or installed on first use), you are ready to complete the installation. Click the **Install Now** button and the Office installation software copies all the files from the CD-ROM to the place you've designated on your local drive. After the installation is complete, Office will let you know. You may be asked to restart your computer, which you should do.

Icons for your Office components are placed on the Programs menu activated by the Windows Start button. Office also provides you with the Office toolbar that can be used to start any of the Office components. The Office toolbar should appear on the Windows Desktop after you have restarted your computer. If the Office toolbar does not appear, add it to your installation. Adding Office components to your installation is discussed in the next section.

Adding and Removing Office Components

No matter what type of installation you do (the typical or custom installation), after you start using your software, you may find that you would like to add components that were not installed during your initial run-through with the software. This doesn't pose a problem. Just insert the CD-ROM back into the CD-ROM drive. A window automatically opens. Click the **Add or Remove Features** button and then select components that you want to install (or remove) in the Select Features interface window.

 To add a component to your computer, you need to change it from its current Installed on First Use status or Not Available status. Click the particular component (remember: to view the components under a particular application such as Word or Excel, click the plus (+) symbol next to that application) and select **Run from My Computer** on the menu.

 To remove a component from your computer, click that component in the features list and select **Not Available** on the menu.

After you've selected items to install (or remove from your computer), click the **Update Now** button in the Update Features window. The component is added (or removed). When the installation is complete, a notification box appears. Click **OK** to close it.

Repairing Office

Office 2000 has also added a new feature that allows you attempt to repair problems that you are having with your Office installation. You should only use this feature if you are truly experiencing problems with a particular Office application or applications.

Insert your Office installation CD in your CD-ROM. The Office 2000 Maintenance Mode window should appear, as shown in Figure A.5. (If the window does not appear, click the Windows **Start** button and then click **Run**. In the Run box, type **D:\setup.exe**. Make sure that you designate the drive letter of your CD-ROM in the place of the "D" shown. Then click **OK**.)

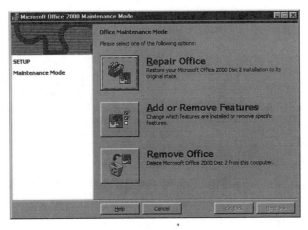

Figure A.5 You can use the Repair mode to fix any problems you are experiencing because of corrupt or missing files associated with your Office installation.

Click the **Repair Office** button. You are provided with two option buttons: **Reinstall Office** does an entire reinstallation of Office. **Repair Errors in My Office Installation** attempts to replace corrupt or missing files. You may find that the reinstallation option is a better choice for getting Office back up and running because all the Office files are reinstalled.

Select your choice of options and then click the **Finish** button. When the Repair feature finishes, you will see a message that says, "Microsoft Office 2000 setup completed successfully." You can now run your Office applications.

In this lesson, you learned how to install Office 2000 and add or remove components from your installation. In the next lesson, you learn how to get the most out of the Office Help system.

Using the Office 2000 Help System

In this appendix, you learn about the various types of help available to you in Microsoft Office programs.

Help: What's Available

Because every person is different, the programs in the MS Office suite offer many different ways to get help with the program. You can

- Ask the Office Assistant for help.
- Get help on a particular element you see onscreen with the What's This? tool.
- Use the Contents, Answer Wizard, and Index tabs in the Help window to get help.
- Access the Office on the Web feature to view Web pages containing help information (if you are connected to the Internet).

Asking the Office Assistant

You have probably already met the Office Assistant; it's the friendly paper clip, (or other character, if someone else has used your computer and chosen a different character) that pops up to give you advice. It appears the first time you start each of the Office programs to ask if you need help getting started, and again when you are attempting certain new tasks. Don't let its whimsical appearance fool you, though; behind the Office Assistant is a powerful Help system.

Turning the Office Assistant On and Off

By default, the Office Assistant is activated, and it sits in your application window, as shown in Figure B.1. You can hide the Assistant by right-clicking the Assistant and then selecting **Hide**. The Assistant will be removed from the application window.

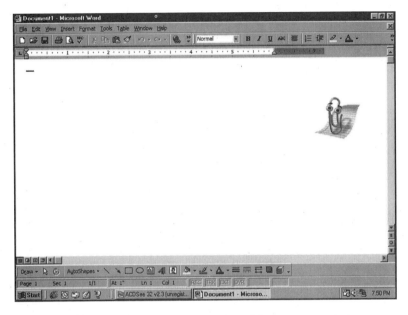

Figure B.1   The Office Assistant appears on top of the program window.

 To return the Office Assistant to the application window, click the **Help** button on the Standard toolbar or select the **Help** menu, then select **Show the Office Assistant**.

Kinds of Help Office Assistant Provides

When you click the Office Assistant, a balloon appears above the Assistant asking you "What Would You Like to Do?" (see Figure B.2). You can do any of the following:

- Type a question in the balloon (in the area that says "Type your question here") and then click **Search** to get help.
- Select one of the Office Assistant's guesses about what you need help with.

- Click the **Options** button to customize the way the Office Assistant works.
- Click outside the balloon to close it (but leave the Office Assistant onscreen).

If you close the help balloon, you can reopen it at any time by clicking the **Assistant**.

Figure B.2 Office Assistant is at your service, asking you what you would like to do.

TIP **Extra Tips Along the Way** Sometimes you see a light bulb above Office Assistant. This means that the Office Assistant has a suggestion for you regarding the task you're currently performing. To get the suggestion, just click the **Assistant**. Then click outside the Assistant balloon when you are done reading the context-sensitive help.

Asking the Office Assistant a Question

If you need help on a particular topic, you can type a question into the text box shown previously in Figure B.2. Follow these steps to see how it works:

1. Click the **Assistant** to open the balloon.
2. Type a question into the text box. For instance, you might type **How Do I Print?** for help printing your work.
3. Click the **Search** button. The Office Assistant provides some topics that might match what you're looking for. (Figure B.3 shows the Office

Assistant's answer to the question How Do I Print? in Word.) The options may be a little different in the other Office applications.

4. Click the option that best describes what you're trying to do. If you were to choose Print a Document, a Help window would appear with instructions for the specified task.

   If none of the options describes what you want, click the **See More** arrow to view more options, or type a different question into the text box.

The Help window that appears (containing the task instructions) is the same window that opens when you ask for help with the Office Assistant turned off.

Figure B.3   The Office Assistant asks you to narrow down exactly what you are trying to accomplish so that it can provide the best help possible.

Getting Help Without the Assistant

If you would like to get your help in a more conventional manner, you can completely turn off the Office Assistant. Click the **Assistant** and in the Assistant Balloon click **Options**. On the Options tab deselect the check box that says **Use the Office Assistant**. This allows you to access the Help system directly.

TIP   **Get the Assistant Back**   If you find that you prefer getting your help from the Office Assistant, select **Help** and then select **Show the Office Assistant** to turn the Assistant on.

After you've turned off the Office Assistant, you're ready to access the Help system. Follow these steps:

1. Select **Help** and then **Microsoft Word Help** (or help in the Office application that you are using.) The Help window appears and explains different ways to get help in your application.

2. Click the **Show** button on the top left of the Help window. The window expands and three tabs appear—**Contents**, **Answer Wizard**, and **Index**— each providing a different way to look up the help or information that you need.

3. The right pane of the Help window looks and acts like a Web browser. Help topics are represented by colored text hyperlinks. Click a link to get specific information on a topic.

After you've opened the Help window, you can then take advantage of the different ways to find information: the Contents tab, the Answer Wizard tab, and the Index tab.

Using the Contents Tab

The Contents tab of the Help system is a series of books you can open. Each book has one or more Help topics in it, which appear as pages or chapters. (Figure B.4 shows the Contents tab.)

To select a Help topic from the Contents tab, follow these steps:

1. Select **Help** and then **Microsoft Word Help** (or the help command found in your current application).

2. Click **Show** to expand the Help window. Then click the **Contents** tab on the left side of the Help window.

3. Find the book that describes in broad terms the subject for which you need help.

4. Double-click the book, and a list of Help topics appears below the book, as shown earlier in Figure B.4.

5. Double-click a Help topic to display it in the right pane of the Help window.

6. When you finish reading a topic, select another topic on the Contents tab or click the Help window's **Close** (×) button to exit Help.

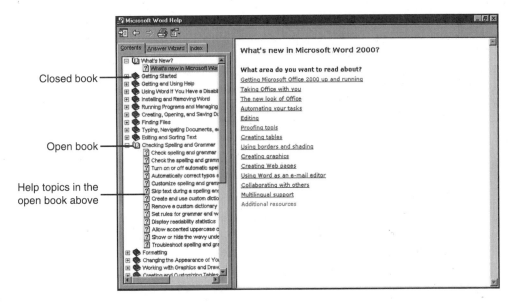

Closed book

Open book

Help topics in the
open book above

Figure B.4 The Help Contents screen is a group of books that contain help information.

Using the Answer Wizard

Another way to get help in the Help window is to use the Answer Wizard. The Answer Wizard works exactly the same way as the Office Assistant does; you ask the wizard questions and it supplies you with a list of topics that relate to your question. You click one of the choices provided to view help in the Help window.

To get help using the Answer Wizard, follow these steps:

1. Select **Help** and then **Microsoft Word Help** (or help in your current application).

2. Click the **Answer Wizard** tab in the Help window.

3. Type your question in the **What Would You Like to Do?** box. For instance, you might type the question "**How do I create a table?**"

4. After typing your question, click the **Search** button. A list of topics appears in the Select Topic to Display box. Select a particular topic and its information appears in the right pane of the Help window, as shown in Figure B.5.

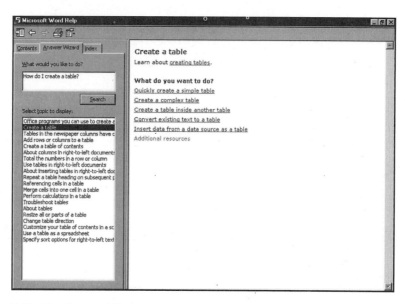

Figure B.5   The Answer Wizard allows you to ask questions about a particular topic or feature.

Using the Index

The Index is an alphabetical listing of every Help topic available. It's like an index in a book.

Follow these steps to use the index:

1. Select **Help** and then **Microsoft Word Help** (or help in your current application).

2. In the Help window, click the **Index** tab.

3. Type the first few letters of the topic for which you are looking. The Choose Keywords box jumps quickly to a keyword that contains the characters you have typed.

4. Double-click the appropriate keyword in the Choose Keywords box. Topics for that keyword appear in the Choose a Topic box.

5. Double-click a topic to view help in the right pane of the Help window (see Figure B.6).

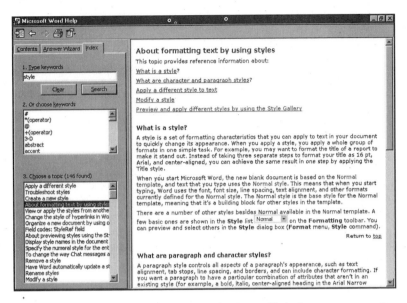

Figure B.6   Type keywords into the Index to find specific help.

Navigating the Help Window

No matter which of the four avenues you choose for finding a Help topic (the Office Assistant, Contents, Answer Wizard, or Index), you eventually end up in the Help window. From there, you can read the information onscreen or do any of the following things:

- Click an underlined word to see a definition of it.

- Click a hyperlink (hyperlinks appear as underlined, colored text—the default color is blue) to jump to more specific help or another topic. These links reside in the right pane of the Help window.

- Return to the previous Help topic you viewed by clicking the **Back** button.

- Move forward through the Help topics that you have viewed by clicking the **Forward** button.

- Print a hard copy of the information by clicking the **Print** button.

- Copy the text to the Clipboard (for pasting into a program such as Microsoft Word or Windows Notepad) by selecting the text and then pressing **Ctrl+C** on the keyboard.

- Close the Help window by clicking the **Close** (×) button.

Close the
Help window
by clicking here.

Click a hyperlink
to jump to another
Help screen.

Click a colored
word to see a
definition of it.

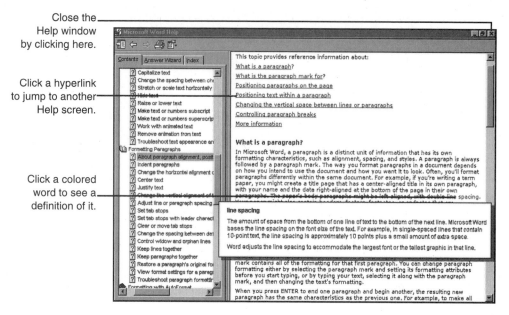

Figure B.7 After you find the information you need, you can read it onscreen, print it, or move to another Help topic.

 TIP **Get Help Online** Office 2000 applications can also provide additional help by taking you to Microsoft's Office Web site. Select **Help** and then **Office on the Web**. You will be taken to the Office support Web site.

Getting Help with Screen Elements

If you wonder about the function of a particular button or tool on the screen, wonder no more. Just follow these steps to learn about this part of Help:

1. Select **Help** and then **What's This?** or press **Shift+F1**. The mouse pointer changes to an arrow with a question mark.

2. Click the screen element for which you want help. A box appears explaining the element.

In this appendix, you learned about how you can get help in your Office applications. In the next appendix, you learn about object linking and embedding, which allows you to share information and objects between the various Office applications.

Object Linking and Embedding

In this appendix, you learn how to share data between applications by using object linking and embedding.

What Is Object Linking and Embedding (OLE)?

OLE (pronounced "oh-LAY") stands for Object Linking and Embedding. It is a Windows feature that enables the Windows applications that employ it to share information directly, without any conversion of the data.

For example, you might create a quarterly report in Microsoft Word that contains an Excel chart. Each quarter, the Excel data in the chart changes. When it comes time to generate the next quarterly report, you could find the most up-to-date version of the Excel chart, and copy and paste it into the report; or you could relax while your OLE link updates the report automatically with the changes made in each supporting document.

What Is Linking?

When you link an *object* to a document or other application file, you are creating a connection between the *source file* and your current document, the *container file*. The object does not reside in the container; it is represented there by a linking code. When you update the object, the update is done in the original source application, and the results of the update are seen in the container. For instance, you can link a Microsoft Excel workbook to a Word document. When you activate the workbook with a double-click, its source application is started (Microsoft Excel), and the file is opened in it.

Object   Any snippet of data that you want to link to another document. It can be as small as a single character or as large as a huge report with many graphics.

Source File   The file from which the information to be pasted originated.

Container File   The file that's receiving the object. If, for example, you're linking an Excel chart to a Word document, the Word document is the container file.

The great thing about links is that you can have the same object linked to several destinations. When you update the file in its source application, the file is updated in all the places that it is linked to. And because the linked object is not actually made part of the container file, the container file does not increase dramatically in size.

What Is Embedding?

Embedding gives you the same results as linking but is a very different process. An embedded object does become part of the destination file, increasing the file's size. It is basically a transplanted copy of the original file. Because the embedded file resides in the destination file, updating the original file in the original application does not update the embedded copy—there is no link between the two.

Embedded objects are dynamic, however, meaning they can be manipulated and updated right in the destination application. When you activate an embedded object (double-click it), the *server application* opens right inside of the current application. In many cases, the menu system of the server application temporarily replaces that of the current application, so in essence, you are running the server application from inside the application that holds the embedded object.

A good example of this would be a PhotoDraw image (such as an employee's picture) embedded in an Access table. Double-click the embedded image, and the Access menus and toolbars are temporarily replaced by the PhotoDraw menus and toolbars. You edit the object, and when you click outside the object window, the menus and toolbars of your container application are returned to you.

Choosing Between Linking and Embedding

You might be wondering when it's best to link and when you should embed. This really depends on the type of information that you want to place in a particular file. Objects, such as worksheets built in Excel or reports written in Word, that are dynamic (the information in them is updated constantly) are best linked to your container file. This enables you to update the object in the application you created it in and still have the current results linked to a number of different containers.

Objects such as scanned photos or video clips of your vacation, which are static and not updated over time, can be embedded into your documents or other application files. This makes the object part of that file. For instance, you might place scanned photos in an Access table field. Or you might place your company's logo on a particular Excel worksheet.

The only other parameter that you might consider when you are trying to decide between linking and embedding is file size. If you are going to embed a very large object into an already large file, you are going to push your computer hardware to real extremes when you open that file and attempt to manipulate it. Very large objects are sometimes best linked because they do not become part of the destination file.

Linking or Embedding with Paste Special

The easiest way to link or embed is with the Paste Special command on the Edit menu.

When an object is pasted into a document with the regular Paste command, the object is dropped in, with no information about its origin. In contrast, when an object is pasted into a document with Paste Special, several pieces of information about the object are stored as part of the container file, including the source file's name and location, the server application, and the location of the object within the source file. This extra information is what makes it possible for the object to be updated whenever the source file is updated.

OLE needs the name of a source file to refer back to later in order to link, so you must save your work in the source program before you create a link with OLE. However, if you merely want to embed, and not link, you do not need a named source file. The only information OLE needs to edit the object later is the name of the *server application*.

Server Application The native application for the object that's being linked or embedded. For instance, if you embed an Excel worksheet into a Word document, Excel is the server application.

Container Application The application that you are linking or embedding the object to. For instance, if you embed an Excel worksheet into a Word document, Word is the container application.

To link or embed with Paste Special, follow these steps:

1. Open the application that contains the object that you want to link or embed (such as Excel, when you want to link an Excel worksheet). Select the item that will serve as the object (for example, click and drag to select the worksheet cells that will serve as the object.)

2. To copy the object to the Clipboard, select **Edit** and then **Copy**.

3. Open the application that is to receive the linked or embedded object and open the specific container file (the file in which you want to paste the object). Place the insertion point where you want to place the object.

4. Select **Edit** and then **Paste Special**, and the Paste Special dialog box appears. (The one for Word is shown in Figure C.1; they are similar in all Office applications.)

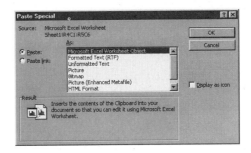

Figure C.1   The Paste Special dialog box.

5. Select the object in the dialog box that you want to place in the current application (in this case, it would be the Microsoft Excel Worksheet Object).

6. Choose **Paste** or **Paste Link**, depending on the type of connection you want:

- **Paste**—Pastes the contents of the Windows Clipboard into the document at the location of the insertion point. The link is not maintained, but you can double-click the pasted material to edit it. (This is embedding.)

- **Paste Link**—This option is available if the contents of the Clipboard can be linked back to its source file. With this option selected, a link is created between the source file and the container file. If you have not saved the source file, the Paste Link option is not available.

7. (Optional) If you want to display the pasted object as an icon instead of as the data itself, select the **Display as icon** check box. This option is only available if you have selected Paste Link. This is useful for pasting sounds and media clips because you can double-click the icon that represents the file if you want to play it later.

8. Click **OK**. The object is embedded or linked into the container file, depending on the options you chose.

When deciding which options to select in the Paste Special dialog box, pay close attention to the notes that appear in the Result area. These notes tell you what happens if you choose OK with the present set of options.

Linking or Embedding an Entire File

If you want to link an entire file to your document—an entire Excel spreadsheet, for example—you can use the Object command. It appears on the Insert menu of most Windows applications.

Unlike Edit Paste, you do not have to open the source file to retrieve the object. You can perform the entire procedure without leaving the application that will serve as the container application. Follow these steps to learn how:

1. Start the container application (the one to receive the object), and then create or open the container file. You use Microsoft Word as the client application in this example.

2. Select **Insert** and then **Object**. The Object dialog box appears.

3. Click the **Create from File** tab at the top of the dialog box. The dialog box changes to show a File Name list box (see Figure C.2).

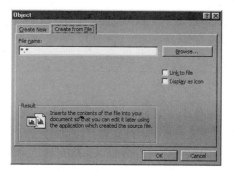

Figure C.2 Use the Object dialog box's Create from File tab to choose an existing file to link or embed.

4. Click the **Browse** button, and select the name of the file you want to insert and link or embed in the container file. For example, use an Excel worksheet. Navigate through the directories and subdirectories to locate the file if it does not appear in the current directory. When you locate the file, double-click it.

5. If you want to link, make sure the **Link to file** check box is selected. This creates an active link between the source file and the destination file. If you merely want to embed, not link, make sure it's deselected.

6. Select the **Display as icon** check box if you want to have the embedded or linked file represented as an icon in the container application.

7. Click **OK**. The dialog box closes, and the source file is inserted into the container file.

Whole Files Only   Remember that using the Insert Object command links or embeds an entire file to the container file. You cannot use this command to link an individual object (such as a range of Excel cells) to the container file. Instead, use the steps in the "Linking or Embedding with Paste Special" section earlier in this lesson.

CAUTION

Creating a New Embedded File

The Insert Object command also can help you create a brand-new file and embed it at the same time. (You can't link with this procedure because to link you must already have a named file from which the object is coming.) Say, for example, that you want to insert an Excel spreadsheet into your Word document, but you haven't created the spreadsheet yet. You can do it all at once with the following procedure:

1. Open the container document and position the insertion point where you want the embedded file to go.

2. Select **Insert** then click **Object**, and the Object dialog box appears (see Figure C.3).

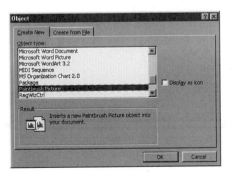

Figure C.3   Select the type of file you want to create.

3. With the **Create New** tab displayed, select the type of object you want to create from the **Object Type** list box.

4. Click **OK**. The application you selected opens within Word, and you can create the object. (Notice that the toolbar buttons and menu commands change to be appropriate for that application.)

5. When you're finished working with the object, click outside of the object window (onto the original application window); you are returned to the container application (the menus and toolbars switch back to those of the application that holds the object) The object is now embedded in your container file.

Editing Embedded Objects

Editing an embedded object is where the greatest advantage of embedding comes into play. You do not have to remember the name and location of the source file that you used to create the embedded object. You double-click the object and the source application starts, enabling you to edit the object.

Follow these steps to edit an embedded object:

1. Open the document containing the embedded object you want to edit.

2. Double-click the object or select the object and then choose **Edit** and then **Object**. The server application of the embedded object starts and displays the object.

3. Edit the object using the server application's tools and commands.

4. Click outside the object on the container document to return to your container application.

CAUTION

Modified Launch   Some objects perform a function or action when you double-click them, instead of opening the source file for editing. For example, Windows Sound Recorder objects play a sound when double-clicked. To edit objects such as this, hold down the **Alt** key and double-click the object.

Editing Linked Objects

After you have created a linked object, you might want to edit and update the information in the object. At this stage, you realize the full benefit of an OLE link because you can edit the object one time, and it is updated in every document to which it is linked.

There are two ways to edit a linked object. The first is to start at the source file, using the server application to make changes to the object. The second is to start at the container file and let the link information lead you to the correct source file and server application. With the second method, you do not have to remember the name of the source file or even which server application created it. In the next sections, you learn how to edit objects using these two methods.

Editing from the Source File

To edit a linked object starting from the source file, follow these steps:

1. Start the server application, and then open the source file that contains the object you want to edit.
2. Edit and make changes to the object.
3. Save the document and close the server application.
4. Switch to (or start) the client application and open the container file. The changes should automatically be reflected in the container file.

If the changes are not reflected, the document might not be set up to automatically update links. Skip to "Managing a Link's Update Settings" later in this lesson to learn how to update the links.

CAUTION

Now You See It, Now You Don't Some client applications enable you to edit or make changes directly to the object that is linked to the container file without starting the server application. This can cause problems because the source file is not being changed, only the image of the object. The changes you make to the image are wiped out when the object is updated via the source file. You do not have this problem with Microsoft Office products, but it might occur with other non-Microsoft applications.

Editing from the Container File

Editing from the container file is quick and easy because you do not have to find and open the server application manually. To edit a linked object from the container file, follow these steps:

1. From the container file, double-click the linked object you want to update. The server application starts and displays the source file. If double-clicking the object does not start the server application, select the **Edit** menu, then select **Links** to open the Links dialog box. Select the link you want to edit and click the **Open Source** button. The server application starts and displays the source file.

2. Edit the object in the source file, making as many changes as necessary.

3. In the server application, choose **File** and then **Save**.

4. In the server application, choose **File** and then **Exit**. You're returned to the container file, which reflects the changes you made to the linked object.

Managing a Link's Update Settings

After you have created a linked object, you can control when changes to the source file are updated in the container file(s). You can update a link manually or automatically. If a link is set to be updated manually, you must remember to follow the update steps each time you change the source file that contains the linked object. With the automatic setting enabled (the default update setting), the changes you make to the source file are automatically updated each time you open the container file.

To set a linked object to be manually updated, follow these steps:

1. Open the container file that contains the object link you want to update.

2. Choose **Edit** and then **Links**. The Links dialog box appears (see Figure C.4). For the linked objects in your document, the list indicates the link name, the pathname of the source file, and whether the link is set to update automatically or manually.

3. Select the link you want to update.

4. Change the **Update** setting to **Manual**.

5. Update the link by clicking the **Update Now** button in the Links dialog box. The object is then updated with any changes that were made to the source file.

6. Click **OK** to close the dialog box.

7. Choose **File** and then **Save** to save the document and the changes to the link settings.

With the link set for manual update, you must repeat steps 5 through 7 of this procedure each time you want the linked object to reflect changes made in the source file.

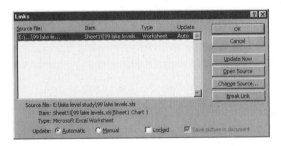

Figure C.4 You can control each individual link in your document.

Locking and Unlocking Links

In addition to setting link update options to manual and automatic, you can lock a link to prevent the link from being updated when the source file is changed. A locked link is not updated until it is unlocked.

To lock or unlock a link, follow these steps:

1. Open the document containing the linked object.

2. Choose **Edit** and then **Links**. The Links dialog box appears (refer to Figure C.4).

3. Select the link you want to lock.

4. To lock the link, select the **Locked** check box. To unlock the link, make sure the check box is empty.

5. Click **OK** to close the dialog box.

Breaking Links

If at some point, you decide that you want a linked object in your document to remain fixed and no longer be updated by its source file, you can break (or cancel) the link. This does not delete or alter the object; it merely removes the background information that directly ties the object to its source file. The object becomes like any other object that was placed by the Windows Copy and Paste operations.

To break or cancel a linked object, follow these steps:

1. Open the container file that contains the object whose link you want to break.

2. Select **Edit** and then **Links** (or **Link Options** in some applications). The Links dialog box appears, showing linked object information.

3. Select the link name of the object you want to break.

4. Click **Break Link** (or **Delete** in some applications). A warning box might appear cautioning that you are breaking a link. Click **OK** or **Yes** to confirm your choice.

In this appendix, you learned how to create and manage OLE links and embedding.

Index

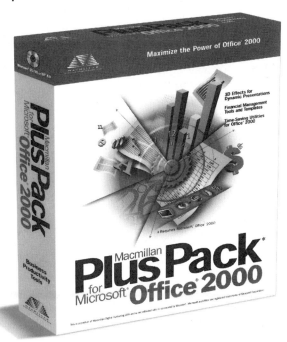

Get FREE books and more...when you register this book online for our Personal Bookshelf Program

http://register.quecorp.com/

 Register online and you can sign up for our *FREE Personal Bookshelf Program*—immediate and unlimited access to the electronic version of more than 200 complete computer books! That means you'll have 100,000 pages of valuable information onscreen, at your fingertips!

 Plus, you can access product support, including complimentary downloads, technical support files, book-focused links, companion Web sites, author sites, and more!

 And, don't miss out on the opportunity to sign up for a *FREE subscription to a weekly email newsletter* to help you stay current with news, announcements, sample book chapters, and special events, including sweepstakes, contests, and various product giveaways.

 We value your comments! Best of all, the entire registration process takes only a few minutes to complete, so go online and get the greatest value going—absolutely FREE!

Don't Miss Out On This Great Opportunity!

QUE® is a brand of Macmillan Computer Publishing USA. For more information, visit *www.mcp.com*